ERWIN R. GOODENOUGH

BY LIGHT, LIGHT

THE MYSTIC GOSPEL
OF
HELLENISTIC JUDAISM

AMSTERDAM
PHILO PRESS
1969

ERWIN RAMSDELL GOODENOUGH:
BY LIGHT, LIGHT.
THE MYSTIC GOSPEL OF HELLENISTIC JUDAISM
FIRST PUBLISHED NEW HAVEN, CONN. 1935.

PHILO PRESS
PUBLISHERS

SINGEL 395
AMSTERDAM C
1969

ΟΙΚΩΙ ΤΩΙ ΕΜΩΙ

λέγεται γὰρ οἶκος καὶ τὸ ἐκ γυναικὸς καὶ
τέκνων σύγκριμα.

τὸ ἐμὸν ὑστέρημα οὗτοι ἀνεπλήρωσαν.

CONTENTS

ABBREVIATIONS

THE text of Philo used, unless otherwise stated, is the Cohn-Wendland edition of the corpus, Berlin, 1896–1930; the last volume, the *Index Verborum* by H. Leisegang, is referred to as Leisegang, *Index*. Works of Philo not included in this edition, because extant only in Armenian, are used in the Latin translation by Aucher as reprinted in the Tauchnitz Edition of Philo (Leipzig, 1851–1853). The titles of Philo's works are so long as to compel a system of abbreviation if they are much used. The following table is for the most part that found in Colson and Whitaker, I, xxiii f. I should like to see it come to be generally adopted by Philonic scholars for our common convenience:

Abr. = *De Abrahamo.*
Aet. = *De Aeternitate Mundi.*
Agr. = *De Agricultura.*
Animal. = *Alexander sive de eo quod rationem habeant bruta animalia.*
Cher. = *De Cherubim.*
Conf. = *De Confusione Linguarum.*
Cong. = *De Congressu Eruditionis Gratia.*
Cont. = *De Vita Contemplativa.*
Decal. = *De Decalogo.*
Det. = *Quod Deterius Potiori Insidiari soleat.*
Deo = *De Deo.*
Ebr. = *De Ebrietate.*
Exs. = *De Exsecrationibus.*
Flac. = *In Flaccum.*
Fug. = *De Fuga et Inventione (De Profugis).*
Gig. = *De Gigantibus.*
Heres = *Quis rerum divinarum Heres.*
Immut. = *Quod Deus sit Immutabilis.*
Jona = *De Iona.*
Jos. = *De Josepho.*
LA, i, ii, iii = *Legum Allegoria,* i, ii, iii.
Legat. = *Legatio ad Gaium.*
Mig. = *De Migratione Abrahami.*
Mos., i, ii = *De Vita Mosis,* i, ii.
Mut. = *De Mutatione Nominum.*
Opif. = *De Opificio Mundi.*
Plant. = *De Plantatione.*
Post. = *De Posteritate Caini.*
Praem. = *De Praemiis et Poenis.*
Prob. = *Quod Omnis Probus Liber Sit.*

Provid. = *De Providentia.*
QE, i, ii = *Quaestiones et Solutiones in Exodum*, i, ii.
QG, i, ii, iii, iv = *Quaestiones et Solutiones in Genesin*, i, ii, iii, iv.
Sac. = *De Sacrificiis Abelis et Caini.*
Sob. = *De Sobrietate.*
Som., i, ii = *De Somniis*, i, ii.
Spec., i, ii, iii, iv = *De Specialibus Legibus*, i, ii, iii, iv.
Virt. = *De Virtutibus.*

BRÉHIER, *Les Idées* = *Les Idées philosophiques et religieuses de Philon d'Alexandrie*, by Émile Bréhier, Second Edition, Paris, 1925.
COLSON and WHITAKER = *Philo, with an English Translation*, by F. H. Colson and G. H. Whitaker, London and New York, 1929–1934. *The Loeb Classical Library* (five volumes out of ten are published).*
HARRIS, *Fragments* = *Fragments of Philo Judaeus*, by J. Rendel Harris, Cambridge, 1886.
HEINEMANN, *Bildung* = *Philons griechische und jüdische Bildung*, by I. Heinemann, Breslau, 1921, 1928, two volumes.
HEINEMANN, *Poseidonios* = *Poseidonios' metaphysische Schriften*, by I. Heinemann, Breslau, 1921, 1928, two volumes.
"HELLENISTIC KINGSHIP" = "The Political Philosophy of Hellenistic Kingship," by Erwin R. Goodenough, *Yale Classical Studies*, I (1928), 53–102, Yale University Press.
JOSEPHUS is quoted by Book and Section as divided by Benedictus Niese, *Flavii Josephi Opera*, Berlin, 1887–1895, seven volumes.
"NEO-PYTHAG. SOURCE" = "A Neo-Pythagorean Source in Philo Judaeus," by Erwin R. Goodenough, *Yale Classical Studies*, III (1932), 115–164, Yale University Press.
PASCHER, *Königsweg* = Η ΒΑΣΙΛΙΚΗ ΟΔΟΣ: *Der Königsweg zu Wiedergeburt und Vergottung bei Philon von Alexandreia*, by Joseph Pascher, Paderborn, 1931 (*Studien zur Geschichte und Kultur des Altertums*, XVII, Parts 3 and 4).
Philos Werke = *Die Werke Philos von Alexandria in deutscher Übersetzung*, edited by L. Cohn, and then by I. Heinemann, Breslau, 1909–1929; five volumes have been published.
SVF = *Stoicorum Veterum Fragmenta*, collegit Ionnes ab Arnim, Lipsiae, 1921–1924, four volumes.

* The translations of Philo which follow have been checked with those of the volumes of this series now available, except the last. Where the authors' rendering could not be improved, as was often the case, it has been reproduced with the kind permission of the Harvard University Press, the publisher. Yonge's translation, although useful for treatises not yet included in the Loeb series, could rarely be accepted for more than a line or two without radical emendation. Responsibility for all translations included is of course mine. Greek writers are quoted in English for the benefit of those whose Greek is laborious.

WACHS. = *Johannis Stobaei Florilegium,* recensuit Curtius Wachsmuth et Otto Hense, Berlin, 1884–1919, five volumes.

YONGE = *The Works of Philo Judaeus, the Contemporary of Josephus,* translated from the Greek, by C. D. Yonge, London, 1854–1855, four volumes.

BY LIGHT, LIGHT

INTRODUCTION

STUDY of the ancient mysteries is complicated by much more than the inadequacy of our data. It can be complicated, and usually has been, by lack of imagination as to the temper of mind of the mystic devotees. This is dangerous ground for an historian, but such a projection is always implicit in our writing, and may become much more accurate by becoming explicit.

Most of us come to the Hellenistic Age after a more or less thorough early training in the point of view of the Classical Age, and in the new field are struck by a sense of contrast. The tendency is then for us, like travellers in a strange land, to analyze the differences while we neglect the similarities, obviously a questionable procedure. Particularly have we tended to contrast the "philosophers" of the earlier period with the "mystics" of the later. We have felt on sure ground with the differences, and when it has been possible to trace Hellenistic mystic imagery to the Orient or Egypt we say that the Hellenistic notion is the oriental point of view simply expressed in the Greek language.

The differences between the two Periods are certainly there, as well as, in the second Period, the oriental imagery. But have we not lost sight of the fact that a native Egyptian of 500 B. c. could much less have written Plutarch's *De Iside,* even if he had had a perfect command of the Greek language, than a classical philosopher could have done? We pass from Classic Greece to the Hellenistic Age with a sense of difference, but if we could trace Isis or Attis, with full knowledge of their native states, out from the original forms into the Hellenistic Age we should find at least just as great changes. The Hellenistic man himself, it must always be remembered, considered himself a Greek.

Further, in our attempt at visualizing Hellenistic mentality, we must always bear in mind the fact that the material borrowed from the Orient or Egypt all passed through amazingly similar types of adaptation. For much as the various mythologies may survive in the Hellenistic accounts, it is not the mythology itself which matters but the mythology as a symbol of metaphysical truth. The mystery is not a path to Isis or Attis; it is a path to Reality, Existence, Knowledge, Life, of which Isis or Attis is the symbol. The value of Isis, that is, is to make the intellectual concept emotionally realizable, something which can be taken out of the cold words of formulation and made radiantly alive within the longing hearts of mankind. So Plutarch can turn from Isis to Iranian mythology, or Greek mythology, and assert their ultimate identity. The point that is often missed is that the union of these is

not in a mystic concept fundamentally arising from one or the other mythology, but in the passionate desire of the Hellenistic man to experience
emotionally the concepts he has learned from Greek rationalism.

The same process is illustrated in Christianity. The early Christians seem
to have been content with the mythological assertion that Jesus was the Son
of God and would return from the clouds to assert his power. As their
thought went on into elaborations it produced more mythology, the stories
of the Virgin Birth. Such a religion in itself meant nothing to the Hellenistic
religious thinkers. Christ almost at once became to them the Logos, the
Sophia, the πνεῦμα, and Christianity a mystic cult with φωτισμός and a
mystic meal. After such a revolutionary change, that is as Christianity became
another and more adequate means of making emotionally real and accessible
the old Hellenistic abstractions, it was ready to conquer the Graeco-Roman
world.

Was all this the orientalizing of Greek thought or the Hellenizing of
oriental mythology? Obviously both. The mystic emphasis of the Hellenistic
Age presents a contrast to the rationalism of the typical, most highly developed, Greek Philosophers. But there is just as great a contrast between a
developed Hellenistic mystery and the original form and meaning of its
mythologies. It is true that the Hellenistic World was wide open to invasions
of eastern religious teachers and doctrines. Men of that age were fascinated
by new mythological formulation and in Gnostic groups dedicated themselves to its ever greater elaboration. Yet the mythology could not remain
long in the Greek world without becoming transformed into typology. The
myths were important only as they helped the Greek thinker with his Greek
concepts.

How far back does this tendency go in Hellenism, the tendency to use
mythology as a basis for an emotional experience of rationalistic concepts;
the sense of failure without divine help to realize the ideal quality of life;
and the conviction that this life is inadequate as a stage for the operation of
justice with men, or for men to accomplish their destiny? The question has
only to be asked for it to become obvious that the tendency was marked as
far back as we can with any certainty trace the various currents of Greek
life. The Mystery of Demeter and the Bacchic groups, and especially the
early and strong influence of the Orphics, though given slight emphasis in
our classical curricula, point to the fact that rationalism was never the solution of life for at least a very large part of the Greeks, and hence that it was
out of the heart of Greek civilization at its greatest period that there came
the tendency to find in a mythological presentation of the divine mystery,
made vivid by initiations and sacraments, the gateway to a larger life. Nor
was this movement long dissociated from the philosophers. The close kinship
of the Pythagoreans with the Orphics, the respect shown the Orphics by the

dramatists, even Aristophanes, and the obviously profound influence they had upon Plato, show, to give only a few instances, that the thought life of Greece early and steadily felt the attraction exerted by the emotional over-tones of Orphism. Aristotle, to be sure, and perhaps the early Stoics, were nearly pure rationalists. But they, far from being representative, are almost unique exceptions in Greek life. Initiations, sacraments, robes, processions, θίασοι, the great constants of the Hellenistic Mysteries, as well as the philo-sophic ideas with which they were fused, all were as idiomatically a product of Classic Greece as its drama and art.

With the collapse of classic Greek civilization, and the absence of great rationalistic metaphysicians to carry on the work of the classic philosophers, not so much a new spirit arose as the spirit which would appear in classic times to have been that of the majority, a spirit overshadowed in our picture of Classic Greece only because of the presence there of the great men who must have been as exceptional and remote then as they would have been at any time since. The Hellenistic Age was the age of the average intellect, with the possible exception of Posidonius and the mathematicians. The amazing thing is, not that in the Hellenistic Age the tone is so different from what appeared from her great men to be the spirit of Athens in her prime, but that, failing to produce giants, the rationalistic temper continued so dis-tinctly and so long to flavor the generally popular civilization. Over that rationalistic remnant swept wave after wave of oriental inundation—only at once to have its oriental character and objective rationalized. More than that, Greek rationalism could penetrate into all the world, and force Syrians, Egyptians, even hard headed Romans, into echoing Greek metaphysics. Not pure metaphysics as Aristotle understood it could thus penetrate and survive. But mystic metaphysics, made vivid to men through mythology, any my-thology, and through initiations into θίασοι with their sacraments, this meta-physic, like a magnificent quicklime, turned everything it touched into its own nature. Not least of all did it do so with the tiny group that proclaimed Jesus of Nazareth to be the Messiah. It is not that the metaphysic of Orphic-Pythagoreanism and Platonism remained unaffected by its borrowings. Strange new terms came into use. The mystic Logos, Sophia, and ὕλη; the "Female Principle of nature" as Plutarch called Isis, and as she appeared in many mythologies to typify creation in sexual language, and to promise the mystic ascent in language just as sexual; and then the fantastic πληρώματα of grades of divinity: all were parts of the new data. Finally there was the great God, Absolute in Being, who had been represented on the hideous cross to gather to Himself, and annihilate in His own death, the sins of humanity. An overwhelming series of waves. The combination was certainly no longer Greek. It was a new compound. Yet for all the strange stuff in the mixture, the new ingredients were transformed more than they transformed the Greek element. For in all intelligent Graeco-Roman circles, mere mythology was not enough. It had to be shot through with Greek rationalism.

The Greek rationalism which transformed the mystic mythologies was, further, not any random type of that rationalism. The Stoics, to be sure, were interested in the mysteries and made some use of them. But what remains to us of the interpretation of the mysteries is, with amazing uniformity, an eclecticism, to be sure, varying in detail, but with a firm basis in Neo-Pythagorean Platonism. Greeks like Herodotus and Diodorus were interested to record oriental mythology as data of oriental history. But men who adopted the mysteries to themselves, or were much influenced by mystic thought, seem almost invariably to have been Neo-Pythagoreans or Platonists.[1] This is not a surprising circumstance upon second glance. For these two schools, so closely related from the beginning, were at their earliest stages the closest of all to the Orphics, and in their version of Orphism developed the first mystic philosophies of Greece. Not that either Platonism or Pythagoreanism was exclusively mystical in its interests. But the rationalistic analysis of the *Republic* could find culmination in the Orphic eschatology of the tenth book as easily as Pythagorean numbers and ethics could culminate in metempsychosis, asceticism, and mystical experience. Plato's charioteer drives his horses not simply through the cosmos, but out into the mystic beyond. Socrates died in Orphic hope.

The great body of literature or tradition which must lie behind Plutarch, Apuleius, and Chaeremon is lost. But it must have been the continuation of this Orphic-Platonic-Pythagoreanism which they themselves are stating in the new typology of Egypt and Iran. The later writers who show mystic influences in their rationalism, or rationalistic influences in their mysticism, Plotinus, Porphyry, Iamblichus, Julian, Proclus, to say nothing of Justin Martyr, Clement, and Origen, have but to be named to show the consistency with which mystic rationalism remained true to the Pythagorean-Platonic type. Records of the early Hellenistic stages of this movement have so completely disappeared that Bevan and Tarn have discussed Hellenistic Philosophy without reference to it. It is, without documents, impossible to state how influential that tradition was in the Hellenistic period. But it is a difficult thing to imagine that the great later tree which supported all these branches stood without roots in the Hellenistic Age.

Into this atmosphere the Jew brought his faith and his Scriptures with their oriental stories and conceptions. He met not Aristotle or Zeno, but the mystic philosophy which was transforming every other oriental mythology

---

1. It must be borne in mind that the most ignorant then as now were probably content with the simplest mythological literalism, and the most mechanical sacramentalism. But we must not judge the mysteries by these people, any more than we like to have our own religion, whatever it is, judged by the type of communicant who is too unintelligent to understand what we consider its real purport.

into a mystery religion. In an environment where the folk religions of Isis and Attis, and later of Mithra and Christianity,[2] were one after the other being made over into mysteries by the Greeks on the model, and with the philosophic foundation, of Orpheus, was Judaism alone to escape? Could and did the Jew keep his orientalism intact, or even be content with occasional borrowings, or did his synagogue too tend to become a θίασος, and his whole tradition a typology of this mystic philosophy? It must at once be said that the thesis of this book is that Judaism in the Greek Diaspora did, for at least an important minority, become primarily such a mystery. There are, as will be indicated, abundant traces of Greek Jews who remained fundamentally oriental, "literalists" Philo calls them. They wrote such works as II and III Maccabees in praise of "normative" legalism. But there is indication of a complete transformation of Judaism in the Greek world that has not been systematically examined.

There is no important writer of antiquity who has been so little studied as Philo Judaeus. True most New Testament scholars, and students of Greek and Roman religious history, have at one time or another, to a greater or less degree, looked in his vast writings for answers to questions that have arisen in the course of their studies. He has been searched for traces of Platonism, of Stoicism, of Rabbinical affinities. The question of how much his Logos doctrine resembled or differed from the Christian Logos has been discussed for more than a century. Writers like Gfrörer, Dähne, Drummond, and Bréhier have attacked the complicated problem of trying to cull out from Philo's allegorical mazes his religio-philosophical "system." Students of the history of religion have indicated many details in his works that reflect the mysteries. To all of these and many others, but especially to the latest *Religionsgeschichtlicher,* Pascher, any student of Philo must be profoundly indebted. My own debt to Pascher will be abundantly apparent. The great work of Heinemann, *Philons Bildung,* is a splendid analysis of the different ingredients that have gone into Philo's composition.

But still the great continent of the Philonic allegory itself remains uncharted for the beginner. Still no one seems to have tried to read Philo, if I may say so, with the grain instead of against it, to understand what Philo himself thought he was driving at in all his passionate allegorical labors. We have insisted that Philo answer this or that question of our own, rather than listen to what he is himself trying to say. Even the attempts of Schürer, Massebieau, and Cohn to give an introduction to the writings of Philo, though they have solved many critical problems about the relation of differ-

2. No one would, I think, dispute that in the liturgy of the *Apostolic Constitutions,* and in Clement and Origen, Christianity had become a mystery religion. The only dispute is as to how early one may assert that the change was made. That Christians were paralleling Christianity and Orphism by the Second Century is clear alike from the writings of the period and the iconography of Christ.

ent treatises to each other, yet leave the reader quite at a loss for the content and purpose of the writings themselves.

So it is not surprising, when a student should try to do just this which seems never to have been done, to read the corpus in an attempt to find what Philo himself wanted the reader to learn, that he should emerge with a novel interpretation. What must provoke initial resistance, especially on the part of those who have been reading Philo for years, without realizing how "cross-grained" their study has been, is that the new interpretation not only involves Philo, but has a significance for the whole problem of the origin of Christianity which most students in that field will not welcome. Yet I am none the less convinced of the truth of the interpretation, and am herewith publishing the first of a series of volumes in which I shall try to prove what has become to me an inevitable thesis.

It will clarify the reader's mind if that thesis is clearly stated at the outset.

It seems to me then that Jews in the Diaspora began very early to borrow ideas from their neighbors. In this connection it must be remembered that their ancestors could never leave the gods of the Canaanites alone. In the earlier period of Israel it had been only the occasional prophet who recognized that the borrowing was not merely a taking over of attractive ideas and practices from the Gentiles, but was apostasy from true Yahvism. The great mass of the Israelites seem never to have suspected that to be Israelites meant to be in opposition to everything, however attractive, that was not peculiarly their own. So long as they were faithful to the requirements of Yahveh they thought that they could satisfy the requirements of other gods as well, and still regard themselves as true Israelites.

It is apparent that after the great revival of Ezra this was no longer possible, at least as regards cult practices. The Jews became a race with a single and exclusive cult. But their nature seems not to have changed. The Pharisees came forward in place of the ancient prophets to insist upon Jewish ideological exclusiveness, the sinfulness of Greek literature and manners. But no cursory reader of their history can miss the point that they had a terrific struggle to pull the Jews away from their fascinated preoccupation with Greek ways and ideas. How far they succeeded in Palestine up to the fall of Jerusalem, our records do not indicate. Yet even the Pharisees were full of foreign notions about angels, determinism, and the future life.

Long before the beginnings of the Pharisaic reaction Jews went over to Egypt in great and increasing numbers, where almost a hundred years before the Chasidim they became so Hellenized that the old Bible was of no use to them in the original Hebrew and had to be translated. The translation which was made showed that even the few who could still read the old language at all had forgotten the original meaning of many of the words, and were primarily thinking in Greek terms. Jewish children now had Greek names.[8] Still the cult was inviolable: that lesson had been learned once and for all. But the cult could put no bounds on the sensitivity, keenness, and range of the Jewish mind.

I do not profess to be able to trace the process in detail. But what shreds of literature we have from Greek Judaism before Philo, and the full achievement recorded by Philo's time, indicate that here again the Jews were captivated by their neighbors' religion and thought. Yet since a Jew could not now simply become an initiate of Isis or Orpheus and remain a Jew as well, the amazingly clever trick was devised, we do not know when or by whom, of representing Moses as Orpheus and Hermes-Tat, and explaining that the Jewish "Wisdom" figure, by translation "Sophia," was identical with that "Female Principle in nature" which Plutarch identified as Isis! All that now needed to be done was to develop sufficient skill in allegory and the Torah could be represented as the ἱερὸς λόγος *par-excellence,* whereby Judaism was at once transformed into the greatest, the only true, Mystery. Moses became priest and hierophant as well as lawgiver. The door was wide open, and the Jews, without the slightest feeling of disloyalty, or the abandonment of their cult practices, could and did take over the esoteric ideology of the mystic philosophers about them, especially and inevitably the Pythagorean-Platonism of Alexandria. Indeed they early claimed, not that they had borrowed it from the Greeks, but that the Greeks originally had taken it from them.

A great mystic conception of Judaism and of life was thereby developed. The stages by which all this occurred are very uncertain. Moses had become Orpheus and Hermes-Tat possibly two centuries before Philo did his writing, certainly not much later than a century and a half before him. But the intermediate steps are lost, and in Philo, while the Jewish Mystery is fully developed, all trace of the process by which the Jews came to ascribe the extraordinary powers to the Patriarchs is lost. Moses now has the power of Hermes, but the explicit comparison is no longer made.

There is much that is uncertain about Hellenistic Judaism. Yet the fact is, it seems to me, that by Philo's time, and long before, Judaism in the Greek-speaking world, especially in Egypt, had been transformed into a Mystery.

The objective of this Judaism was salvation in the mystical sense. God was no longer only the God presented in the Old Testament: He was the Absolute, connected with phenomena by His Light-Stream, the Logos or Sophia. The hope and aim of man was to leave created things with their sordid complications, and to rise to incorruption, immortality, life, by climbing the mystic ladder, traversing the Royal Road, of the Light-Stream.

God, ὁ θεός, as the quotation on the title page says,[4] was to be found by

---

3. Except for "Ezekiel the Tragic Poet," which may well be a *nom-de-plume,* every Hellenistic Jewish writer has a Greek name.

4. *Praem.,* 46: ἀλήθειαν δὲ μετίασιν οἱ τὸν θεὸν θεῷ φαντασιωθέντες, φωτὶ φῶς.

that lower type of divinity, the radiation or emanation from Himself which men of the age frequently called θεός without the article; He was a Light which was discerned by the Light-Rays that He shot forth, as we see the sun, itself a light, by means of the rays that reach us, φωτὶ φῶς.

The Law became a difficult problem. As the Torah, the sacred teaching, it was the ἱερὸς λόγος of the Mystery; but as a set of commands concerned with physical life it was obviously of less importance than the great spiritual reality of the Light-Stream. So again a clever solution was found: the Law, as commandments, was said to be only the projection of the true Law, the Logos, into the material medium of nouns and verbs. It was the material copy of a Platonic original. As such it had its uses, and by most Jews was carefully followed. But its spiritual value was secondary altogether to that of the great Source of the written Law, the Unwritten Law, the unwritten streaming Logos-Nomos of God. Only as one came up into this, the true Law of Judaism, had one fulfilled the Law of Moses.

The Patriarchs, it was said, had had access to this Law, and so had been true Jews before the legislation of Sinai. Indeed they were the model Jews, the Hierophants of the Mystery. One could be a Jew, in a sense, by obeying the copy-law. But the true Jew, according to mystic Judaism, got his Law through the mediation of the Patriarchs, especially of Moses, who had ascended the Stream to the Logos, and were God's "loans" to help other men, Jews and proselytes, to come to the same vision. Indeed some of them, especially Moses, were incarnations of the Logos, and so the saviors of those who would join the Mystery. The great temple cultus was also allegorized as representing a Mystery. But it was the "Lower Mystery," and seems to have been stressed at all only because the Jews did not want to abandon that cultus, and yet, if they kept it, had to see mystic-rationalistic significance in it.

How far such Jews organized themselves into cult groups, θίασοι, I have not been able to determine. The evidence seems on the whole to suggest that they may have had their mystic initiation, baptism, like the Christians later, and a "sacred table" from which the uninitiated were rigorously kept away. The evidence for this is unsatisfactory because scanty and not in agreement. But however much or little the Jewish Mystery may have developed its own cult practices, it seems, as a mystic philosophy, to have been the heart and core of Greek Judaism. At least the remains of the liturgy of Greek synagogues is drenched with this mystic conception of and aspiration for God.

Philo is the chief source for knowledge of details of this Mystery, but he does not stand alone, and there is enough evidence, it seems to me, to warrant assuming not only the existence of the Jewish Mystery, but that in some such way the movement developed. Certainly it is in terms of the Mystery that Philo alone becomes intelligible, for all his writing is oriented about it, and directed toward its explanation.

My general thesis does not stop here, though this is as far as the present volume attempts to go. It seems that, if one admits the existence of this Mystery, it is here that he must look for the origin and explanation of that amazing Jewish art which the Yale expedition, under Professor Rostovtzeff, has just uncovered at Dura. Further if the Mystery did exist, if Judaism in the circles that were using the Septuagint had come to mean what I have indicated, we must look closely at Christian origins for the answer to many problems that have baffled us. Thereby we may expect, perhaps, the unsettling of many theories. But these later aspects of the thesis, the art, and the influence of the Mystery in early Greek Christianity, must await the subsequent volumes of this series. For obviously the first step is to settle the question "Was there ever such a mystic Judaism?" This volume is published as a separate study that discussion may be simplified by being concentrated upon that single point.

The study begins with Philo because he is our only extended source in Hellenistic Judaism. From him the main lines of the Mystery are first described. It appears from his own writings that he is not thinking *in vacuo* in his own age, but represents at least a very considerable minority of his Jewish associates in the Greek world, if not a majority. If he then has not invented Mystic Judaism, once that term has become clear through analyzing his presentation, how far back does it go, and how did the movement develop? This is the problem of Chapter X, followed by a discussion of a body of material, fragments from a mystic Jewish liturgy, which in their present form are apparently later than Philo, but which throw much additional light upon the movement.

In discussing the Mystery the purpose is to be principally descriptive. Earlier approaches to the problem have been made by historians of religion principally interested in the analogies to be drawn, for example, between Philo's Sophia and Isis, or his Powers and similar conceptions in Persia. Such an approach seems to me to be fundamentally secondary. I have not neglected to use all the light possible from oriental religions, though I do not profess to have used all there is. In the primitive stages of the movement, as shown in Chapter X, Jews were obviously looking directly and avowedly to Orpheus and Isis. But Philo, it seems to me, is far beyond so crude a stage of syncretism. He is looking, and with him apparently at least his most intelligent associates, not directly at Gentile mythology but at the Hellenistic mystic philosophy which made any mythology only a typology for its doctrines. The allegories of Philo are then not attempts at making Abraham, Moses, Sophia, and the ark types of Isis or the Persian pleroma, but of the ideas which Greek thinkers were forcing upon all mythology. For Philo the Hellenization of Isis was a foreign thing, a parallel in the true sense of being a line which would never touch his own. Only as notions from Isis had very early come into Judaism or had been completely assimilated into Greek mysticism could they affect him. To begin with the parallels is then misleading, for it implies that Philo himself had, for example, the Isiac mythology in mind as he wrote about Sophia. As a matter of fact it is patent that he would have regarded such an assumption as a violent travesty and insult. The approach to Philo by parallels from other systems is often as unconvincing as the parallels frequently quoted between Paul and Mithra, or Orpheus. In view of the character of Paul, it is at once incredible that he should from such sources have taken practices and ideals directly and *de novo* to weave them into his new faith. In the case of Philo his interest in the thinkers of Greece is as obvious as his dependence upon them. But his attitude toward the mysteries of his neighbors is as scornful as toward their worship of cats and crocodiles. For some of Philo's predecessors two hundred years before him this was not the case. But it is clear that the early stage of syncretism with mythology was quickly lost. Moses did not continue long, we infer, to be developed explicitly as the Jewish Osiris or Musaeus. Rather he became the Greek hierophant ideal, to lead men to Being. The transition is lost, but the distinction between the two attitudes with which Greek Jews approached their environment is unmistakable.

Philo's advanced position, offering Judaism as a solution of common mystic problems independent of the other mysteries, must have presupposed a period when Judaism had at least for a time allowed itself to be compared with the mysteries already recognized by Greek thinkers, that is primarily with Orpheus and secondarily with Isis. After Judaism had, at least in its own eyes, been recognized as a religion offering a way to mystic objectives in conscious comparison with the other mysteries, it could go on to represent itself as the only true Mystery, and deal with its own mythology and the mystic philosophy without further reference to its competitors. It is not for the historian to say that only so could the Philonic stage of the Mystery have been reached, but *a priori* this would seem the natural way, and the records make it highly probable that in such a way Judaism actually did become the type of religion Philo describes.

The transformation in Judaism seems to me as complete as that from the Synoptics to Chalcedon. In both religions the oriental element was never entirely lost, to say the least. But both religions came to be predominately expressions of that powerful genius, the Greek genius as it survived in the Hellenistic and Roman world.

CHAPTER I

THE GOD OF THE MYSTERY

ONE of the most familiar facts about Philo is that to him God was the Absolute, a single and unique Being beyond even the Monad and the number One, as well as beyond the Good and all other categories.[1] Yet, like the God of later Neo-Platonism, Philo's Deity had somehow to be brought into relation with the world, in spite of the fact that He was essentially beyond relation. In the solution of the problem of how the unrelated God could be the God of the universe Philo vividly foreshadows the thought of Plotinus. The sun was taken as the figure, that orb which burns, to all appearances, eternally, yet without need of fuel from outside itself. Independent of the world, a self-sufficient existence, it sends out its great stream of light and heat which makes life possible upon the earth. This stream may be called a stream of light, or of heat, or of life, or of creation. But the stream itself is greater than any of these single aspects, since it includes them all. The aspects are only convenient abstractions for our immediate purpose, for the stream from the sun is not a pluralistic collection of independent elements, but is itself a unit. It is not the sun, yet it is in a sense the projection of the sun to us, or was so regarded by the ancients, in as much as in ancient thought light was a stream of fire coming from a fiery source. Even those schools furthest removed from regarding light as a stream of particles or atoms made it in some sense an ἀπαύγασμα, a radiation or emanation from and of fiery nature.

Such a figure was universally taken in antiquity when the problem of the relation of the Unrelated had to be discussed. From Plato's myth of the Cave on through the latest Neo-Platonists, the Absolute, Plato's τὸ ἀγαθόν, was a solar source which was the unaffected cause of even those shadows which seem to ordinary men to be the only existences. In so far as a concept could be connected with the ἀπαύγασμα from Reality, it had reality. The ἀπαύγασμα could then be a purely ontological theory in metaphysics, or it could inspire the mystical fervor with which Plato's passage is heated. Or it could be, as to Plato, both. For metaphysical or mystical purposes the figure of light was definitely always a figure of speech rather than a literal transference of the details of ancient physical theories of light. But the figure was constantly used, as of course it still is.

The tendency was equally constant to break up the Light-Stream from God into successive stages. As light is brighter at the source, or as one ap-

---

1. See Bréhier's excellent discussion *Les Idées*, 69 ff.

proaches the source, so the Light-Stream of Reality is brighter as one gets away from its more remote glimmerings to deal with it nearer its point of origin. The successive stages of decreasing brilliance were then over and again marked off as distinct grades of reality. Plato had done something suggestively similar in the allegory of the Cave. There was the sun, τὸ ἀγαθόν, then τὰ νοητά, and then the shadows of these, their representation within the cave of the material world. This is a very simple scheme. By Philo's time, largely under inspiration from the Orient, the schematizations were becoming much more elaborate.

Indeed it was by this means that mythology was chiefly used to make vivid and experiential the metaphysical conception. Any formulation of the relation of the Unrelated, whether made primarily with metaphysical or mystical objective, is perforce mythological. Even Aristotle, when faced with the problem of connecting the Unmoved Mover with matter, presented an explanation, the longing of matter for form, which strongly resembles myth. Less rigorous rationalists felt even more consciously that they were trying here to explain the inexplicable, and, like Plato, used myth frankly. The beautiful stories of foreign religions, or of the apparently native Orpheus, could be used quite as easily, and, it was correctly appreciated, quite as accurately, as those made to order like Plato's. It is true that in turning Plato's stages of reality into solar emanations the Hellenistic World went far from Plato's own teachings. There are no hints in Plato that the Forms are "rays" from τὸ ἀγαθόν, or that form in matter was such. All our evidence suggests that this was a mystical element which came from the East into Greek thinking. It may have been introduced by a few great individuals, such as, possibly, Posidonius, or it may have come in gradually as Platonists continued to reach out for fresh parables to explain the grades of reality. But by Philo's time the grades had become emanations, and the Hellenistic mind was quite open to any new mythological formulation which would be helpful to one who wished to visualize and ascend the Stream.

The contrast between the mythology at its origin and the use made of it by Hellenistic schools was that the Isis or Mithra story was mythology in the sense of folk history in its native state, but became, as has been suggested, arbitrary typology, a myth in the Platonic sense of the term, to the Greek. Even Apuleius, when in rapture he has a vision of Isis rising from the sea, prays to her not as to the personal Isis, but as to a conventionalization of the "Female Principle in nature," whom he could address by many names because no one name meant anything literally.

Two main types of formulation of the Stream had arisen, what may be called the Persian type of pleroma, and the Female Principle type. According to the Persian type God is a solar source sending out rays. In the Pseudo-

Aristotelian *De Mundo* the satraps of the Great King are used as figures, for they projected out through the great realm of Persia the Royal Power which was invisibly concealed at its source in the capital. If the King is the sun, the satraps are his rays, his δυνάμεις, lesser manifestations of the single reality, Royal Power. This the Hellenistic writer used as a myth of the Absolute God, sending out His δυνάμεις to be the divine forces and representations in the material world. In oriental religions themselves there were families of deities, theogonies, and, more importantly for our purpose, descending groups of deities. Plutarch names from Persia such a series descending from Ahura Mazda.[2] The first three are the gods or creators, respectively, of εὐνοία, ἀλήθεια, and εὐνομία; the second three are the creators of σοφία, of wealth (πλοῦτος) and "of the pleasures which have reference to what is noble" (τῶν ἐπὶ τοῖς καλοῖς ἡδέων). Beneath these are twenty-four lower deities who were put within the Cosmic Egg, and so represent the forces of deity active within the material world. These are not named. A parallel list of the descending deities, Amesha Spentas, as the Persians called them, is preserved. Pascher[3] is quite right in paralleling Plutarch's list with that in the *Avesta*: 1. Vohu Mano, Good Thought; 2. Asha Vahista, Perfect Righteousness; 3. Khshathra Vairya, Good Royalty; 4. Spenta Armaiti, Pious Modesty; 5. Haurvatat, Health; 6. Ameretat, Immortality.[4] These Amesha Spentas are so much like divine emanations which we shall encounter in Philo that Darmesteter[5] thought their presence in the *Avesta* indicated a Philonic or Neo-Platonic influence, and so a late date for the Persian formulation. Bousset showed the error of such a conclusion, and since his writing the influence of Iranian speculation upon Philo has been generally assumed.[6] However justifiable the assumption of direct Iranian influence upon Philo may or may not prove to be, it is clear that Plutarch's list is only generally similar to the list in the *Avesta*.

In the Mithra-Liturgy there appear to be similar groupings, the "seven

2. *De Iside*, 47.   3. *Königsweg*, p. 214.

4. See also J. Darmesteter, *The Zend Avesta*, (*The Sacred Books of the East*, vol. IV), p. lvi.

5. *Loc. cit.*

6. W. Bousset, "Die Himmelreise der Seele," *Archiv für Religionswissenschaft*, IV, 157, n. 2. See Pascher, *Königsweg*, pp. 209 ff. As Pascher says, the association of Philo's teaching with the Iranian goes back to Zeller (*Philosophie der Griechen*, III, ii, pp. 408 ff.). A review and bibliography of the controversy are to be found in A. V. W. Jackson, *Zoroastrian Studies* (1928), p. 43, n. 18. More fully Wesendonk, *Urmensch und Seele in der iranischen Überlieferung*, 1924, pp. 83–99, has analyzed the problem, with copious references to the literature, of the relation of Philo to the Amesha Spentas and Gayomart. To Wesendonk Philo is an "orthodox Jew" in feeling, influenced by Greek thought. If Persian details are there at all, he argues, they must have come in as part of the general Jewish assimilation of Persian ideas, and not be a contribution of Philo's own. That they were no contribution of Philo I agree. But it does not follow that they must have come to Jews in Alexandria through oriental Jewish assimilation, and could not have been a part of the Gentile Zeitgeist of Alexandria, and so available for direct assimilation there. Plutarch, magical papyri, and the Hermetica show the active presence of Iranian influence.

Τύχαι of the heaven (or the universe, οὐρανός), noble and good virgins, sacred (ἱεραί) and of the same type of existence as μινιμιρροφορ, the most holy guardians of the four pillars."[7] Each is hailed in the Liturgy by its magical name. Beneath these seven goddesses are seven gods with the faces of black bulls, with linen garments and golden diadems, also with magical names. The vision of all these comes after the first experience by which the mystic breathes into himself the Spirit of God.[8] Strengthened by this he addresses God in magical light terms, and begs Him to approach. Immediately he is surrounded by light rays. Then he sees "a younger God, fair of form, with locks of fire, clad in a white chiton and a scarlet chlamys, and with a fiery crown." This is Helios, the greatest of the gods, that is the greatest of the lesser divinities. He is distinguished by the fact that he traverses the Heavenly Road.[9] Above him is still ὁ μέγιστος θεός, to whom the lesser deity is besought to conduct the mystic. First the mystic is conducted through the pleroma described, and finally he comes to the Greatest God. The Greatest is also young, with a light-glance. He has golden hair, is clothed in a white chiton, a golden crown, and wears trousers. He carries a starry symbol and emits stars from his body. This experience of seeing the Greatest means at once death and birth to the mystic, so that now he too is a traverser of the Way which the supreme God has created, established by Law, and made the μυστήριον, the sacrament or secret teaching.

Out of all this material it becomes clear that the Way is important, and the light-mysticism, as well as the general formulation of the supreme God beneath whom is the pleroma. The highest of the lower deities is the mystic guide along the Way through the pleroma to the Greatest. But there is no standardization of the pleroma. The idea of the pleroma is important, but not a specific formulation within the pleroma.

Over against this general organization of the Light-Stream, a type whose origin seems primarily to have been in Persia, stands the Female Principle type of formulation, in which the mysticism of sex is fundamental. According to Plutarch[10] Osiris, the light god and the Logos, has a wife, Isis, through whom he produces Horus, the type of the projection of divine light into the lower realm. Horus would seem to be the Divine Stream as clothed in matter, the Cosmic Logos. Just what Isis typifies does not clearly appear. She is the "Female Principle in nature, the recipient of all coming into being" (τὸ τῆς φύσεως θῆλυ, καὶ δεκτικὸν ἁπάσης γενέσεως). Since she was originally a chthonic deity she would appear to be somewhat analogous to the Mother Nature of our own figurative speech. By fertilizing her Osiris could beget

7. A. Dieterich, *Eine Mithrasliturgie*, 1923, p. 12, ll. 20 ff.
8. Ἕλκε ἀπὸ τοῦ θείου ἀτενίζων εἰς σεαυτὸν τὸ πνεῦμα: ib., p. 10, ll. 23 ff.
9. Ib., 12, l. 11: ἐλεύσεται εἰς τὸν πόλου καὶ ὄψει αὐτὸν περιπατοῦντα ὡς ἐν ὁδῷ.
10. *De Iside*, 53 ff.

the world, though he first begat the World-Principle.[11] At the same time her longing for Osiris, her gathering his fragments together, is a symbol of the whole spirit of mystic ascent, the desire to find the whole of God in place of fragments, and the intense longing for union. It is apparent from the *De Iside* and from Apuleius that the mystic finds the first great step to be union with Isis in her search, and then union with Osiris, as the mystic, now identified with Isis, is gratified by partaking in Isis' own experience with Osiris.[12]

As has been suggested, the important thing about this formulation is not specifically the Isis myth but the concept of the "Female Principle of nature" and the notion of mystic ascent by a sexual mystic union with that "Principle." The idea may have originated in Isis (though in any other fertility goddess as easily), but to the mind of Apuleius the mythology of Demeter and Persephone, or of Aphrodite, of the Phrygian Magna Mater, of Athena, of the Candian Artemis, Hera, Bellona, or Hecate would do just as well. Again as with the Persian type of formulation, one feels that the mythology has been turned by the Greek mind into a typology, and has lost thereby almost all literal significance.

Both of these types of ascent, which to Plutarch were themselves interchangeable, were made into θίασοι by the Greeks after the manner of Orpheus. The temporal priority of Orphism over the mass of Hellenistic mysteries is obvious enough. It was, to be sure, antedated in Greece by the Eleusinian Mysteries, and by the more extreme and crude form of Dionysiac rites. It came forward largely as a reformed and tempered Dionysiac mystery. But more important for Hellenistic religion than the temporal priority of Orphism is Orphism's logical priority. In the Orphic-Dionysiac tradition there was apparently for the first time invented the θίασος, the "local congregation" conception, in accordance with which an Orphic or Dionysiac cultus could be set up wherever there were initiates. The mysteries of Eleusis were definitely localized. The Orphic-Dionysiac groups scattered rapidly and widely throughout the Greek-speaking world. In the classical age itself, then, the Dionysiac-Orphic movement created the θίασος. The Bacchanalian excesses, singularly inappropriate as they seem to our notion of Greek life, were very popular, and of great importance. When one considers the respect shown these rites by the dramatists and Plato, it becomes apparent that, however foreign in origin, the Greeks had made a real place for them in their

11. §53. She would appear also to be Matter, in as much as she can also be fertilized by the Bad one, Typhon; she is the field and matter for both (ἀμφοῖν οὖσα χώρα καὶ ὕλη). But her desire is always toward the Better.

12. The conception of Isis in this sense is best presented by Marguérite Techert, "La notion de la Sagesse dans les trois premiers siècles de notre ère," *Archiv für Geschichte der Philosophie und Soziologie*, XXXIX (1930), pp. 9 ff. Her whole sketch of the conception through the period is very illuminating. Pascher's chapter "Königin Isis" is likewise valuable (*Königsweg*, pp. 60 ff.).

life. An institution which could so affect Greek life as to produce its whole
great tradition of tragedy is obviously not to be regarded as anything but an
integral part of Classic Greece. Here, in a wild way, to be sure, Greeks
learned first to look for an immediate experience of God which would be a
sharing in the divine immortal nature, and so be a foretaste of life after
death. The myth stressed also the notion that the universe was to be explained in terms of a Supreme Deity who has sexual relations with a "Female Principle," Demeter, a chthonic deity, and so produces the Savior God
Dionysus.

Orphism sought to get the same results as the Bacchanalia by a more tempered cultus and a more philosophical mythology. The θίασος, the notion of
the possible share of man in divine nature by cult acts, and the conception
of the cosmic significance of the Savior God as the son of the supreme deity
by the "Female Principle," were kept. But Orphism went on to a more definitely dualistic formulation of the nature of man than appears in our records of the Dionysiac rites in their unreformed state. There seems first to
have arisen here the conception of the uncleanness of matter, and hence of
the necessity for regeneration in the sense of purification. The Orphics seem
to have given the Greeks a "sense of sin" in the later meaning of that phrase,
as well as a way of escape from the cloying contamination of the "wheel."
Its white-clad initiates were free from the burden of the flesh, and were only
awaiting the final deliverance.

Now it must be noticed that in the Classic Age the Greeks had developed
a tremendous sense that unaided humanity is helpless without some sort of
superhuman intervention. Man is sinful by his very nature, and only as he
can get out of that nature into the divine nature can he hope really to live,
since life in the body is death. A divine savior is at hand to give him this life,
the Son of the supreme God and "the Female Principle," and into the very
being of the savior the mystic can rise. The means thereto are at hand, the
sacraments offered in the widely scattered θίασοι. But it is just as important
to notice that strong as was the conviction of the truth of this theory of man,
powerful as were the attractions of the rites, in Classic Greece herself there
were, as represented by the Bacchic and Orphic θίασοι, two mythologies, different though similar, two sets of sacraments. If Plato could treat each with
respect, the less critical "average man" would have done so. What does this
mean for the attitude of the Greek? It can only mean that the theory of man
and of his need for salvation, of salvation as release from matter and union
with divine nature, of the possibility of attaining that salvation through ceremonies, was widely accepted, but that the mythology itself was rather suggestive than definitive. Orphism and the Bacchic θίασοι were not rival
"churches," denouncing each other, and asserting each its own exclusive
truth. Probably a large majority of the Greeks who were initiated into one

were also in the other, and, if their place of residence permitted, into the Eleusinian Mysteries also. The appeal of the Greek mystery was the appeal of a philosophy of life and of a promise through rites to gain an emotional realization of the objective of that philosophy, and not the appeal of a specific mythology.

Indeed the indifference to specific mythological formulations is seen within Orphism itself. This is not the place to treat Orphism as such *in extenso*. But it will be well to point out at least its treatment of the "Female Principle" in nature, a phenomenon which will in itself show conclusively that mythology was a very elastic and typological affair within the Orphic cult group.

We look within the Orphic Hymns for the best revelation of the conceptions lying behind the cult, at least in the Hellenistic Age. Modern scholarship has seriously questioned the relation of this literature to the cult. Traces of Orphic cults in the Hellenistic and Roman times have been disappointingly meager in archaeological remains, especially at Rome, and the hypothesis has been forcibly advanced that the Hymns and the *Argonautica* represent a literary Orphism that existed as a movement of mystic philosophy independent of an actual cult.[18] To this it must first be protested that our knowledge of Hellenistic life, particularly in such centers as Alexandria, is from the archaeological point of view so inadequate as to make an argument *ex silentio* very dangerous. On the other hand absence of Orphic remains at Rome proves little for the East, since Orphism was a type of solution of life's problems which had little appeal to the Roman mind. It has always been a Greek, or Eastern, thing. Even today the difference between the type of piety traditionally Eastern and the piety represented in the Western church is that the Roman tradition so largely lacks the Orphic sense of "contamination," as contrasted with "guilt." Absence of Roman remains of Orphism, then, proves nothing about the possibility of a real cult background for the Greek Orphic literature of the Hellenistic Age. Still the possibility remains that the Orphic Hymns had little real cult association. Granted this, though it is unproved and dubious, it is still true that the type of thought expressed in those Hymns was a continuous and forceful thing. They certainly do not represent the point of view of primitive Orphism. How much they represent the point of view of the Orphism so acceptable to Pythagoreans and Plato is something we cannot say. But they tell their own story for their own age, which is all we need for our purpose, the story of a definite, powerful, and persistent mystic convention of thought.

Here it is that the "Female Principle" is receiving highly important development. Rhea, daughter of Protogonus, wife of Cronos, and mother of Zeus, is mother of Gods and men, and of the earth, heaven, sea, and winds. She is

13. André Boulanger, *Orphée* (Paris, 1925), pp. 53–67.

addressed as the First Author (ἀρχιγένεθλε), Savior (σώτειρα), and saves by her high minded purposes (σωτήριος εὔφρονι βουλῇ).[14] In another Hymn[15] the "Mother of the Gods" is addressed in exactly the same terms, called the spouse (συνόμευνος) of Cronos, but called also the Phrygian Savior (Φρυγίης σώτειρα), that is the Phrygian Magna Mater. Demeter is the All-Mother (παμμήτειρα),[16] which in the next Hymn, also to Demeter, is explained as meaning "Mother of immortal gods and mortal men."[17] In these two Hymns she is of course the goddess who gives the fruits of the earth, but she is also the sharer of Dionysus' hearth, his follower. She is the proclaimer of the "holy marriage of chthonic Zeus." To her is applied the portentous word μουνογενής, "unique of kind," and her coming brings to men the mystic peace and εὐνομία. She is the many-named. It is obviously the same goddess who is addressed as Goddess Earth (Γαῖα θεά), "Mother of the Blessed Ones and mortal men," though in this case without any reference to the specific story of Demeter.[18] Semele, the unfortunate mother of Dionysus, is also the "Universal Queen" (παμβασίλεια).[19] Hippa, the nurse of Dionysus, is identified with the Magna Mater of Phrygia and Lydia, but when she is called "the chthonic mother, Queen" it is obvious that the association may also be with Demeter.[20] Aphrodite is in turn the one who has given birth to all things in heaven, earth, and sea. She is mother of necessity, the throne mate of Dionysus, and the θεὰ βασίλεια recognized in Syria and Egypt, that is she is the Syrian Dea and Isis.[21] Persephone is also μουνογενής, at once a virgin goddess and the mother of Dionysus (called here Eubouleus) and of the Eumenides, and is obviously like Demeter in being the source of earthly fruit.[22]

So far, it is evident, there is a common notion applied to all this list of goddesses. However different they were in details, each is the Great Mother, the Female Principle, the universal Queen. Some, like Persephone, appear to represent only aspects of the activity of the Female Principle. But to most of them the total functions of that Principle are indifferently ascribed, while mythologies foreign to Orphism are freely borrowed, not for their parallelism to Greek mythology, but on the basis of their adaptability to illuminate the significance of the Female Principle.

With this Female Principle goes the notion of bisexuality of the female with power to impregnate. The Hymn to Misa, whoever she was, hails her as male and female (ἄρσην καὶ θῆλυς), double natured (διφυής); so she is identical with Dionysus (Iacchus), and has the seminal power of Dionysus as Eubouleus. But she is also identified with Demeter of Eleusis, with the

Magna Mater of Phrygia, with Aphrodite (Cytheria), and with Isis.[23] Here
the Female Principle has indeed swallowed up all mystic mythology, which
has been dissolved in a conception of Deity that combines the notion of the
universal genetrix with the power of impregnation. It is highly likely that
this power of impregnation would be applied to the mystic impregnation of
the initiate. It is notable for what is to come that this deity is also the θεσμοφόρος, the source of legislation. The male-female is also Pallas Athene, who
is likewise μουνογενής, a virgin, and φρόνησις.[24] The Hymn to Nature expresses the same notion in making Nature "her own Father, Fatherless," and
"universal Mother," the "Father and Mother of all." Nature is all-gleaming
(παναυγές). She is self-sufficient, is Dike, is the "Universal Queen" and all
wise (πάνσοφος). She is eternal Life (ἀίδιος ζωή) and deathless Providence.[25] Dionysus is hailed as Adonis, male and female (κούρη καὶ κόρε).[26]
Within this composite conception was also included the notion that it was
the Fire or Light-Stream. It is with reference to the Light-Stream that I interpret the almost constant allusion to these god-goddesses as the "torch-
bearer," and the fact that Dionysus is specifically born in fire (πυρόσπορος),
is the fire breather (πυρίπνοος) and fire blazer (πυριφεγγής).[27]

In the Hellenistic period, then, the Greeks would have been amazed at the
suggestion that in adopting new mythologies, and new rites, they were any
less Greek than before. A Hellenistic Greek was interested in the religions
of Egypt and the East only in so far as they offered new myths with fundamentally the old significance, and rites that could be adapted to use in a
Greek θίασος. The life that had flowed into him in the streaming cup of
Dionysus might now, under new influences, become the Light-Stream as
represented in the mythology of Isis or Mithra. The Mithraic pleroma might
also appear. But I do not think we shall understand the Greek of the Hellenistic or Roman period if we take any of the mythologies as meaning much
to him in their literal form. None of them was ever made into a creed, and
for none of them was it ever dreamed of asserting an exclusive claim to the
truth.

These were the great types of formulation. There were, as said, the Female
Principle or bisexual type of formulation, and the Oriental pleroma, but

---

23. Hymn XLII.   24. Hymn XXXII.
25. Hymn X.   26. Hymn LVI.
27. Hymn LII. How elaborately later thinking connected this mythology of the hymns with
the Pleroma of the Light-Stream is still most conveniently to be appreciated from Thomas
Taylor, *The Mystical Hymns of Orpheus* (reprinted 1896), a translation, with copious notes
from the very late Platonists. Taylor was quite uncritical, accepted Proclus' thesis that the later
explanations of his school represented the original meaning of the hymns. Yet one is tantalized
by the feeling that such a use of this material as Proclus represents by no means began as late
as the Neo-Platonists. Such thinking as that represented by Plutarch for Isis may well have
been going on before Philo for Orphism, and have been laying the ground for Proclus and his
school. But such a notion cannot, so far as I know, be documented.

both of these had significance only as they threw figurative light upon the
Bacchic-Orphic objective, escape from the toils of the body into immaterial
immortal life. And to a man like Plutarch, they were interchangeable ty-
pologies for the same reality.

This seems to be the mystic background of Philo and his group. In his
thinking about God, as it has been pointed out by Pascher and others, there
are remarkable similarities to Isis and to the Amesha Spentas of Persia,
though Pascher has overlooked the fact that the Philonic Sophia is much
more like the Orphic compound Female Principle than anything specifically
Isiac. But what Philonic Judaism is trying to do is not to find a Jewish Isis
or Demeter, or a Jewish series of Amesha Spentas, it is trying to find within
Judaism a symbolic basis by which it can express and achieve the Greek
mystic goal.

The Greek mystic goal was, it is being argued, a concept inherently independent of its mythological formulations. Fortunately we possess a statement of the concept itself apart from mythological formulation in a fragment from a Neo-Pythagorean writer, Onatas, of whom we know only that
this one fragment bears his name.[28] It is important for our purpose as an
expression of the mystic philosophy that lies behind all the assimilations of
the mythologies, and is for us particularly illuminating because of its basic
similarity to the objective of Philo. There is no need of apology for quoting
in extenso the little read material:

God has knowledge of the affairs of other living beings, . . . unless He is so to
a very restricted number of men.[29] And His Powers (δυνάμιες) are Truth.[30]
These of which He is the herdsman, are manifest and knowable.[31] For God is
Himself mind (νόος) and soul (ψυχά) and the director (τὸ ἀγεμονικόν) of the
whole universe. But His Powers (δυνάμιες) are Truth, and the things of which
they are the herdsmen are the works and the deeds, and the movements that occur
in the whole universe. So God is Himself neither visible nor perceptible, but
rather is to be contemplated (θεωρατός) only by reason (λόγος) and mind
(νόος). But His works and deeds are clearly perceptible to all men. Yet it seems
to me that God is not a unit, although the Greatest and Most Exalted, the Ruler
of all, is One. But the many other [gods] are distinguished with reference to their
function (κατὰ δύναμιν), and over them all He rules who is preëminent in
power, greatness, and virtue. This latter would be the God who embraces the
whole universe, but the other gods who run in the heaven along with the universal revolution are, reasonably (κατὰ λόγον), servants of the First and Conceptual

28. The fragment is found in Stobaeus, I, i, 39 (Wachs. I, p. 48).
29. The text of the first lines of this fragment is very corrupt, and frequently meaningless
In the first sentence the original meaning was probably that God, while unknowable, know
all things: He was perceived by only a very few men.
30. ἀλήθεια here and a few lines below seems corrupt. Perhaps read αἰσθηταί with Meineke
31. Reading ἐντὶ for εἰ.

Those who say that there is one God and not many are in error. For they do not grasp the supreme quality of the divine preëminence. So I mean that they have not understood that the Supreme Principle rules and directs beings similar to Himself, and is more powerful and exalted than the others. The other gods have such a relation to the First and Conceptual God as members of a chorus to the leader, as soldiers to the general, or as comrades in arms within a single troop to the troop leader and captain, for it is their nature to follow after the man who is leading them well. So their function is alike to rule and to be ruled, but those things that are ruled could not be appointed to their tasks if they were deprived of their leader, just as members of a chorus could not be set to singing together, or soldiers to military exploit, if they were deprived of their captain or chorus leader.

Such a nature [as that of the Supreme Leader] has need of nothing whether akin or extraneous to Himself. Accordingly He is not composed out of two things, soul and body (for He is entirely soul), nor out of any contraries (for contraries are wont by nature both to rule and to be ruled). The mixture with the body sullies the purity of the soul, for the soul is unpolluted and divine, but the body is mortal and mixed with mud. In the same way lead sullies gold, and anything spurious sullies what is naturally genuine. In general God gave the body to mortal beings as a result of an eternal and ineluctable necessity. For whatever shares in generation is by nature destitute and impoverished.

God is therefore, as I said at the outset of this discourse, Himself Origin (ἀρχά) and the First. The cosmos and the things that move in every way in it are divine (θεῖος). Similarly the soul is a spirit (δαίμων) for it rules and puts in motion the whole being), while the body, and all its parts, is spiritual. So one must distinguish between God and the divine, spirit and the spiritual.

The ideas here suggested must be clearly vizualized. The word θεός, the author protests, is not to be reserved to the Supreme God. But actually the Supreme God is utterly beyond the lower gods. They have no power to carry out their functions, which are obviously to control the various phenomena of the universe, apart from the supreme and single Leadership. We have little from the fragment as to the exact nature of these lower deities, except that they are "like" the Supreme God. But that is not illuminating, for it is His nature to be unmixed with everything that would sully His character as the pure leader, while they are both rulers and ruled. He is pure soul and mind. The lower gods would seem naturally to be the Powers of the first lines of the fragment, though the text is here too corrupt for the identification to be certain. But the general picture is clear. There is the One God, unmixed, pure, aloof, inaccessible to men except by reason and mind. Beneath Him, subject to His power, are the gods His agents, probably His Powers. Their accessibility is not discussed. They are the shepherds of the works of God in nature, and by means of these works God is first to be apprehended—indeed the mass of men can get no higher. As a result of the

fact that the phenomena of the universe are the works of God, God is represented in the universe, and so even the physical universe can be called "divine." It is a very short step to seeing the whole reach of divinity, which
Onatas insists must not be restricted to the Supreme Being, as a series of
emanations, so that the activity of God within the universe, even secondarily
through His servants, the Powers or lower gods, makes the universe partake
of the divine nature.

Man is a hybrid of soul and body. The body is obviously helpless. By the
soul man can ascend first to knowledge of God as revealed in His works,
and then to a reasoned apprehension of even the Supreme God.

This is exactly the sort of ascent, the philosophical kernel, around which
the mysteries all appear oriented. It is also the kernel to make which vivid
Philo elaborates his own typology. What we must bear in mind in considering Philo's typology is the fact that the objective is to furnish Jews with a
typology for this philosophic mysticism rather than with a direct parallel to
any mystic mythology as such. How Philonic Judaism does this can best be
understood from the details.

The Stream from God Philo accepts without question, and gives varying
formulations. First is that which centered in the "Female Principle." Philo
would not have had far to look, if he had himself made the search *de novo,*
for the Jewish counterpart of this conception. It was right at hand in the Jewish Wisdom who had in Greek become Sophia. It is interesting to see how
variously this figure is developed. One representation is: God the Father produces Sophia. Sophia flows out in a river that is "generic virtue" (ἡ γενικὴ
ἀρετή, ἀγαθότης). This river divides into four streams, the four cardinal
virtues of intelligence, control, courage, and justice.[32] Or again Sophia, while
the daughter of God, is both male and female, and so has the masculine
power of scattering the seeds of intelligence and noble conduct, of begetting
these, in human souls.[33] If God is the Father of the Universe, Sophia is the
Mother;[34] God is the husband of Sophia,[35] the source of Sophia.[36] God and
Sophia are mutually sources to each other of "delight" (ἐντρύφημα).[37] The
relations of Sophia to the Logos are highly complex. Philo speaks of the
Highest Divine Logos who is the source of Sophia,[38] and, two pages later, of
the Sophia as the mother of the Divine Logos.[39] The Logos flows from
Sophia like a river,[40] the same river of Eden that has just appeared as "generic Virtue." The contrast might seem here to be, as Pascher takes it, a contrast between the "Highest Logos," the source of Sophia, and a lower Logos
derivative from her. Into this point we must go later, and will find that

32. *LA,* i, 43, 64, 65.
34. Ib., 109; *LA,* ii, 49; *Det.* 54.
36. *Sac.,* 64.
38. *Fug.,* 97.
40. *Som.,* ii, 242, 245.

33. *Fug.,* 52.
35. *Cher.,* 49.
37. *Som.,* ii, 242.
39. Ib., 108 f.

there is in Philo no real doctrine of a lower Cosmic Logos such as Pascher distinguishes. The figure of the two Logoi, if used at all, is only a slight variant, of no fixed importance in Philo's thinking.[41] For Philo flatly identifies the Logos with Sophia, indeed does so in connection with Sophia as the river of Eden.[42] That is, the Logos can be represented as derived from Sophia, or Sophia as a derivative from the Logos, or the two can be made completely identical. The relationship can be expressed in any form that is immediately convenient. What then does the Sophia mythology mean? In itself and literally, nothing. It is brought in only because Philo and his group want the type of experience which his neighbors are getting through the bisexual "Female Principle of nature." The Stream is evidently the important thing, the fact that there flows from God the effluence of His power and nature, and that in that Stream men may hope to find God. How elaborately Sophia is used in allegorizing the stories of the Patriarchs will appear below. Their experiences with their wives are the Mystic Marriage of man with the divine force and life. But not any specific mythology of Sophia is it worth Philo's while to make consistent.

Important as is the female sexual figure for the Light-Stream in Philo, the formulation in terms of a pleroma is still more important.

It is difficult for us who are not Jews, or for modern Jews, to imagine how intense must have been the emotional associations of the Jews of antiquity with the secret Ark of the Covenant. Hidden away from all men but the high-priest, and approachable even by him but once a year when he must be half blinded by incense, Philo tells us, the ark was the very heart of all that was sacred in the Jewish religion. It had been lost for centuries, but the chamber in the temple which was to have been sanctified by its presence was still as sacred in its memory. It was the abode, the presence, of God in a sense completely unique. Philo speaks of it as though it were still there. If Jews were looking for a symbol of the nature of deity, where more fittingly could they look than to the ark? It is not at all surprising that the figures for the mystic deity should appear from Philo to be here most importantly expressed. The schematization he presents had to express the number seven, because of the Pythagorean foundation of his thought, and by analogy with the Persian conceptions we have been discussing. Philo found the seven parts of the ark to be respectively the box, the law within the box, the mercy seat, the two cherubim, the voice that spoke to Moses from the ark, and the Presence or the One who spoke. Reversing the order of these Philo describes each part as a symbol. The Presence, the One who Spoke, is the highest God, τὸ ὄν. From Him radiate all the lower manifestations. First is the Logos τοῦ ὄντος, corresponding to the voice heard by Moses. From the Logos the

<hr />

41. See below, pp. 101 ff.   42. *LA*, i, 65.

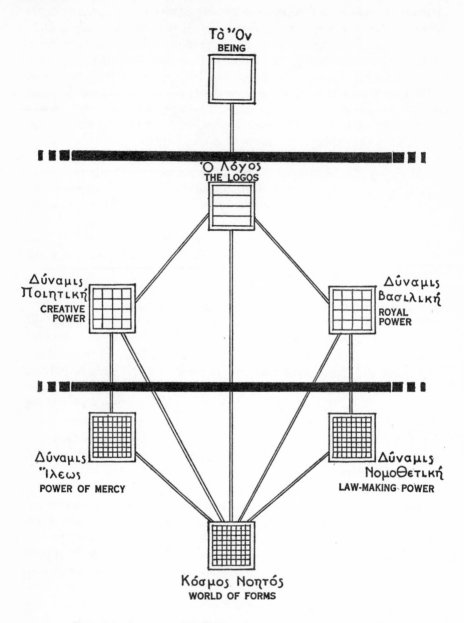

Τò "Ον
BEING

Ὁ Λóγος
THE LOGOS

Δύναμις Ποιητική
CREATIVE POWER

Δύναμις Βασιλική
ROYAL POWER

Δύναμις "Ιλεως
POWER OF MERCY

Δύναμις Νομοθετική
LAW-MAKING POWER

Κóσμος Νοητóς
WORLD OF FORMS

PLATE I. GOD AND HIS POWERS AS REPRESENTED BY THE
ARK OF THE COVENANT

Stream goes on out in two branches, the two cherubim, who are called the Creative Power (δύναμις ποιητική), and the Royal or Ruling Power (δύναμις βασιλική). Each of these is now in turn the source of a further emanation. The Creative Power sends forth the Merciful Power or Benevolence (δύναμις ἵλεως), the Mercy Seat, and the Royal Power sends forth the Legislative Power (δύναμις νομοθετική), the Law within the box, which is also the punishing Power. The seventh and last member of this pleroma, the one typified by the box of the ark, is the Conceptual World (κόσμος νοητός), the Platonic world of forms.

Philo's most important passage describing this schematization of God and the Stream should be quoted. He has explained the significance of the two cherubim as representing the Creative and Ruling Powers of God, with the second definitely inferior to the first. So the Creative Power is equivalent also to the word θεός, the Ruling Power to κύριος, in the common Old Testament reference to God as "Lord God."[43] The cherubim are said to be of beaten gold to express by the gold the fact that they are of the highest being (οὐσία), the pure and unmixed, that is that their οὐσία is divine; the craftsmanship illustrates that they are form, the forms of forms, and so of a conceptual nature (ἐπιστημονικὴ φύσις).[44] These serve in the universe as the guards at its limits (ὅροι). The Creative Power is not only the Creative principle but the guardian of the world against destruction; the Royal Power puts into it the great Law, that of Equality, by which the cosmic peace is preserved since everything is kept within its proper limitations.[45] They are provided with wings because all the Powers of God "desire and struggle for the Road up to the Father"; and their wings overshadow the parts below to indicate the guardianship of these Powers over all that is beneath them.[46]

The next section explains why the faces of the cherubim are turned toward each other, and together toward the Mercy Seat. These words of Scripture, says Philo,

are an extremely beautiful and divine similitude. For it is necessary that the Powers, the Creative and Royal, should look toward each other in contemplation of each other's beauty, and at the same time in conspiracy for the benefit of things that have come into existence. In the second place, since God, who is One, is both the Creator and King, naturally the Powers, though divided, are again united. For it was advantageous that they be divided in order that the one might function as creator, the other as ruler. For the functions differ. And the Powers were brought together in another way by the eternal juxtaposition of the names [i.e., κύριος and θεός] ·in order that the Creative Power might share in the Royal, and the Royal in the Creative. Both incline fittingly toward the Mercy Seat. For if God had not been merciful to the things which now exist, nothing

43. QE, ii, 62; Harris, Fragments, pp. 63 f.   44. Ib., 63.
45. Ib., 64.   46. Ib., 65; Harris, Fragments, p. 65.

would have been created through the Creative Power nor be given legal regimentation by the Royal Power.[47]

Two things are at once becoming clear from the material thus far described, first the definiteness of Philo's schematization, and second the fact that these Powers have not distinct existence, but are only aspects of the single nature and activity of God. They are conventionalizations of the Stream, but only conventionalizations. The Power of God is being visualized in its richness by discussing it in terms of Powers, but the Powers share each other's nature, and though seemingly divided partake in ἕνωσις together. They are functional distinctions of the single Power of God, not existential distinctions.

The next section discusses the meaning of the statement of God to Moses "I shall become known to thee from there."[48]

The purest and most prophetic mind receives knowledge and understanding of God (τὸ ὄν) not from τὸ ὄν Himself, for the mind is not great enough to compass His magnitude, but from His primary and guardian (δορυφόροι) Powers. One must be content with the fact that beams (τὰς αὐγάς) are borne from these into the soul, so that one may be able to perceive the Elder and Brighter by means of the secondary illumination (φέγγος).[49]

The solar character of the figure is at once indubitable, and the object of the whole schematization apparent. A ladder, each rung of which represents brighter illumination, is being constructed, with a mystic-metaphysical rather than cosmic-mythological objective.

Philo now goes on to give the whole scheme. In explaining the words, "I will speak to thee from above the Mercy Seat between the cherubim" Philo says:

Herewith it appears first that above the Power of Mercy, the Creative Power, and every Power, is the Divine Principle; and second that He speaks from between the Creative and Royal Powers. The mind understands this as follows: the Logos of God, which is a Mean,[50] leaves no void in nature, but fills all things and acts as a mediator, and arbitrates between the things that seem in opposition to each other, thus creating love and unanimity. For the Logos is always the cause and creator of fellowship (κοινωνία). The parts of the ark are severally mentioned. We must go over these individually, beginning at the top, if we would understand what they symbolize, for they are symbolic. There is the box of the ark, and the laws treasured within it, and upon it the Mercy Seat; upon the Mercy Seat are the Cherubim, so called in Chaldean, and above and between is the Voice, the Logos, and still above this the One who speaks. Now if any one

47. QE, ii, 66. 48. Exod. xxv, 22.
49. QE, ii, 67; Harris, Fragments, p. 66.
50. This concept echoes the λόγος τομεύς theory which I have discussed in my "Neo-Pythagorean Source," pp. 145 ff.

could accurately grasp the natures of these, it seems to me that possessed by the
most divinely formed beauties he would be able to renounce all other things
which are sought after. But let us see what each of these is. The first is the Being
more primal than the One, the Monad, and the Beginning (ἀρχή). Second is the
Logos of τὸ ὄν, the Essence germinative of things that exist (ἡ σπερματικὴ τῶν
ὄντων οὐσία). From the Divine Logos, as from a source, the two Powers divide
themselves off. The one is the Creative Power, with reference to which the Creator (ὁ τεχνίτης) founded and ordered all things, and this Power is called θεός.
The other is the Royal Power, with reference to which the Creator (ὁ δημιουρ-
γός) rules over the things that have come into being, and this Power is called
Lord (κύριος). From these two Powers others grow out. For the Power of
Mercy, whose name is Benefactor (εὐεργέτις), stems off from the Creative
Power, and the Legal Power, whose proper name is Punisher, stems off from the
Royal Power. Below and around these is the box of the ark, the symbol of the
Conceptual World. The ark has in symbol all things located within the holy of
holies: the immaterial world; the laws which [Moses] has called the testimonies,
that is the Law-making and Punishing Power; the Mercy seat, the Power of
Mercy and the Benefactor; above them the Creative Power, guarantor of Mercy
and Benefaction; the Royal Power, which is the root of the Punishing and Law-
making Power. And there appears the Mean, the divine Logos, and above the
Logos the One who speaks. The aforesaid total seven in number, comprising the
Conceptual World, two kindred Powers, the Punisher and Benefactor, their two
antecedents, the Creative and Royal Powers, which have their kinship rather
with the Creator than with what has come into being; sixth is the Logos, and
seventh the One who speaks. If you want them downwards you will find the One
who speaks first, the Logos second, third the Creative Power, fourth the Rulership (ἀρχή), then beneath the Creative Power, the fifth one, the Benefactor; and
beneath the Royal Power the sixth the Punisher, and seventh the world made up
of the Forms.[51]

The descending emanations are made repetitiously specific. All of this is
the descending Light-Stream of God. Hidden within the holy of holies the
Jews have the true symbol of God's nature. We must bear in mind that Philo
has definitely warned us against conceiving of these as anything but aspects
of God's unity. Yet for his purpose the stages are as set as the Amesha Spentas with which they have often been compared. And his purpose has also
been made clear: they are rather grades, stages, of mystic ascent, than metaphysical realities. We mortals must be content that beams are borne into the
human mind from the secondary existences, the Powers, in the hope that
higher Existence may become apparent by means of the secondary illumination, since the human mind cannot bear the Stream as it comes directly from
τὸ ὄν. We should expect that the mystic ascent would be by successive advances from stage to stage. It must also be noticed that Philo has hinted at a

51. QE, ii, 68; Harris, *Fragments*, pp. 66–68.

distinction between the Creative and Royal Powers, the Logos, and τὸ ὄν, on the one hand, and the three lowest Powers on the other. Beginning with the Creative and Royal Powers the kinship, συγγένεια, is with the Creator, not with the Created Realm. It would seem natural to conclude that the three lowest Powers, conversely, have a kinship with the Created Realm, a conclusion which will soon appear justified. The last Power, the Conceptual Realm, is not in this passage distinctly related with the ones above it. In the diagram I have connected it with all the Powers because of the following passage:

God, who is One, has around Him unspeakably great Powers, which all are helpers and saviors of the Created Realm, and among them are included the Punishing Powers. . . . By the instrumentality of these Powers the Immaterial and Conceptual World was framed.[52]

That is, the Conceptual World would seem not to stem from a particular Power above it, but from all together. Philo tells us also that the Law is put within the box of the ark to show that the κόσμος νοητός is permeated in all its parts by Law.[53]

The explanation of the symbolism of the ark which we have been following, while it is perhaps the most striking one, is by no means Philo's only passage of the kind, nor the only description of Deity as a Being revealed primarily in the Logos and the Powers. In De Vita Mosis, ii, 95 ff., the same symbolism is more briefly explained, but with no mention of the symbolism of the ark itself or of the relation of Law and Mercy to the higher Powers, and with no Logos as the direct source of the two higher Powers. God and His two Powers are the simpler representation of Deity.[54] All seven members of the Pleroma appear in De Fuga, 100 ff., but with no suggestion that the box of the ark is the κόσμος νοητός. In its place the Legislative Power is divided into two, the Negative and Positive Commands, so that the seven are the Negative and Positive Commands, and the Mercy Seat or Mercy as the lower group; and above them the two higher Powers, then the Logos, and finally God. Here the whole series up to and including the two primary Powers are in the visible realm, while the Logos, as "image of God," is invisible and has no share in the realm of things perceptible by the senses. The Logos is the Charioteer of the universe, but with him rides the One who directs the Charioteer, ὁ μόνος, ὅ ἐστιν ἀψευδῶς. One must not jump to the conclusion that Philo thought all the lower members of the series as in any sense perceptible by physical sensation, for the Logos is here the "oldest" of the νοητά, which would imply that there are lesser, or "younger," νοητά, apparently some at least of the lower emanations. Actually, from the discus-

52. Conf., 171 f.
53. QE, ii, 59.
54. See also Spec., i, 307.

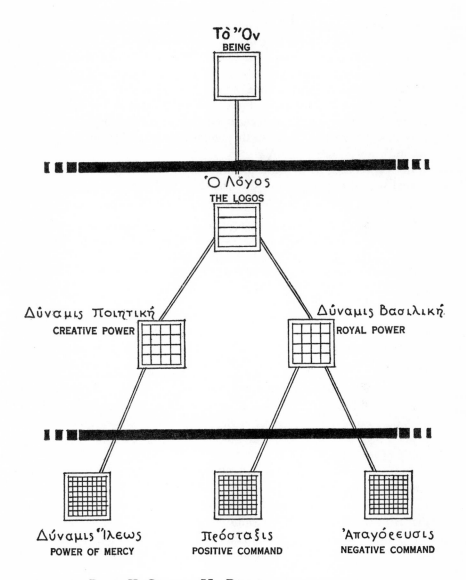

PLATE II. God and His Powers as represented by
the Cities of Refuge

sion immediately following, the line would seem to be drawn between the higher and the lower Powers, as was suggested in the first passage considered.[55]

The passage in *De Fuga* on the symbolism of the ark is a slight digression within a large and highly important discussion of the six cities of refuge, which are taken as symbols of the six emanations below τὸ ὄν, those aspects of Deity to which man may hope to rise. Philo immediately after the digression on the ark returns to these cities and says that three are placed on the hither, three on the further side of Jordan so as to symbolize the fact that the three lower Powers, that is the Negative Commands, the Positive Commands, and Mercy, are contingent upon man, ἐφαπτόμεναι τοῦ τῶν ἀνθρώπων ἐπικήρου γένους, while the three higher members belong to the celestial realm.[56]

In *Cherubim, 27* ff., the same picture of Deity and the Powers appears connected with the symbolism of the Cherubim at Eden. Philo gives other interpretations, but in ecstasy he has learned the following:

The voice told me that while God is indeed one, His highest and chiefest Powers are two, even Goodness and Sovereignty. Through His Goodness He begat all that is, through His Sovereignty He rules what He has begotten. And in the midst between the two there is a third which unites them, Logos, for it is through Logos that God is both ruler and good. Of these two potencies, Sovereignty and Goodness, the Cherubim are symbols, as the fiery sword is the symbol of reason. For exceeding swift and of burning heat is Logos and chiefly so the Logos of the (Great) Cause, for it alone preceded and outran all things, conceived before them all, manifest above them all.[57]

Philo goes on to urge his soul to mystic apprehension of these Powers. When fully apprehended the Powers will, he says, all blend and be seen to be mutually interchangeable, since all are but aspects of the single God. The secondary Powers do not appear at all. The picture is one of God as revealed in the Logos and the two higher Powers, and to go to them is to leave the world of mortality.[58]

Another symbol of the Logos and the Powers Philo finds in the three "men" who appeared to Abraham.[59] Abraham's "lifting up his eyes" is the lifting of the eye of the mind in the vision of a prophet.[60] The three men that Abraham saw typified to Philo the seminal masculine nature of Being rather than the receptive female nature of matter.[61] The one in the middle of the three is called Being (obviously τὸ ὄν), not as a name, for he has no

---

55. The cherubim of the ark appear with the same symbolism as the Powers, divided and united by God Himself, in *Heres, 166.*

56. *Fug.,* 103 ff.

57. Colson and Whitaker's translation.

58. *Cher.,* 31.

59. *Gen.,* xviii, 2.

60. *Deo,* 2.

61. Ib., 3.

name, but to describe his type of existence. The men on either side are symbols respectively of the Creative Power, θεός, and the Royal Power, Lord.[62] This Philo goes on to compare with the symbolism of the cherubim of the ark, the one above them who speaks from the middle, and the Logos that is spoken.[63] He then compares the objects of Abraham's vision to the seraphim of Is., vi. 1 ff. The seraphim, two in number according to the Greek text, and called cherubim by Philo, had each six wings, and, according to Philo, were made of fire, not the consuming destructive fire, but the constructive type of fire by which unformed matter is given form.[64] This fire penetrates all the unformed matter and by its operation separates out the elements.[65] The six wings are themselves interpreted in cosmic significance, for the two lower are the two lower elements, earth and water; the two wings that cover the face are the two elements that are higher, air and fire (heaven). These lower and higher sets of wings, like the lower and higher elements, the Physicist Commentators explain as being in opposition to each other, while the wings that fly are the reconciling principles between them in that they bring the contraries together in the *dux princeps*.[66] So the vision of Abraham was very magnificent, Philo concludes, for he saw the Creator suspending the four elements from Himself, and drawing them up to Himself as though with Body Guards. The Body Guards are His Powers guarding the safety and preservation of His most perfect creation. And God "sends His own form and that of His Powers to us to aid us against the miseries and evils which are the concomitants of every mortal nature."[67]

The Physicist Commentators to whom Philo here refers, and who seem to have been quite specifically scientific in their interests, appear frequently in Philo. Their explanation of the seraphim, who are to Philo identical with cherubim, seems thrust into his general train of thought, but Philo wanted to include it, because though his own interest was primarily in the mystical side by which the vision of God and the Powers meant salvation from material ills and participation in the divine nature, still he was in sympathy with what the Physicist Commentators were trying to do, that is to get science as well as saving doctrine from the Torah. But it is to the saving mystery that he returns. The fiery Power emanations from God account for the formation of the material world,[68] to be sure, but Philo's chief concern is with

62. Ib., 4. 63. Ib., 5.
64. Ib., 6, 7. 65. Ib., 8.
66. Ib., 9, 10.
67. Ib., 12: "Formam suam suarumque virtutum misit ad nos in auxilium adversus dolores et mala, quae prae se fert quicumque mortalis est naturae."
68. Cf. *Opif.*, 23. Here the passive element in creation was too feeble to receive the full effect of God's δυνάμεις; they had to be apportioned according to the ability of matter to receive them. See also *Conf.*, 134–139. In expounding the Neo-Pythagorean theory of creation by bisection Philo hints at identifying the Powers with the λόγος τομεύς, *Heres*, 312.

them as means of escape from material bondage and defect to the pure existence of the immaterial realm, to God. Of that more later.

To be sure the δυνάμεις of God do not always appear to be just these two. One remarkable passage in *De Specialibus Legibus*[69] represents the δόξα of God as the Powers, in themselves apprehensible only by the purest intellect (ἀκραιφνέστατος νοῦς), yet of a sort to represent themeslves in the material world in images or likenesses as they give form and quality to unformed matter. That is they are the "forms" of the Platonic-Pythagorean type, especially of the type of the "limit" which Plato took from the Pythagoreans to be the foundation of his *Philebus*. The forms are "called ἰδέαι because they give individual character[70] to each thing that exists, ordering the disordered, giving limit to τὰ ἄπειρα, definition to τὰ ἀόριστα, shape to ἀσχημάτιστα, and in general attuning together the worse to make it into the better." These Powers cannot be apprehended by material sight, yet Moses burned to go on to apprehend them. The passage is in no sense a contradiction of the scheme typified in the ark, for there the κόσμος νοητός, while only the lowest stage, was still collectively the Powers here discussed.[71]

It is apparently from this point of view that Philo can frequently speak in general of the δυνάμεις of God as being of a great number. In *Quod Deus sit Immutabilis,* 77–81 he describes the Powers of God as pure in relation to God, but mixed in their manifestation to men. For the light streaming from God is too brilliant for us to endure, so the Powers are revealed (apparently in material form) as tempered for our gaze. The Powers he has in mind here are the ἐπιστήμη θεοῦ, σοφία, φρόνησις, δικαιοσύνη, καὶ τῶν ἄλλων ἑκάστης ἀρετῶν, definitely the forms of the virtues.[72] In the *Legatio ad Gaium,* 4–7, Philo speaks of God as incomprehensible in Himself, and to be approached only through His δυνάμεις, which are first the Creative and the Royal, but afterwards those by which He foresees the future and numerous other beneficent, chastising, and corrective Powers.[73]

Such departures from Philo's more usual speech should not deflect attention from the fact that there is hardly a single treatise of Philo in which there

69. i, 45 ff.

70. The manuscript authority seems about equally divided between ἰδιοποιοῦσι and εἰδοποιοῦσι. Against Cohn I prefer the former.

71. The same may be said of *Conf.*, 171 f.

72. The two δυνάμεις in the more special sense appear below in the same treatise, §§109 f. One is struck by the parallel to a list of Powers in a Hermetic tract, γνῶσις θεοῦ, χαράς, ἐγκράτεια, καρτερία, δικαιοσύνη, κοινωνία, ἀλήθεια, ἀγαθόν, ζωή, φῶς: *Corp. Herm.*, XIII, 8 f. These come to the aspirant and cleanse him and articulate him with the Logos (ἀνακαθαιρόμενος ταῖς τοῦ θεοῦ δυνάμεσιν εἰς συνάρθρωσιν τοῦ λόγου). To this Scott (*Hermetica*, I, 245) notes: "The Logos is an organism of which the several Powers of God are the constituent parts; and this organism is built up in the reborn man, as the body is built up of the several members." Scott might have been describing the Logos and Powers of Philo. See Reitzenstein, *Poimandres*, p. 231.

73. The number of Powers seems also indefinite in *Plant.*, 50.

is not at least a reference to God and the two Powers, whether with or without the Logos. God was steadily visualized in this way by him, and it is even the deity which he represents the Jews as worshipping when he writes, for pagan Roman readers, the defense of his embassy to Gaius. Indeed it is just because Philo, and apparently the group he represents, consistently thought of God in these terms that Philo's very monotheism is in danger, and he must insist that God is still the One while represented in the Powers. Philo's form of defense is extraordinary for its premonition of the Christian solution of a kindred problem.

For Philo quotes the verse "He looked and behold three men stood over against him," and comments:

Very naturally, to those who can perceive, this represents that it is possible both for one to be three and three one in so far as they are one in the Logos above them.[74] But this Logos is numbered along with the primary Powers, the Creative and Royal, and produces a three-fold apparition upon the human mind. For the human mind is denied so acute a vision that it can see as a distinct God Him who transcends the Powers assisting Him. So in order that mind may perceive God the ministering Powers appear to be existing along with him, and as it were they make an apparition of three instead of one. For when the mind begins to receive a sure apprehension of Being, it understands itself as penetrating to that stage: mind is itself reduced to monadity, and itself appears as primal and supreme; as I said just above, [the mind] could perceive Being only by means of its association with those primal Powers which exist directly with Him, the Creative Power which is called God, and the Royal Power, which is called Lord.[75]

Then after explaining that the eyes raised are the eyes of the soul Philo continues:

The eye so raised begins by seeing the Rulership, a holy and divine vision, in such a way that a single vision appears to him as a triad, and triad as unity.

For in the highest experience and clearest vision the triad disappears in the one: which makes itself appear without the assisting Powers, and

so the intellect perceives most clearly a unity although previously it had learned to apprehend it under the similitude of a trinity.[76] . . . So speaking truly and accurately, the measure of all things, intelligible as well as sensible, is one God, who in Himself is unity, yet appears in the likeness of the triad on account of the weakness of those who would see Him.[77]

74. The Latin of Aucher reads "eo quod unum sunt secundum rationem supernam," which might mean "they are one by a higher explanation," or "they are unified in the Logos who is above them." The next sentence, where the "ratio" is connected with the two to make a third, shows that the Greek must have carried the latter sense.
75. *QG,* iv, 2.   76. Ib., 4.
77. Ib., 8: "qui in ipsa unitate trinitati similis apparet ob videntium infirmitatem." Yet one

Lebreton, a Catholic writer on the origins of the doctrine of the Trinity,[78] quotes these passages, but thinks their phraseology is so likely to have been given a Christian coloring by the Armenian or Latin translators that he needs mention the passages only in a footnote. But I cannot see why he thus wishes to discard these when he accepts and quotes other passages almost as Christian,[79] where the one God is described as manifesting Himself as a φαντασία, sometimes of one, but sometimes as three, i.e., as the Royal Power, κύριος, as the Creative and Beneficent Power, θεός, while the "one in the middle" is the πατὴρ τῶν ὅλων, ὁ ὤν. Philo compares this appearance of three to a person casting two shadows, though he admits his figure of "shadows" is misleading since there is no such thing as a shadow in deity, and indeed speaks of the "shadow" as "beaming forth" from the central φαντασία (ἀπαυγαζομένων ἀπὸ τούτου σκιῶν). These "shining shadows," an impossible figure for moderns, are possible for Philo's generation because to the Greek a strong light "darkened" a lesser light. So the sun's rising ἐπισκιάζει the light of the stars, and in the same way the coming of the φῶς νοητὸν ἐπισκιάζει the light of human thought.[80] The clearest expression of the idea is a comparison of God to the sun whose rising obscures the stars.

So when the conceptual beams of the shining God, beams unmixed and pure and most luminous, shine in upon the eye of the soul, it can see nothing else; for, when knowledge of Existence shines in, it so excessively illuminates everything as to darken what things had seemed brightest in themselves.[81]

Again when the human mind tries to rise to God the Great King, just before it arrives at that goal "pure and untempered rays stream forth like a torrent, so that by its beams the eye of the understanding is dazzled (σκοτοδινιᾶν)."[82] In spite of this darkening effect of divine light I should guess that Philo could speak of the beaming emanations as themselves comparable to shadows because the light of the central source was so much more brilliant that they seemed rather like shadows than lights in comparison. But really all are one

has to be quite advanced as a mystic to get even a vision of the three. One who is still struggling along in semi-obscurity (ὁ προκόπτων) sees only a dyad, a disconnected thing, divided in itself. The man who has completed the mystical journey (ὁ τέλειος) sees the triad, in unclouded light, its center filled out and complete in nature: QG, iv, 30; Harris, Fragments, p. 32.

78. Jules Lebreton, Les Origines du Dogme de la Trinité, Paris, 1919, p. 195.

79. Abr., 107, 119 ff.

80. In LA, iii, 96 (cf. 100, 102), the Logos is itself a σκιὰ θεοῦ, though Leisegang (Pneuma Hagion, 1922, p. 27, n. 3) points out that this σκιά is a Platonic imitation, as in the parable of the cave. On the Powers as overpowering light-beams see also LA, ii, 30, 58; Immut., 3, 77 ff.; Praem., 37 ff.; Virt., 164; Leisegang, Heilige Geist (1919), 211 ff.; Adler, note in Philos Werke, V, 23, n. 1.

81. Lbr., 44.   82. Opif., 71.

and the same with the source, make together ἕν ὑποκείμενον, and only our being dazzled by φῶς νοητόν makes them appear as three.[83]

The important point for our immediate purpose is that Philo never broke down his monotheism. He might talk in mythological fashion of various personalities and Powers, but the uncreated and eternal world actually was a unit in the person or nature of deity. Indeed in one passage, after speaking of the divine Powers, Philo says:

> The most generic thing is God, and second the Logos of God and the others [apparently the Powers] subsist only with reference to the Logos, but actually they are as good as non-subsisting.[84]

Philo means that to attempt to understand God's nature we must approach it from the point of view of His aspects, but the aspects of God are still only aspects of a nature that is essentially one.

So he addresses the mystic mind as follows about the apprehension of God:

> Oh Mind, receive the uncounterfeited impression in order that as you are instructed concerning the Rulership (ἀρχή) and Goodness (ἀγαθότης) of the Cause you may win the blessed heritage, and may at once know as well the blending and mixture (σύνοδός τε καὶ κρᾶσις) of the supreme Powers. In these Powers together [sc. Rulership and Goodness] God is good by the fact that His dignity as ruler is made manifest, while He rules by the fact that His goodness is made manifest. [This is all so] in order that you may possess the virtues that arise from them, love and piety towards God, and that in your contact with these you may not, by exalting yourself, suffer because of the greatness of the Rulership of the King, and similarly you may not, by dispairing of your better hopes, experience what is undesirable through the Kindliness of the great and bountiful God.[85]

A single reading of this passage in either Greek or English does not make its purport clear. Toward God, Philo is saying, man must take two attitudes corresponding to the two primary Powers. Man must be humble or he will be crushed by God's Ruling Power; he must be full of confident hope (very close to the Pauline Faith) or the Power of God which expresses itself in kindliness toward one who thus hopes will prove anything but the Beneficent. Yet these two Powers are not distinctive themselves, for in nature and function they blend in a single κρᾶσις. They are distinguished only for the solace of mankind, that man may, as a result of their apparent distinction,

---

83. This figure, if not the passage, is familiar in Christian writers about the Trinity, where the Logos is φῶς ἐκ φωτός. The great argument about the relation of the Logos to God hinged upon whether the Logos-ray was a permanent, or a temporary, or only a seeming, effulgence from God. See my *The Theology of Justin Martyr*, pp. 148 ff.

84. *LA*, ii, 86.   85. Harris, *Fragments*, p. 109: Cod. Rup. 195b.

have both humility toward God and steadfast confidence in Him. The Powers, that is, are a human conventionalization.

It is impossible to take this whole speculation of the relation of God to His Powers, of the one and the many, as mere metaphysical hair-splitting. To any followers, however distant, of Pythagoras and Plato this problem would be one of the most important for a personal adjustment to the forces of the universe. And Philo represents it as the very heart of the "mystery religion" through which he himself hoped to find salvation. He writes:

For Abraham went with all zeal and speed and eagerness and bade Sarah (that is Virtue) hasten and knead three measures of meal and make "buried" cakes[86] when God came attended by His two highest Powers, Sovereignty and Goodness; that is, when He, the one between the two, called up before the eye of the soul, which has power to see, three separate visions or aspects. Each of these aspects, though not subject itself to measurement—for God and His Powers are alike uncircumscribed—is the measure of all things. His Goodness is the measure of things good, His Sovereignty of its subjects, and the Ruler Himself is the measure of all things corporeal and incorporeal. It is to serve Him that these two Powers assume the functions of rules and standards, and measure what lies within their province.

It is well that these three measures should be as it were kneaded and blended in the souls in order that, convinced that God, who is above all, exists—God who overtops His Powers in that He is visible apart from them and yet is revealed in them—the soul may receive the impression of His sovereignty and beneficence. Thus too, being admitted into the inmost mysteries, she will learn not to blab or babble them thoughtlessly, but to store them up and guard them in secrecy and silence. For it is written "make buried cakes," because the sacred story that unveils to us the truth of the Uncreated and His Powers must be buried, since the knowledge of divine rites is a trust which not every comer can guard aright.[87]

So the One manifests itself as the three, yet is still always the One, and this sacred or mystic teaching (ἱερος λόγος) is the supreme Mystery, to be told only to one capable of understanding and guarding the secret, worthy of becoming μύστις τῶν τελείων τελετῶν.[88] God is thus at once source of the form and life of the universe, and at the same time is Himself personally that form and life. We are now ready, as far as metaphysics is concerned, for a free shifting back and forth between the Powers and God, and an assertion that to find the highest Powers or the Logos is to find God, together with a

---

86. Gen., xviii, 6.

87. Sac., 59, 60, as translated by Colson and Whitaker in the Loeb series. These editors note: "Philo deduces an allegory from ἐγκρυφίας (so the LXX) which means 'cakes baked in the ashes.'"

88. See on this passage Bréhier, Les Idées, pp. 144 ff. Another reference to the same Mystery is in a fragment from LA, iv, in Harris, Fragments, p. 8, where mention is made of οἱ μήπω τὰ μεγάλα μεμυημένοι μυστήρια περί τε ἀρχῆς καὶ ἐξουσίας τοῦ ἀγενήτου καὶ περὶ ἄγαν οὐδενείας τοῦ γενητοῦ.

sense of relative distinctions which would correspond to the less and more complete mystical experiences.

To the mystical use Philo makes of the conception we shall return. Zeller and many others see quite rightly here a fundamental divergence of philosophy and religion, since philosophy tends to regard principles of mediation between God and Creation as abstractions, while religion is apt to think of them as personalities.[89] It is clear that Philo wanted to keep the Powers as mediators in both senses, since his religion was always ultimately under philosophic control. He brought the two together in what scholars have for some time been calling "Modalism." Not recognizing this, students of Philo have made what seem to me artificial distinctions. For example Lebreton represents Philo's distinction between God and the Powers as being really a distinction between the being and the activity of God.[90] Also Zeller in one passage distinguishes between doctrines of emanation which are schemes for the transmission of divine nature and those which are schemes for the transmission of divine power.[91] So far as Philo is concerned I have characterized such distinctions as artificial because while it is quite true that he, like Plotinus, wanted to represent God as a Being apart and unique, as the Creator and Ruler of a world essentially distinct from Himself, it is just as true that in the thought of both of them even the created world is conceived as held together by God; in a sense the world shares in God's nature as well as power, in God's being as well as in His activity; or as Onatas put it, the world is "divine." So Zeller is quite right when he feels dissatisfied with his own distinction and goes on to characterize Plotinus' system as "dynamistic Pantheism." Philo's doctrine was more dualistic in regard to matter than Plotinus', so that it is never strictly accurate to apply the term pantheism to him, yet these words of Zeller about Plotinus are strikingly descriptive of Philo: "Dieses System ist pantheistisch, denn es behauptet ein solches Verhältniss des Endlichen zur Gottheit, wonach demselben kein selbständiges Sinn zukommt, alles Endliche ist ihm blosses Accidens, blosse Erscheinung des Göttlichen." For in so far as matter manifests any form, Philo felt that the material world was a "blosse Erscheinung des Göttlichen." If this is true even down into the created realm, much more is it true that for all the distinctions Philo draws, the Logos and Powers are modes or aspects of God's nature as well as of His activity. Practically real as the modes are, it is precisely in their being that they are ultimately indistinguishable from God.

In passing, one is forced at least to refer to the development of this conception of the attributes of deity in the Christian heresy of "modalistic mon-

89. *Philosophie der Griechen*, III, ii, 412 f. See Heinze, *Lehre vom Logos*, 291 ff.; E. Caird, *Evolution of Theology in the Greek Philosophers*, II, 201.
90. Jules Lebreton, *Les Origines du Dogme de la Trinité*, p. 197.
91. *Philosophie der Griechen*, III, ii, 561, where he is discussing Plotinus.

archism," or "modalism" as Harnack called it.[92] Here it is at once striking that one of the earliest clear expressions of the doctrine comes out in a fragment from the Gospel of the Egyptians, certainly of Alexandrian origin: τὸν αὐτὸν εἶναι πατέρα, τὸν αὐτὸν εἶναι υἱόν, τὸν αὐτὸν εἶναι ἅγιον πνεῦμα.[93] Another group, the Simonians said: "Hic igitur a multis quasi Deus glorificatus est, et docuit semetipsum esse qui inter Judaeos quidem quasi Filius apparuerit, in Samaria autem quasi Pater descenderit, in reliquis vero gentibus quasi Spiritus Sanctus adventaverit."[94] That is, the unity of God was to be preserved by representing Father, Son, and Spirit as divine modes or aspects, which as modes had no separate existence, but were manifestations due to divine mercy and human frailty. Christian orthodoxy could not tolerate such teaching because the essential thing in its religious life, the worship of Jesus of Nazareth, necessitated the formulation of an expression for his full and ontological divinity as an *individual*. It is highly important, as a background for this speculation, to know that the doctrine that God is One, but with varying manifestations, appears in Philo's writings clearly and is there expressed in terms of the three who are One!

When one raises the question of Philo's sources for this doctrine, one must confess at once that nothing definite can be produced. Bréhier[95] has gone to considerable length to develop the Stoic parallels, recognizing also the emergence of the Greek Δίκη in Philo's δύναμις βασιλική, whose origin seems to him thereby "assez facilement" explained. There is really much to connect Philo with Stoicism, for it is familiar that the Stoics saved their monotheism by insisting that the gods of their fathers and neighbors were only δυνάμεις of the one Logos—God, who pervaded all things. But the Stoics had no definite trinity or special grouping of Powers to correspond to what we have been discussing in Philo. It was apparently a pleasure for the Stoic to think of deity as the πολυώνυμος, and to find various ways of connecting the Logos with new gods.[96] Yet in all this they show no original contribution, but only their susceptibility to the Zeitgeist, as described at the beginning of this chapter.

An immediate source of Philo in making his doctrine take the form it does seems more likely to have been the conception of royalty of the Hellenistic Age, by which the king was deity, and deity king.[97] The identification led to

92. It is a pleasure to record that the similarity was recognized by the learned but ever unknown marginal commentator in my copy of Drummond's *Philo Judaeus*. He compares Philo's conception to Sabellianism.

93. *Ap.* Epiph., *Haer.*, 62, 2. From Harnack, *Dogmengeschichte*, I, 217, n. 2; cf. 206, n. 4.

94. *Ap.* Irenaeus, I, xvi, 1, Ed. Harvey (Harnack, *loc. cit.*).

95. *Les Idées*, pp. 147 f.

96. Heinemann's connecting this with Posidonius (*Poseidonios*, II, 321) does not convince me.

97. On Hebrew royalty see my "Kingship in Early Israel" in *Journal of Biblical Literature*, XLVIII (1929), pp. 169–205. On Hellenistic royalty see my "Hellenistic Kingship."

the most extraordinary mutual borrowing. What was said of God must somehow be said of the King—so the King is νόμος ἔμψυχος because God's nature is the νόμος τῆς φύσεως.[98] On the other hand, God as king acts as judge, leader in war, benefactor, giver of peace, and tends to develop in a cosmic palace[99] a mythological company of vicegerents and councillors.[100] At the same time the conduct of earthly courts symbolizes how we should act toward God.[101] God is the great King, the Logos His ὕπαρχος, ruling according to law and justice.[102] We are reminded again of the extraordinary description of the rule of the Great King of Persia, living remote in his palace, secluded and invisible, but reaching and controlling his kingdom by vicegerents and officers, as it appears in the περὶ κόσμου.[103] Such, says the treatise, is the rule of God, Himself enthroned and inaccessible, but extending His government through the world as He sends forth His δύναμις into all things. This conception of kingship, thought out in slightly different imagery, seems to be the background for Philo's doctrine of δυνάμεις, in which the νόμος appears as the δύναμις νομοθετική or βασιλική. It and the δύναμις ποιητική are the two δορυφόροι,[104] and together constitute God's δόξα.[105] To Philo δορυφόροι conveyed always still its original meaning of a bodyguard of royalty, as when he says ὅπου ὁ βασιλεύς, ἐκεῖ καὶ οἱ δορυφόροι,[106] or specifically they recall to him ὁ μέγας βασιλεύς.[107] Indeed frequently as he speaks of the one Power as being distinctively the Royal Power, it is God, the One, who is King. The matter is made very clear when he says, "*As king* He created the world according to His beneficence (i.e. His Creative Power); but after He had completed it then the world was arranged and set in order under the sway of His Royal Power."[108] So the *creative* act of scattering the λόγοι σπερματικοί is performed by God, in contrast to that stern aspect of His nature usually associated with the Royal Power, because He is a kind and merciful *king*.[109] God is "a King invested

98. There is no remote justification for Heinemann's saying that Posidonius contributed the term νόμος ἔμψυχος for royalty. See his *Poseidonios*, II, 274 ff., especially p. 277: "Fraglos hat er (Posidonius) zu der Neigung der Zeit beigetragen, in dem wahren Herrscher, der zugleich den Weg zur Eudaimonie weisen soll die Inkarnation des göttlichen Logos zu sehen." Far from this statement being "fraglos," it seems to me highly improbable.

99. *Cher.*, 99.

100. *Fug.*, 66. See above p. 13; *Conf.*, 170 ff.

101. *Jona*, 29, 30. This work is questionably Philonic, but the idea here is quite what he would have approved.

102. *Agr.*, 51; cf. *Opif.*, 71; *Cher.*, 29; *Post.*, 101; *Gig.*, 45, 64; *Immut.*, 159; *Agr.*, 78; *Mig.*, 146; *Congr.*, 116; *Som.*, ii, 99 f., 289; *Spec.*, iv, 176; *Legat.*, 3.

103. Chap. vi, p. 398a f.

104. E.g. *QE*, ii, 67; *Legat.*, 6; *Sac.*, 59; *Abr.*, 122.

105. *Spec.*, i, 45.

106. *LA*, iii, 115; cf., *Spec.*, iv, 92, 123, 168.

107. *Spec.*, iii, 111. Reisch in Pauly-Wissowa, *Real-Encyclopädie*, V, 1579, points out that this original meaning had been obscured by Philo's time, but the meaning is very clear for him.

108. *QG*, ii, 75.   109. Ib., 16.

with gentle (ἥμερον) and lawful (νόμιμον) authority (ἡγεμονίαν), who governs the whole heaven and cosmos with justice."[110] Here the ἥμερον and νόμιμον recognizably refer to our two Powers, and God is exercising both attributes as King, has indeed as such "attuned together by unshaken Laws of Nature and into an indissoluble unity the two most beautiful things, namely rulership with providence."[111] These two Powers really correspond to the two chief functions of the Hellenistic king, by which he was described as Εὐεργέτης or Σωτήρ and νόμιμος or δίκαιος. Says Philo, "The form of the creative Power is a peaceable, and gentle, and beneficent virtue; but the royal Power is a legislative, and chastising virtue."[112] Each of these is as much an aspect of the ideal king as the other. The picture is vividly set forth in Philo's description of what he considered the blasphemous antics of Gaius in trying to make himself out as the divine king. Gaius

metamorphosed and transformed himself into Apollo, crowning his head with garlands to represent rays (ἀκτινοειδέσι); he held a bow and arrows in his left hand while he extended graces with his right, as if it were right that he offer good things from his ready store and display the better order which was represented at his right hand, while he subordinated the punishments and allotted them to the more restricted place at his left hand.[113]

God appears in the same light in the discussion of His mercy and severity in Philo, where God saves man by stretching forth His *right hand,* His hand of salvation.[114] The two Powers were, of course, not too sharply distinguished, for in the ideal king, as Philo says here of God, the sovereignty is seen in the beneficence and the beneficence in the sovereignty.[115] It is too much to expect that Philo would be consistent in his division of operation. So in one passage he makes the function of the second Power consist chiefly of punishment of wrong doers,[116] in another the same Power becomes the guardian of ἰσότης, the source of all εἰρήνη and σωτηρία.[117] The way in which ἀρχή is the source of all goods for individuals, cities, and the universe,

110. *Provid.,* ii, 15, *ap.* Eusebium, *Praeparatio Evangelica,* VIII, xiv, 2. Aucher's translation of the Armenian gives a slightly, not essentially, different reading.
111. Ib.
112. *QG,* i, 57. Cf. *Spec.,* i, 307: περὶ τὸ ὄν αἱ πρῶται καὶ μέγισται τῶν δυνάμεών εἰσιν, ἥτε εὐεργέτης καὶ κολαστήριος.
113. *Legat.,* 95: One is strikingly reminded of the Son of Man seated on the throne of his glory at the last judgment as described in Mat. xxv. 31 ff.
114. *Immut.,* 73: τὴν δεξιὰν καὶ σωτήριον χεῖρα ὀρέγων.
115. *Cher.,* 29; cf. *Plant.,* 87, 88: "By virtue of his being a ruler he has a twofold capacity, He can both benefit and injure, changing Himself from one to the other according as He must recompense a man who has done something. But by virtue of His being the Benefactor His desire is only to benefit. The greatest good of the soul would be to doubt no longer concerning the power of the King in either matter, but confidently to abandon the haunting fear of the power of His rulership, and to kindle a flame of that most sure hope of winning and enjoying good things which is afforded by the fact that to be bountiful is His choice."
116. *Mos.,* ii, 99.   117. *QE,* ii, 64: Harris, *Fragments,* p. 64.

is elaborately expounded.[118] Benefaction seems to Philo especially the fruit of the rulership τοῦ βασιλεύοντος θεοῦ.

In Philo's thus representing God as the King with attendant Powers one is reminded of Dio Chrysostom's description of the Court of Hera, who is ruling on the "royal citadel (ἄκρα), the sanctuary of Zeus the King."[119] This ruling of Hera for Zeus at once suggests Philo's Logos, the manifestation of Deity immediately in contact with the Powers. Beside her sit four attendants, two on either side. Δίκη, and Εὐνομία who closely resembles Δίκη, sit on the right; on the left are Εἰρήνη and a male figure, Νόμος, or 'Ορθὸς Λόγος, without whose permission the others can do nothing. Some such picture of divine rulership must lie behind the type of divinity we have been describing. Yet in contrast to Philo, Dio's description is obviously a casual figure for deity. There is no real distinction in Dio between the Powers on the right and left, and while the notion of the legality of the rulership is brought out, the whole would have to be modified as Philo has done to make it symbolize any philosophical conception of divinity.

The figure of royalty was certainly a source of the hierarchy of Powers. But another source is equally apparent, the light mysticism of the mystery religions. Pascher has amply demonstrated the light-symbolism of the hierarchy of divinity which he was discussing. The light-symbolism of Philo's hierarchy of Powers is no less clear. The first passage considered, the allegory of the ark with the cherubim, was clearly a matter of light emanations. For when the question is raised about the way in which a person could get knowledge of God, Philo says that such knowledge cannot come directly from God, τὸ ὄν, but from his primary and guardian Powers (δορυφόροι δυνάμεις):[120]

And it is something with which one must be content that beams are thence borne into the soul, in order that the older and more resplendent [existence] may be visible from the secondary illumination.[121]

The seraphim-cherubim were made of the "constructive fire."[122] The Powers were "beaming shadows." Philo does not refer to the higher Powers specifically in the following passage, but there can be no doubt that the two Powers in which we have been especially interested are included:

118. *Som.*, ii, 285 ff.   119. I, 66 ff.
120. For a combination of solar or astronomical symbolism with δυνάμεις and δορυφόροι, see Proclus, *In Rem Publicam,* ed. Kroll, II, 220, 25 ff., where a certain arrangement of sun and stars makes "the sun as King of all visible things, the imitator of the creative δυνάμεις by virtue of its beams of light: ὑπὸ πάντων δορυφορεῖται τῶν κοσμοκρατόρων. For the use of the term in astronomy, cf. Sextus Empiricus, *Adv. Mathematicos,* V, 38.
121. *QE,* ii, 67 (Harris, *Fragments,* p. 66).
122. The familiar πῦρ τεχνικόν of Stoicism was a material thing. This is a very good instance of Philo's frequent use of Stoic terms with a meaning not at all Stoic.

And therefore it is said in another place, "there is a cup in the hand of the Lord of unmixed wine, full of mixture" (Ps. lxxv. 8). But surely the mixed is not unmixed, and yet there is a meaning in these words most true to nature, and in agreement with what I have said before. For the Powers which God employs are unmixed in respect to Himself, but mixed in respect to created beings. For it cannot be that mortal nature should have room for the unmixed. We cannot look even upon the sun's flame untempered, or unmixed, for our sight will be quenched and blasted by the bright flashing of its rays, ere it reach and apprehend them, though the sun is but one of God's works in the past, a portion of heaven, a condensed mass of ether. And can you think it possible that your understanding should be able to grasp in their unmixed purity those uncreated Powers, which stand around Him and flash forth light of surpassing splendor? When God extended the sun's rays from heaven to the boundaries of earth, He tempered them in this way, that the radiance drawn off from the blazing flame, surrendering its power of burning but retaining that of giving light, might meet and hail its friend and kinsman, the light which is stored in the treasury of our eyes; for it is when these converge to meet and greet each other that the apprehension through vision is produced. Just in the same way if God's knowledge and wisdom and prudence and justice and each of His other excellences were not tempered, no mortal could receive them, nay not even the whole heaven and universe. The Creator then, knowing His own surpassing excellence in all that is best and the natural weakness of His creatures, however loud they boast, wills not to dispense benefit or punishment as He could do, but according to the measure of capacity which He sees in those who are to participate in either of those dispensations. If indeed we could drink and enjoy this diluted draught, wherein is a moderate measure of His Powers, we should reap sufficient gladness, and let not the human race seek a more perfect joy. For we have shown that these Powers at their full height unmixed and untempered subsist only in the Existent.[123]

Philo regarded the Powers as light-emanations, or emanations of the πῦρ τεχνικόν. This would suggest a Graeco-Egyptian or Oriental source for the conception, and indeed striking parallels to his doctrine of Powers are to be found in those sources. In a Hermetic tract it is written:

There are from above the guards (δορυφόροι), two in number, of the universal Providence, one of which is the Keeper of souls, the other the Guide of souls. And the Keeper of souls guards the souls[124] . . ., but the Guide of souls sends forth and assigns to their respective places the souls that become incarnate. The one guards, the other directs, according to the will of God.[125]

The functions of these δορυφόροι are not those of Philo, though in their limited field of operation the Creative Power of Philo would seem like

123. *Immut.*, 77–81. Colson and Whitaker's translation slightly revised.
124. Commentators would fill the hiatus in some way to supply the idea that the keeper of souls keeps those souls not yet incarnate. Cf. Scott, *Hermetica, ad loc.*
125. Stob., I, xlix, 69 (Wachs., I, 464; Scott, *Hermetica*, I, 516).

ψυχοταμίας, the Keeper of souls, the Royal Power like the ψυχοπομπός, the Guide of Souls. At least there are two δορυφόροι of God, in itself a striking fact.

The conception reappears in three magical papyri. In one βαινχωωωχ has not only a father and mother, but two δορυφόροι.[126] Wessely parallels this with Pap. L. 250: ταῖς σαῖς βουλαῖς δορυφοροῦσιν ἅπαντα; and Pap. P. 102: σὲ καλῶ τὸν μέγαν ἐν οὐράνῳ ᾧ... δορυφοροῦσιν οἱ δέκα ἓξ γίγαντες. With these Reitzenstein[127] connects a sentence from a papyrus in the British Museum: οἱ δύο θεοὶ οἱ περὶ σέ, θαθ. καλεῖται ὁ εἷς θεὸς Σω, ὁ ἕτερος ᾽Αφ.[128]

The idea of a God with two δορυφόροι, or more than two, was clearly familiar to popular Graeco-Egyptian thought. The Hermetic Asclepius[129] speaks of εἱμαρμένη and *necessitas* as two Powers which order all things in heaven and earth according to divine laws. Εἱμαρμένη creates the beginnings of all things (*rerum omnium initia parit*), and necessity carries things on to completion. Order (*ordo*) follows these and works out the interrelations of things. The first two of these are more like the Creative and Royal Powers of Philo than anything yet encountered, and it is notable that εἱμαρμένη is *aut deus summus, aut ab ipso deo qui secundus effectus est deus.*

Clearly with this is to be connected a fragment in Stobaeus:[130]

All things come into being by nature and fate, and no place is destitute of Providence. And Providence is the self-perfect Logos of the God of the Heavens; and it has two self-sprung Powers, ἀνάγκη and εἱμαρμένη.

The text describing ἀνάγκη is lost. Εἱμαρμένη, as the text stands, is subject to Providence and ἀνάγκη, the stars are subject to εἱμαρμένη, as are all things in nature and among men. The interest of this passage is that it gives us the two Powers as both subject to God through the Logos, and so it is more than likely that there is some connection between these Powers and Philo's. We are not surprised to find that the Logos itself is πρώτη δύναμις from God in another fragment.[131]

It is in such a source as this, rather than in late Stoicism, that I would find the origin of Philo's Powers. Bréhier[132] has paralleled them with the Stoic

126. BM, CXXIII. Pub. by C. Wessely in *Denkschriften*, Vienna Academy, 1893, Abhandlung II, p. 60.

127. *Poimandres*, 117.

128. Text as by K. Preisendanz, *Papyri Graecae Magicae*, II (1931), p. 25.

129. III, 39; Scott, *Hermetica*, I, 362.

130. I, v, 20 (Wachs., I, p. 82). Scott, *op. cit.*, I, 434.

131. Scott, *op. cit.*, Frag., 28; I, p. 544. With this should perhaps be connected the Aeon, δύναμις τοῦ θεοῦ of Poimander, XI, i, 3 (Scott, I, 208) and the statement in Ib., X, 22b (Scott, I, 202): τοῦ θεοῦ καθάπερ ἀκτῖνες αἱ ἐνέργειαι. The treatment of the δυνάμεις in Kroll's *Die Lehren des Hermes Trismegistus*, 1914, pp. 76 ff. is excellent. He was quite aware of the kinship to Philo's δυνάμεις, p. 77 f.

132. *Les Idées*, pp. 144 ff. esp. 147 f.

χάρις and δίκη, Grace and Justice. He has not a passage to quote to justify his elevating these two into supreme aspects of the Stoic Deity, for his Cornutus reference (ch. xv) only describes the Graces as great Powers along with the whole procession of Greek divinities, all of whom, as the Graces here, are by etymology given significance as aspects (κατὰ τὰς δυνάμεις)[133] of the Stoic pan-Deity. Δίκη will be discussed in the next chapter. It need only be pointed out in general that wherever the Stoics may have borrowed the term δυνάμεις for their particular allegorization of the Olympians, a conception of God as fundamentally a supersensible light-fire source having contact with matter through radiated δυνάμεις was in no sense a part of, or compatible with, Stoicism. Bréhier makes a great deal of the fundamental contrast between the beneficent and punishing functions of the two Powers of Philo. He has done so at the expense of Philo's repeated denial of any fundamental or essential contrast between them.

Inexact as are the Hermetic and magical parallels to Philo's conception, they strongly suggest that Philo's Powers, and the whole picture of Deity of which they are a part, were an adaptation of conceptions from the religious world of Graeco-Egypt and Persia. Certainly they did not come to him from any traditional Judaism we know, or from the philosophical schools of Classic Greece, however much philosophers in Egypt may have attempted to orient traditional deities with such philosophical conceptions as the κόσμος νοητός.

At the same time it is incredible that Philo, who so repeatedly expresses the deepest abhorrence of contemporary mysteries, should deliberately and without precedent have borrowed from them de novo these notions of deity completely at variance with the older Jewish tradition. Had Philo as a complete novelty thus published book after book in which God appears as a Light-Stream manifesting Himself in lower Powers, the Jews of his environment must have treated him as a heretic rather than have regarded him as their leader and chief representative. The probability is much greater that such a borrowing of a foreign conception of Deity was a gradual process, a swing or drift which involved many people and a long time.

In its final form as Philo represents it, it is notable that the borrowed conceptions are thoroughly welded into the Jewish Scriptures. Κύριος and θεός, the Septuagint translation of the two Hebrew words Yahveh Elohim, are regarded with general consistency as representing the two Powers. That they could in themselves have suggested the interpretation Philo gives them is of course impossible. That Jews could suddenly have accepted such an interpretation without long having thought of God, along with their Graeco-Egyptian neighbors, as a Light-Stream is equally impossible.

133. Diog. La., VII, 147.

In conclusion, it is notable that Philo's use of the Powers is on a far higher level than the parallels adduced from magic and the Hermetica. It will be seen that Philo used the Powers in a fundamental way in his mystic approach to God. Yet they are closer in feeling to the Neo-Platonic effort at a philosophical account of God and His relation to the world than to the atmosphere of the popular sources quoted. Popular Gnostic tendencies were philosophically weak in sacrificing the philosophic and Jewish urge for divine unity to a hypostatization of those stages of ascent experienced by the mystic. Philo's Deity is notable because Philo refused to see the Powers as anything but distinct flashes of the single divine nature as apprehended from the human point of view.

There has been much discussion of whether Philo in his use of the Powers was more a mystic than a philosopher. Heinze[134] and Zeller[135] saw the Powers as admissions of failure on Philo's part philosophically to connect an absolute and self-contained Deity with the world; he could make the connection only by using a religious mythology of personal Powers, God's subordinates. Drummond, as it seems to me, fully refutes this explanation, and suggests that the short cut was not in Philo but in the modern interpreters who had failed to take Philo's remarks fully into consideration. For Philo's own theory Drummond speaks strikingly of the Powers as "aspects" of a divine nature which appears to us to have aspects only because man is incapable of apprehending Him at once as a whole.[136] God is Himself ἄδεικτος,[137] His nature, except for the fact of His existence, is ἀκατάληπτος.[138] Bréhier rather returns to Zeller and Heinze, for he is determined to make of Philo not a metaphysician but a man "preoccupied above all with morality and with the ascent of the soul toward the knowledge (mystical) of God."[139] He dislikes Drummond's theory, in spite of what he calls its ingenuity, because as he thinks Drummond "méconnaît la pensée de Philon en la ramenant à une espèce d'idéalisme à la Spinoza, historiquement bien postérieur."[140] Now it is entirely correct, as we shall see later, that this discussion of God and His Powers proves highly valuable in the description of the soul's ascent to God. Of course Philo was not primarily interested in metaphysics. I doubt if any-

134. Heinze, *Die Lehre vom Logos*, pp. 244 ff.
135. *Die Philosophie der Griechen*, III (1903), ii, 407 ff.
136. *Philo Judaeus*, Lond. 1888, ii, 65–155. See p. 95: "He (God) may not do as absolute Being or universal Cause what nevertheless he does as Benefactor or moral Governor. This is a mode of language with which we are not familiar; and yet, if we know a man under strongly marked characters, we might say of him, without danger of being mistaken that it was not the philosopher, but the general, that won the battle, meaning that he succeeded in war, not by his philosophical but by his military abilities."
137. E.g. *Heres*, 130.   138. *Det.*, 89.
139. *Les Idées*, 136 ff., see esp. p. 141.
140. Ib., p. 136. Why Bréhier should object to similarities to Spinoza here is hard to see in view of what he himself says on p. 314.

one in the world ever was so interested. We are all solving in our work our deeper emotional problems and it may or may not be apparent to ourselves or to others what we are ultimately doing. Philo's religious urge is obviously much more apparent than, shall we say, Aristotle's or Kant's. But when we admit that Philo's interest was primarily ethical and mystical, as of course we must, we have by no means justified belittling his serious philosophical purpose. For the mystical urge in Philo was present in a profound mind which was not content without a tremendous effort at grasping and thinking through the intellectual problems arising from his mysticism. And it seems to me that of all problems which Philo was especially anxious to think through the most important was that of the nature of God and of both the possibility of divine relation with men and comprehension of God by men. On this whole problem, which cannot be treated here, Drummond still seems to me the best guide, for description if not for source analysis.

So we shall not understand Philo either by sacrificing his philosophic interest to his mysticism, or vice versa. The fact is that in Philo's Deity we have a conception fit primarily, as will appear, to meet the individual's hope for salvation. But it is a formulation that would sacrifice none of the best philosophic interest of the day in presenting man with a Deity at once the Monad, the Absolute, and the Prime Cause, a God who was the source and sanction of ethical idealism, and the goal of his mystical aspiration.

Philo and Plutarch seem to me to offer the most illuminating comparison. Plutarch turned to comparative mythology, as does Apuleius by implication, to find a schematization for approach to the Greek Absolute. The solution was to Plutarch indifferently the mystic-sexual formulation, or the Persian doctrine of Powers. Comparative mythology meant nothing to Philo. He could not turn from Yahveh to Zeus, or to Dionysus as interpreted by Orpheus, to Osiris, or Ahura Mazda. But he, and the Jews he represents, did recognize the inevitability of the Greek Absolute in any adequate thinking about God, and yet like the Greeks of his day he longed to approach the Unapproachable. How could this be done? The answer of his environment was ascent through mystical-sexual union with the "Female Principle," or by conceiving that the Stream presented itself as a series of quasi distinct stages or aspects. Both of these conceptions of God Philo, and apparently many of his associates, had adopted, and as we go on we shall see how deeply the conceptions penetrated all his thinking. He reveals the fact that Jewish mythologies of Sophia and of the Powers had been created on the basis of the Jewish Chochma and of the mystic symbol of Judaism, the ark. But with Philo this is not true mythology. It is all typology, and the formulations are only human conveniences which quite fade away when one has reached the top of the ladder. Philo would have been insulted if any one had put his typology into the indifferent mixing pot of Plutarch. He himself, for all the similarities that can be pointed out between his formulations and those of his neighbors, found in his typology two definite things, the Road to the Greek Absolute, and a vindication of the unique truth of Judaism. In his exclusiveness he stands out as a Jew. But he is a man of the Hellenistic Age in his attempt to keep typology subordinate to metaphysics. It was for Christian theologians two centuries or more later to subordinate metaphysics to typology.

CHAPTER II

THE HIGHER LAW

BEFORE going on with the Mystery we must stop to ask how Philo could have found room in Judaism for such a deity as that described in the preceding chapter. The God of the Powers, or the God of the Streaming Sophia, is different enough from the God usually associated with Judaism, the Father in heaven who has given His children His will codified in the Law, so that the duty of the Jew was the glorification of God by obeying His Law. How could a man still call himself a Jew when God had become something so essentially foreign to Judaism?

The answer must be found in Philo's attitude toward the Jewish Law, since a Jew's attitude to the Law has always been the criterion of Judaism.

Philo regarded the Jewish Law from the point of view of his entire philosophy of Law. Into this subject we cannot here go in detail. In brief, Philo regarded law as of two kinds, or stages, whether he approached the subject as a politician or as a religious thinker. Law in its ultimate character was the expression of the Life or Being of God, the ordering effect of that Being and His will in and for all existence below Him. When this Law was more or less understood by men of intelligence it was set forth for other men in the material medium of nouns and verbs, and became "laws," always inferior to "Law" which was essentially immaterial. The contrast made itself felt in every place where the Law entered as an entity and force, that is in the private and public life of men, and in the universe. Always, above any concrete legal manifestation was the Law it was reflecting. How this operated in ethics and politics we can not here discuss; but it will clarify our whole exposition of the Mystery to have in mind from the start the relation of Jewish Law to the higher Law. And for this we must first define clearly the higher Law.

Without going into the details of Philo's theory of creation, it must be pointed out that for him creation was the process by which original matter, ἡ ἄποιος ὕλη, describable only by its utter lack of form, quality, or order, was given those attributes by their coming into matter from without, from God. This process could be, and was, expressed through the typical Platonic terminology of the forms, or the same essentially non-Stoic conception could be presented as the making of unordered matter into a great cosmos, the organization of its disorganized parts and nature into a great city with legal regimentation. In the one case it is form that comes into matter, in the other it is Law, but in either case what makes matter into a cosmos is the coming into it of a divine force or effluence; and as there was only one creation of the material world, so the two were to Philo interchangeable ways of saying the same thing. What came into matter from God to make it a cosmos was form or Law or Logos because these were but different approaches in Philo's mind to the same concept.

Creation as the introduction of form need not detain us. On this familiar Philonic notion it will perhaps be sufficient to quote:

For God, being God, knew in advance that a beautiful copy could not come into existence without a beautiful pattern, and that no object of perception could be flawless which had not been modeled after an archetypal and conceptual form. So when God willed to create this visible cosmos He first formed the κόσμος νοητός, in order that He might use the incorporeal and god-like pattern in making the corporeal cosmos like it. The second creation was to be an imitation of the earlier creation, and comprise as many kinds of perceptible objects as there were conceptual kinds in the other.[1]

In the *De Opificio* Philo makes a great deal of this conception that creation was the giving of form to formless matter, but even in that treatise creation in this sense is throughout subservient to the notion that creation was a process of imposing Law upon matter. To Philo the first chapters of Genesis have for their purpose the implication

that the cosmos sings in harmony with the Law and the Law with the cosmos, and that the law-abiding man is forthwith a citizen of the cosmos, for he is one who regulates his actions in accordance with the will of nature, that nature in accordance with which the whole cosmos is ruled.[2]

Philo is here talking of the Jewish Torah which, he is saying, is in harmony with the universe. Behind both Torah and cosmos, however, is φύσις, whose βούλημα is the norm of the universe, what he elsewhere calls the Law of Nature. Into this conception it is necessary to go more deeply. The Platonism sets the tone and is the constant point of view in this treatise. The "Law of Nature," a term usually associated with Stoicism, is used in such a way as in no sense to confuse that Platonism by the introduction of any essentially Stoic point of view. Philo after the passage just quoted goes on to say that Moses, who had gone to the heights of philosophy and the profoundest aspects of nature, recognized that there must, in things that exist, be two principles: first an active cause, the universal mind which transcends all categories, even those of the good and the beautiful; and secondly a passive cause, inanimate and unable to move itself. Stoicism to be sure divided the original fire into two similar principles, but always, as long as it remained Stoicism, insisted upon the ultimate common origin of the two. Philo is opposed to Stoicism precisely because to him the attempt to find an ante-

1. *Opif.*, 16.   2. Ib., 3.

cedent monism behind this dualism was essentially blasphemous. The highest aspects of "Nature" could never in any sense be inherent concomitants of Matter.

Now it is notable that Nature's "will" is the norm of the cosmos, but neither Nature nor her will is in this sense identified with the cosmos. Such will appear to be Philo's generally consistent thought about the Law of Nature.

What then is this φύσις which can thus have a will?

One has only to glance at the *Index* of Philo to see how frequently and variously he uses the term. Φύσις is the material world which natural philosophers study,[3] in which great storms make inner wars,[4] and which supplies men with the "gifts of nature," the fruits of the earth, and clothing.[5] Its parts are the four elements.[6] Again there seems to be nothing specifically Stoic in this usage. True the phrase τὰ ἐν τῇ φύσει is a common one for the natural world,[7] but the expression is found in strongly Neo-Pythagorean passages,[8] and seems often to be merely phraseological,[9] as we speak of the "finest thing in nature," or "in the world" with no specific materialistic connotation. When Philo wishes to be more specific he distinguishes between the μέριστος and the ἀμέριστος φύσις,[10] or the material world is the αἰσθητὴ φύσις,[11] or ὁρατή,[12] or ὑλική,[13] or the term τὰ ἐν τῇ φύσει may include both τὰ αἰσθητά and τὰ νοητά,[14] or even refer specifically to the forms.[15] In one passage he discusses nature as the beginning and end, a passage apparently reflecting Aristotle's language,[16] and says that with men the beginning of perfection lies within our own nature, but the end is God alone, who is ἡ ἀρίστη φύσις. From being the material world itself, φύσις becomes the moving and creating cause in the material world. In creation φύσις first created light,[17] and apparently created the rest of the material world, for Philo speaks of Nature's allotting the scheme of fruit bearing to the different animals and plants,[18] and of her giving the chameleon and polypus their protective colorings.[19] With "divine skill" Nature created man after mixing the elements,[20] gave man the five senses,[21] made him a gregarious creature,[22] and by ἰσότης made him male and female.[23] In the creation and ruling of

3. *Heres*, 152.   4. *Spec.*, ii, 190.   5. *Spec.*, iii, 111; *Praem.*, 99 f.
6. *Mos.*, i, 143; ii, 37, 249; *Spec.*, i, 97; *Prob.*, 43; *Som.*, ii, 122.
7. E.g., *Mos.*, i, 130; *Prob.*, 108; *Abr.*, 58.
8. *Opif.*, 53, 106, 128; *Mos.*, ii, 263; *Spec.*, iv, 231; *Heres*, 180, 235.
9. *Virt.*, 117; *Abr.*, 35; *Decal.*, 111.
10. *Decal.*, 103.   11. *Praem.*, 36.   12. *Ib.*, 26.
13. *Migr.*, 192.   14. *Congr.*, 52.   15. *Opif.*, 129.
16. *Fug.*, 170–172; cf. *Heres*, 121 f. Aristotle, *Phys. ausc.*, ii, 194a 28; *Polit.*, i, 1252b 32; *Meteor.*, iv, 379b 25.
17. *Sac.*, 36.   18. *Congr.*, 4.   19. *Ebr.*, 172.
20. *Spec.*, i, 266. The passage recalls the mixing bowl of the *Timaeus*.
21. *Som.*, i, 27; *Heres*, 184.   22. *Decal.*, 132.   23. *Heres*, 164.

material phenomena Nature used the number seven.[24] That is, in creation φύσις can be used as a synonym for God, as Aristotle did.[25] So it is not surprising that first God and then φύσις gave man his reasoning power,[26] which is a λογικὴ φύσις bound to man by the cement of φύσις. Nature exercises providence.[27] "She gives many gifts to men, yet participates in none herself." For she is unborn, yet gives birth; nourishes but is not nourished; causes growth and decay, yet is herself unchanging; creates but is uncreated. So, Philo concludes, we must separate from our conception of *God* any trace of the created, mortal, changeable, or profane. He has slipped from φύσις to θεός without the slightest sense of change, for φύσις was only a locution for God throughout.[28] In another passage he slips in the same way from God to nature.[29]

With this large variety of meanings for φύσις, it is clear that the term νόμος τῆς φύσεως might have a variety of meanings too. It is quite to be expected that Philo should speak of the Law of Nature as the regimentation of the material cosmos, a Law within the material cosmos, as well as the Law of God since Nature is God. Both types of natural Law are to be found, but there seems little confusion between them. They are distinct types of Law.

By far the commonest type of Natural Law is that which means the rule of God or Nature in their synonymous sense. The cosmos is matter put in order under a divine regimentation.[30] Philo's sense of the law and order of the cosmos is keen.[31] The cosmos is a city, and the Father who begat it directs it "by means of the Law of Nature."[32] Like Plato Philo is willing to concede to the popular rulers of human destiny, the heavenly bodies, a delegated sort of executive power in this divine rulership, but he insists that their power is completely dependent upon God who rules all things in the "city" according to justice and law.[33] As any one would be a fool who went into a well-ordered city and did not conclude that it must have good rulers, so the order of the universe makes unavoidable the inference that it is ruled by God.[34] ἡ μὲν γὰρ μεγαλόπολις ὅδε ὁ κόσμος ἐστὶ καὶ μιᾷ χρῆται πολιτείᾳ

24. *LA*, i, 8–16.
25. *Part. Anim.*, i, 645a 9; ii, 659b 35; *Eth. Eud.*, viii, 1247a 10; *Eth. Nic.*, viii, 1153b 32.
26. *Som.*, i, 102–111; cf., *Cher.*, 39; *Heres*, 302.
27. *Praem.*, 9; *LA*, i, 28; *Spec.*, ii, 205.
28. *Sac.*, 98–101.
29. *Plant.*, 48 f. Cf., *Spec.*, ii, 100, 171–173, 198; *Heres*, 115; *Post.*, 162.
30. *Fug.*, 9 ff.
31. "Per ordinem autem universus mundus et huius partes factae sunt": *QG*, i, 64.
32. *Spec.*, iii, 189; *Opif.*, 143. Cf. *QE*, ii, 42: "magna est mundus iste civitas, ac legitima: necesse est autem istam politicae meliori lege uti, atque aequum est et conveniens, ut sit ei legislator ac legisdator."
33. *Spec.*, i, 13, 14. I prefer keeping πρυτανεύοντος with Cohn to changing to πρυτανεύοντας with Heinemann.
34. *Spec.*, i, 33, 34; *Praem.*, 34.

καὶ νόμῳ ἑνί.[35] Specifically the most orderly city of the ancient world, Sparta, is adduced as the best parallel, and God is called the great Ephor of the Universe, who knows and executes all things in it.[36] God is also the father-ruler,[37] good shepherd,[38] helmsman,[39] and charioteer,[40] with rulership always κατὰ νόμον καὶ δίκην. And the Law of the universe is directly the product of God; it is His providence,[41] but more importantly it is the imitation of His nature.[42] Much of this terminology can be paralleled in Stoic sources. It is just as familiar in Neo-Pythagorean fragments. The meaning of the terms must in any given case be determined not by their meaning in another source, but by their meaning in the writer at hand. If Philo has used Stoic terminology to express his thought, his thought is not on that account Stoic. When Philo speaks of Providence, or of Law, as the βούλημα τῆς φύσεως, as a copy of God the archetype, he means not the law inherent in the "nature of things" but that inherent in the Nature of God, who was in complete and transcendent contrast to "things." If φύσις can mean God to both Philo and Stoicism, yet φύσις means something as different to the two as their conceptions of God are different.

The contrast of the two is most sharply brought out in those passages where Philo departs from his customary usage to speak of a law inherent in matter itself. For he sometimes speaks of a law of nature which conditioned God's act of creation. This law of nature is the law of the nature of matter,[43] not an ordinance of God. So it is not in the nature of creation, he says, to be able to receive benefits in a way comparable to God's power of bestowing them,[44] which limitation would definitely restrict the working of God by setting up an obstacle or situation beyond His complete control. That is, the nature of matter is itself a law not only for itself, but compelling recognition from God, who cannot do with matter what is beyond the law of its nature. There are other traces in Philo of a law of nature quite independent of God's creation. He has much to say of the important powers of the different numbers, powers which God had in mind as He ordered the cosmos;[45] their powers are determined by the "Law of Nature";[46] but he nowhere ascribes the origin of their powers to God's creative act.[47] The providence of God for

---

35. *Jos.*, 29; cf. *Abr.*, 61 where Philo speaks of ἡ ἐν τῇ φύσει τάξις καὶ ἡ παντὸς λόγου κρείττων πολιτεία, ᾗ χρῆται ὁ κόσμος.
36. *Provid.*, ii, 49. God is also the cosmic Ephor in *Opif.*, 11. The Ephor of the universe is frequently Δίκη, as in *Jos.*, 48.
37. *Provid.*, ii, 15.   38. *Agr.*, 51.
39. *Opif.*, 46.   40. Ib.
41. *Provid.*, ii, 82: "Quem ad modum urbs virtuosa per legem dicitur regi, . . . similiter per providentiam regi mundus dicitur."
42. *Spec.*, i, 279: ὁ θεὸς καὶ νόμων ἐστὶ παράδειγμα ἀρχέτυπον.
43. *Opif.*, 8, 9.   44. Ib., 23.
45. Ib., 35, 60, 78, 111, 128; *Heres*, 156.   46. *Opif.*, 13.
47. In this he suggests the *Timaeus*, which always assumes the existence of the παραδεί-

His creation is itself necessitated by a Law of Nature which seems to ante-
cede it, at least logically: "For that the maker should care for the thing
made is required by the laws and ordinances of Nature."[48] Even God's own
kingship He holds φύσεως θεσμοῖς ἀκινήτοις.[49]

These latter usages, in which God's own action is conditioned by a Law of
Nature, are not, it would seem, to be taken as anything but incidental expression. The "Nature," a law of which requires care for creation, for example, Philo would certainly have said was God's own nature. The origin of
the nature of number must be taken as an inadvertent anomaly in Philo as
it is in Plato. The school seems not to have discussed that point, and the idea
of the Creator as having number ready at hand had not been either challenged or explained. Certainly it would have been given no explanation in
the Academy or by Pythagoreans that would have been reminiscent of the
Stoic Law of Nature. The law of matter, while it too appears as a condition-
ing force in Platonism, is in Philo much more akin to the Stoic conception.
Philo uses it as little as possible because it contradicts his own usual notion that
all law is a product of God, and when he does use it, it appears, as in Platonism, to be an emergency device for the purpose of theodicy. Indeed both
Philo and Plato use it slightly, apparently because they were aware that the
logical consequence of a law to which God had to conform in creating the
world is fatalism, and this, abundantly present in Philo's environment, at
least, Philo sharply repudiates, to insist that Natural Law is the Law of
God.[50] Even the heavenly bodies move according to the "ordinances and laws
which God laid down in His universe as unalterable,"[51] with which might
be identified the cause "more ancient," i.e. more primal, than fate or necessity, which drives and steers the universe like a charioteer or pilot, for it has
absolute sovereign authority.[52] Philo is distinctly not a fatalist, however easy
it might be to conclude fatalism from isolated statements. That God is the
cause of all things, but is not the cause of physical imperfection or moral evil
is a position straddling the issue neither original with Philo nor unfamiliar
after him. It was a position inherent in Platonism, and has characterized the
great orthodox tradition of Christianity which shrank from setting up any
ultimate cosmic principle of evil, but which recoiled just as sharply from

γματα, and the system of numerical relationships, as being at hand for the Creator's use, but
nowhere accounts for their origin.

48. *Opif.*, 171; *Praem.*, 42.
49. Frag. in Eusebius, *Praep. Evang.*, VIII, xiv, 3.
50. *Provid.*, ii, 63; *Heres*, 300 f.; *QG*, i, 21 (Frag. in Joh. Damasc., *Sacr. Parall.* 748B,
Mangey II, 653). See Gfroerer, *Philo und die jüdisch-alex. Theosophie*, I, 472 ff.
51. *Opif.*, 61.
52. *Heres*, 301. Cf. Pseudo-Philon., *Jona*, 1: "Quare puto legislationem (dei) sicut in navi
optime a se constructa, superne universorum moderatricem supersedentem, mundum hunc ad
salutem singulorum derigere et singulis quaecumque ubique sint, utiliter consulere." (Tauch.
Ed., VII, 420.)

attributing the causation of evil to God. So we may rightly expect that when Philo is speaking of God, His Nature, and His relations with the world, we shall find him putting all things subject to the Law of God in Nature. But when he turns specifically to the problem of evil we shall find a parallel to Paul's "law of the members," that is mention of a law of the material nature which seems at enmity with God's law.[53] Let that theist who can solve the problem of evil cast the first stone at either Paul or Philo for such inconsistency.

The Law of God, or the Law of Nature, may thus be considered independently of the anomalous natural law of matter. For except only when dealing with the problem of evil, the Law of Nature is the Law that comes from God as a part or aspect of the Light-Stream. God is essentially νομοθέτης καὶ πηγὴ νόμων.[54] The Law is connected with God in the general scheme of the Light-Stream in two ways, first by Philo's identifying it fully with the Logos, and secondly with the δύναμις βασιλική, and its subordinate δύναμις νομοθετική. On each of these a word further must be said.

The identification of the Nomos with the Logos was terminologically again at hand from Stoic sources. Not only did Stoics use the two terms interchangeably, but in their use of ὁ ὀρθὸς λόγος for the Logos they made the meaning of the identification clear. Like many terms now freely called "Stoic," ὁ ὀρθὸς λόγος both as a term and as a description of law antedates their teaching. In view of the evidence given below[55] it is hard to see how Stein is justified in saying that the Cynics first gave the expression philosophical significance.[56] Indeed, as far as its connection with Law is concerned, Clement of Alexandria quotes Speusippos as saying that Law is an

---

53. On this subject see the Appendix.   54. *Sac.*, 131.

55. Sextus (*Math.*, vii, 122) uses the term of Empedocles, but we cannot be certain that it was used by Empedocles. See Heinze *Lehre vom Logos*, p. 60. In Herodotus (ii, 17; vi, 68) it means simply "truth." Leisegang (Pauly-Wissowa, *RE*, XIII, 1058 f.) makes too specific the meaning here. In Plato it is parallel with ἐπιστήμη (*Phaedo* 73a), though I cannot think the two are identical here as does Heinze (*op. cit.*, p. 76). In this passage it seems to mean "formulated reason" (not Burnet's "right account," suggested in his *Phaedo*, note, *ad loc.*), as also in *Critias* 109b. But it means "reason" itself in *Polit.*, 310c. The connection of the term with νόμος first appears in Plato, *Laws*, 890d, where he asserts that the ancient laws which establish the existence of the gods are φύσει since they are νοῦ γεννήματα κατὰ λόγον ὀρθόν. Indeed in *Laws* 659d law itself pronounces the ὀρθὸς λόγος (πρὸς τὸν ὑπὸ τοῦ νόμου λόγον ὀρθόν εἰρημένον). The ὀρθὸς λόγος is a guide of conduct (*Polit.*, 310c). Taylor (*Plato*, p. 415, n. 1) thinks the notion a Platonic invention. Plato's casual way of bringing it in would suggest to me much more a similar popular usage. Aristotle also used the term both as right reason and as the background or source of law. As right reason it is the subjective guide within man (*Eth. Nic.*, 1147b 31; 1144b 26; *Eth. Mag.*, 1208a 9 ff., 19 f.) and so can be identified with φρόνησις (1144b 21 ff.). He gives as a popular definition (πάντες ὁρίζονται) of virtue that it is a ἕξις κατὰ τὸν ὀρθὸν λόγον. This he takes over to his own idea of virtue when he says τὸ μέσον ἐστὶν ὡς ὁ λόγος ὀρθὸς λέγει (*Eth. Nic.*, 1138b 20; *Eth. Eud.*, 1222a 9; b 7). Aristotle also connects it with law, when he says that suicide is παρὰ τὸν ὀρθὸν λόγον ὃ οὐκ ἐᾷ ὁ νόμος (*Eth. Nic.*, 1138a 10; cf. Grant, *Ethics of Aristotle*, I, 257 ff., 487, n.).

56. *Erkenntnisstheorie der Stoa*, 1888, p. 259.

excellent thing as being ὀρθὸς λόγος.[57] The fragment is small, but Clement took it definitely as the source of the similar Stoic notions. All that the Stoics seem to me to have done with the notion was to give it a formulation so convenient that it could be used by all schools: "The universal law (ὁ νόμος ὁ κοινός) is the ὀρθὸς λόγος which pervades all things, and is to be identified with Zeus as he is the leader in the ordering of phenomena."[58] Nomos and ὀρθὸς λόγος, according to the Stoics, alike existed "by nature," and expressed themselves in the mutually complementary realms of private morality and public law.[59] So the Wise Man is he who does everything κατὰ τὸν ὀρθὸν λόγον;[60] uprightness and self-control are defined in terms of it,[61] and sin is its transgression.[62] At the same time the ὀρθὸς λόγος was the foundation of statutory law: "Law, the Stoics say, is an excellent thing, for it is ὀρθὸς λόγος stipulating what is to be done, and forbidding what is not to be done."[63] Dio Chrysostom tells us that nomos, as ὀρθὸς λόγος, was to stand beside the king on his throne.[64] But while nomos and ὀρθὸς λόγος are thus identified in the sense of statutory law, the distinction is usually felt that the civil law is ideally a derivative from the universal Nomos, or ὀρθὸς λόγος, rather than that the civil law is itself in any given case to be identified with the higher principle. As a universal existence the Law of Nature seems to be everywhere present and active, but not everywhere in the same sense. So it is given to all men,[65] but while it does not command the upright man in vain, it has no power to control the wicked.[66] Yet since it is common to men and gods, it is the foundation of a social life between them. Not only, Cicero explains, is *ratio* present in both gods and men, but *recta ratio*, which is law, and so the fellowship of gods and men has the foundation of a common law—which implies a common civil organization (*civitas*). And not

57. *Stromata*, II, iv (ed. Stählin II, p. 123).
58. Diog. La., VII, 88 (*SVF*, III, 4). Heinemann (*Poseidonios*, II, 230 f.) is clearly wrong in thinking that Posidonius first introduced the term into Stoicism. It is Posidonius himself who tells us that the older Stoics used the ὀρθὸς λόγος as the κριτήριον (Diocles, *ap.* Diog. La. VII, 54; *SVF*, I, 631). There is no reason for calling Diog. La., VII, 128 (*SVF*, III, 308), a later ascription, as Heinemann does. On this point Stein, *Erkenntnisstheorie der Stoa*, pp. 253 ff., seems to me still sound.
59. Diog. La., VII, 128 (*SVF*, III, 308). Cf. Stob., II, vii, 10a (Wachs.): καὶ τὸ παρὰ φύσιν δ' εἴληπται ἐν τῇ τοῦ πάθους ὑπογραφῇ, ὡς συμβαίνοντος παρὰ τὸν ὀρθὸν καὶ κατὰ φύσιν λόγον.
60. Stob., II, 66, 14 (*SVF*, III, 560).
61. Stob., II, 96, 18 (*SVF*, III, 501); Clem. Al., *Stromata*, II, 80, 4 (*SVF*, III, 275).
62. Stob., II, 93, 14; 96, 18 (*SVF*, III, 500, 501); Clem. Al., *Paed.*, I, 13, 1 (*SVF*, III, 445).
63. Stob., II, vii, 11d and i (Wachs.); IV, ii, 11. Cf. Marcion *ap.* *SVF*, III, 314; and Alex. Aphrod., *De Fato*, c. 35 (*SVF*, II, 1003). This seems but an adaptation of the definition of law attributed to Pericles by Xenophon (*Mem.*, I, ii, 42): πάντες οὗτοι νόμοι εἰσίν, οὓς τὸ πλῆθος συνελθὸν καὶ δοκιμάσαν ἔγραψε, φράζον, ἅ τε δεῖ ποιεῖν καὶ ἃ μή. See Cicero, *De Legibus*, I, xii, 33 (*SVF*, III, 317).
64. *Orat.*, I, 75 (ed. de Budé).
65. Cicero, *De Legibus*, I, xii, 33 (*SVF*, III, 317).
66. Cicero, *De Republica*, III, 33 (*SVF*, III, 325).

only is the universe a single *civitas* common to gods and men, but as a city is built upon family relationships, so, in the world city, men are agnates and fellow-tribesmen of the gods, by virtue, we understand, of the common possession of the universal *ratio* or *recta ratio.*[67]

The Stoic ὀρθὸς λόγος, as it expresses itself finally in Cicero, then, is identified now with the universal Logos, now with Nomos, and with Nomos in now a civil, now a moral, now a universal mystical sense. If Cicero goes on from this last passage to no mystical flights himself, it is rather because of his own personal character, and not because he has not a philosophy fully capable of mystical inferences. In the Stoic environment from which he took his ideas there must have been many whose natures impelled them to mystical communion and union with the universal principle they found represented in themselves.

Cicero, Lactantius, and Minucius Felix tell us that that equation of natural and divine law, such as we find in Philo, goes back to Zeno himself.[68] The one most striking feature for our present purpose is that λόγος, ὀρθὸς λόγος, and νόμος, both as universal, individual, and political terms are quite interchangeable.[69]

Philo drew in part from much the same philosophical sources as Cicero, and was of a nature to do full justice to the mystical elements of his teachers. One is safe in saying that with Philo the whole conception is developed at least as much for mystical as for political purposes. So with Philo the great Law of God or Nature is the ὀρθὸς λόγος, and in such an identification the Law of Nature becomes a moral as well as physical force. The term νόμος is specifically interchangeable with ὀρθὸς λόγος, as Philo points out.[70] Thus the word ὀρθὸς is frequently omitted and λόγος alone put in formulae where we know ὀρθὸς λόγος must have been understood by both Philo and his readers, as in the familiar definition that νόμος is "nothing else than λόγος enjoining what is necessary and prohibiting what must not be done."[71] In the same definition λόγος θεῖος might be used,[72] while in another passage

---

67. Cicero, *De Legibus*, I, vii, 23 (*SVF*, III, 339); cf. Stob., II, vii, 10a (Wachs., II, p. 48, l. 1) where the term παρὰ φύσιν is defined as τὸ παρὰ τὸν ὀρφὸν καὶ κατὰ φύσιν λόγον.

68. Cicero, *Nat. Deor.*, I, 36 (*SVF*, I, 162, has also passages of Lactantius and Minucius Felix).

69. Even the Stoic necessity and providence were included in the same conception: so Chrysippus defines: εἱμαρμένη ἐστὶν ὁ τοῦ κόσμου λόγος ἢ λόγος (Plut. νόμος) τῶν ἐν τῷ κόσμῳ προνοίᾳ διοικουμένων, *SVF*, II, 913. See a number of interesting parallels in Zeller, *Phil. d. Gr.*, III, i, 161, n. 2. Heinemann, *Poseidonios*, II, 225–323 has an extended exposition of the legal philosophy of Cicero to try to distinguish the Posidonian elements. If his argument frequently runs away from his data, there is much light thrown on Cicero's point of view.

70. ὁ ὀρθὸς λόγος, ὃς δὴ νόμος ἐστίν, *Ebr.*, 142; cf. νόμος ἀψευδὴς ὁ ὀρθὸς λόγος . . . ὑπ' ἀθανάτου φύσεως ἄφθαρτος ἐν ἀθανάτῳ διανοίᾳ τυπωθείς, *Prob.*, 46.

71. *Praem.*, 55.

72. *Mig.*, 130. He goes on to say, λόγος ἐστὶ θεῖος ὁ νόμος; ὀρθὸς λόγος had been used

the law of the universe is defined substantially in the same way, but here identified with λόγος φύσεως,[73] or, just below, ὁ τῆς φύσεως ὀρθὸς λόγος.[74] Again νόμοι are φύσεως ἱεροὶ λόγοι.[75] So with Philo, while the phrase ὀρθὸς λόγος is always to be taken with a legal implication,[76] it is clear that the ὀρθὸς may be dropped at will, and that in Philo's mind the great Law of Nature is only another name for the Logos or one of its aspects. Accordingly the term λόγος appears in many descriptions of natural phenomena where we should expect νόμος.[77] On the basis of this complete agreement of the universal Logos and Nomos I disagree with the latest editors in preferring to read νόμος to λόγος in the following passage:

There is no material thing so powerful that it is able to support the world, but the eternal Nomos of the eternal God is the most secure and stable support of all things. This is extended from the center to the limits, and from the extremities to the center, carrying on the irresistible course of nature, collecting and holding together all its parts; for the Father who created it made it the unbreakable bond of the universe.[78]

The passage of Philo which establishes best the ὀρθὸς λόγος as being universal Law, and at the same time as identical with the universal Logos, is the following: The universe, Philo says, should join in the first verse of the twenty-third Psalm,

for like a shepherd God the shepherd and king leads earth and water and air and fire and all the plants and animals in them, things mortal and divine; and in addition He leads the nature of heaven, the revolutions of the sun and moon, and the variations and harmonious dances of the other stars; He leads them according to

as synonymous with θεός (without the article) just above in § 128. It is clear that θεός, θεῖος λόγος, ὀρθὸς λόγος, and νόμος are here quite interchangeable.

73. Jos., 29.

74. Ib., 31; cf. Opif., 143: ἐπεὶ δε πᾶσα πόλις εὔνομος ἔχει πολιτείαν, ἀναγκαίως συνέβαινε τῷ κοσμοπολίτῃ χρῆσθαι πολιτείᾳ ᾗ καὶ σύμπας ὁ κόσμος. αὕτη δὲ ἐστιν ὁ τῆς φύσεως ὀρθὸς λόγος, ὃς κυριωτέρᾳ κλήσει προσονομάζεται θεσμός, νόμος θεῖος ὤν, καθ᾿ ὃν τὰ προσήκοντα καὶ ἐπιβάλλοντα ἑκάστοις ἀπενεμήθη. See also Prob., 62.

75. Spec., ii, 13. See also the parallelism in Jos., 174: θεὸς ἢ λόγος ἢ νόμος θεῖος. It is significant that none of these has the article.

76. As, e.g., Prob., 97.

77. As for example, τρόπας τέσσαρας, ὧν ἑκάστης ὅρος τρία ζῴδια, γνωριζόμενος ταῖς τοῦ ἡλίου περιφοραῖς κατὰ τὸν ἐν ἀριθμοῖς ἀσάλευτον καὶ βεβαιότατον καὶ θεῖον ὄντως λόγον. ὅθεν ἐνηρμόζοντο καὶ τῷ προσαγορευθέντι δεόντως λογείῳ· λόγῳ γὰρ αἱ τροπαὶ καὶ ἐτήσιοι ὧραι τεταγμένῳ καὶ παγίῳ συνίστανται, Mos., ii, 124 f. Philo has here used λόγος by attraction from the priestly λογεῖον. See also Som., ii, 223, 237.

78. Plant., 8 f. Eusebius, Pr. Ev., VII, 13 quotes the passage using λόγος for νόμος, so all late editors read λόγος with Eusebius. But all mss. agree on νόμος, and it seems more likely that Christians would have changed an original νόμος to λόγος than vice versa. Soulier, Le doctrine du Logos chez Philon d'Alexandrie, Turin, 1876, p. 116 was quite right in pointing out that since the two terms were interchangeable the discussion had little point. Still I think that the mss. reading is preferable.

δίκη and nomos, for He has appointed τὸν ὀρϑὸν αὐτοῦ λόγον καὶ πρωτόγονον υἱόν, who received the guardianship of this sacred flock like a viceroy of the Great King.[79]

It is from this point of view that the λόγος θεῖος can be called the δίοπος καὶ κυβερνήτης τοῦ παντός.[80] One must not be misled, by the fact that the ὀρϑὸς λόγος guides the universe according to (κατὰ) justice and law, to conclude that the two are distinct. Here then are God and His first-born Son, usually called the Logos alone,[81] whose identification with ὀρϑὸς λόγος and nomos is complete. Indeed the ὀρϑὸς λόγος of Philo is the Logos in its legal aspect. The legal implication of the term seems not lost even when it appears as the source of the virtues, especially of justice, the chief virtue. Similarly its legal force is felt when it is given a place in the Pythagorean scheme of the universe according to numbers, in which the ὀρϑός of "right" angles is identified with the ὀρϑός of "right" reason, so that it becomes the constituent element in the square, the Pythagorean symbol of justice.[82] So completely are the universal Logos and the ὀρϑὸς λόγος interchangeable that Philo can speak of the universal σπερματικὸς λόγος as ὁ σπερματικὸς καὶ γεννητικὸς τῶν καλῶν ὀρϑὸς λόγος.[83]

The identification of the Law with the Logos is thus complete. One may read the Logos at any time when Philo is speaking of the Law of Nature: and it must always be borne in mind that the Logos is not the Stoic Logos, a concomitant of the ultimate material substrate. It is rather the Light-Stream coming down into matter. The Stoic terms can be used because the terms are themselves older than Stoicism and have no specific materialistic denotation. Actually the Stoics themselves saw the split between the active and passive agents of the primal fire as taking place so early in the process of creation, and treated the two thereafter in so loosely dualistic a form, that much that they would say of the Logos-Nomos controlling the universe could be said quite as accurately of Philo's immaterial Logos-Nomos coming down from God to matter to introduce form and order. God's Law did in Philo's mind permeate and guide the universe as an immanent principle. But it was from God, not from anything analogous to the Stoic "fire," that it came, and it was always qualitatively distinct from the matter it permeated. It was the immaterial God who was the πηγὴ νόμων.

Philo expresses the interrelation of the concepts much more accurately and clearly when he puts Law into its place in the schematization of the Stream

---

79. *Agr.*, 51.   80. *Cher.*, 36.
81. *Cont.*, 146; *Som.*, i, 215.
82. *Plant.*, 121; see, *Mos.*, ii, 80 with note *ad loc.* by Badt in *Philos Werke*.
83. *LA*, iii, 150. On this passage see Hans Meyer, *Geschichte der Lehre von der Keimkraften*, Bonn, 1914, p. 40. I cannot agree with Heinze, *Lehre vom Logos*, p. 240 f., that this implies an undeniable carrying over of the Stoic materialism.

by its Powers. The Stream, with its legal aspects, has already been discussed in the preceding chapter. Here it need only be stressed that just as the δύναμις ποιητική represented God's creative and providential aspects, so the δύναμις βασιλική expressed the ruling power of God, with the inevitable corollary that He was law-maker. Law itself, or laws, appeared fairly low in the hierarchy, indeed on the hither side of the great line which divided the created from the uncreated aspects of Deity, the aspects apart from the material world and those which could find at least partial representation in matter. But Law was still a higher principle than the κόσμος νοητός, and was definitely present there. Law as it manifests itself in a material medium would by this be definitely inferior to the Law not so manifested, and Law itself is something that could be transcended by the mystic if he rose beyond the great divide to the Higher Powers. The importance of this formulation is that it made Law, even in its lower steps as statutes, a definite step toward higher reality; and as one went beyond to those Powers not characterized by Law he had not rejected the Law but only gone on to the source of the Law. Yet the obligation to rise beyond the particular to the universal, from the product to the source, would have been as essential in the case of Law as in the case of any of the other derivations from God.

One might, and perhaps should, stop here in describing Philo's conception of Natural Law and the Law of God. But there are several cognate notions, figures used by Philo in developing the conception of the Law of God in the universe, which throw so much light upon the variety of its usage, and the way in which it could be linked up with different aspects of his thought, that they must be at least briefly treated.

First of these to be considered is Philo's conception of δίκη. To Philo, as to all Greek tradition, the legal was always the just, and ὁ νόμιμος equivalent to ὁ δίκαιος. Philo does not himself state the familiar Greek aphorism, τὸ νόμιμον δίκαιον εἶναι,[84] but their equivalence was repeatedly assumed in his favorite use of synonymous doublets, and in such statements as that τὰ αὐτὰ δίκαια are equivalent to τὰ κοινὰ τῆς φύσεως καὶ ἀκίνητα νόμιμα,[85] or that τὰ τῆς βασιλείας δίκαια are the same as τῆς βασιλείας δόγματα καὶ νόμοι.[86] Δίκη then must be examined as an aspect of Law. In discussing δίκη, Bréhier points out the most obvious facts.[87] Philo has retained the Greek mythological figure which was first πάρεδρος θεοῦ, seated beside God.[88] Philo seems to have assigned to δίκη a very real function when he says that δίκη looks to the enforcing of the Decalogue, that is Natural Law, which is given out by God without stated penalties, because God Himself is only the source of

84. Xenophon, *Memorab.*, IV, iv, 12. Hirzel has a large collection of similar passages in his *Themis, Dike und Verwandtes*, p. 384, n. 4.
85. *Agr.*, 43.
86. *Mig.*, 196 f.   87. *Les Idées*, 149.   88. *Mut.* 194 ff.; *Spec.*, iv, 201, etc.

"the means of salvation unmixed and not partaking in vengeance," is the "cause of good things only and the cause of no evil thing." So God

offers no asylum for evil doers, but knows that Dike, His πάρεδρος, and the ἔφορος of human affairs will not rest, since δίκη naturally hates evil, and will take the chastisement of sinners as its proper (συγγενές) task. For it is right for the ministers and lieutenants of God, as for captains in war to apply punishments to those who desert the ranks of the Just One; but it is right that the general security of everyone should be ascribed to the Great King, as the warden of peace and the one who furnishes richly and without stint all the good things of peace always to everyone everywhere. For strictly speaking God is the President of peace, but His subordinates are the leaders of wars.[89]

Again the dread visitation of δίκη, the ἔφορος, brings the most terrible punishments to malefactors (such as the profane or incestuous); if her punishments are not inflicted at once, they will be exacted with abundant usury at what seems to her the proper time.[90] A specific example is found in the persistent enmity which δίκη came to take toward Flaccus because he was ἔκνομος;[91] in the way in which δίκη followed the brothers of Joseph,[92] as well as Oedipus and the whole Persian race.[93] For the eye of δίκη sees what occurs in even the most remote places,[94] and as πάρεδρος τῷ θεῷ visits the offenders against the eternal Law of Nature with all the most powerful elements of the universe, especially fire and flood.[95] This is the sort of δίκη familiar to readers of classical literature from Homer on, and not at all, as Bréhier implies, distinctively Stoic.[96] It is obviously at times associated with the δύναμις βασιλική or νομοθετική, but by no means always. As a power of vengeance it appears in Philo for two reasons, as a reflection of current Greek manner of speech, and as another method of theodicy.

The weakness of Philo's theodicy has been shown, and consists chiefly in the fact that, while Philo was convinced of the reality of evil, evil which could not have come from God, he did not actually believe in the existence of any force in the world beyond God's direct control. For δίκη, if sometimes

89. *Dec.*, 176 ff.; *Spec.*, iii, 19. Cf. *Jos.*, 48; *Prob.*, 89; *Mos.*, ii, 162.
90. *Dec.*, 95; *Mos.*, i, 326; *Conf.*, 128. In *Spec.*, ii, 253, he speaks of "myriads" of such ephors.
91. *Flac.*, 102, 104, 106 f., 146, 189.
92. *Jos.*, 170.   93. *Spec.*, iii, 19.
94. *Mos.*, i, 55; cf. *Mig.*, 186, 225; *Conf.*, 116–121; *Spec.*, iv, 201.
95. *Mos.*, ii, 53. Cf. the closing sentences of the fragment quoted by Cohn in the *Editio Maior*, IV, p. 212. The text (§52) speaks of the λόγος τῆς ἀιδίου φύσεως as the object against which sins are committed. Νόμος is clearly meant, and is used in the fragment. If the text has not been altered from what Philo wrote, this is a most striking instance of the complete interchangeability of the two words.
96. Bréhier, *Les Idées*, pp. 147, 149. I need not go into the much discussed history of δίκη. See R. Hirzel, *Themis, Dike und Verwandtes*, 1907, pp. 56–225, and especially the excursus on the πάρεδροι, pp. 412 ff.; Ehrenberg, *Die Rechtsidee im frühen Griechentum*, 1921, pp. 54–102; John L. Myres, *The Political Ideas of the Greeks*, 1927, pp. 167–240.

it acts to relieve God of the responsibility of direct action in punishment, is so completely subordinate to God that δίκη is often said to be inflicted by divine will. For example the destruction of Sodom was brought about by δίκης γνώμη θεία δικασθείσης;[97] the man who puffs himself up in his own conceit makes God his opponent and prosecutor;[98] statements which contravene Philo's entire theodicy. And if δίκη is the all seeing, that is also true of God Himself, who πάντα ὁρᾷ καὶ πάντων ἀκούει.[99] God is also Himself the Ephor.[100] God Himself sees to it that the penalty is restricted not only to the deserts, but even to the endurance of the culprit: this He does, Philo tells us, because His mercy is older than His δίκη—a poetic statement of no literal metaphysical importance.[101] And δίκη itself is not always only the hater of evil. It is φιλάρετος as well as μισοπόνηρος;[102] it sends help to those in distress as well as penalty to the malefactor, as when it sent Moses to help the damsels at the well,[103] and when it brings calamity upon the man who mistreats and kills his slaves, as much to help the slaves as to avenge the sins upon the sinner.[104]

It is interesting that while vengeance and punishments are figuratively, but only figuratively, delegated from God, Philo has no interest in vindicating the justice of God as such. His theodicy is devoted to defending not the justice but the goodness of God. In fact the only passage I have found where God is represented as δίκαιος in any essential way, the δίκαιος is a passing modifier apparently carried over by transposition, and the word is of so little importance that the passage rather gains than loses in clarity by ignoring it.[105] Philo did of course make God personally the judge,[106] and as judge Philo represented God as just in His judgments.[107] But in general God is

97. *Abr.*, 141.

98. *Virt.*, 174.

99. *Spec.*, i, 279.

100. See above, p. 52, note 36.

101. *Immut.*, 76, 80. To Philo this probably meant that the emanation primarily merciful, the δύναμις ποιητική, was more primary an expression of God's nature than the ruling emanation, the δύναμις βασιλική. But we have seen that all such statements have only suggestive value, since the true perception learned that God's emanations were not many or divided, but one.

102. *Conf.*, 128.

103. *Mos.*, i, 55.

104. *Spec.*, iii, 140.

105. The reference to God as δίκαιος in Leisegang's *Index*, p. 368, is a mistake: ἀληθὲς δὲ καὶ δίκαιον μέτρον τὸ τὸν μόνον δίκαιον θεὸν ὑπολαβεῖν πάντα μετρεῖν καὶ σταθμᾶσθαι καὶ ἀριθμοῖς καὶ πέρασι καὶ ὅροις τὴν τῶν ὅλων περιγράψαι φύσιν, ἄδικον δὲ καὶ ψευδὲς τὸ νομίσαι κατὰ τὸν ἀνθρώπινον νοῦν ταῦτα συμβαίνειν, *Som.*, ii, 194. God is not himself here δίκαιος, but προαγωνιστὴς τοῦ δικαίου (*Abr.*, 232), "champion of the just man." This is what is meant also when God is called φιλοδίκαιος (*Heres*, 163). In *Mos.*, i, 260 one escapes from timidity in the battle of life by using τῇ ἀκαθαιρέτῳ τοῦ δικαίου συμμαχία which has traditionally been translated "the invincible alliance of the Just (God)" (so Badt in *Philos Werke*). I see no reason for supplying the word God.

106. *Heres*, 271; *Opif.*, 155; *LA*, iii, 205, as judge He is judge of Himself.

107. *Ebr.*, 111; *Mos.*, ii, 237, 279. So when Philo says that God is unlike man in being able to make a geometrically perfect bisection, and as such is ἀκριβοδίκαιος (*Heres*, 143; cf. *Som.*, ii, 194). I cannot feel that this expresses literally his ultimate philosophy.

ἡ ἀέναος πηγὴ φρονήσεως καὶ δικαιοσύνης.[108] He governs σὺν δίκῃ,[109] or μετὰ δικαιοσύνης.[110] God has the ἐπιστήμη καὶ δύναμις "of the truly good, beautiful, just, pious, and the like,"[111] but these cannot be forced back upon the nature of God, for I think that to Philo God as "just" would be ultimately as anomalous as the conception of God as "pious." The reason for this is not far to seek. Δικαιοσύνη was to any Greek a quality of conforming to laws, and God, as the source of laws, and hence essentially above all law, was hardly to be described by this term. A king might and should be δίκαιος as he harmonized his life with the incoming λόγος-νόμος, but he was above the laws of the realm; so the word "law-abiding" was hardly to be applied to Philo's God, who was above even the λόγος-νόμος. Further the delegation of His justice to Δίκη was a part of Philo's feeling that God must be sufficient in Himself, and self-sufficiency and justice cannot both be inherent in the same person. For justice demands a social environment in which it might be exercised, and the virtues and properties of God must, in Philo's eyes, require no association for their full realization. It is by no means without significance that in the passage just cited where Philo calls God the "ever-flowing source of justice," he has been talking of God as being different from ordinary judges, in that he is not corruptible by bribes. Philo, then, when he would naturally have gone on to say that God is Himself just, instead assures us that God is αὐταρκέστατος ἑαυτῷ, entirely sufficient unto Himself, and then makes Him the πηγὴ δικαιοσύνης.[112] So to Philo, while as we shall see δικαιοσύνη is the great way in which man can imitate and conform himself to God, God Himself is not fittingly to be thought of as having justice as part of His nature.

The confusion is here quite deep, but is not, I think, unescapable. At one

108. Spec., i, 277. As far as I can judge from so small a passage Philo seems to be making an Old Testament statement of the justice of God into a derivative statement that justice is a divine thing, and so deflecting it from its original application to God as an attribute, in the following statement (QE, ii, 10; Harris, Fragments, p. 52; Tauchnitz Edition of Philo VI, 272): πενία καθ' ἑαυτὴν μὲν ἐλέου χρῄζει εἰς ἀπανόρθωσιν ἐνδείας, εἰς δὲ κρίσιν ἰοῦσα βραβευτῇ χρῆται τῷ τῆς ἰσότητος νόμῳ. θεῖον γὰρ ἡ δικαιοσύνη καὶ ἀδέκαστον. ὅθεν καὶ ἐν ἑτέροις εὖ εἴρηται, ὅτι ἡ κρίσις τοῦ θεοῦ δίκαιά ἐστιν. This latter quotation is traditionally referred to Deut. 32, 4; but here the Greek reads δίκαιος καὶ ὅσιος κύριος, which seems exactly what Philo is trying to avoid saying. May Philo have had in mind the lost original of the Apocalypse of John, which twice says ἀληθιναὶ καὶ δίκαιαι αἱ κρίσεις σου (xvi, 7; xix, 2)? Philo's form of reference suggests a non-canonical source. The nearest expressions in the Old Testament are Ps. xix, 10: τὰ κρίματα τοῦ κυρίου ἀληθινά, δεδικαιωμένα ἐπὶ τὸ αὐτό; and Ps. cxix, 137: Δίκαιος εἶ, κύριε, καὶ εὐθὴς ἡ κρίσις σου. But neither is as fitting an original for Philo's statement as the Apocalypse passage.

109. Legat., 336; δίκῃ, Mig., 186.

110. Fragment, in Euseb., Praep. Ev., VIII, xiv, 2.

111. Som., ii, 296 f.

112. Pantasopulos, Elias, Die Lehre vom natürlichen und positiven Rechte bei Philo Judaeus (Diss.) München, 1893, pp. 22 ff., makes this passage and the above mentioned Heres, 163 (see note 105), together with a complete misunderstanding of Som., ii, 172 ff., the basis for stating that Philo regarded God as the model of justice. I do not agree with him.

time we have Philo delegating all acts of discipline to mythological assistants in order to free God of responsibility for evil action, at another God is Himself the sponsor or even the direct agent in such acts. Again we may speak of the justice, severity, and mercy of God, discuss them, yet Philo always evades making them into such fundamental aspects of the divine nature as he makes God's goodness. A complete discussion of the nature of God as Philo considered it is not here in place. The present difficulty, it seems to me, is almost altogether obviated in the mystical ladder, from any one of whose various rungs Philo may be speaking at a given time. Philo did not, of course, solve the problem of evil. But he did think of God as appearing entirely different according to the mystical status of the individual man. God appears to men in a lower mystical stage as the personal guide of a complicated machine, doing all well, in theory, but with some practical difficulties still to be adjusted. On this plane God can be considered as working with assistants, powers, or persons; He can be regarded as the source of a great Law or justice which has become more or less distinct from God Himself, but which is ultimately under His control. The religious attitude of one in this stage is ultimately to be that of obedience to law, and admiration of God's virtues and power.[113]

Quite another vision dawns upon the mind of the man who has climbed above this stage. To one on a higher level the whole process of creation seems rather the unfolding of God's own nature. There is no real objectivization from God, since God is personally the power informing all things, dwelling in all things. All distinctions in God lose their significance, even the distinction between God as acting and God as being. What appear to the lower mystic as actions are now seen to be intimate expressions of that nature of God, which is ultimately self-sufficient and incapable of relation with externals. There are no externals, with the exception of raw matter, which has after all a mere logical existence, since it is only found completely informed by God.[114] So there are in God no actions and no social virtues. Goodness is the only virtue at all applicable to God, and that virtue, at best only approximately applied to God, is associated with Him in its individual rather than social sense; the word is described by being applied to God, not God by the

---

113. For example *Cher.*, 106; and below, p. 93.

114. This appears, for example, in the discussion of God as Space in which the universe moves and exists (*Som.*, i, 63 f.): "God Himself is called 'space' by reason of the fact that He embraces all things, but is embraced by nothing at all and because He is a refuge for all things, just because He is His own receptacle and contains Himself and dwells in Himself. I, however, am not space, but I am in space, and the same is true of every individual thing. For that which is embraced is an other thing from that which embraces, and the divine being embraced by nothing is necessarily its own 'space.'" This discussion of space is the highest of three views: one which considers space as χώρα ὑπὸ σώματος πεπληρωμένη; a second which regards it as the λόγος θεῖος "which God himself has filled completely full with incorporeal Powers." But these both disappear in the third, the true vision of τόπος as God.

word. The perfect mystic finds himself completely assimilated into this nature of God by the vision; his own personality is quite indistinguishable from God's, and it is only when the vision of the truth departs and the ordinary illusion of existence returns that he feels himself as in any sense a distinct existence. In the higher vision, then, there is no room for God as just, merciful, or any of the other words of praise so beloved by Philo's ancestors and compatriots. ὁ θεὸς μόνος ἐστὶ καὶ ἕν, οὐ σύγκριμα, φύσις ἁπλῆ.[115]

Shall we say with Bréhier that this is mysticism rather than philosophy? Yes, if we are willing to say the same of the deity of Plotinus, which differs from Philo's rather in Plotinus' greater powers of analysis and description than in any essential particular. It is philosophy with a mystical urge—and only really philosophic at the top of the "ladder." To this Philo would gladly have agreed. His cosmic mythologies never pleased him. He was constantly indicating higher syntheses, which showed clearly enough his dissatisfaction with much of his imagery. Philo the philosopher really appears undisguised at comparatively rare intervals. His divine Logos, δυνάμεις, νόμος, δίκη, et al., were in themselves only steps to higher conceptions, and had no ultimate validity.[116] For God's nature is that of the monad (ἡ τοῦ ἑνὸς φύσις);[117] He is thus unmixed and unmingled,[118] "for he who thinks that God has any quality . . . injures himself, not God."[119] If justice has no proper place in God's nature, it is still, of course, one of the great principles derivative from His nature. So when Philo says: σωτήριον ἐν τοῖς μάλιστα δικαιοσύνη καὶ ἀνθρώπων καὶ τῶν τοῦ κόσμου μερῶν, γῆς καὶ οὐρανοῦ,[120] it is clearly not the δικαιοσύνη of God which saves men and the parts of the cosmos, but their own δικαιοσύνη, their conformity to His Law and kingship. Δικαιοσύνη is distinctly a virtue of parts of the universe. So δικαιοσύνη, or the quality of conforming to God's Law or Nature, is the highest state of a created being, and truly salvation. Philo had no need to abandon law as a step towards God, but the Law to which he must ultimately aspire would be the Nature of God rather than any cosmic force or code derivative from that Nature. He could no more stop with a code than with the stars.

When Philo wishes to speak of the power of God's Law as a regulative force in the cosmos he is apt to do so in the mathematical terms of the Pythagorean ἰσότης. The importance of ἰσότης as a traditional expression of

---

115. *LA*, ii, 2.

116. So he says of God that κατὰ τὰ αὐτὰ ἑστὼς κινεῖ τὴν σύμπασαν στάσιν, οὐ διὰ τῶν σκελῶν—οὐ γὰρ ἀνθρωπόμορφος—, ἀλλὰ τὴν ἄτρεπτον καὶ ἀμετάβλητον ἐμφαίνουσαν: *Mut.*, 54. He might as well have denied any reality to the δυνάμεις as to the "legs," for neither properly harmonizes with the last phrase.

117. *Exs.*, 162. 118. *Heres*, 183.

119. *LA*, i, 51: ὁ γὰρ ἢ ποιότητα οἰόμενος ἔχειν τὸν θεὸν ἢ μὴ ἕνα εἶναι ἢ μὴ ἀγένητον καὶ ἄφθαρτον ἢ μὴ ἄτρεπτον ἑαυτὸν ἀδικεῖ, οὐ θεόν.

120. Harris, *Fragments*, p. 101, Mang. II, 664.

the Greek sense of justice does not need detailed reviewing here.[121] In early times equality, ἰσότης, was the equal share of one warrior as compared with the others in the spoils and provisions, a matter of equal arithmetic counting. In later times, with the developed caste system of the Greeks, this came to be replaced by a geometric proportionality as the true meaning of ἰσότης: not to every man the same but to every man his due according to his deserts, station, and service. As Hirzel says, it was probably the Pythagoreans who first made this change in meaning explicit.[122] The cry of democracy was always for some sort of application of the mathematical ἰσότης, the demand of all the other forms of the state was for the proportional ἰσότης. So Aristotle could write; "All agree that justice in distributions must be based on some principle of worth,"[123] and "The 'equal' in respect to worth is that every one should have his own,"[124] although he himself admitted that "under certain conditions arithmetical equality must be used, under others equality according to worth."[125]

How ἰσότης became a cosmic principle, or the fundamental principle of the cosmos, Hirzel has eloquently described.[126] "The history of the Greek cosmos, the greatest work of art of the Greeks, is the same as that of their art in general. To a rigid architectonic method of exposition used in primitive times there succeeded also here another method, which not merely formed and ordered dead masses and spaces but expressed life and spirit and sought to subdue both in the masses and forms of beauty. In place of the sensible visible world-harmony emerged the invisible harmony of the opposites."[127]

Philo was quite aware of these aspects of the conception of equality.

For, the term "equal" is used in one way with respect to numbers, as that two equals two, three equals three, and the other numbers similarly; but in another way with respect to spatial magnitudes, whose dimensions are length, breadth and depth. For span[128] may equal span, or cubit cubit, in magnitude, but not in value, as is the case also with things weighed and measured out. A necessary form of equality is also the proportional, by which also a few things can be regarded as equal to many, and small to great. This form of equality also cities are periodically accustomed to use when they bid each citizen to bring an equal amount from his property, not of course equal by count (ἀριθμῷ) but by analogy of the amount of property to the tax rate; so that the tax payment of one hun-

---

121. Hirzel, *Themis, Dike, und Verwandtes*, pp. 228–320. See especially 277 ff., 297 ff., 308 ff. E. Barker, *Greek Political Theory, Plato and his Predecessors*, pp. 46 ff.

122. *Op. cit.*, pp. 277 ff., 315.   123. *Eth. Nic.*, V, 6, 1131a 25 f.

124. *Polit.*, V, 7, 1307a 26.   125. Ib., V, 1, 1302a 7.

126. *Op. cit.*, pp. 308 ff.   127. Ib., p. 313.

128. Παλαιστή, later form of παλαστή, a measure of about three inches. The idea seems to be that a yard of cotton equals a yard of silk, a pound of lead equals a pound of gold, in measure but not in value.

dred drachmas from one man would seem to be equal to the tax payment of a talent from another.[129]

Joseph Cohn, in a note to his translation of this passage, says that Aristotle's discussion lies behind these remarks of Philo. There is no reason for assuming an immediate use of Aristotle's text. The ideas probably antedated Aristotle in Pythagoreanism, and were kept ever familiar in later times.

It is of considerable importance for our purpose, then, that we find Philo using ἰσότης as one of the chief principles in the cosmos, if not the fundamental one. The longest single discussion of this point is found in *Quis Heres*, 130–248, where Philo makes the most of the text, "and he divided them in the middle" (Gen. xv, 10). The immediate agent of the division is the Logos τομεύς, the "Cutter," which begins by dividing all material things down to the "so called indivisible atoms," then goes on to divide the θεωρητά into parts for which Philo finds no names.[130] I have examined this whole passage carefully elsewhere.[131] For our purposes here it is only necessary to indicate that Philo's aim in the entire passage is to point out that this account of creation makes ἰσότης the creative and controlling feature of the universe, cosmic Law, and hence is used by Moses as the basis of all his laws. For "the legal and equal are seeds of peace, and the universal cause of preservation (σωτηρίας) and duration. But inequality and greed give rise to war and are destructive of what things exist."[132]

It is not surprising to find the notion in other writings of Philo, where it is introduced in passing as being an axiomatic part of his philosophy and that of his readers. God is referred to as creating ἰσότης,[133] and in His rulership as always being guided by it.[134] All nature is full of δικαιοσύνη, which means that it is made law-abiding, by the universal presence in it of ἰσότης, the μήτηρ δικαιοσύνης.[135] " 'Equality' put in place all things, both those in heaven and those upon earth, according to unshakable laws and ordi-

129. *Heres*, 144, 145.
130. τὰ λόγῳ θεωρητὰ εἰς ἀμυθήτους καὶ ἀπεριγράφους μοίρας, §131.
131. "A neo-Pythagorean Source in Philo Judaeus," in *Yale Classical Studies*, III (1932), p. 115–164.
132. Harris, *Fragments*, p. 101, See the Tauchnitz Ed. of Philo, VI, 253; cf. *Spec.*, iv, 166.
133. God is ὁ ἰσότητος καὶ παντὸς τοῦ ἀρίστου δημιουργός: *Spec.*, i, 265. In *Spec.*, iv, 187 God is described as calling τὰ μὴ ὄντα εἰς τὸ εἶναι by making τάξιν ἐξ ἀταξίας καὶ ἐξ ἀποίων ποιότητας καὶ ἐξ ἀνομοίων ὁμοιότητας καὶ ἐξ ἑτεροιοτήτων ταυτότητας καὶ ἐξ ἀκοινωνήτων καὶ ἀναρμόστων κοινωνίας καὶ ἁρμονίας καὶ ἐκ μὲν ἀνισότητος ἰσότητα ἐκ δὲ σκότους φῶς ἐργασάμενος. The last two would seem a summary of all the preceding.
134. *Mut.*, 232: οἷς τὰ ἁρμόττοντα·χαρίζεται πρὸς τὰ τῆς ἑκάστου ψυχῆς σταθμήματα καὶ μέτρα σταθμώμενος καὶ διαμετρῶν ἰσότητι παρ' ἑαυτῷ τὸ ἀνάλογον ἑκάστοις. See *Spec.*, i, 295.
135. *Spec.*, iv, 231–238; *QE*, i, 6 (Harris, *Fragments*, p. 47); cf. *Spec.*, ii, 204, where ἰσότης is ἡ δικαιοσύνης ἀρχὴ καὶ πηγή, and inequality is the source of ἀδικία; *Legat.*, 85; *Mos.*, i, 328.

nances,"[136] he goes on to say, and illustrates by the equal divisions of day and night, the phases of the moon, the four seasons, and concludes that in the universe ἰσότης is represented by the cosmic order (κόσμος ἐστίν), in cities by democracy, in bodies by health, and in souls by καλοκἀγαθία.[137] All of this, it should be noted in passing, is δικαιοσύνη, and all is to be called the product of ἰσότης or νόμος τῆς φύσεως indifferently. He has learned of it from those who have investigated natural phenomena most closely, apparently the Pythagoreans.[138] The wealth of nature is arranged on the principle of ἰσότης, and so he who is guided by ἰσότης in money affairs is led into δικαιοσύνη.[139] Thus the study of geometry, by instilling in the mind the conception of ἰσότης, instils δικαιοσύνη at the same time;[140] and of all the numbers, the number four, the first square number, is of course especially symbolical of justice.[141] In general it is only another term for the same conception when Philo, in the passage already referred to, speaks of τὸ φύσει δίκαιον,[142] but makes a distinction between ἰσότης as a principle in nature, and δικαιοσύνη. He points out that even shellfish and storks have social virtues which can only be described as arising from a sense of justice and goes on to say:

It is right that the universe should be composed not of some only of its parts but of them all, however that part in which justice and injustice are found should be preeminently endowed with reason. For both of these pertain to reason. And so it is necessary that reason should be distributed to men and likewise to those animals mentioned.[143]

In discussing the honoring of one's parents Philo points out that lions, hares, and leopards can be domesticated as a result of their sense of gratitude to their keepers; dogs are faithful to death, and storks are exemplary for the care the younger birds give the older ones.[144] But he draws no such conclusion as that therefore they must have a share in reason since they are thus virtuous, while on other occasions he denies that animals could have virtue or vice since they do not have νοῦς or λόγος, the determining factor in all virtue.[145] For us here it is not so important that Philo contradicts himself about the animals as that he has definitely made the distinction between Natural Law and the virtue of following that Law. Ordinarily then he can use the terms ἰσότης and δικαιοσύνη as synonymous, but apparently he had

---

136. *Spec.*, iv, 232.　　　　　　　　　137. Ib., 237; cf. *Conf.*, 108.
138. *Spec.*, iv, 231 οἱ τὰ φύσεως ἀκριβοῦντες ἡμῖν παρέδοσαν.
139. *Cont.*, 17.　　　　　　　　　　140. *Cong.*, 16.
141. *Opif.*, 51; *Plant.*, 122; *Aet.*, 108. See my "Neo-Pythag. Source," p. 151, n. 132.
142. *Legat.*, 213; *Spec.*, iii, 129.
143. *Animal.*, 61.　　　　　　　　　144. *Decal.*, 113 ff.
145. *Opif.*, 73; *Sac.*, 46. Note that there he speaks of ζῷα ἄλογα, τὰ τῶν ζῴων μὴ λογικά, neither of which expressions makes it essential that all animals should be ἄλογα, though that seemed to be his implication.

a real meaning when he did distinguish between δικαιοσύνη and its mother or source, ἰσότης.

Another of Philo's approaches to the cosmic Law of God, or the metaphysical Law, is by describing that Law as the Oath of God. Some of the more striking passages must be quoted:

Justice and every virtue is ancestral law and ancient ordinance. And what else are laws and ordinances but sacred λόγοι of nature, having their fixity and steadfastness in themselves, so that they are indistinguishable from oaths?[146]

God swears not by something else, for there is nothing higher, but by Himself.

Some have said that it was inappropriate for Him to swear; for an oath is added to assist faith (πίστεως ἕνεκα), and only God and one who is God's friend is faithful, even as Moses is said to have been "faithful in all his house." Moreover the very words of God are oaths and laws of God and most sacred ordinances; and a proof of His sure strength is that whatever He says comes to pass, and this is especially characteristic of an oath. It would seem to be a corollary from this that all God's words are oaths receiving confirmation by accomplishment in act.[147]

Since Abraham had faith in God, God responded by giving πίστις back in return to him, guaranteeing by an oath what He had promised to him, speaking no longer as God to a man, but as a friend to a confidant. For His speech is an oath.[148]

If one puts these passages together it appears that Philo is hinting that in giving Abraham His oath He gave him Natural or Divine Law. As Abraham lives by faith in the λόγος or λόγοι of God he is living in that faith that is the πίστις of God. God has met Abraham's πίστις by giving him the supreme πίστις, the very Law and regularity of the divine Nature. It is in this sense that only God and the friend of God is πιστός, for only they have the fixity of the divine nature that expresses itself in the universal Law.

Where did Philo get such a notion of the divine oath as Law? Heinemann says[149] that Hierocles the Platonist is the first to mention the oath as akin to Natural Law, and "hence Philo can hardly be working here from Greek sources." Philo can hardly be working from Hierocles, it is true, but it seems obvious that he was working from Hierocles' sources. There is little likelihood that Hierocles would himself have invented so important a conception. As a matter of fact there is nothing else which Heinemann, or so far as I know any one else, can produce in parallel to Philo's statement. Hierocles, as a Platonist deeply interested in Pythagorean material, belongs precisely to

146. *Spec.*, ii, 13.
147. *LA*, iii, 203 f. Cf. *Decal.*, 84; *Sac.*, 91 ff.
148. *Abr.*, 273.   149. *Philos Werke*, ii, p. 111, n. 2.

that school from which Philo drew most heavily, and a glance at Hierocles' statements[150] makes some interrelation seem to me irrefutable. Hierocles' discussion is interesting in full, but I can quote only excerpts:

Law we have already described as the eternally unchanging activity (ἐνέργεια) of God. Oath, after Law, we would define as the cause which preserves all things in their own state and keeps them so fixed as if they were bound by the faith of an oath (ἐν ὅρκου πίστει); and it preserves the order of the Law (τοῦ νόμου τὴν τάξιν) so that the perfection of the Law of creation is the undeviating quality of the beautiful order in created things. For to see to it that all things endure, as though dispensed by Law, would be the principal work of the divine Oath, which is especially and eternally respected among those people who always think in terms of God.

So to break the law of God is to transgress the πίστις τοῦ θείου ὅρκου.

Whatever the material behind Philo and Hierocles, they, and the Epistle to the Hebrews alone in ancient literature have this peculiar conception of the πίστις τοῦ θείου ὅρκου. As a background for Hebrews, it should be recalled that Philo represents the giving to Abraham of the Oath of Promise as a gift of divine Law itself.

Considerable light is thrown on Philo's conception of the character of Natural Law by the casual references he makes to it for specific applications. The powers of the various numbers are determined by Natural Law.[151] It is a Law of Nature that the thing made comes after the maker (a reference to the priority of the Creator as determining the whole succession of cause and effect in nature).[152] From this it follows that it is a Law of Nature that the maker must have a care for his own creation, a Law which is applied not only to God,[153] but also to men to prevent the exposing of children by their parents,[154] and even to require masters to nourish, at least to the extent of giving them the necessities of existence, all servants born in the house.[155] A fragment of Philo reads: γονέας τίμα· οὗτος γὰρ νόμος θεῖός τε καὶ φυσικός,[156] which follows the Greek notion as expressed by Socrates,[157] and Dionysius Halicarnassus.[158] Similarly rulership is by Nature's Law properly concentrated in a single source. This inference from divine rulership is variously applied. Philo says that it was appealed to by the Roman friends of Gaius to justify his murdering his relatives in order to make himself unchallenged in his sole rulership, an application which Philo by no means approves.[159] His

---

150. *Commentarius in Aureum Carmen*, II, 2. I quote from the edition in Mullach's *Fragmenta Philos. Graec.*, I, 421 ff.

151. *Opif.*, 13.
153. *Praem.*, 42.
155. *Spec.*, ii, 233.
157. Xenoph., *Memorabilia*, IV, iv, 19.
159. *Legat.*, 68.

152. *Plant.*, 132.
154. *Virt.*, 132.
156. Harris, *Fragments*, p. 110.
158. *Ant. Rom.*, VIII, 51.

own theory of rulership accepts the principle, but discussion of that point must be postponed to another study. He does apply it, however, to the human constitution by showing that the rulership of the mind over the rest of the human constitution is established by Natural Law,[160] and hence he can say too that it is a Natural Law that ignorance brings destruction, education brings safety.[161] In these he seems to imply that it is a Natural Law that anarchy must inevitably destroy any kind of order. A still further extension leads him to say that by a Law of Nature foolish people are subjected to the wise,[162] while many who are slaves by civil law are not so by Natural Law.[163] Like traditional Greek formulation of Natural Law, the *status quo* of nature is to Philo guarded by Law. Xerxes failed in his attack because he had aroused divine wrath by bridging the Hellespont and by building a ship canal across the isthmus of Mt. Athos, for in doing so he had broken down the natural boundaries of sea and land.[164] Similarly it is a violation of the Laws of Nature to get more than one crop a year from the soil.[165] Man is also subject to a Law of necessity which requires him as a soul to leave his fatherland for the mortal body,[166] while his body is affected by the changes of seasons according to Natural Law.[167] Murder is against Natural Law.[168] The Laws of Nature seem especially specific in regard to man's sexual life. Concupiscence is given man by this Law to preserve his body,[169] and intercourse for begetting children is a Law of Nature.[170] But adultery, intercourse during menstruation, or with a barren woman, as well as what we still call "unnatural" vice, incest and pederasty, Philo calls violations of Natural Law,[171] while against the crossing of different types of animals, as in the breeding of mules, he formulates the Natural Law that justice is a matter of uniting equals with equals, like with like.[172] Also a man who marries a woman older than himself breaks the Law of Nature.[173] Many of these ap-

---

160. *QG*, iv, 218; *Agr.*, 31. See the Appendix.

161. *Ebr.*, 141 ff.   162. *Prob.*, 30.

163. Ib., 37.

164. *Som.*, ii, 117 ff. The same notion about the bridge over the Hellespont is expressed in almost identical words in Aeschylus' *Persians*, 735 ff. It would appear that Philo was drawing upon this passage were it not that he has obviously got his reference to the canals near Mt. Athos from the same source as his protest against the bridge. The Greeks had the same feeling about canals as Philo expresses: see Herodotus, I, 174; Hirzel, *Themis, Dike und Verwandtes*, p. 221.

165. *Spec.*, iv, 212.   166. *QG*, iv, 74.

167. Fragment *ap.* Eusebius, *Praeparatio Evangelica*, VIII, xiv, 23.

168. *Decal.*, 132; cf. Empedocles, *ap.* Arist., *Rhet.*, I, 13, 1373b 14 ff.

169. *QG*, ii, 46.

170. *Praem.*, 108; *Animal.*, 48; *QE*, ii, 19. See the Appendix.

171. *Spec.*, iii, 19, 32, 37 ff.; 47 ff.; *Animal.*, 49.

172. *Spec.*, iv, 204; iii, 46 ff. Cf. Fragment 14 in Harris, *Fragments*, p. 53; μιγνύναι τὰ ἄμικτα οὐχ ὅσιον. Heinemann in his note to *Spec.*, iv, 204 points out that this is rabbinic.

173. *QG*, i, 27; an inference from the fact that while all other animals were created simultaneously male and female, Eve was created after Adam.

plications of the Law of Nature to sex are Jewish, but Philo is building upon a Greek foundation as expressed by Socrates that begetting of children must not be done between people closely related, or of improper age, else the law of the gods brings the natural penalty of misbegotten children.[174] It is θεῖος νόμος to honor virtue for its own sake.[175] In the same realm Philo says that it is a Natural Law that one who curses a good man becomes himself accursed, he who blesses a good man is himself blessed.[176] For human beings there are two great tribunals, and only two, in nature, the one which tests impiety toward God and the other which has regard to misanthropy among one's fellow men.[177]

These applications of Natural Law are by no means complete, but show the varied use Philo made of it. In one passage he gives a more comprehensive discussion.[178] The High Priest, by the Mystery of Aaron, is an incarnate representation of the Logos, and so must be in harmony with the Laws of Nature. As such his mind must be filled with piety by constant preoccupation with good and useful thoughts and his life filled with good works. So his hands must never have worked ἀδικία by accepting bribes, by sharing in the spirit of rapine, by being spotted with innocent blood, or by having done deeds of πήρωσις, ὕβρις, τραῦμα, βία, or any thing else reprehensible in the sight of σοφία or νόμοι, or of σοφοὶ καὶ νόμιμοι ἀνδρές, but only what is honored by them.[179]

So the Law of Nature is a conception which appears in every aspect of Philo's thinking. It is a creation of God or an expression of His Nature or will, while it is conveniently and on occasion spoken of as a principle independent of God to account for evil. But as the expression of God's rulership it is the governing force in all nature, and guides the conduct of men, as a whole and by specific application, into all goodness. Accordingly the chief approach of man to God is through His radiant νόμος τῆς φύσεως. God Himself is higher than even the differentiation of His radiation which men call Law. When the mystic has achieved the full experience he will have transcended God's legal activity as he does God's Creative Power. But natural science and Law are still the great avenues which lead man to the place where creation and creative activity, laws and Law, are alike subsumed in the Logos, and in τὸ ὄν which towers in brooding mystery even beyond the Logos.

174. Xenophon, *Memorabilia*, IV, iv, 19 ff.; cf. *Cyrop.*, V, i, 9–11.
175. *LA*, iii, 167.   176. *QG*, iv, 219.
177. *Decal.*, 111. It was according to divine law to worship the gods in Xenoph., *Memorabilia*, IV, iv, 19; Pomponius, *ap. Digest*, I, i, 2.
178. *Spec.*, I, 202 ff.
179. For a fuller discussion of the Temple and Priest see Chapter IV.

CHAPTER III

THE TORAH

In the discussion of Philo's view of the Higher Law of God, the Law of Nature, nothing was found that was not familiarly Greek in its foundation. The Stream in which that Law finds its place is of composite origin, but the legal terminology and its implications are those of Greek thinkers, especially of the schools of Plato and Pythagoras, with details found in Aristotle which Aristotle may well have taken from those schools. However the prominent position given to Law in the Stream, and in Philo's thinking in general, the emphasis laid upon it, are the result of the Jewish attempt to represent Law, and, by implication, the Jewish Law, as the guide to mystic salvation. The Jews had much of the best Greek thought with them in seeking salvation in Law. The Stoic ideal of living according to nature was realized in the fulfilling of the Law of Nature. Aristotle, Plato, and Solon, to give only the more familiar examples, thought that the best way of educating a people in the higher life and leading them into adequate achievement of their possibilities was in providing them with a legal system which would best train them in δικαιοσύνη by being true Law κατὰ δίκην. Yet in Philo's writings there is a stress laid upon Law as the approach to salvation that goes beyond these writers, in degree if not in kind.

When one turns to Philo's notion of Jewish Law it is clear that Jewish apologetic fervor has been the inspiration of this intensified stress upon Law in general. By magnifying Law, and by orienting Jewish Law with Natural Law as the Law of God, the Jew could present his religion as the solution of the Greek problem, or of the mystic search of the Hellenistic Age.

No more patent fact springs out of the pages of Philo than his loyalty to Judaism. He was loyal to the Jewish group in Alexandria, loyal to the race as a whole,[1] but most of all loyal to the Jewish Law, and his treatment of the Law is so Jewish that his writings are frequently only intelligible when the Jewish attitude toward the Torah is kept in mind along with the Greek conception of νόμος.

So much has recently appeared to explain the Jewish view of the Torah in Philo's day[2] that now only a word is needed on the subject. The Jewish Torah was regarded essentially as God's revelation of Himself to Israel, Israel's treasured "Teaching" on sacred subjects. Opinion at the time was divided among Jews as to whether that Torah was essentially limited to the

1. *Spec.*, iv, 179–181. Franz Geiger, *Philon von Alexandreia als sozialen Denker*, pp. 102 ff.
2. I have in mind the familiar writings of Herford, Moore, Montefiore, Abrahams, Schechter, etc.

Scriptures, or included the sort of legalistic and doctrinal tradition that later developed into Talmudic Judaism. But in either case it was agreed that Judaism rested upon the Torah, which itself was God's revelation of His existence and character, and of His will for man. The Septuagint translation of the word Torah by the Greek word νόμος was peculiarly unfortunate, as Herford has well pointed out,[3] for it has led later generations to believe that the Jewish Law was primarily a code of commands and prohibitions. The Torah to which the CXIX Psalm was dedicated was a long way from being merely a book of laws, though it included a code. For the Torah included also the revelation of God as the God of Israel, who had created the world, painstakingly fashioned man, called the great patriarchs to found the Jewish race, watched over the race in Egypt, and led them out miraculously to give them the Promised Land. Such a God had in His great mercy revealed to the Jews His will for human conduct, but the specific laws had their authority from being a part of the greater Torah which included them, rather than from being that Torah themselves. The specific laws were specific, and to be specifically followed, but not as an end in themselves. Obedience to the commands carried value only as it sprang from a love for the whole revelation and the God thus revealed, and from a desire to please Him by accepting and fulfilling the entire Torah. Understanding and interpretation might and did vary, for the Torah as a whole was thought to be beyond formulation. One could obey the laws, and try to understand, and only by doing both was one living according to the Torah.

Much as Philo departed from the ordinary lines of traditional Jewish Midrash, in trying to use all his gifts and faculties to understand the depth and height of the treasures of Jewish revelation, he was a writer of Jewish Haggada or Midrash, expounding always the Torah of God. It is Torah, or as he calls it, νόμος, as the revelation of the truth that is his constant concern in all but his occasional political writings.

That the Jewish νόμος meant to him the divine revelation of truth is easily demonstrated. He of course refers to the specific laws as νόμοι throughout his writings, but constantly quotes non-legalistic parts of the Pentateuch as ὁ νόμος or οἱ νόμοι, or as ἡ νομοθεσία. The fact that Potiphar, a eunuch, had a wife is "law";[3a] the stories of Rebecca at the well,[4] of the tower of Babel,[5] of the Flood,[6] of Creation,[7] of the curse of Cain,[8] of Abraham's migration,[9] and divine visitation,[10] of the activities of the Amorites,[11] of the appointment of Aaron as Moses' spokesman,[12] of Balaam's cursing,[13] of Phinehas' thrust-

3. *The Pharisees*, p. 54.
4. *Post.*, 132.
6. *Ib.*, 23.
8. *Det.*, 155.
10. *Det.*, 159.
12. *Mig.*, 169.

3a. *LA*, iii, 236.
5. *Conf.*, 5.
7. *Opif.*, 77.
9. *Mig.*, 177.
11. *Immut.*, 99.
13. *Conf.*, 159.

ing his spear through the womb of the Midianitish woman,[14] all these are Law. In a word, even those parts of the sacred books are Law which are attacked as fables by unsympathetic Greeks.[15] Such a use of νόμος is meaningless in Greek; it is a purely technical term used by Jews to indicate the Hebrew conception of Torah. It is in this general sense that the Law is a teacher, instructing men "to worship Being, who is greater than the Good, more simple than the One, and more primal than the Monad."[16] By having taught the Jew human sympathy (ἀνθρωποπαθεῖν) it teaches him not to seek the punishment of his enemies.[17] It is from the Law that Philo has learned that the happy man is the man who uses sound judgment for good ends.[18] From the Law the haughtiest tyrant could learn humility in learning that men all have a common origin and nature.[19] When Philo speaks of the Patriarchs as νόμοι ἔμψυχοι, as νόμοι ἄγραφοι from whom the written laws are derived,[20] he does not mean that the Patriarchs are bundles of commands which were written down by Moses, but that they were an unwritten representation of God's revealed nature and will, and that the Pentateuch only set forth in writing what was more perfectly revealed in their characters. There is no thought of deducing the specific commands from the incidents of the lives of the Patriarchs. It is the Law in the larger sense which they brought to men.

Occasionally Philo feels the Greek meaning of his term in referring to the Pentateuch. The transition from the Hebrew to the Greek sense is not always superficially apparent. At the beginning of the De Abrahamo, when he is writing a transitional paragraph from the De Opificio to the subject before him, he explains that the first book of the sacred laws is Genesis, and sketches a few of the variety of subjects he finds therein discussed. The first of these subjects was the creation of the world, says Philo, and since this has now been canvassed in the preceding treatise we can go on to discuss the laws, postponing consideration of the particular laws until we have discussed the more general laws, the Patriarchs. That is, one could infer that the story of creation was not a part of the Jewish law unless one looked back and saw that the creation story was not an introduction to, but itself the beginning of the Jewish Law, and had been so treated in the De Opificio.[21] At the close of the same series of writings, as he introduces the last book (the De Praemiis et Poenis), he says that the λόγια delivered by Moses are in three parts, the story of creation, the historical part, and the legislative. Here the legislative is restricted still further to the Decalogue and the particular laws, and the part dealing with the patriarchs is the historical part; the word

14. *Post.*, 183.   15. *Conf.*, 2 f.   16. *Cont.*, 2.
17. *Flac.*, 121.   18. *Post.*, 80.   19. *Decal.*, 40.
20. *Ib.*, 1.
21. See also *Mos.*, ii, 37: κοσμοποιία ἡ τῶν νόμων ἐστὶν ἀρχή.

λόγια has taken the place of νόμοι for the whole. That is the Greek sense of νόμος has for the time quite driven out the Jewish sense. In one passage of the *Allegory*[22] he betrays a consciousness of this double meaning, for while he refers to the whole Pentateuch (here specifically Gen., vi, 7) as Law and the product of the lawgiver, he explains that the parts of the Law concerned with injunction and prohibition (οἱ ἐν ταῖς προστάξεσι καὶ ἀπαγορεύσεσι νόμοι) are the laws in the proper sense of the term (κυρίως εἰσὶ νόμοι), that is in the proper sense of the Greek word as distinguished from the peculiar Jewish usage.[23] So far as I know this is the only passage where Philo betrays his sense of the inaccuracy of the Jewish usage; in general he refers to the entire Pentateuch as νομοθεσία, or νόμος, as an established *terminus technicus*. But the reader must always bear in mind that the word in such a connection means Torah and not the Greek νόμος, or our word law.

When one takes up the problem of Philo's attitude toward the Jewish νόμος, then, one is faced by the fact that Philo himself thought of that νόμος in two senses, as the νόμος in general, the Jewish Torah, and as a body of specific commands. His attitude toward the one need not, and, it will be found, does not fix his attitude toward the other.

It is almost as obvious that only the Pentateuch is Torah to Philo as that the Pentateuch as a whole is such. In the first place it is striking that in the course of the entire *Exposition* there is not a single reference to any Jewish writer or document but Moses and the books ascribed to him.[24] The Judaism Philo was presenting to Gentiles did not bring in the histories, the poetry, or the prophecy of Judaism. When writing for Jews in the *Allegory,* in the *Quaestiones,* and in the *De Exsecrationibus* he could occasionally quote these other writings, though on the whole surprisingly little, but they were no part of the Torah Philo gave his prospective converts.

His forms of quoting books of the Bible outside the Pentateuch, where he refers to them in his writings for Jews, are worth noting. On the whole the commonest introduction is simply by the title of the book quoted, as he might quote from Homer.[25] A quotation from Judges is introduced by φησί, with no explanation of the force of the word on the context.[26] Sometimes a quotation appears simply as representing the opinions of the "men of old."[27]

22. *Immut.*, 51–53.
23. Leisegang (*Philos Werke*) and Colson and Whitaker have both missed the point in their notes *ad loc.*
24. In a single passage, *Virt.*, 62, Philo's words reflect the "Wisdom" language of Proverbs, viii, 22 ff., a passage quoted in *Ebr.*, 31. But nothing is given to suggest to the reader whence the thought came.
25. Job thus quoted in *Mut.*, 48; Psalms in *Mut.*, 115; *Mig.*, 157; *Immut.*, 74; *Gig.*, 17; *Conf.*, 52; *Som.*, i, 75; ii, 242, 246; *Fug.*, 59; Proverbs in *Ebr.*, 84; *QG*, iv, 129.
26. *Conf.*, 130. Cf. the quotation from I Samuel in *Mut.*, 143.
27. I Sam. so referred to in *Mig.*, 38; I Kings in *Immut.*, 136–139. In §136 the passage from I Kings is called an "imitation" of a conception in Leviticus.

But frequently there is a phrase which shows that Philo thought the book he was quoting was inspired. He says that he is an admirer of the oracular utterances of the books of Kings.[28] He says it would be well to believe that "the Lord is my shepherd," for the author of the twenty-third Psalm was not an ordinary man, but a prophet.[29] He quotes as witness for an argument ὁ θεσπέσιος ἀνήρ who wrote the ninety-third Psalm.[30] Again as witness he quotes Is. v, 5, 7, saying that it was spoken under inspiration (ἐπιθειάσας) by one of the ancient prophets.[31]

These passages would lead one to conclude that Philo regarded the rest of the Old Testament as inspired, but not as Torah. The basis of Philo's distinction would seem to be that in the Mystery, as we shall see, one could become inspired (Philo felt himself inspired at times),[32] and that certain great men of past generations had achieved that experience, but none in such a way as to put their writings on a level with the writings of Moses himself. Of Jeremiah he says, for example, in introducing a quotation, that he was not only an initiate but a hierophant in the Mystery, to such an extent that in his inspiration he could utter an oracle ἐκ προσώπου τοῦ θεοῦ.[33] There is a definite mystic circle, a θίασος, which was also the prophetic circle. Jeremiah again is τοῦ προφητικοῦ θιασώτης χοροῦ.[34] Zechariah and the author of the sixty-fourth Psalm were each τις τῶν ἑταίρων Μωϋσέως;[35] the author of Proverbs was τις τῶν φοιτητῶν Μωυσέως,[36] or τις τῶν ἐκ τοῦ θείου χοροῦ.[37] The author of the thirty-sixth Psalm was also a member of Moses' θίασος, who was entirely absorbed in the divine possession. The author of the thirtieth Psalm, because he felt his weakness in sophistic argument, prayed God to silence his opponents: he was τις τῶν Μωυσέως γνωρίμων.[38]

The inspiration of these men was certainly not to be classed with that of Moses, nor were their books, valuable as they were, Torah or Nomos. Occasionally words are taken from the histories or prophecies and quoted as "an oracle" of God,[39] but it will be noticed that in each case such words are represented in their context as spoken by God in the first person, and Philo explains in one passage that God spoke the words through the prophet as an oracle.[40] He is thus implying not that the book quoted is an "oracle" as a whole, but only these divine utterances. In only a single instance, so far as I can discover, is a quotation introduced from a book outside the Pentateuch as "scripture": Samuel is quoted as ὁ ἱερὸς λόγος.[41] However this unique

28. Conf., 149: ἄγαμαι καὶ τῶν ἐν βασιλικαῖς βίβλοις ἱεροφαντηθέντων.
29. Agr., 50. The eighty-third Psalm was written by τις προφητικὸς ἀνήρ, Heres, 290.
30. Plant., 29.   31. Som., ii, 172. Cf. Exs., 158.
32. Spec., iii, 1 ff.; Mig., 34 f.; Cher., 27.
33. Cher., 49, 51.   34. Conf., 44.
35. Ib., 62; Som., ii, 245.   36. Cong., 177.
37. Ebr., 31.   38. Conf., 39.
39. Plant., 138; Mut., 139, 169; Conf., 166.
40. Fug., 197.   41. Ebr., 143.

departure from his custom is to be explained, another passage makes abundantly clear that Samuel was not regarded as on a level with the Pentateuch, for he quotes the same chapter of the same book in another place as simply from "the first book of Kings," and says that the passage agrees with τὸ ἱερώτατον Μωυσέως γράμμα.[41a] The reader could not have missed the contrast in his feeling about the two writings. One other passage likewise is at variance with Philo's usual attitude. In *QG*, iv, 147, Philo says that there is attributed to God (he means, obviously, attributed by Scripture) three senses in their higher form, sight, hearing and smell. To justify his statement he quotes Genesis on the senses of sight and smell, but Psalms lxviii, 34 (lxix, 33), for the sense of hearing, as though the Psalms were on that plane of equality with the Pentateuch that elsewhere he so consistently denies. One might devise ingenious explanations for this departure, but whatever the explanation, the fact remains that it is a single instance of departure, and cannot seriously alter the impression of his remarks when taken as a whole.

On the whole, then, it would appear that what inspiration the later writers had was in Philo's opinion an inspiration quite inferior to that of Moses, if their contact with God was not in some sense mediated by their membership in Moses' θίασος. Traditional Judaism for Philo was Moses-centered in a way that is in striking contrast with the Apologetic and Christian literature of his day. He has not excluded the Messianic hope from his belief. Rather there are good reasons for believing that his expectations in that direction were active and eager.[42] But his writings are conspicuous for their omission of prophetic words and of the prophetic point of view. This is quite intelligible in writings directed to Gentiles, but more striking that it should be so largely absent from the writings for Jews. Philo's Judaism was the Judaism of the Torah, and for him the Torah was the Pentateuch.

Philo's attitude to the Scriptures seems just as much in contrast with the Jewish tradition in Palestine which we know as with early Christian writings. It has frequently been pointed out that early rabbinical tradition made Moses and his inspiration unique as compared with the other inspired writings. He is said to have uttered every inspired prophetic writing as well as his own, and Philo's representing the inspiration of the other sacred writers as in a sense derived from Moses may be an echo of some Palestinian tradition we do not know. Philo, like what was apparently Palestinian tradition of the time, also divided the sacred Scriptures into Law, the Prophets, and the Hymns and other Writings,[43] and viewed these all as inspired. But he sharply departs from the Jewish tradition preserved to us in the way he

41a. *Immut.*, 6.
42. This point must be elaborated on another occasion.
43. *Cont.*, 25. Cf. the Prologue to Sirach, νόμος καὶ προφηταὶ καὶ τὰ ἄλλα τὰ κατ' αὐτοὺς ἠκολουθηκότα.

reserves the word νόμος, Torah, for the Pentateuch exclusively. Paul[44] can quote Isaiah, the Fourth Gospel[45] can quote the Psalms, as νόμος, and historians of rabbinical tradition agree that the word Torah was applied to the whole body of writings accepted as inspired, on the ground, apparently, that they were all revealed teaching about God.[46] But this Philo does not do. He seems to have a sharper sense of the secondary character of the other writings than did rabbinical tradition, so much so that when the writer of *De Jona* (44) quotes the Psalms as νόμος, the fact is only another indication that Philo could not have written it. Rabbis would frequently quote for proof a verse from each of the three divisions.[47] Philo never.

This extreme concentration on the Pentateuch is accentuated by the absence of any sense of a verbal tradition that could be appealed to alongside the written Law. Heinemann has examined the question carefully, and has concluded that Philo's references to the "unwritten Law" cannot be taken in any case as a reference to the "oral tradition" of Pharisaic Judaism.[48] The most cursory examination of Philo will bear him out. Heinemann has found some traces of the content of tradition, especially in the *Hypothetica,* the laws of temple cultus, and of oath, but these seem taken, he establishes, from sources which had used the tradition rather than from the tradition directly. On point after point the tradition would have helped Philo out of awkward situations had he known it. The amazing thing is, as Heinemann well demonstrates, that for Philo Judaism had no history or development or fundamentally important literature between Moses and his own time, a matter that is the more astonishing in that Philo is liberal in references to the history and literature of other peoples, especially of the Greeks.[49] Heinemann's handling of the matter is so convincing that one need only say that it is demonstrated that Philo knows nothing of Jewish oral tradition, certainly nothing of it as Torah, an inspired parallel to the Pentateuch.

When one visualizes this surprising reactionary attitude which saw the authority for Judaism only in the Pentateuch, however it might be interpreted, and which functioned in complete independence of the Pharisaic-rabbinical tradition, one is struck by the possibility that Philo's attitude was influenced by the Sadducees. It is interesting to compare what little else we know of the Sadducees with Philo's positions. The points where Heinemann finds him in agreement with Palestinian tradition, the actual usages of the temple cultus, the strict conception of the oath, the dating and nature of certain offerings, the use of God's name in the temple, the regulation of the

---

44. I Cor. xiv, 21.   45. John x, 34.

46. E.g., G. F. Moore, *Judaism,* I, 248, 263. Strack in *Realencyclopädie für Protest. Theologie u. Kirche,* IX (3d ed.), 767, ll. 35 ff.; Weber, *Jüdische Theologie,* 81.

47. Moore, *op. cit.,* I, 239; Heinemann, *Bildung,* 528.

48. In *Hebrew Union College Annual,* IV, 149 ff.; *Bildung,* pp. 10, 476, 528, 540.

49. Heinemann, *Bildung,* 526 f.

temple ordeal for a woman accused of adultery, are all matters that were largely the concern of the Sadducean group as high-priests. We know that the appeal of the Sadducees was primarily to men like Philo, that is to the wealthy and to men of great social distinction.[50] Philo certainly belonged in that category. Heinemann has pointed out that in the strictness of his penal code[51] and in his treatment of the Talon[52] he is distinctively reminiscent of Sadducean legal practice.

We know further that the Sadducees denied the Pharisaic doctrine of predestination ("fate" as Josephus calls it) which Paul brought over into Christianity.[53] It is at least, then, in harmony with the Sadducees that Philo consistently, in its Stoic form, repudiates determinism, to make man a free moral agent. Eaton has interpreted Josephus as representing that the Sadducees repudiated "divine providence." But this is quite another matter, as Philo himself shows by keeping the doctrine of providence while he rejects determinism. The Sadducees denied the resurrection of the body,[54] an idea which also does not appear in Philo. He does not go so far as they in saying that souls perish with their bodies,[55] but his Greek notion of immortality, and all his ethical teaching, are quite without a sanction of rewards and punishments at a divine tribunal after death. The present life with its heavenly possibilities is Philo's great concern: virtue and mystic endeavor alike have their goal in a eudaemonism whose continuance into the next life is relatively incidental. The Sadducees rejected the angelology of the Pharisees.[56] Just what the angelology of the Pharisees was we do not know with any certainty, but it seems likely that it expressed itself in that type of angelic mythology found in Jewish writings of the period and in early rabbinical writings,[57] where the angels had become such fixed personalities as, in many cases, to have names and distinct functions. Philo knows nothing of such an angelology; his angels are only δυνάμεις of God, and not of a sort remotely to provoke or admit individual mythological elaboration. He could not possibly have made room for a literal Gabriel or Michael in his thinking, and

50. Josephus, *Ant.*, XIII, 298; XVIII, 17. See Finkelstein, "The Pharsees" in *Harvard Theological Rev.*, XXII (1929), p. 189, n. 6. I do not feel that Jerome's remarks about Philo in *Vir. Illust.*, XI, are necessarily authentic. His story of Philo's trip to Rome under Claudius is marred by an account of his meeting Peter there and praising the work of Mark in Alexandria. But Jerome has the trip to Gaius right, and it may be that the other trip also occurred, and that the only addition to fact is the story of Philo's relations with Christian leaders. Jerome's statement that Philo was *de genere sacerdotum* is accordingly not to be taken too finally. Yet considering everything it seems very likely correct. If it is true, Philo's Sadducean tendencies would be fully explained at once.

51. Heinemann, *Bildung*, 210, 229.　　52. Ib., 379.
53. Josephus, *BJ*, II, 164; *Ant.*, XIII, 173.　　54. Acts xxiii, 8.
55. *Ant.*, XVIII, 16; *BJ*, II, 165.
56. Acts xxiii, 8. The passage is very unsatisfactory evidence and stands alone, but is universally so interpreted. See e.g., Finkelstein, *op. cit.*, 235-240.
57. See G. F. Moore's *Judaism*, I, 401 ff.

allegorized away all resemblance of the Cherubim to that Palestinian tradition which seems to have been accepted and developed by the Pharisees.

These are all the points we know definitely about the Sadducees. Our evidence for them is so slight that it is impossible to prove that Philo was in any sense influenced by them. But it is at least striking that Philo agrees with every one of the positions they are known to have taken, while if he was possibly not of priestly family he was at least of the same general social class to which they made their appeal. It is, of course, impossible to turn the argument and read any of Philo's positions back into the Sadducees, for he was obviously influenced by many other currents. What their attitude was toward Greek civilization, for example, we do not know, though we suspect it was more liberal than that of the Pharisees. But whatever else was in Philo, his general approach to Judaism seems to have been colored by the Sadducees, and indeed he seems as close to them as Paul to the Pharisees. In no point is the resemblance more striking than in the fact that his devotion to Judaism limits itself to an intense loyalty to the Pentateuch as Torah, to the temple, and to the nation, but to nothing else, whether later literature or oral tradition.

The Pentateuch as Torah then teaches Philo his Judaism. It is very interesting to note that Philo's Judaism, in contrast to Palestinian Judaism, was specific in doctrine as well as in prescription for conduct. The Torah "taught" the Palestinian Jew that God had created the world and man, and was particularly close in His relation with the Jews. Nothing else, except that the Torah was God's revelation, was it required that a Jew believe, and this was rather assumed than presented as formal *articulus fidei*. But Philo lived in an environment where a man's beliefs could not so readily be assumed, and so he had to formulate Jewish positions for proselytes who would have come from almost any Hellenistic circle. The Torah as he conceived it taught Greek philosophy, to be sure, but in spite of Philo's eclecticism, it taught, and could be allowed to teach, only certain doctrines of Greek philosophy. That ultimate reality was a material φύσις of any sort, for example, could not for a moment be allowed. Orthodoxy, a notion of appalling history, first came into the Jewish thought world in Philo's environment.

Philo revered the Torah on the ground that it was a revelation of the existence and nature of God, and of God's higher Law of Nature. In spite of his endless concern with details of the letter, he studied the Law for what he could make of it as a whole, rather than for its literal content. He could logically have had this attitude to the whole without retaining respect for the letter as such. What did Philo think of the specific laws as obligations?

The giving of the specific laws was, he thought, an act of great mercy on the part of God and showed profound understanding of human needs on the part of Moses. It was not enough to lead the Israelites out of the bondage to flesh which Egypt represented. Of course the men who are to receive sacred laws must first be cleansed just as physicians must first check a patient's disease before they can by food build up his strength.[58] The medicine may keep the disease from killing the man, but a state of health is dependent much more upon the building power of proper nourishment. So Moses led the people out where they would be free from taint and be impressed with the fact that the laws he was to give them were "the clearest oracles of God."[59] Then he gave them divine νόμοι καὶ λόγοι as their food[60] by means of which they might not only live but live well.[61] Philo loved the individual laws because they were full of gentleness and humanity, and taught men to be so.[62] In the De Specialibus Legibus, as he takes up each law to explain it to the Gentile beginners, his enthusiasm never wanes. It was not only in composing the Torah as a whole, but in drawing up each law that Moses wrote with his eyes upon the πολιτεία τῆς μεγαλοπόλεως.[63]

Philo was not content with thus praising the individual laws. He was very careful to obey them. In his great address to the Gentiles on the subject of the Legation to Rome Philo explained:

All men are guardians of their own customs; but this is true of the Jewish race in a peculiar sense. For the Jews regard their laws as God-given oracles, they are trained in them as a discipline from early age, and they have the commandments impressed like images in their souls. Accordingly, as their minds are constantly confronted with a clear vision of their shapes and forms, they never cease admiring them.[64]

The keeping of the Law is here an essentially valuable thing ex opere operato. The same appears much more clearly in the two little companion writings, the De Benedictionibus and the De Exsecrationibus, writings which, I have elsewhere argued, are no part of the Exposition (Cohn printed them as parts of De Praemiis et Poenis), but are addresses, or together constitute an address in two parts, to Jews, possibly to Jewish farmers.[65] Here Philo talks as a revived Deuteronomist.

In the De Benedictionibus his theme is that the ἐντολαὶ καὶ προστάγματα of the Law should be in the Jew's mouth, heart, and hands. The blessings of the Messianic Age, which he now describes, are the reward of "those who obey God, and who always and everywhere observe His commandments and who harmonize the commandments with each part of their lives" (§98). Happiness results from complete fulfilling of the Law, for happiness is the

58. Decal., 10–12.   59. Ib., 15.
60. Ib., 13.   61. Ib., 17.
62. Spec., ii, 105, 107.   63. Mos., ii, 51.
64. Legat., 210 f.; cf. Decal., 15.
65. §153 ff. See "Philo's Exposition of the Law and his De Vita Mosis," Harvard Theol. Rev., XXVII (1933), pp. 109–125.

truest wisdom and prudence, and wisdom means the service of God, prudence the proper regulation of human life (§81). The spoken commandments are incomplete: only as they are translated by men into action in
every phase of life does their beauty emerge from darkness into light (§82).
In the Messianic Age no one "of those who have ordered themselves according to the Law" (τῶν κοσμουμένων τοῖς νόμοις) will die prematurely
(§110). The man ἀμαθὴς καὶ ἔκνομος has no share in reason or number, but
the man who coöperates with training and the sacred laws gets precisely
that, which is fulness of days in quality and quantity (§§111 f.). Such a
man gets his reward also in the public recognition of his virtue, a goal that
Philo here puts forth as entirely valid and commendable (§§112 f.). The man
who tries to be virtuous, that is who sets the sacred laws before him as the
guide of the speeches and actions of his life, will even be rewarded by good
health (§§119 f.). These, Philo concludes, are the εὐχαί for the good men
who fulfill the laws in their acts (τοὺς νόμους ἔργοις ἐπιτελοῦντες) (§126).
He then proceeds to discuss the curses of the ἔκνομοι καὶ ἄθεσμοι (§126).

The treatise De Exsecrationibus is on exactly the same level. The curses
are directed against "those who disregarded the sacred laws" (§138), "who
leave the straight roads leading to truth" (§148), for "the men of noble
descent who have adulterated the coinage of their birth" (§152), "who have
despised the sacred laws of justice and piety and been seduced by polytheistic
opinions" (§162). Philo suggests a symbolic meaning of some of the laws
he specifically mentions. The recurring seven days and seven years of nature
should teach men the true rest periods. Men should be aware of the deeper
significance of such laws as those concerning salt, contracts, the altar of
mercy, and the common hearth, for all were established through the number
seven.[66] The men Philo is denouncing have violated these laws, especially
by being such greedy landlords that they have refused the Sabbath to men
and the sabbatical year to the soil in their eagerness to get every penny.
Such men will be destroyed.[67] Here is a glimpse into a type of Hellenistic
Judaism based upon a Deuteronomic conception of the Torah strange for
Philo, though its existence in Egypt is to be inferred from the type of loyalty
the Alexandrian Jews displayed under persecution. It is purely "normative"
in its regarding obedience to the specific laws as an end in itself, the cause
of all blessings, but whose neglect would bring the most hideous catastrophes.
Philo is perfectly in sympathy with this attitude; he can preach it vigorously,
though it will appear not fully to represent his own. But this much is clear.
Much more as he may have seen in the Law than his audience, he could
not have preached such a sermon without rank insincerity had he not him-

---

66. On these laws see my Jewish Jurisprudence, pp. 54 f., 224.

67. Philo is clearly here speaking of Jewish landlords and not Roman. He seems to be referring to a contemporary group.

self believed that the Laws were in themselves good, and the observance of the specific commandments a literal obligation for the Jew.

Such a conclusion is borne out when Philo is seen turning to another group of Alexandrian Jews who called themselves Allegorists. These men carried to its logical conclusion the notion that Scripture contains a deeper meaning than the literal, indeed that the true meaning can be found only by allegory. Having found the deeper meaning they went on to say that the literal meaning was useless and carried no obligation. How large an influence this group had in their environment there is now no way of telling, though presumably, from the notorious strictness of Jews as they appeared to Romans, and the extreme loyalty they showed to their traditions at Alexandria under Gaius, it would seem that the extreme Allegorists must have appealed to only a limited circle. Philo definitely belongs to the majority in rejecting their conclusions, however much allegory he may have taken from them. He says:

There are some who, regarding laws in their literal sense in the light of symbols of spiritual matters, are overpunctilious about the latter, while treating the former with easy-going neglect. Such men I for my part should blame for handling the matter in too easy and off-hand a manner: they ought to have given careful attention to both aims, to a more full and exact investigation of what is not seen and to a blameless stewardship of what is seen. As it is, as though they were living alone by themselves in a wilderness, or as though they had become disembodied souls, and knew neither city nor village nor household nor any company of human beings at all, overlooking all that the mass of men regard, they explore reality in its naked absoluteness. These men are taught by the sacred Word to be mindful of good repute, and to let go nothing that is part of the customs fixed by divinely empowered men greater than those of our time. It is quite true that the Seventh Day is meant to teach the power of the Unoriginate and the non-action of created beings. But let us not for this reason abrogate the laws laid down for its observance, and light fires or till the ground or carry loads or institute proceedings in court or act as jurors or demand the restoration of deposits or recover loans, or do all else that we are permitted to do as well on days that are not festival seasons. It is true also that the Feast is a symbol of gladness of soul and of thankfulness to God, but we should not for this reason turn our backs on the general gatherings of the year's seasons. It is true that receiving circumcision does indeed portray the excision of pleasure and all passions, and the putting away of the impious conceit, under which the mind supposed that it was capable of begetting by its own power: but let us not on this account repeal the law laid down for circumcising. And further we shall be ignoring the sanctity of the Temple and a thousand other things, if we are going to pay heed to nothing except what is shown us by the inner meanings as resembling the soul. It follows that, exactly as we have to take thought for the body, because it is the abode of the soul, so we must pay heed to the letter of the laws. If we keep and observe these, we shall gain a clearer conception of those things of which these are the symbols; and besides that we shall not incur the censure of the many and the charges they are sure to bring against us.[68]

The figure that the literal law is the body, the spiritual significance of the Law is the soul leads Philo on from this to several further allegories (Leah, women's service in the Tabernacle, the women's fire kindled against Moab, the prayer of Isaac, the High Priest as Logos) and he concludes that there are three things required by the Torah, "the necessaries, the clothing, and the fellowship,"[69] which are the higher obligation of natural or divine law, the physical garment of the higher principle in the specific laws, and the careful study by which one may come to see that the lower law is a reflection of the higher.[70] That is, one must seek to grasp the higher Law while he fulfills the literal command and tries to understand the relation between the two, by which the act of obedience becomes in each case a symbol of some aspect of the higher Law.

Philo is then undeviatingly loyal to the literal commands, and yet, for all his loyalty to the letter, his legal regularity was that of a symbolist. The sacramental or ritualistic symbolist has, as the real source of his ideas, not the rite itself, but a philosophy not necessarily, or usually, derived from the cult act. The appeal of the cult is in itself the appeal of emotional or aesthetic association rather than of idea, and the act is respected along with ideas essentially foreign to it because it is interpreted as a symbol of those ideas. The modern sacramental symbolist is often, though not always, quite as unaware as Philo that the symbolism which combines his two loyalties is a paradox. This is said not as a reflection on the symbolists, for no one can reproach the man whose solution of practical life can be analyzed as ultimately a paradox. To hold to an inspiring cultus while one's mind is open to philosophical speculation is one of the most sensible of dualistic solutions of life. Nonsense appears only as one attempts, not to assert, but to work out in elaborate detail, their symbolic identity. Beneath Philo's great mass of nonsense the patient student comes to perceive a fundamentally practical and sane, not to say beautiful, spirit.

Philo was a fastidious observer of the Law. Yet, except in the little address *On Blessings and Curses,* his legalism was not the legalism of "normative" Judaism. Apart from the controversy between Pharisees and Sadducees over the validity of the oral tradition, all that we know of normative Jewish piety, especially as that piety was immortalized for all classes in the great Psalter, indicates a sense of the ultimate and inherent value of obedience to the Law

68. *Mig.,* 89–94. Cf. *Cont.,* 78 for this conception of the Law as an animal with body and soul.

69. Ex. xxi, 10.   70. *Mig.,* 105.

quite in itself. The difference between Philo in his three great commentaries and this type of legalism lies in an ultimate divergence as to the meaning and content of virtue. The normative point of view developed inevitably into rabbinism, which had primarily the legist's, not the philosopher's, approach to law and life. Many philosophers of significance have enriched the stream of Jewish tradition, but their speculations have not been in the main current. That main current has from the beginning been channeled by the Jewish assumption that virtue was a matter of exactly, and sincerely, fulfilling the commands of God, and the Jew has always been proud of the privilege of doing so. By Jews the Law has chiefly been treated as lawyers treat law, with the written code as a precedent for application rather than as a principle of ethics in the philosopher's sense. The Jew got his reward in the assurance that God was pleased with him for his obedience, and would mercifully help him back into the path if he had faltered but wanted sincerely to be reinstated as an obedient child.

Philo in general betrays none of this attitude to the Law, because his ethical motivation is primarily Greek. True he could deal with the prescriptions of the code which touched the legal field as we usually conceive it, the field of crimes, contracts, torts, and inheritance. But when Philo left the court, or was not addressing a popular audience, he left his lawyer's approach to law behind, and became the ethical philosopher in the Greek sense. The validity of circumcision, of the food regulations, of the laws of purity, was based upon their being Law of God, to be sure, but, as has appeared in the foregoing quotation, also upon their symbolism for the life of true virtue in the Greek philosophic sense. When he talks of virtue the Jewish virtue of obedience is never mentioned. In contrast with Jewish obedience, Greek ethical thought began with the life of reason, itself in a sense divine, as the force which should guide and rule the lower aspects of a man's life. Not what a man did was so important as the equilibrium he was able to maintain, whereby mind was free from sensuous domination, and ready to escape to God or Nature. It was an ethic grown out of a mystical metaphysic. The typical religious Jew has always lived, as far as possible, guided by the clear light of the personal God's specific instructions. The religious and philosophical Greek lived in the dim radiation of cosmic rays which his reason tried to use as a light for life, or in the blinding light of ecstasy. In place of specific law the Greek had the great cardinal virtues and the ethical mean, to be achieved by self-control. In a word, while to the Jew God was the loving Father and virtue a summation of acts, to the Greek God was a metaphysical entity and virtue a state of being.

To expound Philo's attitude toward ethics is outside the present investigation. Here it can only be said that Philo's attitude was that of the Greek. As such, however he might preach to the Jewish mob, or sincerely repudiate as shocking the easy dismissal of literal obligation to which extreme Allegorists were led; however much he might spend his life in symbolic representation and fulfillment of the laws, to him a body of precepts demanding obedience was essentially opposed to the fundamental postulates of his ethical thought, or had only marginal significance.

Mention has been made of the importance of the king in Hellenistic thinking as a link between man and the cosmic or divine Law, and so as being the integrating force in society to make it into a state. The king himself was thus important because the Greeks could think of the legal structure of the state in no other terms than as a divine institution. The laws of the state might be made by enactment of the βουλή, but the Greek world was always keenly aware that a law was good according as it was a specific application of δίκη. So it was always subject to oracular veto. In common parlance the just man in the state was the man who obeyed the law, and he was just in the eyes of the gods who obeyed the laws of the gods. No one ever questioned the fact that the law of the state was valid only as it expressed the will of the gods to men,[71] much as they might dispute the machinery by which laws were to be enacted. When the Sophists presented an astonished world with their thesis that νόμος and φύσις, far from being complementary terms, were sharply opposed to each other, the inevitable consequence was to take men's interest away not from φύσις but νόμος. For without the sanction of φύσις, νόμος became automatically worthless. Law was valuable to a Greek, whether he was always fully conscious of it or not, according as it explained to him φύσις, or the will of the gods, and he was really self-deceived in supposing that δικαιοσύνη was essentially the quality of being νόμιμος with reference to laws of the state; more deeply still the Greeks were thinking of δικαιοσύνη as lying in a man's conformity to nature, long before the Stoics crystallized the phrase.[72] This was a constant assumption in the tragedies. The letter of our civil codes we respect: to obey it is δίκη. Yet here is a situation, as in the *Antigone,* for example, where man must recognize a higher δίκη or νόμος directly at variance with the law of the king or state. To do the higher δίκη involves the tragic clash with human νόμος. The basic protest was against the fact that the letter did not, as it should, represent δίκη or the higher Law.

On this ground the tradition arose of which Hirzel[73] has given the classic exposition, the tradition that the written law is as such inferior to the un-

71. This is in spite of such practical definitions as the one of Demosthenes, that law is συνθήκη κοινή of the city. The passage prefaces this by stating that law is a gift of the gods, *Contra Aristog.*, I, 15, 16; Xenoph., *Memorab.*, I, ii, 42.

72. The argument of the Sophists as to the contrast of νόμος and δικαιοσύνη with φύσις is quite unintelligible if it was not made in opposition to a proverbial connecting of the two.

73. R. Hirzel, "Ἄγραφος Νόμος," in *Abhandlungen der sächsischen Gesellschaft*, Philol.-Hist. Classe, XX.

written law. The unwritten law might be regarded as the unformulated custom of the city, or it might be identified with the νόμος τῆς φύσεως, or it might be both at the same time. But in any case the letter of the law, although it should be strictly enforced, must be checked by ἐπιείκεια, an appeal from the letter to a broader and more vital δίκη, if νόμος is to function as a vehicle of δικαιοσύνη rather than of injustice. The feeling of the inadequacy of written law as a guide to true δικαιοσύνη increased with the decline of the classic states and their submergence under Hellenistic monarchies. The Cynics flouted the laws of the state altogether: the Stoics tolerated them while they looked for a higher regimentation in Natural Law.

It would have been natural, in view of the general trend, for Platonists and Pythagoreans to have developed a theory that the written law was only a reflection or image of the Idea-Law, and to have tended like the rest to regard the written law as valuable only for those lower natures which could not rise to, and be guided by, the ideal. Our information is so slight about Platonism in Philo's day that there is little significance in the fact that nothing of the sort, to my knowledge, is at hand. But we do know that later Platonism was expressing itself in exactly this form. To Proclus the νόμοι ἄγραφοι in the usual sense of their meaning were inadequate. For the Greeks thought of them usually as being τὰ ἔθη; but customs, says Proclus, though they are ἄγραφα, are still νόμιμα rather than νόμοι. Οἱ ἀληθεῖς νόμοι need no writing, but abide within the souls of those who live according to them, and who are therefore νόμοι ἔμψυχοι, in contrast with animals who obey νόμοι φύσικοι, and with ordinary men who obey νόμοι πολιτικοί. At this point there is a break in the manuscript which goes on with what is obviously a discussion of the νόμοι ἀληθεῖς, or the Cosmic Law which lies behind them. The passage is so much closer to Philo than the Stoic material that is ordinarily adduced in parallel, and Proclus is in general so little read, that I quote the following:

In the case of the [divine and heavenly] elements Law is seen to be eternally [present] in the same things and unchangeably aligned according to a single [logos]; among men it rules according to the appointed seasons; among animals it fulfills the way of life that is natural for each. So then this Law must be regarded as divine,[74] the link between the necessary laws[75] which the Creator of the

---

74. θεός without the article.

75. This God who is συνοχεύς τῶν εἱμαρμένων νόμων is probably the same as Julian's Gallus who is the primal dampness, "not itself material, but the last immaterial cause which precedes matter. It [or he] is ὁ νοερὸς θεός, the συνοχεύς of the material and sublunar forms, united with the cause that is ordained for matter, yet not united in the sense that one thing is united with another, but like a thing that is gathered into itself" (Julian, V, 165D). Αἰτία is here νόμος, and what Julian is doing is to see a law inherent in material nature which is subsumed in a spiritual Law. The law inherent in matter is the "necessary laws" of Proclus. Both are attempts to combine Stoic Natural Law with a Platonic ultimate immaterial world

Timaeus (41e) wrote into souls, and the laws which extend into every polity of the universe. . . . On account of this God let us be bold and say that a great destiny allotted in the world underlies the force of customs everywhere, and that many things come to pass according to it even in our own souls. And just as the true laws are images of the cosmic laws, although some laws go amiss and others being only rough sketches are a sharp remove from the originals (ἀποπτώσεις ἐκείνων), so the customs in our lives are some of them likenesses of those in the universe (ἐοικότα τοῖς τῶν ὅλων), while others are only copies (εἴδωλα) of them. But there is an undeviating force which sways our destinies and the honors and dishonors of the universe.[76]

The meaning of the passage is on the whole clear. To any Neo-Platonist the fact that human law, even in its best form, was but an image of a spiritual reality would have meant *ipso facto* that the earthly written law was inferior to the spiritual Law, and that the man of spiritual ambition must rise above the codes and traditions of men to the true Law. It was good Platonism to contrast "reality" with its inferior imitation in nouns and verbs, for that had been precisely the ground for Plato's rejection of the poets.[77] The fact that this conception is found in Proclus in connection with the conception of νόμοι ἔμψυχοι in whom abide οἱ ἀληθεῖς νόμοι makes it apparent that Proclus is throughout drawing upon the tradition that lay behind Philo's thinking. For that Proclus is giving here an idea originated by Philo cannot seriously be suggested. There must then have been a familiar notion on which Philo was drawing which discussed the written law as a Platonic image of the true law of God and nature, with the implication that as an image the written law was inferior to the heavenly or ideal law, however accurate an image it might or might not be. When Philo insists that the Torah is an image of this higher law he is using a double edged sword. If the Jewish law is an accurate copy of the divine Law it is of course superior to the laws of Gentile peoples, which, in Proclus' terms, are only rough sketches of heavenly law if they do not miss it altogether. But at the same time Philo is indicating that the written law, even the Torah, is inadequate for a spiritually minded man, who would aspire, like Proclus, to become a νόμος ἔμψυχος, not by obeying copies, but by getting οἱ ἀληθεῖς νόμοι to abide within his soul.

Was Philo himself aware that his very praise of the Torah was in terms which indicated its inadequacy? Philo's own description of the Torah in this sense must be examined before the question can be answered.

---

and Law above matter. Philo shows (*Spec.*, ii, 124) that he knew this term, or its equivalent when he says that it is a "law of necessity" that no mortal or earth-born thing can become immortal. That is, it is a condition and limitation of the mortal and material world, a fact which not even God the Creator and His Law can contravene.

76. Proclus, *In Rem Publicam*, ed. Kroll, II, 307, ll. 15 ff.

77. *Rep.*, 601a.

One of the most interesting statements in this connection is the following:

> Moses thought that it was beneath the dignity of the Torah to make the founding of a city actually built by hands the point of departure for his writing; he looked up with the most accurate eyes of the mind to the magnitude and beauty of the universal legislation, and considered it too immense and divine for any earthly limitation. So he began with the creation of the Megalopolis, considering that the Torah was to be a superlatively accurate image (εἰκών) of the polity of the universe.[78]

To this Platonic description Philo goes on to add that each individual law, in Pythagorean expression, is "directed toward the attunement of the universe," or "sings on pitch with the Logos of eternal nature."[79]

Again he says that the laws of Moses are "the finest of all laws, truly divine. . . . They are stamped with the seal of nature herself."[80] In calling them ὡς ἀληθείως θεῖοι νόμοι Philo would seem to be identifying them with οἱ ἀληθεῖς νόμοι, collectively θεός, described later by Proclus. But his classing them afterwards as the product of the seal of nature, one of his favorite metaphors for Platonic imitation, shows that such was not in his mind. They are such excellent imitations that they are divine, but are not themselves the νόμος-λόγος-θεός. Indeed Moses, like the other Patriarchs, but to a degree that completely surpassed the rest, was himself the incarnation of the divine virtues, a νόμος ἔμψυχος, and the virtues which, by being in him, made him νόμος ἔμψυχος were obviously οἱ ἀληθεῖς νόμοι of Proclus. The legislation of Moses was but the projection of ἀπεικονίσματα καὶ μιμήματα of these virtues or laws, which, as patterns for the legislation, he bore about like images in his soul.[81] God Himself is in another passage the παράδειγμα ἀρχέτυπον of the laws, the conceptual sun behind the visible sun, giving forth from the invisible source beams that are visible.[82] The distinction is succinctly stated in the following:

> Δικαιώματα are different from νόμιμα. For the former exist by nature, the latter by imposition. For what exists by nature is older than what exists by imposition, so justice (τὸ δίκαιον) is older than law (νόμος).[83]

Philo must have had the Jewish Law in mind as he wrote this. Beyond the νόμιμα or νόμοι, even of the Jews, was the eternal and natural δίκαιον to which they should aspire.

In spite of all the machinery he describes by which Moses prophesies the laws, Philo seems fundamentally to have considered the code to be but an

78. *Mos.*, ii, 51.   79. Ib., 52.
80. Ib., 12, 14.   81. Ib., 4–11.
82. *Spec.*, i, 279.
83. *Sitzungsberichte der preussischen Akademie der Wissenschaft*, 1932, p. 79 (H. Lewy, "Neue Philontexte in der Überarbeitung des Ambrosius"); also *QG*, iv, 184.

imitation of the true laws incarnate in the Patriarchs.[84] The law that is in them is the ἄγραφος νόμος,[85] and by virtue of this they are themselves νόμοι ἄγραφοι.[86] This contrast between the unwritten laws and the written Philo freely applies to the written Torah, and no Greek-speaking person could have missed the fact that Philo had a model of Law that stood much higher in his esteem than the Mosaic Code itself. In describing the Code as an image or copy of this higher Law, Philo could not have been unconscious of the fact that, by his own philosophy, every copy belies the original in the very deceit of its resemblance.[87] He could ultimately have been no more content than Proclus with copy-law, even if that copy were the Torah.

As a matter of fact he was not. It is one thing to recognize that an apologist has defended the value of some aspect of an institution to which he is in general loyal, and indeed that he is conscientious about observing its forms, and quite another to suppose that that aspect is really the source of his loyalty. The history of the Church is full of men, many of them mystics, for example, who are loyal defenders and obedient servants of an ecclesiastical organization or cultus which at bottom had only a symbolic, if not an essentially quite extraneous, relation to their real religious life. Philo had no more sympathy with the Allegorists in their abandoning of the literal Law than Erasmus with the Lutheran abandonment of the Church. And yet his spiritual aspirations are as little to be explained by the literal Law as Erasmus' piety by Church organization or scholastic theology. The very passage that has been quoted,[88] where Philo so sharply rejects the Allegorists' abandonment of the letter of the law for its deeper meaning, shows that Philo was quite at one with them as to the real purport of the Law. The letter is only the body; it is the inner meaning that is the soul. Keeping the letter is valuable chiefly for its giving the man who observes the Law a good reputation among his compatriots, and because the observance itself helps one better to understand the symbols (σύμβολα).[89] The purest and most keen eyed class of men, those distinguished by σοφία rather than discipline (ἄσκησις), pierce through beyond any impartation of knowledge in the form of nouns and verbs to the words of God that are seen as light is seen.[90] The man who is equipped to be his own guide by the fact that reason has conquered sense, and by the fact that he has become one of those who "see" God, or in other words the νόμος ἔμψυχος of Philo and Proclus, acts first and then listens.

84. *Abr.*, 3–6. On this see more fully the following chapter.
85. Ib., 16.
86. Ib.; 275 f.; *Decal.*, 1; *Virt.*, 194. Philo knew the "customs" of a city as their νόμοι ἄγραφοι, but while he regards them as superior to the codes (*Spec.*, iv, 149 f.) they have for him as little ultimate value as the various civil codes (*Heres*, 295).
87. *Praem.*, 29: πᾶσα εἰκὼν ὁμοότητι εὐπαραγώγῳ ψεύδεται τὸ ἀρχέτυπον.
88. *Mig.*, 89 ff. See above, pp. 82 ff.
89. Ib., 88 ff., espec. 93.   90. Ib., 46–52.

That is, he acts according to his inner light and uses the Law (the divine words and sacred admonitions) which he "hears" only as a check.[91]

As one goes up in the mystic flight, he learns that the written laws are not for him. Isaac, who we shall see symbolized to Philo one of the highest of the mystic types, is described at the height of his initiation: he has walked out in the twilight to be with God, leaving behind his human qualities and becomes possessed by God; at this time he learns and teaches us

> that the sacred books of the Lord are not monuments of learning or of what is to be seen, but are the divine command, the divine Logos, which admonishes the negligent, and which is nigh at hand, though as if it were not there. But it speaks without the projection of words, and talks to any one without uttered sound, not at all withdrawing from those who speak with it or from intimate disciples, but on the contrary bringing them boldness with incorporeal realities. and an imparting of discourse about the intelligibles contained within itself.[92]

The interesting point for our purpose in this, a part of a long description of Isaac's having the vision of the true Virtue, is the fact that Philo has gone out of his way to state that the lesson of the matter is that the holy books of the Lord are not things which can be studied or seen, that is, are not the written books, but are the Logos with whom the true mystic has immediate contact.

Pointing in the same direction, and intelligible when read in view of the same mystic abandonment of the written Torah for immediate experience of God, or for initiation into the Mystery by Moses the hierophant, is a passage[93] which follows a long discussion of the Powers of God. For the ordinary wicked man, Philo explains, such a person as Moses is God, who in this capacity is made equivalent to the lower Ruling Power of God. The man who is advancing from wickedness to virtue has the higher Power, the Benefiting (elsewhere the Creative) Power, and the man who is fully advanced has the Ruling and Benefiting Powers both together, that is, we understand, the Logos in whom both meet, as his God. Such a person has become the "man of God," by virtue of which achievement, it would appear, Moses could be God to the wicked, for Philo[94] describes Moses as an ἀντίδοσις θείας προνοίας. How is one then to achieve such an exalted position? "If you want to have God as the lot of your mind," Philo answers, "you must first make yourself into a lot worthy of him. And you would become so if you would run away from all hand made and voluntary laws." From this Philo returns immediately to elaborating what he has said about the two Powers of God.

91. *Conf.*, 55–59, espec. 59.

92. *QG*, iv, 140. It is difficult to believe that the last sentences of the paragraph read in Aucher's Latin as Philo intended.

93. *Mut.*, 26.   94. Ib., 25.

But the odd digression in the passage stands. The man who is going to achieve this exaltation is one who must run away from hand made laws. It would be a complete break in the sense to see, with Pantasopulos,[95] the passage as a rejection of civil law for Jewish Law. What Philo is rejecting is the very idea that a written law, even the written law of the Jews themselves, could be a possible help in the higher reaches, at least, of this mystical ascent. We can understand the little digression only if we regard Philo as stopping in the middle of his description of the spiritual rise through the Powers to God in order to remind the reader that this sort of spirituality has nothing to do with worship through obedience to any written law, and requires its abandonment. The Law might well be kept as a series of observances, but not with the idea that observance in itself could lead to God. In that sense one must run from the laws. Such a parenthetical remark would be quite in point, if, as we are coming to see, Philo really felt that the written Code was not an objective basis for the higher Mystery, and had definitely to be transcended for the true experience of God.

The remark is actually a reminder of the great passage in the preceding treatise of the *Allegory* where Philo has described this "running away" from the Law of statutes to the Powers and the Logos. For that passage and for a final judgment on Philo's attitude toward the precepts of the Code we must wait until we have gone on to study the Higher Mystery itself. So far there has appeared ample ground for suspecting that Philo might well have revered the Code, and obeyed it, while it had nothing, as statutory law, to offer his higher spiritual life. True the Jewish laws are

the clearest image of the polity of the cosmos. At least if any one is willing to examine the powers of the specific laws he will find them aiming at the attunement of the universe and pitched in harmony with the Logos of eternal nature.[96]

But the whole objective of Philo's life was to get beyond all material images, beyond the material cosmos itself, and come through to the spiritual originals, at last to the Logos or God as the ultimate spiritual original, of all things. So there is no reason to think that highly as he praises the Jewish Law he did not include even its statutes when he wrote:

When the prudence of the acute and seeing Nature enters the soul as though it were coming into a country all the racial laws that are in it grow insanely angry and withdraw from worthy thinking, since bad things cannot live and stand along with good things.[97]

Only in comparison with "acute and seeing Nature" could Philo have

95. Pantasopulos, E. A., *Die Lehre vom natürlichen und positiven Rechte bei Philo Judaeus,* 1893 (Diss.), p. 15.
96. *Mos.,* ii, 51 f.   97. *QE,* ii, 22.

called any great body of racial laws "bad." But in contrast with the higher reality, even the Jewish Code could become an impediment, a thing to be run away from, and bad.

Philo, it seems to me, is quite aware of the fact that he is thus discounting the value of Jewish laws, but expresses his inner feeling only casually because of his fear of the "Allegorists'" position which had abandoned the Code altogether. This Philo did not at all want to be understood as recommending. He was perfectly sincere in praising Moses for eulogizing the careful legalism of the Levites, and in saying that ὁ ἀστεῖος was always the guardian of the words and covenant of God (καὶ λόγων καὶ διαθήκης θεοῦ φύλαξ).[98] "Abraham did all my law,"[99] is discussed. Law, he admits, is a matter of the divine Logos enjoining and prohibiting specific conduct. "Doing the Law" is then for the Sophos "doing the Logos," that is following God, which is all an allegory to show that the soul should comply with divine teaching, whose point is the honoring of God.[100] That is, at just the place where a legalist would have found opportunity to stress the value of obedience to the Mosaic Code Philo makes the passage really a praise of obedience to what we might call the "inner light." The traditions of the noble deeds of the past given by histories and poets are well enough for beginners, he says in another connection, but that, as well as all other knowledge we get through the ears, is banished when the "sudden beam of self-taught wisdom" shines in upon the eye of the soul. "Words" are then of no significance. Philo would not be misunderstood. We must not neglect this traditional wisdom the fathers have handed down to us, he goes on to explain. But it is swept away by the higher wisdom. "God's pupil" (φοιτητής, γνώριμος, μαθητής) has no need of expositions that mortals have given.[101]

The Torah was then actually to Philo a source of instruction in specific conduct, an inspired formulation of God's purposes for the beginner, and for the vast majority of men who never get beyond the beginner's stage. It was binding upon the man of higher experience in so far as he had still to live among his fellows. But it was no longer as statute Philo's norm and objective. The value of the Torah for the man of higher experience was in its revelation of the experiences of the Patriarchs in becoming νόμοι ἔμψυχοι, an understanding of which could be achieved only by allegorizing the actual words. The aspiration of Philo centered in the hope of reproducing their experiences of God in his own life. The great value of the Torah was, then, that it gave an exposition of the nature of God and of the mystic way to Him. That is, the Torah was essentially to him what he so often liked to call it, the ἱερὸς λόγος of the Mystery. He still dedicated his life to the Law revealed by Moses, but to him that Law was the unwritten Logos of God.

98. *Det.*, 68.   99. Gen. xxvi, 5.
100. *Mig.*, 130 f.   101. *Sac.*, 78 f.

A better summary of Philo's attitude toward the Law could not be found than the following statement of Eusebius:

The whole Jewish nation is divided into two sections. While the Lawgiver meant to lead the multitude on gently by the precepts of the Laws as enjoined according to the literal sense, the other class, consisting of those who had acquired a habit of virtue, he meant to exempt from this sense, and required them to give attention to a philosophy of a diviner kind, too highly exalted for the multitude, and to contemplation of the things signified in the meaning of the Laws.[102]

So Philo could at once be a loyal Jew and at the same time abandon the very foundations of what Professor Moore taught us to call "normative Judaism." There is no reason to think that Philo was alone in doing so. His writings were designed to show to Jews already sympathetic with this procedure or to Gentiles looking for mystic ultimates, the true purport of the Torah, its mystic teaching. We can now follow him into the Mystery which he found there.

102. *Praep. Evang.*, VIII, x (378b, c). Eusebius goes on to identify the second class with the "Jewish philosophers" as described by Philo in his account of the Essenes. But Philo shows that Eusebius' distinction had wider implications.

CHAPTER IV

THE MYSTERY OF AARON

To Philo, we have seen, the revelation of God, and the Way to God, fell into two stages, stages metaphysically connected, but so different from each other that they can almost be called contrasting. There was the Way of the unwritten Law and Logos, or of Sophia, a Way that was characterized by its utter lack of contact or association with material existence. And there was the Way represented by those Powers that could be projected into, and represented in, the material world, the Way, we have seen thus far, of the written Law. It has already appeared that the second Way was one which Philo found very inferior to the first. Yet the secondary Way was not necessarily closed, in the sense that it prohibited those who took it from ever reaching the higher Way. True the mass of Jews lived their lives throughout on the basis and in the light of the written Laws, and it was hopeless to expect more of them. The "Allegorists" regarded the lower road as a blind alley, one that had to be abandoned if one hoped for the truth. But Philo saw in the life of the letter, as it may be called, that is the life guided by those glimmerings of Reality reflected in material media in general, a life which, when properly developed, had great, though not the greatest, possibilities. The highest function of the lower Way was that it might become an introduction to the higher Way, for as man traversed it he might come to recognize the distinction between the illumined material and the illumination itself, and so have suggested to him the possibility of living by the immaterial illumination.

Such a contrast was often expressed in Philo's environment by two successive initiations within a single Mystery. So it is interesting that in several passages Philo speaks of a "Lesser" Mystery in contrast with a "Greater." He points out that initiation under Moses is initiation into the "Greater Mysteries."[1] He speaks of the fact that those who were initiated into the Lesser Mysteries before the Greater had with the help of Reason, the softener, worked up the wild passions as one does in preparing food. The method for doing this was revealed through inspiration.[2] The point of contrast between the Lower and Higher Mystery is that the person on the lower stage cannot approach God (τὸ ὄν) without the aid of something that goes out from Him, that is through His creative or ruling activity.[3] This appears to mean that the Lesser Mystery was an apprehension of the Powers, or of a Power, of God rather than an apprehension of pure Being, which lower apprehension will also appear a regular stage of mystical experience.

1. *Cher.*, 49. 2. *Sac.*, 62.
3. *Abr.*, 122.

These few references to the Lower and Higher Mystery would seem to indicate that while the Higher was a definite experience, the term "Lower" could be used for several lower stages. But they suggest even more definitely that Philo thought of the Lower and Higher Mystery as an acceptable figure, at least, to express his own thought of the two ways of approach to God.

Actually there are two distinct stages of the Mystery in his teachings, sharply contrasted with each other as the Lower and the Higher, though not usually by that name. For general convenience we may distinguish them as the Mystery of Aaron and the Mystery of Moses. The Mystery of Aaron got its symbolism from the great Jerusalem cultus, the temple and the priesthood, and was a worship of God from the point of view of the material world. The Mystery of Moses abandoned the material world and led the worshipper above all material association; he died to the flesh, and in becoming reclothed in a spiritual body moved progressively upwards through the κόσμος νοητός, the Powers, and at last ideally to God Himself, being identified at each stage with the spiritual existence of that stage. The objective symbolism of the Higher Mystery was the holy of holies with the ark, a level of spiritual experience which was no normal part of even the high-priesthood. Only once a year could the high-priest enter there, and then only when stripped of his distinguishing robes, clad in simple white, and when so blinded by incense that he could see nothing of the sacred objects within. The Mystery of Aaron was restricted to the symbolism of the Aaronic high-priest, and hence was the worship of a deity or spiritual realm whose existence the high-priest recognized but could not share. In a striking passage Philo contrasts this type of priest with Moses, who put off his physical nature and went into the darkness naked, and so had communion in a constant way with the Monad, as a result of which he became the true initiate (μύστης), hierophant of the rites (ἱεροφάντης ὀργίων), and teacher of divine things (διδάσκαλος θείων).[4]

The significance of this contrast between the two types of Mystery will appear more distinctly as we go on. The concern of the present chapter is with the Mystery of Aaron.

The Mystery of Aaron is presented three times by Philo more or less *in extenso*. He describes it in the *De Vita Mosis,* his primer for proselytes. He goes over the ground again in the *Exposition,* but not so thoroughly, since he throughout assumes that the reader, still a Gentile inquirer into Judaism, will already have read the primer; yet he adds many new details of interest. Again in the *Quaestiones in Exodum* he reviews the subject, this time for Jews of the inner group. In all three accounts the fundamental idea is quite the same. As the symbol of the Immaterial World, of the Light-Stream, was the secret ark of the covenant, the symbolism for the Lower Mystery was

4. *Gig.,* 52–55. Cf. Pascher, *Königsweg,* pp. 168 ff.

based upon the parts of the tabernacle and the functions of the high-priest visible to the ordinary worshipper, or, at least, to the priesthood.

In discussing Philo's symbolism it will be well to follow each of the three accounts separately, and to take the details in the order in which they as objects would have been observed by one coming into the sacred precincts and advancing to the sanctuary. The description of the tabernacle in Exodus is the basis of Philo's remarks rather than the temple of Herod. The sacred precincts were the enclosed outer court, walled off but not covered, within which stood the tabernacle with two chambers, the inner court and the holy of holies. In the outer court stood the altar of sacrifice and the laver of purification. As the interpretation runs in the first passage,[5] the outer court with its laver of purification and altar of sacrifice represents the preliminary requirements for entering the Mystery. In the account we are considering the laver is not mentioned, but the altar symbolizes the proper intention of the man who approaches to sacrifice (ἡ προαίρεσις τοῦ προσφερόντος), since the spirit in which a man offers his sacrifice determines its validity.[6] The altar is his εὐσέβεια, the first requirement of mystical advance. That is, the whole subsequent experience is possible only for one who begins with a devout frame of mind.

The candidate for further progress looks, as he stands reverently in the outer court, toward the tabernacle which shows him only its general shape and proportions, and five outer pillars. The five outer pillars are, of course, the five senses, and very fittingly for Philo's purpose, since the senses are, he explains, the means of connection between the mind and the outer world of matter. For the tabernacle is going to be found to represent the whole gamut of human perception from τὰ αἰσθητά to τὰ νοητά, and the proper place of beginning is with the senses, facing outward but connected with what is within. The proportion of the tabernacle is elaborately described in terms of the number of "pillars," fifty-five, including the five outer ones, the Pythagorean symbol of the perfection of the decade,[7] or fifty without them, symbol of the right-angled triangle, creative beginnings.[8]

As one enters the inner court he observes its walls and roof made up, or covered, as they are by great curtains embroidered in bright colors. On the floor of the chamber stand three objects, the altar of incense, the seven-branched candlestick, and the table, bearing, in this passage, bread and salt, in another the twelve loaves. The curtains, made of linen, and embroidered with the three colors hyacinth, purple, and scarlet, represent, by the linen and the three colors together, the four elements.[9] The three objects on the floor are also each symbolic. In the center is the altar of incense, symbol of

5. Mos., ii, 71–135.   6. Ib., 94, 106 ff.
7. Ib., 78 f. See Badt's note ad loc. in Philos Werke.
8. Ib., 80. See Badt's note here also.   9. Ib., 88.

the gratitude (εὐχαριστία) of earth and water[10] or of all the things of the earth.[11] The seven-branched candlestick is on the south, representing the heavens[12] by specifically representing the sun, moon, and five planets, with the sun at the center.[13] The table, on which Philo says was bread and salt, stands at the north, symbolizing the nourishing and fertilizing power of the north wind,[14] by which we may fairly see the projection of the λόγος σπερματικός, or πνεῦμα θεοῦ, into the material world.[15] The symbolism does not appear at first glance. The inner court as a whole represents the first stage of spiritual progress, the stage where the material world as a whole was experienced. The details stand for the four elements, the altar of incense for earth and water, the table and its burden for air, and the candlestick for the heavenly fire, the source of light. The curtains are also the four elements. All of these are represented, however, as being in a mystical state. The two lower elements are rising in prayer and worship. The air is the πνεῦμα which feeds and nourishes the soul, and the heavenly fire appears at once as the great system of order of the planets and as the source of light, the symbol of the mystical higher light. An experience of the cosmos, then, would involve an apprehension of the world as it is in adoration of its Creator and as a symbol of the great spiritual forces. It was on this stage that the priesthood of Aaron ordinarily moved, since the holy of holies beyond was closed to it.

The holy of holies itself contained the ark, which Philo here explains as a symbol of God and the Powers in the way described above.[16] He tells us that another symbolic interpretation was in his day also current (τινές φασιν),[17] namely that the cherubim of the ark represent the two hemispheres. But Philo does not think this the best explanation. It is notable that Clemens Alexandrinus, who has reproduced the description of the tabernacle as here presented detail by detail, stops at describing the ark in terms of the Powers. He says: "The things recorded in connection with the holy ark symbolize the details of that κόσμος νοητός which is concealed and hidden away from the multitude."[18] So instead of reproducing this allegory Clement goes on to the other interpretation which Philo suggested but with additions. For he says that some interpret the cherubim as the two Bears, others as the two hemispheres, and notes that the wings, apparently six for each after the order of Ezekiel's seraphim, made together the zodiac. Clement has "loaves" on the table, not bread and salt. It would look as though Clement were draw-

10. *Mos.*, ii, 101.   11. Ib., 105.
12. Ib., 105.   13. Ib., 102 ff.
14. Ib., 104.
15. The idea is clearly that the north wind was the rain bearer, and so a symbol of heavenly nourishment and fertilization.
16. *Mos.*, ii, 99. See Chap. I.   17. Ib., 98.
18. *Strom.*, v, 6 (Stählin, vol. II, p. 349, ll. 18 f.).

ing from another Hellenistic account of the Mystery of Aaron, one which Philo also knew, rather than upon Philo himself.

Josephus too, while he interprets the symbolism of the curtain and the candlesticks quite in the same way, and comes out with the same fundamental conception of the temple symbolism as a whole, differs from Philo on too many details to have taken his material from Philo. The three courts or chambers of the temple represent to him earth, sea, and οὐρανός. Instead of bread and salt upon the table were twelve loaves, symbolic of the zodiac. The altar of incense had thirteen kinds of spices, furnished by sea, earth, and air, and symbolized the offering of the elements to God: this is ultimately like Philo, but with quite a different treatment of detail.[19]

It would seem that there was considerable variety in the way in which Jews made the objects in the temple represent the mystic rise from material confusion, through the cosmos as philosophically and mystically interpreted, to the κόσμος νοητός and God. But the very variety of detail is essentially important to us precisely because so strong a unity of purpose carries on through the variety, and hence suggests a single and a considerable movement with wide divergences. All alike see the chamber as a symbol of the worship of immaterial Reality by the material elements. The chamber represents the worship of God by the cosmos. It will be increasingly clear that the Mystery of Aaron brings the worshipper to share in this great cosmic praise and worship of God.

The significance of the priesthood which ministers in the cosmic temple Philo explains by pointing out the symbolism of the priestly robes. Immediately after his explanation of the temple in De Vita Mosis, Philo goes on to tell of the priestly dress. First he describes the dress,[20] then he gives the symbolism.[21] The regalia as a whole, he says, is "a likeness and imitation of the cosmos, its details are likenesses and imitations of the details of the cosmos."[22] This is quite what was to be expected after the symbolism of the temple.

The robe Aaron wears represents the four elements. It is of hyacinth color to typify air, for air is naturally black.[23] This hyacinth robe stretches from the shoulders, where, as will appear, are the heavenly symbols, to the feet. There, at the ankles, is a border of promegranate-shaped tassels, flowers, and bells.[24] The flowers represent earth, the tassels water, and the bells typify the attunement of these two. These all appear on the tunic which represents the sublunar sphere and its elements. The mantle over the shoulders represents heaven, that is the outer circle of the universe, for several reasons. First, on

19. Antiq., III, 179–183; BJ, V, 207–221.   20. Mos., ii, 109–116.
21. Ib., 117–135.   22. Ib., 117.
23. Philo repeatedly says this: Mos., ii, 88; Opif., 29. See the note in Philos Werke to this later passage.
24. On the difficulty of harmonizing this with the Hebrew text, see the note in Philos Werke to Mos., ii, 119.

either shoulder the priest wears a large emerald.[25] Some propose to explain the emeralds as the sun and moon (and this is the school Josephus follows at this point[26]), but Philo thinks a better explanation is that they represent the two celestial hemispheres, for they are equal and unchanging in a way the sun and moon are not. In accordance with this interpretation it was inevitable that six names should be engraved on each stone, representing the six signs of the zodiac proper to each hemisphere. The zodiac appears in more detail on the priest's breastplate. The breastplate has four rows of three stones each, making together the twelve signs of the zodiac, but properly divided into four rows to stand for the four seasons of the year into which the whole circle of the zodiac is divided.[27] As a whole this breastplate, called in the Septuagint the λογεῖον, represents that permanent, fixed, and truly divine λόγος (ratio) which appears in the realm of numbers. This λόγος is the ratio of numbers, but is also the governing rule by which the changes of seasons occur. That is, we conclude, it is the Natural Law of the heavenly world which the breastplate represents as a whole. The different signs or animals of the zodiac are further symbolized by the different color of each stone, since the different color of each sign is a matter of cosmic significance.[28]

The breastplate has further important significance, but here we approach the most difficult element of the interpretation. For Philo says:

The breastplate is double not without reason; for both in the universe and in man the Logos is double. In the universe, then, there is one Logos which has to do with the immaterial and prototypal forms, from which the κόσμος νοητός is made, and also the Logos which has to do with visible things which are imitations and likenesses of those forms, of which the sensible [world] is constituted. In man there are respectively the λόγος ἐνδιάθετος and the λόγος προφορικός, the one of which is in a sense the source, the other the stream flowing from it. The location of the former is in τὸ ἡγεμονικόν, but the seat of the uttered λόγος is the tongue, mouth, and all the other organs of speech.[29]

Philo would seem here to be definitely projecting a λόγος ἐνδιάθετος and προφορικός from the human to the divine realm.[30] It is true that he does not say that there is a divine λόγος προφορικός and ἐνδιάθετος to correspond to the double human logos, but certainly such a meaning is implied. There has been much discussion over why Philo did not make the comparison explicit, and set up a double divine Logos to correspond to the double human

---

25. There is some dispute as to whether the gem called σμάραγδος by the ancients was actually what we call the emerald. See Liddell and Scott, *ad verb.*

26. *Antiq.,* III, 185.   27. *Mos.,* ii, 124 f.

28. Ib., 126.   29. Ib., 127.

30. A reference to Heinze's still classic *Die Lehre vom Logos,* 140 ff. is sufficient for this very familiar Stoic notion.

logos, as was done by later Christian writers, since he seems to suggest it.[31] Gfrörer[32] and Heinze,[33] from different reasons, think that the implication is quite sufficient that Philo did think of the double Logos, and that it is a matter of chance and of no importance that he did not make the comparison more explicit. Drummond[34] insists that while there is a double divine Logos, the comparing of the lower divine Logos to human speech involved too sharp a suggestion of human organs to be applicable to Deity. He thinks that Philo was aware of this and hence compares the double divine Logos with the double human logos, but does not make the comparison go further to an actual divine λόγος προφορικός. Zeller denies the existence of a double Logos at all in Divinity, and says that there is only the double manifestation or activity of the Logos, the Logos in its relation with the κόσμος νοητός, and the same Logos in its relation to the material world.[35]

So have students of Philo varied in their judgments.[36] The question has become highly important for our subject because Pascher has based much of his discussion of the Mystery elements he treats in Philo upon precisely this distinction. He sees, in contrast with the Logos of the Powers, a cosmic Logos. The one is the Logos-Monad, the other the Logos-Dyad, so described because in being clothed with material the second Logos is not simple and single immaterial substance as is the higher Logos. In his opinion the second or Cosmic Logos of Philo is the Stoic Logos, the Logos that is the law of material nature by the fact that it is the formal principle immanent in matter. So to Pascher the temple cultus and the priestly dress indicate that this type of worship, the Mystery of Aaron, is an ascent to and an identification of the mystic with the cosmic Logos of the Stoics. In building up his argument for the two forms of Logos, Pascher does not use this passage,[37] but relies upon deductions from the general purport of the argument of the Monad and Dyad,[38] as Bréhier[39] erects the ὀρθὸς λόγος into a similar cosmic principle. Both arguments are to me quite unconvincing. The high-priest is certainly represented by Philo as the Logos, as will shortly appear, and yet the high-priest is not qualified to enter the holy of holies as his fixed and proper sphere. In a striking passage this is explained as being based upon the

31. See my *The Theology of Justin Martyr* (Jena, 1923), pp. 151 ff.
32. *Philo und die jüdisch-alexandrinische Theosophie*, I (1835), 177 f.
33. *Op. cit.*, p. 232.   34. *Philo Judaeus*, II, 172.
35. Zeller, *Philos. d. Griech.*, III, ii (1903), pp. 423 f. To him the distinction "auf die Frage bezieht . . . nach den Objekten, mit denen er (the Logos) sich beschäftigt." Zeller's refutation of Heinze's argument is very convincing.
36. A. Aall, *Geschichte der Logosidee*, I (Leipzig, 1896), 197, and Soulier, *La doctrine du Logos chez Philon d'Alexandrie* (Diss., Leipzig, 1876), 92 ff., agree with Zeller and Drummond; F. Keferstein, *Philos Lehre von dem göttlichen Mittelwesen* (Leipzig, 1846), p. 36, with Heinze.
37. Though he does so later, *Königsweg*, p. 144.
38. *Königsweg*, esp. pp. 33–37.   39. *Les Idées*, pp. 92 ff.

fact that the λόγος προφορικός is not fixed, but is a Dyad, while only the λόγος ἄνευ φωνῆς is a Monad.[39a] In contrast to such a mediator as the high-priest stands Moses.

Another passage also deals with the high-priest as Logos. In so far as he is the Logos, the high-priest cannot wear robes which indicate that his father was νοῦς, his mother αἴσθησις:

because, I think, he has had indestructible and most pure parents, God as his Father, who is also Father of all things, and Sophia for his mother, through whom all things (τὰ ὅλα) were born. And I explain his head's being anointed with oil by the fact that his mind (τὸ ἡγεμονικόν) is permeated with the illumination of brilliant light, so that he is rightly represented as "putting on the garments." And the oldest Logos of God (ὁ πρεσβύτατος τοῦ ὄντος λόγος) has put on the universe as a garment (for he has wrapped himself in earth and water and air and fire and their products), and the individual soul puts on the body, and the mind of the wise man puts on the virtues. And the stipulation that he "shall never put off the mitre" from his head indicates that he shall not take off the royal diadem. This diadem is the symbol not of absolute rule but of a marvelous vicegerency. "He does not tear his garments" for the Logos of God (ὁ τοῦ ὄντος λόγος) is the bond of all things, as has been said, and holds together all the parts, and prevents them by its constriction from breaking apart and becoming separated.[40]

Pascher very rightly sees this conception of the Logos, born from God and Sophia, as a mystic-mythological conception, not a philosophic one, and his parallels with Isis are striking.[41] This must not, however, blind us to the fact that if mythological systems had a cosmic Logos, Philo has gone a long way, while he borrowed the mystic notion of the Logos as the ruler of the universe, to avoid setting up a distinct mythological cosmic Logos himself. A second glance at the passage will reveal that it has nothing to tell us of the usual symbolism of the priesthood, and indeed is explicitly contrasted with that symbolism. Just before, Philo has been allegorizing the great passage on the cities of refuge as stages of religious experience.[42] In the three higher stages man has gone beyond the river and is in mystical union with the Powers or with the Logos, that is, as will appear, he is in the Higher Mystery. Philo now has to explain the scriptural statement that the soul that goes to one of these cities must stay there until the high-priest dies. What high-priest is indicated, asks Philo. In answer Philo specifies that it is not the high-priest whose robe signifies his double origin from the immaterial and material realms, not the high-priesthood assumed by a man, but the high-priest-

39a. Gig., 52.
40. Fug., 108-112; Pascher, Königsweg, pp. 61 ff.
41. Apuleius, Metam., XI, c. 24.
42. See above, pp. 28 ff., and below, pp. 249 ff.

hood of that Logos whose origin and nature is entirely immaterial in origin. In other words, Philo is clearly saying that it is not the Aaronic high-priest about which he is talking, but the Logos, ὁ πρεσβύτατος τοῦ ὄντος λόγος, certainly the "highest" Logos by Bréhier's and Pascher's distinctions. Nothing could be more inaccurate, then, than to carry what Philo says here of the Logos as priest over to apply to the Aaronic priesthood. Philo is led by the contrast to go on to explain that this "highest" Logos put on the four elements as a garment, and became the binding force within them. But he has already said that it was not this combination that he was calling Logos, and nothing that follows justifies calling the new combination a "Second Logos." The new combination is the cosmos.[48] It is because the high-priesthood was so fixed a symbol of the cosmos to Philo and his readers that he is forced to make the distinction and explain the relation here.

The conception of a double Logos in Pascher's sense also does violence to what Philo seems to have in mind by comparing the two stages of the heavenly Logos to the λόγος ἐνδιάθετος and the λόγος προφορικός of man. When Philo says that the Logos in τῷ παντί and the Logos of human nature is in each case διττός, that is not to say that there are δύο λόγω. When διττός means "two" it is written διττοί and used as a dual. The passage says in plain Greek only that the Logos, a singular thing, is of twofold aspect. The whole point of the λόγος προφορικός and ἐνδιάθετος of Stoic distinction was not to make two λόγοι but to make clear that the λόγος projected in speech was only a projection of thought, and that speech was only a derivative manifestation of thought. The divine Logos does, to be sure, appear to men as a duality, but that is only because the one Logos, the Logos in its proper purity and the Logos as an immanent principle in the material universe, together a monad, has the power of presenting itself along with matter which is in no sense an inherent part of itself. The Logos remains a monad, for it is not the Logos in the world that is the dyad but the world as consisting of matter with the Logos, just as the dyad speech is made up of human logos plus sound. When the logos goes out from man and becomes mixed with sound we have speech; when the Logos of God goes into matter we have the great cosmic dyad, the World. It is, if I may coin such a word, the very monadity of the Logos that makes it the bond of the universe, a fact that has abundantly come out in the discussion of the λόγος τομεύς. Pascher seems wrong throughout, then, in his assumption of the two Logoi, monad and dyad. There is one Logos which can combine with matter to make the dyad, and that dyad is the material world.

While we are on this subject, it may be well to consider briefly another

---

43. Philo does say here that the Logos puts on the cosmos, but explains that he means the four elements. It is obviously only the Logos "holding them together and keeping them from dissolution" that makes the elements into the cosmos.

passage, where the high-priest is described in terms of the word logos. Here,[44] the human reason is compared with the high-priest. The high-priest dwells always among the holy doctrines, but cannot enter to consort with them (πρὸς αὐτὰ φοιτᾶν) more than once a year. This, Philo explains, is because the λόγος προφορικός as a dyad is unstable; only the logos without utterance, the monad, can have the vision of τὸ ὄν. Again, the high-priest is being compared with the λόγος προφορικός of human speech, but again not in such a way as to suggest a cosmic dyadic Logos. The priest in the cosmic robes, that is the Logos clothed in the material elements, is the cosmic dyad, the λόγος προφορικός, and nothing here is contrary to our conclusion from other passages that that λόγος προφορικός is the cosmos.

Philo seems to me through all this to be working still from the point of view of deity as sun-radiation. There is a distinction between the sun and the radiation, between God as above the monad, and the Logos-monad. But again and again Philo insists that the various stages of radiation, the Powers and κόσμος νοητός, and now the Logos in the material garment, are all to be called Logos. Only the beginner sees the distinction, though to one in any but almost the highest stage the vision of the Logos and the two chief δυνάμεις still appears as three. The true vision is not that of the aspects, but to see, and so become one with, the Logos in its purity, the monad. Philo's language frequently echoes mythical and gnostic conceptions of definite stages of a divine pleroma. But to isolate these occasional passages from the thought of Philo as a whole, as it seems to me Pascher and also Bréhier have essentially done, is to illuminate the figures on which Philo was drawing, but not the thought of Philo itself. The true understanding for us of Philo's thought, like the vision to which he aspires, is to see his Logos, through all its various aspects and figures, as One.

Yet that vision of the Logos as One was not to be attained at a single leap by ordinary man. From the confusion and multiplicity of the world of our senses, it is a great step in advance to come to the vision of the cosmos as a great dyad, the Logos clothed in matter. Hence the importance of the symbolism of the temple, the importance of the priesthood which God had Moses confer upon Aaron, the importance of the Mystery of Aaron. It was far from being, as we shall see, the Highest Mystery. The priesthood of Moses has already appeared a vastly superior thing. But the priesthood that would lead men into the cosmic harmony was a divinely instituted boon for humanity. On that stage we still must linger for further details.

The section in the *De Vita Mosis* which describes the breastplate as the symbol of the twofold representation of the Logos is followed by a discussion of the Urim and Thummim. Philo agrees with the Septuagint in calling them δήλωσις and ἀλήθεια. The priest had these, says Philo, because the

44. *Gig.*, 52.

Logos of Nature is itself both true and the revelation or manifestation of all things.[45] The two human logoi are copies of these and each has respectively one of these virtues: reason must be true, speech must be a clear manifestation. Again Philo is comparing the great Logos to the two human logoi of Stoicism. But these are not two Logoi of God or Nature. The λόγος τῆς φύσεως, which would be by Pascher's and Bréhier's reasoning the λόγος προφορικός, has itself both these virtues. It is in the human realm that he will allow himself even figuratively to speak of δύο λόγω. Philo's objective in the interpretation of the Urim and Thummim is clear. The Logos in the material world is itself the truth, and at the same time, as it clothes itself in matter, is a magnificent manifestation of the truth to men.

Upon his head the high-priest wears a cidaris, to signify, as here interpreted, his superiority to all kings.[46] This, Philo points out with his usual caution, means not the high-priest as an individual, but καθ' ὃν χρόνον ἱερᾶται, during the actual time he is exercising his office.[47] Philo is not going to be caught saying that the priest at Jerusalem is a higher person than the Roman emperor. What Philo intends is to remind the reader of the familiar fact that the king or emperor was himself subject in his rule and law to the Logos and Law of Nature. In so far as the priest represented this, his sovereignty must be superior to kings', for while the king was also a revelation of that Law and Logos, he was so not in the complete and pure sense that the priest was. We have already seen[48] another interpretation of this cidaris, that it betokened the fact that even the rule of the Logos in Nature was only a marvelous vicegerency. The real ruler, we assume, is God Himself. There are still other interpretations of the cidaris to which we shall come.

Above the cidaris, Philo goes on to say, is the golden plate on which the four letters were engraved; by these letters the name of God (τοῦ ὄντος) was, they say, indicated because nothing that exists (οὐ . . . τι τῶν ὄντων) can endure without calling upon God. For the attunement of all things is the Goodness and the Power of His Mercy.[49]

The priestly robes have for their crowning symbol the fact that the Goodness and Merciful Power, that is the δύναμις ποιητική and its secondary manifestation, the Merciful Power, are the aspects of the Logos which hold the created world together, and on which the very existence of creation not only

45. Mos., ii, 128 ff.   46. Ib., 131.
47. Ἱερᾶσθαι ordinarily means to be a priest, and the clause would normally mean "during the time when he was priest." The priesthood of Aaron and his early successors was for life, so that this clause would have no meaning when applied to him, for then his superiority to kings would have been for life. The clause must then be translated as I have done, following Yonge and Badt in Philos Werke, or else taken as a reference to the rotation of priesthood practiced in Philo's day.
48. See above, p. 102.   49. Mos., ii, 132.

depended but still depends. This was the Power, it will be recalled, that was
θεός, and hence the world must constantly invoke θεός, its savior or preserver. In passing it is notable that Philo has not forgotten to indicate by
inserting the φασί that his explanation is a traditional one in his Jewish
environment.

The purpose of all this imagery is indicated in Philo's own summary that
follows:

> The high-priest, adorned in this fashion, is dressed for the religious rites so
> that when he goes in to offer the ancestral prayers and sacrifices, the whole cosmos
> may go in with him by virtue of the symbols (μιμήματα) which he wears: the
> long robe reaching to his feet a symbol of air, the pomegranate of water, the
> flowered hem of earth, the scarlet of fire, the ephod of the οὐρανός; he wears in
> type the two hemispheres in the jewels on his shoulders, with the six characters
> engraved on each; symbols of the zodiac are the twelve stones upon his chest
> arranged in four rows of three stones in each row, while the breastplate as a whole
> represents the principle that holds together and rules all things. For it was neces-
> sary that he who was consecrated to the Father of the world should use as a para-
> clete His Son[50] who is perfect in virtue to secure remission of sins and an abun-
> dance of indestructible good things. Yet perhaps it is also to teach in advance one
> who would worship God that even though he may be incapable of making him-
> self worthy of the Creator of the cosmos, he yet ought to try unceasingly to be
> worthy of the cosmos. As he puts on its imitation he ought straightway to become
> one who bears in his mind the original pattern, so that he is in a sense trans-
> formed from being a man into the nature of the cosmos, and becomes, if one may
> say so (and indeed one must say nothing false about the truth), himself a little
> cosmos.[51]

One further section sets out in figurative but clear language that the
preparation for this experience is purification from all material and fleshly
concern, from any bondage to pleasure.[52]

The significance of the Jewish priesthood and temple has been here set
forth with unmistakable meaning. It is a worship designed for those who are
not worthy of association with God, or of mystical union with Him, or deification, and is a transformation of the worshipper into the Cosmic Being,
made up of Logos and Matter, to be sure, but still oriented in a great harmony through God's Powers of Goodness and Mercy. Such a person shares
in the cosmic communion of the world with the Creator, not as an individual, but as one who has at last achieved the ideal now popularly associated
with the Stoics, of living according to Nature, of being in harmony with the
great sweep and course of the universe. We shall have to bear in mind as the
Mystery of Philo becomes more clear the problem of whether we are dealing

---

50. That is the κόσμος, as Badt rightly points out *ad loc., Philos Werke.*
51. *Mos.,* ii, 133–135.   52. Ib., 136–140.

with a Mystery proper, in the sense of an organization with formal initiation, or a mystic gnosis of the Hermetic type. In the latter type there seem to have been no rites of initiation, but definite levels of spiritual experience, so that the person who had no such experience, or only the lower type, was given only the lower teaching. This is the sort of Mystery Paul and the author of Hebrews make of the Christian teaching when they refuse meat to babes and will give them only milk. Paul is very cautious, as in I Corinthians, not to go into the deeper teaching with those not ready to receive it. It is impossible that Paul's distinction between "adults" and "babes" was based upon a sacramental distinction between those who had and those who had not been baptized. Apparently there were definite levels of spiritual achievement which he could recognize, and which he always bore carefully in mind.

Without yet attempting to answer the question as to which type of Mystery Philo is teaching, it must here be pointed out that the robe and cosmic experience of the high-priest seem something in which the individual can definitely share. In the foregoing quotation Philo has said that the significance of the priestly worship is to

teach in advance one who would worship God that even though he may be incapable of making himself worthy of the Creator of the cosmos, he yet ought to try unceasingly to be worthy of the cosmos. As he puts on its imitation he ought straightway to become one who bears in mind the original pattern, so that he is in a sense transformed, etc.

The implication of those words would seem to be, not that the high-priest alone puts on the robes but that there is a Mystery in which any one who would worship God may also put them on. The language may just as well be figurative, however, and we cannot decide at this point in which way we should take it. But it is clear that whether the ordinary aspirant went through a ceremony of investiture or not, the experience of the priest was in some way open to all who properly aspired.

I have begun my discussion of the significance of the temple and priesthood with this passage from the *De Vita Mosis* because it is from a book written for Gentiles, a simplification of some of Philo's more elaborate symbolism, presented here purposely in a way to be intelligible to one who knew nothing of the doctrine before. It may be well to stop for a moment with the interpretation of the same material made for slightly more advanced Gentiles, but men who still apparently had not yet definitely become proselytes. Here it is at first surprising to find that the account is much less elaborate than the one in the *De Vita Mosis*. This is not to be wondered at, for throughout the *Exposition* Philo assumes that the reader has already read,

108 BY LIGHT, LIGHT

or has available, the *De Vita Mosis;*[53] so of the ground already covered Philo has a relatively slight sketch. But he reaffirms the main interpretation, and adds many important details.

As to the significance of the Jewish temple, he says that it is a symbol of the true temple, ὁ σύμπας κόσμος, whose sanctuary is the οὐρανός, the holiest part of the substance (οὐσία here in the sense of material) of things that exist. In this temple the stars are the votive offerings (ornaments, or the images of God, ἀναθήματα)[54] and the priests are the sub-deacons of the Powers, the angels, whose natures are unmixed with matter. He mentions the temple in another passage briefly to say that there are two temples of God, the human soul (ἡ λογικὴ ψυχή) and the κόσμος. In the κόσμος the priest is the Logos, ὁ πρωτόγονος αὐτοῦ θεῖος λόγος.[55] We need not worry about the fact that the priests in one passage are the angels, or as Philo elsewhere calls them, the λόγοι, and in the other passage are the Logos. In either case they are the Logos seen in relation to particular matters, so that they could easily be described as singular or plural interchangeably.

The Jewish temple, the one made with hands, was God's concession to the laudable desires of the people for a more definitely available sanctuary, though God allowed only one such shrine to be built, for since there is only one God, He can have but one temple.[56] The journey to this single temple has the double advantage of testing by the rigor and inconvenience of the journey the good faith of the worshippers, and at the same time of bringing together Jews from every quarter of the world and uniting them, as they get to know each other and sacrifice together, in a fixed fidelity based upon their common interest and conceptions.[57]

Philo goes on in the *De Specialibus Legibus* briefly to describe the temple,[58] here obviously the contemporary temple, and speaks of the holy of holies as at the center, completely shut off from the public view, and indeed seen by no one, for when the high-priest enters once a year he must so envelop himself with the smoke of incense that he can see nothing while he is there.[59] The temple has no sacred grove.[60] It is supported by the offerings

53. See my "Philo's Exposition of the Law and his De Vita Mosis," in *Harvard Theological Review,* XXVI (1933), pp. 110–125.

54. A parallel passage throws some light. Philo in *Opif.,* 55, speaks of the creation of the material world after the image of the κόσμος νοητός: after the pattern of the conceptual light "God made the stars perceptible by the senses. They are divine images (ἀγάλματα), exceedingly beautiful, which he set in that purest temple of the material substance (σωματικὴ οὐσία), the heaven."

55. *Som.,* i, 215.

56. *Spec.,* i, 67. Philo could have had no dealings with the temple at Leontopolis. Apparently Judaism in the Diaspora was far indeed from being a unit. But it is notable, as Heinemann (note, *Philos Werke, ad loc.*) has pointed out, that Josephus reproduces the same argument for a single temple (*Ap.,* II, 163; *Antiq.,* IV, 200).

57. *Spec.,* i, 68–70: εἰς βεβαιοτάτην πίστιν ὁμονοίας.

58. Ib., 71.   59. Ib., 72 f.   60. Ib., 74 f.

of the Jews from all over the world. Illuminating as is this section for our knowledge of the relation of Jews in the Diaspora to the temple, and suggestive as it is of the Mystery, it adds little to our knowledge of the Mystery itself.

Philo goes on to describe the priests and their garments[61] but again only summarizing or assuming knowledge of the description given in the *De Vita Mosis.*[62] The robe of the high-priest represents the elements, the garment over the shoulder the οὐρανός; the stones on the shoulders are the hemispheres, the twelve stones of the breastplate the zodiac, and the breastplate itself the Logos. The Urim and Thummim are different here as specifically representing the manifestation and truth of heaven. Falsehood cannot enter heaven, for it is the function of heaven, especially of the sun, to illuminate and reveal, though the heavens furnish guidance to mariners with their stars, and the portents of the heaven foretell the weather. The dress of the high-priest is then a copy of the universe (μίμημα τοῦ παντός). Besides the value of such a robe for its mere impressiveness Philo gives three reasons for its cosmic significance. First, that the priest might, by constantly seeing it, make his own life worthy of the universal nature (ἄξιον τῆς τῶν ὅλων φύσεως), that is, as Philo has given it before, make himself so in harmony with the cosmos as himself to become a microcosmos. Second, he wears the robe that in his ministrations the whole cosmos may worship with him. "For it is most proper that the one who is consecrated to the Father of the universe should offer to Him also the Son, the universe, in worship of the Creator and Begetter." Third, the Jewish high-priest is distinguished in that while priests of other religions function only for their own circle, the Jewish priest is a mediator for all mankind, and not for all mankind only, but also for the very universe itself. Jewish worship has cosmic significance.[63]

The fundamental interpretation of the temple and high-priesthood as a cosmic worship, a Mystery of the Cosmos, here appears as opening a good many possibilities of significance at which Philo only hints. If these hints were developed at more length an extraordinarily rich religion, with appeal to many types of mind, would be presented. The varieties of interpretation found in Philo, as well as those of Josephus, and Clement, obviously show that we have here various actual interpretations from different types of thinkers. It is notable that one interpretation is definitely an attempt to get philosophical physics and metaphysics, the second seems of mythological-gnostic background, the third mystic in the true sense. Let the individual

---

61. Ib., 82–97.

62. Ib., 82 f. The trousers (περισκελῆ) appear as the περίζωμα (εἰς αἰδοίων σκέπην). Cf. Suidas, *s.v.* περίζωμα, τὸ ὑπὸ τὰ αἰδοῖα σκέπασμα. On sacramental use of περίζωμα see Plutarch, *Aemil. Paul*, xxx, iii, 1. The tunic (χιτών) is explained as serving the purpose of the ζώνη in *Mos.*, ii, 143 f., where three articles, χιτών, περισκελῆ, and ζώνη, are mentioned.

63. *Spec.*, i, 95–97.

take his choice! The Mystery, like all great religions, was in itself comprehensive.

Philo's passage on the priesthood in the first book of *De Specialibus Legibus,* brief as it is, is a digression. Philo's business in this writing is to prove that the various special laws of Judaism do, contrary to all appearances, have importance as practical legislation of the very highest type. So he goes on to details of the legislation for the priesthood from this point of view: the fact that the priest must drink no wine, be physically perfect, must marry a virgin of priestly family, must limit his time of mourning. In connection with this last it is notable that Philo considers that the high-priest may not go through the usual signs of mourning, because he must

share in a nature greater than human, and approach much nearer the divine nature, indeed, to tell the truth, be a creature bordering upon both natures (μεθόριον ἀμφοῖν), that men may appease (ἱλάσκωνται) God through some mediator (διὰ μέσου τινός), and that God may have some underservant (ὑποδιάκανός τις) to use in abundantly stretching out His favors (χάριτας) to men.[64]

This is the first appearance in our material of the notion of the θεῖος ἄνθρωπος, the man who is between the human and divine natures because he shares in both, and who is hence in a position to mediate the salvation of God to men. It will by no means be the last. Philo indeed seems to be ascribing to Aaron the type of priesthood he usually reserves for Moses. But the point of this passage is that Aaron and his successors are really still of two natures. True they have a share in the divine nature, but have it only as the cosmos has it, still mixed with the lower nature. The higher priests will appear to have put off this lower side altogether, and hence to have become θεῖοι ἄνθρωποι in a sense that not even this passage ascribes to the high-priest.[65]

The *De Specialibus Legibus,* then, like the *De Vita Mosis,* sketches a high-priesthood which is essentially that of the dyad, as Pascher calls it. The mystic in rising to the state of the high-priest rises from multiplicity to the dyad, made up of Logos and matter. Himself a microcosm, he is at one with the macrocosm.

The remainder of the first book of *De Specialibus Legibus* goes on to speak of the particular sacrificial laws. Into them we need not go in detail. The whole spirit in which the sacrifice is offered is stressed as being of far more importance than the animal offered. Philo explains to the Gentile reader the cheerfulness with which Jews pay the temple tribute,[66] and the fact that the motive of the sacrificer alone determines the value of the sacri-

64. *Spec.,* i, 116.
65. Philo goes on from this level to the higher priesthood in *Som.,* ii, 181–189. There the priest is not only mediator, but himself an offering and source of grace. See below, page 255.
66. *Spec.,* i, 144.

fice.[67] He praises the laws for their conformity with Natural Law,[68] for the fact that the laws display a plan and a philosophic basis (τὸ προμηθὲς καὶ φιλόσοφον)[69] for the ascetic control[70] and general moral elevation of their purport and influence, especially as they inculcate justice in the minds of those who obey them, so that the faithful man is a model of social conduct. The goal of this worship is a life which merits no accusation since it has been attuned to the Laws and Commands of Nature.

For the meaning is that in the first place the mind of the one who offers sacrifice, after it has been disciplined with good and beneficial intentions, is to be made holy (ὡσιῶσθαι), and afterwards the life is to consist of the noblest deeds.[71]

So his hands and feet become the servants doing what things are honored by σοφία and νόμος, and by wise and law-abiding men.[72] As he is purified in the ceremonies he no longer walks upon the earth, but soars into the air.

For in truth the soul of one who loves God springs up from earth to heaven and with its wings flies about, longing to be put in order with and to take part in the great dance of the sun, the moon, and that most sacred and perfectly attuned company of the other stars. God their captain and general has the kingship over them, one that cannot be opposed or taken away. Through this kingship each individual thing is ruled in accordance with justice.[73]

The notion of the flight is still definitely a union with the cosmos, not a flight beyond it. And the prayer which Philo goes on to teach men[74] is a cosmic prayer, in which we thank God for the universe as a whole, and for its parts, heaven and the heavenly bodies, earth and its planets and animals, the seas and rivers, and the air and its changes, the seasons. In praying for men, one should pray for them as a whole, as well as for the races and individuals; and in praying for individuals, for them as a whole as well as their parts. This is the type of prayer of one who has come to know and be at one with the universe, which is both a whole and an assembly of parts. It is by no means here or anywhere else a prayer to the universe. The Stoic who could pray to the universe Philo viewed with quite as great horror as he

67. Ib., 257 ff., esp. 271, 277, 290.   68. Ib., 178, 191, 202 f.
69. Ib., 262.   70. Ib., 149.
71. Ib., 202 f.   72. Ib., 204.
73. The language recalls the *Phaedrus* (246c) of Plato. R. Jones ("Poseidonius and the Flight of the soul through the universe," *Classical Philology*, XXI (1926), 97 ff., especially 103 for this passage) has successfully laid the ghost of Posidonius in connection with this familiar thought. The untimely death of Jones has cost Greek Philosophy one of its clearest and sanest minds. Would that he had lived to complete the comprehensive work on Posidonius he was so capable of producing! I am not so sure, however, that in this case the notion can be dismissed as simply borrowed from the *Phaedrus*. It seems to me to have gone through a good many hands, and to be closer to the type of Neo-Platonic Mystery preserved in Iamblichus *De Mysteriis*, v, 15 than to Plato.
74. *Spec.*, i, 209–211.

viewed any other manifestation of atheism. The cosmic experience was one in which man learned to pray with, not to, the universe. Such actual prayers will be presented in Chapter XI.

The immediate object of the sacrificial system seems to have been the conciliation of the Merciful Power of God. Philo mentions this three times.[75] Apparently when one gets beyond the literal fulfillment of the Law into the philosophic appreciation of God's relation to the universe including man, the suppliant's appeal is to this Power rather than to the lowest Powers, the Power of Negative and that of Positive Commands. To that we shall return.

In one striking passage,[76] Philo suggests a distinction between the old and the new sacrifices; he sees in the eternally burning fire on the altar a unification of the two.[77] He does not explain himself specifically as to which is the old, which the new. But the higher sacrifice he has in mind he makes clear. Philo gets this type, in contrast to the ceremonial sacrifice, by allegory; that is, what he has been doing all along here is not allegory at all. For the higher type of sacrifice is one in which the altar is the grateful soul of the wise man compounded of perfect and undivided virtues. Upon this altar the sacred light (not fire as above) is kept unquenched. This light is Sophia, for what sensible light is for physical sight, that ἐπιστήμη, a usual synonym for mystical Sophia, is to the reason in its perception of τὰ ἀσώματα καὶ νοητά, whose beams always shine forth unquenched. Whatever the explanation of the "new" and "old," Philo is putting in here a hint that there is a Higher Mystery, the gate to whose understanding is allegory.

The closing sections of the first book of the *De Specialibus Legibus* are highly important, but to them we shall return after considering the *Quaestiones in Exodum,* the most detailed source of all for the explanation of the Mystery of the temple and priesthood.

Here Philo has been talking of the Mystery of the ark and the holy of holies, a passage which must be discussed in connection with the Greater Mystery. He turns from this to talk of the other parts of the tabernacle or temple, remarking that he is turning from the symbols of the incorporeals to the symbols of those things that are *in sensu.* The first symbol in this realm is the table, type of the material world,[78] which is separated into parts.[79] It is useless to go through all the details again, but the additional ones must be noted. It is made clear that Philo is drawing his material from other men, the Allegorists.[80] The candlestick is made all of gold because the heaven is made up of a single element, the "fifth" in contrast to the constitu-

---

75. *Spec.*, i, 229, 265, 294.						76. Ib., 286–288.
77. Ib., 286: τάχα μέντοι καὶ διὰ τοῦδε βούλεται τὰς παλαιὰς ταῖς νέαις θυσίαις ἁρμόσασθαι καὶ ἑνῶσαι.
78. *QE*, ii, 69.						79. Ib., 70.
80. Ib., 71. They seem referred to in the *putatur* of §76 (ed. Tauchnitz, p. 366, l. 7).

tion of the rest of the universe from the four elements.[81] The branches of the candlestick go off at an acute rather than a right angle because the zodiac cycle is of such angles.[82] Each branch of the candlestick has three cups as the three signs of the zodiac in each season, and the other ornaments and details of the candlestick are likewise given cosmic symbolism.[83] As the incorporeal world is represented by the ark, the substance of the sensible world by the table, the heaven by the candlestick, so the tabernacle is designed to show the nature and substance of the sublunar world and its four elements.[84] The ten curtains of the tabernacle indicate the usual significance to him of the decade,[85] their four colors, as previously, the four elements.[86] They are joined together to show that out of material multiplicity the cosmos is a unit,[87] and the fact that there is one tabernacle, not several, has the same meaning,[88] while the pole binding all together signifies the fact that the elements are held together by an indissoluble bond,[89] the harmony they achieve from being a copy of the incorporeal pattern.[90] The veil which divides the tabernacle indicates that the outer chamber is dedicated to the sublunar world, the inner to the aetherial essence,[91] and its colors likewise indicate the elements.[92] The holy of holies separated off by the veil represents the intelligible world.[93] The altar of sacrifice calls properly for the offering not of victims and flesh, he elaborately points out, but of a pure life.[94] The olive oil of the lamp is the supply for the light of wisdom, and indicates the encyclical studies.[95] The lamp is to be kept burning from evening to morning to symbolize the stars.[96]

Aaron and his sons have been initiated for the divine ministry and have become greater kings than the Great King; like all kings they must thus be priests and serve God if they are to rule others.[97] He comments interestingly upon the two robes the high-priest is to wear, the great regalia of the sacrifices and the white robe he puts on for his annual entrance into the holy of holies. The one is a robe of honor and glory,[98] the other of something greater. The one is proper for material ministration, for honor and glory are the things held in esteem in the material realm. Also they signify that the high-priest is honored by men, and glorified by participation in divine things. This is the literal significance. The inner meaning is that the priest represents true opinion.[99] It is notable that the priest in these robes does not

81. Ib., 73.   82. Ib., 75.   83. Ib., 76–81.
84. Ib., 83.   85. Ib., 84.   86. Ib., 85.
87. Ib., 86.   88. Ib., 88.   89. Ib., 89.
90. Ib., 90.   91. Ib., 91.   92. Ib., 92.
93. Ib., 93 f.   94. Ib., 99–101.   95. Ib., 103.
96. Ib., 104.

97. Ib., 105. "The Great King" was the usual classical way of referring to the King of Persia, and became proverbial for the highest type of kingship. The priestly function of the king will appear somewhat expanded in the treatment of Moses below.

98. Exod. xxviii, 2.   99. QE, ii, 107.

represent truth or wisdom. The higher significance of the white robe is not here explained.

Philo now goes on to the symbolism of the great robe of the high-priest, and while the interpretation in general follows the lines we have found elsewhere, he adds many details of interest. The two shoulder pieces of Exod. xxviii, 7 are the two aspects of religion, piety to God and kindliness to men.[100] The two stones on the shoulder are again the hemispheres with the six signs of the zodiac on each.[101] The breastplate is logos;[102] it is double because there are two kinds of λόγος, ἐνδιάθετος and προφορικός; also because logos is directed doubly toward divine and human things. The symbolism is elaborated on several details, but throughout it is the human logos he seems here to have in mind.[103] The four rows of three jewels each on the breastplate are again the four seasons with three signs of the zodiac for each season.[104] They are enclosed in gold as the elements are encircled by ether.[105] The names of the Patriarchs are associated each with one of the stones because the twelve Patriarchs themselves represent stars. Their names are engraved on the stones like seals, for the virtues of the Patriarchs are like the forms, in that their virtues are stamped upon their successors.[106] Here is a notion, slightly developed, that will appear to be one of Philo's most important concepts in the Higher Mystery.

As Philo closes his description of the robes of the priest he continues to emphasize the cosmic symbolism of the details.[107] But there is a brief excursus on the Logos as head of the world, on the fact that the world is subject to him and beneath him, but he himself is seated by God the Father.[108] How much of this is a Christian interpolation, whether the whole passage or only the gloss (eo quod Christus dominus est) it is difficult to determine. The whole seems dragged into the context, but that, of course, so frequently happens in Philo that it is impossible to discard any passage for its tangency. The last few sections deal with the plate of gold on which is engraved the sacred four letters. This is a symbolum incorporeae intelligibilisque formae materiae,[109] that is, the Logos[110] or the world of forms.[111]

Closely as the symbolism of the Quaestiones in Exodum has followed the general plan of interpretation of the temple and the high-priest in Philo's other writings, there is a striking divergence of detail. Sometimes the difference of detail may be regarded as sufficiently explained by Philo's own love of fanciful extemporization, but there are just enough references to the interpretations of "others" to make it much more probable here also that Philo's variations arise from his attempt to reproduce several current interpretations, rather than that he is just letting his imagination run wild.

100. QE, ii, 108.
101. Ib., 109.
102. Ib., 110.
103. Ib., 111.
104. Ib., 112.
105. Ib., 113.
106. Ib., 114.
107. Ib., 117–120.
108. Ib., 117.
109. Ib., 121.
110. Ib., 122.
111. Ib., 123 f.

There was certainly a variety of traditions as to the details of the Mystery of Aaron, but all the traditions agree on this point, at least, that the service of the Jewish priesthood, and all the temple except the holy of holies, was a Cosmic Mystery in which the initiate or worshipper rose to join in the hymn of the universe to its maker.

For Philo's attitude toward the Mystery of Aaron one passage is highly revealing. He has twice explained the Mystery for Gentiles, in the *De Vita Mosis* and the *De Specialibus Legibus*. But at the end of his discussion in the latter treatise he significantly says that the foregoing has been a discussion of the laws established for the purpose of promoting piety by means of commands and prohibitions. It is all a part, that is, of the Judaism of the letter. He says he must now go on to discuss the legislation which would produce piety by means of philosophic teaching and advice. What he goes on to say has no reference to the Mystery of Aaron, but the Mystery of Moses, the Mystery of God and the incorporeal Powers.[112] Here, for the first time in the whole discussion of the Mystery, the Gentiles are considered. The passage is important for the Higher Mystery, and its contents will be discussed later. In this connection it need only be pointed out that as great a Mystery as Philo has shown the Lesser Mystery to be, Gentiles are not invited to share in it, as they obviously are in the Higher. This is entirely in accord with the spirit of the *De Specialibus Legibus*. Philo is trying to bring the Gentiles into the Mystery of Moses, into what he here calls the "philosophic" Judaism, and he has no interest in making literal Jews out of them. For their benefit he goes through the whole body of literal commands, including the Mystery of Aaron, and describes it all to them, explaining its majestic origin and value. But never does he ask his Gentiles to look for salvation in fulfilling the letter of Jewish Law. For Philo had, as we shall see, himself moved beyond that type of Judaism into the "philosophic" Judaism as he had himself become an initiate of Moses. For high as the Mystery of Aaron could lift men, even up to cosmic proportions, it still left them material creatures, shut off, as was Aaron himself, from sharing in the realm of the incorporeal. The Aaronic initiate knew that the immaterial world was there beyond, but he was always shut in by material incense from any mystical union. True understanding of the Torah by allegory had revealed to Philo the higher experience, and it was to this higher experience Philo would have conversion to Judaism lift the proselytes. Here it need only be emphasized that Philo has specifically pointed out to his readers that the Mystery of Aaron was a part of literal Judaism, quite distinct from the higher worship offered men by Moses.

In several passages Philo has appeared to be equating the high-priest not with the cosmos specifically, but rather with the Logos,[113] and so many times

---

112. *Spec.*, i, 229 f.   113. See above, pp. 100 ff.

has he done this that commentators take the high-priest to be a fixed symbol with Philo for the Logos. This seems to me on the whole to be misleading. The high-priest is the Logos, but the Logos as present in the cosmos. As the Logos is the ἡγεμονικόν of the universe, so the highest office of the priest is his representation of the most important part of the cosmos, the Logos. But never does Philo forget that the priest in his great robes is the Logos as clothed in matter. He is not a "second" Logos, as we have concluded above, but the highest Logos, the only Logos, yet that Logos *only* as it presented itself in relation with the elements.

A glance at the passages, in addition to the passages already discussed, where Philo calls the high-priest the Logos, will confirm this statement. In one passage[114] Philo makes the identification. As a type of the Logos the high-priest wears a regalia which in its highest part, the gold signet on his head engraved with the name of God, represented τὰ νοητά; in its lowest parts it signified the elements. The signet is specifically the symbol of the ἰδέα ἰδεῶν, which we recognize as the "higher" Logos of Pascher. The worship in which the high-priest leads is elaborately described as the cosmic hymn; the priest, by his double presentation of τὰ νοητά and τὰ αἰσθητά brings man to recognize that the material world is formed after the likeness of the immaterial. This is far indeed from the Higher Mystery, where things of sense are left behind altogether, far indeed from the Logos as elsewhere described. Yet as before I can see no justification for speaking of a "second" Logos, that of the dyad clothed in matter, as distinct from the cosmos. What the priest represents here again is the Logos clothed in matter, that is the cosmos, and he is designated as most significantly typifying the Logos, because for religious purposes that part of the cosmos was overwhelmingly the more important.

In one more passage[115] the high-priest is again the Logos. The Bible, significantly called here ὁ ἱερὸς λόγος, points out the details of his ceremonial duties and vesture, with brief indication of their cosmic symbolism.

For the cosmos is a temple in which the high-priest is ὁ πρωτόγονος αὐτοῦ θεῖος, λόγος, . . . of which the one who offers up the ancestral prayers and sacrifices is a material (αἰσθητόν) imitation. He is commanded to put on the aforesaid tunic as a copy of the universal cosmos (οὐρανός), that the world may worship together with man, and man with the universe.

He puts off this robe and is clothed in luminous white linen for the inner service.

The high-priest is Logos here, as in all these passages, by the familiar figure of the part for the whole. Philo here lets us see more clearly why he speaks of the part for the whole. In the universe the priest is the Logos, as

114. *Mig.*, 102–105.   115. *Som.*, i, 214–219.

that is the bond that connects the material world with God. Relatively the elements are of slight significance. So the high-priest in his great robes is a representation of the Logos, but not of the Logos alone; he symbolizes the Logos in the cosmos, or the cosmos as a whole, and again the worship to which he brings men is to a share in the cosmic worship of God. Of course in sharing in this worship the essential step is to bring the human mind into harmony with the Logos that dominates matter, and so much did this outweigh all other aspects that Philo could call the high-priest the Logos, or its imitation, although officially in his robes he was the cosmos.

In his section on the Mystery of the high-priest Pascher has concluded that on the level of the Aaronic Mystery Philo is almost purely Stoic. He thinks that the fundamental notion of the Mystery, the lifting of the initiate to move in time and sing in tune with the cosmos, was derived from that source. This seems to me highly unlikely. Such phrases as "living according to nature," upon which Pascher bases his claims, were too generally in the air to denote any definite borrowing from Stoicism. The point is that the Mystery of the Cosmos, as Philo presents it, is essentially foreign to Stoicism in that union with the cosmos was itself but a stepping stone to the vision of the Creator. The Stoic saw union or harmony with the cosmos as harmony with the ultimate. Philo sees it only as a way of joining in with the hymn of all creation to the Creator who is infinitely beyond the world. It is a worship of one of the lower manifestations of God, His Merciful Power, and he assumes throughout that no greater sin could be conceived than that of confusing the created with the Creator. To adapt the Stoic conception to Philo's theism was a large task, and I cannot think that to Philo or to any other Jew it would have suggested itself as a desirable thing to attempt. If there were other mystic teachings which made the cosmic worship the first stage in the approach to God, represented that step as a Lower Mystery, and as a stopping place only for those who could go no higher than worship through visible symbols, then there would have been incentive for Jews to have exercised their ingenuity to fit that scheme into the Torah by identifying the lower stage with the rites at the temple. Was there at hand a conception of the ascent to God through the universe which could have attracted the Jews to such adaptation?

If it has seemed necessary to reject Pascher's interpretation of the Logos dyad and the Cosmic Mystery as being essentially Stoic, it must be pointed out in gratitude that he has yet asked the above question and undoubtedly given the right answer to it. As he has pointed out, the whole conception would seem to have come to Hellenistic Jews originally from that Egyptian thought which we associate with Isis and the Hermetica, however uncertain we may be as to the exact connection between these two expressions of Egyptian piety. Rather than simply refer the reader to Pascher, his arguments and evidence, with some expansion, must here be reproduced.

The Hermetica show strikingly the place of the cosmic worship in the general rise to the Higher Mystery. One striking passage[116] describes the mystic as rising up through one planetary circle after the other until he at last reaches the circle of the fixed stars, where he sings with the stars the great hymn to the Father. He is made like them, and can hear also the δυνάμεις, which are above the οὐρανός, likewise singing their hymn to God. Then the soul rises up, becomes one with the Powers, a Power himself. At the end he enters into God.

Since Pascher lays no stress upon the importance of the Powers in Philo's Mystery he has under-estimated the extent of the parallel here to Philo's whole scheme. The cosmic stage at which one becomes a part of, and sings with, the universe as a whole is quite a part of the Hermetic preliminary to approaching the Powers.

There are other striking Hermetic passages which Pascher does not quote. Man appears to be made in the image of the cosmos and has συμπάθεια with it, the δεύτερος θεός, as well as a conception (ἔννοια) of the First God. Man, while ultimately from God, is immediately from and in the cosmos in the same way as the cosmos is from and in God. Man's first step, by this, would then logically be to come to the realization that he himself is thus ὑπὸ τοῦ κόσμου καὶ ἐν τῷ κόσμῳ.[117] Another Hermetic passage is strikingly suggestive of Philo's formulation of the mediating work of the high-priest as a cosmic priest:[118]

God, the Master of eternity, is first; the cosmos is second; man is third. God, the Maker of the cosmos and of all things that are therein, governs all things, but has made man as a composite being to govern in conjunction with Him. And if man takes upon him in all its fullness the function assigned to him, that is, the tendance which is his special task, he becomes the means of right order to the cosmos, and the cosmos to him; so that it seems the cosmos (that is, the ordered universe) has been rightly so named, because man's composite structure has been thus ordered by God. Man knows himself, and knows the cosmos also, provided that he bears in mind what action is suited to the part he has to play, and provided that he recognizes what things he is to use for his own ends, and to what things he in turn is to do service, rendering praise and thanks in full measure to God, and revering God's image (the cosmos), not unaware that he himself is a second image of God. For there are two images of God; the cosmos is one, and man is another, inasmuch as he, like the cosmos, is a single whole built up of diverse parts. For you must note that man, in order that he may be fully equipped on both sides, has been so fashioned that each of his two parts is made up of four elements; and so, in respect of the divine part of him, which is composed of other

116. *Poimandres*, 24–26a; Pascher, *Königsweg*, p. 58.
117. *Corp. Herm.*, VIII, 5; cf. X, 14b.   118. *Asclepius*, I, 10; Scott's translation.

and higher "elements," so to speak, namely, mind, intellect, spirit, and reason, he is found capable of rising to heaven; but in respect of his material part, which consists of fire, water, earth, and air, he is mortal, and remains on earth, that he may not leave forsaken and abandoned all things that are entrusted to his keeping. Thus it is that man, though in part divine, has been made mortal also in part, being placed in a body.

There can be no mistaking the similarity of Philo's cosmic Mystery with these Hermetic statements. Pascher has quoted from Plutarch's *De Iside* a passage so striking that I must repeat it after him:

The vestments of Isis are of various colors; for her power is extended over matter, which becomes and assumes all sorts of forms (πάντα γιγνομένην καὶ δεχομένην), namely light and darkness, day and night, fire and water, life and death, beginning and end. In contrast the vestment of Osiris has no shadow or diversity, but has a simple and single nature, the light-form (φωτοειδές). For the primal principle is pure, and the First and the Conceptual is unmixed. On this account initiates put on this robe only once, and lay it down again, keeping it out of sight and touch. But the Isis robe they frequently wear. For the objects of sense, which are always in use and ever lie ready to our hand, are subject to various developments and in the course of their constant changes take on now this form, now that. But the principle of knowledge of the nature that is conceptual, pure, and simple, flashes through the soul like lightning and offers itself in a single moment's experience to apprehension and vision.[119]

The passage he quotes from Apuleius is almost as striking.[120]

Thus in the Aaronic Mystery Hellenistic Judaism has drawn into Jewish worship the point of view of Isis and the Hermetica. Yet there is one important point to be recalled. However much Philo and his school were attracted to adopt the ideas and spiritual ascent of thoughtful Egyptians, they are strikingly different in avoiding precisely that mythological formulation of divinity which Pascher has made the center of his presentation. God was one: He worked and revealed himself through His light emanations, to be sure, but always Philo is careful to deny ultimate reality to any distinctive manifestation of God. If, as Bréhier has insisted, Philo is primarily religious rather than philosophical in his writings, he could yet have had no sympathy with that travesty of philosophy, the type of mythological presentation to which we give the collective name of Gnosticism. For all his Hermetic and Isiac roots, he is closer to Plotinus than to any mythological conception of Deity.

How long had Jews in the Diaspora, especially in Egypt, been so much under the influence of mystic thought that they interpreted their holy temple

119. Chap. 77, p. 382c; Pascher, *Königsweg*, p. 53.
120. *Metam.*, xi, 23 f.

and priesthood in such terms? Little as we know of the history of such a development, Philonic scholars have long been aware that this allegory must be as old as the Book of the Wisdom of Solomon. For there it is stated:

Upon *his* long *high-priestly* robe was the whole world *pictured*,
And the glories of the fathers *were* upon the graving of the four rows of
    precious stones
And thy majesty *was* upon the diadem of his head. (xviii, 24.)

The little statement is priceless, since, as Pascher[121] points out, for the author to have said this much he must have had much more to go with it.

For some time before Philo, then, the Mystery of Aaron had been developing. The extraordinary variety of detail and interpretation which Philo shows, and which betrays a variety of ultimate sources, would then come from a widely current mode of thought.

In closing it must be pointed out that the Aaronic Mystery may not at all have arisen simply from Egyptian suggestion. Traces of oriental solar astrology in the later books of the Old Testament, especially in connection with angelology, have frequently been pointed out, especially by Gressmann[122] and Bousset.[123] They show that Jews had long before Philo, and in Palestine itself, been influenced by this type of thought. The fact that Josephus presents the Mystery of Aaron but not the Mystery of Moses suggests that the cosmic interpretation of the temple cultus was familiar in Palestinian Judaism as the Higher Mystery was not. The similar notions in the Hermetic tradition may well have been of oriental and not Egyptian origin, and the Mystery of Aaron originally a product of Palestinian syncretism. As to this we can only say that, lacking any early distinctive Palestinian tradition, the matter must be left undecided. What the Hermetic parallels definitely show us, since it is unthinkable that they owe the notion to Judaism, is that the Mystery of Aaron was, at least originally, a syncretistic product of some kind, originating in those mystic ideas that later became popular in Egypt also.

121. Pascher, *Königsweg,* p. 51.
122. *Die hellenistische Gestirnreligion* (*Alt. Orient,* Beiheft 5), 1925, passim, esp. pp. 20 ff.
123. *Die Religion des Judentums,* 3rd ed., 1926, pp. 320 ff., 475 ff.

CHAPTER V

ENOS, ENOCH, NOAH, AND ABRAHAM

IT has already appeared that Philo is by no means satisfied that the Jewish Law, as a literal revelation of the will of God, can be an adequate approach to Deity. The Deity he worships is one that has projected His life into the universe and His will for man into the "elements of nouns and verbs." But as the mystery of Aaron was throughout described as secondary to the Mystery of the ark and the holy of holies, so the literal Law was a thing designed for men in a material and essentially inferior state of being. The best plan in interpreting Philo's conception of what lay beyond the precepts and beyond the Mystery of the cosmic priesthood is to follow Philo's own method of presenting the higher Mystery to Gentile readers in the great *Exposition* and the *Life of Moses*. For to Philo the way of approach to God in His immaterial aloofness had been revealed in the lives of the Patriarchs. They had become the νόμοι ἔμψυχοι, the incarnations of the will of God and of the life and nature of God (for Philo knew no distinction between God's being and will), and as they had lived without the code in immediate experience of God, so they became at once the patterns for the code and the revelation of the higher and direct way to God by which they themselves had achieved union with Him. The exposition of the mystic higher teaching of the Torah was to Philo largely an exposition of their lives. So we shall try to come into the Mystery as Philo would have initiated us, by first understanding the significance of the individual Patriarchs.

It is clear that Philo would not have taken us at once even to the Patriarchs. The *Exposition* does not begin with their stories, but with the *De Opificio Mundi*, in which the Mosaic account of creation was treated, not as an introduction to the Law in its higher sense, but as the beginning of the Law, its first part. For entrance into the Mystery the ideas developed there constitute the first essential step. Philo is not just beginning at the first part of Genesis, for he omits much of the Torah in the *Exposition*, and could have omitted this had it not been an important part of his presentation. The fact is that before one can go into the Mystery there are certain philosophical points of view which the initiate must understand and accept, else what follows will be meaningless. Hence the point of beginning with the creation story is that Philo must first sketch the cosmogony, philosophy, and doctrine of God which the Mystery presupposes.

It is obvious that Philo wrote the *De Opificio* to demonstrate that the cosmogony and philosophy of Moses was that taught by the Platonic and Neo-Pythagorean philosophers. With many details from the *Timaeus* Philo ex-

plains that the first chapter of Genesis teaches that the material world has
been created after the pattern of the immaterial, created through the instrumentality of the Logos, but by God, the uniquely existent, as the Prime
Cause. The book closes (§§170–172) with a doctrinal summary in which
Philo insists that the story of Creation brings out four points. First against
the atheists, both those in doubt about God's ruling,[1] and those who denied
His existence altogether,[2] Philo affirms that God exists and rules the world.
Second, against polytheists, he affirms that God is one. Third, against various
schools[3] he affirms that the material world had a beginning in its present
form. Fourth, against the atomists of all periods, that there is but one cosmos,
which exhausts all matter, rather than a plurality or infinite number of
κόσμοι. Fifth, against the Epicureans, that God exercises providence in the
world. We know from his other writings, as has been said, that providence
here is not the Stoic providence which implied determinism, but only what
we might call an immanent presence and coöperation of God in the created
world, and especially with man.

This thoroughly Platonic-Pythagorean creed (both schools agreed on all
these points) is a necessary part of the Torah, the starting point of what is
to Philo the Jewish life. For "he who has begun not by hearing these things
but by learning them with his understanding, and has stamped in his soul
these marvelous and priceless forms (εἴδη) (that is the five articles of this
"creed"), . . . will lead a blessed and happy life, for he will have become
moulded by doctrines of piety and holiness."[4]

It is natural that Philo should have had to emphasize a correct conception
of God from the Jewish point of view for converts. The Torah must for
them have been made to teach something explicit along the lines of conceptions which could be assumed among traditional Jews. Philo's writings for
Jews are throughout concerned with expounding the nature of God and His
relation to man and the created world: for Jews His existence and creative
and ruling power need exposition, not proof. But for Gentiles God's very
existence has to be proved,[5] and theology crystallized into a creed.

To the credal prerequisites for the Mystery which Philo laid down for

1. These would seem to be especially the Epicureans.
2. J. Cohn (Philos Werke, ad loc.) suggests that Philo is referring here to the Sceptics. Yet
they denied not the existence of God but the possibility of our knowing about Him. The reference if not to popular and unphilosophic atheism, is possibly to the early atomists and other
philosophers of φύσις whom Aristotle criticized because they explained creation or reality
without a moving Cause (Metaph., 984a ff.).
3. Aëtius (Plac., II, iv, 11; Diels, Doxogr., 332) lists Xenophanes, Parmenides, and Melissus,
to whom must of course be added Aristotle, as saying that the world is ἀγένητος καὶ ἀίδιος.
The Pythagoreans were divided on the subject. See my "Neo-Pythag. Source," p. 144.
4. Opif., 172.
5. See the elaborate proof in Spec., i, 32 ff.; Abr., 69 ff. To Jews Philo says that only one
who is drunk can deny that God is the Creator and Father of the universe: Post., 175. The
approach is different in the Exposition.

Gentile converts, and which must have applied also to Jewish members of the Mystery, he returns at a later part of the *Exposition*. That passage is of interest here. It will be recalled that much of the *De Opificio* had been devoted to describing how the material world was created after immaterial patterns, though this is not made one of the prime statements of creed at the end. In the other passage, however, he makes good the omission. He is discussing the dangerous perversions, misleading doctrines and practices, which must be avoided by one who would enter the Mystery of the Powers he has briefly been describing. The passage that concerns us begins at *De Specialibus Legibus*, i, 315.

The first perversion is that of false prophets who would lead one to worship the gods of the Gentiles. The false prophets are clearly Jews, and in preferring pious Gentiles as incomparably superior to such Jews Philo is, I am sure, not talking at random. There were evidently such Jews about him, who urged the people to break down their exclusiveness and join in the popular celebrations, temples, libations, and sacrifices. Philo would here again lynch such a person, as in §§54 ff.[6]

Just as realistic is Philo's denunciation[6a] of the people who would enter into mystic initiations. Their secret rites are an abomination. When nature has revealed the secrets of philosophy to all who would see them in the stars, seas, air, and seasons, and in the animals and fruits of the earth, who are men to shut themselves off with the secrets of the universe and give them out to anyone, and only to anyone, who will pay for the initiation? The secrets should be given out to anyone worthy to receive them (πᾶσι τοῖς ἀξίοις). So "let no follower of Moses initiate anyone, or himself be initiated."[7] At first glance this passage would seem to indicate only that some Jews were being initiated into the pagan mysteries, people whom, like those going to idolatry, Philo wanted to exclude from the Mystery of Moses. But the last sentence quoted (μηδεὶς οὖν μήτε τελείτω μήτε τελείσθω τῶν Μωϋσέως φοιτητῶν καὶ γνωρίμων) has quite a different possibility of interpretation. It seems to me more natural that the reference should be to Jews who were celebrating a Jewish Mystery. That is aside from our present purpose, and we shall return to the subject.[8] In any case it is notable that Philo criticized them not for keeping secret the true doctrine of God and the cosmos, but in equating that truth with certain rites, and in making the prerequisite for admission not the character or aspirations of the applicant, but ability to pay the initiation fee.

Who then may approach for the mystic teaching? Who are οἱ ἄξιοι? This is the question that Philo now proceeds to discuss, at least from the negative

6. Even Heinemann (*Bildung*, 225 ff.) admits the literal meaning of these calls to lynching for apostasy to idolatry.

6a. *Spec.*, i, 319 ff.   7. Ib., 319–323.   8. See below, pp. 259 ff.

point of view. Certainly those incurably sunk in sin are excluded from "flee-
ing for refuge" to the fellowship.[9] The principle of exclusion Philo sees
established in the laws forbidding *castrati* to enter the temple.[10] The fact that
these and that harlots and bastards (who cannot be sure who is their father)
are excluded opens the way for Philo to inveigh against the various types
of atheists. For atheists do not know their Father, God, and so are excluded.
Once started on this, Philo gives us five types of people whose philosophy
would exclude them from sharing in the Mystery.

The *castrati* are those who reject the Platonic-Pythagorean doctrine of
Forms.[11] As the *castrati* have made themselves into ἄμορφος ὕλη, these
people would take away all the formal principles of the universe. The difficulty is, as Philo sees it, that if the Forms are not recognized, God must
have personally shaped matter in creation, and could not have had the
Powers, which are Forms, through which to work. That is, the first requirement for admission is for the candidate to recognize the deity of Philo as He
works through the Powers and Forms. What looked at first like a miscel-
laneous collection of allegorical fancies suddenly emerges as something very
like a definite credal requirement.

The second group to be excluded are the atheists. First those who reject
not only the Forms but the very existence (ὕπαρξις) of God, saying that one
talks of Him only for the benefit of ordinary men to keep them from doing
wrong, on the ground that the notion of an ever present and all seeing God
makes men cautious.[12] One is reminded of the striking poem ascribed to
Critias by Sextus Empiricus.[13] Sextus' introduction to the poem is still closer
to Philo than the poem itself. It is impossible to say definitely whether Philo
is simply making a literary gesture in including this category, or is reflecting
some popular sceptical flippancy whose language had become fairly conventionalized. Since throughout this passage he seems to have realities in mind,
I should suspect the latter to be true. The widely divergent traditions of the
authorship of the poem suggest a general popularity, and wide circulation,
so much so that its real origin had been forgotten. In any case Philo rules
such people out. They are also *castrati*.

The third group to be ruled out are the polytheists, who in calling many
gods "Father" show that they are children of a harlot and have no way of
knowing which of many possible ones was their father.[14]

The fourth and fifth excluded types he discusses together, since both have
variant forms of the same disease, self-love (φιλαυτία)[15] The two seem at
first to be the Stoics and Epicureans. The former are the people, he says,

---

9. *Spec.*, i, 324.　　　　　　　　　　　　10. Ib., 325.
11. Ib., 327 f.　　　　　　　　　　　　　　12. Ib., 330.
13. *Adv. Mathem.*, IX, 54. (Diels, *Fragm. Vorsokrat.*, II, 4th ed., pp. 320 f.) The ascription
is in some doubt, as Diels shows.
14. *Spec.*, i, 331 f.　　　　　　　　　　　15. Ib., 333 ff.

who have deified reason (ὁ λογισμός, νοῦς), the latter who have deified the unreasoning part, the individual senses. Philo has an extended digest of the arguments of both. Those who deify the mind dwell upon the fact that it has marvelous powers, and penetrates into all things, and has solved the practical and theoretical problems of nature. This is at first highly suggestive of the Stoics, and yet the attack is hardly a direct one, for Philo must have known that νοῦς and λόγος were no less divine terms to himself than to them. It would seem that he rather has in mind people of the type we now call "rationalists," who put their ultimate trust for knowledge upon the human mind. The description of those who delight in and refine each sense as the ultimate likewise might suggest Epicureans, but, as Heinemann has pointed out, is by no means recognizably specific.

The point of the whole section appears in the last paragraph of the book:

We the disciples and pupils of the prophet Moses, shall not give over our quest of τὸ ὄν, for we recognize that knowledge of Him is ultimate happiness and a blessed life, even as the Torah sets forth a necessary and philosophic teaching when it says that those who worship God are alive. For atheists are truly dead in their souls, but those who are ordered by the order that comes from the true God (ὁ ὤν θεός) shall live an immortal life.[16]

The element of exclusiveness is made very sharp. The line was not drawn between Jew and Gentile, or, apparently, between wise and foolish, though the Mystery was obviously designed to be preceded and helped by encyclical studies. Only an honest desire, coupled with the correct philosophical point of view, could bring one in, and in the end no more was needed. After that the teaching would apparently be revealed slowly according to the individual's capacity.

While on the subject of Philo's requirements for admission to the Mystery and its teaching it may be well to refer to the fact that there is definite evidence that these requirements are to be taken literally, and that there was a Mystery of such definite organization as to make "exclusion" much more than a figurative expression. That matter must wait for further discussion.[17] But here we may anticipate at least by saying that admission meant a definite renunciation of pagan religions in both the traditional and mystic forms, and purification through the "sacred laws" of Judaism; it implied also piety and holiness to the true God and evidence of such a character that the initiate would be fit for admission.

Philo begins his *Exposition* of the true Judaism to Gentiles, then, by setting before them the philosophic postulates on which the whole Mystery is founded. It is impossible to go on, he insists repeatedly, unless these be not only understood, but accepted.

16. Ib., 345.   17. See below, pp. 259 ff.

The *Exposition* assumes the success of the introduction in properly orienting the mind of the reader. Philo may now take the reader into the Mystic
teaching as set forth in the great Torah of Moses. The Mystery itself is revealed to Philo in the Patriarchs, as has been said. The next treatise after the
De Opificio, the *De Abrahamo*, begins the review of their lives in which he
explains how in them the true Way to God has been revealed. We shall
follow Philo by studying these patriarchs for their mystic significance.

By way of introduction to their lives as he interprets them it may be well
to recall that Philo was neither the first nor the last man to look to human
personalities as the source of revelation of divinity. The great philosophers
before him had tried to offer man reason and abstract principles as the saving force which would lead to the truth and the greater life. But the Hellenistic Age, as has been pointed out, had rarely followed these great philosophers in their loyalty to abstractions and in their demand for reason. Everywhere the tendency was to put even ethical concepts into a concrete form.
The mystery religions were engrossing the age with their graphic representations of ethical and metaphysical truths. Isis or Cybele were apprehensible
in a way that the ideal καλόν, or the φιλανθρωπία θεοῦ, was not. Ἰσότης
would do as an abstraction for the classic philosophers, but became a goddess in Hellenistic Syria.

A marked part of this tendency was the increasing regard for what was
called the θεῖος ἄνθρωπος, the human being who had by his virtue raised
himself, or been raised by God or the gods, to relations with deity so far
beyond those of ordinary people that he had become in a sense divine. Such
men were inspiring as models, but still more useful in popular eyes as
mediators and saviors for other men. The lives of the great sages of the past
came to be regarded as being of more importance than their teachings, because by idealizing the philosophers as θεῖοι ἄνθρωποι people could more
readily copy the concrete personality than they could make practical judgments in ethics by applying principles alone. This change, like the other
distinctive aspects of the Hellenistic Age, seems to have been more a failure
of the Age to produce great intellectual successors of the early giants, whose
writings would continue to overshadow in our eyes the writings of men
who only reflected the point of view of the masses, than any change in the
masses themselves. From the greatest periods of Greek thought it is apparent
that the crowd was as unable to follow abstractions, and as eager for concrete and personal representations of truth, as in the Hellenistic Age. When
Empedocles went about among crowds who kept demanding of him a sign
or a miracle, he himself met them with what they wanted by proclaiming:

$$\text{ἐγὼ δ' ὑμῖν θεὸς ἄμβροτος, οὐκέτι θνητός.}[18]$$

18. Frg. 112 (Diels).

The picture is not essentially different from the idealized portrait of Apollonius of Tyana, the later lives of Plato, and Porphyry's life of Plotinus.

For it is the way of the multitude at all times to get their ethical standards from a picture, engraved in their hearts rather than in their minds, of an ideal personality whom they can follow and imitate. The bravery of William Wallace, the chastity of St. Francis, the purity of the Virgin Mary, the mystic achievements of Buddha, the patriotic devotion of Washington, such are the inspirations of most of us, not Bravery, Purity, or the Good. The Hellenistic World would have found room for either Plato or Plotinus, but such great men were not born. So it was the timeless mob that gave the age its color, and which was never fully satisfied until it found the ideal θεῖος ἄνθρωπος in Jesus of Nazareth.

In looking for a personal incarnation of the virtues and divine life to which he aspired, Philo was, then, in harmony with the popular aspiration of his day and of all days. But it must be recalled that even the greatest philosophers had gone far toward admitting that abstract truth is best revealed in a personality. Plato and Aristotle felt that the highest law would be found only in a state which had a personal representative of divine law as an absolute ruler if such a man could be found. Aristotle said: "Equity is . . . the having an eye not to the law but to the law maker."[19] A general study of the phenomenon of the θεῖος ἄνθρωπος is most to be desired. Here I shall only point out that the Pythagoreans, with their reverence for the hazy figure of Pythagoras, were especially active in building up the conception, to make room for their reverence for Pythagoras, and to justify their conception of the king. Delatte[20] gives us the two following quotations:

The Pythagoreans posited alongside God and man a distinct third class in their reverence for the king or the Wise Man, on the ground that Homer had first posited the king as being between gods and men, but had represented the king as yielding in honor to the Wise Man.[21]

Delatte suggests that this is an expansion of a notion which Iamblichus[22] reports from Aristotle:

Aristotle records in his work on the Pythagorean philosophy that in their secret teachings they preserved some such distinction as follows: of the reasoning animal there is God as one sort, man as another, and a third that is of the sort represented by Pythagoras.

Reverence for the θεῖος ἄνθρωπος, and the feeling that the problems of

19. *Rhet.*, I, xiii, 17, 1374b 11.
20. *Études sur la littérature Pythagoricienne*, pp. 120 f.
21. *Schol. in Homer, Il.* (W. Dindorf, III) A, 340.
22. *De Pythagorica Vita*, VI, 31.

personal salvation were to be solved in such a figure, could have come to Philo, then, both from the multitude and the philosophers, especially from the Pythagoreans. It will appear that in the peculiar intimacy with which he associates that notion with the conception of the νόμος ἔμψυχος his inspiration must largely have come from the Pythagoreans, though whether directly or indirectly is another matter. The striking parallel to his thought as found in Proclus has already been discussed.[23]

The great personalities of the Patriarchs could not have been so important to Philo had he not been able to orient them with both his loyalty to the Torah and to the Greek metaphysics and soteriology. From the Greek point of view he saw the Patriarchs as incarnations of what Proclus calls οἱ ἀληθεῖς νόμοι, and so as the true νόμοι ἔμψυχοι, θεῖοι ἄνθρωποι, for whom the people of the day had long been wistfully looking. It was Philo's triumphant boast that what the Greeks sought in ignorance, the Jews had actually produced. If one really wanted to know what the true sophos was or would be like, he need not speculate, but only study the records of the characters of the Jewish Patriarchs. Philo's Judaism was as much gratified in the lives of the Patriarchs as his Greek mysticism and ethical aspiration. For the Jewish Law as a whole was in his eyes an attempt to describe the ideal way of life of these first great protagonists.

In the *Exposition, De Abrahamo* follows *De Opificio;* it begins:

As well as we could we have analysed in our former treatise how the creation of the world was disposed. But since it is now necessary in due order to investigate the laws, we shall postpone the consideration of the detailed laws, which are in a sense copies, in order to investigate those more general laws which one might call their antecedent archetypes. These latter laws are those men who have lived irreproachably and nobly, whose virtues have been promulgated in the sacred scriptures, not merely to praise them, but in order to exhort those who read them, and to lead readers to the like aspiration. For these men were incarnate and vocal laws (ἔμψυχοι καὶ λογικοὶ νόμοι), whom Moses has celebrated for two reasons: because he wished first to show that the laws of the code are not at variance with nature, and second that those who wish to live according to the established Laws (of the Torah) are not confronted with a tremendous labor, in as much as these original men readily and easily used the legislation even in its unwritten form, before a beginning had been made in writing down any of the particular laws. So one could properly say that the laws of the Code are nothing but memoirs of the life of the ancients, discussions of antiquities, namely the deeds and words

23. See above, pages 87 f. In normative Jewish tradition the Patriarchs followed the "unwritten law," but it was the Pharisaic traditional law, not the Greek Law of Nature, which they had: see II Baruch lvii. In Jubilees the various Patriarchs are represented as teaching details of what Philo called the "Specific Laws." The difference between Philo and normative tradition is beautifully clarified in this one point of contrast.

of their active careers. For they were not pupils or disciples of anyone, nor did they learn what to do or say from teachers, but they were people who heard for themselves (αὐτήκοοι) and taught themselves (αὐτομαθεῖς), clove to what was in accordance with nature (ἀκολουθίαν φύσεως ἀσπασάμενοι), and, on the supposition, as is indeed the fact, that nature herself is the primary Law (πρεσβύτατος θεσμός), they shot their whole lives through with the fine order of law (ἅπαντα τὸν βίον ἡὐνομήθησαν). They did nothing reprehensible of their own volition, while for chance offences they loudly implored God and propitiated Him with prayers and supplications in order that they might share in a perfect life purged of both deliberate and involuntary offences.[24]

Philo now considers the Patriarchs in detail. There are seven great types of achievement in the Pentateuch, though Philo, who might well have emphasized this number, does not do so. Enos, Enoch, and Noah are the first triad, Abraham, Isaac, and Jacob the second, and Moses stands out by himself with all the conspicuousnesses Philo likes to give to the One that makes the six into seven. The only reason why Philo does not bring out this grouping more sharply, it seems to me, is that to do so would be to cheapen the other Patriarchs, many of whom he wants occasionally to use as types of mystical perfection.[25] But it is quite likely that Philo had the number seven clearly in mind when he raised to prominence just the seven he selected.

The first triad is in the *Exposition* of relatively slight importance, and is discussed merely as an introduction to Abraham. Each represents a stage in the mystic's ascent. Enos, the first on the list, symbolizes Hope. As such he is given the honorable place of fourth in the great line of human genealogy, a number, Philo tells us, honored alike by Moses and those who "cleave to the immaterial and conceptual substances."[26] Further a man who is hopeful excludes fear, and thus shows that he is looking to good rather than evil, which two things (by Pythagoreanism) were completely irreconcilable.[27] Hope is thus something highly advantageous which every lawmaker tries to put into the souls of his free subjects; but Enos, without any such leadership, "trained himself in this virtue by means of that unwritten and self-taught Law which nature has ordained."[28] Enos is Hope because

24. *Abr.*, 2–6.   25. As Shem in *Sobr.*, 52–58, 65.
26. *Abr.*, 13.
27. In itself the reference to people who admire the ἀσωμάτους οὐσίας καὶ νοητάς, as well as the notion that good and evil, as opposite entities, are incapable of intermingling, might seem a reference to Platonism as easily as to Pythagoreanism. But since the οὐσίαι here are the numbers, and since Plato must have derived his sense of the irreconcilability of forms of opposites from the Pythagorean notion of opposites, the reference seems more natural to Pythagoreanism.
28. *Abr.*, 16. In his other writings Philo adds little to this discussion of Enos. See *Det.*, 138 ff.; *QG*, i, 79 f.

an attitude of hope is the first step in mystic achievement, is the "doorkeeper which nature has put at the gates leading into the Royal Virtues within."[29]

Enoch typifies the next step, repentance for sins and improvement.[30] He is the man who leaves ignorance for instruction, cowardice for courage, and the like, because he is aware that the true regimentation of one's character involves "a genuine and well-lawed rulership which justly dominates all things, in contrast to the bastard and falsely called rulers."[31] He aims at a tranquil stability of soul by aspiring for the φαντασία τῶν καλῶν. But he has not yet achieved this. The dominant note of his character is his constant desire to get away from sin and sinful associates, a state of μετάνοια. It is a stage of convalescence, not health, for the convalescent is primarily getting away from his illness. He is not yet the perfect man standing very close to divine power.[32] Here appears a theme which will seem increasingly important in the Mystery, the conception of the mystic as a fugitve or emigrant from the confused world of sin inhabited by the great mass of humanity. This element is stressed even more strongly in Philo's summary of the Patriarchs at the end of the *Exposition*.[33] But it is clear that Philo thinks a person can live throughout his life on what is an essentially transitional stage. Such is the life of the recluse and student, living away from men, always seeking the truth, but never having reached the solution of his problems. It too is the life of the tribes of Israel, who have abandoned the sinful Egypt, but who wander year after year in the desert of struggle.[34]

Of Enoch Philo tells us in the *Quaestiones* that his repentance was specifically the purifying of himself from all injustice, and his reaching the plenitude of perfect virtue.[35] Enoch's translation was from the realm of the visible into an incorporeal idea, appreciable only by the intellect,[36] an end that came alike to him and Elijah. In the *Allegory*[37] it would appear that the experience of Enoch was not so unusual, but simply represents the fact that those who are lovers of virtue escape from the sinful life of the mob and are not found in it and by it, since God has translated them into immortal γένη. That is, the experience would be that of one who has left the life of men to achieve transformation in the mystical ascent. It must have been in some such way as this that Enoch would have been commonly presented, since his actual translation could have offered no hope for any of his followers.

29. *Abr.*, 15.
30. Ib., 17: ἡ ἐπὶ τοῖς ἁμαρτανομένοις μετάνοια καὶ βελτίωσις.
31. Ib., 25. These νόθοι καὶ ψευδώνυμοι ἀρχαί must be the parts of the body or soul, or sense perceptions. See the Appendix.
32. *Abr.*, 26. 33. *Praem.*, 15–21.
34. See below, Chapter VIII. 35. *QG*, i, 83.
36. Ib., i, 86: "ex sensibili visibilique loco ad incorpoream et intelligibilem ideam."
37. *Post.*, 41–43.

Noah, the last of the first triad, represents Justice. As such he has conquered his lower passions, and has left once and for all the "confusion" of sinful society and of the life of conflict with his own lower nature. In possessing justice he possesses all the other virtues, and is at the same time pleasing to God. What could be a clearer demonstration of καλοκἀγαθία? By means of his justice, then, that is his conquest of the lower passions and perfection in virtue, he has won God's favor, and with it the ultimate objective, εὐδαιμονία.[38]

The reward of such an achievement is that Noah was exempt from the general calamity of the sinful race, and became the founder of a new race of men.[39] Philo's account of the flood which destroyed Noah's contemporaries is one of his most brilliant descriptive passages.[40] From all this Noah was spared, thereby showing that the one righteous man is of more value than all the rest of corrupt humanity.[41] And yet, like the other two members of this triad, Noah's perfection in δικαιοσύνη was only a partial perfection as compared with that of the great triad to come. Philo explains the relative imperfection by saying that Noah's achievement was that of having left sin and come to righteousness, while the Patriarchs who followed were perfect from the beginning.[42] The first triad had virtues analogous to those of childhood, the second to those of people who are fully developed for the second struggle, the ἀγών, in which they will win a victory over the opposing passions.[43] But I do not think this really represents the point of Philo's contrast, for of the later triad, only Isaac was thus perfect from the beginning. The real point appears in the review of the Patriarchs in *De Praemiis et Poenis,* 24–26, where it seems that, in contrast to the first triad, the second was able to rise above the circle of the earth and arrive at heaven. Abraham was the first to get to truth, which, as we shall see, means the abandoning of everything material and created.[44] Noah would by this contrast appear to be the man who achieved the lower height of self-discipline and control, the domination of his lower members by his reason, but not the higher life in which those lower members are themselves forgotten or left behind as reason turns to the immaterial realm for its sphere of activity.[45] Noah's achievement might be compared to that of the "merely moral man" so often preached against by Protestant clergymen. The "moral man" has indeed done much to live the life he does. His superiority to the mass of sinners is freely recognized, valued more highly by Philo than by the Protestants, it

38. *Abr.,* 32–35. 39. Ib., 46. 40. Ib., 40–45.
41. As is brought out in the later summary of the Patriarchs, *Praem.,* 22.
42. *Abr.,* 47.
43. Ib., 48. It will be well to remember the sacred ἀγών with the passions.
44. *Praem.,* 27–28.
45. Though this is hinted at in the sacred ἀγών with the passions, which will appear to be not a wrestling match but a race in which the victor runs away from the passions.

may be added, but both agree that morality which is an end in itself is definitely inferior to a life in which morality is regarded as a by-product of the
experience of God.

In view of the difficulty of understanding exactly what was Philo's contrast between Noah and the Patriarchs of higher achievement it is worth
seeing what Philo says on the subject in some of his other writings. In the
Allegory[46] the question of Noah's achievement is canvassed. Noah's having
found grace with God is described as meaning that Noah discovered that
all things, earth, air, fire, sun, stars, heaven, and all animals and plants, are
the grace of God. "God has given His good things to the universe as a whole
and to its several parts," which He has done not because He judged the
universe worthy of such a gift but by virtue of His own Beneficent Power.[47]
Philo gets this explanation, he says, from the fact that Noah was pleasing
to "the Lord God," that is to the two Powers represented in that double
title, the Creative or Beneficent Power and the Royal Power. This was the
height of Noah's achievement. Moses in contrast was pleasing to the One
whose body-guard these two Powers are, and which can be conceived of
apart from them only as pure Being.[48] The wisdom of Noah was only a
likeness of Moses' wisdom, and so while Moses got grace from ὁ ὢν αὐτός,
Noah had it only from the subject Powers. Philo's route for arriving at this
goal has been circuitous, but the end result is clear. In contrast with Moses,
Noah went only as far as the Powers. And so the conclusion is clear for the
Mystery. The true goal for us all is to rise like Moses to ὁ ὢν or to ὁ τοῦ
ὄντος λόγος. But if that is too great to be thought of, then "without turning
go to God's Powers and make yourself a suppliant to them, until they accept
the constancy and genuineness of your service and appoint you to take a
place among those who are well pleasing to them, even as they did with
Noah."[49] The descendants of such a man are the virtues.[50] In another brief
and isolated passage Noah is of praiseworthy constitution and origin, apparently one of the class that stands next below God. He has discovered that
grace comes only from God and not from any aspect of creation.[51] Four
other treatises of the *Allegory* take their departure from texts about Noah,
De Agricultura, De Plantatione, De Ebrietate, De Sobrietate, but actually
they leave their texts so far behind in general discussions of the subjects that
nothing much is added to our knowledge of the interpretation of the
Patriarch himself. One small passage is, however, of the greatest importance.
The ark, we learn, in which Noah took refuge, and into which all the wild
animals were brought, was "a figure of the body which has been compelled

46. *Immut.,* 104–110.
47. Accepting Wendland's conjecture for reading §108.
48. Ib., 109: Moses was pleasing τῷ δορυφορουμένῳ πρὸς τῶν δυνάμεων καὶ δίχα
αὐτῶν κατὰ τὸ εἶναι μόνον νοουμένῳ.
49. Ib., 116.   50. Ib., 118.   51. *LA,* iii, 77 f.

to make room for the untamed and savage pests of the passions and vices."[52] This figure must be recalled when we come to the catacombs and find the great consistent type of deliverance of the sainted soul from the body to be Noah emerging white robed from the ark.

In discussing the Mystery it is going to prove impossible to represent Philo as consistent in his symbolism. The Mystery itself becomes consistent although the place in the Mystery of many Old Testament types is not always by any means certain. It is notable that both in the *Allegory* and in the *Exposition* Noah was restricted so that he could recognize God only through cosmic tokens, in contrast to Abraham who went on to the Truth, and to Moses who went on to ὁ ὢν αὐτός. The passage in the *Allegory* would make it clear that Noah went beyond the cosmic tokens to the Creative Power, while the *Exposition* would suggest that he did not get to the immaterial world at all. I should myself be inclined to think that Philo has understated himself in the *Exposition* rather than overstated himself in the *Allegory*. Noah, as a great model Patriarch, must, in Philo's mind, have got beyond the universe to at least some experience of the Immaterial. This figure is much more elaborately worked out in our third and chief source for Noah, the *Quaestiones in Genesin*.

Here it appears that the career of Noah illustrates the great battle between the flesh with its appetites and the soul or mind, the contrast between men who are of the flesh and those who are sons of God.[53] For the men of flesh are the enemies of those virtues which constitute the road to God and lead one along it.[54] Noah's ark is elaborately developed as representing the body,[55] in contrast to the Ark of the Covenant which symbolizes as a whole the κόσμος νοητός.[56] In contrast with the wicked race that must perish, Noah, as endowed with virtue, is the heir of the divine substance, and so has himself become a treaty between God and good men (men of reason) to be their possession and glory.[57] That is, he is their savior, or high priest. The figure Philo has in mind, then, is of the soul of the mystic in his body, the ark. The flood itself is the washing away of the sins.

The flood is a symbol of spiritual dissolution.[58] When therefore we wish by the grace of the Father to discard and wash away all the sensible and corporeal things with which like swelling ulcers the intellect was infected, the muddy slime is cleaned off as though by a flood at the coming of a sweet flow and a drinkable stream.[59]

---

52. *Plant.*, 43.
54. Ib., 99.
56. *QG*, ii, 4.
58. This *spiritualis dissolutio* seems to me not to represent Philo's original, which from the context must have been some word for "cleansing."
59. *QG*, ii, 15.

53. *QG*, i, 92, 99.
55. *QG*, ii, 1–7; cf. *Plant.*, 43.
57. Ib., 10.

Philo does not tell us what this purifying stream from God is, but it is obviously the flowing into men of God's grace, the spiritual drink of the divine fluid that will constantly reappear as a part of the mystic's experience.

Yet Noah is still in the ark, as one who, though now purified from every sin, is still not developed positively so that his intellect is put into such a condition as to be wholly incorporeal.[60] When the flood subsides he sends out the raven, the last vestige of dark folly in his soul.[61] He then begins to send out his virtue, the dove, which goes out from him like the radiation of the sun, without diminishing the source.[62] So long as there was no one to receive this virtue, it returned to him who sent it out. But later it could stay away (because by the allegory there are those who can receive it), and so Noah's virtue has become a common good to all who will receive the emanations of wisdom.[63] At last Noah himself is ready to come forth from the ark, the body, and in so doing symbolizes the intellect that wishes to spring upwards because of the desire for heavenly things. He, as the intellect, accordingly bursts through every sort of (bodily) concupiscence, with the result that by getting away from that which has been an obscuring veil the intellect can direct its senses to naked and incorporeal natures.[64] So Noah comes to the uncreated Essence itself, to which he has always been the friend.[65]

This is the main experience of Noah. But as the story develops further, Philo adds a few details of interest. During his stay in the ark, that is during his period of purification, his business had been to purify himself of the body absolutely. So he had been kept, like all the other inhabitants of the ark, from sexual intercourse, but after he went out the command was that they increase and multiply; which means that the purified and glorified intellect returns to the body to regiment it completely with the new virtue.[66] This salvation of the body had been pointed out earlier as the ultimate ideal. The proper intellect benefits the body by cutting off its worst desires, and the body is saved with the soul.[67] So long as man is indulging in sins the body is a corpse that has to be borne about; but when God makes the soul "dry," he quickens also the body by animating it with a purer soul.[68] The best figure for this complete renewal and use of the body is toward the end, where Noah is the farmer cultivating the body.[69]

Throughout Philo has been careful to orient the experience of Noah with

60. QG, ii, 25.   61. Ib., 35.   62. Ib., 38–40.
63. Ib., 44.   64. Ib., 46.   65. Ib., 16.
66. Ib., 49.   67. Ib., 11.

68. Ib., 12: "Quoniam si vini potu, ciborum exquisitione, feminarum ardenti desiderio et omnino molli lubricaque vita utamur, cadaveris gestatores sumus in corpore. Si vero miseramus deus avertat vitiorum illuviem et aridam reddat animam, incipiet vivificare atque animare corpus mundiori anima, cuius sapientia est moderatrix." This conception alone makes clear Paul's "redemption of the body" in Romans viii, the experience which Paul has not yet achieved. See the Appendix.

69. QG, ii, 67.

the God of the Mystery, God who expresses Himself in the Logos with the two Powers. The ark of the body is contrasted with the ark of the immaterial Essence, the Ark of the Covenant.[70] The purging flood was sent by the Ruling Power of God, though that Power did not act apart from the Beneficent or Creative Power.[71] Having passed through the stage where the Royal Power with its punitive and purging action has been predominant, and become now pure, Noah directs the sacrifices he makes after his emergence from the ark to the Creative and Beneficent Power.[72] His offering is his purified sense life, the offering that represents the final achievement of one who has gone the whole course of the divine plan.[78] But as before the Creative Power was present in the activity of the Royal Power, so now the latter is there with the Creative Power to receive the sacrifices.[74] Philo never wants to be caught making the Powers into distinctive beings in the Gnostic sense, however helpful they may be in explaining the mystic ascent.

Since he has been worked upon by both Powers Noah is made into a microcosm and a man of God alike. For he had in himself the elements and creative factors of the world, but also qualities peculiar to God Himself.[75] Noah's experience is summed up in that he is represented as having been made into the equal, not of the second Adam who was made from clay in the second story of Creation, but of that Primal Adam who was the Form of the material Adam, and who was himself immaterial and in the likeness of the Logos.[76] This is the sort of Man, it will be recalled, to whom Law could not come as commands. He had risen above this as above all other earthly things. And those who become Wise Men (like Noah, we understand) develop souls that can completely dominate their bodies.[77]

So the story of Noah and the flood is a revelation of the Royal Road to God, the road of Sophia,[78] the Road of the Mystery. It will be recalled that he had also, in the *Exposition,* been represented as one of the νόμοι ἔμψυχοι, though little was made of him as such.

Great as Noah can be represented, when Philo is briefly schematizing for Gentiles Noah is relatively inferior, like Enos and Enoch, to the next great triad of Patriarchs. Abraham, Isaac, and Jacob are the fully perfect men. True they too are distinguished from each other in that Abraham represents virtue derived from instruction, Isaac virtue from natural endowment, and Jacob virtue achieved by effort,[79] but as a matter of fact each man laid

70. Ib., 4. 71. Ib., 16. 72. Ib., 51.
73. Ib., 52. 74. Ib., 53. 75. Ib., 75.
76. Ib., 56. 77. Ib.
78. *QG,* i, 99. The Law of Wisdom appears in *QG,* ii, 41, and the story of Noah is the Law of Wisdom in Ib., 12.
79. *Abr.,* 52: Ἀβραὰμ σύμβολον διδασκαλικῆς ἀρετῆς ἐστιν, Ἰσαάκ, φυσικῆς, Ἰακώβ, ἀσκητικῆς.

claim to all three types of virtue and only was distinguished by the virtue that was predominant in his particular case. For actually each of the three types of virtue is impossible without the other two.[80]

For the Mystery a highly important statement follows. Not only are each of the three men all of virtue with especial emphasis upon one virtue, but they are more than individual men. They are, as virtues, each a χάρις of God, are together the three χάριτες, which are δυνάμεις of God. So the expression "God of Abraham and Isaac and Jacob" means God who through His Powers gives gracious and perfect gifts to the soul.[81] This sounds at first like the merest fancy. But it will be of interest to see how literally Philo meant just that, that the great Patriarchs had become so identified with the Powers of God that they became a medium for the giving of God's higher gifts to men.

For Philo goes on to explain that this august triad was made into "a royal priesthood and holy race."[82] This race has got the name of Israel, that is "Seeing God," and is distinguished by the fact that it has the vision of God at the end of the mystic Road, the highest possible achievement, to which vision God draws the soul up the Road by the action of the divine Powers.[83] This is not a reference to the race of Israel, but first to the Patriarchs, and then to those who got the vision, whether Jew or Gentile, and only to those. For the true successors of the Patriarchs, who have themselves been thus elevated, are not those descended from them in the flesh but their spiritual successors.

We have at last got the general distinguishing feature of the great Patriarchal triad. Whatever was the achievement of the first triad, the second triad is marked by having come through with the help of the Powers to the end of the mystic Road, and by having been given the vision of God. As such they are not only themselves holy, but are a "royal priesthood," a phrase which Philo does not here elaborate, but which comes clearly to mean that they have priestly power in the Mystery to bring others up to their own experience. Philo is now ready to go on to consider the three Patriarchs individually.

First Abraham.

Abraham was zealous for piety, the highest and greatest virtue, and so he eagerly followed God and obeyed His commands, on the supposition that the

---

80. *Abr.*, 53. οὔτε γὰρ διδασκαλίαν ἄνευ φύσεως ἢ ἀσκήσεως τελειωθῆναι δυνατὸν οὔτε φύσις ἐπὶ πέρας ἐστὶν ἐλθεῖν ἱκανὴ δίχα τοῦ μαθεῖν καὶ ἀσκῆσαι οὔτε ἄσκησις, εἰ μὴ προθεμελιωθείη φύσει τε καὶ διδασκαλίᾳ.

81. *Abr.*, 54.

82. Ex. xix, 6. I omit the καί between βασίλειον and ἱεράτευμα, as Cohn suggests, to agree with the Hebrew and LXX.

83. *Abr.*, 56–59. Note especially the last sentence: ἐκ τῶν αὐτοῦ δυνάμεων ἀνακρεμάσας τὴν ψυχὴν ὁ θεὸς ὁλκῇ δυνατωτέρᾳ πρὸς ἑαυτὸν ἐπισπάσηται.

commands were not merely those published by speech and writing, but just as much those indicated by the more evident signs of nature which the truest of the senses (sight) apprehends rather than the untrustworthy and uncertain sense of hearing. For anyone who observes the order in nature and the cosmic polity which is beyond any verbal description learns, though not a word has been said, to make his life εὔνομον καὶ εἰρηνικόν by paying close regard to the imitation of τὰ καλά.[84]

So Abraham is to be described as the νόμος ἔμψυχος. In developing such a thesis, Philo is somewhat limited by the actual story of Abraham's life as it is told in Genesis. But he schematizes the material cleverly for his purpose. The νόμος ἔμψυχος is one who has found God, and committed himself to Him in so complete a way that his life flowers in perfect virtue of inner adjustment and outer act. It is to be noted that for Philo the act or attitude of Abraham which made him into this higher type is described as his following God, obeying God's commands, conforming himself to the material universe which he could learn from observation, and imitating τὰ καλά. To call this all Stoicism is obviously a mistake. "Following God" is a Neo-Pythagorean concept[85] as much as conforming oneself to the material world is Stoic, while "obeying God's commands" is a recognizable Jewish notion alongside the Platonic conception of imitating τὰ καλά. Of the lot it will appear that the Platonic and Neo-Pythagorean conceptions are the ones Philo is chiefly following.

The migration of Abraham from his home in Chaldea at the call of God is taken by Philo as the migration from erroneous opinion about the character of God to recognition of the truth. The Chaldeans, he says, were people engrossed in astronomy to such an extent that they had no notion of ἡ ἀόρατος καὶ νοητὴ οὐσία, recognized only the visible οὐσία, and so identified God with the world itself. Abraham migrated out from this into the discovery that above the world was its Creator and Ruler, and that the order of nature was not an inherent property of the material world, but the work of God.[86] Philo repeats his point so often that his general meaning is unmistakable in spite of some difficult details.[87] The philosophy he is ascrib-

---

84. *Abr.*, 60 f.

85. See for example Hippodamus, *ap.* Stobaeus, IV, xxxix, 26 (Wachs., V, 910, ll. 19 ff.).

86. *Abr.*, 70. In all types of Judaism Abraham is celebrated as the hero who broke from polytheism for monotheism. The material has been collected in Beer, *Leban Abrahams* (1859), Chapters I and II. See also *Jewish Encyclopedia*, I, 84–87, and Box, *The Apocalypse of Abraham*, pp. 88–94. Abraham's legendary conflict with his father may be a reflection of Zoroaster's similar conflict. See A. V. W. Jackson, *Zoroastrian Studies* (1928), p. 19; *Zoroaster* (1901), pp. 26 ff.

87. The most difficult passage is in *Abr.*, 69, the statement: Χαλδαῖοι γὰρ ἐν τοῖς μάλιστα διαπονήσαντες ἀστρονομίαν καὶ πάντα ταῖς κινήσεσι τῶν ἀστέρων ἀναθέντες ὑπέλαβον οἰκονομεῖσθαι τὰ ἐν κόσμῳ δυνάμεσιν, ἃς περιέχουσιν ἀριθμοὶ καὶ ἀριθμῶν ἀναλογίαι κτλ. The whole passage, beginning from ἃς περιέχουσιν and continuing six lines, is written

ing to the "Chaldeans" is strange enough. It may be that he is referring to Babylonian tradition, but Babylonian scholars would be amazed to learn that the Babylonians taught that τὸν κόσμον αὐτὸν εἶναι θεόν,[88] to the exclusion of any personal divine agencies or rulerships. Philo is of course right in saying that the Chaldeans were interested in astronomy and saw great power in the stars as controlling πάντα. But when he says that Abraham, in going from them to Canaan, went from materialistic pantheism to theism he is attacking not the Chaldeans but the Stoics and scientists of his own environment.

It is Philo's passionate sense of the contrast between theism and materialistic pantheism, expressed here and frequently throughout his writings, that distinguishes him preëminently from the Stoics, including, in my opinion, Posidonius,[89] and which marks him, for all his Stoic traces, as fundamentally a Pythagorean Neo-Platonist.

When Abraham left materialistic pantheism he went to Charran, the land of the senses, to begin at the bottom to observe the world for himself.[90] But the senses are useless without the mind to interpret their perceptions. When Abraham's mind had thus been freed of false opinion, so that it could consider the world, he at once concluded that there must be a mind behind the visible universe as there is one behind the material aspects of a man. First he got this as a conception, since he could not with his physical sight endure the contemplation of the divine Light-Rays.[91] And yet his getting the right conception was followed by God's revealing Himself to Abraham, for the right conception had removed the veil that made such a vision impossible, though even then God had to take the initiative in revealing Himself to Abraham, since without special action of God no man can get the Vision.[92]

in by a late hand in one of the best mss., and the clause ἃς . . . ἀναλογίαι is omitted in the Armenian translation. The insertion of that clause makes nonsense of the passage, for it is incredible that Philo thought of ἀριθμῶν ἀναλογίαι as material entities, while the passage is quite coherent without it. For the statements in the text above see *Abr.*, 70 f., 77 f., 84, 88. See also *QG*, iii, 1; *Mig.*, 178 ff.; *Som.*, i, 47–60; *Cong.*, 49.

88. *Abr.*, 69.

89. Evidence that Posidonius left the Stoic pantheism for a genuine theism is marshalled by Heinemann. *Poseidonios*, II, 308–312. The only material he can quote of any cogency is the pseudo-Aristotelian *De Mundo*, which, I have indicated elsewhere, is by no means to be taken indiscriminately as evidence for Posidonius' teaching. See my "Neo-Pythag. Source," pp. 153 ff. Heinemann's "evidence" only goes to prove that there is no reason for thinking that Posidonius ever took such a step. It is true that Diogenes Laertius (vii, 134) does represent Posidonius as teaching δύο ἀρχαί, τὸ ποιοῦν καὶ τὸ πάσχον· τὸ μὲν οὖν πάσχον εἶναι τὴν ἄποιον οὐσίαν τὴν ὕλην, τὸ δὲ ποιοῦν τὸν ἐν αὐτῇ λόγον τὸν θεόν. Whatever this might be made to appear to mean, it could not have meant any departure from the regular Stoic doctrine, since Diogenes Laertius simply lists Posidonius after Zeno and Chrysippus as teaching this doctrine, and in general the same doctrine of the panmaterial God (vii, 148). The only positive direct evidence available, then, puts Posidonius in his doctrine of God directly with the founders of Stoicism, whose pantheistic materialism is here and elsewhere sufficiently attested.

90. *Abr.*, 72 ff.   91. Ib., 76.   92. Ib., 79.

This vision was a "running up" of his mind to a φύσις higher than the visible φύσις, the φύσις νοητή, which he saw, and with it the Being who is ruler and creator of both these natures.[93] So his name was changed, to signify that he had become the Sophos.[94]

The next step is the union of Virtue with Abraham's own nature which is now oriented in his νοῦς. Philo is discussing the saving of Sarah from the lustful advances of the king of Egypt. He thinks well to omit Abraham's apparent timidity in representing her as his sister, for he insists that Abraham typifies the virtuous mind (apparently because of his having achieved the correct notion of God) whose union with Virtue is here given divine protection.

Here we meet for the first time in the story of the Patriarchs the peculiar bisexual functions of the Female Principle,[95] and confused as the passage at first appears to be, it must be quoted:

The marriage in which pleasure unites people achieves the union of bodies; but the marriage which Sophia consummates unites Perfect Virtue with minds (λογισμοί) that aspire for purity. These two kinds of marriage are in contrast to each other. For in the physical marriage it is the male who sows the seed and the female who receives it. But in the union that takes place within souls Virtue, although she might seem to be the wife, has by nature the power of sowing seeds of good intentions and virtuous speeches, and expositions of doctrines that are profitable for life, while the reason, though apparently the husband, actually receives the sacred and divine seeds. Perhaps what I have said is put in a false light by the verbal difficulty that νοῦς is grammatically a masculine word and ἀρετή feminine. But if one will take off the darkening veil of words and look at the bare facts he will perceive clearly that Virtue is masculine by nature in as much as it sets in motion and dispenses and introduces[96] noble ideas of noble actions and utterances, and that the reason is moved and trained and benefited and in general put into a passive role, which passivity is the only condition in which it can be saved.[97]

This explanation, Philo specifically tells us, is *not* original with himself. He has learned it from "men versed in natural philosophy (φυσικοὶ ἄνδρες) who interpreted this passage ingeniously."[98] It is notable at once that marriage with ἀρετή is marriage with Sophia. The two terms are interchangeable for the Female Principle formulation of the Light-Stream. Abraham's spiritual advance is going throughout to be developed according to both formulations, that of the Female Principle and that of the Powers. By this passage, advance is a matter of the mystic marriage. The human mind must

93. *Abr.*, 88.   94. Ib., 81 ff. Cf. *Praem.*, 58.
95. See above, pp. 17 ff.
96. The word is ὑπηχεῖ, "cause to echo," or, "reecho." For Philo's peculiar use of the word see Leisegang, *Index, s.v.*
97. *Abr.*, 100–102.   98. Ib., 99.

put itself into such an attitude of passivity that it becomes female as over against the masculine activity of Sophia or ἀρετή. The impossibility of one's achieving Sophia in any other way than by thus playing the female rôle is well brought out by Philo's interpretation of the humiliation of the king of Egypt. He desired to have relations with Sarah, as Sophia or ἀρετή. But he is the lower mind, the νοῦς φιλοσώματος. He, as an assertive, masculine activity aspired to Sophia. But Sophia, or ἀρετή, will have nothing to do with a person in whom the lower mind is so strong that it cannot be completely subdued. It is Abraham, the man who had made so good a start by getting his own νοῦς in a proper attitude toward God, who gets Virtue herself by humiliation of the lower mind.[99]

Philo does not pull this allegorizing together, but its meaning is clear. The man who has come to the right opinion about God humiliates himself, and is then given Virtue, the divine principle, which fills his mind with good seeds, develops it into being itself virtuous, and puts the lower mind into complete subjection. Virtue does not wait until this battle between the two minds has been fought out, but comes into a man when she sees that with her help the battle can be hopefully joined. The result is that now the man who has come into right conceptions of God has been met by divine power, and has come through to a properly integrated personality in Virtue.

Abraham is now ready for the next step, the vision of God, and to receive God as guest within himself. The section[100] is one of the least coherent of the treatise, with many digressions into which we need not go. The description centers about the coming of the "three men" to Abraham's house, and the consequent destruction of the cities of Pentapolis. One important passage repeats that God does not come into the soul of a man unless it is properly regimented under the mastership of the mind, while, as in the relation with Sarah as Virtue, the mind is developed by God's, or the divine Powers', coming into it:

For how could the divine Powers ever have endured to enter (a human habitation or soul) at all, unless they had known that like the well organized crew of a ship all the inhabitants were obedient to a single command, that of the master who is in a sense their pilot? And how could they have given the impression of being feasted and entertained if they had not recognized that their host was akin to them and a fellow servant who had run for refuge to their own master? Further it must be understood that at their very entrance all the parts of the household increased in goodness, for there was breathed upon them a breath of perfect virtue.[101]

The three visitors are the two Powers, the Ruling and the Creative Powers

99. *Abr.*, 103, 106. 100. Ib., 107–176.
101. Ib., 116.

of God, with their connecting principal, elsewhere spoken of as the λόγος.[102] These appear as three to the beginner, though to the man who is more advanced the two Powers are recognized as only aspects of the One, and a vision of them as one is vision of ὁ ὄντως ὤν.[103] The value of the threefold appearance is that some men who cannot rise to the full vision can yet aspire to the good things of God and be richly rewarded as he comes to appreciate the Creating and Benefiting Power of God. One who cannot rise even to this height can at least appreciate that God punishes evil through His Ruling Power, and can thus propitiate God and thereby escape punishment.[104] But Abraham is the man who rises above both of these lower incentives to aspire to God for His own sake.

After a considerable digression on the significance of the five cities of the plain, Philo goes on to the next great event of Abraham's life, as he sees it, his sacrifice of Isaac. The birth of Isaac, which might have given him large grounds for allegory, does not fit into his explanation of the development of Abraham's own character. It was probably discussed more fully in the lost De Isaaco. He describes the sacrificial scene with great feeling and power, dilating upon the extraordinary love which Abraham had for Isaac as the son of his old age and as his only son, and as a boy of great inherent loveliness. The boy represented ultimately "laughter," he says,[105] and "laughter" means that highest εὐδαιμονία for which the good man aspires, and which is the ultimate goal of all Pythagorean and Platonic morality and mysticism. Yet it is not the natural property of man, for man is a creature of sorrow while God alone has natural εὐδαιμονία.[106] Man must then be ready to sacrifice his own aspiration for εὐδαιμονία in a complete dedication to make himself subject to God. God will, as He did to Abraham, give him εὐδαιμονία, but it must come as a gift from God, a reward, while man centers his attention not on the quest for happiness but on the complete dedication of himself, including all his joys, to God. Even so, man never has happiness in the full and unmixed sense in which it appears in God.[107]

102. See above, pp. 25, 30 ff.   103. Abr., 119–125.

104. Abr., 126–130. See especially §129: δέχομαι γὰρ καὶ τὸν τῆς εὐεργέτιδός μου δυνάμεως βουλόμενον μεταλαχεῖν εἰς μετουσίαν ἀγαθῶν καὶ τὸν φόβῳ τὴν ἡγεμονικὴν καὶ δεσποτικὴν ἱλασκόμενον ἐξουσίαν εἰς ἀποτροπὴν κολάσεως.

105. Abr., 201.

106. Abr., 202. The contrast appears strikingly in Hippodamus (ap. Stob., IV, xxxix, 26; Wachs., V, 909 f.). ἁ μὲν γὰρ εὐδαιμονία τελειότας ἐστὶ βίω ἀνθρωπίνω . . . ὁ μὲν ὤν θεὸς οὔτε μαθὼν παρά τινος τὰν ἀρετὰν ἀγαθὸς ἐγένετο οὔτε ἐπισυναρξάμενος αὐτῷ τᾶς τύχας εὐδαίμων· φύσει γὰρ ἦν ἀγαθὸς καὶ φύσει εὐδαίμων καὶ ἀεὶ ἦν καὶ ἐσσεῖται καὶ οὐδέποκα ὑπολείψει τοιοῦτος ἐών, ἄφθαρτος ἐὼν καὶ φύσει ἀγαθός· ὁ δὲ ἄνθρωπος <οὔτε τᾷ φύσει ἀγαθὸς> οὔτε τᾷ φύσει εὐδαίμων, . . . Hippodamus puts human happiness in τύχη, though he clearly makes it a concomitant of virtue, while Philo makes it a gift of God rewarding virtue, but the contrast of man and God is strikingly similar in each. On happiness as the goal of life and the end of virtue see also Euryphamus, ap. Stob., IV, xxxix, 27 (Wachs., V, 917 ll. 12 ff.).

107. Abr., 203–205. It must at least be noted that Philo in this is quite in accord with the

With this description Philo feels that he has represented the fulness of Abraham's character as concerns his relation to God. Beginning with an apprehension of the existence of God as a true doctrine Abraham went on to regiment his own nature so that the mind was completely dominant, and free to look up to God. He was met with two dispensations: he was solidified in his virtuous life by the immediate action of Virtue within him, the mystic marriage, and then he was able to go on to a mystic vision of God in His true nature. To God as He was now fully apprehended he dedicated his life completely, even to the abandoning of the quest for happiness, and was finally rewarded by being given happiness in God. Many more things could be said on the subject, says Philo, but this is adequate.[108]

But piety, the right relation with God, fundamental as it is, is not a complete picture of the life of such a character as Abraham. Along with piety is the problem of the relation with other people.

For piety and love of one's fellow men (φιλανθρωπία) belong to the same nature, and so we must look for each in connection with the same individual, his holiness toward God and his justice toward men.[109]

The remaining part of the treatise is accordingly devoted to showing how Abraham excelled in the four cardinal virtues of justice, courage, self-control, and wisdom.

Abraham's justice appeared in his allowing Lot to choose the part of the country he preferred.[110] As this concession was made also in the interest of peace, Abraham is likewise shown to be a man of peace.[111]

So then ὁ ἀστεῖος is not only peaceful and φιλοδίκαιος, but is also brave and warlike; not for the sake of fighting—for he was not contentious and strife-loving —but with a view to guaranteeing peace for the future which his adversaries were destroying.[112]

The bravery of Abraham appeared in his fighting with the kings to rescue Lot.[113] Philo has the story in the main correctly, but he loses sight of the recorded events, and of the lesson of bravery he is trying to draw from the

best teachers of the Christian experience, who have always insisted that the deepest joys of life are to be found by abandoning the conscious quest for happiness in an all-consuming aspiration for a pure character and the right relation with God. Such teaching is psychologically sound. Enduring happiness is a by-product from some interest which is in itself so engrossing that it dominates and thus harmonizes the entire personality. By striving immediately and consciously for the harmony we can never achieve it.

108. *Abr.*, 208.

109. Ib. It will be noticed that δικαιοσύνη is here often a generic term for virtue.

110. Ib., 208-209.

111. The incident also typifies for Philo the victory of the higher mind over the pleasure loving mind in the individual.

112. *Abr.*, 225.   113. Ib., 225-244.

life of the first man and founder of our race: some regard him as νόμιμος, but my argument has shown that he was himself unwritten νόμος καὶ θεσμός.[123]

The last contrast is striking. It was apparently a common thing among the Jews of Philo's day to regard Abraham as one who obeyed the Law, νόμιμος. But Philo is not content with this conservative statement. Abraham was more than νόμιμος, he was νόμος ἔμψυχος, and as such a savior of men. Philo does not say, and there is no reason to infer, that he was the *first*, and alone, in this opinion about Abraham. He says he has proved a position different from that held by some others, not from that held by all others.

Abraham, like the earlier Patriarchs, is being represented to the Gentile reader of the *Exposition* as a saving force by virtue of his having been νόμος ἔμψυχος, or the νόμος καὶ θεσμὸς ἄγραφος. He was, too, a merciful χάρις from God, with permanent power to benefit men. His great mystical achievement of having left the world of passion to rise, pure of body, to a vision of God through His Powers is an achievement at once inspiring to others, and of immediate power to help others along the same Road, the Road to a life lived beyond the written law in the Law of God, which is the Nature of God. This conception of Abraham's character is made unmistakable in Philo's works for Jews.

In the *Quaestiones in Genesin* Philo takes up the story of the Patriarch, and develops it by giving a brief commentary on the narrative verse by verse. Sections of the account permit him to trace a consecutive development in Abraham's character, but many details throw him into irrelevant digressions from the main thought. It is certain, too, that our manuscripts are very defective, for one cannot imagine that Philo would have skipped great blocks of the story when he deals with such labor with every detail of the sections treated. The commentary as we have it takes up Abraham at Genesis xv, 7, thus omitting the story of the call of Abraham from the Chaldeans. It is certain, however, that the explanation of that call had followed the main lines of symbolism used in the *Exposition*.[124] Abraham is already out of Chaldaea, then, and conversing with God when the story begins. The early stages of his development are lost. It will be useless to try in this summary to present the details. Abraham prays to the lower Power, the Royal Power, for a sign[125] and is commanded to make the sacrifice. This is elaborately discussed for the significance of the sacrifice, which is explained, apparently,

123. *Abr.*, 275 f.
124. The loss of this section is to be deplored because it might well have described the faith of Abraham on that stage in a way which would have been closer to the remarks of Paul than we dare without evidence supply; it might also have told us more of the significance of Melchizedek and so have thrown light upon the letter to the Hebrews and the mosaic of the scene in Santa Maria Maggiore.
125. *QG*, iii, 2.

according to the Scientific Commentators to whom Philo occasionally alludes. The whole is made into the cosmic worship on a Pythagorean foundation. After the sacrifice, at sunset, Abraham's bodily nature sets and the
Spirit of God takes possession of him.[126] But this is not extraordinary since
the soul of the Wise Man is not a proper habitant of the body anyway, but
a stranger to be released and return to God by the subjection of the body.[127]
In the full experience, as in the case of Noah, the rays of God, i.e., we understand the Logos, or probably here the Royal Power, come in to unite the
divided personality of soul and body.[128] The barrenness of Sarah is like the
period when Noah could not beget: until the soul is fully purified it cannot
beget.[129] Sarah is Virtue, and in the preliminary stages man can have no
fruit from her. But he can profitably have relation with and get results from
the encyclical disciplines. Thus Philo interprets Abraham's relation with
Hagar.[130] There is a sense of achievement in this begetting that sets itself up
as equal to the real begetting by Virtue,[131] and the encyclicals, Hagar, have
therefore to be humiliated by Virtue, Sarah.[132] The flight of Hagar is essentially Abraham's own experience as he is temporarily led astray by this sense
of achievement and only brought back to Virtue and Sophia by a miracle
of the Logos who is guiding him.[133] Abraham's first vision of the Powers
occurred on the occasion when his name was changed. It is the "Lord God"
that appeared to him, hence the two Powers. In this experience he is definitely purified from sin, made into conformity with the two Powers, that is
he is made according to the likeness of God, the Creative Power, in the
same sense as the Cosmos is in that likeness, and is made a citizen of the
world by the Royal Power, Lord.[134] The last vestige of his offenses fall from
him.[135] Abraham has now in turn risen from earth to heaven, then to the
κόσμος νοητός, and thence to God, not as He is, but as He represents Himself in Intelligible Virtue herself. So he becomes a force for other men in the
way of both the divine Powers, benefiting them and disciplining them.[136]
The new name meant that he had risen from knowledge of the cosmos to
Wisdom about the Intelligible Existences; he had become "wholly eye," and
was

surrounded by light which knows no darkness, and which reveals the very form
of light as by a flash of lightning, taking God for his leader and guide to the
comprehension of the knowledge of Essences and to the formulation of explanations.[137]

126. *QG*, iii, 9.   127. Ib., 10.   128. Ib., 15.
129. Ib., 18.
130. Ib., 20. This is consequent only when we understand ἀρετή to be merely another word
for σοφία, as in the *Exposition* (see above, p. 139).
131. Ib., 23.   132. Ib., 25 ff.   133. Ib., 27.
134. Ib., 39 f.   135. Ib., 41.   136. Ib., 42.
137. Ib., 43.

His union here would appear to be with Sophia, in the sense in which Sophia appears in Pascher's schematization of the Royal Road. So, in accordance with this, he is now able to beget with seed from God, to become the re-deemer and intercessor for all nations before God. Having himself become filled with Sophia he can beget by her.[188]

Now he returns to what we may call the "redemption of the body" theme and gives one of his clearest statements of what that means.[189] After the mystic experience God rewards the philosophic soul by

conferring a benefit upon it, namely the possession of perpetual rulership of all terrestrial things, with the result that he will never be dominated by the body, but always be its prince and ruler, and will keep it as his slave and attendant.

A passage on circumcision follows, in which the rite is treated from many different angles. Mystically it is a symbol of the "redemption of the body," the stage where not only the spirit but the body is under the regulation of the Divine Logos so that every excrescence of sense is pruned away.[140]

The change of Sarah's name indicates that she too has been transformed from being the part to the whole, from the corruptible to the incorruptible, so that instead of representing the human attempts at the virtues that must die with the individual she is changed into Virtue herself.[141] In contrast with the barrenness of the mortal virtue, Virtue is fertile and brings forth a nation.[142] The Third Book closes with a strong statement of the power of the good man to save not only himself and his friends, but strangers, and to give them a share in his virtue and piety.

The Fourth Book of the *Quaestiones in Genesin* opens with the incident of Mamre. Here the same experience as before is fundamentally repeated, with great detail of description. God, he explains, cannot be comprehended by man or the cosmos, so He sends a glory, properly Form, as He showers incorporeal rays about the whole soul. Led by these rays, through the me-dium of Form, the intellect is born as the prototype. The oak itself is Sophia, the mediator in the vision between God and man. By clever comparison to the olive tree Philo makes the oak, Sophia, also a symbol of the Light of the universe. Under the tree, then, Abraham, imitating the quiet of God, sits and gets the vision as a symbol of the coming of incorporeal rays of Light.[148] The vision takes the form of the Three Men.[144] They are not men because Abraham worships them,[145] and he addresses them in the singular for he now sees that the Three are One. He asks them to stay with him, "for it is the end of happiness to be near God, as God fills the whole soul with his incorporeal light."[146] The feeding of the Three Men leads Philo to speak of

138. Ib., 44. 139. Ib., 45. 140. Ib., 51.
141. Ib., 53. 142. Ib., 54. 143. *QG,* iv, 1.
144. Ib., 2. 145. Ib., 3. 146. Ib., 4.

the fact that there is a sacred food of the intellect, consisting of "the Laws and Forms of Sophia," to take which is to feed on divine things (*vesci divinis*).[147]

The Triad now come into Abraham's house, and that is the coming of God and His Powers into a man of purest soul, perfect virtue, and proper speech, all of which qualities of the host hasten to greet and serve the divine visitors. Homer had said that all things are to be divided into threes, and the Pythagoreans had made the triangle an element in the knowledge of all things, the prime measure of both corporeal and incorporeal existence.

So, truly and properly said, the measure of all things, intelligible as well sensible, is the one God who, though a unity in Himself, appears as a trinity because of the weakness of the observers.[148]

For as the eye, when it is weak, often sees "double," one object as two, so the eye of the soul is at first unable to see one as one, but gets the vision of three, apparitions of the primal ministering Powers. It was this clear vision of God as One that Moses prayed for. Knowledge of the Father and his Powers is hidden from the many, Philo explains, in view of the Mystery, and must not be told to them, for he who reveals the secret to those who are untutored and unworthy destroys the law of perfection of the holy Mysteries. Happy is the man who entertains such a guest, for from this guest flows out a perpetual flow in which the souls of prophets and angels delight as they eat the food of the voluntary law of pure Sophia that comes from God.[149]

In this section we begin to see clearly at last that the divine radiation of Light is to be called Sophia or Law interchangeably, as it had been Spirit above.[150] Philo can call this radiation by one or by a combination of the terms as the exigencies of a given allegory may demand. I cannot see room in the picture for Sophia as a distinct principle in contrast to the Powers. Philo is too specific in denying the Powers any independent existence to have kept Sophia as such. To follow his thought we must begin with, and never lose sight of, the Radiating Deity, and recognize that various terms are only means of describing the nature of that radiation.

Sarah laughs at the promise of the Triad that she is to bear a son, and that laughter typifies the joy of the ultimate mystical achievement, for it is the joy of the nearness of God, the ecstasy of receiving the rays.[151]

After this experience God keeps none of His plans hidden from Abraham, for the soul can now see the plan of God fully in the world, to see which is the goal of the contemplative life and of all virtue.[152] Because Abraham has

147. *QG*, iv, 6.   148. Ib., 8.
149. This remarkable conception is expounded in Ib., 8. See also, §§9, 10, 12.
150. *QG*, iii, 9.   151. *QG*, iv, 16, 18, 19.
152. Ib., 21.

seen the incorporeal Light he becomes a dynamic force to excite a desire for virtue in others,[153] and is a priest above the madness of the wicked.[154]

With this the most important part of the story of Abraham for our purpose is done. The story now shifts to Lot at Sodom who was a character quite inferior to Abraham.[155] Lot saw only the "two" Powers, not the Logos between them,[156] though it was the Logos who gave him the instructions later.[157] The Powers do not want to enter his house as they did the house of Abraham,[158] and when Lot fed them it was not the secret cakes of the Mystery which he gave them, because he was "not yet perfectly purified."[159] Lot is told to save himself by leaving the corruption of Sodom to go to the hills, that is to Sophia, where he would "change the mortal life into the life of immortality."[160] But he is not ready for such a step, and goes instead to a small city, symbolizing that he is making progress, but has not yet got away from material existence.[161] He was really saved by the virtue, not of himself, but of Abraham, by which the conception of the saving power of the Patriarch is well brought out.[162] It is the Royal Power that rains down the sulphur upon Sodom,[163] and it was to that Power that Abraham had addressed his prayer for the preservation of Sodom.[164] That is, for Philo, Lot is by no means one of the great Patriarchs, though we shall see reason for thinking that Lot was so regarded by other Jews in the Mystery.

A few details of the rest of the discussion of Abraham are worth noting. After the vision of the Triad Abraham went to the "South" to live. This means, says Philo, that he lived in the country of the Virtues, nourished by divine laws, rejoicing always in the Father, and irrigated from the perennial fountain of the Logos; that is he lived in full the contemplative life.[165] The incident of Abraham's passing off Sarah as his sister to Abimelech,[166] and of Abraham's later marriage to Keturah,[167] only made Philo writhe in insignificant allegory, and the sections that treated the great chapters of Genesis on the birth and sacrifice of Isaac are lost.[168] The Sophos is a stranger among men,[169] he is seeking dominion over the body,[170] he is a king ordained by God over other men.[171] His body is to him a corpse, as dead as a bronze statue,[172] which must be suppressed,[173] but if properly mastered it can be made as faithful as the soul, for the soul can so dominate it that the body shows forth an imitation of the powers of the soul—the idea again of the re-

153. Ib., 22.   154. Ib., 23.   155. Ib., 24–58.
156. Ib., 30.   157. Ib., 48 f.   158. Ib., 33.
159. Ib., 35.   160. Ib., 46.   161. Ib., 47.
162. Ib., 54.   163. Ib., 51.   164. Ib., 53.
165. Ib., 59.   166. Ib., 61–70.   167. Ib., 147.

168. In a later section (§122) he states that Abraham's age at the birth of Isaac shows that he was entirely beyond material things and corruption, that is he had reached a stage that made it possible for him to sow the seed of happiness (Isaac).

169. QG, iv, 74.   170. Ib., 75.   171. Ib., 76.
172. Ib., 77.   173. Ib., 78.

demption of the body.[174] Abraham was a prophet and imposed law, divining what things are to be, and what are to be done. For law is an invention of Nature, not of men.[175] So, full of days, he was added to his people, that is, as Philo interprets it in one place, Abraham was added to the incorporeal substances;[176] here he was added to his successors, apparently as their permanent possession for salvation.[177] By way of summary two brief statements may be quoted:

> The man who is at once a lover of virtue because of his own nature, and a diligent cultivator of it [by the mystic ascent, we understand, which Philo is describing], is the most human physician of our race, and is truly its guardian and the one who drives out evil from it.[178]
>
> The wise man is the savior of the race, the intercessor before God, the one who seeks pardon for the sins of those akin to him.[179]

Philo has, by following the story of Genesis line by line, not been able to dramatize the life of Abraham so effectively as he did in the free composition for the Gentiles. But the richness of detail is evident with which the character of Abraham had been elaborated to make it conform to the Mystery, and to represent him as a saving force for men to come. Particularly has the light symbolism come out with increasing emphasis, and the conception that Abraham was nourished by the stream of divine rays, which was symbolized by Sophia or the Powers, and which was at the same time a law. By this, while I have not noticed the term νόμος ἔμψυχος in the story of Abraham in the *Quaestiones,* the term as used in the *Exposition* is more clearly explained. Abraham's nature, in being changed into the likeness of the Immaterial Essences, is changed into the Light Substance which is the Law of Nature. We must not look to Stoicism, then, for the meaning of the Law of Nature as Philo conceives it. It is not in the material world that Philo would find such a Law, but in the nature of the divine Stream, which incidentally coming into matter, makes it into a Cosmos, but which the higher mystic gets not as a cosmic derivation but directly from the immaterial Source. The conception is that found in the *Hermetica* and in the *Avesta,* in the Pseudo-Aristotelian *De Mundo,* and in Neo-Pythagoreanism, rather than in the Stoics of any period.

The picture of Abraham is again drawn, and in still greater detail, in the *Allegory.* But this exposition, while it generally follows the career of Abraham, brings in parallel illustrations from all the other Patriarchs, so that it will be well to reserve that body of material as a whole for the summary of the Mystery.[180]

---

174. *QG,* iv, 83 f.   175. Ib., 90.   176. *QG,* iii, 11.
177. *QG,* iv, 153.   178. *QG,* iii, 10.   179. Ib., 44.
180. See below, Chap. IX.

But a few passages can well be brought in here as adding definitely to the portrait. It is strange that in the *De Abrahamo* no mention has been made of Melchizedek. The section that might have treated that part of Genesis is lost from the *Quaestiones*.[181] In the *Allegory* he is mentioned in only two passages. He is the Logos, heir of Being,[182] and the ideal king.[183] He grows wine that produces in men the Sober Intoxication of divine ecstasy.[184] As in the *Legum Allegoria* he was listed among those without antecedents, so in the *De Congressu*[185] his priesthood is that of the "self-taught." But neither passage throws any light upon the significance of Abraham's coming to Melchizedek for the Patriarch's spiritual development.[186]

Abraham does not appear specifically as the νόμος ἔμψυχος in the *Allegory*, but the conception is described in fact if not in name. For the fact that Abraham "went as the Lord had spoken unto him"[187] showed that he fulfilled the height of philosophy, he lived according to Nature. Living according to Nature, he explains lest his readers think he has the Stoic conception of the term, takes place when the mind enters the path of virtue and moves in the course of the ὀρθός λόγος, and so follows God.[188] In such a case "the actions of the wise men are indistinguishable from the λόγοι of God." Abraham "has kept all my law."[189] But since Law is the divine Logos, in executing (ποιοῦν) the Law Abraham has executed the Logos. It is in this sense that the actions of the wise man are the λόγοι of God. A study of the deeds of Abraham is, thus, a study of the λόγοι-νόμοι, the ὀρθός λόγος, the great ultimate Law of God.[190] The passage is one of the best explanations we have of the νόμος ἔμψυχος conception, though the term does not appear.

181. A fragment from the lost section is preserved in Harris, *Fragments*, p. 72, col. 1; from Cramer, *Catena in Heb.*, p. 580, e cod. Paris. 238. But it answers none of our questions.

182. *LA*, iii, 82. 183. Ib., 79 ff.

184. Ib., 82. 185. §99.

186. The letter to the Hebrews suggests that the Philonic interpretation was a current one, but the archeological material suggests that by another interpretation Melchizedek was priest according to the Cosmic Mystery, and that Abraham's being accepted by Melchizedek indicated his having reached that stage in his development. Melchizedek remains one of the many points on which we need more light.

187. Gen. xii, 4.

188. This is another instance of Philo's talking in a theistic and Pythagorean way of "following God," or "living according to Nature," in a sense that is definitely not Stoic. See above, pp. 50 ff. The man is happy, says Hippodamus (*ap.* Stob., IV, xxxix, 26; Wachs., V. 910 ll. 19 ff.), who follows the gods; he steers his actions by virtue as a pilot his craft by the stars. "So he not only follows God, but aligns the human good with the divine." The good man is such διὰ τὰν γνῶσιν τᾶς χρήσιος. Iamblichus (*Vita Pythag.*, 137; Diels, *Fragm. Vorsokr.*, 45 D2) says that Pythagoras and his followers ἅπαντα ὅσα περὶ τοῦ πράττειν ἢ μὴ πράττειν διορίζουσιν, ἐστόχασται τῆς πρὸς τὸ θεῖον ὁμιλίας, καὶ ἀρχὴ αὕτη ἐστὶ καὶ βίος ἅπας συντέτακται πρὸς τὸ ἀκολουθεῖν τῷ θεῷ καὶ ὁ λόγος οὗτος ταύτης ἐστὶ τῆς φιλοσοφίας ὅτι γέλοιον ποιοῦσιν ἄνθρωποι ἄλλοθέν ποθεν ζητοῦντες τὸ εὖ ἢ παρὰ τῶν θεῶν, κτλ. See also §§174–176. Philo always says "following nature" in the theistic and Pythagorean sense, rather than in the Stoic sense.

189. Gen. xxvi, 5. 190. *Mig.*, 127 ff.

In another passage Abraham is the type of the fact that εὐνομία is achieved by eliminating the passions, purifying oneself from sins, and leaving the false notions of the Chaldeans (the Stoics) for the true doctrine of God.[191] Abraham has discarded all kinship to the flesh,[192] and has come to stand unchangeably very near to the divine power.[193] He has fully realized the ideal of the Sophos.[194]

So in Abraham are all the people of the world blessed. As the Sophos he radiates "most brilliant and star-like beams of virtues."[195] He is associated with Moses in a brilliant description, to which we shall return, of the soul of such a man as being a spark from which the dark souls of later generations can be kindled.[196] God has showered by grace (χαρίζεσθαι) His gifts upon the Patriarchs, and *through them* upon others.[197]

That is, Abraham as one who is raised above men into the immaterial life of God, and who hence has become a savior and mediator of the higher Law to men, appears to be the Abraham of the *Allegory* as well as of the *Exposition* and *Quaestiones*.

191. *Heres*, 289.   192. *Det.*, 159; *Cher.*, 31.
193. *Post.*, 17 f., 27.
194. *Sobr.*, 55 ff. This passage is quoted as a source for Stoicism by Arnim, *SVF*, III, 603. But I doubt that the explanation of εὐγενής, in itself a Stoic term for the Sophos (*SVF*, III, 394), is here used in the Stoic sense where it is made to mean "Son of God."
195. *Heres*, 88.   196. *Mig.*, 118 f. See below, p. 231.
197. *Mig.*, 127.

CHAPTER VI

ISAAC AND JACOB

THE great *Exposition* went on after the treatise *On Abraham* to expound similarly the careers and characters of Isaac and Jacob. Unfortunately these two treatises are lost, and we have not a single fragment.

Isaac was obviously developed as a still higher type of existence than Abraham, higher also than Jacob, so the loss of the *De Isaaco* is much to be deplored. But it is possible to gather at least its general point of view. In the *De Praemiis et Poenis*, the closing treatise of the *Exposition*, Philo summarizes the contents of the earlier books. A comparison of the summary of the *De Abrahamo*[1] with the treatise itself shows that without the treatise we could have known very well its general purport from the summary, though of course with great loss of detail. It is with some confidence then that we turn to the summary of Isaac:[2]

After Faith [i.e. Abraham] Joy (χαρά) is set forth as the reward of him who gains without a struggle the natural virtue (τὴν ἀρετὴν ἐκ φύσεως) and wins the victory. For he was named, as the Greeks would say, Laughter (γέλως), but as the Chaldeans called him, Isaac. But laughter is a visible and corporeal token of the invisible joy of the mind. And it happens that joy is the best and most beautiful of the good states, the one by which the soul is entirely filled with contentment (εὐθυμία), rejoicing in God the Father and Maker of all things, and at the same time rejoicing in deeds that without evil are done [in the universe,][3] even though they may not be pleasant, on the ground that they are virtuous actions, and rejoicing in the permanence (διαμονή) of the universe. For just as a physician in great and dangerous illnesses sometimes cuts away parts of the body to effect the health of the rest of the body, and as a pilot, when storms arise casts out cargo with a view to the safety of the people aboard; and yet no blame is attached either to the physician for having mutilated the patient, or to the pilot for what he has cast overboard, but rather both are praised for having looked to and insured what was advantageous instead of what was pleasant; in the same way we must ever marvel at the nature of the universe and be delighted at anything that is done in the world as being done without voluntary evil, putting our attention not on the question whether some particular circumstance results in personal unpleasantness, but rather on the fact that after the manner of a well-lawed city the world is guided and piloted safely. So then Isaac was blessed no less than his predecessor,

---

1. *Praem.*, 28–30.   2. Ib., 31–35.

3. The context goes on to show that Philo's reference is not to individual activities but to cosmic events. One is to find joy in God as Father and Creator of the universe, and in the universe itself, first as whatever happens is designed for the good of the whole, and second in the permanence of the universe. Both Yonge and Heinemann miss the point here in their translations.

for he was free from anxiety and dejection; he enjoyed a life without pain or fear, and he experienced not in the least any of the bitterness or wretchedness of life because his soul in every part was preoccupied by joy.

From this section it would appear that the *De Isaaco* developed as its central theme the fact that Isaac was so completely at one with the power behind the cosmos that he typified joy. But the passage does not give the full significance of this joy. Philo would appear from many passages in the *Allegory* to be at one with classical philosophers in making εὐδαιμονία the ultimate gɔal of all endeavor, though he sharply distinguished, as did all schools but the Cyrenaic-Epicurean, between εὐδαιμονία and ἡδονή.[4] Philo interprets Isaac[5] as representing the type of character which is so exalted and perfect that he is the embodiment of εὐδαιμονία, since he is completely, naturally, and without effort at one with the law of God or nature. What he means by εὐδαιμονία Philo makes plain elsewhere, with reference to Isaac, in the thoroughly Aristotelian definition: "Happiness is the exercise of perfect virtue in a perfect life."[6] With this Aristotelian point of view he combines the mystical one that happiness is a gift of God, demanding, first, death to the passions,[7] after which happiness comes as a child or offspring of virtue.[8] Philo is so convinced that εὐδαιμονία comes as the crown or reward of virtue from God that he frequently is near to denying Abraham's paternity, and representing Isaac as the direct child of God through Sarah, to whom virginity has been miraculously restored. "God is the creator of laughter that is good, and of joy, so that we must consider Isaac not as the product of generation but as the work of the One without Beginning" (οὐ γενέσεως πλάσμα τὸν Ἰσαάκ, ἔργον δὲ τοῦ ἀγενήτου νομιστέον).[9] For if "Isaac"

4. For their emphasis upon eudaemonism he need have looked only at his Pythagorean models. See Euryphamus, *ap.* Stobaeum, IV, xxxix, 27 (Wachs., V, 917); τέλησς δὲ καττὸν βίον, αἶκα εὐδαίμων γένηται· ἀ γὰρ εὐδαιμονία τελησότας καὶ συμπλάρωσίς ἐστι τῶν ἀνθρωπίνων ἀγαθῶν. Cf. Hippodamus, *ap.* ib., §26: καττὸν βίον δὲ τέλησι τοὶ μὴ μόνον ἀγαθοὶ ἐόντες ἀλλὰ καὶ εὐδαίμονες. ἀ μὲν γὰρ εὐδαιμονία τελειότας ἐστὶ βίω ἀνθρωπίνω (Wachs., V, 909, ll. 19 ff.).

5. For Isaac as Happiness see also *LA*, iii, 86 f.; *Mut.*, i, 130–176; *Abr.*, 200 ff.; *QG*, iii, 53; iv, 17.

6. *Det.*, 60. The definition is an epitome of Aristotle's remarks about happiness. See *Eth. Nic.*, 1098a 16: τὸ ἀνθρώπινον ἀγαθὸν ψυχῆς ἐνέργεια γίνεται κατ' ἀρετήν, εἰ δὲ πλείους αἱ ἀρεταί, κατὰ τὴν ἀρίστην καὶ τελειοτάτην. ἔτι δ' ἐν βίῳ τελείῳ. The "human good" is of course εὐδαιμονία as the context shows. See also *Eth. Eud.*, 1219a 38: ἡ εὐδαιμονία ζωῆς τελείας ἐνέργεια κατ' ἀρετὴν τελείαν. Three lines below (1219b 2) it appears that χρῆσις is interchangeable here with ἐνέργεια.

7. *Cher.*, 8.

8. *LA*, ii, 82: τέτοκεν ἡ ἀρετὴ τὴν εὐδαιμονίαν Ἰσαάκ.

9. Compare the ideal king of Ecphantus: "He is like the rest [of mankind] indeed in his earthly tabernacle (σκᾶνος), inasmuch as he is formed of the same material; but he is fashioned by the supreme Artificer, who in making the king used Himself as the Archetype." Quoted in my "Hellenistic Kingship," p. 76. The confusion of parenthood, by which a hero's father would be called now God, and now a human being, is an echo in Philo of one of the commonest elements in Hellenistic religions. See A. D. Nock, *Conversion* (1933), pp. 232 f.

means "laughter," according to the true witness of Sarah, God is the maker of laughter, and God would most accurately be called the father of Isaac. "And He gives the wise Abraham a share in His own title, and by cutting off pain He gives to Abraham gladness, the offspring of Sophia."[10]

Some of the virtues are ever virgins, but some are changed from being women to being virgins, like Sarah: for "it ceased to be with her after the manner of women" (Gen. xviii, 11) when she first conceived Isaac, τὸ εὔδαιμον γένος.[11]

Moses represents Sarah as conceiving at that time when God visited her in her solitude (Gen. xxi, 1), and yet bringing forth, not to the One who made the visitation, but to the man who aspires to achieve Sophia, whose name is Abraham.[12]

In another passage Abraham rejoices that he is to beget Isaac, but he is apparently in error, for the Torah clearly indicates to Philo one of the holiest secrets of the Mystery for initiates, namely that it is "the Lord who begat Isaac."[13] As a result Isaac is not

a human being, but is a synonym of that best of the commendable emotions, joy, laughter; he is the unprojected son of God who gives him to souls that are entirely devoted to peace as a soothing and comforting presence.[14]

How far this allegory of Isaac as the son of God by a virgin was carried out in the *De Isaaco* it is impossible to know, and that impossibility makes it also impossible to judge how literally Philo believed that Isaac as the ancestor of the race was the miraculous son of God. There is at least a possibility that Philo developed the idea in a way so closely parallel to Christian doctrine about the birth of Jesus that Christian copyists suppressed the text.[15] But it seems clear that as Abraham was to Philo a great savior of the race by being an incarnation of the cosmic order, and so bringing *faith* to man, Isaac, as a still higher representative of the same order, brought them that εὐδαιμονία which transcends human effort.

Another contribution which he made was the fact that he reached so exalted a state not by effort or instruction, but as one "self-taught," τὸ αὐτο-δίδακτον καὶ αὐτομαθὲς γένος,[16] ἡ αὐτομαθὴς σοφία.[17] Indeed Isaac is the

---

10. *Det.*, 124. 11. *Post.*, 134.
12. *Cher.*, 45. 13. *LA*, iii, 218 f.

14. *Mut.*, 131: ὁ ἄνθρωπος ἀλλ᾽ ὁ συνώνυμος τῆς ἀρίστης τῶν εὐπαθειῶν, χαρᾶς, γέλως, ὁ ἐνδιάθετος υἱὸς θεοῦ τοῦ διδόντος αὐτὸν μείλιγμα καὶ εὐθυμίαν εἰρηνικωτάταις ψυχαῖς. Εὐπάθεια is used here in the sense of the Stoics. The πάθειαι are condemned, but these εὐπάθειαι, χαρά, εὐλάβεια, and βούλησις are commended. See Diog. La., vii, 115 (*SVF*, III, 431).

15. It is interesting to note in this connection that in the story of Abraham in the *Quaestiones* the section dealing with the birth and sacrifice of Isaac has again disappeared. The coincidence is at least suggestive.

16. *Mut.*, 1, 88, 255; *Ebr.*, 60, 94; *Sobr.*, 65; *Mig.*, 101; *Som.*, i, 194.

17. *Det.*, 30. The phrase is also used of Adam in *Opif.*, 148, where it is synonymous with, or closely allied to, kingliness. Cf. *Immut.*, 4.

stock example of those who have "dispensed with the instruction of men and become apt pupils of God, and so have received τὴν ἄπονον ἐπιστήμην, and have been changed into τὸ ἄφθαρτον καὶ τελεώτατον γένος."[18] He is the exponent (κανών) of φυσικὴ σοφία[19] or of φυσικὴ ἀρετή,[20] in contrast with Abraham whose wisdom and virtue were διδασκαλική, and to Jacob in whom these were ἀσκητική. What Philo meant by the αὐτομαθὴς καὶ αὐτοδίδακτος σοφός he carefully explained:

He has not been improved by investigation, drill, and labor, but from his birth he has discovered ready prepared Sophia from above showered down from heaven, which he sucked in neat as he feasted, and so was in a constant state of that sober intoxication which goes with correctness of reason. For it was not a human being who was brought forth but a most pure concept, one noble by nature rather than by practices. . . . The self-taught genus is a new entity, one greater than reason and truly divine, and it subsists not by virtue of human ratiocination, but by divine madness.[21]

This self-taught knowledge, Philo continues, is so quick as to be something timeless. God is its expounder, and Himself sows the seed in one who is by nature ready to receive it. It is a knowledge which rises spontaneously. In another passage Isaac typifies

self-taught knowledge which comes by nature, and in contrast to the instructed knowledge of Abraham he needed only the grace of God, not at all His admonishment, for Isaak by nature achieved τὸ καλόν, and by means of the endowment showered upon him from above he was good and perfect from the beginning.[22]

So God taught Abraham, but begat Isaac, gave one the rank of pupil, the other that of son, though both were ἀρχέτυποι τῆς παιδείας ἡμῶν τύποι.[23] Isaac is the unique example of complete natural goodness; he is τὸ μόνον ἀπαθὲς εἶδος ἐν γενέσει.[24]

The De Isaaco must have contained much of this exposition of Isaac as the αὐτομαθής, for this conception is alluded to in connection with Isaac in the De Praemiis et Poenis (§§36, 59), the De Abrahamo (§52), and the De Josepho (§1), though again how far it developed these allegorical expositions it is impossible to say.

What benefit the moral achievement of Isaac had for future generations is not elaborated, but is strongly hinted. Philo spoke of the possibility of receiving "the inheritance of Isaac," the αὐτομαθής, a blessed event which

18. Sac., 7.
19. Mos., i, 76. Cf. QG, iii, 59. From Plutarch, Bruta Ratione Uti, 991 f., we learn that to be αὐτομαθής is to be taught by nature.
20. Abr., 52.
21. Fug., 166 ff.
22. Som., i, 160–162.
23. Ib., i, 173. Cf. ii, 10; Cong., 35, 38.
24. Det., 46.

would put an end to all spiritual labor, and result in the abiding presence of God, the bounteous one.[25] Again those who are but midway on the road to perfection, characterized chiefly by their perseverance (ὑπομονή), cannot yet see God, ὁ τῆς σοφίας ἡγεμών, but can apprehend Isaac, ἡ αὐτομαθὴς σοφία.[26]

The Self-Taught is nourished by no one, but is the nourishment of others, inasmuch as he is competent to teach others though unable himself to be taught.[27]

The picture of Isaac that emerges in the detailed commentary of the *Quaestiones* adds some striking features not only to the character of the Patriarch, but to the whole problem of the basic conceptions of the Mystery. For Pascher has rightly noted that the chief source of our knowledge of the Mystery in terms of the Sophia formulation, or what I am calling the Female Principle formulation, of the Light-Stream is the great allegory of Isaac in the *Quaestiones*.

This Allegory begins with the same conception of Isaac as that in the *Allegory* and *Exposition:*

Isaac is mind, master instructor of himself, and educated by himself, himself distinguished from indistinct things (distinctus ab indistinctis), rejoicing always and daily in the Father, in God, and in all His works; not discontent with what is made in the world, completely satisfied that all things are done according to nature by divine providence for the salvation and preservation of the universe.[28]

The story of Isaac, as an allegory of the mystical achievement of those "who hasten to immortality,"[29] is centered about his marriage. Such a man could not take a Canaanite woman as his wife, for Canaan means "stupid." He could not himself go to Chaldea, for that would be a desecration: it would indicate that he had gone back to the error of thinking that astronomy was the highest approach to contemplation of the invisible and incorporeal nature. His wife, like Abraham, must be an emigrant out from such a conception.[30] Actually the servant gets him a wife from the house of Nachor, which means Quiet Light, the light of the soul, Sophia.[31] At evening, the symbol of the setting of the material light of the corporeal nature, the servant comes to the divine fountain, Sophia, which flows out like water.[32] Rebecca who meets him there is Perseverance, that is, she suffers neither decrease nor increase, since she is Sophia, the daughter of God, and mother of all things, especially of those people who are completely purged in soul.[33] The pitcher

25. *Mig.*, 29 f.   26. *Det.*, 29–31.   27. *Mig.*, 140.
28. *QG*, iv, 88.   29. Ib., 103.   30. Ib., 88 f.
31. Ib., 93. I am consistently translating *sapientia* as "Sophia."
32. Ib., 94. So I understand the cryptic "quae (sapientia) secundum virtutem sumit aquae similitudinem." Cf. *Fug.*, 194–196.
33. *QG*, iv, 97.

she carries contains the *aquam rerum,* that is, *legem, voluntatem, et contemplationem,* which are seen *secundum sapientiam.*[34] She was virgin and beautiful, virgin from any corruptible seed of desire in her mind, the sort sowed by man; yet she received the pure seeds of divinity which the Father of All sows from above within us, the incorporeal and intelligible seeds.[35] As she fills the pitcher, so must man fill his soul from the fount of God, the eternal Sophia;[36] like the servant running to Rebecca we must run up to Sophia to be filled with that true Sophia which God extends out as from a generous fountain.[37] The drink he gets is compared to the manna of the wilderness, obviously another symbol for the same experience.[38] As he drinks he recognizes that it is not his own Sophia but the Sophia of God that he is getting. After this drink he is no longer a boy, but a man matured. He understands the nature of his master, clever Sophia, and so stands quiet while the divine Logos speaks within him, speaks without vocal organs, explaining to him the Road which leads to virtue and immaterial prosperity.[39] The figures have become badly confused, and likewise, if we were not prepared, the sexes. Sophia is plainly identical with, or brings with her, the divine Logos. But this only means that here as elsewhere there is no metaphysical importance in the mythological allegory of the Stream as either the feminine Sophia or the masculine Logos.

"In accordance with the divine Mysteries" Philo allegorizes the earrings and bracelets the servant gives Rebecca. They typify the fact that the material universe is harmonized and ruled by the Logos as the mind in man should affect his material parts, and that Rebecca can comprehend the unity of the Logos.[40] The servant asks for a place in the home of Rebecca's father, i.e., with the divine Logos, where one may abandon all mortal and corruptible things.[41] Yes, she says, in her father's house the beasts are separated from the place where the human beings, the rational as contrasted with the material, can find rest.[42] So the man praises God that in going to the house he is to receive the Word of Virtue,[43] that is the Logos-Sophia. At this point Philo stops to throw Abraham into the picture by explaining the fact that when the servant addresses the "God of Abraham" the servant is implying that Abraham has been the intercessor through whom he is getting this mystical experience. And indeed Philo generalizes by stating that any man who tries to reach the heights in any other way than this which nature had ordained will only work his greater ruin. Apparently Abraham is the inter-

34. *QG,* iv, 98.   35. Ib., 99.   36. Ib., 100.
37. Ib., 101.   38. Ib., 102.
39. Ib., 107 f. Further on (§125) Philo speaks of the Road of Truth to Virtue as being *intelligentia et sapientia.* It is proportional, equal, secure, and short. The whole is an allegory of the Road (§131).
40. *QG,* iv, 110.   41. Ib., 111.   42. Ib., 112.
43. Ib., 113.

cessor stated by nature to be the unique medium of approach.[44] For in Abraham are present the pure forms of justice and truth,[45] and Abraham is the servant's "City of Refuge," law, and judge.[46] In contrast to Rebecca, temporarily Reason, Laban is sense-perception, so while she looks after the man, he tends to the beasts.[47] In this connection we are reminded that Philo is throughout talking of the Mystery, for he distinguishes the sorts of teaching to be given to those with ears purged and those not purged. There is a good teaching for both, he says, but to the good man is given instruction that elevates him to heavenly greatness and sublimity, and so makes him master of terrestrial things.[48] The experience of the servant is in a sense epitomized in the following:

They understand the true adoration who drink from that fountain not to be approached and touched because it is incorporeal. Such are equipped with wings and soar aloft; they fly about the Father and Creator of the universe and call Him Blessed, Founder, Omnipotent, God of Truth, the One who in true essence fills all things with His Powers (*virtutes*) for the salvation (or security) of the universe.[49]

Rebecca is given to the servant who hastens by the right course to give her to the Seft-Taught,[50] and happy is he to whom Virtue comes as wife.[51] She brings as servants the qualities that make for steadfastness.[52]

Open thy spiritual eyes, Oh Mind and behold him who is thy example, Isaac, Laughter free from sadness: he rejoices uninterruptedly and continually beyond all things made by God. For thou shalt see him preserved from indiscriminate and turbulent thoughts, making his way with no uncertain steps to Sophia, who is immune from great evils, from ignorance and disorder. See him in true and proper way entering into converse with Sophia at the well, that is, at the marvelous and divine fount which is called the fount of Vision.[53]

Such an experience is again a vision of the super-sensible world of Him who is, and of the Forms,[54] as well as an escape from empty opinion.[55] Isaac had gone out, on the evening when Rebecca was to arrive, to meditate in the field. So "he who is removed from the consideration of visible things has it as his reward that he begins all alone to live a solitary life with the invisible God." It is a life with the Form that surpasses the Good, Sophia, and the Best. Such a person is a God-bearer (*deifer* = θεοφόρος), that is, he is inspired or deified, for he has been *initiated into the divine things* to the extent that he is almost wholly possessed by God. He is instructed by the divine Law (certainly not the laws of Moses!) in how properly to produce fruits

44. Ib., 114.
47. Ib., 117–119.
50. Ib., 129.
53. Ib., 138.

45. Ib., 115.
48. Ib., 121.
51. Ib., 134.
54. Ib.

46. Ib., 120.
49. Ib., 130.
52. Ib., 136.
55. Ib., 139.

that are the immortal foods of the soul. It is at evening when this happens, that is, as usual with Philo, at the setting of the light of visible opinion. Then:

He is taught that the monuments of Sophia and of Vision *are not the holy books of the Lord* but the divine command and the divine Logos, which warns one who would fall away, and which is itself very near, yet as though it were not there.[56]

It speaks without projection of words, and gives the mystic confidence with the incorporeals, and converse about the Intelligibles that are themselves concealed. It is the Father of Sophia that is now teaching him.[57] Rebecca comes to him and gets down from the camel as Sophia comes down to the mystic.[58] She is veiled as are the inner secrets of the Mystery (*quicquid est intus et in adyto*), to be revealed only to one who desires Sophia, but not to the unskilled or uninitiated.[59] The wedding chamber is the house of Sarah, Sophia, Mother of the Self-Taught, Isaac, but herself having no mother. The house is itself here the ὀρθὸς λόγος (*recta ratio*) of Sophia, which has become the wedding chamber for the marriage of the Self-Taught with the eternal Virgin, Perseverance, "from whose love," Philo prays, "may I never cease."[60] Now Isaac is consoled for the loss of his mother, for in Rebecca he has found Sophia again, and not as an old woman, but as one who is eternally young in incorporeal beauty.[61]

Here ends the amazing allegory of Isaac, the Self-Taught, who achieves the mystic marriage with Sophia the ever Virgin, daughter of God, daughter of the Logos, wife of God, mother of the Logos, scatterer of the seeds that ennoble man, man's mother and man's own wife in mystic rapture. A greater jumble of sexes and incests could not be imagined, for at the end it is evident that Isaac has married his own mother. The whole is an approach to the incorporeals and to God, and is but another figure, we feel, for the union with the Logos. The God who reveals Himself in the Powers has not once appeared. The Sophia and Logos are adequate symbols of the Light-Stream.

Pascher has an illuminating discussion of the place of Sophia in the mysticism of Philo,[62] although his conclusions are not always convincing. He quotes the important passage, *De Fuga*, 108–112, in which it appears that the Logos is the Son of God by Sophia, surrounded by light and wearing the cosmos as a robe. He is the sub-ruler under God of the cosmos and is the bond which holds it together. According to *Quaestiones in Genesin*, iv, 97, as Pascher indicates, Sophia is herself the daughter of God and the first-born mother of all things. From the fact that Philo parallels Sophia with the source of the stream which waters Eden, Pascher concludes that she is to

---

56. *QG*, iv, 140.   57. Ib., and §141.   58. Ib., 142.
59. Ib., 143.   60. Ib., 145.   61. Ib., 146.
62. *Königsweg*, pp. 60 ff.

Philo a goddess of the Earth, like Plato's "nurse," but he has apparently not noticed that the stream here irrigates the plants and shoots of souls that love virtue.[63] It will be noticed that Sophia and God mutually find delight in each other. But as the Logos was the stream from Sophia, her son in the one passage, he is the source and she the stream in *De Fuga*, 97.[64] Pascher[65] would explain this contradiction by his theory of Philo's twofold Logos, the higher Logos, the Monad, who is the source of Sophia, and the lower Logos, the Dyad, which is their son, and wears the cosmic robe. But we have seen reason to question Pascher's second Logos. My own explanation would be to admit Philo's contradiction, and account for it by the fact that the mythologies had no absolute value in Philo's mind in any case, but were all only figures of speech for his very real conception of the great light-streaming God. Terms for stages in the Stream were of relative unimportance, for actually there were no stages. The whole Stream was the Logos, and it might be called Sophia just as well. If one began with the Logos symbolism, as in the Logos and Powers formulation, Sophia could fit in incidentally as a lesser manifestation of the Logos. If one began with the Sophia symbolism, the Logos could be her son streaming into the cosmos. The point which the story of Isaac brings out most sharply is that we have here two distinct mythologies of the Light-Stream, each of such importance that it has forced itself into the exegesis.

Pascher's service has been distinguished in his analysis of the possible sources for the Sophia mystery, and in finding close parallels in our fragmentary Isis remains. Interesting as is his material, I do not think he has said the last word on the matter. Beside not agreeing with him in connection with the existence in Philo's thought of a Cosmic-Logos distinct from the Monad-Logos, I feel that he has not recognized the problem of the two types of Mystery, that of Sophia and that of the Powers, and that he had similarly confused the Persian sources with the Isiac. Plutarch has actually three sources, not two, for the mythology of his *De Iside*, one Egyptian, one Persian, and one Greek, the three fused and interpreted in mystic philosophy of Greek origin. How much the combination of the three mythologies, or their interpretation, is his own work it is now impossible to say, but the writings of Philo seem to me to indicate that they were all in process of combination at least by his time. Philo keeps the Mystery of the Powers almost entirely distinct from that of Sophia. In a few passages[66] there is a passing attempt at fusion, but when regarded from the point of view of the Patriarchs as mystic types it is at once apparent that for all of Sarah's marriage with Abraham she, and the Sophia *motif* of which she is part, constitute a mystic mythology of ascent parallel to that of the Powers. The Powers

63. *Som.*, ii, 242.
65. *Königsweg*, pp. 68 f.

64. And God the source in *Sac.*, 64.
66. As *Fug.*, 97.

do not appear at all in the story of Isaac because either mythology was indifferently interchangeable with the other, indifferently because neither had more than figurative value. In the allegory of Abraham, it will be recalled, Philo used both formulations in parallel simultaneously.

In comparison it is worth repeating that while Isis is in Plutarch the daughter and wife of God, mother of the Logos, one who is female in her relations with God, male in her power to scatter divine seeds in the initiates,[67] it is in Persia that Plutarch finds the conception of Light, Ormuzd, radiating out seven Powers: εὔνοια, ἀλήθεια, εὐνομία, σοφία, πλοῦτος, and ὁ τῶν ἐπὶ τοῖς καλοῖς ἡδέων δημιουργός.[68] These seven are not Philo's seven Powers, though in each case it is seven, and many of them are strikingly reminiscent of Philo. Sophia appears here, but not at all in the rôle which she obviously played as Isis, where she could not remotely have been conceived as fifth removed from the Source of the Light-Stream. If Plutarch is to be taken as guide (and we have no other) it would appear that the Powers in Philo had their origin in an attempt to reconcile Jewish thought with Persian conceptions, and that the Sophia figure had the same relation with Isis. The spectacle of Philo, Plutarch, and the Hermetica, in all of whom the three elements are present, suggests strongly that in Egypt the Persian description of the Light-Stream was being regarded as a parallel with the Isiac (perhaps they had been so regarded since the days of Ikhnaton or of the Persian conquest of Egypt), and that both were in the process of assimilation by Greek thinkers. Pascher insists that Philo is in the same line as Plutarch in his handling of the material, that he knows more of the higher mysteries than Apuleius cared to write down, and that hence he has much to tell us of the higher reaches of the Isis Mystery.

On the lower stage, which Apuleius could tell us about, Isis herself first appeared to him in a robe representing the cosmos.[69] At the procession the next day it is notable that the initiates of both sexes wore *linteae vestis candore puro luminosi*.[70] It must have been with this same significance of light that the principal priests wore white garments,[71] and that when Apuleius was transformed from being an ass he was first naked and then clothed with white linen, in accordance with which robe he must look joyful.[72] This was apparently in anticipation, for at the first stages of the initiation he was given a robe representing the heaven, the "Olympian Stole." He had a flaming torch in his right hand and his head was "crowned with white palms,

67. On this Pascher quotes the striking passages, *Fug.*, 48–52, an allegory of Rebecca, and *Abr.*, 99–102, an allegory of Sarah. It is notable that Philo goes out of his way to indicate that the latter allegory is one he has learned from other commentators and is not original (as I am confident little of Philo is) with himself.
68. *De Iside et Osiride*, 47. See above, pp. 13 f., 46.
69. *Metamorphoses*, xi, 4.   70. Ib., 10.
71. Ib.   72. Ib., 14 f.

whose leaves stuck out after the manner of rays. So I was adorned like the Sun."[73] The prayer that follows is addressed to Isis as the cosmic deity.[74] What happened at the later stages we do not know, except that it was an initiation into the rites of Osiris, father of Isis, and that the priests of this rite wore the white linen robe also.[75] A passage from Plutarch already quoted[76] throws light upon this confusion. There we learn that the Isis robe was definitely a cosmic one, and the Osiris robe the φωτοειδές. Apuleius has deliberately been so vague in his description that he gives the reader no clear conception of the mystic rites. But Apuleius in general agrees with Plutarch in this: the priests of Isis wore the cosmic robe, those of Oriris one of white linen. Plutarch, inadequate as he is, is our only guide to the conceptions behind these robes and rites. He represents their significance in terms so philosophic that it is impossible to sift out the original, purely Egyptian, notions, those held by the ordinary native initiate. But it seems to me that his interpretation, so much like the mystic ideas of Philo, reflects what Isis had long come to mean to many Greek initiates in Alexandria.

That is, Philo is definitely giving us a picture of ascent through Sophia which is clearly the Hellenistic dream of ascent through the Female Principle; and since we know that Female Principle best from Plutarch's account of Isis and from Apuleius, Philo's similarities to the ascent there through Isis are striking. What must always be borne in mind, however, is that the Hellenistic dream of the Female Principle may well have been much older than its imposition upon the Egyptian legend of Isis. There are many things which Plutarch feels he must *read into* Isis, and these may well have included the whole notion of the Female Principle as savior. To say that Philo was looking to Isis as interpreted by such men as Plutarch is thus dangerous. It is just as possible, and indeed much more likely, that Philo himself felt highly antipathetic to the Isis myth and initiates, however they explained their faith, but powerfully attracted by that Hellenistic notion of the Female Principle which also thrust itself upon Isis. We might recall that a similar tendency existed in Orphism to make Greek goddesses into bisexual saviors, a tendency which there is no reason to ascribe to the influence of Isis. We have met the Orphic material before[77] and shall meet it strikingly again.[78]

What is clear is that a pleroma conception of the Light-Stream, apparently of Persian origin, and a Female Principle conception, of whatever origin, have both forced themselves upon the Judaism Philo represents, and that he is content with treating them, like Plutarch, as parallels, without adequately fusing them, partly because the two notions were not fused in his environment, and partly because of their relative unimportance to him anyway as

73. Ib., 24.
74. Ib., 25.
75. Ib., 27.
76. De Iside, 77. See above, p. 119.
77. See above, pp. 16 ff.
78. See below, pp. 270 ff.

mythologies. As types they were helpful, and as figures of the ascent. But it must always be remembered that the lower stages melted into one as soon as the mystic had reached the Source and could see the Stream from above.

For the mystic significance of this Sophia cycle Pascher[79] quotes *De Cherubim,* 42–52. This passage, not to go into the points on which I agree or disagree with Pascher, gives a number of instances in which God has fertilized women in the Pentateuch. Sarah, Leah, Rebecca, Zipporah, represent Sophia or Virtue, each of whom at her impregnation "receives the divine seed from the Cause, but brings forth to one of her own lovers, who is preferred above all others who seek her favor." A passage in Jeremiah (iii, 4) makes the idea behind all this clear, says Philo, for from that passage he concludes that God,

the incorporeal dwelling place of the incorporeal forms is the Father of all things, for He begat them. As the husband of Sophia God drops the seed of happiness for the race of mortals into good and virgin soil.

When God begins to consort with a soul He makes what was before a woman into a virgin (for God can have relations only with virginity) by removing the passions. The seeds He scatters are the Forms of the immortal and virginal Virtues (Virtue and Sophia are here parallel, as frequently). So must the mystic, if he would experience this impregnation, abandon his sense life and cling to Wisdom (ἐπιστήμη).

By this the rise of the mystic would seem to be that at first he purifies himself of bodily allegiance and so becomes virgin. In that state he clings to Sophia, who, as Pascher points out, is now playing a masculine rôle in impregnating the soul. In this union the soul becomes identical with Sophia (as feminine), and so can receive the Seeds of God direct in a higher marriage with the Cause. Such would be the scheme behind Philo, but it is not thus clearly stated for the simple reason, I believe, that such a presentation would, for him, be taking the mythological element too literally and seriously. As Philo has softened the mythological element in the Logos-Powers cycle because it violated his monotheism, so he has not cared to mark out too clearly the function of Sophia as a hypostatic personality. I doubt, that is, if Philo is himself doing more than using the terminology of the mysteries as a figure to bring out his much more philosophic conception of the ascent, and to allegorize the wives of the ancient heroes. For the possibility is before us here, as in the other cycles and mysteries, that he is drawing not at all directly upon the Isis cycle, but upon a long tradition in which the assimilation of mystic *motifs* had been aged and refined.

The great significance of Isaac, as it is brought out in the *Quaestiones in Genesin* has been expounded in his mystic marriage. It will have appeared

79. *Königsweg,* pp. 88 ff.

that now in discussing the pregnancy and delivery of Rebecca Philo is still showing the significance of the soul made pregnant from God through Sophia by that elusive changing of sexes which runs through the cycle. Rebecca is made pregnant "with the Forms of Sophia, which like the day and sun totally illuminate the thought and mind."[80] The first thing this Light does is to discriminate good from bad, so the two sons in her womb are abundantly described as representing these two principles. They are celestial light fighting with terrestrial light,[81] the immaterial forms against material forms,[82] virtue against vice,[83] one the immortal part of the cosmos above the moon, the other the mortal part below it.[84] The struggle between them is primarily the story of Jacob, and will be treated later. A few later sections are of interest in connection with Isaac. Isaac is forbidden by God to go to Egypt, for that realm is the body;[85] he is to migrate to the land God will show him;[86] he is given, as a Sophos, dominion over all earthly things.[87] When Abimelech saw Isaac having intercourse with Rebecca he was too imperfect to apprehend that what he was seeing was the mystic union where the mortal joins himself to the immortal forms which are in the likeness of God, and so the attainment of supreme happiness.[88] When Isaac digs anew the wells of Abraham he is clearing the way to vision of the rays of light of Sophia.[89]

One section is very interesting, because it shows how Philo is avoiding the Logos-Powers cycle for the Sophia cycle in interpreting Isaac. He comes to the question "Why did the Lord when he visited Isaac show that He was God?" (Gen. xxvi, 24). This, which would have thrown Philo at once into a passage on the Powers if found in the Abraham story, he here explains by saying that "Lord" is the name of a ruler and governor, "God" a name used because of benefits. God is truly made manifest in the latter way because he *gives out Sophia* not as a king to subjects, but as a benefactor among friends.[90] I see no suggestion here for connecting the two cycles. With every opportunity to do so, Philo has not attempted it.

Isaac's losing his sight is, "according to the allegorists," the falling away of human sight as the prophet gets spiritual vision. He has become the instrument upon which God plays using the Logos as a plectrum, and so he

80. *QG*, iv, 158.   81. Ib., 157.   82. Ib., 160.
83. Ib., 163.
84. Ib., 164. It is notable that in this allegory, which could easily have been made into the cosmic struggle of the East, Philo keeps to Greek religious motivation.
85. Ib., 177. Cf. *LA*, ii, 59.   86. *QG*, iv, 178.   87. Ib., 182.
88. Ib., 188.   89. Ib., 193.
90. This passage occurs in *QG*, iv, in a section not preserved in the Armenian, but only in the anonymous translation of a part of the *QG* published in Basel, 1538. This section Aucher inserted between §195 and §196 of his edition. There are eleven paragraphs, and the above is taken from paragraph 4. The paragraph is obviously an abridgement, and there may have been originally more about the Powers than now appears.

gives off a finely attuned sound in which Laws are made known.[91] He is anxious to bless the wicked son because he knows the good son is already taken care of, but the wicked one can be saved only by Isaac's prayers.[92] For the blessing of Isaac, as the blessing of a prophet, is the blessing of God.[93] Further on Philo warns the reader that the story has nothing to do with men at all, but with symbols of souls and their parts.[94] One wonders how Philo meant this. It might be taken to mean that he is denying any mystic importance to the careers of the Patriarchs as historic figures, and seeing in them only an allegory of the ascent of the soul. Yet so many other passages insist upon the importance for Israel and the human race of the fact that these Patriarchs actually did live their great lives, did become the νόμοι ἔμψυχοι and hierophants for men, that I do not believe the passage reflects more than a passing mood of Philo. Isaac who hunts out the sinful man to ennoble him with the blessing of God[95] was to Philo a symbol, but one cannot avoid thinking that Philo looked to him as a living and permanent reality.

The career of Jacob is likewise allegorized according to the Mystery, though his character is not so exalted as either Isaac's or Abraham's.[96] In the *Exposition* Jacob is contrasted with his father and grandfather in that he represents ἀρετὴ ἀσκητική, virtue won by ascetic discipline.[97] "He was gentle and a lover of mankind, a lover of the beautiful and good, of equality and humility. He ranked in the better order, was a protagonist of reason and the opponent of folly."[98] The treatise *De Jacobo* is lost, and we have to gather its substance, as in the case of the *De Isaaco,* only from the summary in the *De Praemiis* and from casual references. In the *De Praemiis* Philo summarizes his view of Jacob as ὁ ἀσκητής[99] by saying that he has had experience of every part of human life, and has spared no pains or labor to track out the great object of desire, truth. Humanity and the cosmos he found veiled in ultimate darkness, because they were ἀόριστος. Some people have pierced this darkness by happy guesses to come to a belief in a single God and Creator. Jacob went much beyond these people, for his eager desire for illumination was met by God Himself, who suddenly made shine upon him an incorporeal beam purer than aether. By this beam the conceptual world

91. *QG,* iv, 196.   92. Ib., 198.
93. Ib., 212.   94. Ib., 230.
95. Ib., 167.
96. The list in *Ebr.,* 94, leaves him out altogether.
97. *Abr.,* 52; *Praem.,* 49–51. Cf. *Mos.,* i, 76.
98. *Praem.,* 59.
99. §§36–51. The term is a constant epithet of Jacob, appearing in various forms throughout Philo's writings: e.g., *LA,* ii, 89; iii, 18; *Sac.,* 5, 17, 46, 64, 81; *Det.,* 45; *Post.,* 59; *Agr.,* 42, etc., throughout the *Allegory.* In the *Exposition: Abr.,* 52; *Praem.,* 27. See also *Mos.,* i, 76.

was revealed to him as it is guided,[100] though even he saw of God only ὅτι ἔστιν, not οἷός ἐστιν.[101] The experience was achieved, Philo insists, not by inference from a study of phenomena, but by direct revelation. For as the sun and stars are seen by their own light, so God, being His own effulgence (ἑαυτοῦ φέγγος ὤν), is seen by means of Himself alone, with nothing assisting or coöperating. "Those men are on the way to truth who apprehend God by divinity, a light by its light."[102]

Relatively little as Philo gives us of Jacob in what remains of the *Exposition*, it is clear that, like the other Patriarchs, he was explained to Gentiles in terms of the mysticism of the Light-Stream. In looking to the allegorical writings of Philo for material about Jacob, it may be well to fit the passages together from the *Quaestiones* and the *Allegory* according to the Biblical story of Jacob's life, for the material in the *Allegory* is very scattered, and the *Quaestiones in Genesin*, as we have it, breaks off early in Jacob's career.

Jacob, as has been indicated, is, even in the womb of Rebecca, the figure of all that is good as opposed to Esau, evil.[103] So from the beginning, his life is one of struggle.[104] The pottage for which Esau sells his birthright is fleshly desire, not actual pottage, "as say the silly detractors of Scripture who follow only the nouns and verbs."[105] The deceit of Isaac by Jacob throws Philo into a desperate allegory which attempts to represent Jacob as still the virtuous type throughout the incident,[106] the main point of which is summed up in the conception that, clothed in Esau's garment of external righteousness (even the worst men, says Philo, have some good points), Jacob gives Isaac the food of the Mystery (*cibum mysterii*).[107] The blessing that Isaac gives him is that he is a soul filled with Sophia and bedewed with Virtue, gifted with the Incorporeals, and bearing the fruit of virtue, virtuous conduct.[108] He is to have the dew of heaven, the Logos, and the fatness of the earth, control by the mind of the sense-life and the lower judgments. He, as master of Esau, is master of the lower parts of the soul according to the Law of the more just Nature.[109] When Jacob is in danger from Esau he wisely runs away, as all men should run from vice.[110] He is advised to go to Laban, which means that in the mystic advance a man may well spend some preliminary time in

100. *Praem.*, 37: καθαρωτέρα γὰρ αἰθέρος ἀσώματος ἐξαίφνης ἐπιλάμψασα αὐγὴ τὸν νοητὸν κόσμον ἀνέφηνεν ἡνιοχούμενον.

101. Ib., 44.

102. Ib., 45 f.: ἀλήθειαν μετίασιν οἱ τὸν θεὸν θεῷ φαντασιωθέντες, φωτὶ φῶς. Cf. *Mig.*, 39 f.

103. Cf. *LA*, iii, 88 f.

104. *QG*, iv, 163. Cf. *LA*, iii, 190 f.; *Sac.*, 17, 81, 135; *Ebr.*, 9 f.; *Cong.*, 62, 129, 176; *Virt.*, 208–210.

105. *QG*, iv, 168–175.

106. Ib., 203–211.

107. Ib., 213; cf. *Immut.*, 92; *Heres*, 251–256.

108. *LA*, iii, 192–194; *Mig.*, 101.

109. *QG*, iv, 214–218.

110. *Fug.*, 23 ff.

getting to understand his physical nature.[111] There he is to marry Sophia[112] rather than one of the daughters of folly, the Hittite women.[113] Here the *Quaestiones in Genesin* break off, and the rest of the story of Jacob must be reconstructed from the *Allegory*.

Jacob's dream on the way to Laban is very elaborately expounded in *De Somniis*, i, 2–188. It will be unnecessary to follow Philo through the devious ramifications of this allegory. It is taken as the chief of Philo's second type of dreams, that in which the mind comes so to move along with the universal mind that it becomes possessed by God (ἐξ ἑαυτοῦ κατέχεσθαι καὶ θεοφορεῖσθαι), and gets the power of prophecy.[114] There are three preliminary points to be discussed before he comes to the dream proper. Jacob is described in the Biblical account as having gone up from the Well of the Oath to Haran, and as having then "gone into a place" and lain down until the sun rose. Jacob's coming up from the Well of the Oath is the first point to be explained. The well is of course Wisdom (called σοφία or ἐπιστήμη),[115] but it is also the fourth element, the heaven in the external world and the mind in man.[116] Each of these is in its own world the highest element, mysterious in nature, the highest representation of deity, and the part fit to sing best the praises of God.[117] That is, Philo is making it very clear that the mystic experience of Jacob at this stage is the achieving of the lower Cosmic Mystery which we have discussed as the Mystery of Aaron. The fact that Jacob is on his way to Haran is indicative, in the second place, that he is still, while only a sojourner in the life of the senses, not freed altogether from them. He has yet to come to a masterful comprehension of the life of the senses, though he is by no means going to remain there.[118] The "place" where Jacob goes is the third preliminary point. This indicates that Jacob has not arrived at God, but has only come to the comprehension that there is a Deity beyond the material world, though that Deity was still quite incomprehensible to him.[119] What he finds is not God but the intermediate divine Logos (ὁ μέσος λόγος θεῖος). Indeed it immediately appears that what he experiences as ὁ μέσος λόγος was not the Logos in its entirety, but the λόγοι, that is, the manifestation of the Logos in terms of recommendations and teachings which have become to him like sacred laws.[120] In short, what he saw was a vision not from God but from God's attendant Powers.[121] This vision could only mean that when the inexpressibly brilliant Light of the supreme and invisible God shines in the soul the secondary beams of λόγοι, and, even much more those of sense, grow dim.[122] This leads Philo into a remarkable passage on God as light.[123] God is only by remote approximation

---

111. *QG*, iv, 239 f. Cf. *Fug.*, 46 ff.; *Mig.*, 213 f.; *Ebr.*, 46 ff.; *Som.*, i, 46.
112. *QG*, iv, 243.   113. Ib., 241 ff.   114. *Som.*, i, 2.
115. Ib., 6–13.   116. Ib., 14–34.   117. Ib., 35–40.
118. Ib., 41–60.   119. Ib., 61–67.   120. Ib., 68 f.
121. Ib., 70.   122. Ib., 72.   123. Ib., 73–119.

to be compared with the sun, since nothing visible can be compared with His invisible nature. Actually, while God is compared to light, and is light, the archetypal pattern of all light, still more accurately God is "older and more exalted" than any pattern, and it is God's Logos which is the archetypal pattern of light, with God something too abstract even to be described by that figure.[124] To have access to that Light in the holy and sacred Mysteries (αἱ ἅγιαι καὶ ἱεροπρεπεῖς τελεταί) one must discard the light and knowledge of the senses[125] So the Logos as Light brings the mystic complete refuge and salvation from his enemies (the impulses of the flesh).[126] God as Light sees and knows all things; and when we bring our secret sins to Him in repentance He purifies us and gives us inner peace by taking the sting from our consciences.[127] After a long allegory that adds little to the argument, Philo sums up his discussion of the Light of God. The point is that there are two grades of Spiritual Light, that of the archetypal and incorporeal beams of the reasonable source of God who brings man to perfection in initiation,[128] and who is available only for those who entirely leave the flesh behind; and that of the copies of these beams, the immortal λόγοι, popularly called the angels. It was this lesser type of vision that was given Jacob at this stage of his career.[129]

Jacob's hard bed and pillow seem quite appropriate to the man eager for virtue.[130] The man whose ultimate objective is to get the vision of God and rest upon the Logos begins by applying to his head, i.e. to his mind, one of the incorporeal intelligences, one of the λόγοι, which teaches him what he should know at this stage in preparation for the great wrestling match to come.[131] So he dreams his dream. The ladder[132] is the air reaching to the sky, and upon it Jacob sees the λόγοι of God, those ambassadors of God who are "the eyes and ears of the great king."[133] They are pure souls and extensions of the universal mind into the universe.[134] The Scriptural name "angels" is much better for them than the "demons" of the philosophers, since they are truly messengers from God to men, and from men to God.[135] God and the Logos are with them in their work of saving souls from drowning in their bodily constitution.[136] God is Himself accessible only to the souls completely purified from the body, but these λόγοι come into the minds of

124. Ib., 75. 125. Ib., 77–84. 126. Ib., 86.
127. Ib., 87–91.
128. Ib., 115: αἱ ἀρχέτυποι καὶ ἀσώματοι ἀκτῖνες τῆς λογικῆς πηγῆς τοῦ τελεσφόρου θεοῦ.
129. Ib., 115–117. Philo admits that some allegorizers here have interpreted the passage as meaning that Jacob has got the full vision of the Logos-Beams. He cannot fit such an interpretation into his general concept of Jacob's development (§§118 f.).
130. Som., i, 120–126. 131. Ib., 127–132. 132. Ib., 134, 144.
133. Ib., 140. The Persian origin of the symbolism is unmistakable.
134. Ib., 135. 135. Ib., 141. 136. Ib., 147.

those still unwashed and cleanse them with their beautiful teachings.[187] The ladder illustrates also the fact that at this stage the mystic is in a very vacillating stage, up and down between the higher and lower things.[188]

The dream has thus far taught us a good deal about Philo's conception of Jacob. In spite of the representations of Jacob as a man of virtue in contrast with his brother Esau, Jacob is a man who has actually a long way to go before he can get the vision of God, and be worthy of the Higher Mystery. He begins at first definitely in the Cosmic Mystery, and indeed in this description of the dream we have a great enrichment of the Cosmic Mystery as represented in Aaron and the temple. Further the relation of the Lower Mystery to the Higher in the life of the aspirant is made much more clear, and Philo's conception of the saving activity of God is unmistakable. For God reaches down by His λόγοι to the "great unwashed," meets them on their level, and gives them the sort of help they need at that stage. The familiar assertion that Philo, in contrast to Christianity, thought that spiritual rewards awaited only those who had in some way already purified themselves is a complete misconception. With the exception of Calvin's doctrine of "irresistible grace," Christianity, as well as Philo, has always regarded God as powerless to help a man who does not first want to be helped. Philo went no further than this in what he required of an aspirant.

It is notable also that Philo is shifting, with his λόγοι and Λόγος, from the Sophia formulation of the Light-Stream to the Logos-Powers formulation. In the case of Abraham the Sophia *motif* came in as a parallel to the other, while Isaac was described entirely in terms of Sophia. Jacob is interesting in that two conceptions of the Light-Stream are being blended even more closely than was done with Abraham to describe his mystical struggles. The God of the Powers emerges sharply in the God who is at top of the ladder and speaks to Jacob, and who is God, not as present in the universe, but as the incorporeal Being outside the heavens.[189] Philo points out that God is the "Lord God" of Abraham, but the "God" of Isaac in Gen. xxviii, 13, and curiously that it is Abraham, not Isaac, who is there called Jacob's father. Abraham was, as one who is "taught," in need of the two Powers, those of Rulership (ἡγεμονία) and Beneficence (εὐεργεσία), since he needed both legislative guidance and benefactions of grace to get along on his level. Isaac, the "self-taught," needed only the latter. Jacob is aware that Isaac's is a higher level, and prays that he may some day reach it.[140] But he is just now much closer to Abraham, and needs both. The vision of the God of the Powers is, as yet, only something which "he dreams about in an indistinct way" (ἀμυδρῶς ὠνειροπόλει). Only after the later vision does he become the "See-er," "Israel," and the son of Isaac.[141] Still, even now, he

137. *Som.*, i, 148.   138. Ib., 149–156.   139. Ib., 157 f.
140. Ib., 159–165; cf. *Plant.*, 90.   141. *Som.*, i, 166–172.

needs no longer fear,[142] for he is promised the ultimate possession of virtue,[143] and in his final stage as the man purified by perfect virtue he is going to be a saving influence among the nations of the earth, his fine flavor permeating into and ennobling the lives of others as the odor of spices goes far out to sweeten the lives of men.[144] God will be with him, and lead him back to the land of his dreams.[145] Yet his present inadequacy is finally indicated by the fact that when he awoke he thought that "God was in the place,"[146] showing that the true nature of God, which could not be subject to space in any sense, was quite beyond his comprehension.[147]

The dream of Jacob, to which Philo has devoted almost a whole book of the *Allegory*, has told us a great deal of Philo's conception of the Patriarch, of the spiritual struggle which he represented in the Mystery, of the relation of the Lower Mystery to the Higher; and it has brought us back again to the God of the Powers. For Jacob seems really to have experienced the Cosmic Mystery, and in doing so has had an intimation, but no more than that, of the existence of a realm beyond into which he has not yet penetrated. Before he is to be ready to go on to the immaterial realm, he has still much preparation to make.

Jacob has now to proceed to Haran and the house of Laban, the region of sense and matter.[148] His problem about getting Laban's daughters in the order he desires represents the point ever at issue between the man who understands Natural Law and the man who does not. The two daughters are respectively the encyclical studies and philosophy, and the "devotee of Sophia" (ὁ σοφίας ἀσκητής) knows that they must be taken in that order, not, as sophists insist, vice versa.[149] Treatment of this part of Jacob's life is sporadic and fragmentary. We know that Philo used the fact that "God opened the womb" for Leah as a symbol of divine and virginal impregnation, whose progeny was really the son of God, and only attributed to the earthly husband.[150] We too, if we turn from matter, can become pregnant in the divine Stream of beauty.[151] Isaac as the "Self-Taught" had had a sufficient mate in Sophia alone, but Abraham, and much more Jacob, had to have more alliances than this one. So Jacob needed two wives and two concubines to help him through the various aspects of his complicated struggles.[152] There is no suggestion that his relations with these, even with Leah, were the mystic marriage such as Isaac had experienced.

142. Ib., 173. 143. Ib., 174–176. 144. Ib., 177.
145. Ib., 178–183.
146. The text is dubious here. I read τῷ for Wendland's τῳ.
147. *Som.*, i, 184–188. 148. *Abr.*, 212–214. 149. *Ebr.*, 47–53.
150. *LA*, iii, 181; *Cher.*, 46; *Mig.*, 95 f.; *Cong.*, 7, 123; *Mut.*, 255.
151. *Post.*, 135. It is notable that Rachel, who is sense perception, does not provoke Philo to this allegory, though Genesis says the same of her. For further notes on the progeny of Leah see *Plant.*, 134 ff.; *LA*, i, 80 ff.
152. *Cong.*, 25–38.

In becoming a shepherd for Laban, Jacob is a type of the fact that the good king and wise man is a shepherd,[153] that is, he is a type of the Greek, Persian, and Egyptian ideal of the "Good Shepherd." But he cannot tend all sorts of sheep, which means that he has nothing to offer as a spiritual guide to all sorts of people. It is unreasoning men who need such a shepherd, but some people, or some aspects of one's constitution, are willfully and stubbornly unreasonable, and these are the hopeless part of the flock assigned to the sons of Laban.[154] They must be eliminated by the ascetic. But other parts of man, and other types of men, are only ignorant, and by careful training can be taught to align themselves with the higher life. To these Jacob is the shepherd.[155] For the general allegory of Jacob this shepherding represents him doing the work for which he came to Haran, the purifying and disciplining of the body to make him ready for the Greater Mystery to come.

The deceit by which Jacob got the better part of Laban's flocks is twisted by main force, even to the point of quite misrepresenting the Biblical story, in order to make the incident typify the true effect of Jacob's mystic shepherding. As Philo tells the story, the device of the rods produced not striped or mottled sheep, but white ones: that is, his effect upon the flock was to make them manifest the pure white of truth instead of the motley hue of those not yet developed in the Mystery.[156] In another passage the mottled sheep are explained as the symbols of the mind which has become impressionable to the marks stamped in by the Seal.[157]

Now that the flocks have come increasingly into Jacob's possession, Laban becomes angry, and Jacob is warned in a dream to run away. This dream and its interpretation are of great significance, since in connection with it Philo gives us one of the clearest of his pictures of the Mystery as a whole. For Jacob's dream is this time a vision of the Mystery in its various stages. It is described in *De Somniis*, i, 189–256. God's approach to man is still the approach of God, though it be made, as here (Gen. xxxi, 11–13), through an attendant angel.[158] To some the mystic word (ὁ ἱερὸς λόγος) is a command, like that of a king; to others it speaks what is helpful as a teacher to a pupil; to others it brings great benefit as a counsellor; but to still others it speaks as friend to friend, and in this sort of conversation it imparts many secret things which no uninitiated person may hear.[159] Jacob's experience here, like that of Moses at the bush and of Abraham at the sacrifice of Isaac, is of this highest type in which God speaks to him as a friend. For the dream opens by Jacob's being addressed, like these, by name.[160] So Jacob is at last marked

153. *Agr.*, 39–42.
154. The allegory is here immediately concerned with the control or shepherding by reason of the lower elements of the human constitution, but his thought was in general no less clear of the obligation of the sage thus to help other men, as *Agr.*, 42, shows.
155. *Sac.*, 45–48.   156. *Plant.*, 110.   157. *Heres*, 180.
158. *Som.*, i, 190.   159. Ib., 191.   160. Ib., 192–195.

as one of the φιλικὸς θίασος, the mystery group based upon friendship with God;[161] that is, he here begins to enter the final experiences that have set the other Patriarchs off from mankind.

In the dream Jacob is commanded to look and see, which means that now for the first time he can see with the eye of the mind, an organ up to that time clouded.[162] What he saw was the rams and he-goats mounting the females in the flock, some pure white, some variegated, some with ash-colored spots. The ram and he-goat, as leaders of their respective flocks, represent the two kinds of Logos, the one which purifies the soul and empties it of sin, the other which nourishes it and fills it full of rightful action. The females represent those aspects of our nature, or those people, who are rushing with zeal to δικαιοσύνη.[163] The intercourse which Jacob dreamed about was, then, the intercourse of the Logos with souls that are fertile and virginal, an intercourse which both purifies and nourishes; it is the intercourse of Perfect Virtue with well-grown souls. It is not the intercourse of our irrational natures, our bodies, but the scattering of the seeds of Sophia. The offspring of this mystic marriage are of three sorts, white, variegated, and striped.[164] This is not, what it would first appear, a mixture of the Logos-Powers formulation of the Stream with Sophia. It is throughout the Sophia formulation, a formulation by which the Logos could appear to represent Sophia in masculine aspect, but one which had no room for the Powers.

The three types of offspring of the Logos or Sophia by human souls are the three grades of experience familiar to us from the three courts of the temple. The white sheep are the souls who are in the Highest Mystery and so are excessively white,[165] for they are like unblurred light and the brightest possible effulgence, such as is a beam of the sun on an unclouded day at noon.[166] The variegated (ποικίλα) are marked not with a motley of forms and characters like the spots of unclean leprosy an emblem of the unstable life of the fickle mob, but are shaped with seemly lines and stamped images of a sort to produce together musical concord. The harmony and marks, he explains at length, are those of the cosmic forms, made known through the encyclical studies. But these forms, as copies, are the work of Bezaleel, the master-builder of the tabernacle (Ex. xxxi, 2 ff.), in contrast to Moses who deals with the archetypal natures, and to Sophia who marks out a variety of forms, and so makes the cosmos into the great ποίκιλμα. The man who is in the stage of being an aspirant (ὁ ἀσκητής) has for his objective the forms

---

161. Ib., 196. One recalls the obvious cognate: "No longer do I call you servants; for the servant knoweth not what his lord doeth: but I have called you friends; for all things that I have heard from my Father I have made known to you" (John xv, 15). In §193 this group of Patriarchs is referred to as τὸ τῶν φίλων συνέδριον.
162. *Som.*, i, 199.   163. Ib., 198.   164. Ib., 198–200.
165. Not λευκοί but διάλευκοι, as Philo points out in §201.
166. *Som.*, i, 202.

as they appear in the sky and on earth, that is, in the cosmos, the house of Sophia.[167] It is quite clear that in contrast to the experience of pure Light of the first group, this group stands for the men who are in the stage of the Cosmic Mystery.

The third type of sheep in the vision are those with ash-colored spots (οἱ σποδοειδεῖς ῥαντοί). The significance of these also is to be found in their symbolism of the Road to καλοκἀγαθία. They represent the beginning of Sophia, where the beginner is sprinkled with ashes and water to remind him of his own humble and unworthy nature. For he is himself, and in himself, made of such elements, and so he must begin by sharply visualizing his lowly estate, and by putting off all arrogance, the sin which God hates most of all.[168] So before the priest can advance to the cosmic sacrifice he must first be reminded of "human nothingness" (ἀνθρωπίνη οὐδένεια) by being sprinkled with water and ashes. He must know himself.[169]

The man who has not yet achieved perfection (ὁ ἀσκητὴς ἅτε μήπω τέλειος) deals with these three stages, or conceives them, imperfectly. One sees them in their perfection in the ordinance of the high-priest. This comparison seems at first one between Jacob, as the man who is ὁ ἀσκητής, and so has not gone through the whole experience, and the high-priest, who does go through it all. But what Philo seems to be contrasting is the inadequacy of Jacob's dream symbolism to make clear the three stages of the Mystery as contrasted with the perfect symbolism of the complete temple service. Unless Philo is here quite inconsistent, the high-priest, as such, was not one who had achieved final perfection in any way comparable to Moses. So here Jacob's representation of the Mystery, as he got it in a dream when still not perfect, is contrasted with the representation Moses gave us in the three stages of the temple worship. The first stage is the purificatory sprinkling with ashes in the outer court. The second stage is the putting on of the cosmic robe to sacrifice in the inner court. By putting on this robe the highest element in man's ψυχὴ λογική, i.e., we understand, the ἡγεμονικόν, the logos in man, is united with the ἡγεμονικόν of the cosmos, the divine Logos, son of God, so that man in his highest aspect worships God together with the highest aspect of the cosmos. The third stage is that of the "purely white." For this the priest puts off the cosmic robe and puts on one of white linen

which is a symbol of vigor,[170] of incorruption (ἀφθαρσία), and of the most brilliant light (αὐγοειδέστατον φέγγος).[171] . . . By these figures it is represented that there is no one guilelessly and purely worshipping τὸ ὄν who has not

167. *Som.*, i, 203–208.
168. This sin is ascribed to Laban in *Cher.*, 67–74. Laban thought that his children and cattle were his own, not knowing that as men we own nothing.
169. *Som.*, i, 209–212.
170. Εὐτονία seems to have been a synonym of ζωή.
171. *Som.*, i, 216 f.

first had to exercise a set determination in pouring contempt upon human matters, things which only bait, weaken, and ruin him. Next he sets as his objective incorruption, despising the presumptuous images made by mortals, and finally he is illumined by the unshadowed and brilliant light of truth, and is no longer attracted by those cousins of darkness, false opinions.[172] . . . So when the mystic teaching (ὁ ἱερὸς λόγος)[173] has purified us with the sprinkling vessel prepared for our sanctification, and has marked us with the variegated stripes by the secret formulae of true philosophy it leads into what is seemly and then makes us distinguished (διασήμους), conspicuous (ἐπιφανεῖς), and shining (λαμπρούς).[174]

Such a man has no longer anything to fear from Laban, for God has appeared to him.

Philo now proceeds to analyze the theophany itself.

God came to Jacob, says the Hebrew text, and said to him: "I am the God of Bethel." Some of the Septuagint manuscripts read this as obviously Philo's manuscript read, "I am the God who was seen by thee in the place of God." What or who, then, is the God of the vision, and does the text suggest two Gods? Philo indignantly repudiates the latter suggestion and asserts his monotheism. There is only one God here or anywhere else who is called ὁ θεός; it is the Logos that is θεός without the article.[175] Only the incorporeal souls that attend God can see God in His essence. He takes on the appearance of angels for the benefit of those still in the body: more accurately He does not change His unchangeable nature, but presents His radiating effluence, his δόξα, in a changed form. Yet this that is presented is not a copy, but is itself the archetypal model.[176] Popular legend speaks of God as appearing in various forms all over the world to different people, and this is true to the extent that God has to appeal to ordinary men in a form far from His true one.[177]

In this one case it was the Logos that was the angel, appearing to Jacob because he was not yet able to see the true God. This seemed to him to be God, as people unable to look at the sun or moon think the rays from these bodies are themselves the bodies.[178] His mind has indeed been strengthened to the extent that it can now see the Leader of the Powers (ὁ ἡγεμὼν πασῶν τῶν τοιούτων δυνάμεων).[179] The pillar which Jacob had set up before had been dedicated to the image of this appearance, i.e., to the element of stability

---

172. Ib., 218. A brief discussion of Joseph follows as the man who without preliminary purification, or the ultimate experience, just put on the middle cosmic robe (§§219–224). Joseph is himself a fascinating study in Philo's political theory, but his career has no connection with the Mystery.

173. Perhaps here, as often, this means the Bible. But I think the reference is clearly to the ἱερὸς λόγος of the Mystery he is describing.

174. Som., i, 226. It will be recalled that in Polybius X, v, 1, the λαμπρὰ ἐσθής meant the Roman toga candida.

175. Som., i, 229.   176. Ib., 232.   177. Ib., 234–237.
178. Ib., 239.   179. Ib., 240.

in the cosmos.[180] It was the dedication of the results of encyclical studies.[181] In a word, it had been the Cosmic Mystery. Now he has come through in the Higher Mystery to a vision of the Logos, the Leader of the Powers. Philo closes the allegory of the dream with an exhortation to his soul to go to Jacob, and from him to learn to conquer the passions, and so be able to take one's flocks (one's lower nature which has now become a flock quite rational and beautiful) and lead them back to the house of our Father.[182]

The dream suddenly stops here without mentioning the fact that God at the end commands Jacob to leave Laban. Philo is treating the dream as an epitome of Jacob's whole experience and significance, and for that it is highly valuable. In the fuller treatment of Jacob it must have been rather a preliminary vision and call, for not until he had left Laban did he himself have the ultimate experience. And it is to be noted that even in this isolated treatment Philo does not say that Jacob put on the white robe of light as a result of the dream.

For it was Jacob's flight from Laban that represented his final leaving of the life of material things to go into the higher Mystery. Philo devotes several pages to the flight in *Legum Allegoria,* iii, 15–27. The wise man may face the lesser temptations, but when the objects of sense threaten him as a whole, he can only run away.[183] His flight is over the river of the objects of sense,[184] that is, he is definitely now leaving the world of matter and sense for the spiritual world, here the world of virtue. One is reminded at once that in the great allegory of the Cities of Refuge the divine Mystery in its higher experiences lay beyond a river, the Jordan, in exactly the same way. The effect upon the life of the body, when the soul thus deserts it to run away beyond the river, is to leave it robbed and impoverished. For Jacob has taken with him the only virtues that were in the realm, his wives, Laban's two daughters, which stood, as we have seen, for the encyclical studies and the quest for Sophia. With these gone, Laban, as the body, protests that there is no longer left to him intelligence of any kind, but only ignorance.[185] Even the passions themselves have gone, for in leaving the body Jacob stole the teraphim of Laban and hid them. That is, the passions are now dead.[186] Only the man can do that to his lower nature whom God is leading into a vision of Himself in the unutterable Mysteries.[187] Jacob is now going into the final Mystery (τελειωθῇ) and so leaves the house of the senses for that of the soul in its higher aspects.[188]

However Philo may have dealt with the subsequent events in his extended analyses of the career of Jacob, little is left to show. Various fragments of

180. *Som.,* i, 241–249.   181. Ib., 250 f.   182. Ib., 255 f.
183. *LA,* iii, 15–17.   184. Ib., 18.   185. Ib., 20.
186. Ib., 21–27.   187. Ib., 27.
188. *Mig.,* 214. See note *ad loc.* by Colson and Whitaker.

the next three chapters of Genesis are mentioned, but in general the robbery of Laban, the terror of Jacob at the coming of Esau, and the last descriptions of the family before the story of Joseph begins, add as little to Philo's respect for the Patriarch, apparently, as to ours. It is surprising that for all the numerous references to the great wrestling scene, and the obvious fact that the career of Jacob is here to have its consummation, the incident itself which gave him title to be one of the greatest Patriarchs is not fully explained. Still there is sufficient to show that Philo must have gone on in the fuller stories of Jacob to make this the great scene to which he has been all this time coming. It was in this scene that the "man of effort" (ὁ ἀσκητής) became the "man who sees God." In this last stage of the struggle for virtue he changes hearing for sight, words for deeds, and progress for perfection.[189] Here is one of the best groups of passages for Pascher's theory that the Lower and Higher Mysteries were distinguished respectively as the Mystery by which one hears about divine things, becomes a "Hearer," and the Mystery in which one gets the Vision, becomes a "See-er." Jacob came to see τὸ ὄντως ὄν.[190] He has all along been wrestling with his lower nature, and his reward is the vision of that which is alone worth seeing.[191] The fullest description of Jacob's vision of God is in the De Praemiis, 43–46, and is especially important because it probably gives us a digest of the lost De Jacobo, that is, of Philo's more deliberate explanation as contrasted with the many casual and baffling references in the Allegory. Here Philo uses Jacob as the type of those rare men who have gone beyond the "heavenly ladder," the Lower Mystery, beyond the contemplation of God through His works, to the immediate comprehension of God ἐξ ἑαυτοῦ. Jacob has seen God, οὐχ οἷός ἐστιν, ἀλλ' ὅτι ἔστιν, not the nature of God but the fact of His existence. He has seen this not by inference from any of His created works, but "has been called by the One Himself who is willing to reveal His own existence to the suppliant." Philo feels that this needs some explanation, so as usual falls back upon the figure of the sun. God, like the sun, is perceived by His own Light. That is, Jacob's vision was apparently a vision of God not fully or directly, but in the Light-Stream. It was a vision of God in as much as the Light-Stream, the Logos, is God in His primary extension. But it was not the complete comprehension of God, for that, he specifically says, is impossible. That is, it is apparently only another way of stating the fact that he has risen, like Abraham, to the Logos, or like Isaac, is fully "married" to Sophia. Both figures appear in the Allegory. By such a vision, he says, one becomes united or identified with the object of the vision.[192] So the vision appears to have united him

189. Ebr., 82. Cf. Som., i, 129, where his ears are changed into eyes; Fug., 208; Conf., 72; Mig., 38 ff. In Conf., 146 f., Jacob sees God, and his "sons" are hearers.
190. Ebr., 83.   191. Mut., 81f.; cf. Praem., 51.
192. So I understand Post., 92: ὁ γὰρ ὁρῶν τὸν θεὸν ὑπὸ ἐκπρεπεστάτου κάλλους ἀγόμενος τῷ ὁρωμένῳ προσκεκλήρωταί τε καὶ μεμέρισται.

with the Logos, for by having seen "God as source (τὸν θεὸν ἀρχεγονώτα-τον ὄν) he has become the First Begotten of the One without beginning" (τοῦ ἀγενήτου γέννημα πρώτιστον),[193] and Israel, the one who sees, is a proper name for the Logos.[194] At the same time Philo says that Jacob "saw the divine light, that is, Sophia. . . . Man sees the Wise thing through Wisdom. And Sophia is not simply the organ of sight after the analogy of light, but she sees herself."[195] That is, Jacob sees Sophia by becoming identified with Sophia. The passages are not altogether satisfactory, but enough is here to make it clear that in the experience Jacob at last reached the height of the Mystery, was identified with the Logos or Sophia, and so got, to a certain extent, their vision of God.

We are quite in the dark as to how Philo explained the angel with whom Jacob wrestled. In one passage Philo has been talking about the fact that God has no name, or at least none that can be told to man. Not even the ministering Powers tell us His proper name, says Philo. For example, when Jacob was wrestling with "the Invisible," he said: "Tell me thy name," but the "Invisible" refused.[196] Was this "Invisible" one of the Powers, refusing to tell God's name, or God Himself refusing to reveal His own? Precisely on this question we should like a more adequate statement from Philo himself. Either answer would fit a part of this passage. It may well be that Philo did conceive of Jacob as going beyond the Powers to the Absolute, τὸ ὄν, in this experience, and for that very reason makes no point of it in the general discussion of the *Allegory,* since such an experience was not a regular part of the Mystery formulation, and it is that formulation that the *Allegory* is dedicated to expounding.

The shrunken thigh is the reward of Jacob's having his lower nature finally reduced to subjection.[197] But the end of his experiences is not by any means the total prostration of the body. We have had hints before that the final stage of the Mystery, after the mystic has abandoned the body to rise to a spiritual apprehension of God, is a return to the body to live the rest of one's earthly life so much its master that the body itself becomes a spiritual vehicle as the perfect servant of the spirit. To illustrate an allegory of Jacob's dying words (Gen. xlviii, 15) Philo gives us a new interpretation of the relation between the inner court of the tabernacle and the holy of holies. The former is a symbol of the "without," the latter of the "within." So the ark was gilded within and without. And the high-priest has an inner robe of white linen, an outer one that is embellished. Apparently Philo is here thinking of the high-priest as wearing the white robe under the cosmic robe, and this combination seems here the ultimate attainment for man. For from the

193. *Post.,* 63.
195. *Mig.,* 39 f.
197. *Som.,* i, 130–132; *Praem.,* 47 f.

194. *Conf.,* 146.
196. *Mut.,* 14.

time of the wrestling with the angel Jacob has the strength both of the im-material world in his soul, and of the created world, especially of man, in the body and the outer parts of the soul.[198] Perhaps this obscure passage may throw some light later upon some of the iconographical problems. At least we are certainly forced again to see that the Mystery for Philo was not com-plete until the glorified soul had been so brought back to face the problems of fleshly control and ethics, that in the end the Mystery solved, not hindered, the development of a fully rounded life in the flesh.

So the race Israel is benefited by the experience of its prototype. Indeed Philo can boast to the Romans that in the possession and practice of the Mystery of the Powers Israel has deserved to be called the "Race that Sees God." In their experience the frustrations of philosophy have been done away, its dreams fulfilled. For philosophy has never been able to manifest the Powers, since these are beyond reasoned inference from phenomena; far less could it contemplate the Divine Being who is beyond all beauty and goodness as we can formulate or conceive the terms.[199] These are now the objects of Israel's vision.

198. *Mut.*, 41–46.   199. *Legat.*, 4–7.

CHAPTER VII

MOSES AS PRESENTED TO THE GENTILE INQUIRER

At this point it may be well to remind the reader of the general line of thought we are following, for Philo's details have a way, in his own writings and in writings based upon them, of obscuring the general drift of an argument. In expounding the Mystery which seems to underlie Philo's writings we are taking the method Philo himself used in presenting "true Judaism" to the prospective proselyte. So after a few preliminaries, the explanation of Philo's notions of God and of Natural Law, of the lower Cosmic Mystery, and of Philo's attitude toward the Code, we have been approaching the Higher Mystery as Philo asked the Gentiles to do, through the great Patriarchs in whose stories the Mystery seemed revealed. There was much that he saw in Abraham that he does not bring out for beginners in the *De Abrahamo*, additional details which were found richly used in the *Allegory* and the *Quaestiones*. In the absence of the *De Isaaco* and *De Jacobo* we have had to rely almost entirely upon the more allegorical writings for the careers of these two Patriarchs, though the invaluable summary in the *De Praemiis et Poenis* has shown that these lost works only elaborated the fundamental conception of the Patriarchs in the *Exposition*. In following the Patriarchs, then, we have been following that method of presenting the Mystery which was originally Philo's own.

One important detail should be pointed out. Philo's allegory is proving to be very far indeed from sporadic. There is an extraordinary unity of purpose that emerges. One can take the story of a Patriarch, skip from the *Allegory* to the *Exposition,* and then to the *Quaestiones,* and however slightly a passage may treat a given incident in one of the careers it fits with amazing precision into the story of the Patriarch as generally allegorized for the Mystery. Philo's allegory does not always run true, but the astonishing thing is to find that it does run true in the great majority of cases. There is obviously a fixed, almost stereotyped, interpretation of the Pentateuch which predetermines his interpretation of any given text. And that stereotyped interpretation is the turning of the sacred narrative into the ἱερὸς λόγος of the Mystery according to a very precise formulation. For a man like Jacob, of whom we have no connected allegory, the various references to and allegorizations of the incidents in his career fit together into as orderly a picture as do the connected accounts of the others. This fact must be borne in mind as one of the most significant evidences for the existence and importance of the Mystery. Philo himself could hardly have developed this great allegory of the

Mystery *de novo*, and then broken it up into the myriad incidental allusions and fragments that he offers. Were the interpretation original with himself he must have presented his thesis with demonstration and argument, else his readers would have been at as great a loss to understand his purpose as moderns have been. On the contrary he assumes throughout the *Allegory* and *Quaestiones*, as he writes for sympathetic Jews, that they will understand his objective since they too are initiates. Without some preliminary knowledge of the Mystery for a guiding thread they could not possibly have understood his purpose. As we go on into the character of Moses the same phenomenon will become still more striking.

It has repeatedly appeared that for the Mystery the hero and hierophant of greatest importance was Moses. Yet in the *Exposition* there was no *De Mose*, although the general review of the Patriarchs in the *De Praemiis et Poenis* includes him after the others as the greatest of all. Actually the brief review of his career in that treatise is so much like the *De Vita Mosis* that I have elsewhere argued that Moses was not represented by a separate treatise in the *Exposition* only because on another occasion Philo had already written the *De Vita Mosis*, and supposed that the reader would have read it before receiving the *Exposition*.[1] It may well be that we too should have begun with it. As will shortly appear, its whole argument and presentation are closer than even the *Exposition* itself to the thinking of a Gentile. Moses is equated more explicitly with such current conceptions as the ideal King and the Hellenistic θεῖος ἄνθρωπος than was done in the case of the other Patriarchs. So marked is this difference that scholars have in general been blinded to the fact that the *Exposition* is likewise intended for Gentiles, though for Gentiles more advanced in their comprehension of the Jewish point of view. On the whole it has seemed best to reserve Moses for his logically proper place, as the great climax, rather than present him as the first example of the Mystagogues. So our next task is to set forth Philo's ideas of Moses, ideas so exalted that one might have called the whole Mystery "the Mystery of Moses." The *De Vita Mosis* was written "for those who ought not to be ignorant" about one who was in every way supremely great and perfect.[2]

The first book is designed to show Moses as the ideal king. Philo does not say so at the outset, but as he tells the story of Moses' youth and development he brings out by point after point the fact that Moses' character was the perfect representation of the ideal of kingly character, and at the end declares that he has been showing what Moses did κατὰ τὴν βασιλείαν.[3] Bréhier did the great service of recognizing the parallelism between Philo's conception of royalty and the Pythagorean kingly fragments, and indeed the

1. See my "Philo's Exposition of the Law and his *De Vita Mosis*," *Harvard Theological Review*, XXVII (1923), pp. 109–125.
2. *Mos.*, i, 1.   3. Ib., 334.

De Vita Mosis is one of our best sources for the notion. But as I have shown elsewhere that these fragments seem to represent the current Hellenistic ideal of kingship rather than the peculiar notions of a school,[4] the βασιλεία in terms of which Moses is described was quite in accord with the assumptions of Philo's Gentile neighbors. It will be noticed that Philo claims that he is drawing not only on the Bible but also on the oral tradition of the Jewish elders for his story and interpretation.[5] The interpretation is, then, he definitely states, not original with him.[6]

According to the *De Vita Mosis*, the great Lawgiver, who came from a distinguished ancestry,[7] was from his birth a child of finer aspect than ordinary people (ὄψιν ἐνέφαινεν ἀστειοτέραν ἢ κατ᾽ ἰδιώτην).[8] It was on this account that his parents tried to save him, and it was his εὐμορφία καὶ εὐεξία which appealed to the princess when she had found him. After he had been weaned he returned to the palace more developed than normal for his age (τελειότερος τῆς ἡλικίας).[9]

So he was thought worthy of a royal upbringing and training, and did not, like a mere child, delight in teasing, in laughing, and in other childish amusements, . . . but modestly and with dignity (αἰδῶ καὶ σεμνότητα παραφαίνων) he addressed himself to what he could see and hear that would benefit his soul. From the first, various teachers came from different countries, some on their own accord from the neighboring districts and the sections of Egypt, some brought over from Greece by large fees. In no great time, by the fine endowment of his nature, he had surpassed the powers of these teachers, for he anticipated their instruction and seemed to be using recollection rather than to be learning new things; and he went on quite by himself to penetrate into what was obscure. For great natures make many fresh contributions to knowledge.[10]

As good athletes need little training, and the best trees little cultivation, "the εὐφυὴς ψυχή anticipates instruction and is improved by itself rather than by its teachers."[11]

What Philo is doing, obviously, is to represent Moses, like Isaac, as the "Self-Taught," an idea which seems to have been the inspiration of the legend of the boy Jesus with the doctors in the temple.[11a]

A complete list of Moses' studies is given. After he had mastered the usual fundamentals, arithmetic, geometry, and music, both the theory and the practice, which he learned from Egyptians, they went on to teach him

4. See my "Hellenistic Kingship."   5. *Mos.*, i, 4.
6. For traces of this tradition in Hellenistic Judaism outside of Philo see Chapter X.
7. *Mos.*, i, 7.
8. Ib., 9. On beauty of form in the ideal king see my "Hellenistic Kingship," p. 72.
9. *Mos.*, i, 19.   10. Ib., 20 f.
11. Ib., 22.
11a. The notion may well be ultimately Iranian, since the same experience is narrated about Zoroaster. See A. V. W. Jackson, *Zoroaster* (1901), p. 31.

their priestly lore as hidden in the hieroglyphs. He had astronomy from the Egyptians and Chaldeans both, to get their different theories; Assyrian literature from native teachers; the Greeks taught him the rest of the encyclical disciplines. In all these studies he did not become a partisan of any single school, but sought everywhere and only for the truth, "since his mind was incapable of receiving any falsehood."[12]

To this comprehensive instruction he added the training of his mind to rule the body, to such an extent that he was the model of Plato's *Phaedrus,* a charioteer with the horses so completely in control that he could bring out their valuable potentialities without danger from their violence. The result was that his life was characterized by a perfect ἁρμονία of thoughts, ideals, words, and actions.[13] Naturally, says Philo, those who beheld him were astonished at such a novel spectacle, and asked themselves "what sort of mind this was that inhabited his body and was ἀγαλματοφορούμενος, whether it was human or divine or a mixture of the two, for he had no resemblance to ordinary men (οἱ πολλοί) but towered above them and was exalted to greater majesty (πρὸς τὸ μεγαλειότερον ἐξῆρθαι)."[14]

Philo has introduced a problem to which we shall return. Here he has only raised the question of the divine nature of Moses' mind without answering it. But while it is uncertain here whether Philo himself thought of Moses as θεῖος or μικτός, it is obvious that Moses did not seem to him to be ἀνθρώπειος. It is clear already that much as Philo had in mind the ideal king in the Pythagorean or current Hellenistic sense as he described the earlier Patriarchs, he is here developing the parallel much more thoroughly. Moses was distinguished in body and mind beyond οἱ πολλοί, and was exalted to majesty most of all in the ἁρμονία of life between these two aspects of his nature.

But in all his royal education he did not, like many of the ambitious Jews the readers knew, forget his Jewish loyalties.[15] Philo describes elaborately the enslavement of the Jews in Egypt, with pointed allusions to the courtesy due a foreign bloc in a country,[16] and relates that Moses used all his influence with the authorities to mitigate the Israelites' hardships. When Moses had killed one overseer, his enemies flocked to the king and incited him so against Moses that flight was the only recourse.[17] In Arabia, instead of relaxing and enjoying the tranquillity of his retreat or trying to ingratiate himself with local leaders, he went on with his self-training.

He had within himself a teacher, λογισμὸς ἀστεῖος, which trained him both in theory and practice for the best types of life, attuning theory and practice together, and directing him to reality rather than appearance. For only a single objective

12. *Mos.,* i, 23 f. 13. Ib., 29. 14. Ib., 27.
15. Ib., 31. 16. Ib., 32–39. 17. Ib., 40–47.

lay before him, the ὀρθὸς τῆς φύσεως λόγος, ὃς μόνος ἐστὶν ἀρετῶν ἀρχή τε καὶ πηγή.[18]

This was at the same time to "follow the wholesome impulses of his soul."[19] Like the typical king, Moses was oriented in the Law of Nature, the ὀρθὸς λόγος.

The incident of Moses with the daughters of Jethro at the well is told to show how Moses regarded justice as an unconquerable power, and acted as its inspired and irresistible instrument.[20] The appearance and βούλημα of Moses combined brought the rude shepherds to obey him,[21] and at once impressed Jethro.[22]

With all these elements from current descriptions of the kingly nature, Philo naturally made capital of Moses' having been a shepherd in Arabia. He points out the value of shepherding as a part of kingly training, in the same way that hunting trains a warrior. A king is honored by the title "shepherd of his people," and Philo concludes that, though the suggestion may seem ridiculous to his readers, a king's training ought to include the experience of being a practical shepherd of sheep.[28]

Then came the burning bush and the beginning of Moses' activities as ruler. The bush itself contained what might appear an image, θειοδέστατον ἄγαλμα, but without stopping for metaphysical allegorization, Philo is here content to call this εἰκὼν τοῦ ὄντος simply an angel.[24] The divine representation began to exhort Moses to undertake the care of the Jews. He was to give them their freedom, and lead them out of Egypt, in all of which God would be his aid.[25] The story of the commission adds nothing important to the Biblical narrative until the question of Moses' ability in public speaking arises. God tells Moses that He is the creator of the windpipe and all other organs of speech, and at His will all things will become articulate, and so when Moses speaks "it will be as though a stream of words flowed from a pure fountain smoothly and evenly without impediment." Aaron is to be simply an interpreter, "telling to the multitude what he gets from you while you tell him τὰ θεῖα."[26]

Philo's brilliant description of Moses' return to Egypt and of the plagues need not detain us. The exodus at last begins with Moses as the ἡγεμών. Moses

18. Ib., 48. Cf. *Plant.*, 121. 19. *Mos.*, i, 50. 20. Ib., 50–57.
21. Ib., 57. 22. Ib., 59. 23. Ib., 60–62.
24. Ib., 65–70. The image was not the fire, for in the midst of the flame was μορφή τις περικαλλεστάτη, . . . φῶς αὐγοειδέστερον τοῦ πυρὸς ἀπαστράπτουσα, ἣν ἄν τις ὑπετόπησεν εἰκόνα τοῦ ὄντος εἶναι.
25. Ib., 71.
26. Ib., 84. On the king's speech (λόγος) as a streaming projection of his royal nature by which he imparts the benefits of that nature to his subjects see my "Hellenistic Kingship," pp. 92–95.

had received rulership and kingly power not like those who force themselves into rulership by shock troops, infantry, and cavalry, and by powerful fleets, but because of his virtue and fineness of character, and kindliness toward all men, . . . and further because God who loves virtue and nobility gave it to him as a well deserved reward.[27]

It was given also because of the nobility of his soul, his magnanimity, and his hatred of evil.[28] This is the beginning of a very important passage on the kingship of Moses. Upon taking office, Philo tells us, Moses renounced a number of the interests that spoil the rule of kings. First he put from himself all ambition to found a dynasty through his sons.

For by using his will power, which was guileless and pure in all things small and great, he like a good judge subjected his natural love for his children to the impartiality of his mind.[29]

For his sole objective was the good of his subjects. On the same ground he was unique among rulers in refusing to make himself personally rich, and in eschewing those external trappings of royalty universally deemed valuable by kings and their councillors alike. He chose rather the wealth of Nature, and lavishness in that of which kings ought truly to have the lion's share (πλεονεκτεῖν), namely abstemiousness (ἐγκράτειαι), endurance (καρτερίαι), self-control (σωφροσύναι), keenness (ἀγχίνοιαι), comprehension (σύνεσις), technical skill (ἐπιστῆμαι), toils (πόνοι), discomforts (κακοπάθειαι), contempt for pleasure (ἡδονῶν ὑπεροψίαι), justice (δικαιοσύναι), instinct for the best (προτροπαὶ πρὸς τὰ βέλτιστα), legal censures and punishments for sinners (ψόγαι καὶ κολάσεις ἁμαρτανόντων νόμιμοι), and praise and honors, again according to Law, for the righteous (ἔπαινοι καὶ τιμαὶ κατορθούντων πάλιν σὺν νόμῳ).[30] As Moses renounced material wealth for these higher values, God rewarded him with

the wealth of the whole earth and sea, of the rivers and all things else that are either elements or mixtures of elements. For as God thought Moses worthy to share in the portion He had reserved for Himself, He committed to him the entire cosmos as a possession fit for His heir. Wherefore each of the elements was made subject to Moses as master and altered its inherent properties to become subject to his commands.[31]

Philo goes on to say that the good man is always given a share in the treas-

27. *Mos.*, i, 148; cf. *Praem.*, 54. Bréhier has rightly pointed out that this is a definite rejection of the Pythagorean theory that one of the functions of the king was to be a military commander. See *Les Idées*, p. 21.

28. *Mos.*, i, 149.   29. Ib., 150 f.

30. Ib., 152–154; cf. *Praem.*, 54. See Ecphantus, quoted in my "Hellenistic Kingship," p. 76: the king "claims the lion's share of the better elements of our common nature."

31. *Mos.*, i, 155 f.

ures of the world as he becomes a κοσμοπολίτης, but Philo's notion that Moses took a share in God's cosmic rulership had a deeper inspiration than this. The ideal king was in the Hellenistic world thought to be a man or deity so attuned to God that he brought his subjects cosmic peace, good crops, freedom from natural calamity. To be sure Philo had to give some account of Moses that would justify the stories of the nature miracles: but the account he gives was one quite in harmony with the thought-forms of his age. It should throughout be borne in mind how close Philo is coming to deifying his hero. Gentiles could have found no more exalted phrases to describe the kings whom they actually worshipped. Yet Philo has not yet gone far enough. "What, then?" Philo asks:

Did Moses not enjoy the benefit of a still greater κοινωνία[32] with the Father and Creator of all things in that he was deemed worthy of the same appellation? For he was called θεὸς καὶ βασιλεύς of the race. And he is said to have "entered into darkness (γνόφος) where God was" (Exod. xx, 21), that is into the unseen[33] and invisible substance which is the immaterial model of all things, and to have apprehended things unrevealed to mortal nature. And he put himself and his life forward into the middle like a well executed sketch, thus setting forth an extremely beautiful and divinely formed object as a model for those who wished to copy it. And happy are they who have stamped this image upon their own souls, or who have even tried to do so.[34]

Philo goes on to describe how the people are wont to copy, for good or ill, the ways of their rulers.[35] All this can now be summarized with Philo in the sentence:

And forthwith since Moses was to be also the lawgiver, long before that event he himself became the incarnate and vocal law (νόμος ἔμψυχός τε καὶ λογικός) by divine providence which appointed him for the future into a lawmaker without his being aware of it.[36]

32. It will be recalled that the ideal king got his laws by his association through life with Zeus in the *Minos,* 319 ff. The treatise is, as Taylor thinks, of late Fourth Century origin.
33. The mss. and editors agree upon ἀειδῆ, formless, but I have read ἀιδῆ. Philo seems reflecting here, directly or indirectly, the language of Plato's *Phaedo* 79a, where, by a singular coincidence, if nothing more, the Codex Bodlianus reads ἀειδῆ for ἀιδῆ. We are driven to the alternative that either ἀειδῆ has a meaning "invisible" not recognized in the lexicons, or that the text must be changed as I have done. For that the οὐσία which was τῶν ὄντων παραδειγματική was itself "formless" is nonsense.
34. *Mos.,* i, 158 f. On the king as the model see the pseudo-Aristotelian *Rhetorica ad Alexandrum,* 1420a 19, as quoted in my "Hellenistic Kingship," p. 92.
35. Victorian England itself produced Victoria and her standards, to an extent, but perhaps no more than Victoria herself colored her age. There are also to be remembered the England of the later Stuarts, and Versailles in its prime.
36. *Mos.,* i, 162. The translation of νόμος λογικός by "vocal law" is justified by the common Hellenistic notion that the king's business was to make articulate the divine realm and will into which he could penetrate. See for example the statement ascribed to Philip of Macedon in Stobaeus, xlviii, 21 (Wachs., IV, p. 254): Φίλιππος ὁ βασιλεὺς ἔλεγε, δεῖν τὸν βασιλέα

Moses is now fully a king by choice of the people and of God who arbitrated and approved.[37]

The story of the exodus continues, and Philo becomes so interested in the narrative that Moses appears only occasionally. At the passage of the Red Sea Moses was able to encourage his people during their terror by allocating (διανείμας) his νοῦς to associate invisibly with God, and his λόγος, here his speech, to encourage the people.[38] He spoke the truth about everything.[39] God was merciful to the Israelites in the desert because of His inherent

equity and benevolence, but too because God wished to honor the one He had ordained as their leader, and still more to set forth clearly to all how much Moses had of piety and holiness both in things visible and in things hidden.[40]

Moses was careful of every type of honorable obligation, even to letting the Edomites go unpunished for their unfriendliness.[41] He was a man

who did not vaunt himself in the authority of his rulership, but who cared for his people, honored justice and equality, and always dealt with a miscreant not with a view to his shame, but to the chastisement which would make for his improvement.[42]

For the most part Moses is lost in the story of the adventures of the Israelites. The character of Philo's intended audience is amply revealed in Philo's selection of events and way of telling the story. None of the set-backs, defects, and weaknesses of the race is told, except in those cases where the revolts and lack of faith were at once corrected by Moses' miraculous power to give them food and water. Only the sin of the young Hebrews with the daughters of Moab is told, but there to glorify the character of Phinehas, and with it the ultimate virtue of the race and the glory of the Jewish priesthood. Miracles are everywhere softened, given a rational explanation, or omitted. At the dividing of the Red Sea Moses' rod is mentioned but the reader is given to understand that the sea was parted by a stormy south wind of the kind which is known to produce the phenomenon, while the Egyptians were overwhelmed in the waves by a change of wind to the north.[43] The wood which Moses threw into the waters of Marah

perhaps only showed a power given it by nature, a power perhaps unknown, or perhaps it was endowed with that power now for the first time to meet the emergency.[44]

μνημονεύειν ὅτι ἄνθρωπος ὢν ἐξουσίαν εἴληφεν ἰσόθεον, ἵνα προαιρῆται καλὰ μὲν καὶ θεῖα, φωνῇ δὲ ἀνθρωπίνῃ χρῆται. Also Cicero, De Legibus, III, i, 2: "magistratum legem esse loquentem, legem autem mutum magistratum." This is Philo's νόμος ἔμψυχος καὶ λογικός in reverse order.

37. Mos., i, 163.	38. Ib., 173.	39. Ib., 196.
40. Ib., 198.	41. Ib., 243.	42. Ib., 328.
43. Ib., 176, 179.	44. Ib., 185.	

The Manna was a shower of very fine light grain,[45] and Moses explains that
if the air under God can produce rain, it is not strange that it should at
God's command produce food. He parallels with the fact that Egypt by the
rising of the Nile gets its rain from the ground.[46] The rock in Horeb or
Rephidim which flowed water when struck by Moses' rod could do so either
because the vein of an already existing spring was opportunely cut open, or
because water was put there for the first time.[47] Balaam's ass sees the vision,
but Philo omits entirely the conversation between Balaam and the animal.[48]

The book is designed for Gentile readers who believe in divine providence,
but who will be critical of tales that are too "tall," especially in the case of a
foreign people.

Philo has concluded his first book, in which he proposes to tell of Moses'
acts in the kingly rôle.[49] As he summarizes his findings at the beginning of
the second book he says that by Moses' education and rulership, by events in
Egypt and during the wanderings of the people, by his labors and by his
distribution of rewards to his soldiers, Moses has appeared to be the true
philosopher-king of the political theorists.[50] The second book is designed to
show that he was also the ideal lawgiver, priest, and prophet. These three
are all really parts of his kingly office, for the perfect ruler must include them
with the kingly office,

that he may by his legislative power command what ought to be done and prohibit what ought not, by his priestly power manage divine as well as human
matters, and by his prophetic power foretell what cannot be apprehended by
reason.[51]

The king then must command and prohibit, and as this is the function of
law (ἴδιον νόμου) the king is at once the νόμος ἔμψυχος and the law is the
βασιλεὺς δίκαιος.[52] Now the office of lawgiver demands four qualities of
character,

social mindedness (φιλανθρωπία), which teaches him to project into society
judgments for the public good; justice (δικαιοσύνη), on the ground that equality
must be honored and each man get his due; love of good (φιλαγαθία), by which
he should receive the things naturally fine, and furnish them abundantly to be
freely used by all who are worthy; hatred of evil (μισοπονηρία), by which he
should prosecute those who have dishonored virtue and condemn them as public
enemies of the human race.[53]

45. *Mos.*, i, 200: κέγχρος, which means specifically millet, but which also means any fine
grains. It is impossible to determine whether Philo here meant to identify manna specifically
with millet or not. It may be that Philo's text of the LXX read κέγχρος for κόριον at Exod.
xvi, 14.

46. *Mos.*, i, 202.   47. Ib., 211.   48. Ib., 269 ff.
49. Ib., 334.   50. *Mos.*, ii, 1 f.   51. Ib., 187.
52. Ib., 4.   53. Ib., 9 f.

Moses revealed in his legislation that he was the only man who fully achieved all four of these virtues, for the laws were copies and imitations of these virtues, whose ideal prototypes he bore about like statues within his soul.[54]

With this as his account of Moses, Philo goes on briefly to show that the Jewish Law is in harmony with nature, that it has had great influence upon all other legislation, that Moses surpassed all lawmakers in beginning the statement of the Law not with the creation in his own mind of an ideal city, but with God's creation of the great natural order. The inevitability of penalty for infractions of the natural order leads him into a rather extended account of Noah and the destruction of his generation by the Flood. With this the discussion suddenly ends. The section is obviously fragmentary, for its ending is inconclusive.

Philo's remarks on Moses as lawgiver have been brief, but his conception is quite clear. Moses, the ideal king, had as his essential quality the fact that he was νόμος ἔμψυχος, an incarnation of the great Law of Nature. This Law of Nature, it must be recalled from the second chapter, was not an abstraction, but a spiritual entity, ultimately identical with the Logos. Its existence in itself might be conceived as an effluence of spiritual force and νοῦς from God; or as the ideal world of Platonism. Thus to be the incarnation of this νόμος was to be the incarnation not only of the divine force which ruled the world but of the Platonic ideas, as expressed in Philo's phrase that the ideal virtues were "ideal prototypes borne about like statues" in Moses' soul. The king as the ideal lawmaker was νόμος λογικός (law become articulate) as well as ἔμψυχος. He could transmit his great personal endowment to the people, for while he could not transfer his nature fully into their souls, he could give them his life to copy, and fragmentary facsimiles of the paradigmatic law written within him. In doing so Moses began with an account of the creation of the world, then set the Patriarchs, the great νόμοι ἔμψυχοι, before them, then the fundamental principles of the Decalogue, then a code of actual legislation, then an explanation of the place of the ideal virtues in the Law and the divine sanctions of the whole. In doing all of this he was making λογικός, vocal or articulate, the νόμος within him, for that νόμος had more complete representation in the doctrine of creation, and of the relation of man to God and nature, than in any individual commandment. The entire Pentateuch was thus to Philo, as to the Jews in Palestine, the Law of God given by Moses. The relative inferiority of the actual legislative code has already been discussed.

The treatise goes on to describe Moses as the priest. Philo ignores the difficulty that it was Aaron and not Moses who was made the priest. Moses was the priest *par excellence* who taught Aaron what he had himself learned

54. Ib., 10 f.

from God. All that Philo says about the priest and his raiment was meant to be understood primarily and fully of Moses.

First as to the connection of the priestly office with the royal:

A king and lawmaker ought to supervise divine as well as human matters; for without divine wisdom (ἐπιφροσύνη) the affairs of kings and their subjects go awry. Hence the ideal king and lawmaker must have a share in the chief-priesthood, in order that with perfect sacrifices and perfect comprehension of the worship of God he may entreat for the averting of evils and for participation in good things for himself and his subjects from Him who is merciful and harkens unto prayers. For how could He who is propitious, and who deems those properly worshipping Him to be worthy of privilege, not answer such prayers?[55]

The royal office was of course originally almost universally associated with, or dependent upon, priestly function, and Philo may have assumed that his readers not only knew the tradition of the Egyptian and Homeric kings,[56] but understood the interest Augustus had taken in the priestly office in connection with the founding of the Principate. In most of the praises of the king extant from Philo's period the ruler is in general not exhorted to perform the priestly offices because the priestly duties had been so generally relegated to professional priests. The king had primarily to see to it that the priests carried on their functions rather than himself to conduct sacrifices. But in representing Moses as the priest Philo had had to do violence to the Biblical record, in which Moses founds the priestly office, to be sure, but is not himself otherwise connected with the priesthood. Philo's motive for representing the royal νόμος ἔμψυχος as a priest is, however, not far to seek. This element was an important part of the Pythagorean formulation of royalty which Philo is himself following. Diotogenes lists three aspects of the kingly office, military command, legal administration, and the priesthood. In explaining the latter Diotogenes says:

The third duty, that is, worship of the gods, is no less fitting for a king. For the Best must be honored by the best man, and the Governing Principle by one who is a governor. So, just as God is the Best of those things which are most honorable by nature, likewise the king is best in the earthly and human realm. Now the king bears the same relation to the state (πόλις) as God to the world; and the state is in the same ratio to the world as the king is to God. For the state, made as it is by a harmonizing together of many different elements, is an imitation of the order and harmony of the world, while the king who has an absolute rulership, and is himself Animate Law, has been metamorphosed into a deity among men.[57]

55. *Mos.*, ii, 5.

56. In *QE*, ii, 105 Philo makes the following trenchant observation: "mihi videtur priscos reges simul et pontifices fuisse, palam per suum ministerium facientes, quod oportet eos, qui aliorum dominantur, per se colere deum officiose."

57. Stobaeus, IV, vii, 61 (Wachs., IV, pp. 263 ff.). See my "Hellenistic Kingship," pp. 66–68.

The priesthood of Moses was by current notion a necessary part of his kingship, then, and not at all a digression from Philo's representation of him as the Animate Law. Moses was fit for the priesthood because of his piety, his natural endowments, and the development of these endowments by philosophy, as a result of which he was "one who loved God and was loved by Him."[58] So ideal a person had however still to be initiated (μυσταγωγεῖν) into the Mysteries. He was first purified by complete abstinence from all that had to do with the body, and in this condition went up upon the sacred mountain.[59] Here he was not only given a vision of the immaterial forms,[60] but had them stamped upon his mind.[61] In view of such an endowment Moses was the true High-priest.[62] Philo now goes into the long description of the tabernacle which Moses built after this sacred model, a description we have discussed in connection with the Mystery of Aaron.

This cosmic priesthood and perfection[63] was, it must be recalled, pre-eminently the endowment of Moses. For practical purposes he passed on the prerogatives to Aaron and his sons, and Philo describes in detail their installation, or what he calls their "initiation," into the priestly office.[64] But it was Moses who was their "good guide," and who continued to be the real intercessor for the people. This was illustrated in the circumstance of Moses' second consultation with God on Sinai. Philo has changed the story all about from the way it appears in Exodus and Leviticus. It will be recalled that the Biblical narrative describes the incident of the golden calf at the end of Moses' first sojourn on Sinai. It was only after that matter was settled that Moses went back for further instructions and returned to build the tabernacle, make the robes, etc., and consecrate Aaron and his sons. The burning of the sacrifice of Aaron by heavenly fire followed elaborate sacrifices by Moses and Aaron not thus consumed. Philo reverses the two groups of events. According to his account it was after the first visit of Moses to Sinai

58. *Mos.*, ii, 66 f. 59. Ib., 68–71. 60. Ib., 74.
61. Ib., 76. 62. Ib., 75 f.
63. The immediate purpose of such an interpretation of the ritualistic law, which is the same as that given more elaborately in the *Exposition,* is obviously to remove it altogether from the Gentile reader and prospective convert as a literal obligation which he might feel called upon to fulfill. Philo himself went to Jerusalem, as did, probably, all the other Alexandrian Jews who could possibly do so. But for a Gentile this could hardly be represented as an essential part of the faith he was being urged to accept. The passage here and in the *Exposition* may represent the attitude of many Jews of the Diaspora to the Jerusalem cultus, but the interpretations of that cultus as presented to Gentiles must be used cautiously as a basis for concluding the inner attitude of the Jews themselves. Philo was probably quite sincere in thus explaining away the necessity of the actual cult on the ground that it was only a symbol of a spiritual offering. But it has been generally true in religious history that those most zealous in a symbolical interpretation of religious rites and sacraments have also been deeply loyal to their actual and physical observance. How much this was true of Philo may be seen in his description of the horror with which he reacted to the news of the proposed violation of the temple by Gaius: *Legat.,* 186 ff.
64. *Mos.*, ii, 153: ὀγδόη ἦν τῆς τελετῆς . . . αὐτόν τε καὶ τοὺς ἀδελφιδοῦς ὠργίαζεν.

that the tabernacle, cultus, and priesthood were instituted, confirmed by the heavenly fire which consumed the first offering; he puts the incidents connected with the golden calf after Moses' second retreat to the mountain. One motive for this revisal of the Biblical order of events is obviously to put the tribe of Levi, who were especially consecrated as a result of their loyalty in this crisis, in a secondary position to the high-priesthood.[65] But another motive seems to have been the emphasizing of Moses' supreme efficacy as the priest of Israel even after the priesthood of Aaron had been instituted. The inference is that Moses' mediation was of a type vastly superior to that offered in the temple cultus. For after God had told Moses on the mount that the people had made the golden calf and were in revolt, Moses,

in as much as he was the mediator and intercessor (μεσίτης καὶ διαλλακτής), did not depart at once, but first he offered supplications and prayers for the people in which he begged for the pardon of their sins. Then when the guardian and intercessor had propitiated God (ἐξευμενισάμενος ὁ κηδεμὼν καὶ παραιτητὴς τὸν ἡγεμόνα) he went down.[66]

This was going on, by Philo's rearrangement of events, when the priesthood of Aaron was temporarily in complete collapse. Philo does not, for Gentiles at best only beginning in Judaism, draw the conclusions here which seem implicit. It remains for his remarks about Moses in other treatises to confirm the impression here that Philo did think that Moses, the perfect Mystagogue, was the eternal priest of Israel and of the world, offering a mediation of which the temple cultus was only a cosmic reflection.

Philo has now developed the character of Moses as king, legislator, and priest. The remaining section describes him as the supreme prophet of Israel.

Moses' prophetic utterances took three forms. In the first he spoke ἐκ προσώπου τοῦ θεοῦ, that is produced directly an utterance of God, by which the divine virtues of mercy and beneficence were set forth in their great totality (ὅλα δι᾽ ὅλων). These virtues of God are the means by which all men can be trained in preparation for καλοκἀγαθία; yet though the salvation was offered to all, the Road to εὐδαιμονία was opened especially to the feet of God's saving race (τὸ θεραπευτικὸν αὐτοῦ γένος).[67] Philo passes over this first type of prophecy on the pretext that such utterances are beyond his

---

65. If Philo was himself a Sadducee and "of priestly race" he would have been especially interested in thus subordinating the Levites. See above, pp. 78 ff.

66. Mos., ii, 166.

67. Ib., 189. One of Philo's many clever little turns to attract Gentiles to Judaism. He admits that all men may make some progress toward καλοκάγαθία, but implies that they are struggling along ineffectively. In Judaism, the healing race, the ideals of men are fully realized, and here is the path to εὐδαιμονία, that state which to thoughtful Gentiles was the constant if remote objective.

praise.[68] His real reason is that they had little bearing upon the character of Moses as a prophet. For he says that these utterances are made by Moses by ἑρμηνεία rather than by προφητεία, and that these are quite different things.[69] The passage cannot be taken as marking a real refinement in Philo's theory of inspiration. Philo did not want to discuss Moses' relation to the direct utterances of God, but did want to ιdiscuss the other aspects of Moses' prophetic character. So by calling the prophecy ἐκ προσώπου τοῦ θεοῦ by another name than prophecy, he can continue the discussion without reference to this particular type. The distinction, however, is not of real significance for him.[70]

The second type of prophecy is when Moses asks God for an oracular response and gets one; in the third type he himself gives utterance out of a state in which he is possessed by God, and it is by virtue of the third type that he is preëminently called a prophet.[71]

Under what he calls the second type of prophecy, the procuring of an oracular response from God in an emergency, Philo selects four instances for his Gentile readers, obviously with intent. The first[72] is the incident from Leviticus, xxiv, 10 ff., where it is commanded by God that the man who had blasphemed the name and word be stoned by the whole congregation, an incident which had been made a precedent for general procedure in such cases. Philo tells the story with his usual flourish, and describes how this is

---

68. *Mos.*, ii, 191. 69. Ib.

70. There is no reason for thinking that Moses' function as ἑρμηνεύς in *Mos.*, ii, 191, in spite of ib., 213, was understood to be exclusive of the Decalogue (as Badt understands, *Philos Werke*, I, 341, n. 2), for Moses was the only source of record for this as for God's other direct statements. It seems impossible to understand what Philo could have meant by this distinction, for he does not explain it here, and elsewhere in Philo's writings (*Immut.*, 138; *Det.*, 39; *Heres*, 259; *Mut.*, 126; *Spec.*, iii, 7; iv, 49; *Legat.*, 99) προφήτης and ἑρμηνεύς are entirely synonymous, as even in the *Mos.* itself (i, 277). The closest he comes to making the distinction elsewhere is in *Praem.*, 55: ἑρμηνεὺς γάρ ἐστιν ὁ προφήτης ἔνδοθεν ὑπηχοῦντος τὰ λεκτέα τοῦ θεοῦ, which in itself might be taken as meaning: "the ἑρμηνεύς is the προφήτης when God makes His utterance echo out from within him." But in the parallel *Spec.*, i, 65: ἑρμηνεῖς γάρ εἰσιν οἱ προφῆται θεοῦ καταχρωμένου τοῖς ἐκείνων ὀργάνοις πρὸς δήλωσιν ὧν ἂν ἐθελήσῃ, the θεοῦ is certainly a possessive genitive, "the ἑρμηνεῖς are the prophets of God who uses their organs," etc., and the passage from *Praem.* can well be taken in the same way: "The ἑρμηνεύς is the προφήτης of God who makes the utterances echo from within." Such would better accord with Philo's general usage, by which this sort of inspiration is the common description of a prophet, as for example *Heres*, 249. It is hard to see any reason, also, for excluding the Decalogue from the points covered by these three types of prophecy in view of the fact that Philo introduces the section by the words: πάντ' εἰσὶ χρησμοί, ὅσα ἐν ταῖς ἱεραῖς βίβλοις ἀναγέγραπται, χρησθέντες δι' αὐτοῦ (*Mos.*, ii, 188), and since in *QG*, iv, 196 he says that that state wherein God is the actor and the prophet is the instrument in the state by which God's laws are published. Badt's paralleling (*Philos Werke*, I, 341, n. 3) the distinctive sorts of prophecy with Philo's classification of types of dreams (*Som.*, i, 1 f.; ii, 1 f.) is interesting but not illuminating.

71. *Mos.*, ii, 191. Though this is exactly the description of the prophet as ἑρμηνεύς elsewhere. See the preceding note.

72. *Mos.*, ii, 183–208.

interpreted by Jews so strictly that it led to what must have appeared to Gentiles as the lynching of such malefactors; but he is careful also to point out that it kept the Jews respectful in their attitude toward the images regarded by Gentiles as their deities. The passage is obviously directed to make his readers from outside Judaism understandingly tolerant of the Jewish lynching of apostates, but is addressed to Gentiles not so far along in their Jewish sympathies as the similar passage *De Specialibus Legibus,* i, 51–55, where even the proselytes are invited to participate in an apostate Jew's execution.[73]

The second instance of prophetic question and answer selected by Philo gives Moses the authorization for stoning Sabbath breakers.[74] Philo has selected this incident to get a pretext for introducing a defense of the Jewish Sabbath, a description of the synagogue services, and of the Jewish strict withdrawal from labor. It does not appear that Jews still stoned Sabbath breakers, for there is no application of the law to contemporary life here as in the case of blasphemy. But the Gentile reader is given a highly attractive picture of the metaphysical justification and practical inspiration of the Sabbath as Jews observed it.

The third instance of prophecy by question and answer is a very interesting explanation of the fact that Jews in the Diaspora, cut off from participation in the passover and its sacrificial rites in the temple, were excused from this important part of Judaism by God Himself.[75] The story as told in Numbers ix, 6–14 relates simply that God made provision that those who were unclean or away on a journey on the regular day of the Passover might celebrate it a month later. Philo alters the story to make the point at issue not the uncleanness resulting from a dead body, but the preoccupation of a family when it is mourning the loss of one of its members. The oracular response of God not only covered, he says, this case, but implied general directions to apply to people who should be prevented by other causes from joining in the rites at Jerusalem. Philo gives a free paraphrase of the scriptural command about "mourners" being allowed to sacrifice a month later, and goes on to represent God as saying that the same applies to those who are kept away from the sacrifices not only by a journey but *by distant residence,* for those should not be deprived of their full standing since a single country cannot

73. In speaking to Jews on the subject of idols Philo is by no means so benignantly tolerant. In *QE,* ii, 5, he gives two reasons for not blaspheming the pagan gods: first, the heathen are very angry when their gods are questioned, and this makes for war, while the purpose of the Law is to teach Jews to know the way to peace; second, if one curses the gods the heathen will likely retaliate by cursing the God of the Jews, so that the Jew who curses heathen gods is in a sense guilty of cursing his own God because he has provoked others to do so. This puts the matter on an entirely different footing among the Jews themselves from what it is represented to Gentiles.

74. *Mos.,* ii, 209–220. See Num. xv, 32–36.   75. *Mos.,* ii, 231–232.

contain the race, but has to establish distant colonies in every direction. Philo has suddenly shifted ground. These distant residents could usually appear as well on the day fixed as a month later. The point is that most will not appear at all, yet thereby Philo is assuring the Gentile reader, they do not lose their ἴση τιμή.

Philo's fourth[76] selection of a prophecy by question and answer is not so obviously of immediate concern to a Gentile sympathetic to, but still outside, Judaism. It relates the case of the inheritance of Zelophehad which the daughters wanted. Philo tells this story, but his point is at the end where he explains the general law of inheritance in such a way as to make it, contrary to the Scriptures but in accordance with Greek law of Egypt, include the father as the first ascendant heir.[77] Since the other three instances of this type of prophecy were so obviously selected as of immediate importance for the problem of the Gentile reader, this matter of Jewish inheritance must have likewise been a prominent matter of discussion. Perhaps the subject had recently been thrown up into importance by a famous case in which Jews were in such disagreement that Philo felt obliged to defend for Gentiles the interpretation that had prevailed.

Whatever the motive for the fourth selection, it is clear that the group as a whole is made up of attempts to explain aspects of Judaism that would early have to be cleared up for Gentile readers. As Philo himself admits, they throw little light upon Moses' character as a prophet, for it was in the third type of prophecy, that in which Moses was immediately inspired by God for utterance, that this character became properly manifest. The emphasis in this section is upon the fact that Moses foretold the future accurately: he foretold the salvation of the Israelites and the destruction of the Egyptian host at the Red Sea;[78] the raining of manna with the remarkable double supply on the sixth day, and total lack of supply on the seventh day;[79] the fidelity of the Levites at the time of the golden calf;[80] the destruction of the apostates by earthquake and fire from heaven;[81] and finally the circumstances of his death.[82]

Of these only the last brings out material on Moses worthy of note. The death of Moses was a "change." Moses was summoned, perhaps "recalled" (μετακληθείς), by the Father to leave the mortal life and be made immortal (ἀπαθανατίζεσθαι). Moses had been a dyad, σῶμα καὶ ψυχή, but now was wholly transformed (ὅλον δι' ὅλων μεθαρμοζόμενος) into the nature of a monad, that is into Mind with especially sun-like brilliance (νοῦς ἡλιοει-

76. Ib., 233–245. See Num. xxvii, 1–11.
77. I have dealt with this problem in my *Jurisprudence of the Jewish Courts in Egypt* (1929), pp. 58, 61 f.
78. *Mos.*, ii, 246–257. 79. Ib., 258–269. 80. Ib., 270–274.
81. Ib., 275–287. 82. Ib., 288–292.

δέστατος). In this new state he prophesied the fate of each tribe, some of which prophecies are yet to be fulfilled.

This section, with definite reference to the *Vita Mosis,* is elaborated in the *De Virtibus,* 51 ff. Here Philo, in the course of discussing the great Greek virtues and their fundamental relation to the specific laws, comes to social-mindedness (φιλανθρωπία), and, using Moses as the great type of this virtue, speaks of his last days as its supreme exemplification. The passage ties back all he has said about Moses in the *Vita Mosis* with the objective he has had throughout, namely to show Moses as the great νόμος ἔμψυχος who presented his own life as a good model, like an archetypal drawing, Cicero's way of expressing the notion of the νόμος ἔμψυχος. For upon his soul was clearly stamped the divine seal of καλοκἀγαθία.[83] Here at the approach of death he acted differently from any other person, whether king or private citizen, and was solely concerned that the succession to his honors and to the rulership should go not necessarily to his sons or nephews, but to the persons God should designate. In such a matter he will not trust his own wisdom. For the man selected is to be the pilot and governor of the people and must have greater than human wisdom for the task. That is, Moses' successor, since he must be endowed by God, must be selected by Him.[84] When God had designated Joshua, Moses presented him to the people. In this, as in all else, Moses was to be the "norm and law for all later political leaders, who should look to Moses as the archetypal pattern," specifically as respects dealing with successors, but also, we infer, in matters of rulership in general.[85]

This matter completed, Moses began his final song of praise while still in the body.[86] In order to sing this song with absolute perfection he gathered a mighty company. But Philo's description is too remarkable for paraphrase:

He gathered together a divine company, that is the elements of the universe and the most important parts of the cosmos (ἄθροισμα θεῖον, τὰ στοιχεῖα τοῦ παντὸς καὶ τὰ συνεκτικώτατα μέρη τοῦ κόσμου), namely earth and heaven, earth the hearth of mortals and heaven the house of immortals. In the midst of these he composed hymns in every type of mode and interval, in order that men and ministering angels might hear, men as learners that he might teach them a similarly grateful attitude, and the angels as critics to watch how, judged by their own technique, he made not a single false note. The angels would also be strengthened in their faith (διαπιστοῦντες) if a man clothed in his mortal body could have a power of song like the sun, the moon, and the sacred choir of the other stars, and could attune his soul to the divine musical instrument (ὄργανον), namely the heaven and the whole cosmos. But Moses the hierophant, when he had taken his place (ταχθείς) in the aether, mingled, along with the choral hymns of praise to God, true emotions of good will to the Nation. He reproved them for their

83. *Virt.,* 51 f.
85. Ib., 70.
84. Ib., 61 ff.
86. Ib., 72.

past sins, gave them warnings and corrections for the present, and advice for the future based upon good hopes which were bound to be fulfilled.[87]

In Moses the gulf between mortal and immortal, the cosmic and the human, has been bridged. A man has sung the perfect song while yet in the body, and even the faith of the angels has been strengthened. Yet this great person, even as he was in the height of his grandeur, could not forget his loving kindness to the people, and while he rebuked them for their sins, he gave them such instructions and advice that the future became full of hopes which must be fulfilled. When Moses had finished the song he began to be changed

from mortal existence into immortal life (ἐκ θνητῆς ζωῆς εἰς ἀθάνατον βίον), and noticed that he was gradually being disengaged from the elements with which he had been mixed. He shed his body which grew around him like the shell of an oyster, while his soul which was thus laid bare desired its migration thence.

Even then he tarried long enough to offer final prayers for Israel.[88]

Such was the character and career of the "most holy man who ever lived."[89] As νόμος ἔμψυχος he was the model to his people for their government, laws, and cultus, and not to his people only, but to all people. But he was more than that—he was their intercessor with God, a function which he continued even after his disembodiment. Like all the νόμοι ἔμψυχοι (of whom with the possible exception of Isaac he was the greatest, for he began where Abraham left off[90]), and like the Christian conception of Jesus, Moses was the model, the leader: he set the eternal verities before men in his utterances and commands, but his life was greater than any of his utterances. His followers might well obey his injunctions but much more copy his spirit, imitate his life, for his life was the true life. The Christian conception of Jesus goes farther and represents the Master as not only giving the great precepts and example for life, but as being the intercessor for men whose intercession and reconciling power did not end with his death, but goes on eternally through his eternal divinity and relationship with the Father.

Did Philo think of Moses, who in life had all these virtues and was the incarnate representation of the divine forms as well as of the cosmic law; who was the intercessor and savior of his people throughout life even to the point of mingling at his final deification the cosmic hymn with loving intercession for his people: did Philo think that such a Moses had finished his great work and was done, so that the race had left only the sacred laws he had taught and the inspiring memory of his personality? It does not seem so, in spite of the fact that this is all the Moses that is presented to Gentiles making their first inquiries about Judaism. The saving power of the earlier

87. Ib., 73–75.   88. Ib., 76–79.
89. Mos., ii, 192.   90. Post., 174.

Patriarchs has appeared a permanent χάρις from God to mankind,[91] and it would be strange if Philo did not think in the same way of Moses. Actually when we turn to the allegorical writings where the Mystery is being more explicitly set forth, the references to Moses and to the great emigration from Egypt make it clear that he was the savior of Judaism *par excellence*.

91. See above, p. 136.

CHAPTER VIII

THE MYSTIC MOSES

IN one passage where Philo is talking about Moses he tells us that the difficulties of the scriptural passage under discussion are too great for the present and must be left until he shall come to investigate "the whole prophetic life, at such time as we are fit to be initiated into it."[1] Colson understands by this "the whole life of the prophet." In either case it is clear that Philo has much more to say of Moses than he tells in the *Allegory*, and if Colson is correct, he planned writing a special study of the subject. We do not know whether such a document ever was written. If it was, its loss is the most serious of any of our Philonic losses, for obviously it would have taken us into the Mystery quite beyond what is given in the *Allegory*. Further there are left only a relatively few sections of the *Quaestiones in Exodum*, and the *Quaestiones in Leviticum* is represented only by two small fragments, if we may rely upon even these quotations as rightly ascribed.[2] So the only approach to the Moses for whom it will appear Philo makes such extraordinary claims is by a collection of the passages in which he is more or less incidentally described in the *Allegory*, and in the fragmentary material of the *Quaestiones in Exodum*.

When this material is put together, however, it shows that Philo had quite as consistent and standardized an allegory of Moses and of the migration of the Israelites from Egypt as has appeared in the similar collection of material for Isaac and Jacob. As in their case, the best outline will be to treat the passages according to the order of the Biblical narrative, and to put the material from both sources together as either may illuminate the successive events.

Moses is like Isaac and unlike Abraham and Jacob in that he is the Self-Taught, and there is no drama of his leaving the body, going through great struggles of discipline, and finally achieving the vision. Rather he is a special type of incarnation:

When God lent Moses to earthly things and permitted him to associate with them, He endowed him not at all with the ordinary virtue of a ruler or king with which forcibly to rule the soul's passions; rather He appointed him to be god, and decreed that the whole bodily realm and its leader, the mind, should be his subjects and slaves.[3]

1. εἰς τὴν τοῦ προφητικοῦ βίου παντὸς ἐξέτασιν, ὅταν αὐτὸν ἱκανοὶ γενώμεθα μυεῖσθαι: *Gig.*, 57.
2. Harris, *Fragments*, p. 75. Schürer doubts the ascription of the fragment, since Eusebius knew only the *Quaestiones in Gen. et Exod.*
3. *Sac.*, 9.

The Patriarch as a special divine incarnation has been suggested in the miraculous conception of Isaac, who entered Sarah's womb not from Abraham but from God, but nothing so explicit has appeared as this about the birth of Moses. Philo also contrasts Moses and Noah. Noah went out of his way deliberately to build himself an ark, that is to provide himself with a body, says Philo, but when Moses was floating on the river in the little ark of bulrushes he wept for his imprisonment and for all others so shut in, so much did he long for immaterial nature. For Moses was excellent (ἀστεῖος) at his very birth.[4] He was a stranger in the body.[5] The picture of the childish omniscience of Moses given in the De Vita Mosis is then a definite part of the conception. While Abraham and Jacob had so much to learn, Moses was fully aware of the immaterial world and its nature at birth. The final achievement of Abraham was but the starting point for Moses.[6]

It was on this level as the complete mystic that Moses lived his entire life. True he attacked the Egyptian, who was Epicureanism with its doctrines of pleasure and atoms,[7] but that is only the attack of truth against falsehood, not an episode in Moses' development. Moses was, indeed, the divine representation sent into the confusion of Egypt, bodily life, to straighten matters out; he was never himself tinged with the Egyptian taint. So he is definitely contrasted with Jacob who deserted Laban, sneaked away from him, to go to the mystical experience.[8] When Moses left Egypt it was to go only temporarily to the Well of Wisdom in Midian for strength to fight the battle with the passions. It was there too that he got his commission to carry on the fight,[9] for apparently Moses was in some doubt as to whether to desert the body, Egypt, or to make a campaign against it. The whole experience of Midian was then not one of endowment, but of commission.

In Midian his first experience is to see the rude shepherds trying to prevent the seven daughters of Raguel-Jothar from watering their sheep. This incident is elaborately allegorized. Raguel-Jothar is the mind, whose seven senses are trying to give spiritual nourishment to the perceptions, the sheep, and bring them into his service, make them fullfil their natural function, but are prevented from doing so by that all-pervasive evil spirit of the Greek World, φθόνος. Moses rushes in and protects the senses from this attack, with the result that the mind is now able to regulate the lower life.[10] The mind that is able thus to rule its flock is one that has used the shepherd and king of the mind mentioned by Scripture in the words "The Lord is my shepherd," the divine Logos. Mind, Raguel-Jothar, is surprised at the way in which the senses now function in bringing the sheep back quickly and properly at his

4. Conf., 106.		5. Ib., 82.		6. Post., 174.
7. Fug., 148. The account in LA, iii, 37 f. is not so clear, but seems an equally objective act for Moses.
8. LA, iii, 16 ff.		9. Ib., 12–15.		10. Mut., 110–114.

behest, and asks them how it occurred. They tell him that it is Moses who
stepped in.[11] Moses is not explicitly equated with the Logos, but the allegory
is definitely one of the saving activity of Moses who can come into the struggle of a mind and quell the adversary; he is clearly the agent, if not the exact
equivalent, of the saving Logos.

The daughters have been operated upon by reason (τὸ λογικὸν εἶδος), but
as mere senses they do not apprehend what has affected them. They leave
Moses to rush back to their father. Jothar, the mind, reproves his daughters,
the senses, for having left Moses after he has done so much for them, and
bids them summon him that he may eat with them, that is may feed on their
improvement and even bring the winged and god-bearing and prophetic
thing, Zipporah, to them.[12] It is notable that the account in Exodus does not
state that Zipporah was one of the daughters who were tending the sheep,
though that is usually inferred. Philo sees fit to assume that she was not with
them, and so makes her represent something entirely different from what
he sees typified in them.

For the marriage of Moses to Zipporah must be, like all Philo's allegories
of the marriages of the Patriarchs, the mystic marriage with Sophia. But in
this marriage Moses did not, like Abraham, Jacob, and Aaron, have to make
a choice of Sophia before marrying her, says Philo. He was like Isaac in
being *given* Sophia or Logos as his spouse because Sophia was a fitting endowment of his own "Self-Taught" nature.[13] That is, Sophia was his natural
companion and endowment, not something acquired by effort and aspiration. It was God Himself who joined them in this marriage.[14] And Moses
found her already pregnant from God when he married her,[15] one of the
many illustrations we have encountered of the fact that ἀρετή as Sophia has
intercourse with God, and thus brings forth progeny to God, not men. Moses
was so much greater than the other Patriarchs, even than Isaac, that while
they all had to pray God for this impregnation of their wives, Moses found
his wife already pregnant without having to ask for it. Philo tells us that in
getting into the matter of the mystic marriage he is dealing with one of the
inmost secrets of the Mystery, and cryptic as are his remarks about it, he
warns the reader against babbling the story to the uninitiated.[16]

What is the secret that lies behind these cryptic utterances? To understand
it we must recall the concept of the mystic's rise through the Sophia formulation of the Light-Stream. In this there have appeared to be two successive
marriages. In the first the mystic strips himself of all positive characteristics,
that is of his masculinity, and presents himself in feminine receptivity to
Sophia. Sophia comes to him now herself as the male, and sows within him
her seed. In the higher marriage the sexes are reversed. He as masculine now

11. Ib., 115–117. 12. Ib., 119 f. 13. *Post.*, 75–78.
14. *LA*, ii, 67. 15. *Cher.*, 47. 16. Ib., 43–46, 48.

has relations with her as feminine. In Moses' marriage he is not feminine in the sense that he is being taught by Sophia, receiving her seeds. He, the self-taught, is meeting her as a male meets a female. But he finds her already pregnant by God, for God is her true spouse. How then could Moses marry her? Only, and here is the guess as to the meaning of the "secret," because Moses has reached so high a stage of mystic union with God that he can function as God with Sophia. His union with Deity is so complete that he can take God's place with her. Philo does not say this. But I strongly suspect that this was the hope of Mystic Judaism, as it expressed itself in terms of the Sophia formulation, just as it appears likely, from Pascher's evidence, to be the highest stage in Isis. There one finally becomes identical with Osiris, the Spouse of Isis. Here one becomes identical with God, the Spouse of Sophia. And the mystic intercourse as male with Sophia as female is the sweet token of one's ultimate deification.

Moses now begins to be shepherd of the flocks of Jethro, who appears in this allegory in his more usual bad odor. The flocks, which represent the thoughts and commands of the bad shepherd, have to be put into order by Moses, led into justice. This he does for Jethro like the ὀρθὸς λόγος.[17] His relation to Jethro is indeed like Jacob's to Laban, but is much better a type of the way in which the Good Shepherd will come in and shepherd our flock. The allegory is an extended one of the divine power of salvation, and the divine care God exercises for those who come to Him.[18]

The experience at the burning bush is variously explained. In one passage Moses seems to be attempting as a man to solve the principle of cosmic causation when he approaches the burning bush with his shoes on. He is warned off the holy ground of causation (ὁ αἰτιολογικὸς τόπος) by God who has reserved knowledge of this for divine natures. He does better when at Sinai he makes the vision of God his objective, though even here he can only partially succeed.[19] In another passage it is pointed out that God addresses Moses as a friend, since He calls him by name.[20] God could not appear to Moses as He is, for that vision can be had only by incorporeal souls. He told Moses that His name is "I Am Being," "that he might recognize the existence of the things which it is impossible for a man who is not with God to apprehend."[21] In two passages it appears that while Moses could not learn the name of God, he learned the fact that it is God's nature to Be. For human convenience God is to be named the God of Abraham and Isaac and Jacob, that is κύριος ὁ θεός of three natures, teaching, perfection, and discipline.

17. *Sac.*, 50 f.
18. *Agr.*, 42–54.
19. *Fug.*, 161–165.
20. *Som.*, i, 194 f.
21. *Som.*, i, 231 f. The text here is obviously corrupt, and Wendland's conjectures do not help. To make the sentence fit the context it must have read: ἵν' ὧν ἀδυνατὸν ἀνθρώπῳ καταλαβεῖν μὴ ὄντι περὶ θεόν.

The three Patriarchs are symbols of these three "natures" according to which God is κύριος ὁ θεός.[22] When we look from this curious statement to *De Abrahamo*, 51–55, we notice that on the basis of the same allegory each of these three natures is a "power," δύναμις, in which the Patriarchs shared. Each Patriarch had all three "powers," though predominantly sharing in only one. They are also χάριτες for they have become divine gifts to men. In a third passage we are told that at the bush Moses was engaged in "investigations of God and His most sacred powers,"[23] a statement that would naturally be taken as referring, as Philo does in almost every one of his writings, to the three great Powers of the Mystery. The passages lead us strongly to suspect that this God of three powers, κύριος ὁ θεός, is none other than the God of the Mystery, who was also the God of the Powers, and that if we had more explicit information it would appear that Jacob represented the δύναμις βασιλική, Abraham the δύναμις ποιητική, and Isaac, in between the two, the Logos. Such may well have been the revelation to Moses at the bush, the revelation of the Mystery in three terms. I do not feel that the suggestion, slight as the evidence is, can be too lightly discredited, since the same allegory of the incident is seen to have appeared in both the *Allegory* and the *Exposition,* and hence must be taken as something more important in Philo's sources and thinking than its cryptic exposition would superficially indicate.[24]

The rod which is transformed into a serpent during this scene at the bush is discipline, which when thrown away becomes a serpent, pleasure. Moses' first instinct is to run from it, but God recalls him, for the Perfect Man (ὁ τέλειος) must not run from pleasure like the man not yet made perfect, but must grasp it by the tail and turn it again into discipline.[25] Still the picture is of the experience and lessons of the man already perfect, not of one being perfected. Moses' life is throughout the life of the perfect man turned to war against the forces of evil in the world.

Yet Moses feels himself unable to speak well enough to fulfil the mission on which God is sending him. Several explanations of his inability to speak

22. *Mut.*, 11 f.

23. *Mig.*, 76. αἱ περὶ θεοῦ καὶ τῶν ἱερωτάτων αὐτοῦ δυνάμεων.

24. Identification of each of Philo's seven great Patriarchs with one of the seven Powers has already seemed a possibility. And while the identification of each Sephira with a Patriarch in the Kabbalah (see below, pp. 367 f.) proves nothing for Philo, it does not at all weaken the possibility that Philo did so with his Powers. By this Enos would have been the κόσμος νοητός, Enoch the Legislative Power, Noah the Merciful Power, or possibly Noah would have been the Legislative Power, and Enoch, the middle of the three, would have been the highest of the three, the Merciful Power. In the next triad Abraham would have been, from the above, the Creative Power, Jacob the Ruling Power, and Isaac the Logos. Moses would have been left to represent τὸ ὄν. We have no proof that Philo made any such identifications, but from such scattered hints as the above it would seem not at all unlikely.

25. *LA*, ii, 88–93.

are given. One is that the sort of speech needed with the type of man Moses must face is sophistic rhetoric, but such rhetoric vanishes from one who has had a vision of the truth.²⁶ Also Moses has become stamped by Sophia, and so is made into λόγος ἐνδιάθετος. He is the source of speech, πηγὴ λόγων, but not himself "utterance."²⁷ He is in ecstasy and so has become a resistless stream of the beauties of Sophia, but that stream is never formulated in words.²⁸ The promise is that Moses will receive a stream of God's λόγοι, which he will pass on to Aaron to express in utterance.²⁹

With his vision of God thus clarified, and with the practical assistance of Aaron, Moses now goes to Egypt to begin his great work. He returns to Pharaoh, to struggle with him and ultimately destroy him. Pharaoh represents all that is bad in human nature, a lover of pleasure who knows not God;³⁰ he is one who "rejects both parents," divine and human restraint,³¹ and hence, with Egypt his country, represents the body in its worst form.³² Captive in this country is the "mind fond of seeing," Israel, which at this stage is rather the mind capable of seeing. This mind must be led out of Egypt if it is to get the vision, and it is Moses who, with Aaron, has the power to do this for man's higher nature.³³ The salvation he brings the Israelites is one "where the helping principle (τὸ συμμαχικόν) of its own accord comes wholly from the outside to shield us after our own faculties have been quite destroyed."³⁴

So the passover is a constant symbol with Philo for the abandoning of the life of the passions and the beginning of the journey to ὁ σωτὴρ θεός.³⁵ The lamb of the passover symbolizes the "forward step" one is about to take.³⁶ It represents the beginning of a hard and bitter task,³⁷ and requires the girding up of the loins.³⁸ The allegory of the passover in the *Quaestiones in Exodum* is the same. The ceremony indicates the passing over from ignorance to wisdom, and the emigration of the soul from the body, of mind from the senses, under the inspiration of prophetic spirits.³⁹ The passover and its perquisites

are signs of the good soul desiring perfection: for it is first necessary to eradicate the sins, but then, when these have been expunged, to carry out and practise daily virtues.⁴⁰

26. *Sac.*, 12 f.
27. *Det.*, 38–40.
28. *Heres*, 4.
29. *Mig.*, 76–85, especially 80.
30. *Ebr.*, 19.
31. Ib., 77.
32. *Mut.*, 205, 209; *Som.*, ii, 258–260, 266 f., 277; *Sac.*, 69.
33. *Mut.*, 207–209; ὁ μὲν γὰρ τοῦτο δυνηθεὶς Μωϋσῆς ἐστιν οὗτος.
34. *Som.*, ii, 267.
35. *Heres*, 192; *Sac.*, 63; *Mig.*, 25.
36. *LA*, iii, 165. Philo allegorizes πρόβατον according to its possible relations with προβαίνω.
37. *Cong.*, 161 f.
38. *LA*, iii, 154.
39. *QE*, i, 4.
40. Ib., 8.

As the people are thus united in the one great collective act of migration they are made one; from being a multitude, or a tribe, or a people, they become an "ecclesia," a church, united not so much in body as in mind, intent, and spirit.[41] The passover is held at evening because of the usual significance of evening, the time of the fading of material light at the coming of immaterial illumination.[42] The passover is eaten with unleavened bread and bitter herbs as a symbol that they have left the pride of material life, and have gone over from desire to apathy, from wickedness to virtue; by speculations of wisdom they have migrated to the happy state of immortal life.[43] The migration is to lead to the vision of the incorporeals.[44]

When the death Angel smote the eldest sons of the Egyptians it did not smite Israel, for Israel is not to be overwhelmed, but is to "emerge as from the depths."[45] So the Exodus is an allegory of how Moses can lead the soul out from its lower aspects and complications to the vision of God. It is the story of Moses as the great hierophant and savior of the Mystery.

An illuminating passage from this point of view is *De Confusione Linguarum*, 88–97. Here Moses describes Pharaoh as king of Egypt, the lower bodily mind which is in revolt against God. Not only is that mind engrossed in the complicated structures of pleasure, but it takes the higher mind with its possibilities of Vision and enslaves it. The higher mind groans heavily at this subjection and cries to God the only savior. In answer God commands, "Send forth the people that they may serve me." The type of service to which τὸ ὄν calls them is not a menial one; it consists in

going up to the aetherial heights with their reasonings, setting before them Moses, the type of existence beloved by God, to lead them on their way. For there they shall see the place which indeed is the Logos, where stands the undeviating and unchanging God, and also "the things beneath His feet, like the work of a brick of sapphire, and like the form of the firmament of heaven,"[46] that is the sensible world, which he is indicating by these words. For it well befits those who have become the comrades of Wisdom[47] to desire to see τὸ ὄν; but if they cannot do so, at least to see His image, the most sacred Logos, and below the Logos the most perfect sensible product, this cosmos.[48]

41. Ib., 10.   42. Ib., 11.   43. Ib., 15.
44. Ib., 22. §23 is an allegory of the destroying angel, in which the angel is obviously the Persian Ahriman. There are two *Virtutes* (probably the Greek was δυνάμεις) who come into every man at birth, the benefiting and the destructive power. These together made the material world, and a great cosmic struggle is going on between them, one that is reënacted in every man. Only by the good Power shutting out the bad altogether can the soul achieve its proper end. The passage is unique, so far as I recall in Philo, but is very important for showing his knowledge of Persian thought, and his acceptance of its postulates, to the point of working it into his Old Testament allegory.
45. *LA*, ii, 34.   46. Exod. xxiv, 10.
47. Ἐπιστήμη is clearly here, as throughout the Mystery, the synonym of Σοφία.
48. *Conf.*, 95–97. I have followed Colson's admirable reconstruction of the text and have

As the story of the Exodus goes on it becomes evident that this is the allegory which lies consistently behind the great mass of isolated references to the details. The Israelites are to go through, or come to understand, the three stages of the Mystery, first the cosmic stage, second the Immaterial Stage which is collectively represented in the Logos, and third τὸ ὄν. The last stage is inaccessible to humanity, but it is Moses, τὸ θεοφιλὲς γένος, who will lead us to the two others.

In leaving Egypt the Israelites made the great mistake, Philo points out, of taking with them all sorts of herds, a mixed or manifold company of "beastlike and unreasoned teachings," or "opinions."[49] It is the dragging influence of the "manifold" as contrasted with the single.[50] This vestige of "confusion" which remained even after Israel had left Egypt accounted for the fact that the tribes wandered in the desert forty years instead of quickly coming through in three days to the "inheritance of Virtue" to which the threefold light of perception of things past, present, and future could otherwise have brought them.[51] They had still, even after leaving bodily Egypt, to "knead the savage and untamed passion by the aid of Logos the Softener, softening it as though it were food." This passion which must still be softened is compared to the dough the Israelites brought from Egypt and baked in the desert.[52] So by softening down the passions with Logos as they were taught to do by divine inspiration they could bake the cakes of the Lesser Mystery, and thus partake of those secrets into which one must be initiated before he is ready for the secret cakes of the higher Mystery, the mystery of God as revealed in the three Powers.[53]

The Israelites brought with them those hampering vestiges of the somatic nature, but the destruction of the Egyptian host was the destruction of the body, the death of the lower mind and its six sensuous manifestations.[54] The tribes had come to the point where this was possible by the fact that the Logos, the Cutter, had already begun to make the division between the higher and lower aspects of human nature by standing between the two hosts as the pillar of fire, a saving force for the one, destructive for the other.[55] This death of the body, Philo is careful to point out, is not physical death, but is the destruction of unholy doctrines and of the words that come from them.[56] The hymn that is sung when the Egyptians, the passions, perish is the song of a mind that is beginning to see, led by the keenest vision,

---

translated the μεθ' ὃν of §97 as "below whom" since Philo is going from the higher to the lower in his list so that the sense is better rendered by "below" than by the literal "after."

49. *Mig.*, 151 f.   50. Ib., 153.   51. Ib., 154 f.
52. *Exod.* xii, 39.   53. *Sac.*, 59–62, especially 62.
54. *Ebr.*, 111; *Conf.*, 70; *LA*, ii, 102; iii, 172.
55. *Heres*, 203 f. The context before and after this section makes it clear that the cloud is only another illustration of the λόγος τομεύς.
56. *Conf.*, 36.

Moses the leader, and by the purified senses, with Miriam as leader. "Horse and rider he threw into the sea" is the song sung to God at the destruction of the body and the bodily mind.[57]

The years of wandering in the wilderness, in spite of the high favor of God, are typical of the struggle of a man who has renounced the lower life, and migrated out from it as the place of his settled abode, but who is still so hampered by what might be called "somatic survivals" that he is unworthy and unable to come through to a higher experience. It is the familiar ground where most men of mystic aspirations live. So Paul, for example, for all that he is no longer "dead in his sins," and has had moments or hours of mystic exaltation, had to drag about with him the dead body, which, for all it was dead to him and he to it, was a heavy weight that had still not been entirely cast off or "redeemed." One wonders whether Paul ever got the experience for which he, and the Spirit with him, are groaning, "to wit, the redemption of the body." That is, there may seem confusion in Philo's representing the Israelites as having drowned the body and passions in the Red Sea, and yet still being obliged to fight them for the forty years of wandering. The confusion is quite common in any experience, where man is trying to move out completely during his present life from bodily to spiritual orientation. In a sense the body is dead. Something has freed the spirit in man to look beyond it and its needs, and occasionally there may come the Rapture of the great Illumination. But live from day to day on that plane? Never to feel "that the evil we would not, that we do"? Never to be almost suffocated by the desires to which we had in a sense died? Philo is like Paul in being too much a realist in his mystic life not to know that most of the lives of even the greatest mystics is spent wandering in the wilderness between the Red Sea and the Promised Land, or, as Paul has it in Romans, between death to the body in Baptism and the Redemption of the Body. It is one thing to sketch the ideal stage by stage, and to see that ideal realized in the great Savior or Saviors: it is quite another to realize it consistently in oneself.

Far then from marking Paul or Philo as "confused" in their mystic presentation, their very apparent contradiction arises from the vividness of their mystical experience and understanding. Even Jesus humbly asked, "Why callest thou me good?" It is for smaller men than either Paul or Philo, the "perfecti" of all ages and religions, to claim consistent achievement of the goal.

During the period of struggle the mystic is aware that there are "showers of refreshing," miracles of grace to support the soul on the way. There is little chronological significance in the incidents here. Each is a miracle of the mercy of God, to help in some emergency of fleshly temptation. The

57. *Agr.*, 78–83.

manna of the wilderness is repeatedly explained in the sense of such a merciful dispensation. The great passage on the manna is in *Legum Allegoria,* iii, 162–176. There it is stated that Pleasure, the snake of Eden, is condemned to eat earth,[58] but the food of the soul is heavenly: it consists of the λόγοι that God pours out like rain from the exalted and pure element (φύσις) which men call "heaven."[59] Only a day's supply of such food is given at a time, and for several reasons, chiefly because man is not capable of receiving the grace of God in a single torrential rush, and because by daily rationing we are constantly reminded of our dependence upon God. He that would have God's grace otherwise, lacks hope, faith, and sense.[60] By allegory it is evident that this food is illumination,[61] nourishment on the heavenly ἐπιστῆμαι, wisdoms.[62] More than the λόγοι and ἐπιστῆμαι, the food is the Logos and Sophia,[63] the heavenly Light-Stream itself as well as its lower and plural manifestations.[64] The manna is white because of its being itself the light that illumines the soul.[65] Only Moses can tell one what is the nature of this heavenly grace in the soul. Ordinary men feel their souls brightened and sweetened by it, but cannot know what it is. Moses as hierophant and prophet tells us it is the Logos.[66] It comes after a testing time when there has been a scarcity of food, and the soul has grown so faint that the lower leaders of the soul want to give up the struggle and return to Egypt, the passions.[67] We ordinary men do, indeed, get this spiritual food in portions (διὰ μέρους): the souls of the more perfect get the Logos as a whole.[68]

There is some confusion in the passage as to whether he means that the manna is the Logos or the lesser logoi. He calls it both here. The contrast between the ordinary man in the wilderness getting food in portions and the perfect getting the Logos as a whole is expanded to represent two mystic stages. The one stage is purificatory, supervised by the lower divine agencies and angels and logoi. The higher stage is where God acts directly to give the Logos as a whole.[69] It is probably the former which he has in mind when he says that it falls only in the wilderness of passions and wickedness.[70] Philo is confused here because ultimately the distinctions of personalities or agencies within the Logos or Light-Stream had no significance. The logoi or angels are only lower manifestations of the single Stream. The difference between the experience of the Stream in its lower manifestations and that in

58. *LA,* iii, 161.　59. Ib., 162.　60. Ib., 163 f.
61. Ib., 167. Cf. *Fug.,* 139.　62. *LA,* iii, 168. Cf. *Fug.,* 137.
63. *Fug.,* 138; *Mut.,* 259 f.; *Cong.,* 170–174; *Heres,* 191. In *Det.,* 114–118 the divine food is the Rock, Sophia, or the Manna, the Logos, and these, Philo insists, are synonymous. From this food came two cakes, one of honey that sweetens the life, the other of oil, spiritual illumination.
64. *LA,* iii, 169, 175.　65. Ib., 171.　66. Ib., 173.
67. Ib., 174 f.　68. Ib., 176.　69. Ib., 177 f.
70. Ib., 169.

its higher is important, indeed, but there was no real merit in the figure of higher and lower personalities to represent the contrast. What Philo has in mind by the two experiences of the Logos and the logoi, as it seems to me, is, in the one case the Higher Mystery, where one had the Logos at its source, and in the other case the Lower Mystery, where men are using the lower agents of the Stream as revealed in the laws, advices of Judaism, and in the cosmic order.

After leaving the passions of Egypt the Israelites came to the bitter waters of Marah. The bitterness was their apprehension for the future, that timidity which drives many easily discouraged people back to pleasure.[71] The Israelites would indeed have been lost and returned to Egypt had not the Savior thrown into their lives, their souls, a bit of wood, a sweetening thing, to make them see that toil was sweet. This Savior was the Creator, the δημιουργός, a strange term even for Philo to apply to Moses; though in the narrative it is he who is the Savior and throws in the wood at God's command.[72] The wood or tree cast into the waters was the Tree of Life, says Philo, the tree that brings immortality, and hence it is Goodness and her body-guards, the specific virtues.[73] Again it is apparent how Moses is acting as the Savior-Hierophant for the wanderers.

The Israelites now go on to Elim, with its twelve fountains and seventy palm trees. These fountains are the springs of learning, the right and most nourishing Logoi, by which one is introduced to Virtue. Since they are twelve in number they are parallel in symbolism with the zodiac[74] and the Cosmic Mystery of the high-priest's robe.[75] The palm trees are the Mystery of the seven, that is, we understand, of τὸ ὄν with the six Powers, and of the seventy elders who received the divine and prophetic spirit.[76] Hence the distinction is that those who are learning make use of the wells of preliminary instruction, those who are adorned with complete virtue are crowned with palm leaves and fillets.[77] Israel, at this stage, Philo points out, was not ready to camp by the palms, but only by the springs of the Lower Mystery.

The incident is given little more than parenthetic attention in the *Allegory*, and might easily escape notice if it were not that it seems to be certainly what lies behind one of the most difficult of the frescoes in the Dura Synagogue. In the *De Vita Mosis*, i, 188 ff. the twelve trees are a symbol of the twelve tribes, the seventy palm trees of the seventy elders. In the fresco, which will be reproduced and more fully discussed in the next volume, the twelve tribes take the place of the twelve palm trees encircling the fountains. Each tribe is represented by a figure standing before his tent, the tent

71. *Cong.*, 163 f. 72. *Post.*, 155–157. 73. *Mig.*, 36 f.
74. *Fug.*, 183 f. 75. Ib., 185. 76. Ib., 186.
77. Ib., 187.

of the biblical encampment, and the twelve man-tent units are arranged in a circle like that of the zodiac around a central spring from which flow twelve streams, the twelve fountains of the Bible conceived as a unit. Moses it is, apparently, who stands by the central fountain, a huge figure in a peculiar checked garment, touching the fountain with his wand and thereby, apparently, causing its twelve streams to flow out one into each of the surrounding tents. With these details are shown the altar, censers, and candlestick of the Mystery of Aaron, while the reality beyond is fittingly indicated only by an arch through which nothing can at this stage be seen. The fresco stands beside another which represents the significance of the temple as administered by Aaron. The fresco would seem to agree with Philo in representing the scene at Elim as the incident when the tribes were taken into the Lower Mystery. With this harmonizes the fact that the twelve springs at Elim represented both the twelve tribes and the twelve signs of the zodiac in early rabbinic tradition.[77a]

Again the Israelites are discouraged and mutinous because of their thirst and the hardships of the journey, and again God through Moses comes to their rescue. This time it is the first incident of the water brought forth from the rock by Moses' rod, the rock of Horeb.[78] Philo explains this twice. The soul, represented by the Israelites, is disorganized in the desert

and is gripped by the thirst of the passions until God sends down the stream of His own precipitous Sophia and quenches the thirst of the soul with unwavering health. For the precipitous (ἀκρότομος, literally, sharply cut) rock is the Sophia of God which He cut off as the peak (ἄκρα) and first of His own Powers, and from which He quenches the thirst of the souls that love God.[79]

The passage is too slight to emphasize particularly except for the general identification of the rock and its stream with Sophia. The picture of the sharply cut peak at the top of the Powers suggests the way in which all the Powers head up in the Logos or Sophia, as I have illustrated it in the Diagrams on pp. 24, 29. It is at least possible that Philo has in mind this peaked triangle of Powers.

More elaborately he allegorizes the words, "Behold I will stand before thee there upon the rock in Horeb":[80]

77a. See D. Feuchtwang, "Der Tierkreis in der Tradition und im Synagogenritus," *Monatsschrift für Geschichte und Wissenschaft des Judentums*, LIX (1915), pp. 241–267, esp. p. 243.

78. Exod. xvii, 6. It is notable that Philo follows the general Jewish conspiracy of silence about the second incident of the rock (Numb. xx, 10, 11), the rock of Meribah, where Moses was commanded to speak to the rock, but instead struck it in anger, and so was forbidden himself to enter the Promised Land.

79. *LA*, ii, 86. The phraseology comes from the reference to the incident in Deut. viii, 15, where the detail that the rock was ἀκρότομος is added. The Hebrew word is taken by commentators to mean flint.

80. Exod. xvii, 6.

This is equivalent to saying "I who am made manifest and am there, am there and everywhere. I have filled all things (yet stand and remain in a fixed condition (ἐν ὁμοίῳ) since I am unchangeable) before either you or any phenomena came into existence. I am seated upon the highest peaked (ἀκροτάτη) and eldest Power, that of Rulership, from which the creation of phenomena is rained down and the stream of Sophia flows."[81]

The two passages together do not make a picture clear in details, for the rock is in one case the highest Power, Sophia; in the other it is again the Power that is most sharply peaked, but this time that Power is ἀρχή, the source of Sophia. But the two are more alike than dissimilar, for in both cases the rock is the highest Power as the flowing source of Sophia to men, with God, in the second passage, above the peak of Powers. He may be understood to be so in the first passage also. It is quite evident that the Biblical scene was one that would appeal to men interested in striking illustrations of the mystic impartation of the Stream through the mediation of Moses as the Savior, and actually we shall find Moses at the rock to be one of the most common of our iconographical survivals.

When Moses by holding up his hands brought victory to the Israelites over Amalek he showed that the soul can triumph over mortal things only as the mind is borne aloft above them.[82] His hands are supported in the effort by Aaron as Speech and by Hor as Light or Truth (φῶς, ἀλήθεια).[83]

The next incidents in the story are described rather with the purpose of showing the character of Moses and his relations to God than to illuminate the migration. So Moses who "sits alone" outside the camp[84] is the Sophos withdrawn from the tempestuous sea of humanity, contemplating τὸ ὄν. Thus he is constituted κατὰ τὸν μονάδα, in accordance with the Monad, in marked contrast to the high-priest, logos. For the logos without speech is constant and one, but logos projected with voice is not one but two, logos and sound, and so is not fixed and stable. Hence the high-priest, who represents logos in speech, λόγος προφορικός, can have only occasional recourse to the sacred doctrines, only once a year, in fact, when he goes into the holy of holies. Moses sitting outside the camp is really then a type of the perfect mystic who, having gone beyond the experience of the Logos in the Cosmos, comes to the higher doctrines of the Mystery, and can live simply and continuously on that level.[85] Indeed he is that Logos itself.

In this passage the man of puffed up conceit, ὁ περισσὸς τῦφος, Moses' father-in-law, Jethro, is amazed when he finds how Moses lives, and reproaches him.[86] In another treatise Philo discusses the same scriptural passage and with the same interpretation. Jethro is again ὁ τῦφος, the Egyptian

81. *Som.*, ii, 221. 82. *LA*, iii, 186. 83. Ib., 45.
84. Exod. xvii, 4. 85. *Gig.*, 51 f. 86. Ib., 50.

Proteus,[86a] rebuking Moses, ὁ σοφός. Jethro thinks he has said something fine in saying that "the Lord is great beyond all gods."[87] By these very words he shows that he does not perceive God, for if the Light, those unmixed and purest and most brilliant conceptual beams of the Light-Bearing God, had come to him, the lesser lights would have been so eclipsed that he could not have made this comparison. He has not got from the Many to the One. In contrast Moses teaches men the true Law, and urges them to leave Jethro's "empty opinion": he urges men to come, under his guidance, to the "true faith dear to man,"[88] which we may suppose involved the inflooding of the Light-Stream.

It is hard to think that there could be any higher vision or communion with God than this, but certainly the descriptions of Moses on Sinai are meant to imply the supreme human experience of God. References to the experience are of course frequent, and need not all be discussed. The most beautiful message Moses has for his mystic followers (τοῖς γνωρίμοις) is

that they love God, hearken unto Him, and cleave unto Him.[89] . . . Vivid is the invitation Moses gives them to honor the Thrice Desired,[90] the One worthy of love: for he says, "cleave to Him," thereby bringing out the continuity and successiveness and unbrokenness of the attunement and union that come from appropriating God to oneself.[91]

Moses' own yearning to see and be seen by God was so intense that he left the people at the foot of Sinai to press on into the thick darkness where God was,[92] that is into the unapproachable and invisible conceptions (ἔννοιαι) about τὸ ὄν.[93] For God is not Himself localized by the darkness or by any other time or place, for He transcends the material universe though He Himself made it and has filled the world with Himself. What are in the world are His δυνάμεις, His Powers, which hold the universe together according to the ratios (λόγοι) of harmony.[94] In trying to get beyond these Powers to the essence of Being (τὸ τί ἐστι τὸ ὄν κατὰ τὴν οὐσίαν) man is seeking the invisible, a quest that is doomed to failure though the attempt brings the greatest boon, since perhaps the highest achievement we can hope

---

86a. The identification of Jothar with the "Egyptian Proteus" is the only survival I have found in Philo of the primitive identification of biblical figures with pagan deities, a process described in Chapter X. Just what the identification orginally meant it is difficult from this phrase to reconstruct. "Egyptian Proteus" is Homeric (Od. iv, 355, 385; cf. Legat., 80). But Proteus in Egypt was a king who received Dionysus, and he figures importantly in Orphic mythology (Hymn, XXV, Abel, Orphica, p. 72). Frazer suggests (Diodorus, The Library, Loeb Classics, I, p. 326, n. 1; III, v, i, ad loc.) that the visit of Dionysus to Egypt was part of the identification of Dionysus with Osiris.

87. Exod. xviii, 11.   88. Ebr., 36–45.   89. Deut. xxx, 20.
90. τριπόθητος. One is reminded of Trismegistus.
91. Post., 12.   92. Exod. xx, 21.   93. Post., 13 f.
94. Ib., 14.

for is "to see that God is invisible."[95] Now the hierophant, Moses, was aware in advance of the inevitable failure of his attempt to see God.[96] For his approach, like Abraham's, must be through the Powers, since God has so separated true Being from what is created that we cannot touch Him even with the pure and immaterial projections of the intellect.[97]

In a very similar way Philo in another passage discusses Moses' ambition to see God, and his failure. Moses recognized that the highest possible gift to mortals was to see, or get knowledge of, "the bodies and things that are below Being" (τὰ μετὰ τὸ ὂν σώματά τε ὁμοῦ καὶ πράγματα), that is God's "back parts." Imperfect as was this experience, the fact that Moses had achieved it meant that he had penetrated into "the invisible and immaterial substance" (ἡ ἀόρατος καὶ ἀσώματος οὐσία), and had beheld "the unseen nature" (ἡ ἀειδὴς φύσις).[98] The Sophos, as typified by Moses in this experience, can only hope to know the things attendant and consequent upon God, for he would be absolutely blinded by the streaming Light if he tried to see the Dominant Nature itself.[99] These things which are μετὰ τὸ ὂν are definitely the Powers. One can come to see God only through the Powers that range the universe, Philo says. God in his Being (ὁ κατὰ τὸ εἶναι θεός) cannot be seen by mortals; only His existence (ὕπαρξις) can be apprehended. The substance (οὐσία) or quality (ποιότης) of God is inaccessible. So when Moses saw the "back parts" of God he saw the Powers that follow upon and attend Him (αἱ ἑπόμεναι καὶ ἀκόλουθαι δυνάμεις), and inferred God's existence from these resultants (ἐκ τῶν ὑποτελουμένων) of His nature.[100]

While on the mount Moses was an incorporeal listener to the divine music of the Cosmos. His incorporeality was a result of the experience, since the music made him forget to eat for forty days;[101] he not only listened to the music, but himself became a part of it. For it was on the mount that he came to "stand with" God, share His immutability.[102] Hence his soul became a lyre in such perfect attunement with the virtues that as he plucked and swept the strings he produced the most beautiful of all symphonies, the symphony of a life in which ideal virtues are perfectly expressed in actions.[103] By the fact that Moses could live so long upon the vision of divine things, and without material food, he showed his complete renunciation of the body. In this he is contrasted with the man of gradual improvement.[104] Since now he has "gone out from the body" Moses can

95. Ib., 15.
96. Ib., 16.
97. Ib., 17–20.
98. Mut., 7–10.
99. Fug., 164 f.: αὔταρκες γάρ ἐστι σοφῷ τὰ ἀκόλουθα καὶ ἑπόμενα καὶ ὅσα μετὰ τὸν θεὸν γνῶναι, τὴν δ' ἡγεμονικὴν οὐσίαν ὁ βουλόμενος καταθεάσασθαι τῷ περιαυγεῖ τῶν ἀκτίνων πρὶν ἰδεῖν πηρὸς ἔσται.
100. Post., 165–169.
101. Som., i, 36.
102. Post., 28 f.; Conf., 30–32; Sac., 8.
103. Immut., 23–26.
104. LA, iii, 141–143.

go into the darkness where God is, the invisible region (ὁ ἀειδὴς χῶρος). Entering there he abides while he is made perfect in the most sacred Mysteries (τελούμενος τὰς ἱερωτάτας τελετάς). And he not only becomes an initiate (μύστης), but also the hierophant of the rites (ἱεροφάντης ὀργίων) and teacher of divine things (διδάσκαλος θείων), which he will reveal to those whose ears have been purified (ἃ τοῖς ὦτα κεκαθαρμένοις ὑφηγήσεται). With him then the divine spirit that leads along every Right Road abides.[105]

In pitching the tent outside the camp Moses has run away from himself to the knowledge of the One (ἡ τοῦ ἑνὸς ἐπίγνωσις), and this sort of running is a noble race (δρόμος).[106] His being outside the body in this way is analogous to the fact that the high-priest strips off the robe, the garment of opinion and fantasy of the soul, and, leaving it behind for those who love external things, goes into the holy of holies.[107] Moses is also in contrast to Noah, who was pleasing to the Powers; for Moses was pleasing to ὁ ὢν αὐτός, the One who is attended by the Powers, and so Moses gets grace directly from God.[108]

In the *Quaestiones in Exodum* Philo has the same conception of the experience of Moses on the Mount. At first he took with him Aaron, Nadab, and Abihu, that is the purest intellect went up with true speech, a will for piety, and divine aid or truth. But proper as it is that one should start the journey to God with these, nothing but the pure intellect in man can go on to the vision. Philo has in mind here the supremacy of Moses to the other men, and at the same time the unique superiority of the intellect in man's constitution. The other men, the attributes preparatory for the vision, could not stand the rays from God, but there are a few individuals who like salamanders can live in fire, the very inner region of God.[109] On the Mount God stands, for there is no motion possible for Him, but He sends out His Powers to indicate His essence.[110] The glory of God appeared as flame; this was not God Himself but His Powers, and it was not really fire but only appeared to be so.[111] Moses, in going up into this, goes beyond the heaven into God, and there himself abides.[112] He is so united with Deity that his own logos now is in the form of light, and expresses itself, its beauty, not in words but things.[113] Moses was thus called up upon the mountain

that the mortal race might not be cut off from the incorruptible *facies,* and that the divine and holy essence of things might not be exposed among the mob. He was taken up upon the high mountain that was absolutely forbidden to others.

105. *Gig.,* 54 f. The text is translated as it stands. I am convinced that τῆς has been lost before πάσης or should be understood there, and that the meaning was that Moses acts with the Spirit to lead one along the "whole Road," the entire way to perfection.

106. *LA,* iii, 46–48; cf. *Ebr.,* 100.   107. *LA,* ii, 54–56.

108. *Immut.,* 109 f.   109. *QE,* ii, 27 f.; cf. *Mig.,* 166.

110. *QE,* ii, 37.   111. Ib., 47.

112. Ib., 40.   113. Ib., 44.

The clouds which the people saw were just a sign of the intelligibles, a figure to be used in teaching them.[114]

Clearly it was through these experiences that Moses came to be the hierophant supreme of Israel, though he has been acting as such in anticipation since the incident of the Bush. He has the secrets; his is the Spirit that guides men on the Road. He can now give Israel leadership in two ways, as mystagogue and as lawgiver. In preparation for the production of the machinery of the Lower Mystery, the building, that is, of the tabernacle, God has already so exalted Moses that Moses himself needs a mediator between his person and material representations. This mediator is Bezaleel, the master builder of the tabernacle. Bezaleel is a copy, stamped with the Logos to be sure,[115] but one who gets his stamp only through the medium of created things.[116] Moses on the contrary was initiated into the greater Mystery[117] so that he apprehended both God and the Logos. He has direct vision of the Cause itself, while Bezaleel, who appears to be in the Lower Mystery, gets his vision only from the created shadow. Hence Moses produces the archetypes of the tabernacle, Bezaleel the material copies of the archetypes.[118] The same idea appears in another treatise where Moses' experience has made him "keeper and guard of the rites of Being" (ὁ ταμίας καὶ φύλαξ τῶν τοῦ ὄντος ὀργίων), and so producer of the archetypes. Bezaleel can produce only copies since he had been deemed worthy of the secondary things (ὁ τῶν δευτερείων ἀξιωθείς). The point of the contrast is that some men have given to them a brighter Light-Stream, that is one nearer the source, than others.[119]

It is notable that the *Allegory* has little or nothing to say of Moses as the author of the specific laws. The *Quaestiones* mentions the giving of the law briefly, but only to interpret that legislation as a spiritual impartation of *lex voluntaria*,[120] which has its source in Sophia.[121] Legislation in the traditional Jewish sense has no importance here. The legislative office came to Moses according to the *Allegory* along with the prophetic office and the gift of Sophia, so that he was "parent mind." Again there is no thought of representing the legislation as such as being of importance.[122] For all that occasional allegories of much of the legislation appear scattered through the *Allegory*, the Code of Commands as such, and Moses' function as legislator of specific laws, play no part in the Mystery. The Mystery presented in the *Allegory* is obviously moving beyond the specific commands in that realm which we have found many times suggested as the realm of the true Judaism. For the significance of Moses as legislator we are wholly dependent upon the *Exposition*.

114. Ib., 52. 115. *LA*, iii, 95 f. 116. Ib., 102.
117. Ib., 100.
118. See the whole passage, ib., 95–103.
119. *Plant.*, 23–27; cf. *Som.*, i, 206 f.
120. *QE*, ii, 34. 121. Ib., 36. 122. *Cong.*, 131–135.

While Moses was thus being initiated in a way quite beyond the experience of anyone else, what of his flock at the foot of the mountain? They were having different experiences. They are represented as having been in ecstasy at the appearance of God on Sinai, and later at the descent of fire at the sacrifices, but this was an ecstasy of consternation.[128] The great voice from Sinai, as in the *Exposition*, was "seen" by them, since that voice was the outflowing of the Light-Stream of the Logos.[124] As they had the vision of the Logos they ate and drank, because such a vision is food to the soul and gives it immortal life.[125] But they really had little immediate experience at Sinai of the great revelation. Over and over again it is brought out that the people were not ready, and that the mountain had little for them except as it was brought to them by Moses. Moses and God talked together in reciprocal streams of utterance. He as the Sophos took God as his teacher; but the less perfect, Israel, must take Moses.[126] He alone could bear the divine annunciation of Sinai as a whole. God can speak to the mass of men only through Moses, for He must always thus temper His benefactions to the capacities of the recipient.[127] Moses as a friend of God is the intercessor for the people, and not only speaks for God to the people, but speaks boldly to God for men in need.[128]

Actually the people were so perverse, still so tied to the body and its passions, that they were unable to receive the revelation even as mediated by Moses. They projected their still lingering passions into the formation of the golden calf. But the calf, as the vestige of the passions, must be destroyed: we must destroy our bodies, burn our pleasures, pulverize the "gods" of the material realm, if we may hope to share in the higher things.[129]

Had we in the *Allegory* a connected account of the incidents following the destruction of the calf,[130] it would undoubtedly have interpreted these incidents as the provision of the formal Mystery for the people. It is to this provision that the *Quaestiones* at once goes on, describing the significance of the ark as representing the Higher Mystery. This material we have already discussed. But the form of the *Quaestiones*, where the treatment of each individual text is the important matter rather than the connected exposition of the Mystery as such, makes the point not so clear as a stated allegory of the life of Moses, or one of the migration, would have done.

One of these incidents is too important for Philo to omit, the incident of the sacrifice of Moses. By an incredible explanation of Lev. vii, 34, Philo represents the sacrifice of Moses, in which he put only the beast's breast upon the altar, as signifying that Moses is beyond any labor with the passions, for

123. *Heres*, 251.   124. *Mig.*, 47.   125. *QE*, ii, 39.
126. *Heres*, 17–19.   127. *Post.*, 143; cf. *Som.*, i, 143.   128. *Heres*, 21.
129. *Post.*, 158–169; *Ebr.*, 95–100, 124–126.
130. See above, pp. 191 f.

he has cut them off altogether; but Aaron who sacrifices the shoulder with the breast is one who is still laboring with the passions. So Moses is the perfect man (ὁ τέλειος), while Aaron is the attendant and minister of holy things, the man still in the great battle with his lower nature.[181] Similarly the belly, the symbol of pleasure and appetite,[182] is washed by Moses in his sacrifice,[183] for while he cannot do wholly without food, he is freed from all dependence upon the belly, as his forty days' fast on the mount showed. In contrast Aaron cannot wash the whole belly, for he must be content if he can control the passions by reason, and cannot once for all dominate them and put away their desires.[184] This whole contrast seems part of a great contrast that may well have existed in the tradition of the Mystery, between the type of sacrifice Aaron could offer and that of the Higher Mystery.[185]

Obviously also a part of the installation of the Mystery is the explanation of the choice of the Seventy Elders.[186] Age has nothing to do with one's having a claim to the title of Presbyter, says Philo, in spite of the fact that ordinary men think that it is men of senior age whom one must regard as hierophants. The true Elder is a man whom the Sophos alone knows. The Sophos (Moses) rejects all men with the spirit of youthful rebellion in them whatever their age, while those are Presbyters in heart and in mind who are his mystic disciples (γνώριμοι).[187] These elders were ordained by fire from Moses' Spirit. For the fact is that they could not be elders in the true sense of the term (πρὸς ἀλήθειαν)

unless they partook of that all-wise spirit. For it is written "I will take of the spirit that is on thee and lay it upon the seventy elders." But do not think that this taking of the spirit is a matter of cutting off a piece or severing. Rather it is like the process of taking fire from fire, for though one fire should light ten thousand torches it would remain absolutely undiminished itself. Such is the nature of Wisdom (ἐπιστήμη). For it makes experts of all the followers and disciples (φοιτηταὶ καὶ γνώριμοι) but is itself no whit diminished. Indeed they often contribute to its improvement, as springs are said to be improved by drawing water from them. For the report is that the springs are thus made sweeter. So the frequent giving of instruction to others involves practice and discipline for the instructor, by which he is brought to the perfection of knowledge. If, then, it were Moses' own spirit, or the spirit of some other created being, which was to be distributed to such a great crowd of disciples (γνώριμοι), it would be diminished by the process of cutting it up into so many pieces. But now the spirit that is upon him is the Wise Spirit, the divine Spirit, the Spirit that is uncut and unsevered, excellent, the Spirit that is filled in every part with all things.[188]

131. *LA*, iii, 133–137.   132. Ib., 138–140.   133. Lev. ix, 14.
134. *LA*, iii, 141–159.
135. So it is not surprising that this sacrifice, culminating in the descent of fire from the Glory of God, is one of the scenes chosen for representation at Dura.
136. Numb. xi, 16.   137. *Sobr.*, 16–20.   138. *Gig.*, 24 ff.

That is, the Spirit which was on Moses, and which passes on to his γνώρι-μοι to make them Presbyters in the true sense, is none other than Sophia or the Logos, the Light-Stream. The idea is introduced at a part of the narrative which makes it seem that we have a glimpse into the organization of the Mystery. For the passage seems to reflect a real doctrine of what might be called "patriarchal or Mosaic succession." The similarity of the conception to the very early doctrine that the presbyter or bishop in the Christian Church was a successor in just this way to the spirit that Jesus had given to the disciples is, to say the least, striking. As we come through the Philonic testimony to the other literary testimony and to the iconographical evidence for the Mystery it will appear most likely that the Mystery may have had a considerable organization which centered in its Presbyters who got their authority from being γνώριμοι Μωύσεως. Evidence for the character of that organization is precisely what we most lack, so that the loss of a consecutive account of this part of Moses' activity is deeply to be deplored. Much as these two passages stand off alone by themselves, it is impossible for me not to feel that, appearing twice in two remote parts of the *Allegory*, they represent a very fixed convention of "succession of elders" within the organization of the Mystery. That is a large generalization, not justified, perhaps, by the evidence we have as yet considered, so I will leave the matter only with emphasizing that the passages, exactly as they stand, are strikingly similar to the Christian doctrine of "succession." Of that there can be no doubt.

In spite of the founding at Sinai of the formal institutions of the tabernacle and the ark, the Israelites can still not give up their love of the body, and must yet wander in the desert.[139] The next great event is the coming of the tribes to the borders of Palestine, and the sending of the spies to report on conditions in the Promised Land. This seems to represent the people as at last ready for a preliminary glimpse, a foretaste, of the Higher Mystery. The scouts sent out for the people are the ὀρθὸς λόγος of the human mind sent out into the country of Virtue along the "road of Philosophy." Here the mind finds Virtue or Sophia, a great tree or vine, but at this stage is unable to appropriate it fully. It can only break off a fabulous bunch of grapes from the vine and bring it back. The vine is also supreme happiness, εὐφροσύνη, of which the scouts are able to bring back a portion. Indeed the joy of God is especially manifest at the time when people are beginning to turn from their sins to "follow of their own will the laws and injunctions of nature."[140]

There is nothing inspiring in Israel's being forbidden entrance to Palestine at this time, so Philo does not discuss it, and again describes the wandering of the Israelites in the wilderness under the leadership of Moses.

139. *Mig.*, 154 f.; *Heres*, 79 f.
140. *Som.*, ii, 170–177; cf. *Mut.*, 224: the spies could not bring back the whole tree of virtue, so brought back a single virtue.

One extended and elaborate allegory is built upon the incident of the Israelites' asking passage through the country of the Edomites and being refused. They do not want to stop with the Edomites, for they are on their way to the mountain country.[141] Here Israel, as contrasted with the Edomites, is the company of true followers of Moses[142] going on the Royal Road of Sophia to God[143] under the guidance of the ὀρθὸς λόγος.[144] It is quite true that such people only want to go through the land of the Edomites, the people of this material world, for what use have a people fed and watered from heaven for the food and hand-dug wells of the world. There is no point, as Jesus explained to the woman of Samaria, in drawing up water by ropes from a well made by men when heaven itself gives us its unmixed draughts, sometimes with an angel as cupbearer, sometimes without even that mediation between God and the thirsty soul.[145] Only the grapes, the virtues treasured also by human ideals, will they not scorn to use.[146] The road is the flight for refuge to the uncreated (ἡ ἐπὶ τὸν ἀγένητον καταφυγή).[147] It is the straight Road, ethically, of the mean.[148] Through the allegory, Moses is the hierophant of the journey.[149] The incident is a favorite one with Philo. In another reference this Royal Road is commended to kings, and is again the road of the mean, but the mean is recognizably that of the Pythagoreans rather than of Aristotle.[150] Again it is the Road of true philosophy, the Road of the Logos to God, on which Moses leads us.[151]

High as the Israelites, who are on the Road of Sophia or the Logos, may be in contrast to the Edomites, they still have far to go, and still must struggle with the love of matter and pleasure. This is of course Philo's interpretation of their being attacked by the serpents, which are, like the serpent of Eve, the pleasures that bring the death not of the body but of the soul.[152] At the command of God Moses makes a serpent of the opposite kind, the serpent of self-mastery (σωφροσύνη). Since the command is to make it "for

141. Numb. xx, 17–20.
142. *Immut.*, 144, 148.
143. Ib., 142–145, 159 f.
144. Ib., 152 f.
145. Ib., 153–158.
146. Ib., 154.
147. Ib., 160.
148. Ib., 162 f.
149. Ib., 156; see the continuation of the allegory to §183.
150. *Spec.*, iv, 168. The assumption that every mention of the ethical mean indicates Aristotelian influence is not at all warranted, since the conception is, through Plato's *Philebus* and by many details in Aristotle, traceable to the Pythagoreans. In this passage Philo definitely connects the mean with the symbolism of the number three in a way that shows he is thinking of the mean as it would have reached him in the Pythagorean tradition. Certainly, in view of his marked dependence upon Pythagorean ethics as a whole, when he refers (*Mig.*, 146 f.) to the teachers of the "mean," the "Royal Road," as being those who "follow the mild and social forms of philosophy," the description seems more to resemble Pythagoreans than Aristotle.
151. *Post.*, 101 f.
152. *LA*, ii, 77. In §§84 f., Philo points out that they were bitten in the wilderness, and says that pleasure can attack one there quite as well as in the city. He goes on to one of his rare and most appealing personal passages, saying that running to the desert has solved no problems for him personally. He was as apt to be "scattered" by desire there as anywhere else, while God could give His grace quite as easily while one is surrounded, but alone, in a multitude.

thy self," the self-mastery Moses shows them for their salvation is peculiarly his own self-mastery. The serpent is of brass because this is as near to the golden virtue present in Moses as the people could come. Salvation from pleasure, then, is to look upon the beauty of σωφροσύνη, the "serpent of Moses," and, "in seeing this, one beholds God Himself. Let him look and mark it well!"[153] This is not a casual allegory, as its substantial repetition in another treatise shows.[154] The mystic looked to the virtues of Moses, and in doing so looked upon God. A more definite statement of Moses' power as a divine savior could not be made.

The Israelites are soon back in sin, this time with the daughters of Moab. Phinehas is now the hero, representing the "Seeing Race," the higher mystic who fights sin with the Logos Cutter (λόγος τομεύς), and is, as always in such encounters, victorious. So he is become "the peaceful and manifest priest of God."[155] It will be recalled that it was this performance of Phinehas which caused his being consecrated "everlasting priest." As a son of Aaron, the Biblical implication is of course his holding the Aaronic high-priesthood. Philo seems to understand it of the higher priesthood of the upper Mystery both in this passage and in another treatise.[156]

Through this later part of the wanderings of the tribes Moses is still the savior and hierophant. He prays to God for us that we may have the ὀρθὸς λόγος as a shepherd within our personal constitutions.[157] It is still he who can lead the soul out from the bodily regions,[158] for he gives himself in place of the divine providence.[159] When Moses stands between God and the people in Deut. v, 5, it is the Logos mediating for us.[160] In connection with this text of mediation Philo says that immutability appears in four kinds, first the immutability of τὸ ὄν, second that of ὁ τοῦ ὄντος λόγος, third that of the Sophos, and fourth that of the man making progress by effort. Aaron typifies (with the Aaronic priesthood, we understand) the last type. He is still in the cosmos, and so, though he has made much progress, he has not yet left the material world. The class above him is the Sophos, who is Moses, the type of priesthood represented by the holy of holies. This is the priesthood that really can stand between man and God in the sense that Moses is said to have done.[161]

The migration, as Philo describes it, never gets into the Promised Land.

153. *LA*, ii, 78–81. Is not the "gold," the real virtue of Moses of which he could show the Israelites only a brazen copy, an echo of the succession of metals in Mithras, or of the earlier Iranian-Babylonian sources of Mithras? By this, gold is the symbol of the highest mystic achievement, the "seventh" stage. The statement of Philo would then imply that the "golden" stage of virtue at the top of the ladder was not properly to be exhibited to the multitude, even to a multitude on an early stage of the Road. This is precisely Philo's meaning. He has certainly learned of the "golden" virtue in this sense from neither the Bible nor Aristotle.

154. *Agr.*, 95–101.	155. *Mut.*, 106–109.	156. *Ebr.*, 73–76.
157. *Post.*, 67 ff.; *Agr.*, 44.	158. *Mut.*, 209.	159. Ib., 25.
160. *Heres*, 206.	161. *Som.*, ii, 227–237.	

That is always the unattained goal. Perhaps this is because to Philo the Pentateuch alone was the Torah, as we have seen, and other people would have continued the story with Joshua as leader. Yet the story would have had to stop somewhere, for the history of the Israelites in Canaan could hardly by the most imaginative treatment have been allegorized to typify the soul in its ultimate spiritual achievement. Furthermore to go on from here would have involved discussing why Moses was unfit to lead the people on to the end, and Joshua must have emerged as one greater than Moses. This could not be allowed. So Philo ends the story without taking the tribes into Canaan.[162]

I strongly suspect that the mystic allegory of the migration stopped there also. In place of their coming into Palestine, the supreme achievement of the Israelites in the desert under the leadership of Moses is in Philo centered in a peculiar incident, not really in the Bible at all, because it is made up of two scenes put together. Numb. xxi, 16–18, according to the translation of the Septuagint, reads:

They went then to the well. This well is the one the Lord mentioned when he said to Moses, "Gather together the people, and I will give them water to drink." Then Israel sang this song at the well:
> Lead ye the song to it:
> This Well, the rulers have dug it,
> The kings of the nations have hewn it out,
> In their kingdom, in their lordship.

This is the well or stream of Sophia, says Philo, to be dug only by those who are so beyond the common herd that they are kings and leaders. The song adjures "lead ye the song," ἐξάρχετε; but Philo says that at the well it was Moses who led the song. The song's theme is no longer that of the Red Sea, where the destruction of the passions is celebrated. Now it is the greater, the long anticipated, step, the achievement of Sophia that is being hymned.[163] The song is the song of the initiation into Sophia, where Moses, as hierophant, now leads the people. Ordinary people cannot dig the well of Sophia, but only kings, and not kings whose power rests upon conquest, but those who have become kings, after the familiar teaching of the day, by conquering their own lower natures. And who are such kings? Philo does not explain. Instead he identifies those who are sharing in the song to Sophia at the well with the warriors and their captains who are mentioned later as being organized and numbered. For the leaders who dug the well prove to

162. I recall only one possible exception to this statement. The promised land with its cities, houses, pits, vineyards, and olive gardens (Deut. vi, 10 f.) is allegorized as the great gift to the fully perfect. This allegory appears twice (*Immut.*, 94–96; *Fug.*, 175), but there is no suggestion in either passage that the Israelites got there.
163. *Ebr.*, 112 f.

have associates and disciples (φοιτηταὶ καὶ γνώριμοι), those who were numbered and marshalled, and of whom it is said that not one of them was off pitch, but each brought his gift to the Lord, every man what he found. These disciples and followers are also joining in the song of victory to the perfect and dominant Powers. They are perfectly attuned in their courage, neither rash nor afraid, perfect indeed in every virtue. The gift they bring is the gift each man finds at his birth, the whole universe.[164]

Another and much briefer passage, again in quite a different treatise, has the same contrast between the well of this scene and the Red Sea. At the Red Sea the song celebrated the destruction of the passions.

But the rout and destruction of the passions, while a good, is not ultimate good (τέλειον ἀγαθόν): the discovery of Sophia is the surpassing good (ὑπερβάλλον καλόν). When this is found all the people will sing, not according to a single part of music, but according to all its modes and melodies. "For then," he says, "Israel sang this song at the well," that is to say at Wisdom (ἐπιστήμη), which had formerly been hidden (since it is deep by nature) but now has been sought out and found by all. For the law of Wisdom is that she shall irrigate the fields of reason in the souls of men who are lovers of vision.[165]

In these passages it is to be noticed that there are three great events marked off as the great stages of the migration. First is the leaving of Egypt, second the destruction of the passions at the Red Sea, and third the consummation at the well. This is particularly to be borne in mind as, in a subsequent study, we approach the scenes painted at Dura. Here there are three great scenes from the migration, first the leaving of Egypt, second the destruction of the Egyptians at the Red Sea, and third a picture where a group of warriors are arrayed behind a desert waterhole, beside which stands Moses in mystic garb, pointing to the well with his rod. The symbolism of the pictures fits perfectly with the symbolism of the migration as Philo schematizes it. For Moses Sinai was of great importance. But it meant nothing immediately to the lives of the Israelites as a whole, and is omitted altogether from this particular group of the pictures.

This is to get ahead of the story. And yet the story of the migration is ended. All that is left is to tell of the death of Moses. The fact that Moses did not go into the Promised Land is not to be taken, as some people do, says Philo, as a sign of his humiliation. Philo refers to the record that Moses was allowed a vision of Canaan, and explains that apprehension of the highest things is a matter of vision, with the conclusion that Moses came to possess the Land in his vision more truly than those who later entered it.[166] Moses, it will be recalled, had from the first been a special loan to men, to

164. *Ebr.*, 112–118.   165. *Som.*, ii, 270 f.   166. *Mig.*, 45 f.

serve as the God over our lower natures.[167] When such a Moses was about to die he was translated back to God by the Logos. Hence no one knows his grave:

For who is able to perceive the translation to ὁ ὤν of the perfect soul? Indeed I do not suppose that the one who is having the experience is himself aware of his change to better things, inasmuch as at that time he is in a state of ecstasy (ἐπι-θειάζειν).[168]

He is regarded by God as being quite as important as the entire Cosmos.[169]

Many difficulties are unexplained in what Philo has told us. He has here just skipped the hard places, such as why Moses' death occurred at the age of one hundred twenty years, and it is these and many other points that he hoped to discuss in the treatise on Moses' life as a whole "at such time as we are fit to be initiated into it."[170] Yet when the many passages are put together it is possible to make a remarkably rounded picture of the life of Moses as the great savior and hierophant of the Mystery.

The description of Moses' death both here and in the De Vita Mosis[171] has suggested strongly that to Philo Moses was a God. Before closing the study of Moses some attention must be paid to this question.

It would be easy to collect a group of passages to prove that Philo thought of Moses only as "the perfect man," or the perfected man. "The perfect man," Philo says, as we have seen, was a middle type of existence, for he has been exalted above ordinary humanity, and has become a middle type of existence between the unoriginate and the corruptible natures (μεθόριον τῆς ἀγενήτου καὶ φθαρτῆς φύσεως).[172] When it is recalled that Moses was, even in comparison with the other Patriarchs, "most perfect" (τελειότα-τος),[173] it might be assumed that this was all he meant to ascribe to Moses. Moses pleased God and so was worthy of grace directly from God, in con-trast even to Noah whose virtue was a "copy," and so was rewarded only through God's Powers.[174] From these and from many other passages Moses would appear only as a man who in spite of his special gifts from God, even the gift of a portion of the divine Logos,[175] was in no sense divine.

But on the question of the divinity of Moses Philo falls into one of his frequent vacillations between points of view which cannot be reconciled. This time the hesitation is between the monotheism on the one hand, which

---

167. See above, p. 199.
168. Sac., 8–10.   169. Ib.
170. Gig., 56 f. See above, p. 199.   171. See above, pp. 195 ff.
172. Som., ii, 234. But in ib., 189, Moses seems different from the high-priest in that the priest is this middle type of existence, while Moses is actually called God. But Philo does not develop the idea. See above, p. 202.
173. Ebr., 94; Heres, 260–263; LA, iii, 103.
174. Immut., 109; cf. Som., ii, 232.   175. Heres, 24.

Philo had from his Jewish ancestry and from the Neo-Pythagorean and Platonic traditions in philosophy, and on the other the popular tendency to deify great figures and heroes. The problem of how one might be a mono-theist and yet ascribe deity to various persons and divine principles was one of the great problems of the age. Ordinarily the solution was made, as by the Sabellians in Christian tradition, in line with the growing Neo-Platonic solu-tion, that the one God had a body-guard, was δορυφορούμενος by Powers which were emanations of His own nature; they could be called θεοί, though in contradistinction to ὁ θεός. With this linguistic trick monotheists could justify gratifying their emotional urge to divine personalities and representa-tions less remote than the abstraction τὸ ὄν. Philo, as has appeared, was entirely a creature of his age in this as in most else. The philosopher's rever-ence for the Absolute as the single Deity was strengthened by the Jewish insistence upon the one God, and in many passages Philo defends this posi-tion by denying to the Logos any independent operation or existence, and to Moses any divine nature that was not a gracious gift to one who was essentially a man. Were Philo put to the question to state his theoretical position he would unquestionably have stood by this interpretation of Moses as being only a man inspired, indeed inhabited, by the Logos.

But Philo did not live by theory. Under the stress of his emotions he made statements about the divinity of Moses which cannot be reconciled with the "gifted man" presentations of Moses' character, and these passages must be taken as being quite as representative of Philo's position as the others.

First a passage must be considered as a whole which has already been discussed in part.[176] The passage begins with a discussion of virtue as a gift ordinarily made to virtuous men to take the place of the evil natures which they have eliminated from themselves, or God has taken from them. Types of this are Abel, Abraham, and Jacob, who are "added to" something better in the process, that is to fellowship with the company of angels. Isaac too abandoned the bodily elements, yet he is not added to a host, but to a γένος, and this signifies the highest One.[177] Into this incorruptible and perfect γένος such people as Isaac are not added so much as translated (μετανίστανται).[178] An unfortunate lacuna of four lines in the papyrus text of the passage brings us without introduction to the following:

But there are some whom He has advanced higher, and has made able to soar beyond all εἴδη and γένη, and has stationed beside Himself. Such is Moses to whom He says, "stand here with me."[179] So when Moses was about to die he did not "leave" in order to be "added" like the others, for there was no room in him for either adding or subtraction. But he was translated by the Word (ῥῆμα) of

176. Sac., 1–10.
178. Ib., 7.
177. Ib., 6. On γένος see below, note 187.
179. Deut. v, 31.

that Cause[180] by which the whole universe was created. Thus you may learn that God regards the Sophos as of equal honor with the world, for by the same Word (λόγος) He both made the universe and takes the perfect man from earthly things up into Himself. But by no means, when God gave him as a loan to earthly things and suffered him to dwell with them, did God attach to him any common virtue of a ruler or king, the type of virtue by which one gains forcible control over the passions of the soul. Rather God ordained him as deity (εἰς θεόν), and decreed that all the region of the body and its dominant mind should be subject and slave to him. "For I give thee," He says, "as a god to Pharaoh;"[181] but a deity [here Moses] is not susceptible of subtraction or addition, for deity is a plenum and is perfectly balanced (ἰσαίτατος) in Himself. Therefore it is said that no one knows his tomb, for who would be competent to apprehend the perfect soul's translation over to Being (πρὸς τὸν ὄντα). Nor do I think that the soul itself which had the experience was conscious of its being improved, because at that moment it was in a state of inspired frenzy (ἐπιθειάζουσαν).[182]

Taken by itself this passage could only mean that Moses was a deity who was made incarnate by a special decree of God. This incarnate deity had a full human complement, body plus even the dominant mind (νοῦς ἡγεμών),[183] but he dominated these as a master over slaves. The supreme divine gift to other men is strength of this dominant mind to rule the body; it is especially the greatest divine gift to kings. But Moses was a dominant principle even over the mind. His death did not involve a change of the essential Moses, for he was so purely divine as to be changeless. That is, the human element was so little a part of Moses that its loss was no change. He was merely restored to τὸ ὄν.

Leisegang protests that this is by no means to be taken as a literal expression of Philo's view of Moses. He quotes several parallel passages in which Philo comments upon Moses as being a "God to Pharaoh." Some of them are mere psychological allegories of the mind ruling the body, but one of them is very important. Philo has just explained that God alone is truly Existent (ἐν τῷ εἶναι):

The case of Moses is in agreement with this. For when Moses was appointed "God of Pharaoh" he did not actually (πρὸς ἀλήθειαν) become so, but was only accepted as such by opinion (δόξῃ). For I know that deity gives and bestows, but I cannot conceive of God as being given. But it is said in the holy books, "I give thee as God to Pharaoh." Anything that is given is passive, not active, while true Being (τὸ ὄντως ὄν) has to be an active principle, not passive. What then is to be inferred from these facts? That the Sophos is said to be God of the fool but he is not actually God, no more than the counterfeit tetradrachm is a tetradrachm.

180. Deut. xxxiv, 5. The LXX has ῥῆμα, which Philo is understanding as λόγος.
181. Exod. vii, 1.   182. Sac., 8–10.
183. An interesting premonition of the later Dyophysites. Philo, it would appear from this passage, would not have sympathized with the Monophysites.

When he is compared with τὸ ὄν he will be found a man of God, when he is compared to the fool he is thought by all seeming and appearance to be God, though he is not so actually and essentially (τὸ εἶναι).[184]

Leisegang is quite right in pointing out that when Philo is thinking in terms of his monotheism he was bound to contradict the deity of Moses, because it was inconsistent with his general philosophy. But I still think Philo meant what he said when he wrote the preceding passage. Philo is not to be read by those looking for detailed consistency. The point to be decided is not whether Philo contradicts his statements of Moses' divinity but whether he repeats them often enough so that one may assume that it really represents one of his attitudes toward Moses.

In one passage he points out that every man possessed by the love of God and who worships only τὸ ὄν is called not ἄνθρωπος but θεός; he is not the God of nature to be sure, but he is ἀνθρώπων θεός.[185] Again Philo discusses why Moses was called up upon the mount on the seventh day.[186] In that connection Philo makes several points. The first reason for which Moses was called up is in order to show that his calling up, which meant his election to the "seeing genus" (ὁρατικὸν γένος), was analogous to the creation of the world. This genus[187] was elected and adorned just like the universe itself, "so that like the genus, and equally so, Moses manifested an orderliness in accordance with the *recta lex ac norma*[188] of the God of nature who is immutable, not determined by space, and unmoved." The "calling up" of the prophet was indeed

a second birth better than the first; for the first birth took place in the flesh and had corruptible parents, while the second birth was unmixed and simple, had its seat in the soul which was changed from begotten to unbegotten; and it has no mother, but only a Father, who is also Father of the universe. Wherefore the "calling up," or, as we called it, the divine birth, made him eternally virgin like the nature of the seven. He was called up on the seventh day and differed in this from the protoplast. For the protoplast (created on the sixth day) was made out of earth and had a body. But Moses (called up on the seventh day) was without

184. *Det.*, 161 f. Leisegang's other passages are *LA*, i, 40; *Mig.*, 84; *Mut.*, 19 (the reference to *LA*, iii, 13, must be an error). The first two of these are allegories of psychology again, and have little to tell about Philo's notion of the historical Moses.

185. *Prob.*, 43.

186. *QE*, ii, 46. A few scattered sentences of the Greek are preserved. See Harris, *Fragments*, 60 f. In the translation I follow the Greek where preserved.

187. The γένος is not Israel in general, as Harris takes it, *ad loc.*, but the "true Israel," the company of mystic initiates as above, p. 224 (*Sac.*, 6). In using "genus" for γένος I am frankly avoiding translation. My pupil, Dr. Benedict Einarson, has called my attention to the obvious parallels in Plato: *Repub.*, 501e, τὸ φιλόσοφον γένος; *Tim.*, 19d, τὸ ποιητικὸν γένος; 19e, τὸ τῶν σοφιστῶν γένος, etc. See also Soph., *Antig.*, 1055, τὸ μαντικὸν γένος. The interpretation he suggests here is "professional class."

188. The Greek must have been ὁ ὀρθὸς νόμος καὶ λόγος.

body. Accordingly the number six is assigned as proper for the earth born, but the most sacred nature of the seven for the other.

This, it will be recalled, refers not to Moses' translation at death, but to his experience of God on Sinai.

In one of the passages adduced by Leisegang it is being explained that God is God only of the righteous, while He is Lord and Master of the wicked.[189] So God would not be God to Pharaoh, who was the last word in depravity, but made Moses his God. There is nothing here to tell of what that appointment meant to Moses himself, but the treatise does illuminate the point further on. For Philo comments[190] upon the fact that Moses was the "man of God."[191] God is utterly unchangeable (ἄτρεπτος), but the perfect man (ὁ τέλειος) is the man of God as he gives blessings to the people.

Oh thou who art worthy to be this extremely beautiful and holy substitution, namely to substitute thyself for divine providence! But do not think that he is "man" and "man of God" in the same sense: for he is "man" as God's possession (κτῆμα), but "man of God" as an object of boasting and a benefit (αὔχημα καὶ ὠφέλημα).[192]

The idea that Moses is a substitute for God is clearly running through Philo's mind. He acts for God in relation with Pharaoh and with the Israelites alike, and to the latter he is their pride and their great blessing as the mediator of God's blessings.

Moses is also "many named," the πολυώνυμος.[193] He is called "Moses" because he is the interpreter of the divine oracles, "man of God" because he prays for the people and blesses them, and "God of Pharaoh" because through him Egypt is punished for its crimes. None of these functions, Philo says, is within the power of ordinary humanity. The transcription of beautiful laws is the business of one who is reaching for divine things and has them always in his hand.

And praying and blessing are not the function of an ordinary person, but of a man who disregards his kinship with creation, and who has dedicated himself to the Guide and Father of all things. For one [sc. the ordinary man] must be con-

---

189. *Mut.*, 19.   190. Ib., 24 ff.
191. Deut. xxxiii, 1.   192. *Mut.*, 25 f.
    193. Ib. 125 ff. The word was frequently applied to deities by classical writers to indicate that their many aspects were shown in their being worshipped by many names. The Stoics made much use of the notion, as in the famous passage of Diog. La., VII, 135: ἕν τε εἶναι θεὸν καὶ νοῦν καὶ εἱμαρμένην καὶ Δία· πολλὰς τ'ἑτέρας ὀνομασίας προσονομάζεσθαι. Philo uses the term to describe God and the Logos: *Som.*, ii, 254; *Conf.*, 146; *LA*, i, 43; *Dec.*, 94. See my *Theology of Justin Martyr*, p. 173. The sage is πολυώνυμος in *Ebr.*, 92, where Philo seems to me to have Moses in mind as priest, prophet, law-maker, and king. The term is, of course, not distinctively Stoic. Philo's use of the term may, and very likely does, have its ultimate origin in the Orphic usage. See above, p. 18.

tent to be allowed to make use of the formula of blessing; but actually to procure the good for others is the function of a greater and more perfect soul, and one that is truly filled with God (ὡς ἀληθῶς θειαζούση).¹⁹⁴

Moses is called θεός in as much as he is σοφός, Philo goes on, and as such is the natural ruler of the fool, even though the fool be a king. For God wants even the most wicked men to have an intercessor (παραιτητής) who will plead for them and so mitigate their punishment. Moses is in all this still a human being, but he is given strikingly the office of mediator between man and God, interpreting God's will to them, bringing them the blessing of God, and averting the worst of God's wrath.

But Philo goes farther than this. Moses was called up to the top of the mount, he says, "alone":

because the prophetic intellect, since it has been initiated into divine things and is the *deifer,* is like unity, mixed with absolutely none of these things which exhibit a share in duality. But he who clings to the nature of unity is said to approach into God with a certain familiarity of kinship (*cognativa quadam familiaritate*). For when he had left all mortal categories behind, he was changed into divinity (*transmutatur in divinum*), so that he might be made akin to God and truly divine (*ita ut fiat deo cognatus vireque divinus*).¹⁹⁵

When Moses on the mount was told by God "Stand thou here with me," the words indicate that God gave Moses a share in His own nature, the quality of fixed unchangeableness.¹⁹⁶ And yet Moses, like the other σοφοί, the Patriarchs, was different from ordinary men from the beginning. For he was the great example of a soul sent down to dwell in the body, which never becomes naturalized to its new abode, but which, even while in the body, was really living in the conceptual virtues which are indistinguishable from the divine λόγοι. Such souls come down to the earth at all only because they have a great love of learning and seeing.¹⁹⁷

Was, then, Moses θεός in Philo's mind? The answer must be yes and no. He is contrasted with God in His pure existence. There was only one Deity in the strict sense for Philo. But if Moses was thus contrasted with God, he was quite as sharply contrasted with any man but the Patriarchs, and with all of them but Isaac, by the fact that his humanity was ultimately meaningless in his almost completely divine nature. Philo would probably have been quite unable to have made his conception of Moses much more consistent than these various passages represent it. The uncertainty is, as has been stated, that of Philo's age. It seems to me that what Philo had in mind was the Pythagorean notion of the τρίτον γένος,¹⁹⁸ which was sufficiently vague

194. *Mut.,* 127 f. 195. *QE,* ii, 29.
196. *Post.,* 28 ff.; cf. *Gig.,* 47 ff.; *Immut.,* 23; *Conf.,* 30 f.
197. *Conf.,* 77–82, 105 f. 198. See above, p. 127.

for Philo to use, and the phrases already quoted come to mind as a parallel. Philo said in one place that he would for the time leave the matter open whether to call Moses' mind human or divine or a mixture of the two.[199] The perfect man was a middle type of existence between the unoriginate and the corruptible natures.[200] We recall that the Pythagorean king, as that τρίτον γένος, could be spoken of as one who was metamorphosed into a deity among men (θεὸς ἐν ἀνθρώποις παρεσχαμάτισται),[201] and also as an alien and foreign thing which has come down from heaven to man.[202] The latter idea appears in Philo's passage about Moses' being different from ordinary men from the beginning.[203] That is, Moses was the θεῖος ἄνθρωπος of current dreams, or, since Philo preferred to use the Biblical phrase, the ἄνθρωπος θεοῦ. What precisely that meant Philo's contemporaries and successors seem to have defined as little as Philo. The important thing, in their minds, was not the aligning of the conception with metaphysics, but the great fact that in the θεῖος ἄνθρωπος the gulf between man and God was bridged. If philosophers had tried to work out the notion, they must have ended in as great philosophical absurdities as did later Christian attempts to do so. But the age needed, and sought everywhere to find, the union of divine and human nature that a θεῖος ἄνθρωπος could offer. Philo triumphantly tells the world, Jewish and Gentile alike, that the longing has been met in the Patriarchs, especially in Moses. So while Moses was not ὁ θεός, for that would have been irreverent nonsense to Philo, yet θεός he frequently seemed to him, and as such Moses was Israel's, and all mankind's boast and succor.[204]

What was this great succor (ὠφέλημα) which the life of Moses had brought to man? Of course one of his great benefits to the race was his foundation of the Jewish Law. As the legislator Moses is the Good Shepherd of the mind, leading it out from appearance to reality, that is to the universal principles of justice, or the universal and unchanging Laws of Nature (αὐτὰ δίκαια, τὰ κοινὰ τῆς φύσεως καὶ ἀκίνητα). Without his leadership in this sense men live in all the divergencies manifest in the civil law of various cities, which are founded only upon seeming and probability. In contrast to these the συναγωγὴ κυρίου is not as sheep that have no shepherd.[205] Again "the seeds of human legislation were sown" by the fact that Moses, ὁ καθαρώτατος νοῦς, has gone beyond any material or created manifestation of God to cleave to God alone, and so has received God Himself for his por-

199. *Mos.*, i, 27. See above, p. 183.
200. *Som.*, ii, 234. See above, p. 223.
201. Diotogenes. See above, p. 190.
202. Ecphantus, quoted in my "Hellenistic Kingship," p. 77.
203. *Conf.*, 77–82, 105 f. See above, p. 228.
204. *Mut.*, 26. See above, p. 227.
205. *Agr.*, 43–49.

tion.[206] The *Exposition,* as we have seen, has similarly glorified Moses as the ideal lawgiver, himself the "norm and Law," the "archetypal pattern" whom all other lawmakers should copy.

For the advice of a good man can raise up those who are prostrate in spirit, and, lifting them up to a height beyond seasons and circumstances, can establish them there, for he puts into them a noble and intrepid mind.[207]

The saving power of Moses and the Patriarchs is not limited to the giving of the written code. The influence of their personalities persists to Philo's own day. After a brilliant description of the freedom and virtue of the ideal Sophoi, Philo stops and notes[208] that some people might well ask who these ideal persons are or were that he is describing. In former times, he answers, there were people alive who used God alone as their guide, and lived according to Law, ὁ ὀρθὸς λόγος.

These men were not only free themselves: they filled also those they met with a free mind, and even to our own day there are still men who are as though they had been stamped as images from an original model, the καλοκἀγαθία of the Sophoi.

True such men are rare, and live for the most part in seclusion from the mob, he continues. Sometimes they turn aside from the crowd to spend their time in contemplation of Nature (here God) and in prayer, so that if possible life may be improved. For one man's virtue is a benefit to all. Failing this they protect themselves from corruption by retiring altogether from men. Those men contemporary with Philo, exalted as they are, cannot have been the Jews in general. One did not have to seek long in Alexandria for a Jew. They were the few who went quite beyond ordinary Judaism to what seemed to Philo the essential and only true Judaism. Their life and religion were based upon what we would call a salvation which they had received from the great Models, of whom Moses was the chief, and which consisted not in obedience to the precepts, but in reproduction of the divine experience and characters of the model Sophoi.

This salvation, or true essence of Judaism, appears in the Mystery of Judaism, which is by no means the religion of the Jews in general. Philo has just reviewed the catalogue of the Patriarchs when he goes on to say:

Ye initiates, whose ears have been purified, receive these things as the truly sacred Mysteries into your souls and babble them not to the uninitiated, but guard them as a treasure which you share among yourselves. Gold and silver, corruptible substances, are not stored therein, but the finest of the true possessions,

---

206. *Cong.,* 131–134. The transition from Moses to Levi makes this passage at first puzzling. See Colson and Whitaker, *ad loc.* The praise of Levi is also a praise and description of Moses, as the descendant of Levi.

207. *Virt.,* 70 f.   208. *Prob.,* 62 f.

knowledge of the Cause, and of Virtue, and of that Third which is begotten of these. If ye meet with any of the initiated press him closely and cling to him lest he conceal from you some newer Mystery. Cling to him until ye have mastered it clearly. For I myself have been initiated by the God-beloved Moses into the Greater Mysteries. Yet when I saw the prophet Jeremiah and recognized that he was not only an initiate but a capable hierophant I did not shrink from his company.[209]

So Philo goes on to tell of the secret of God's intercourse with the Virgin Sophia which he learned from Jeremiah.[210] Moses is the lawgiving Logos (θεσμοθέτης λόγος), the guide (ποδηγέτης), "for he is the nurse and nurturer of good works, words, and intentions," and so exhorts man to leave that mother who deals in everything absurd, to leave the passions, and come to God the savior, who leads the soul that comes to Him out into unanticipated liberty.[211] In contrast with those who infer God from His shadow, the Logos and the universe, stands Moses who was the "purer and more perfect mind initiated into the Great Mysteries (τὰ μεγάλα μυστήρια μυηθείς)," and who lifted his eyes directly to God. The ordinary type of good man is represented by Bezaleel, Aaron, and Miriam, who learned from Moses while Moses learned from God.[212]

Philo describes the function of Moses and Abraham, as intercessors and saviors of men:[213]

Households, cities, countries, tribes, and regions of the earth have enjoyed great happiness when a single individual has taken heed of καλοκἀγαθία,[214] and especially when God has given this individual along with the good character an irresistible power (δύναμις ἀνανταγώνιστος), to serve him as musical instruments or constructive tools serve a musician or craftsman, or as sticks of wood serve a fire.[215] For in reality the just man is the foundation prop of the human race. And he brings everything he has into the common stock and gives it without stint for the benefit (ὠφελεία) of those who will use it: what he himself lacks he asks from God who alone has unlimited wealth. God thereupon opens up the heavenly treasure, and pours down a torrent of τὰ ἀγαθά like rain and snow, so that all the earthly channels are filled to overflowing. And God is accustomed to give these things and not to turn away from His own suppliant Logos.[216] For

209. *Cher.*, 48 f. 210. Ib. 211. *Mig.*. 23 ff.
212. *LA*, iii, 100–103. 213. *Mig.*, 120 ff.
214. Cf. Posner's note *ad loc.* in *Philos Werke*. The idea is common to both Stoicism and Judaism.
215. The text is here divergent and difficult. The simplest emendation is to read ὕλη for ὕλην, and understand the whole as I have translated.
216. That is, Moses and Abraham are here God's suppliant Logos. Moses is frequently identified with the Logos, as Drummond recognized (*Philo Judaeus*, II, pp. 191 f., 227 f., 268). Frequently the identification is made to clarify the conception of the Logos, but here it seems to be made to explain the significance of Moses and Abraham. The fact that a scriptural quotation, used by Philo as proof-text, has ῥῆμα instead of Logos does not seem to me, as to Colson

when Moses on one occasion besought Him as a suppliant, it is recorded: "I am compassionate upon them according to thy word." This statement has obviously the same force as the one [to Abraham], "All the tribes of the earth will be blessed in thee."

Philo goes on to explain that God has mercy upon all men when a spark of virtue is left in one man to rekindle the others in whom the fire has gone out. This spark can be fanned up and made not only to give light to the blind, but to kindle and make blaze what is shrivelled, and to make all things like itself.

So we must pray that the just man may forever abide (διαμένειν) in the human race for the curing of illnesses.

For so long as he is healthy we must not abandon hope of complete salvation (σωτηρία), because the savior God extends His all-healing medicine, the Power of Mercy to the suppliant and worshipper, and bids him use it for the salvation of those who are ill. The suppliant spreads it as a salve upon the wounds of the soul which folly and injustice and all the other evils like a sharp weapon have inflicted.[217]

Philo explains more fully elsewhere how this kindling from the soul of the wise man, especially of Moses, can take place. He says that Moses had the divine Spirit which he passed on to the seventy elders. The "spirit" in his case was "pure knowledge, which every wise man naturally shares." Moses did not lose the spirit in giving it to others, but passed it on as fire can light a great number of torches without itself being diminished. The Spirit which was on Moses and is thus communicated is "the Wise Spirit, the Divine, the Unsevered, the Indivisible, the Admirable, the Spirit which fills all things full of itself." This Spirit is one that benefits (ὠφελοῦν) not injures, and in being shared with others loses none of its "comprehension, understanding, and Sophia."[218]

The *Exposition* throws some light upon the representative character of the Saviour-Sage, by which Moses as suppliant causes God to be compassionate not on himself alone, but on the whole people, as all the race is blessed in Abraham. For in the beautiful Exordium in which he urges the Gentiles to convert, he describes how Moses, the most holy, calls men to a life of piety and δικαιοσύνη. One should not be discouraged if he has been a sinner, for sinlessness is a peculiarity of God (ἴδιον θεοῦ), and perhaps also of the

and Whitaker, *ad. loc.*, to prevent the reference in the passage from being a reference to the Logos.

217. *Mig.*, 124.

218. *Gig.*, 22–27. This passage has been considered in connection with the consecration of the "elders." See above, pp. 217 ff. It seems to be a general description of the experience of the initiate into the Mystery as well as that specifically of the presbyter.

divine man (θεῖος ἀνήρ), here obviously Moses. The prudent man will repent of his sin, and such people Moses summons. He brings them together
and initiates them. He gives them a teaching that will bind them together in
love, teachings that exhort them to reject the ideas with which they were
brought up, and to be diligent and humble seekers for truth, for so is
εὐδαιμονία to be found.[219] For in Moses the whole race has been accepted
by God. God took Moses as His own, and with him the nation, for since
Moses was the true worshipper and suppliant, even though he was a single
individual, he was δυνάμει the whole race, for he was "equal in importance
to the whole race."[220] Philo describes Moses as one with whom the Divine
Spirit permanently abode[221] because he had divested himself of the created
world and presented himself naked to God, fixed his γνώμη in him.[222]

Then he began to worship God. He entered into the darkness, the invisible region, and there abode, initiated into the most sacred Mysteries. And he came to
be not only μύστης, but the hierophant of rites and the teacher of divine things
which he will expound to those whose ears have been purified.[223]

In one passage Philo has been developing his contrast between those who
have God both as Lord and God, that is as a source of both beneficence and
discipline, and those who use no discipline and come to God only as the
Beneficent One. This is the higher state, possible only for the initiate. He
continues:

And is it not likely that even those whose minds are blinded to these and similar
things should become keen of sight when eyes are given them for the most sacred
oracles, so that they discover their true nature and do not stop as though anchored
in their literal meaning? Oh thou hierophant, though the eyes of our soul are
closed because we do not desire to see, or cannot do so, still do thou uphold us
and help us and not cease to annoint us until thou hast initiated (μυσταγωγῶν)
us into the hidden meaning of the sacred words and revealed those locked beauties that are invisible to the uninitiated. This it is meet for thee to do.
But you souls who have tasted of divine love, rouse yourselves as from a deep
sleep, dissipate the mist from your eyes, put away your slow and hesitant timidity,
and hasten to the magnificent spectacle, that you may apprehend all the spectacles
and sounds which the President of the Games (ὁ ἀγωνοθέτης) has prepared for
your benefit (ὠφελεία).[224]

This is not an address to one who is dead and gone. Philo sees in Moses an
active and present power, and the prayer to Moses for guidance, light, and
annointing, is precisely such a prayer as Christian mystics have for centuries
been addressing to Christ.

219. *Virt.*, 175–178.   220. Ib., 185 f.   221. *Gig.*, 47.
222. Ib., 53.   223. Ib., 54.   224. *Som.*, i, 164 f.

A passage occurs almost in passing which summarizes and fully confirms the fact that Philo was looking to the Patriarchs as the saviors for the race and the individual of Judaism. Philo has been describing the character of the Jewish race as contrasted with the other races, and compares their isolation to that of an orphan. But God has compassion upon them, he says, because the Jewish race, as a sort of first fruits of all mankind, has been set aside to the Creator and Father.

And the reason of this dedication is to be found in the highly prized justices and virtues of the founders (ἀρχηγετοῦντες) of the race, virtues which endure like immortal and everlasting plants that bring forth the fruit of salvation and benefit to their descendants in all things even though they may happen to have sinned, unless their sin is quite incurable.[225]

It has been asserted that the Christians transformed the Stoic doctrine of the Sage on two essential points: for the Stoic the Sage was a hypothesis, while for the Christian the Sage was a reality in Jesus Christ; again for the Stoic the Sage was perfect in himself, while for the Christian the Sage, Jesus, was a dynamic force for others.[226] But if the Stoic Sage was not dynamic, the Pythagorean Sage-King was so; and in any case a transformation on either count was not original with Christianity. Philo saw in the great νόμοι ἔμψυχοι, preëminently in Moses, the realization of the pagan dream, and so perfect a realization that the blessing, the ὠφέλημα, the σωτήριον of their characters were still available to the race in general, but especially to those who would allow themselves to be initiated in the Greater Mysteries. Moses, who was often thought of as entirely deified, was the God-man whose supplication with God had not been in vain. His Spirit, the Spirit of Wisdom and Truth, could still be imparted to an aspirant, with the result that the new initiate could thereafter live the life of εὐσέβεια and δικαιοσύνη, and achieve the ultimate goal of pagan, and later Christian, endeavor, εὐδαιμονία.

225. *Spec.*, iv, 180 f.
226. Casey in *Harvard Theological Review*, XVIII (1925), p. 63.

CHAPTER IX

THE MYSTERY

WITH so much detailed allegory of the Patriarchs did Philo present the Mystery. The Torah has been changed into a great allegory, an allegory made up not of detailed and disconnected flights to reconcile the scriptural narrative and laws piecemeal with Greek Philosophy and mysticism. But behind the disconnected presentation there lies an elaborate schematization of the characters and words of the Bible according to a single objective. Fancy in individual points is certainly to be found in Philo. Yet there is a great unity of thought and purpose running through the allegory that cannot be denied. The conception that unites the whole is the Mystery, with its philosophical and cosmological assumptions and its mystic goal. Philo's philosophy, which is eclectic, is by no means sporadically eclectic: it is the philosophy of an eclectic Neo-Pythagorean-Platonist, one with many Stoic and Cynic details, especially in ethics, but quite consistently antipathetic to the Stoic, Cynic, or Skeptic fundamental points of view. From the Cyrenaics or Epicureans he will have not a word on any subject. The basic Neo-Pythagorean-Platonic philosophy has been fused with mystic notions from the Orphics, Persia, and Isis. The fusion was probably made not by Jews for the first time, but by thoughtful Greeks who had found the Mystery of Isis in their environment as attractive a thing as Orpheus and Dionysus had proved to be in Greece itself. The early steps in this direction are lost to us. Plutarch, who was born probably within a year or two of Philo's death, shows us how men in his time were laboring on exactly this problem, the problem of restating Isis and Persian mystic conceptions to conform to a Philonic type of philosophy, that is to a fundamental Platonism, much enriched by Pythagorean notions, with Stoic details but with a strong dislike of Stoic fundamentals. The Light-Stream of Persia and that of Isis, for all their different formulations, seem to Plutarch but different approaches to the true nature of the Light-Stream, and it is in Platonism and Neo-Pythagoreanism that he would find the intellectual approach to the same Reality. He would indeed be a rash man who considered Plutarch able to conceive *de novo* this great unity in the three sources of teaching. The problem is at least as old as Philo, and the fact is that Philo, a deeper thinker than Plutarch, shows the solution much more nearly worked out than does Plutarch fifty years later. It is necessary only to refer to the Hermetica as evidence for general interest in the same problem.

It seems that it would also be very rash to say that Philo himself was in any real sense a pioneer in the problem. He is much too elaborate, too sure, too mature, to be working on the problem for the first time. His assumptions, for example, that Sophia and the Logos are identical, that mystical ascent by marriage with Sophia is quite the same as ascent through Powers of the Logos, these are too assured and unargued to be the suggestions of a pioneer. And similarly Philo's confidence in identifying these conceptions with his Platonic and Pythagorean postulates is not a confidence that a pioneer could have achieved. The working out of such a blend of mystic mythology and philosophy into this great system must have required many years, indeed many generations, to have reached such assurance, such complete freedom from any necessity for justification, as Philo shows.

Indeed Philo shows this whole mystic philosophy, with its still recognizable components, in an advanced stage of assimilation into even the fourth milieu, Judaism. This assimilation too seems much too mature to be the product of Philo as an innovator. He speaks of the Mystery as a commonplace to his readers. He is offering them nothing new, but is rather like Chrysostom or Jerome, an expounder of the deeper significance of concepts that are the accepted positions of the men of his environment. In his writings which explain the Mystery for Jews he is not by any means conscious of presenting them with something essentially new. It is assumed that his readers are for the most part thinking in terms of the Mystery, are themselves initiates. In being initiates they are not disciples whom Philo has himself "begotten in Moses," as Paul wrote those whom he had "begotten in Christ." Mystic Judaism is the ready made environment of his writings, not the product of his original genius. In the *Exposition* he tries to bring Gentiles into that Mystery without betraying in a single line that he had originated it. He is drawing constantly on the "Allegorists" for his interpretations. Who these were, how much their works had already appeared in writing, I cannot say. Of this we can be sure, however, that the Allegorists were a group of people many of whom had gone to the logical end of the mystic position and had lost all sense of obligation to fulfil the letter of the particular laws.[1] In leaving their obligation to the material world they had left behind for babes the representation of divine will in the material medium of nouns and verbs, and were living by and in the Law of the immaterial realm alone. With this extreme conclusion Philo does not agree. To be sure the Law by which the mystics live is the Law of the Logos. But the details of the Jewish Code are still of great importance for the life of ordinary people, he insists, and since even the highest mystic does actually have to live in a sense in the material realm, it is a good thing to set the example for weaker brothers by complying with the restrictions still binding upon them.

1. *Mig.*, 89–94.

All of this difference of point of view implies, indeed specifically denotes, the existence of the Mystery quite independently of any Philonic invention. The paralleling of Persian and Egyptian traditions about God as the Light-Stream may well have been a living force in Egypt consistently after the great work of Ikhnaton in that direction, so that the Greeks may have had these two presented to them in parallel immediately upon their settling in the country. The adjustment of this doubly-conceived Mystery to Greek thought may well have begun from the first contacts in Alexandria, if not before. As Plato and the Pythagoreans were the most sensitive of all Greek philosophers to Orphic conceptions, it is not surprising that it should have been followers of these schools who took the mystic teachings of Egypt most seriously.

It is quite possible and probable, then, that for two centuries or more before Philo the Jews in Egypt, especially in Alexandria, found in their environment that type of thought ready made which we can only describe by an extended hyphenization, a Persian-Isiac-Platonic-Pythagorean mystery. This ready made blend was the nearest thing to Judaism in their environment, for it alone was a philosophy built upon the personal apprehension of an exalted and monotheistic Deity. The Jews had early lost their sense of the meaning of the Hebrew original of the Scriptures, and with it the connotations of the Hebrew words for God. They thought of God in the Greek language, and must have been linguistic antiquarians to have kept the word God in their own use of it from meaning the Light-Stream. Personal in His love for them God might remain; the great lawgiver to the Jewish nation He did remain. But the tribal Yahveh he could not remain, or even the strongly personal deity of Amos and Hosea, when it came to explaining His nature in the Greek language. With the early stage of this process we shall deal in the next chapter. The great conscious syncretistic movement we shall there describe was at an end by Philo's time, and he can assume that in his generation the true meaning of the Torah is the revelation of the Royal Road of the Light-Stream. In Philo the Mystery is not only fully developed, but ripe with the ripeness of very many years. So mature is the Mystery that it may well have lost all localism and been quite as familiar among the Jews of Rome and Tarsus as in Alexandria itself. For all of its definitely Egyptian origin, it is quite likely that, when a Jew went with this sort of Judaism from Alexandria to Ephesus or Tarsus in 50 B.C., or 10 A.D., he would have been heard with the same respect and credence that greeted Apollos in Christian Ephesus or Corinth a few years later.

Into the Mystery we have followed Philo by his own route, the route of the lives of the Patriarchs. It may be well before we leave Philo to look back at the ground we have traversed, and fix the Mystery in our minds by studying it from a new vantage point.

The Patriarchs, and especially Moses, are the great revelation of the higher Way. Sometimes Philo groups them to show that each reveals a different aspect of the struggle to rise, or of mystic achievement. But each Patriarch is really one who has achieved the end of the Mystery. The first triad of Patriarchs, for example, is Enos, Enoch, and Noah. Each of these represents a preliminary stage; Enos, Hope, Enoch, Repentance, and Noah the achievement of δικαιοσύνη by the destruction of the passions. These men may thus be treated as preliminary steps on the mystic ladder, or any one of them may be referred to as representing the ultimate experience. But Noah is emphasized much more than the other two since his being confined in the ark represented the soul shut up in the body with the passions through the time of purification, and his coming out of the ark the great experience of delivery from material bondage that he might rise to saintliness for himself and saving power for others.

It is through Abraham, Isaac, and Jacob that the Mystery is first fully developed. Abraham and Jacob are treated from the point of view of ascent through the Powers to the Logos, though the Sophia-marriage theme is developed in connection with their marriages. Abraham goes out from Chaldea, as Jacob runs from Esau, to typify the first step, the running away from the life of dependence upon matter, from the life of unrestrained response to passions and perceptions, from the life of confused thinking in which matter is regarded as the ultimate. This step is also represented in the allegory of the migration of the Israelites by the departure from Egypt. The flight is only one step in the preliminary emancipation from matter; the second step is a definite renunciation of the somatic life, what Paul would call dying to the body but what Philo more correctly calls killing the body.[2] This is the stage in the migration represented by the drowning of the Egyptians in the Red Sea. The corresponding stage in the story of Abraham is lost, if it was included, through the fact that the section of the *Quaestiones* which might have given it is not preserved. But it may well have been omitted from the story of Abraham, for this step may be identified, according to the necessities of tracing spiritual progress through the recorded incidents in the lives of the Patriarchs, with either the flight from the body or the going up to the great final experience after the period of discipline.

Abraham now goes through a series of experiences. The passage dealing with Melchizedek is not found in the *Quaestiones,* and the few references to him in the *Allegory* leave the significance of the incident rather undetermined in Abraham's general spiritual development. It may well have been the stage where he experienced the Cosmic Mystery. After this he has several

---

2. Philo also called it dying to the body, or to mortal life. One fragment reads: ἐὰν δὲ ἀποθάνῃ μέν τις τὸν θνητὸν βίον, ζήσῃ δὲ ἀντιλαβὼν τὸν ἀθάνατον, ἴσως ὃ μηδέποτε εἶδεν ὄψεται; Harris, *Fragments,* p. 72, at the bottom of the first column.

visions of, or conversations with, God. These are carefully schematized. The first[3] is his experience of the Royal Power, when he has a marvellous in-flooding of the divine Light. At the same time he is progressing according to the Sophia cycle. He has married Sarah, who is Virtue, but as yet she is the virtue achieved by human effort, as high a type of virtue as at this stage Abraham could claim. It is no wonder that he finds her sterile, for such virtue is always sterile. So he begins to lay the foundations of higher advance, like Jacob with Laban, by studying the encyclicals. This is represented by his relation with Hagar, and a bastard achievement, Ishmael, or a preliminary one, can be effected through such a relation. That is, the fruits of encyclical study are bastard, or at best preliminary, in comparison with the fruits of true knowledge, Sophia. The encyclicals must, after serving their purpose, be humiliated, put in their proper place, as Hagar was humiliated for presumption.

With the encyclicals mastered, and Ishmael, their profit, achieved, Abraham can go on to a higher vision of the Powers, and this time, in the incident of his name being changed,[4] he sees both Powers, the Creative as well as the Royal. Here the last traces of his sin fall from him. He is again bathed in Light, and now becomes a saving power for other men. But the union is not only with the Powers, it is also union with Sophia, the preliminary union by which he is himself given potency to beget. For he presents his human nature to Sophia, not as masculine but as feminine; it is Sophia who is temporarily masculine and fills Abraham with seeds. Having now himself become full of seeds he can as masculine return to Sophia, now feminine, and make her pregnant. But before this happens there are a few other preliminaries. He must return with his new powers to become the complete master of the body, a step symbolized by circumcision. The body is no longer dead to him, or he to it, but it has become his perfect servant, the perfect spiritual medium.

Abraham's union with Sophia on the higher plane, where he is masculine and she feminine, is the experience of begetting Isaac. His spouse is no longer human virtue, but divine Virtue, or Sophia, as indicated by Sarah's changed name, and this divine Virtue is very fertile when approached by one with Abraham's new powers. The experience is figured in the oak of Mamre under which Abraham sits, and in the later relations with Sarah. Here he comes to the height of the Mystery by both formulations. He is united with Sophia and at the same time sees beyond the two Powers to the Third who unites the two, the Logos, and in seeing the Third sees that the Three are One. They bring their incorporeal light into his house, his self. He is united with them in the full mystical union. His saving power for others has in-

3. Gen. xv.   4. Gen. xvii, 1 f.

creased at each advance he has made. His body is in a sense as dead to him as a bronze statue, but in another sense it is now made as fruitful, in its subservient capacity, as the soul.

The story of Abraham is especially enlightening for the Mystery, for its stages of progress are most clearly worked out according to the pattern of the Powers, and at the same time the different stages in ascent according to the Sophia formulation are carefully kept in parallel. The two are clearly distinct formulations of the ascent which Philo as a child of his age believed identical, even though the fusion of the two was at least very imperfect. They are still *parallel* formulations to him.

The story of Jacob is the next best account of the ascent of the soul in the Mystery. Jacob runs from Esau, as has been said, and there begins his development. In his early encounters with Esau he had represented preliminary struggles of a naturally well intentioned man against fleshly evil and pleasure, but he finds that his only real safety is in flight, for, if he stays to fight his lower nature, it will overcome him in the end. He has obviously had some contact with the Mystery already, and has shared the mystic meal with Isaac and received Isaac's blessing. But in his dream he appears to have experienced the Cosmic Mystery for the first time, and to have had that shadowy premonition of the immaterial world which went with the Cosmic Mystery. He here gets only the Logoi, and is given complete salvation from his enemies, the impulses of the flesh. This is of course what the Israelites experienced at the Red Sea. It is interesting that the dream is explained at once as a preliminary revelation of the Logos-Powers and of Sophia. Again the two strands are clumsily intertwined, but distinct.

Like Abraham, Jacob has still much to do. He must go to Laban's household as Abraham went to Hagar, to learn the encyclicals, to get the first marriage with the disciplinary studies, and to learn to rule his own lower nature, the sheep, and to become a shepherd of men. At the end of this discipline he is ready to go on into the Mystery itself. His first experience is the dream of the sheep of different markings, by which he comes to see the different offspring of Sophia or the Logos in contact with men. The first are the white sheep, those clothed in the blinding white of the Higher Mystery. The second are those marked with the Forms like the Cosmos, and are the people in the cosmic stage of the Mystery. The third are the beginners in the stage of repentance and first purification. These three types, he says, correspond to the three experiences of the temple, the outer court of purification, the inner court of the cosmic robe and Cosmic Mystery, the holy of holies with its white robe of light; only, says Philo, the symbolism given by Moses is better than that Jacob got in a dream.

From this vision of the Mystery Jacob goes on to its experience. But here our fragmentary account of his story fails us, and the great scene where

Jacob wrestles with the angel and becomes the "man who sees God" and "perfect" is not preserved. Yet we have enough hints to see that here Jacob reached the height of the mystery by both formulations, like Abraham, and became united with the Light-Stream as both Logos and Sophia. Like Abraham, the epilogue to the mystical experience of Jacob is his return to the body to dominate it and use it as a perfectly functioning medium of the spirit.

The other great allegory of the mystical ascent is the story of the migration of the Israelites. They too left Egypt, the realm of the body, and destroyed its passions in the Red Sea. Then they began a long period of wandering, the period when they were learning self discipline to prepare themselves for the mystic achievement. But Philo never takes them into the Promised Land.[5] They are throughout the symbol of life as lived by most men who are trying to live nobly, are aspiring for the mystic experience, but never get sufficiently disciplined to be able to go on into "perfection." They do, however, seem to have gone through the two mystic stages. At Elim it is hinted that they enter the Cosmic Mystery, and they come into the Higher Mystery of union with the immaterial world in the strange scene Philo describes as "the song at the well." Here by a combination of two incidents, the marshalling of Israel as an army of warriors in companies under the captains, and the scene where the Israelites under Moses stop to sing at the well, he represents the tribes as singing the song of triumph at final mystical attainment.

The great importance of the migration, then, is not so much to show the Mystery itself, as to depict Moses as the hierophant of those who are struggling for mystical "perfection." The thing of real importance is the great dominant figure of Moses, the God-man and Savior.

Moses himself is like Isaac in being of a specially unique type of being, needing no preliminary stages at all, but living from early years the "perfect" life. Isaac had not to go through a period of discipline, he had to have nothing in preparation. All he had to receive was the consummation in the mystic marriage with Sophia. As "self-taught" he was one already born with the knowledge that saves.

Moses similarly is from the first the "Self-Taught." He is a loan from God, a special incarnation, for the benefit of the race. The encyclical studies mean nothing to him: rather the boy Moses can teach the doctors of every land what their knowledge never suggested to them. Problems are all exter-

5. It should be noted that in one passage Moses does lead the Israelites from Egypt, sense, to Canaan, vice, for he has revealed to them that what was innocent sense-act in Egypt is, by the higher standard, vice. This notion is identical with Paul's insistence that "when the law came, sin revived." "I had not known sin except the Law had said *thou shalt not*," etc. See *Heres*, 83–87.

nal to him. He is never purified. At the early stage when he is at the burning bush he already "takes pleasure by the tail" in the way of the final "redemption of the body," a thing which the other Patriarchs dared to attempt only after the last experience of the Mystery. He is concerned throughout, rather, with the problem of trying to go beyond the second great divide, that between the Logos and τὸ ὄν. At the bush he is trying to find the name of God, that is His nature, and is, incidentally to his own experience, given his commission as supreme hierophant.[6] On the mount he is again attempting to see τὸ ὄν Itself, and again with only partial success, though he gets higher than any other human being. But here his commission as hierophant is perfected, and he is given the whole divine scheme for the salvation of men. For ordinary men he is given the specific laws to guide them in their trials. For higher types of men he is given the two Mysteries, one of which he commits to Aaron, in the other of which he remains as the permanent great high-priest, so that those of all generations who come into the Higher Mystery are initiates, disciples, followers, of Moses. In this sense it is that to Philo the Mystery is preëminently the Mystery of Moses.

Four scenes might well represent the great significant aspects of Moses' mystic career: the scene at the Bush; the scene on Sinai; Moses as the giver of the mystic Torah; and the assumption of Moses. For in this last scene he is taken back to God to sing the great song. It is precisely three of these scenes that I see in the panels at Dura, while in the mutilated fourth panel I strongly suspect that the scene was the getting of the Law on Sinai, the missing fourth.[7]

It will be recalled that this highly consistent allegory of the Patriarchs has appeared not only in the connected discussions of Abraham and Moses in the *Exposition* and *De Vita Mosis*, but also in the *Quaestiones*, and in a combination of the isolated allegories of the various anecdotes of the Patriarchs taken from their contexts in the *Allegory* and arranged in the order of the Biblical narratives. That is, the allegories of the events in the lives of the Patriarchs, far from being sporadic as they appear on first reading, are always true to a definite plan from which Philo rarely if ever deviates. That plan seems not at all the creation of Philo, but a settled tradition of interpretation which Philo is freely drawing upon, but not inventing. Such a settled tradition, presented with the confidence and lack of argumentation conspicuous

6. Philo thinks of Moses at the bush as traditional Christianity thinks of the baptism of Jesus. It was not a time when anything fundamental happened to the nature of Jesus; such a notion is Adoptionism and heresy. It was a time of public confirmation of Jesus, of his definite call to begin upon the work God had sent him to do. The public announcement theme is missing in Moses' solitary experience with God, but it was like Jesus' experience as marking the beginning of his call to his active career.

7. This whole matter of the interpretation of the Dura frescoes must receive separate treatment, as I have indicated in the Introduction.

in Philo, could come only from one who is perhaps the greatest exponent, the finest flower, of a wide and established movement, not from one who is essentially a pioneer.

The Patriarchs experienced the Mystery: it is Moses who formulated it and still presents it to men in the Torah and in his person. As Moses formulated it, under God's revelation and guidance, in what did it consist?

First it consisted in a great mystic philosophy of God and of His relation to the material world and to man. According to this philosophy God is in His Being the Absolute One, of whom nothing in human formulation can be predicated. Over against God is matter in that Platonic-Pythagorean sense which Aristotle adopted. Essentially matter is formless. Actually since God's creative act, matter is unknown in its original condition, for it has become infused with form. The form with which it is infused is the lowest of the various emanations from God, or rather the lowest point in God's single emanation. For Deity, while in His Being He is the self-contained Absolute, radiates from Himself a great stream of Light-Power. This Stream is, Philo feels, best compared to solar radiation, since the sun is the best physical type of God's existence. For the sun is unchanging from century to century, completely self-contained, needing no fuel or sustenance from the outside, but its being is such as to give forth warmth and life to the earth. The sun is itself unaffected, and, by the science of the day, undiminished by its radiation, yet all the earth is dependent upon it. So God, although in His Being He is completely self-contained and self-sufficient, shoots forth a great stream of radiation, immaterial, of course, yet on that account all the more real. This Stream as a whole may be called Logos or Sophia, or Virtue, or occasionally πνεῦμα. As such it is God in extension, God in relation, θεός, or Son of God, yet not ὁ θεός, not God in the fully proper sense of the term. As this Stream goes out from God it takes on differentiations of function, which from the human point of view seem almost existential differentiations. The Stream as a whole is the Logos. Then the Logos is itself differentiated into what Philo and other Greeks in Egypt and elsewhere called "Powers." The first two Powers distinguish the Creative and Royal or Ruling functions or aspects of the Stream. These two with the Logos itself make not three but one, though in the mystic ascent they appear as three to a man approaching them from below. Below these are secondary differentiations or Powers, the divine actions of mercy, the divine legislative activity, and the Platonic world of forms. The latter three are "within the created realm," that is they not only exist as immaterial entities, but are the aspects of the radiation of God which can come into the material world and express themselves there. So by whatever theory of "imitation" or "participation," or Logos-Cutter "division" Philo may approach the problem of creation, original matter is made into the cosmos by the representation of the forms in matter. The cosmos is also guided by the great legislative force of God which God sends down into the material world to be the Law of Nature, and the world is sustained by the Power of Mercy by which God acts within the material world to preserve it. By the fact that these lower manifestations of the Logos-Stream from God are present in the material world, the Logos may be said in so far to have put on the material robe, and to be present in the material cosmos. The great Stream is ultimately a unit, and the part may at any time be called by the name of the whole. Yet the fact remains that above the material world, for all that it includes an infusion of the Stream, the Stream exists in its unmixed purity, the three which are really One. "Above," I say, but that is rather a matter of qualitative gradation than of space, for spatial categories have nothing to do with immaterial reality, and indeed the very Powers that represent themselves within the visible cosmos are themselves separable from matter and not exhausted by their representation. The Forms, for example, are to be found in matter as the three great Powers, or τὸ ὄν, are not: yet the Forms properly exist in the κόσμος νοητός, and not in the κόσμος αἰσθητός. The same is true of the other lower Powers, God's Law and Mercy.[8]

Such is the Deity, and such the relation of the material world to Deity visualized in the Mystery. As this system was the inner secret of the Mystery, so it has been revealed to men by God, through Moses, in that secret and most holy symbol of the Jewish religion, the Ark of the Covenant. The symbols of the ark represent the seven great manifestations of God: the box of the ark is the world of forms; the tables of the law within the box are the Power of Law; the mercy seat is the Power of Mercy; the two cherubim are the two higher Powers, the Creative Power and the Royal Power; the voice which came to Moses is the Logos; while the One who is present and utters the voice is τὸ ὄν. This is the inner secret of Judaism, then, the true *Wesen* of Judaism, the fact that it has hidden away at its heart the symbolic revelation of the true nature of God.

But the Mystery was more than a doctrine, a philosophy, or even than a concrete and holy symbol of the nature of Deity. For the Mystery was also a great revelation to man of his own nature, of his need of salvation, and of the Royal Road by which men could rise above matter into the immaterial realm. And through its great Savior or Saviors Mystic Judaism was a dynamic source of what later came to be called "saving grace." Not only could Mystic Judaism point the way: it could give men strength to walk along it, or to run along it as a fugitive from the allurements of matter and sense to the peace and safety of immaterial reality.

8. It is obvious that the essential difference between this conception and Neo-Platonism is not in the names for the different stages of the Light-Stream, but in the fact that matter is still visualized as only the recipient of the Stream, and in no sense its own lowest manifestation.

It is interesting to see that the central theme of the *Allegory* is the development of the Mystery. A section of it from the *de Confusione* through the *de Fuga* may be analyzed for the light it throws on Philo's method of presenting the Mystery. Philo's purport is easy to miss by the fact that he is in a sense riding two by no means congenial horses at once. He visualizes the stories of the Patriarchs as a revelation of the Moses Mystery, and writes to develop this theme for Jews who are interested but need detailed instruction. At the same time, in order to prove his point, he feels compelled to treat the account in Genesis word by word to show its bearing for his general purpose. In the *Quaestiones in Genesin* he assumes knowledge of the Mystery as a whole and can devote himself freely to writing simply a reference work of interpretation, verse by verse. But in the *Allegory* he is trying at the same time both to give a connected account, and to orient each verse as it comes, and so does neither very clearly. He is driven to digression after digression, and to interpreting many verses in terms of details that should logically appear at a later point in his argument. The intention of the work as a whole is, however, indicated by the titles he gives to the successive studies. If one follows these as representing what Philo considered the key notion of each book, there is a definite development of thought.

In the *de Confusione Linguarum* Philo has been chiefly concerned with a description of the nature of human sin, the mixing of values. "Confusion" is the punishment of the race for its rejection of the doctrine of providence, its shutting the soul down to the level of the senses and passions, and its self-sufficiency as contrasted with the humility it should have before God. The next two treatises, the *de Migratione Abrahami* and the *Quis Heres,* raise the question of the general qualities of the man who emerges from this human welter. The *de Migratione* praises, in contrast to the wicked, the man who has gone out of lower to higher things. Such a man lives by the vision, not by verbal instruction, that is he is beyond the Law as given in nouns and verbs, and has access to the real Law, which was given from Sinai in the "vision that was seen."[9] His qualities are thereby fully developed; he is given a marvelous speech by which he can help others (i.e. he becomes a hierophant to instruct others in the Mystery); he is given a great reputation among men, but greater still he is made worthy of esteem. As a result of this experience he becomes a saving force in society. He lives the life of Law, not, obviously, the Law of the Mosaic Code, but the Law of the Logos which he has received.[10] As a result his own acts are the logoi or νόμοι of God. When Abraham has at last advanced to the place where he can leave Lot, his lower nature, quite behind, he is ready, not to follow the Logos, but to walk by his side, that is to become mystically identified with the Logos.[11]

9. *Mig.*, 47–52.   10. Ib., 127–131.   11. Ib., 173–175.

This all implies that the man who has "migrated" has gone out from the realm Pascher identified as the lower stage of the Mystery, where one is preoccupied with a mystic comprehension of the universe, to the higher spiritual realms, first Haran, the place of the mind, and then to God Himself. It is a going out from the senses.[12]

The basic principle and chief objective of the Mystery has now been sketched. The treatises that follow go into details. The *Quis Heres*[13] takes up the question of what sort of man is competent to undertake this journey out from humanity and to become the heir of divine things. The first verse of the Biblical section here to be treated leads Philo off into a digression on the different manners of speaking to God. This disposed of, Philo, by an elaborate and devious consideration of Masek[14] concludes that the man whose life is characterized by the blood-soul, as contrasted with the life of mind or reason, cannot be the "heir" of divine things.[15] The "heir," the mind, must come out of the body, the senses, and speech, and indeed his very self in so far as he renounces his own thought processes. A man who has made this migration becomes the "Seer," the one who sees God,[16] for he has gone out of himself, a thing which you (uninitiate) readers do not understand, but which is perfectly intelligible to us who are mystic pupils of Moses.[17] Abraham has been brought out to see the stars, but he has gone far beyond the physical heavens and stars, that is beyond the Stoic notion that the world itself is God, and his migration is from the created to the uncreated, a step taken by the aid of Sophia.[18] This whole process is one in which God is the giver and the initiate only the receiver, and what he takes he still owes to God and must give back to Him. Everything is now concentrated in God, sense, speech, and mind, and all should properly be used for God. God is the beginning and the end.[19] The flight to God is a ransom by which our minds, slaves fugitive to God, are set free.[20] At this point Philo puts in the long discussion of the Logos as at once the Divider and the principle of unity, a section so important by itself that it is represented by a sub-title at the beginning of the book. The point of the section, itself drawing heavily upon a Pythagorean prototype, is a discussion of the basic idea of the whole Mystery, the great cleft between the material and immaterial worlds. A large number of instances of the presence of a fundamental division in the universe finally lead Philo to the conclusion that the incense of the temple cultus is the praise rising to the Creator from the cosmos as made up out of the four elements.[21] Between these two is the Logos, simultaneously their divider and

---

12. *Mig.*, 198–215.
13. A treatise on Rewards originally stood before the *Heres*.
14. See Gen. xv, 3 (LXX).   15. *Heres*, 40–62.   16. Ib., 69–80.
17. Ib., 81–85.   18. Ib., 96–99.   19. Ib., 100–122.
20. Ib., 123 f.   21. Ib., 196–200.

mediator. The two parts divided are complementary and make a single whole, but they need the Logos to turn the six into seven, to unite all into a single entity.[22] God, the infinite immaterial, is described in contrast to the finite universe. Philo now returns to the description of the migration of the "heir." He has begun with discarding the evil tendencies and notions of the soul[23] and then he goes into the "ecstasy." Various kinds of ecstasy are described. But the ecstasy of Noah, Abraham, Isaac, Jacob, and especially Moses is the prophetic ecstasy, in which the light of one's own mind "sets" before the brilliance of the divine illumination, the coming of the divine Spirit. In this state the prophet speaks the view of Another.[24] The migration is one out from the body and the passions.[25] After considering a number of details Philo sums up. It is the Sophos who is the "heir." He rises to the promised land, the land which is Sophia, so that he gets "a sure and abiding vision of the Sophia of God," and the Cutter separates him off from what is evil. The process begins with the perfection of the parts of the body and ends in the attainment of the divine Sophia.[26]

So far Philo has been describing the ideal. The reader must have felt that the *Quis Heres* left him little ground to hope that he could share in such a Mystery. The next treatise, the *de Congressu*, begins at the bottom to explain how a novice might have a mystic experience through the Preliminary Studies. The normal beginning for one who is not like Isaac miraculously endowed with a special nature is in the Pythagorean encyclicals.[27] But highly valuable as these are, they are represented by Hagar, who was, as an Egyptian, of material nature and must mark only a temporary stage.[28] By an elaborate allegory of Rachel and Leah and Jacob's two concubines he concludes that the beginner must provide himself with two types of mind, one which peacefully appropriates τὰ πρεσβύτερα καὶ ἡγεμονεύοντα ἀγαθά, and the other by which he fights off evil. In addition he must take care of his body and train himself in rhetoric: but these are the concubines.[29] Isaac, the type quite beyond ordinary men, needs only one wife, for he can go direct to Virtue and Sophia.[30] Philo is now led by the idea of allegorizing wives and concubines into a section which adds little to his main point except that the aspirant must marry himself to true knowledge, not to opinion or false-

22. Ib., 201–229. For fuller discussion of this conception see my "Neo-Pythagorean Source."
23. Ib., 239–248.   24. Ib., 263–266.
25. Ib.. 267–274.   26. Ib., 313–316.
27. Colson and Whitaker (IV, 452) note that this is a Stoic encyclical. They give no references, and seem quite unjustified. The school that was famous at the time for its encyclical preparation was the Pythagorean, while no such preparation was demanded from young Stoics. Justin Martyr, for example, without an encyclical education, claims that he was a student in both Stoic and Platonic schools, but could not be admitted into a Pythagorean school because of this lack. See my *Theology of Justin Martyr*, pp. 57–60.
28. *Cong.*, 14–23. See Colson and Whitaker's interesting note in Vol. I, p. xvi, note f.
29. *Cong.*, 24–33.   30. Ib., 34–38.

hood, if he is to be a man of Vision of the Highest.[31] Sarah, who is throughout Virtue or Sophia, herself gave Hagar to Abraham; so the Encyclicals are truly delightful as a preparation, so long as it is borne always in mind that they are not to be the true wife.[32] Even these preliminary studies cannot begin in the frivolous period of youth.[33] The ten years Abraham lived in Canaan before he took Hagar symbolize this, but lead Philo off on a long digression on the number ten.[34] The following section is confusing because while the women of these stories are generally equated with Sophia, their being made pregnant is the receiving of Sophia. This confusion is clarified by Pascher's analysis. Sophia is, as we have seen, really bisexual. She receives the seed from God as a female, but at the same time has power to impregnate her offspring, to scatter divine seeds. What Philo means is that one must, after the encyclicals, take Virtue or Sophia to himself and become pregnant from the divine seeds she will sow in him. This is the point of the treatise. It is one of Philo's most rambling books, and takes in a great number of incidental subjects. The mystic at this stage must go to Philosophy which alone can interpret the encyclicals, as for instance in its perceiving the real nature of geometrical concepts.[35] And there is elaborate suggestion that this stage is going to be one of toil, and of temptation to return to the life of flesh.

The *de Fuga et Inventione* goes on from the treatise that has outlined the preliminary studies and the stage of affliction.[36] Philo is now ready to discuss the stage in which one makes the great escape. Flight, he finds, is from three motives, shame, hatred, fear. The flight of Hagar from Sarah is one of shame, and occurs when a person gets a sense of his unworthiness as compared with true virtue, and is so apalled that he runs from virtue.[37] To this type of flight Philo returns at the end of the treatise. Much more important for his present purpose are the other two types of flight, those inspired by hatred and by fear. The flight of hatred is the flight of the soul or mind from the material universe, from the senses, along the Road to Virtue. It is still an uninstructed and instinctive flight.[38] The type of flight based upon fear comes when one really understands the danger to which the soul is subject from the material world and the senses, the fear lest the lower may overcome the higher in himself. A considerable digression points out that this does not imply actually the abandonment of wealth or political office, since such rejection of earthly responsibility on the part of good men would leave the masses helpless in the hands of the wicked. We must fulfill our temporal obligation.[39] And yet at the beginning one flies alike from the best, because we cannot endure it, and from the worst, as disgusting and terrible.

31. *Cong.*, 38–62.

32. Ib., 71–80.

33. Ib., 81–88.

34. Ib., 89–120.

35. Ib., 139–150.

36. *Fug.*, 2.

37. Ib., 5, 6.

38. Ib., 7–22.

39. Ib., 24–38.

In such a temporary state the soul is engaged in trying to understand the material and sensuous world. After a little one is ready to leave this stage (the one apparently in which Philo elsewhere puts the encyclical studies of the universe) and to return to Virtue-Sophia. Jacob, who is the type throughout this section, accordingly marries Sophia-Virtue, who here as elsewhere is the androgynous figure, a female who scatters seed of her own nature in her temporarily feminine husband.[40]

So far the figures have been somewhat confused. Philo seems by these three flights to indicate that the first stage of flight is a recoil from sin by reason of a rebuke from conscience as representation of the Good. After the sin and shame comes a hatred of sin and a flight from it, a great putting away of one's sinful acts. In itself this is not sufficient. Man must next study the whole nature of sin as represented in the material universe and as urged upon him by his senses. Without such an understanding he cannot go on, but he will temporarily be concerned with the lower rather than the higher, be living in a suspense between the two. The next stage is the ascent to Wisdom-Virtue, and the being impregnated with Sophia in the mystic marriage with her. At this point the ascent in terms of Jacob and the flight to Sophia breaks off. Mangey suspected a lacuna in which the higher stage would be more fully described, and though Wendland thinks not, it is very likely that such a passage did follow.

Up to this point the imagery has been chiefly that of the Female Principle type. But now[41] Philo takes up a new Biblical setting, and develops quite a different picture of the Mystery. Here he deals with the Cities of Refuge. The Biblical passage is marred for Philo's use by the fact that the fugitive to the cities is a murderer, and so Philo confuses his real intent by a desperate allegory to show why the fugitive is a murderer. Apart from this element, Philo's argument is based upon the conception that life and death are matters of the presence or absence of virtue. To live to virtue we must first die to sin, exchange mortality for an immortal life, go from the creature to God.[42] God Himself is described not in terms of the Light-Sophia hierarchy but of the Logos and the two Powers, the Creating and Ruling. Man has been created partly by God (apparently in this section God is completely the equivalent of the Logos) and partly by the lower Powers, for the One made man's reason, the other his sensuous aspects. The true fugitive then is one who flees to an immaterial country, that is to God Himself, Who comprehends but is not comprehended (περιέχων οὐ περιέχεται), and is the refuge of all the universe.[43] This country which God inhabits is His own wisdom (ἐπιστήμη), and He inhabits it as a native while the fugitive can never be more than a resident alien.[44]

40. Ib., 50–52. 41. Ib., 53. 42. Ib., 58–64.
43. Ib., 75. 44. Ib., 76.

Philo goes on to devote some space to the character of the fugitive again. He must be pure from the sin of thinking that God is in any sense the cause of evil, and he cannot be a lover of self.[45] Suddenly Philo breaks into the adjuration:

Drive them out, then, Oh ye initiates and hierophants of the divine mysteries, drive out the souls that are mixed and just miscellaneously tossed together, those that have been mingled in confusion, the souls that are hard to purify or wash clean.[46] Such souls go about with their ears unstopped, their tongues unchecked, and thus bear with them the ready instruments of their own misery that they hear and prattle forth all things which must not be heard or spoken.[47]

In contrast those who know about sins, who have a proper mouth, may use the Cities of Refuge from unintentional sins.

Philo's preparation has been elaborate. Now he has at last finished talking about the Mystery in general, and has given what sounds like the formula of expulsion of uninitiates. At this point he should go on to tell the Mystery in its inner detail. In my opinion that is precisely the significance of what follows. For Philo goes on at once to the mystic significance of the Cities of Refuge.

The Mystery which is presented as the Mystery of the Cities of Refuge is really the Mystery of the ascent to God through His Powers. Philo discusses the cities under four main topics: why the cities chosen should have been cities from the tribe of Levi; why six cities were chosen and what they represent; why they were divided into three on each side of the Jordan; and why the fugitives were to return at the death of the High-Priest.

First the cities were cities of the tribe of Levi because the Levites are types of the true fugitives. They have done what the fugitive must do, stripped themselves of their bodies, of their unreasoning element (τὸ ἄλογον), by which is meant the senses, and of their power of speech (ὁ προφορικὸς λόγος). Thus only their κατὰ διάνοιαν λόγος, their higher reason, is left; they now live in a state that is according to monadity (τῇ κατὰ τὴν μόνωσιν διαίτῃ) and so can aspire purely and without distraction to the One.[48]

Second Philo discusses why there should have been six cities selected, and what is their meaning. The six cities are the Logos and his descending Powers; that is the first city is the Logos itself, the second the Creative or

45. *Fug.*, 80–84. Plato's *Theaetetus* 176 is quoted, and evidently the thought of the *Theaetetus* has much influenced the entire passage. Parenthetically he puts in here (§78), ἀλλ' οὐ ζωὴ μέν ἐστιν αἰώνιος ἡ πρὸς τὸ ὂν καταφυγή, θάνατος δ' ὁ ἀπὸ τούτου δρασμός.

46. The language is that of mystic θίασοι, and seems at the same time connected with Pythagoreanism, or was at least used by those who, in such matters, first used the common vocabulary, says Plutarch, *De Fraterno Amore*, 488B, C.

47. *Fug.*, 85.

48. Ib., 88–92. In §§93 f. he also mentions briefly the priestly significance of the Levites, but makes little of it.

Beneficent Power, the third the Royal or Ruling Power, the fourth is divine Mercy, the fifth and sixth together the legislation of God, for the fifth represents the body of specific positive commands in the Torah, the sixth the negative commands.[49] The cities are beautifully arranged, Philo says, for all grades and sorts of people who aspire to be free from sin. So far as the Mystery is concerned, Philo's real understanding of the unintentional homicide is that the homicide represents the man who aspires to be free from sin. The "unintentional homicide" who may flee to the city is figuratively a man who wants to do what is right and is looking for strength to do so. The willfully malicious have no more place in the Mystery than the willful murderer in the city of refuge. Yet among the people who want to do right there is every grade of spiritual gifts, and each aspirant must be treated according to his distinctive capabilities.

So he [Moses] urges the man able to run very swiftly to stretch out without stopping for breath to the most exalted divine Logos who is the source of Sophia, in order that by drawing from the flowing source he may discover for himself the prize of eternal life instead of death.[50]

Philo is very specific. It is not the Logos as found in the cosmos to which the fugitive aspires, but the Logos in its unmixed purity, the source of Sophia, and for one who has achieved this height, the prize is the putting away of mortality and the putting on of eternal life (ζωή) in the Logos. One has but to change the term Logos to Christ to have the famous passage in which Paul "stretches forward to the prize," the prize of putting off mortality for immortality.[51]

Philo goes on:

And the one not so swift [Moses urges] to fly for refuge to the Creative Power, which Moses calls God,[52] since by this Power the universe was arranged and set in order. For the one who apprehends that the universe was created has come into possession of a great good, knowledge (ἐπιστήμη) of the Creator, knowledge which at once prompts a created object to love the Creator.[53]

Philo's second place of refuge is at once the Creative Power and the ἐπιστήμη of God, which, since ἐπιστήμη is commonly a synonym of Sophia, and Sophia has just been mentioned as a derivative of the Logos, suggests the stage where the fugitive is identified with Sophia in the other formulation of the Mystery. Here the prize is, then, that one learns really to love God, in a mystic union with His Sophia.

The one who is still less facile [Moses urges to fly] to the Royal [Power]. For

---

49. Ib., 94f. 50. Ib., 97. 51. Philip. iii, 8–16.
52. θεός without the article. 53. *Fug.*, 97.

if the child is not regimented by good will for the Father, the subject is at least regimented by fear of the ruler, by Necessity which chastens him.[54]

Life on this stage is lived in a great sense of the majesty and force of the divine way, in a realization that one is bound by Necessity. We recognize the distinction at once between the religion of the level of the Creative Power and that of the Royal Power when we notice that in the latter the religious impulse is based upon a mystical appreciation of the majesty of God and the servitude of man. In the former the mystic has risen to a religious experience based upon the love of God for man and of man for God. It was just such an advance the Arminians later tried to make in moving out from the stern majesty of the God of Calvin to the loving Father they preached.

Philo goes on:

But for the man who cannot reach these objectives (ὅροι) which have been described, because they are too remote, other and nearer goals (καμπτῆρες) have been established, those of the Necessary Powers (δυνάμεις ἀναγκαῖαι), namely Mercy, and the injunctions that prescribe what must be done, as well as the injunctions that prescribe what must not be done. For though he may have sinned formerly a man who assumes that Divinity (τὸ θεῖον) is not implacable, but is merciful by the kindliness of its nature, straightway repents in hope of pardon. And he who conceives of God as a Legislator is happy in obeying all God's injunctions. And the last type of man will find the last refuge, that is simply the avoidance of evil, even though he may not be able to share in the more desirable goods.[55]

The description of the three lower Powers as ἀναγκαῖαι is obscure, and I have no suggestion to make as to its meaning. Otherwise the statement is clear and highly illuminating. The man who cannot cross the river must live by the extensions of Deity made especially for man into the material realm. These are two-fold, the merciful activity of God which reaches down to men, and the Law in its positive and negative aspects which God has projected into the material of nouns and verbs in the Torah for human guidance. The distinction between the positive and negative commands was familiar in Judaism. Women as a lower order were exempt from obligation to many of the positive commands.[56] Indeed no person was so sunk in material life that he could not understand a prohibition from some specific act. It demanded more understanding to grasp and fulfill such positive commands as to love one's neighbor than the negative command not to kill him. Still higher was such an appreciation of God as to understand that He was merciful and forgiving to one who had erred, but who sincerely wanted

54. *Fug.*, 98.   55. Ib., 98 f.   56. G. F. Moore, *Judaism*, ii, 129.

to be forgiven and reinstated. All six of the cities represent a remarkable classification of the different mystic stages, or types of religious capacity. But it is highly significant that the group of Powers on the lower side of the river, the Laws and Mercy of God, represent an epitome of traditional Judaism as it has been presented to Jewish lads of all ages. The Jew had the Law, positive and negative, mercifully given him by God, and believed that God was kindly desirous of granting pardon to one who was sincerely trying to fulfill the Law, but who inadvertently, or by sudden temptation, failed to keep it. The mercy of God went on and offered hopes for the Jewish race, later for the Jewish individual, in the future. Normative Judaism has always centered in the merciful God who gave men the guidance of His Law.

The interesting thing is that while Philo recognized normative Judaism, and could thus epitomize it, he put that Judaism definitely on the hither side of the river, and found his own true aspiration quite beyond. Normative Judaism was of divine institution, but its appeal was directed only to men who could not go into the Mystery. The Mystery was no less Judaism than was normative Judaism for Philo; rather it so far transcended normative Judaism as to make normative Judaism at best a propaedeutic, something which need not detain the swift runner at all in his rush for God. How differently Philo regarded the importance of the two sides of the river will appear shortly.

Parenthetically it is in view of these lower stages that Paul's perplexing conclusion to his description of the flight to the goal becomes clear. He has described the objective of the τέλειοι, and then continues:

Let us who are perfect have this objective in our minds (φρονῶμεν); and if you have some other objective in mind, God has revealed this also to you. But on the level to which we have attained, by that standard let us order our lives.[57]

Paul has not described the lower refuges, but he has recognized that not all men are of a nature to come through to the highest; they must content themselves with what Philo called lower δυνάμεις, and live in harmony with the level of spiritual life they are competent to reach.

It is very important that Philo goes on to parallel in a brief digression the schematization of Powers as he found it in the Cities of Refuge with the Ark of the Covenant, the symbol he usually employed for God and the Powers. For in the ark, he explains, the positive and negative specific law was inside the box. Mercy was represented by the mercy seat, the Creative and Royal Power were the cherubim above them, while still above these two Powers was the Presence, the invisible divine Logos, which here is the

57. Philip. iii, 15, 16.

εἰκὼν θεοῦ, the oldest of all the νοητά, the nearest to God of all the Powers, so close that there is no interval between them at all. The Logos is the charioteer driving the Powers, and He who utters the Logos is the passenger in the chariot telling the Logos where to drive. So, Philo concludes, the mystic who is entirely pure even from involuntary offences may have God Himself (αὐτὸν τὸν θεόν) as his inheritance and dwell in Him alone, but those who still, even though against their will, commit offenses, have the six Cities of Refuge for their way of salvation.[58]

Philo has little to say of the mystic who goes beyond the cities to God Himself, for it was an achievement that he reserved for his greatest heroes, if even Moses did actually achieve it. But he is careful to bring in at least an allusion to the supreme level of mystic aspiration, else his picture of the Mystery would be incomplete. The digression has then not only brought in this additional element, but it has definitely linked the scheme of the cities with the inner symbol of the Mystery, the Ark of the Covenant.

Philo has more to tell of the cities. He has yet two of his main points to discuss.

He goes on to the third question, why the cities were divided with three on each side of the Jordan. The three beyond Jordan are the Logos and the two Powers, far removed from the human race, and with them the universe as a whole has fellowship. But the three that are contingent upon the human race with its proclivity to sin are the lower three Powers, Mercy and the two types of Specific Laws. For, he explains very significantly:

What need is there of a prohibition for men who are not going to do wrong? Or of positive commands for those whose nature is not erring? Or of Mercy for those who have no sin? But our race [the human race] has need of those by the fact that it is naturally inclined to both voluntary and involuntary sin.[59]

Again we have it obviously implied that even the divine scheme of Judaism as it was usually taught was one designed essentially for lower souls who had not the spiritual gifts, while just as obviously those who had the gifts had no essential benefit from legalistic Judaism. Here certainly is the point of departure of the allegorists. It was not that in contrast to the legalistic literalists they saw a more philosophic meaning in the Torah by means of their allegory, and so rejected the letter as mythological and juvenile. The conflict was much deeper. They read into the Torah by allegory a distinctly non-Jewish type of salvation, and so they left the letter behind because in the Mystery which allegory had revealed they had become superior to the letter of spiritual accomplishment. They had crossed the river Jordan, and in one stage or another of the Mystery had no need of the laws. Philo went

58. *Fug.*, 100–102.   59. Ib., 105.

with them into the Mystery, though he himself still feels the importance of keeping the laws.[60]

The rest of the book adds little to our picture, and need not be followed in detail. The fourth point about the cities brings out that they are really not temporary refuges, but may be inhabited by the fugitive so long as he keeps himself in contact with the Logos-Priest. With this ends the section on flight. The discussion of discovery is concerned again with defining the types of persons who can rise to these heights. The highest type is the Self-Taught like Isaac, who finds without seeking. The next type seeks and finds, while two lower types are not within the possibilities of mystic achievement at all. What is found is illumination and sweetening of the soul,[61] and the contemplative life (θεωρητικὸς βίος), a life which achieves unmixed joy and the noetic beam that comes as from a flame.[62] The third main division of the book discusses the symbol of the well or fountain. The ἡγεμονικόν, the encyclical studies, the senses, Sophia, and God are discussed as fountains, and it is pointed out that we must not abide by the lower fountains but go to Sophia who will lead us higher. The book ends in an allegory of Ishmael, the type of product from one who has not yet reached the height. Such achievement is at best a sophistic affair.

The *Allegory*, for all its rambling, has, then, for its main theme the presentation of the Mystery.

In this Mystery the great high-priest is Moses. The true priesthood is a matter of learning that nothing material is excellent, but that God as the Primal Cause deserves worship and honor.[63] The Aaronic priest can alone of men enter the inner sanctuary because "in him alone resides the winged and heavenly yearning for those forms of good which are incorporeal and imperishable."[64] The true high-priest "has received a drink of the eternal graces, and repays this preliminary draught by pouring out himself as the full libation of unmixed wine."[65] His wife is a virgin (Philo must have had in mind the marriage with Sophia) and his offspring are λόγοι, ἐπίσκοποι and ἔφοροι of the affairs of nature, or are λειτουργοὶ θεοῦ, hastening to kindle the flame. This they do by uttering λόγοι περὶ ὁσιότητος, which come forth like sparks from flint.[66] Their father, Moses, the true high-priest, is completely self-sufficient, able to do and to know all things by himself. He subsumes in himself the entire race. He is less than God, but greater than man, partaking of both natures. His is preëminently the priesthood of the holy of holies, and as such he is not a man.

60. See above, Chapter III.
62. Ib., 176.
64. Ib., 136.
65. *Som.*, ii, 183. The χάριτες is here probably to be understood as χάρις.
66. Ib., 184–186.

61. *Fug.*, 139.
63. *Ebr.*, 75.

Was he then God? I would not like to say, for the archprophet Moses was actually given this title as his lot when he was called the God of Pharaoh. At least he was not man, but had a share of each extreme as though one were the pedestal, the other the head.[67]

Such a Priesthood had the Jews in Moses, the Nature beloved of God, who could lead them on the great Royal Road of the Mystery.[68] Its symbolism has appeared throughout. It is the Mystery of the holy of holies, whose symbol is the white robe of the man who has "put on immortality." It is the Mystery of the sacred marriage with Sophia; of the fugitive rushing past city after city of the divine Powers until he comes at last to the Logos. If pictures were devised to illustrate the Mystery artists might have made use of almost any scene of the Old Testament, for scarcely an inch of the Pentateuch, at least, has escaped Philo's allegory. But preëminently such pictures must have centered in Noah's coming out of the body, as his ark was called; in the meeting of Abraham with Melchizedek or with the Three Men; in the courtship and marriage of Isaac; in the flight and the dream of Jacob, his departure from Laban and the wrestling with the angel; in Moses the self-taught youngster who got his commission at the burning bush and who became the great mystagogue of the Exodus, who got the Law from God and gave it to Israel, and who was at last taken to God to sing His praises forever in the great song of the heavenly bodies. Through it all the coming of a white-clad mystic to Sophia or to the three Powers must have been symbolized, and the contrast between the White Robe and the Robe of Aaron would appear, though these robes might be put together on the true priest as Philo sometimes describes him.[69] Also the contrast would be shown between one who wore the white robe and the mass of people who did not.

Is there evidence that any such organization of the Mystery existed as would have produced such an iconography?

First it may be asked what was Philo's attitude toward the plastic arts. In one passage, an isolated statement in an irrelevant context, Philo stops to say that in talking about the Giants Moses has not turned into a myth-maker. Moses is too much a follower of truth to stoop to myths. It was on this ground, Philo adds, that Moses banished painting and sculpture from his commonwealth, since their attractive and charming artistry belies the truth.[70] The statement is not elaborated. In itself it seems only to mean that Moses took the same attitude toward plastic artists that Plato took toward the poets, and forbade all use of their arts. If this is Philo's general position, and he thought art and Judaism fundamentally opposed, it is curious that there are no other passages that say so since he has a good deal to say about

67. Som., ii, 187–189. On the deity of Moses see above, pp. 223 ff.
68. Conf., 95 f.		69. As in Mut., 43 f.		70. Gig., 58 f.

art. True he denounces artistic productions sharply in a strongly Cynic rejection of all the refinements of life. The quest for beauty in material objects
is a perversion of the true quest for immaterial beauty.[71] From the Platonic
point of view he depreciates their value, because they are the creations of
deceitful false opinion done by men who have never seen τὰ πρὸς ἀλήθειαν
καλά.[72] They are only copies of the works of φύσις, and are not φύσεις
themselves.[73] But he admires their beauty and considers that many pictures
and statues done by Greeks and barbarians, and set up to ornament the cities,
are more beautiful than even living men and women.[74] Indeed their beauty
is one of the most dangerously seductive of the appeals of paganism.[75] He
knows the symbolism of the pagan iconography, and what that symbolism
means to pagans, so much so that Gaius' adopting the symbols of the gods
for himself seems to Philo a real desecration.[76] He even warns Jews not to be
disrespectful to pagan idols,[77] and is proud to point out to Gentiles that
Jews respect their "gods" although they reject them as objects of worship.[78]
He is not uncritical in his artistic judgments. He not only knows the inferiority of copies to the original masterpieces,[79] but speaks with assurance of
how the hand of a given master is to be recognized in works of different
types and sizes.[80] So far from taking advantage of the texts against the
making of images for a general denunciation of art,[81] he either allegorizes
any specific meaning from the texts, making the "images" allegories of the
worship of wealth,[82] or he interprets the scriptural prohibition as applying
only to images of pagan gods that can be used for idols.[83] Certainly against
decorative works of art, or symbolic ones, there is no invective that seems to
have any literal significance (for I cannot take Philo's Cynic asceticism literally), except against images that are supposed to represent Deity and are
used for cult purposes. An iconography of the Jewish Patriarchs and their
Mystery, in which God was symbolically represented by a hand, would not
violate Philo's position in the least.

True Philo does not mention such a Jewish iconography. But it is highly
noteworthy that he does leave room for such an iconography, and shows a
sympathy for works of art which is quite in contrast with our other records
from the Jews of the time.

For example Josephus wrote:

The Greeks and certain other peoples believe it to be a good thing to set up

71. *Som.*, ii, 52 ff.; cf. *LA*, ii, 75.　　　72. *Gig.*, 15.
73. *Mig.*, 167; cf. *Plant.*, 27.　　　74. *Abr.*, 267.
75. *Spec.*, i, 29.　　　76. *Legat.*, 98 ff.
77. *QE*, ii, 5.　　　78. *Mos.*, ii, 205.
79. *Opif.*, 141.　　　80. *Jos.*, 39.
81. As Exod. xx, 4 and Lev. xix, 4.　　　82. *Spec.*, i, 25 ff.
83. *LA*, iii, 22; *Decal.*, 7, 66 ff., 76, 156; *Spec.*, i, 21 f., 56; *Virt.*, 221; *Cont.*, 7.

images, and then they take pleasure in depicting their fathers, wives, or children; some moreover have pictures of persons who are in no way related to them, and others do so by reason of fondness for their slaves. So then what wonder is it if they seem similarly to honor lords and masters likewise. Furthermore it is not as though our legislator were prophetically commanding that the power of the Romans was not to be honored, but as though he recognized that this was a thing useful to neither gods nor men, and since [artistic representations] are proved by their inanimation to be inferior to animate beings, much more to God, he forbade the making of images.[84]

The difference between this statement of Josephus and Philo's attitude toward works of art is at once striking. While Philo says nothing of pictures of Moses, or any Jewish Patriarch, at least his remarks do not make their tolerance completely out of the question as do those of Josephus. The passage is by no means unique in Josephus. "It was unlawful that there should be any such thing in the temple as images, or busts, or the representation of any living thing whatever,"[85] Josephus wrote of the golden eagle put on the temple by the Romans. That the law was more general than this application he shows later: "It was not lawful for them [the Jews] to put an image of God, much less of a man, in the temple, or even in any profane part of their country."[86] As Kleinert remarks,[87] Josephus carried his ideas from later Judaism back into the earlier period, and naïvely gave as one reason for the fall of Solomon's house that he made the images of brazen oxen (the cherubim) in the temple, and of lions about his throne.[88] If Josephus is any guide to sentiment in Palestine at the time, as he is universally taken to be, it is significant that when speaking to local Jews in Galilee he justified his coming up to Tiberias by saying that he was to lead them in destroying Herod's palace because it had been profaned by being decorated with images of animals.[89] Indeed the populace was so sensitive on the matter that they raised a great protest against the prizes Herod offered in his games. These were sets of armor hung on some sort of wooden framework, and the Jews thought that images of men were being foisted upon them under the cover of the armor. Herod had to take the leaders of the Jews and show them the crude wooden framework, objects that made them laugh, before their sensibilities were appeased.[90]

It has been generally thought from these passages in Josephus that all Jews had by the time of Christ so entirely got away from the primitive idolatry as to be completely averse to artistic representations of any animate beings, and especially of God. The discovery in Dura of a synagogue filled

84. *Cont. Ap.*, ii, 74 f.   85. *BJ*, I, 650.   86. Ib., II, 195.
87. In Herzog-Hauck, *Realencyclopädie für protestantische Theologie*, 3d Ed., III, 221. See also Schürer, *Geschichte des jüdischen Volkes*, 4th Ed., II, 89 f.
88. *Ant.*, VIII, 195.   89. *Vita.*, 65.   90. *Ant.*, XV, 267–279.

with great frescoes forces us to conclude that the Judaism of Dura had many elements in it that normative Judaism would have repudiated, at least in Josephus' time. Certainly the Dura type of Judaism drew upon a tradition that regarded pictures differently from Palestine as Josephus describes it. The leaders of the Jews who made an official inspection of the trophies to make sure that human figurines were not hidden under the prize armor would hardly have returned to synagogues decorated like those of Dura. Philo has shown an interpretation of the Jewish Law that forbids the use of idols, to be sure, but by no means the use of art in general. When "those who make molten images," without any distinction are condemned with sorcerers and witches as practising the arts of Satan,[91] and when Jews are later forbidden even to look at idols, Philo knows them by each of their charming details. The only passage, so far as I know, in any way kindred to Philo's statements is in the other great classic of Alexandrian Judaism, the *Wisdom of Solomon*.[92] Here image making was represented as being the beginning of the gods themselves. The author suggests that some father who had a picture made of his dead child came to revere the picture because of its beauty, and so deified the child and founded a mystery for him which later got legal support. Thus the gods arose out of artistic representations. Similarly men made statues of distant rulers to do them honor, and again the beauty of the statue leads to deifying the subject glorified by art. The author goes on to a denunciation of the sins that result from idolatry.[93] That is, *Wisdom*, like Philo, detests idolatry, but is keenly sensitive to the appeal of art. Still *Wisdom* does not go so far as Philo does in the appreciation of art.

Philo's position as regards images has been pointed out in partial answer to a question: Is there evidence in Philo that the Mystery was so organized in Hellenistic Judaism that it might have produced such an iconography as that at Dura? This first answer has been inconclusive, but at least it has appeared that Philo has an attitude toward art which might conceivably have admitted its development, while the non-Alexandrian, the known normative tradition, could not have tolerated it.

Other material is interesting as to the question of whether Philo was speaking of a definite type of Jewish cultus, or only of a mystic interpretation of the Scriptures. It has appeared in many passages that the language of cult groups, initiations, cult robes, secret doctrines is his normal medium. Even the mystic food has been mentioned, the *cibum mysterii* which Jacob gave to Isaac,[94] and the "buried cakes" which Sarah prepared and Abraham shared with the three visiting Powers, and so was admitted into the final Mysteries (αἱ τέλειαι τελεταί).[95] Both these passages are so allegorized as to give no

---

91. I Enoch. lxv, 6.   92. xiv, 12–21.   93. xiv, 22–31.
94. *QG*, iv, 213. See above, p. 167; for the high-priest's robe, p. 107.
95. *Sac.*, 60.

direct inference of a mystic meal in a cult. And yet that there might well have been a definite Mystery appears in the conclusion:

It is written "make buried cakes" because the mystic teaching (ὁ ἱερὸς μύστης λόγος) about the Unbegotten and His two Powers must be concealed, since not everyone is able to guard the deposit (παρακαταθήκη) of the sacred rites (θεῖα ὄργια).[96]

A similar declaration is:

Further in a most excellent way Moses mentioned the "buried cakes" after the three measures, not only because knowledge and understanding of the Sophia of the Father and His two higher Powers are hidden from the many, but also because a matter of this kind must be concealed and not shown to all. It cannot be told to all since he who reveals the Secret to the imprudent and unworthy destroys and overthrows the law of perfection of the holy Mysteries.[97]

Still more striking is the fragment:

It is not permitted to speak out the sacred mysteries to the uninitiated until they shall have been purified with the perfect purification. For the uninitiated and the facile person (ὁ ἀνοργίαστος καὶ εὐχερής), since he is unable to hear or see immaterial and conceptual nature, is deceived by the thing which is made manifest to his sight and so casts reproach upon the irreproachable. To declare the Mysteries to the uninitiated would mean the destruction of the laws of the most sacred Mystery.[98]

Here it is hard to think that Philo had not some definite ritualistic criterion. We have "laws" of the sacred Mystery (θεσμοί, leges), something that could be made "manifest to the sight," and a "deposit of sacred rites," all in connection with the Mystery of God and the Powers, and certainly not a reference to the Jerusalem cultus. Figurative use of terms from the mysteries had been familiar from Plato's time for describing a philosophic mysticism, but this seems to go beyond the figurative. Still more definite is the following in its reference to a mystic Judaism:

It is strange that there should be a law in cities forbidding one to divulge the mystic secrets (μυστικὰ μυστήρια) to the uninitiated, but that the true mysteries (αἱ ἀληθεῖς τελεταί) which lead to piety and holiness, should be revealed to ears full of wickedness. One must not share everything with everyone, that is not teachings and practices which are especially sacred. For there are many prerequisites which must be satisfied by people who aspire to share in these things. The first,

96. Sac., 60.   97. QG, iv, 8.
98. In R. Harris, Fragments, p. 69; the fragment appears twice in Dam., Par., and also in the Cod. Reg., and is assigned by both to QG, ii. É. Bréhier (Les Idées, p. vii, n. 2) declared this fragment to be identical with the foregoing, QG, iv, 8, but they are obviously only parallel and similar statements.

greatest, and most essential prerequisite is piety and holiness with respect to the one and true (ὄντως ὄν) God, after they have put off their endless straying to statues and idols, images in general, and to mystic rites that are no rites, mysteries that are no mysteries. The second thing is that they must be purified with the sanctifying purifications in body and soul through the laws and customs of the fathers. Third they must furnish a reliable pledge that they are worthy of being welcomed into our fellowship in order that they may not, like intemperate youths, get drunk from surfeit and superabundance when they partake at the sacred table, and so be changed for the worse:[99] to such people it is not permitted.[100]

That this is a Jewish group is clear not only from its tolerably reliable ascription to Philo but by the reference to the purification διὰ νόμων πάτριων καὶ ἠθῶν. What aspect of the Torah this meant I shall not risk guessing, but it is too familiar a form of reference in Philo to the Torah to be taken as anything else. It is interesting that the purification is to take place διά, by means of the Torah, rather than κατά, according to it. The plain implication of the passage as it stands is that over against the "mysteries that are no mysteries, the τελεταὶ ἀτέλεστοι," stood in Judaism a Mystery, one without idols, but with purificatory rites that accomplished what the others promised but failed to perform. This Mystery was a very secret one, to be revealed only to those who had given pledge of being worthy. And it involved a sacred table, communion at which was *ex opere operato* a dynamic force. If it involved terrible danger to one who was unfit to receive its operation, certainly it was as powerful to benefit those who came to it properly. One is strikingly reminded of the Corinthians who partook of the bread and cup of the Lord in an unworthy manner, and so ate and drank to their damnation. For our immediate purpose the point is that Philo's words seem as strongly to reflect an actual "table" as do Paul's an actual bread and cup. Too much cannot be made of an isolated passage, especially when that passage is a fragment torn from its context. It is conceivable that if we had the context we should see that Philo is speaking of what Gentiles are to be allowed to partake of the Passover, and that the mystic comparison is all rhetoric. For only proselytes who had gone through the traditional purification, circumcision and baptism, and the presenting of an offering to the Temple, were admitted to the paschal ceremony.[101] It must be recalled that Philo lived before the destruction of the temple, and that the paschal meal was still a feast which could be celebrated only in

99. ἐναλλοιώθωσιν seems to mean, "fall into a condition of change" in contrast with the ideal "unchangeableness." See a Hermetic fragment from Stobaeus in Scott, *Hermetica*, I, 384, l. 27. Scott translates it here "changing from one thing to another."

100. Fragment, in Harris, *Fragments*, p. 75; Mangey, II, 658 f. Harris omits the first sentence as given by Mangey without giving a reason for doing so. The fragment is found in both Cod. Coislin (276, f. 205) and Damascenus, *Parall.* (782). In the former it is attributed to *QE*, i.

101. G. F. Moore, *Judaism*, i, 330 f.

Jerusalem, so far as we know.[102] This would make the requirements of Gentile admission to the Passover of minor concern to Jews in the Diaspora, yet Philo's range of observation is so great that he might have been speaking on that subject in the lost context. The fact remains, however, that if the paschal meal is behind these words of Philo, it is a frank turning of the rite into a "Mystery," shrouded with secret meaning and sacramental power, one that goes quite beyond the conception of the meal in normative Judaism. Indeed if Jews were to have made a Mystery of their own, nothing would be more to be expected than that they should have done so by putting mystic meaning into the traditional rites of Judaism. And the further fact remains that the passage seems to imply a more regular ceremony, a more usual mystic celebration, than the annual Passover. What seems highly probable in the passage, and together with this in the other passages just cited, is that the Jews actually did have a Mystery of their own in contrast to the false mysteries of paganism, a Mystery with secret objects "manifest to the sight" of the initiates, governed by a body of laws with its own ἱερὸς λόγος, and πράγματα ἱερά, θεῖα ὄργια. Together these constituted a solemn παρακατα-θήκη, an entrusted deposit, which only the initiated could properly receive and guard. There is also a hint that the Jewish θίασοι were under πρεσβύτε-ροι ordained into a mystic "patriarchal succession."[103] The prejudices of this type of Judaism were by no means so active against pictorial art as those of their cousins in Palestine, and included denunciations only of objects of art regarded as actual representations of Deity and used as objects of worship.

The fact is that some such mystic Judaism would have to be presupposed to account for the pictures revealed at Dura. The mystical character of the frescoes is something that must be pointed out in the next study of this series. Here I can only indicate that within the Judaism of the Diaspora, as Philo reveals it, there are unmistakable indications of such a group or tendency as we should have been inclined hypothetically to assume in accounting for the newly found Jewish art. And it is in Philo that the basic character of that Judaism is exposed.

To be sure there are other stray details which perhaps should be introduced into the picture of this mystic Judaism. There are the Therapeutae, meeting for the sacred meal every Sabbath, clad in white garments, their hands concealed under their robes, consuming the most holy food, bread, salt, and hyssop, after they had been feasted spiritually upon allegorical commentary on the sacred Laws.[104] These seem to be the hermits contemporary with Philo, whom he mentions as being the only living men who realize the ideal

102. G. F. Moore, *Judaism*, ii, 40 f.   103. See above, pp. 217 f.
104. See the *Vita Contemplativa, passim.*

life of the Patriarchs, and who bear in their souls the images stamped upon them from the lives of the archetypal σοφοί, men who take God alone as their guide and live strictly according to the Law, that is according to the ὀρθὸς λόγος of nature.[105] Philo seems to have felt himself very close to the Therapeutae, though we do not know the nature or extent of his connections with them. He may have been with them only temporarily, as was Josephus with the Essenes, or he may have visited them frequently, and kept what we might now describe as a sort of lay brother affiliation with them. In our ignorance of the Therapeutae, and of the extent of their influence upon Philo and Alexandrian Judaism in general, it seems we can only surmise that they may have contributed much to the mystic thought he is expressing. There are also again to be recalled the "allegorists" who likewise allegorized scripture but who went too far for Philo by severing the body, the letter of the law, from the soul, its allegorical intent; the Law was to Philo properly an animal made up of both.[106] Certainly these allegorists were not Philo's ideal, but they too may have been the source of much of his thinking, and have had organizations where, the letter being no longer binding, pictorial representation of sacred themes may have arisen.

That is, I would not like to appear to the reader to be unaware that it is difficult if not impossible to estimate the significance of Philo's writings as witness to Hellenistic Judaism in general. But of some things we may be sure. First there is revealed in Philo an elaborate transformation of Judaism into a mystic philosophy, one that ultimately drew for its sources largely upon Orpheus, Isis, and Iran, as these were interpreted by the mystic philosophers of Greek background. This mystic philosophy with almost monotonous reiteration brings all the incidents of the Pentateuch into an account of the Mystic Royal Road to God through the Powers or through Sophia. The white robe, the sacred table, the stages of progress, are all thoroughly standardized, and seem in Philo's pages to be the reflection of a great tradition. With this mystical doctrine went a surprising leniency to pictorial representation, and several striking hints of actual mystic organization and initiation. Further we know that Philo was a man considered thoroughly sound by his contemporaries, who selected him as their ablest and most fitting representative in one of the greatest crises of their history.

It seems that Philo must hereafter be treated as the great source from whom we learn of a Judaism so thoroughly paganized that its postulates and its objectives were those of Hellenistic mysteries rather than those of any Judaism we have hitherto known. For all its passionate Jewish loyalty, it

105. *Prob.*, 62. I take these to be the Therapeutae since the Essenes seem to be introduced later as additional examples of Stoic Liberty, with no such reference to the Patriarchs. On this doctrine see above, pp. 83 ff.
106. *Cont.*, 78.

was not fundamentally a Judaism with Hellenistic veneer: it was a Hellenism, presented in Jewish symbols and allegories, to be sure, but still a Hellenistic dream of the solution of the problem of life by ascent higher and ever higher in the Streaming Light-Life of God.

CHAPTER X

THE MYSTERY IN NON-PHILONIC WRITINGS

A READER who has followed the argument to this point, and who is familiar with the writings of Judaism, must have been impressed with the great difference between the Judaism here expounded and any type of Judaism which he has elsewhere encountered. In spite of the fact that Philo's statements and mode of presentation almost invariably imply that he was drawing upon a rich tradition which had long been elaborated before him and which would already be familiar to his readers, his conceptions of God, of salvation, of the Logos and Sophia, of the Patriarchs, of the Royal Road are as strange as his doctrine of the higher Law which transcends the Torah. Must this mystic Judaism remain indicated to us only from Philo's allegory and with no external support? It does not seem so.

First there are in some of the writings of the "apocryphal" class passages that are striking when read with Philonic ideology freshly in mind. In the Pseudo-Philonic *De Sampsone* the hero is developed as a type of "strength" in a way analogous to Philo's making the Patriarchs individually types of different virtues, though the mystic element we are looking for is absent.

More extended traces of analogy are to be found in the Pseudo-Philonic *Biblical Antiquities:*[1] ix, 10, the birth of Moses was prophesied to Miriam in a dream by a "man in linen garments"; xii, 1, Moses when coming down from Horeb was covered with *"invisible* light, for he had gone down to the place where is the light of the sun and moon: the light of his face overcame the brightness of the sun and moon, and he knew it not"; xii, 7, when the Israelites were punished for worshipping the calf, those who had been drawn into the affair against their will were distinguished from the others by the fact that their faces shone; xii, 9, God is light; xix, 16, Moses is gloriously changed and then dies, the angel choir ceases for the day, and God buries him with His own hand "in the light of the world"; xx, 2 f., when Joshua puts on Moses' "garments of wisdom and girdle of knowledge," he is changed and his mind "kindled"; xxii, 3, Light abides with God; xxiii, 6, God showed Abraham the "torches of fire by which the righteous which have believed in me shall be enlightened"; xxxvii, 3, "and when the truth enlightened Moses it was by a thorn bush that it enlightened him"; li, 3, 5, the words of Samuel are going to "enlighten the people," and the "light of the righteous," apparently their souls, is not destroyed by God; liii, 2, Samuel as a boy of eight

---

1. The Latin translation is very difficult to procure. I have been dependent upon the version by M. R. James, published by SPCK, 1917.

years is unable to "see the fire" as Moses did, so he can only hear God's voice; lxiv, 6, Samuel, when called up by the witch of Endor, has not the "form of a man; for he is arrayed in a white robe and hath a mantle upon it, and two angels leading him." The frequent recurrence of light mysticism makes it very tempting to interpret the vision of Samuel clothed in the white robe with two attendant angels as a vision of the Logos and the two Powers. Some such may have been the original meaning of this whole series of "light" passages, though they are again scattered through a book which is otherwise quite uninteresting in its unoriginal repetition of ordinary Jewish points of view.

The ultimate origin of the material may be indicated in the first analogy cited, the fact that the birth of Moses was prophesied to Miriam in a dream by a "man in linen garments."[2] In the Egyptian religion the appearance of Isis and Osiris in dreams to give prophetic messages or warnings was a constant feature,[3] while linen was so much the distinctive garb of Osiris that the linen towel with which Jesus girt himself at the Last Supper at once suggested Osiris to men of the Second Century.[4] We may be pardoned if these linen garments of the angels and Patriarchs suggest the same to us, and if we think they may have had the same association in Hellenistic Judaism. The *Biblical Antiquities* impresses one as being the production of an author, himself a Jew of the normative type, but one to whom the mystic type of Judaism was sufficiently familiar so that its phrases continuously recur. God as "invisible light" and the experience of the Patriarchs as one of "illumination" is really no part of the author's own thought. The frequent recurrence of the phrases makes it all the more necessary to assume an important group in Judaism to whom these conceptions were vital and significant, a group so important that their phrases crept—unawares, I might say—into the language of a man more conservatively Jewish than they.

The *Assumption of Moses* has some points of analogy to the mystery in its glorification of Moses.[5] When Moses is represented as saying, "He designed and devised me, and He prepared me before the foundation of the world, that I should be the mediator (*arbiter*) of His covenant" (i, 14), the statement is striking, but iii, 12 shows that the author thought of Moses as mediator only of the "commandments," and "pre-existence" is too familiar a bit of apocalyptic machinery to be pressed here in isolation.

A book that seems contemporary with Philo, *II Enoch*, is, so far as we can judge from the defective text that has come to us, a Hellenistic, indeed an

2. *Bib. Ant.*, ix, 10.
3. See T. Hopfner, *Fontes Historiae Religionis Aegyptiacae* (hereafter abbreviated as *Fontes*), Index, s. v. *somnia*.
4. Lucan, IX, 153–161 (*Fontes*, II, 186, ll. 16 ff.); Tertul., *De Corona*, 8.
5. The passages are collected and summarized conveniently by Charles in his *Apocrypha and Pseudepigrapha of the Old Testament* (hereafter abbreviated as *Apoc. and Pseud.*), II, 412.

Alexandrine, apocalypse.[6] As such it is drawing upon many sources different from those of Philo. Still it is interesting to see that the view of God as Light had become so proverbial in Hellenistic Judaism as to be axiomatic even in an apocalypse. This appears most clearly in the account of creation, which seems to follow, at least in this one detail, the Platonic conception of creation ἐκ τῶν μὴ ὄντων, a phrase which here as often means not "nothing," but "what has yet no being," that is formless matter (xxiv, 2). With this conception is combined the oriental mythology of creation from the primal egg (xxv, 1–3; xxvi, 1–3). The Egg, Adoil, is filled with Light when God first calls him into existence "out of the invisible" (xxv, 1, 3). God was Himself in this great light (*ibid.*), "and as there is born light from light, there came forth a great age, and showed all creation, which I had thought to create." God established a throne for Himself and then sent the Light to dwell above the throne, to be the highest of all things (xxv, 4, 5). God then went on to finish creation. The final picture is of God with the Light *above Him*, which can only mean *superior* to Him in dignity. The story of creation which follows has little to our purpose, except that before the Fall Adam could see into the open heavens, and behold the angels singing and the "gloomless light" (xxxi, 2). Large conclusions cannot be drawn from so small a passage and so indirect a tradition. But at least it is interesting that as the text stands the highest reality is Light, and creation is done by a divinity that was "in the midst of the Great Light." The association of God with Light is undeniably a part of the Judaism of this author, as well as of Philo.

IV Maccabees has little of the Mystery in the sense that it includes the Logos or Sophia. But it is strikingly similar to Philo in other respects. For example while the Mosaic Law is the basis of the heroes' religion and loyalty, it is revered from quite a different point of view from that of the author of *III Maccabees*. In the latter, obedience to the Law is motivated by a sense of racial duty, on the ground that by obedience alone can Israel retain her position as the "Chosen People" protected by God. In *IV Maccabees* the motive is stated:

The Law teaches us self-control, so that we are masters of all our pleasures and desires; it teaches us to practise courage, so that we can willingly endure pain; it teaches justice, so that in all our usages we act equitably; and it teaches piety, so that with due reverence we worship the God who alone is (μόνον τὸν ὄντα θεόν). Therefore we eat no unclean meat: for believing our Law to be given by God, we know also that the Creator of the world in His act of legislation was sympathetically disposed toward us by nature. He has commanded that we eat the things that will be fitting for our souls, and He has forbidden us to eat meats that will be contrary to our souls (v, 23–26).

6. See the introduction by Forbes and Charles, *Apoc. and Pseud.*, II, 425 ff. I have had to depend upon the text as there given, since I do not read Slavonic.

That is, the Law given by God is part of a great συμπάθεια, in which God and our souls are working together with material things. Some of these would help us to the great virtues, some would hinder us from such achievement. The Law simply explains the Way of Nature, and the natural properties of things. We follow the Law and the religion of the Jews because such a religion "saves into eternal life with God" (xv, 3). Through the Law man's reason can become pious (xvi, 1), can be called "of the type of Isaac" (ὁ Ἰσακεῖος λογισμός) (vii, 14), and so the man himself become a φιλόσοφος θείου βίου (vii, 7). The motive of obedience has changed from the typically Jewish into the Philonic motive: by the Law we come into the true regimentation of our inner lives with the cosmic συμπάθεια, into the true Philosophy, achieve the character revealed in the greatest Patriarchs. Philo at Rome was fully prepared to die hideously for the Law: but his motives and loyalties were those of *IV Maccabees,* as contrasted with those of *III Maccabees.*

With the *Wisdom of Solomon* we come to still more definite testimony to the fact that Philo's Judaism was not of a type peculiar to himself. *Wisdom* has already been found to know the Mystery of Aaron,[7] and to take an attitude toward images more like Philo's than that of any other Jewish writer.[8] An extended analysis of the book is quite impossible here, but some of its more striking points must be mentioned. Use of *Wisdom* has become much complicated by the enormous variety of opinions about the unity of the book. From writers who insist that the book is a unit, though written perhaps at different times by the same author, opinions have been urged breaking the work up into from two to seventy-nine parts, with variety of authorship and date.[9] As Professor Porter quietly remarked, "The analyses do not agree." Since we are here interested in the work only as a possible source of data to establish the existence of ideas in Judaism similar to those of Philo about the Mystery, there is no need to express one more opinion as to whether the work was written by one or many hands. Few commentators, however, have failed to be impressed with the difference between the ideas preceding chapter xi, 1, and those following it, and these two sections are here treated independently.

The reader who turns to *Wisdom* from the Philonic material is at once struck by the fact that there are two references to the "Mystery." In the first reference the "Mysteries (μυστήρια) of God"[10] are the reward of immortality awaiting the righteous. The basis of this reward is that the "just man" (ὁ δίκαιος), who, like all men, is made for incorruption (ἀφθαρσία) and in the

---

7. See above, p. 120.   8. See above, p. 259.
9. For convenient summaries of the matter see: Holmes' introduction in R. H. Charles, *Apoc. and Pseud.,* I, 521 ff.; A. T. S. Goodrick, *The Book of Wisdom,* pp. 72–78; F. Focke, *Die Entstehung der Weisheit Salomos,* 1913, pp. 1 ff.
10. *Wisd.,* ii, 22.

likeness of God's own distinctive qualities (εἰκὼν τῆς ἰδίας ἰδιότητος),[11] is kept by God from the wiles of the devil, and tried in His fiery furnace. This experience is itself the blessed visitation,[12] or is followed by the blessed visitation, with the result that the righteous shine out and become sparks kindling others, apparently with the divine fire. Such people are to be given rule over others. This is unmistakably a representation of the doctrine of immortality, in terms of a light transformation, as a mystic teaching. It gets still more importance when considered with the second reference to μυστήρια.

The second reference[13] is much more important. Solomon is represented as the hierophant, a fact that is interesting for its similarity to Philo, as well as for its dissimilarity. For the author or authors of *Wisdom* Solomon definitely takes the place occupied by Moses in Philo's thought. *Wisdom* does not describe the Patriarchs as a series of hierophants whose chief was Moses, though in the great allegory of the Patriarchs[14] they are all symbols of ὁ δίκαιος because of the special action of Sophia in the career of each. This may have been because the book is so much older than Philo that the elaborate allegory of the Pentateuch had not yet been worked out, or it may simply mean that it was not within the author's purpose in so brief a work to try to tell all he knew. Either conclusion from the silence would be dangerous. Yet the fact that the Patriarchs and Moses do not appear as hierophants must not hide it from us that a striking analogy to their experience and function in the Mystery as Philo describes them is found in the picture of Solomon as mystic and mystagogue in *Wisdom*. The passage must be examined somewhat in detail.

"Solomon" begins the section by promising that he will tell the nature of Sophia and his experience of her:

What Sophia is and how she had her beginning I will proclaim,
    And will not hide mysteries from you;
I will trace her out from the beginning of her coming into being,
    And will bring out into the open her gnosis.[15]

The first step in this bringing εἰς τὸ ἐμφανὲς τὴν γνῶσιν αὐτῆς is for "Solomon" to tell how he came to know it. To prevent any misunderstanding he first explains carefully that he is himself a mortal of the mortals in

11. See the interesting note to the passage for text and interpretation by Goodrick, *op. cit.* Goodrick prefers the reading ἀϊδιότητος for ἰδιότητος (both have ms. support), and so translates "God created man to be imperishable."

12. *Wisd.*, iii, 7. See Siegfried's note *ad loc.*, Kautzsch, *Apokryphen und Pseudepigraphien des alten Testaments.* Goodrick's note is also very valuable, though I cannot agree with him in referring the καιρὸς ἐπισκοπῆς to the future judgment, for the subsequent rulership of the saints appears to indicate rulership in this world. But his interpretation is by no means an impossible one.

13. *Wisd.*, vi, 22 ff.   14. Ib., x.   15. Ib., vi, 22.

origin, experience, and destiny.[16] But "Solomon," if mortal in his constitution, was certainly not like ordinary men. He was a "naturally gifted" child, a παῖς εὐφυής, which latter word is so freely used by Philo for one competent to receive the Mystery, or specifically to receive ἡ αἰθέριος σοφία, that it may be regarded, at least for Philo, as a settled *terminus technicus*.[17] Another way "Solomon" has of saying the same thing is to state that he was at the beginning a "good soul" joined to a "flawless body."[18] But "Solomon" recognized that even so he could get Sophia only as a gift of God,[19] and accordingly he prayed mightily to God for her.[20] In another passage he explains that he loved her from his youth up and sought her for his bride,[21] a suit in which it is implied that he succeeded.[22] The many pages that have been written to prove or disprove the connection of Sophia in this treatise with the thought of Philo would seem to have missed their decisive point. Here, if nowhere else, is the idea of mystic ascent by marriage with Sophia, an idea we have found *passim* in Philo, unmistakably enunciated. It is the formulation of the Jewish mystery according to the Female Principle, and it is quite natural from what we have seen of Orphism and Isis that this formulation should appear before that of the Mithraic Powers.

The great prayer of "Solomon" is given, as a result of which this marriage was consummated.[23] God is exhorted to send Sophia down from the throne of His glory to be Solomon's companion and guide. The result is that he has learned all the secrets of the universe,[24] and has become immortal,[25] and a friend of God,[26] the king perfect in judgment.[27] While much of this ideology is Jewish, its *double entendre* with the Greek νόμος ἔμψυχος is obvious.[28] It will be recalled that the perfection of the Patriarchs in the Mystery was most commonly indicated by the fact that they had become νόμοι ἔμψυχοι. Perhaps the line of development by which this came to be the distinguishing achievement of the Patriarchs was brought about because the Mystery was first formulated in the tradition of Solomon's becoming the ideal king and νόμος ἔμψυχος through receiving Sophia. As he had done, so had they. Hebrew speculation on Wisdom would be the easy starting point for

16. *Wisd.*, vii, 1–6.

17. Ib., viii, 19. As such it was one of the qualities of Abraham (*LA*, iii, 196; *Mut.*, 68); and is the standing epithet of Reuben to connect him with the Mystery (*Som.*, ii, 33, 37; *Mut.*, 98; *Sac.*, 120); it is the quality of a mystic capable of receiving ἡ αἰθέριος σοφία (*Fug.*, 138, 176; *Sac.*, 7, 64; *Spec.*, iv, 75); and in general of one fit for the Mystery (*Mut.*, 212 f.; *Mig.*, 164 f.; *Heres*, 38; *Cong.*, 82; *Agr.*, 158). In *Mut.*, 102 Philo remarks: τὸ εὐφυὲς ἄμεινον τοῦ μανθάνοντος—τὸ μὲν γὰρ ἔοικεν ὁράσει, τὸ δὲ ἀκοῇ.

18. *Wisd.*, viii, 19 f.	19. Ib., viii, 21.	20. Ib., viii, 21 ff.
21. Ib., viii, 2.	22. Ib., vii, 22.	23. Ib., ix, 1–12.
24. Ib., vii, 17–21.	25. Ib., viii, 13–17.	26. Ib., vii, 14, 27.
27. Ib., viii, 9–12; ix, 12.		

28. I have tried to account for the similarity of the two traditions in my "Kingship in Early Israel," *Journal of Biblical Literature*, XLVIII (1929), pp. 169–205.

assimilating the Female Principle. It is implied that "Solomon's" experience is one typical of that of all men who have "gained knowledge of God's counsel,"[29] specifically the Patriarchs from Adam to Moses.[30] He does not say that they all became νόμοι ἔμψυχοι, but it is natural that others should have said so from what he wrote. At least they were all "saved by Sophia,"[31] and became "friends of God" and "prophets."[32]

What is this Sophia, "marriage" with whom was so determining a factor in the lives of "Solomon" and the Patriarchs? Sophia is in the first place "Spirit," πνεῦμα,[33] that mysterious conception of the late Greeks which, beginning as wind, came to betoken the immaterial quality of divine substance. In Stoic circles πνεῦμα never lost its material association; in philosophies that thought of ultimate reality as immaterial, while it was freely used, as in Philo, for that Nature which is elsewhere abundantly specified as immaterial, πνεῦμα itself was so often even in that connection described with its material attributes that in itself it presents one of the most baffling problems of late Greek and early Christian terminology. In the Hellenistic Jewish and Christian literature it becomes complicated by its obvious association with the Hebrew *ruah*. In a given passage there is often little appeal for its meaning beyond the reader's impression. My own impression here is that the Spirit-Sophia is immaterial, in spite of the verbal difficulties. Since Sophia is definitely herself πνεῦμα, I take it only as literary ποικιλία that the Spirit, where more elaborately described in a later passage,[34] is said to be "in" Sophia. The attributes of the πνεῦμα within Sophia are obviously intended to be the attributes of Sophia herself. As such she is said to be

thinking (νοερόν), holy (ἅγιον), unique in kind (μονογενές), manifold (πολυμερές), fine (λεπτόν), mobile (εὐκίνητον), lucid (τρανόν), unpolluted (ἀμόλυντον), clear (σαφές), inviolable (ἀπήμαντον), lover of the good (φιλάγαθον), keen (ὀξύ), unchecked (ἀκώλυτον), beneficent (εὐεργετικόν), lover of man (φιλάνθρωπον), fixed (βέβαιον), unfailing (ἀσφαλές), care-free (ἀμέριμνον), all powerful (παντοδύναμον), all surveying (πανεπίσκοπον), one that spreads out through all spirits that are thinking, pure, and especially fine.

It is interesting to take these words and to try to trace out their origin, as

---

29. *Wisd.,* ix, 17.

30. It is interesting in this earlier and less analytical list that Lot and Joseph were included, as they appear to be in the iconographical tradition, though Philo puts them at best much beneath the great exemplars.

31. *Wisd.,* ix, 18.

32. Ib., vii, 27. Both of these are familiar as one of the special signs in Philo of the final mystic achievement. Holmes parallels both Plato (Laws, iv, 716D, ὁ μὲν σώφρων θεῷ φίλος) and a Stoic dictum in Philodemus (SVF, ii, 1124). For some reason he is more impressed by the Stoic than by the Platonic parallel.

33. *Wisd.,* i, 6.   34. Ib., vii, 22 f.

has often been done by editors.[35] The Stoic associations of many of them are striking, and into others it is easy to read ideas from other philosophies. For our purpose it is sufficient to find that this Sophia-spirit is a concept with these striking divine qualities, and then to enquire what such a list of qualities implies as to the concept of Sophia that lies behind them. Stoic as many of the terms may be, as in Philo the Stoic details are subordinated to the God, Himself utterly different from the God of Stoicism, whence Sophia with these qualities emanated. For such a Sophia, who would have been the ultimate Deity of Stoicism, is here not the ultimate deity, but only ἀτμὶς τῆς τοῦ θεοῦ δυνάμεως καὶ ἀπόρροια τῆς τοῦ παντοκράτορος δόξης εἰλικρινής, "the breath of the power of God and the clear effulgence of the Glory of the Almighty."[36] Nothing here would justify the assertion that the δύναμις θεοῦ is an antecedent of the Powers of Philo, but at least it is apparent that behind Sophia is a God who is the source of an effulgence that can be compared to breath or a Light-Stream. Indeed, Sophia is herself an effulgence from everlasting Light (ἀπαύγασμα φωτὸς ἀϊδίου), and as such she reflects to men as in a mirror His ἐνέργεια, an εἰκών, image, of His goodness.[37] She is fairer than the sun and superior to the stars, but indeed upon comparison with light she is found to be something anterior.[38] This last word, προτέρα, is very interesting. Sophia is certainly a light emanation, yet the author does not want to have her confused with physical light. She is radiant and unfading (λάμπρα καὶ ἀμάραντος),[39] her beam is sleepless (ἀκοίμητον τὸ ἐκ ταύτης φέγγος).[40] Yet she is to be chosen ἀντὶ φωτός, instead of light. She is then light, but not in the sense of physical light which fades. She is something anterior. The "immaterial light" familiar in Gnostic, Philonic, and Neo-Platonic thought seems certainly what the author has in mind, though that term does not appear.[41] Accordingly I would understand the words already quoted, fine, mobile, lucid, unpolluted, clear, inviolable, to be descriptions of Sophia as light. For it appears in vii, 10, 29, that one of the most important contrasts between Sophia and ordinary light is that ordinary light can fade away.

Such must be the fundamental thought of Sophia; she is the Light-Stream from God's glory. As such she is the Orphic μονογενές, "unique in kind.[42]

35. I see no point in the fact that there are twenty-one titles here. Editors have made this number a standard comment. Ancient writers introduced numerological speculation often enough without our forcing it upon them.
36. *Wisd.*, vii, 25. 37. Ib., vii, 26.
38. Ib., vii, 29. 39. Ib., vi, 12.
40. Ib., vii, 10.
41. τὸ ἄφθαρτον φῶς does appear in xviii, 4, but in connection with Law, and very likely from a different writer. It could only with uncertainty be brought over to apply here to Sophia.
42. Holmes's "alone in kind," is certainly the right meaning here and elsewhere, not Goodrick's "singly born." The word never meant "only born" except when used with such a word as "son" or "daughter," and then the combination meant rather "only son" than "only born"

We are again reminded of Philo by the fact that she is unchanging (βέβαιος), and sharp (ὀξεῖα). That she is νοερά, herself initiated into the wisdom of God (μύστις τῆς τοῦ θεοῦ ἐπιστημης),⁴³ makes her further like the Logos-Sophia of Philo, which is the νοῦς of God, as does her rôle of being God's creative agent, ἡ πάντων τεχνῖτις,⁴⁴ and her function of holding the universe together⁴⁵ and ruling it.⁴⁶ It is in connection with creation that the parallelism shows her to be identical with God's Logos:

"Who makest all things by (ἐν) thy Logos
And foundest man by Thy Sophia."⁴⁷

The identification is complete, though here it throws more light upon the word Logos than Sophia. For that God made all things by His Word is something Jews had been saying for years without meaning by the "Word" this effluent Stream. The Logos of God is being identified with Sophia, but here the identification is timid and tentative. It would seem that it was through the Sophia conception that Jews first introduced the Stream into their religion. The Stream never ceased to be the Sophia, though later the masculine Logos was often preferred. Here *Wisdom* shows us the early stage where the enrichment of thought made through the term Logos seems to be only beginning.

It is thus not surprising to find Sophia closely identified with the giving of a higher Law. The Law is referred to in the latter part of *Wisdom* in connection with a phrase already mentioned, "the incorruptible light of the Law,"⁴⁸ which was given to the race of men. It would be daring to claim for this phrase, in spite of the distinctively Greek conception in the adjective ἄφθαρτον, more than the familiar Jewish notion that the written Law was a light to the feet.⁴⁹ But in the first half of the book, the part we are drawing upon exclusively for the Sophia doctrine, the indication is much more plain that Sophia brings to men an immediate impartation of the Law. Two passages seem to refer to a Law of Sophia, where the written Torah could not have been understood.

The first of these is in the prayer of "Solomon" for the gift of Sophia. He prays that Sophia, the throne-mate of God, be sent to him "because I am . . . inferior in understanding of judgment and laws."⁵⁰ God has made him king, "Solomon" goes on, in spite of his inadequacy for the task, has bid him build the temple "in imitation (μίμημα) of the holy tabernacle which

or "only begotten son." On the Orphic usage see above, p. 118, Albinus (Alcinous), *Introduction,* 12.

43. *Wisd.,* viii, 4.   44. Ib., vii, 22.   45. Ib., i, 7.
46. Ib., viii, 1.   47. Ib., ix, 1.
48. Ib., xviii, 4. See note 41, above.
49. Ps. cxix, 105; Prov. vi, 23; *Test. Levi,* xiv, 4; xix, 1, etc.
50. *Wisd.,* ix, 5.

Thou hast prepared in advance from the beginning."[51] The only way in which "Solomon" can hope to fulfil this obligation is for God to help him by sending down Sophia to him, for she was present with God at Creation and knows what is pleasing to God and what is right in His Laws (τί εὐθὲς ἐν ἐντολαῖς σου).[52] Only with her presence and help can "Solomon" hope to be acceptable in his deeds and in his judgments.[53] This cannot be a reference to any written Law. Sophia comes down and tells the person especially endowed with her inspiring company what are the Laws of God in a way not otherwise revealed.

The second passage seems just as clearly a reference to Laws which can only be learned through the mystic association with Sophia:

For the beginning is the truest desire for her instruction;
  Concern for her instruction is love [of her];
And love [of her] is the keeping of her Laws;
  And adherence to [her] Laws is the assurance of incorruption (ἀφθαρσία).
And incorruption brings one near to God.[54]

The steps here are those of a mystic ladder of Law. One begins with desire of Sophia's instruction, which leads to love of Sophia, which in turn leads to the keeping of her Laws (apparently those first learned by her "instructions"); the keeping of her Laws leads to a change into an incorruptible nature, which brings one near to God. The formulation is not exactly that of Philo, but the conception is basically identical, and there can be no doubt that the Laws are mystic revelations rather than the statutes of the Torah. One has only to glance at a normative Jewish work like *Sirach* to see the contrast.

He that taketh hold of the Law findeth Sophia.[55]
All these things [of Sophia] are the book of the covenant of God most High
The Law which Moses commanded as an heritage for the assemblies of Jacob.[56]
All Sophia is the fear of the Lord,
  And all Sophia is the fulfilling of the Law.[57]

Here Sophia is given as a result of obedience to the written Torah, as she always is in normative Judaism.[58] The Law given by Sophia in *Wisdom* is a totally different thing. In the one case the man begins with obeying the written Law, and so is given Sophia; in the other he prays God for Sophia, and when she comes to him she gives him Law. She certainly does not present him with a roll of Torah.

51. *Wisd.*, ix, 8.   52. Ib., ix, 9.   53. Ib., ix, 12.
54. Ib., vi, 17–19.   55. *Sirach*, xv, 1.   56. Ib., xxiv, 23.
57. Ib., xix, 20. See Box and Oesterley, *Apoc. and Pseud.*, I, 305 f.
58. Cf. *Baruch*, iii, 9—iv, 4, especially iv, 1.

As to the origin of this conception I feel that the Female Principle is again the ultimate source. Isis, the great Stream of loving and protecting life to men and the universe, is also the giver to men of higher civilization and the one who gave them law in place of ὕβρις. As such she was Thesmophoros or Thesmothetis, the goddess of justice, δικαιοσύνη.[59] Indeed in the official description of Isis it is said "I am Isis the queen of every region the one educated by Hermes; and whatsoever I have legislated (ἐνομοθέτησα) these things no one can abrogate."[60] The Orphic male-female deity was also the source of legislation.[61]

The relation which this Law given by Sophia bears to the Torah is not suggested in *Wisdom*. But the two types of the Law seem definitely present in the book: for ii, 12, is a reference to the traditional Jewish Law as certainly as the two passages we have been discussing are not.

This is in brief the "Mystery of Sophia" which "Solomon" proclaims. Other details could be added, such as the similarity to the Logos-Sophia of Philo in her relation to the beginner and mystic; her identification with the pillar of fire that led the Israelites.[62] But enough has been said to warrant assuming that *Wisdom* shows the Mystery in one of its earlier and most fascinating stages. Sophia is here definitely a streaming Light from God to reveal to the mystic the true Law of God that alone can make the recipient kingly.

The second part of *Wisdom* has almost no mention of Sophia. It goes on with allegory of the Patriarchs, especially of the plagues in Egypt, many details of which are suggestive of Philo. In general the second part betrays no such fundamental similarity to the Mystery of Philo as does the first part. But a few details are striking.

It has already been noted in connection with the discussion of the Mystery of Aaron[63] that *Wisdom* knew this Mystery. The author has been speaking of the destruction of the Egyptians. He now says that the Israelites when in the desert also experienced death.[64] But the Wrath did not long continue, for it was opposed by a blameless (ἄμεμπτος) man.

He conquered the Anger, not by strength of body, not by the force of arms,
But by Logos did he subdue the Chastiser,
In recollection of the oaths and covenants of the Fathers.
For when the dead were now fallen in heaps upon one another,
He stood between and cut off the Wrath
And obstructed his [the Wrath's] path to the living.

59. For references see Roeder in PW, *Realencyclopaedie*, IX, 2119.
60. Diodorus, I, 27; Hopfner, *Fontes*, p. 106, ll. 22 ff.
61. The Orphic deity is θεσμοφόρος and brings εὐνομία; above pp. 18 f.
62. *Wisd.*, x, 17.   63. See above, p. 120.
64. *Wisd.*, xviii, 20.

For upon the robe that reached to his feet was the whole world,
And the glories of the Fathers upon the carving of the four rows of stone,
And thy magnificence was upon the diadem of his head.
To these the Destroyer yielded, these were the things feared,
For it was sufficient merely to put the Wrath to the test [sc. by presenting
him with these symbols].[65]

Commentators have long recognized that this description of Aaron's robes was to be understood in the light of Philo's and Josephus' accounts of their significance. But I have not noticed anyone who has pointed out that Aaron, in presenting the Avenger with those robes to frighten him away, presented him with the Logos. It seems clear to me that the story of Aaron's intervention is but an elaboration of the first statement that the Punisher was subdued not by strength of body or force of arms, but by the Logos. In the section immediately preceding it was the Logos who in sharp personification slew the eldest sons of the Egyptians.[66] Now when another Death Angel, or whatever he might be called, attacks the Israelites, the Logos, as committed to the Israelites in the oaths and covenants of the Fathers, that is in the priestly office, intercedes and saves them by his mere exhibition. It is very interesting that Philo interprets the incident in the same way as *Wisdom*,[67] one of the few places where we can check our impression that Philo's allegory came to him already stereotyped. The Mystery of Aaron has seemed to be a different mystic tradition in Judaism from the Light-Stream Mystery of the Logos-Sophia. But the passage, which seems to me unquestionably to antedate Philo and Josephus, is of the greatest value in showing how much Philo is drawing upon a more ancient tradition.

Wisdom has been treated sufficiently for our purpose, which is to show from the various survivals of Hellenistic Judaism that Philo's mysticism is not by any means to be understood as his own invention. The importance of *Wisdom* is the fact that it shows a definite and elaborate Mystery of Sophia, one that is certainly non-Philonic in origin, and is in all probability distinctly pre-Philonic in time.

But we have learned this also from the material we have thus far examined: there was definitely a Hellenistic Judaism, of the type most familiar in *II* and *III Maccabees,* whose orientation was in a strict regard for the letter of the Law, and whose chief glory was its observance. Other groups were so concerned with the apocalyptic hope and imagery that the Mystery appears, as in the *Assumption of Moses* and in *II Enoch,* in only casual details. That we should have had some survivals of a normative legalism in Hellenistic Judaism was to be expected from Philo's constant reference to the "literalists," by whom the mystic meaning he found in the Torah was rejected. The

65. *Wisd.,* xviii, 22–25.   66. Ib., xviii, 15.   67. Philo, *Heres,* 201.

apocalyptists are important for their echoing ideas which associate themselves at once in our minds with the Mystery, but which are obviously phraseological reflections from a type of thinking about Judaism essentially foreign to their own. *Wisdom* has done still more, it has shown us Mystic Judaism itself, or at least some aspects of it, at a stage apparently earlier than Philo's, yet definitely in the same line of development. Solomon and Sophia are the heroes, not Moses or Isaac and the Logos. But the Sophia is the Light-Stream, quite the same fundamentally as Philo's Logos, and Sophia as an equivalent of the Logos-Stream is by now so familiar in Philo himself that the conception of Sophia in *Wisdom* can be accepted as a predecessor of at least a large part of the Philonic Logos. That is, *Wisdom* has shown us not *a* mystic Judaism, but *the* mystic Judaism we are investigating, though in an earlier stage than that which Philo reveals.

We do not need to stop even here. Thanks to Eusebius there are still preserved a number of strange fragments from the writings of very much earlier Hellenistic Jews. Schürer has listed them and discussed them, but so far there has been no conception of Hellenistic Judaism in which they could take a natural place. There are two main sources for this material, the writings of Aristobulus and of Alexander Polyhistor.[67a]

Aristobulus addressed his work to Ptolemy VI Philometor, so was writing approximately 160 B.C. Eusebius quotes him in two passages.[68] From these fragments we get some highly important information. The fragments are taken from a great ἐξηγήσεις τῆς Μωϋσέως γραφῆς, *Exposition of the Writings of Moses*, a title strongly reminiscent of Philo's so-called *Exposition*, and appears, as Schürer has indicated, to have been similar to it in method. The book, being addressed to Ptolemy, was designed, like Philo's *Exposition* for Gentile readers, and seems from what Clement says, to have been dedicated to proving "that the Peripatetic philosophy was derived from the Law of Moses and the other prophets."[69] But Schürer is entirely right in saying that even the fragments left us show that, while tradition is united in pronouncing Aristobulus an Aristotelian,[70] his philosophic interest included more than that single school. We can see for ourselves that for him Pythagoras, Socrates, and Plato as well as Aristotle, and even Homer and Hesiod,

67a. The dates of these writings, as Schürer has assigned them, have been widely challenged. Bousset, for example (*Religion des Judentums* (1926), pp. 19 ff.) rejects Schürer's early dates for dates in the first century B.C. Others would make them much later, or take them, especially Aristobulus, for Christian forgeries. I confess that Schürer's arguments still seem to me the most convincing, though certainty is impossible.

68. *Praep. Evang.*, VIII, x; XIII, xii. Other quotations, as Schürer indicates, are included in these passages.

69. *Strom.*, V, xiv, 97. Judaism in immediate contact with Iran developed the same apologetic. There all oriental science was said to have been first taught by Abraham. See Bousset, *Religion des Judentums* (1926), pp. 73–75, 196.

70. See Schürer, *op. cit.*, p. 516, n. 50 for the reference.

drew upon Moses for their doctrines. Indeed in what of his writings we have he seems more interested in Socrates and Plato than in Aristotle, and more colored by Pythagoreanism. That is, he is an eclectic filled with the idealism and ethics of the same schools as those which most influenced Philo. Further examination reveals that he also was a direct predecessor of Philo in his regarding Judaism as a Mystery.

He has a considerable allegory of the number seven.[71] The seven is a symbol of the logos in man, by which man has knowledge of things human and divine. The plants and animals of the cosmos revolve in a cycle of sevens. He concludes his discussion of the week (the seven days) with the following passage:

Homer says:
And on the seventh day we left the river Acheron.
This indicates that [we went away] from the forgetfulness and evil of the soul, [and that] the aforesaid things [i.e. the forgetfulness and evil] were abandoned on the true Seventh, the logos, and that we received Gnosis of the Truth, as aforesaid.

If my understanding of the text is correct Aristobulus is saying that if man abandons the forgetfulness and evil of the soul he can, through his logos, receive the higher Gnosis. This is as clear a parallel to Philo's Mystery as could be desired, at least to a part of it.

Another aspect of the Mystery also appears in Aristobulus' treatment of Sophia. The creation of the first day, he says, was the creation of Light, which means Sophia, ·

since from her all light proceeds. And some members of the Peripatetic school nave said that Sophia is appointed (ἔχειν τάξιν) to be the lantern; for by follow-.ng her men can make themselves free from trouble (ἀτάραχοι) throughout their ives. More clearly and beautifully did Solomon, one of our forefathers, say that ͻophia existed before heaven and earth, which agrees with what has been said ,efore.[72]

ᴦhat is, the famous statement of Proverbs viii, 22, 27, is definitely taken out ͻom its Jewish setting and equated with Sophia as the pagan Light-Stream, ᴉe source of all light and the guide of the individual. One does not know ͻow much earlier than Aristobulus was the date of the first suggesting of this ɪentification. But Aristobulus shows that it was indeed a long tradition ͼfore *Wisdom* and Philo.

Still more of the Mystery doeȿ Aristobulus show. He quotes at consider-ͻle length an Orphic poem of great interest. He admits that he has made ιme changes in it. But fortunately we are in a position here to check him,

71. Eusebius, *Praep. Ev.*, XIII, xii, 12–15.   72. Ib., 10 f.

for the same verses are preserved in apparently their original pagan form as a quotation from the tract *Testamenta* of Orpheus.[73] This work of Orpheus, says the author of the Pseudo-Justinian *De Monarchia* (ii), introduced three hundred and sixty gods; but

he [Orpheus] appears to repent of his error in that he wrote the following:[74]

I speak to those who lawfully may hear:
Depart and close the doors all ye profane.
But thou, Musaeus, child of the bright moon,[75]
Lend me thine ear; for I have truths to tell.
Let not the former fancies of thy mind
Deprive thee of the blessed number ten.[76]
But look unto the Word Divine, and fix
In Him your mind. The intelligible sphere
Of your own heart set straight; tread well
The Road; look only on creation's Lord.
One He is, the Self-Begotten: all
Begotten things arise from One; He
Towers up above creation. No mortal eye
May pierce to Him, yet He Himself sees all.
He from His goodness gives to mortals Evil,
Sending both chilling wars and tearful griefs;
And other than the great King there is none.
Yet Him I cannot see, for clouds forever
Gird Him round about; and mortal eyes
Have only mortal eyeballs, weak, too weak
To see great Jupiter reigning over all.
He sits established in the brazen heavens,

73. The material has been excellently analyzed by Lucien Cerfaux, "Influence des Mystères sur le Judaisme Alexandrin avant Philon," *Muséon*, XXXVII (1924), pp. 36–48 (cited hereafter in this chapter only as Cerfaux) where earlier literature is discussed. Cerfaux calls this "Le Hiéros Logos Juif," but that seems too sweeping. In the Jewish Mystery the ἱερὸς λόγος was always the Scriptures. Cerfaux's article has merely touched the whole problem, not probed it. His treatment of Philo shows no sense of the material that could be marshalled, and his conclusion is accordingly of little value. But he has incidentally suggested many interesting points, which I am glad to be able to use.

74. The author of the Pseudo-Justinian *Cohortatio ad Gentiles*, xv, introduces the same lines by saying: "Orpheus, who was as one might say, your most elaborate polytheist (πολυθεότητος ὑμῶν), and the first teacher, latterly proclaimed to his son Musaeus, and the other legitimate auditors (οἱ λοιποὶ γνήσιοι) concerning the one and only God." The first distich, missing in the *De Monarchia*, appears in the *Cohortatio*. A few of the lines are quoted by Clemens Alex., *Stromata*, V, xiv, 123.

75. I have inserted here two introductory lines from *Cohort. ad Gent.*, xv.

76. To translate φίλη αἰών "blessed number 10" seems a bit strained until one looks at Iamblichus, *Theologumena Arith.*, 59, where it is stated that the Pythagoreans called the αἰών the 10, as a symbol of cosmic perfection. In the same passage the idea occurs that God περιγένηται the cosmos. The figures throughout seem to me Pythagorean. The phrase really means that one's preconceptions must not hold one back from *perfection*.

Upon His golden throne; He plants His feet
On the broad earth, and stretches His right hand
To all the ends of ocean, and around
Tremble the mountain ranges and the streams,
The depths, too, of the blue and hoary sea.[77]

This fragment is in itself a very interesting Orphic piece, one that seems to me genuinely pagan. It is the sort of paganism, however, that one can recognize as what must have been at the bottom of Mystic Judaism. God is the great Ruler of all, utterly beyond creation in His being, but permeating all creation with His powerful rulership. He is invisible to mortals. Yet a Road leads to Him, the Road of the Divine Logos, or of the κόσμος νοητός. The reward is the perfection of the "dear aeon" possibly, as I have dared to translate it, the number ten, or seven.

Now it must be recalled that Aristobulus, in quoting these verses, admits that he has made some changes in them. He actually says that he has taken out from them "the name of Zeus which runs through the poems; for it is to God that their thought is sent up, and for that reason I have so expressed it." Aristobulus has certainly cut out the name of Zeus! He has completely altered the fragment into a call to the Mystery of Moses. The lines must be quoted in his new redaction, with the new matter italicized for convenience:

I speak to those who lawfully may hear:
Depart, and close the doors, all ye profane,
Who flee the ordinances of the just,
The law divine announced to all mankind.
But thou, Musaeus, child of the bright moon,
Lend me thine ear; for I have truths to tell.
Let not the former fancies of thy mind
Deprive thee of the blessed number ten.
But look unto the Word Divine, and fix
In Him your mind. Direct your heart
To the intelligible sphere, tread well
The Road; *and have regard to Him alone*
Who is the immortal Framer of the World:
For thus of Him our ancient story speaks:
One He is, *the Perfect in Himself,*
All else by Him *made perfect.* Though He
Is *ever present* in His works, He yet
Remains by mortal eyes unseen, *by Nous*
Alone discerned. He from his store of good
Ne'er[78] sends dire evil down to mortal men.

77. Many of these lines are taken from the translations of Dods and Reith, and of Gifford.
78. That God can be the cause of evil was, as we have seen, frequently denied by Philo.
is interesting to see how Aristobulus has corrected this passage to make it accord with
Hellenistic Jewish thought by inserting the negative.

Both love and hatred wait upon His steps
And war and pestilence and tearful grief:
For there is none but Him. All other things
'Twere easy to behold, could'st thou but first
Behold Himself; here present upon earth,
The footsteps and the mighty hand of God
Whene'er I see, I'll show them thee, my Son.
But Him I cannot see, so dense a cloud
In tenfold darkness wraps our feeble sight.
Him as He rules no mortal could behold
Save one, a Chaldee sprout unique from heaven:[79]
For he was skilled to mark the sun's bright path,
And how in equal circle round the earth
The starry sphere on its own axis turns,
And how the winds career o'er sea and sky;
And how the might of force-born fire shines forth.
But God, *in contrast, on high*[80] heaven unmoved
Sits on His golden throne, and plants His feet
On the broad earth; His right hand He extends
O'er ocean's farthest bound; *the eternal hills*
Tremble in their deep heart, nor can endure
His mighty force. Himself a heavenly being
In all respects, He perfects earthly things,
And is Himself beginning, mean, and end.
So runs the story of the men of old,
So tells that man from Water born,
Taught by the two-fold tablet of God's Law,
Nor dare I otherwise of God to speak:
In heart and limbs I tremble at the thought,
How He from heaven all things in order rules.
Draw near in thought, my son; but guard thy tongue
With care, and store this doctrine in thy heart.[81]

A number of points at once become clear from this fragment. Orpheus is regarded as having drawn his mystery entirely from Moses, and as having dared, at the end, to teach nothing contrary to what Moses has learned from God and transmitted in the Torah. The Orphic ideology has been slightly toned down, but ever so slightly, and the teaching it embodied is ascribed to Moses. Abraham, as the one who saw God ruling, is again strikingly reminiscent of Philo's treatment of Abraham. The Patriarchs, the "Men of Old," with Moses at the head, are the sole revealers of the mystic doctrine of

79. εἰ μὴ μουνογενής τις ἀπορρὼξ φύλου ἄνωθεν Χαλδαίων. The meaning of μουνογενής has already been discussed. Here its sense of "unique" is obvious, since Abraham was not "only begotten" in any way. Ἄνωθεν is more general than I have translated it.
80. It is notable that Aristobulus has taken out the *bronze* heaven.
81. *Praep. Ev.*, XIII, xii, 5.

the Logos-Road to God. The Mystic element is not toned down; rather the presentation of the account as a secret to be revealed only to Musaeus and those worthy to be associated with him is intensified by the closing lines, lacking in the original.

Aristobulus has taught us a good many surprising things. Two hundred years before Philo, if we may accept with Schürer the traditional date, Jews had begun to transform their Jewish doctrine of Wisdom into the mystic doctrine of Sophia as the Light-Stream. They had turned to philosophy, especially to Plato and Pythagorean numerology, and justified themselves in retaining their Jewish loyalty by insisting that an allegorical reading of the scriptures showed that Moses was the true source of all Greek philosophic lore. They had also turned to the mysteries and regarded salvation as escape from the lower tendencies of the soul in a higher Gnosis through Logos. Since they could not join the mysteries of paganism they were making a counterattack by claiming that Orpheus himself admitted that he could teach only as Moses had revealed the truth to him, that the Orphic poems were full of adulation of the Jewish Patriarchs, and even, by implication, that the true Judaism was the Mystic Road of the Logos to God. That is, all the essential features of the Mystery as Philo reveals it are to be found in Aristobulus. But obviously we are on an earlier stage. Philo can and does insist that the philosophers learned from Moses. But by his day there is little reference to the mysteries. Jews have so long regarded themselves as having the true Mystery that the crude paralleling of Moses and Orpheus is no longer necessary. Jews could, in Philo's day, simply assert that they had the true Mystery, and explain it as revealed in the Torah. They did not care what Orpheus or Isis taught because they had got beyond the early stages of assimilation, though they still were thinking along the same mystic lines as the pagan mysteries. In the early stage, when Judaism was consciously borrowing pagan notions, its technique could not be so assured. Even at this stage Aristobulus shows the same difficulty as Philo, in that his version of Judaism is not favored by those people "devoid of power and intelligence," who cling to literal Judaism.[82]

Additional light is thrown upon the Mystery at the early syncretistic stage by the *Sibylline Books*. The point of view of these books is fundamentally that of normative Judaism. The Jewish objective may be described in Greek terms as "practicing justice and virtue,"[83] but that means in reality "fulfilling the command of the mighty God."[84] The Jew's trust is in the holy laws of the mighty God,[85] and his happy anticipation is of a time when good law shall come to men from the starry heavens, and lawlessness be done away.[86]

82. *Praep. Ev.*, VIII, x, 5.
84. Ib., 246.
86. Ib., 373 ff.

83. *Sib.*, III, 234.
85. Ib., 284.

So "let us all ponder the law of the Most High God."[87] But it is to be noted that, granting that this book belongs basically to "normative" Judaism in its orientation about the Law, even here, a great many syncretistic features appear. The literary form, putting the highest message of Judaism into the mouth of a pagan Sibyl, is itself an acceptance by Jewish thinking of the Greek mythological figure. The rest of Greek mythology seems quite as much accepted, for most of the genealogy of the gods, in general after the model of Hesiod, is included in the story of the early part of world history.[88] More important is the description of God early in the book.

Ye men who have the form of God, moulded in His likeness (ἐν εἰκόνι) why do you vainly wander and follow not the straight Road as ye bear always in mind the immortal Creator? God is One, the sole ruler, ineffable, dwelling in the ether, self-sprung, invisible Himself but seeing all things. No stone carver's hand did make Him, nor does some model formed from gold or ivory by the varied skill of man represent Him. But He, Himself eternal, hath revealed Himself as One who is and was before, yea and shall be hereafter. For who being mortal can gaze on God with his eyes? Or who could bear to hear even the mere Name of the mighty heavenly God who rules the world? Who by His Logos created all things, the heaven and the sea, the tireless sun and the full moon, the twinkling stars, mighty mother Tethys, springs and rivers, unquenchable fire, days and nights. He is the God who fashioned the tetragram Adam, the first man fashioned, who completes in his name east and west, south and north. He too fashioned the form of mortal men and made the beasts and things that creep and fly.[89]

The Sibyl turns to denounce Egyptians for their abhorrent worship of snakes and cats.

A most interesting section. Behind it lies scriptural allegory of the Philonic type, as shown in the acrostic of the four letters of Adam's name.[90] The Jewish reverence for the Name is stressed. Yet creation is by the Logos, the Road consists of bearing in mind the immortal Creator, who is described in purely Greek terms. Indeed the terms are not only Greek, but to a considerable extent definitely Orphic. One is struck by the similarity to the original Orphic form of the poem which Aristobulus adapted.

"Tread well the Road; look only on creation's Lord," says that poem; "Why do ye vainly wander and follow not the straight Road, as ye have always in mind the immortal Creator?" asks the Sibyl. Each then goes on to describe that God. He is One (εἷς ἐστ', Orphic; εἷς θεός ἐστι μόναρχος,

87. Ib., 719; see also ll. 686, 573 ff.   88. Ib., 105–158.
89. Ib., 8–28.
90. The acrostic reappears in *II Enoch*, xxx, 13, as Geffcken points out *ad loc.* (Sibyl). It is obviously of Greek-Jewish origin, for the four names are rearranged in the Sibyl passage *metrica causa*. The notion was derived from the fact that the first four letters of ἀντολίη, δύσις, ἄρκτος, and μεσημβρίη, spell Adam. See the note *ad loc.* (*II Enoch*) by Forbes and Charles, in Charles, *Apoc. and Pseud.*

284 By Light, Light

Sibyl). He is "Self-sprung" (αὐτογενής, Orphic; αὐτοφυής, Sibyl). "Invisible Himself, He sees all things" (οὐδέ τις αὐτὸν εἰσορᾷ θνητῶν, αὐτὸς δέ γε πάντας ὁρᾶται, Orphic; ἀόρατος ὁρώμενος αὐτὸς ἅπαντα, Sibyl). The Sibyl, after the Jewish reference to idols, adds the declaration of the eternity of God, then goes on to ask "For who, being mortal, can gaze on God with his eyes?" (τίς γὰρ θνητὸς ἐὼν κατιδεῖν δύναται θεὸν ὅσσοις): the Orphic poem asserts "all mortals have mortal eyeballs in their eyes, too weak to see God ruling over all (πᾶσιν γὰρ θνητοῖς θνηταὶ κόραι εἰσὶν ἐν ὄσσοις, ἀσθενέες δ᾽ ἰδεῖν Δία τὸν πάντων μεδέοντα). The last phrase, the notion of God ruling over all, is brought in by the Sibyl immediately in connection with the Jewish statement of the impossibility of one's bearing to hear the Name "of the great heavenly God who rules the world" (οὐρανίου μεγάλοιο θεοῦ κόσμον κρατέοντος). If the Sibyl goes on to speak of creation by the Logos, the Orphic poem has bid its initiates look unto the λόγος θεῖος.

There can be no question at all that the Sibylline forger, if he did not have this very Orphic poem before him, was following a definite Orphic convention of description of God.[91] He like Aristobulus is making Jewish changes and insertions. But the passage belongs to that type of Judaism represented by Aristobulus, a Judaism which was drawing heavily upon Orphic sources for its basic conceptions, and was patently revising Orphic texts to make Jewish mystic utterances. For both Aristobulus and the Sibyl the true Road was the looking to a superficially Judaized version of the God of the Orphic mystery.

Before leaving the Third Book, it should be pointed out that here is met the device, after such assertions about God, of going on to list the details of creation as a part of describing Him. With this device we shall have frequent meeting. That it is an Orphic form of prayer or hymn is clearly attested.[92]

The Third Book of the *Sibylline Oracles*, if it can be taken as a unit, shows how, even with Jews still centering their lives in the Law, God had Himself become a Mystic conception. If the book is a compilation, the same

91. God as ἀθέσφατος is also Orphic. See Kern, *Orphic. Frag.*, frg. 248b. God as "dwelling in the ether" (αἰθέρι ναίων) is to be paralleled with the fact that the Orphics thought that the ether surrounded the universe (Kern, fr. 165). In the Orphic poem recorded by Eusebius (*Praep. Ev.*, III, ix) from Porphyry, where Orphic notions are put into accord with Stoic pantheism, the ether is God's mind (νοῦς) with which He hears and ponders all things (Kern, fr. 168). Ether "crowns" God in fr. 248b. Φάνης, the Orphic Light-Stream, is so called, says the *Etymolog. Mag.* (Kern, fr. 75), "because he first became visible in ether" (πρῶτος ἐν αἰθέρι φάντος ἐγένετο). A fuller statement appears in the following (fr. 86): "No one has ever seen the First Born (πρωτόγονος) with his eyes, except sacred Night alone. All the others marvelled at seeing the unhoped for beam (φέγγος) in the ether which streamed from the frame of immortal Phanes." The πρωτόγονος is himself αἰθερόπλαγκτος, roaming in ether (fr. 87).

92. Kern, Frag. 248.

is true of the Judaism of the compiler, while the Judaism of each part is sufficiently attested.

The Fourth Book is exclusively a list of the woes that have come upon past civilizations, and a warning to men to cease their strife and recognize God. Neither legalistic nor mystic elements appear to identify the work with either main branch of Judaistic thought in the Diaspora. Yet the fact that the Sibylline form of utterance is used suggests that it belongs to the syncretistic school, and the complete rejection of sacrifices and temples marks its Judaism as dubiously normative.[92a]

The Fifth Book is regarded by editors as predominantly of the Second Century after Christ, and contains some Christian traces. For our purpose the only verses of interest are those which connect the Sibyl with Isis. In line 53 the Sibyl is Ἴσιδος ἡ γνωστή. Text and meaning are both uncertain. Granting the text, it is questionable whether γνωστή should be understood as simply "the familiar friend," as Lanchester takes it, or "the one initiated into the gnosis." In either case the Sibyl is closely allied with Isis. But at the close of the book (lines 484-503) the end of Isis and Sarapis is mentioned, with dignity and sorrow, as the inevitable concomitant of the triumph of the religion of the immortal God. A man *clad in linen* is to lead the Egyptians to the true worship in the new temple in Heliopolis. As the converts hymn the incorruptible God, θεὸς ἄφθιτος, and give Him sacrifices there, they are to receive incorruptible life (ἄφθιτος ⟨εμ⟩βιοτεύειν). Judaism, led by the man in "linen garment," is to supplant Isis as the future religion of Egypt.

Besides these three books, there are two important Sibylline Fragments that seem certainly Jewish, and which are very interesting. The first fragment is worth quoting entire:[93]

Ye mortal men and fleshly, who are naught,
How quickly are ye puffed up, seeing not
The end of life. Do ye not tremble now
And fear God, Him who watches over you,
The One who is most high, the One who knows,
The all-observant witness of all things
All-nourishing Creator, who has put
In all things His sweet Spirit and has made
Him leader of all mortals? God is one;
Who rules alone, supremely great, unborn,
Almighty and invisible, Himself

92a. *Sib.*, IV, 8, 24 ff. Noted by M. Friedländer, *Judentum im vorchrist. griech. Welt* (1897), p. 58.
93. Quoted in Terry's translation: M. S. Terry, *The Sibylline Oracles*, New York, 1899, pp. 257 ff.

Alone beholding all things, but not seen
Is he himself by any mortal flesh.
For what flesh is there able to behold
With eyes the heavenly and true God divine,
Who has His habitation in the sky?
Not even before the bright rays of the sun
Can men stand still, men who are mortal born,
Existing but as veins and flesh on bones.
Him who alone is ruler of the world,
Who alone is forever and has been
From everlasting, reverence ye him,
The self-existent unbegotten one
Who rules all things through all time, dealing out
Unto all mortals in a common light
The judgment. And the merited reward
Of evil counseling shall ye receive.
For ceasing the true and eternal God
To glorify, and holy hecatombs
To offer Him, ye made your sacrifice
Unto the demons that in Hades dwell.
And ye in self-conceit and madness walk,
And having left the true, straightforward path
Ye went away and roamed about through thorns
And thistles. O ye foolish mortals, cease
Roving in darkness and black night obscure,
And leave the darkness of night, and lay hold
Upon the Light. Lo, he is clear to all
And cannot err; come, do not always chase
Darkness and gloom. Lo, the sweet-looking light
Of the sun shines with a surpassing glow.
Now, treasuring Wisdom in your hearts, know ye
That God is one, who sends forth rains and winds,
And mournful cares, and storms of snow, and ice.
But why do I thus speak them one by one?
He guides heaven, rules earth, Himself exists.

Again we are in the Orphic atmosphere of the Third Book, and it is conspicuous that, unless we have documents mutually dependent, the ideas are definitely conventionalized. Instead of beginning with a denunciation of men for not having followed the Road by gazing upon God, this fragment opens with a similar denunciation because men have not kept their eyes on the βίου τέλος, the end of life. The author probably has the Road in mind for it appears further on. This denunciation is followed as in the Third Book and the Orphic original of Aristobulus, by a description of the nature of God. He is again Creator, one who knows and cares for all things; He is

One, is here ἀγένητος instead of αὐτοφυής or αὐτογενής, though αὐτογενής also appears below; He "alone rules," and is the παντοκράτωρ, while in the Orphic poem Zeus is ὁ πάντων μεδέων. The familiar ἀόρατος ὁρώμενος αὐτὸς ἅπαντα reappears, again elaborated with reference to the weakness of human eyes of flesh. On this an interesting variant appears in the form of the question, how could human eyes see God when they cannot even gaze upon the sun? The implication that God is a light brighter than the sun is warranted by what follows. Men are given their trial in common light (ἐν φαὶ κοινῷ). Instead of meeting this test, and giving sacrifices and honors to God, the people have strayed to the worship of chthonic demons, which would seem probably a reference to Isis, though perhaps to the Orphic Persephone or Demeter. Such wandering was to leave the right Road (ὀρθὴ τρίβος εὐθεῖα), to rove in darkness. The darkness one must leave and instead seize the Light. The Right Straight Road is thus the Road of the Light. God Himself (as Light) is clear (σαφής) to all; the sweet light of the Sun (which is certainly here God, not the sun already mentioned as similar to but beneath God) shines out in a way that surpasses everything (ἔξοχα). From God Himself the poem goes on to mention His manifestations, as before were mentioned His creatures, the rain and wind and the rest.

New in emphasis is the fact that the Road is the Light of God in contrast to the common light of the sun, a darkness. But the Orphic Phanes,[94] discussed above, shows that the idea is still purely Orphic, while the whole plan of the poetic fragment is in general only a metrical variant of the Orphic original of Aristobulus. With this are two other new elements, the "sweet spirit" and "Sophia." "God has put his sweet πνεῦμα in all things and made it the leader of all mortals." One's instant reaction is to suggest "Stoic influence," and perhaps that explanation is the true one. But it has no certainty. The Stoics did not invent the word πνεῦμα, and I do not recall a case where the one God of all is said by Stoics to have put his Spirit into all things. God is Himself the Spirit in Stoicism. Further the mystic suggestion of the Spirit as the Guide of mortals is not Stoic. The πνεῦμα seems here a variant of the Ophic Φάνης, as that identification, we know, was made by the Orphics. Orpheus calls the divine spirit Phanes.[95] One also recalls the Orphic couplet: "Men complete all things through the mighty help of the immortal God, through the wise impulse of the Spirit."[96]

In spite of the fact that σοφός appears here, σοφία seems in the Sibyl the Hellenistic Jewish σοφία. As we treasure Sophia in our hearts we may *know*.

The second Sibylline fragment of importance for us is the third fragment

94. See above, note 91.
95. θεῖον πνεῦμα, ὃν Φάνητα Ὀρφεὺς καλεῖ: Clem. Rom., *Homil.*, VI, 5: Kern, fr. 56 (p. 134).
96. Didym. Alexandri., *De Trinitate*, II, 27: Kern, fr. 340. The date is indeterminable.

in Geffcken's edition. It is not sufficiently important to be quoted entire. In general it begins like the others with a description of God as the One, the All Ruler, and the Creator of the most elaborately listed parts of the universe. Again He dwells in the ether. He rewards the good and punishes the bad. Hence one must not deify cats and brute beasts (κνώδαλα), or moth eaten, spider-webbed idols, serpents, or any such like objects. While these "gods" pour out only poison upon their worshippers, God is in contrast Life (ζωή), and He pours out eternal Light incorruptible, and joy sweeter than honey upon men. So men must follow the Road (τρίβος) and forsake idolatry with its dire end, for those who fear God inherit eternal Life, dwell ever in Paradise feasting on sweet bread from the starry heaven.

Again, that is, we have an exhortation, after Jewish-Orphic lines, to forsake idolatry and choose the true Road that leads to the One God of the Streaming Light. For the end of the Road is Paradise.

The Road itself appears to be Orphic. True the doctrine of the two Roads is traced in Judaism back to Jeremiah (xxi, 8) and Deuteronomy (xxx, 15). The doctrine of the two ways as being the choice between light and darkness, however, appeared in *II Enoch,* xxx, 15,[97] immediately in connection with the acrostic of Adam's name already mentioned as belonging to the group of ideas we are considering as Orphic-Judaism. The Road, we have seen, is also given important emphasis in the Orphic original of Aristobulus. The idea was probably originally Orphic. The very early golden plates of Orphism made it important that one "journey on the right."[98] In Orphism this seems to have represented the journey of the soul which belongs originally to the γένος ὄλβιον, the blessed race, and is struggling to return to its former state. So it tries to get away from the wheel and come through to the mystic goal.[99] In other tablets what seems to be the same experience is a matter of avoiding coming to the well on the left and reaching instead the well of Memory on the right.[100] This well is a flowing source to quench

97. See the note by Forbes and Charles *ad loc.* in Charles' *Apoc. and Pseud.*
98. Χαῖρ⟨ε⟩, χαῖρε, δεξιὰν ὁδοιπορ⟨ῶν⟩: Kern, fr. 32, f, 5.
99. Kern, fr. 32 c, d.
100. The significance of this "Well of Memory" may be that the person is at last given full recollection of his former state, and is thus restored to the personality he was. It is notable that in Philo, *Plant.,* 129, Memory is sharply personified as the inspiration of man's powers of praising God. One recalls the Platonic "Recollection" of the Phaedo. Only as one retains his pristine knowledge of τὰ νοητά can he adequately praise God. The whole conception of "memory" as a means of mystic achievement might well have come to Plato from Orphism. It will be recalled that in the Myth of Er, after the souls have chosen their lots and the Fates have sealed them in those lots, the souls drink of the waters of Indifference in the plain of Forgetfulness, and those who drink forget all things (*Rep.,* 621a). Then they are ready for reincarnation. The "Well on the Left" of the Orphic Tablets would most naturally be Forgetfulness in contrast to Memory, the "Well on the Right." The soul trying to get back to heaven would try to drink from "Memory," in contrast to the drink of Forgetfulness that preceded incarnation. Plato's whole doctrine of "Reminiscence," and the notion of memory as the help

spiritual thirst, and is suggestive of the imagery of Philo, where the Road and the Stream seem interchangeable figures for spiritual ascent, as well as the imagery of this last Sibylline Fragment, where God is the Stream of Light which men approach by the Road.

Another great source of knowledge about pre-Philonic Hellenistic Judaism is the group of fragments taken by Eusebius from Alexander Polyhistor, of the early First Century B.C. Alexander, among a great number of books on the geography and history of various countries, wrote one book about the Jews. He drew for his material largely from Greek-Jewish writers, though somewhat from Greek opponents of the Jews, and indeed his text as quoted by Eusebius is largely a series of such quotations. The material he quotes was obviously regarded by Eusebius as at least of second-century origin. I still agree with Schürer in seeing no good reason for doubting the tradition. The sources of Alexander show the same discrepancies as those already described. Demetrius, of the time of Ptolemy IV (222–205 B.C.) wrote a "literalist" chronology;[101] Eupolemus wrote in the middle of the Second Century a more embellished account, but apparently still "literalist" in its point of view.[102]

Cleodemus or Malchus, another writer quoted by Alexander, seems possibly to suggest a mystic tendency, but nothing definite can be said of him. For from him, of whom we know only that he antedated Alexander, only a single brief fragment remains.[103] In it he relates that the sons of Abraham by Keturah helped Hercules in his fight against Libya and Antaeus, and that Hercules married the daughter of one of these sons, and by her had a son Sophron, the ancestor of the Sophacians. The content of Cleodemus' volume can hardly be judged by this fragment, but at least we can see that he was writing as one who saw a definite relation between Greek and Jewish stories.[104]

Other sources quoted by Alexander, however, seem directly in the line of the Mystery. Ezekiel, of whose date we know only that he antedates Alexander Polyhistor, was what Clement calls "the poet of Jewish tragedies."[105] How many tragedies he wrote we do not know, for all of the quotations in

to Mystic achievement, seems to have come from this Orphic notion. Incidentally the Orphic Road appears strikingly in the same myth (*Rep.*, 619b, 621c).

101. Eusebius, *Praep. Ev.*, IX, xxi; xxix, 1–3. Clem. Alex., *Strom.*, I, xxi, 141. Schürer, *Gesch. des jüd. Volkes*, III (1909), pp. 472 ff.

102. Eusebius, *op. cit.*, IX, xvii; xxvi; xxx–xxxiv. Clem. Alex., *Strom.*, I, xxiii, 153. Theodotus, in Eusebius, IX, xxii, the poetic historian, seems to have been a Samaritan and not to bear upon our problem. He was also literalistic in his treatment.

103. Josephus, *Antiq.*, I, 240 f. Taken thence by Eusebius in *Praep. Ev.*, IX, xx. See Schürer, *op. cit.*, p. 481.

104. An anonymous fragment in Eus., *Praep. Ev.*, IX, xvii, xviii, shows interest in the connection of the Patriarchs with astrology. The author was probably also a Samaritan.

105. *Strom.*, I, xxiii, 155: ὁ Ἐζεκίηλος ὁ τῶν Ἰουδαϊκῶν τραγῳδιῶν ποιητής.

the Alexander fragments are from a single play, *The Exodus*. In the fragments we have a portrait of Moses that strikingly supports the mystic Moses. He had, says Ezekiel, a royal education:

> The princess then through all my boyhood years,
> As I had been a son of her own womb,
> In royal state and learning nurtured me.[106]

When Moses was in exile in Midian he had, according to Ezekiel, a marvelous vision. He seemed to see on Sinai a great throne reaching to heaven upon which was a man of noble countenance wearing a diadem and holding a sceptre in his left hand. The throne, except that it is now placed on Sinai, is exactly the divine throne we have met in the Orphic fragment. We have not left the Orphic atmosphere at all, though Moses is being assimilated into the conception as not even Aristobulus had done. For, according to Ezekiel, God, the great king, with His right hand, beckoned Moses to come and take His place on the throne, to make which possible the great King Himself descended. Indeed the King even gave Moses His diadem and sceptre. From this seat the entire cosmos was opened to Moses' view, the circle of earth, the regions under the earth, and the heavens above. The stars come in a great host to do obeisance at his knees. As he counted them he awoke.[107] Here is unmistakably the divine kingship of Moses set forth, a kingship not only over men but over the entire cosmos. He is in the place of God! His father-in-law interprets the dream for him, explaining that it means he is to be a great king, the judge and guide of mortals, with vision of the past, present, and future.[108] Ezekiel has indeed shown us a mystic origin for Philo's kingship of Moses. The conception of God has come directly from Orphic sources,[109] and the idea is, as Cerfaux has pointed out, the astral mystery of Egypt. Moses' nature is taken up to associate itself with the nature of the stars. One recalls Philo's description of the ascent of Moses, in which Moses' supreme moment was when he was united with the heavenly beings and bodies in the great hymn of the cosmos to God.[110] It is quite to be expected that the symbolic representation of Moses with the heavenly bodies should reappear in the iconography.

In the incident of the bush, as described by Ezekiel, God explains to Moses that as a mortal he cannot see His face, but must only listen to the words. The fire in the bush is the Divine Logos shining out upon him:

$$\text{ὁ δ' ἐκ βάτου σοι θεῖος ἐκλάμπει λόγος.}^{111}$$

106. Eusebius, *Praep. Ev.*, IX, xxviii (438a, b). τροφαῖσι βασιλικαῖσι καὶ παιδεύμασιν ἅπανθ' ὑπισχνεῖθ', ὡς ἀπὸ σπλάγχνων ἐών.
107. Ib., chap. xxix (440a–c). 108. Ib., 440c.
109. Cerfaux, p. 55 has some interesting remarks upon the solar mysticism of the vision.
110. See above, pp. 196 f. 111. Eusebius, *op. cit.*, 441a.

The rest of the poem as Eusebius has preserved it is only a free treatment of the details in Exodus. But here we have it unmistakably that Moses was the great king who ruled as from the throne of God, and that at the burning bush he met the Divine Logos. These are striking details to find in a work that is traditionally dated in the Second Century before Christ. It seems also important that Jews were so hellenized by that date that they were using Greek dramatic forms, if not, as is probable, dramatic presentation, to set forth their traditions. Cerfaux[112] has paralleled the drama of Ezekiel with the mystery drama of Adonis written by Philopator. He thinks, and not without reason, that we may reasonably suppose that the tragedies of Ezekiel were actually performed, like those of Philopator, in connection with the Jewish Mystery.

Artapanus, likewise of the Second Century b.c., tells us still more of the Orphic elaboration of Moses and brings in for the first time specifically Egyptian *motifs*. He tells us that Moses was called by the Greeks Musaeus. He was the teacher of Orpheus, and when he had grown up he taught men many things.

For he invented ships, and machines for laying stones, and Egyptian arms, and contrivances for irrigation and for war; and he invented philosophy.[113]

The account goes on to describe how he divided Egypt into nomes, and established a god for each nome, with its proper priests, who were also given their special districts. He it was who invented the priestly writing. All this, it is explained, was to make the king of Egypt for the first time secure in his rulership. Moses' measures were so popular that he was beloved by the people, while his teaching the priests the hieroglyphics led them to name him Hermes, that is the Egyptian Tat-Hermes, and honor him as a god. Because of his popularity the Egyptians as a race adopted circumcision from him. Cerfaux has pointed out that in making Moses the giver of all inventions Artapanus has made him recognizably parallel to Isis, who did the same thing, and to Horus or Hermes.[114] Investigation has led me to add Osiris. For the parallels are indeed striking. If Moses was the inventor of ships, Isis was the inventor of sails,[115] and the patroness of sailing and sailors.[116] Osiris gave the Egyptians their laws and taught them the worship of the gods.[117]

112. p. 54.

113. *Ap.* Eusebium, *Praep. Ev.*, IX, xxvii, 4.

114. P. 49, n. 2. Reitzenstein, *Poimandres*, 181 f., rightly takes this Second Century reference to the Egyptian Hermes as evidence for the early date of the Hermetic tradition.

115. Hyginus Mythog., *Fabulae*, CCLXXVII; Cassiodorus, V, 17 (*Fontes*, III, 349; V, 719).

116. Papinus Statius, *Silvae*, III, ii, 101 f.; Claudianus, *De Isidis Navigio;* Juvenal, *Satirae*, XII, 26–28; Lucian, *Navig.*, 5, (*Fontes* II, 209; IV, 595; III, 282; III, 314).

117. Plutarch, *De Isid.*, 13. Cf. Diodor. Sic., I, 15 (*Fontes*, I, 96).

Isis was also the Lawgiver.[118] Osiris established the worship of the other gods and prescribed the rites for each.[119] Isis and Osiris taught men the τέχναι, gave them ὅπλα, and the instruments of agriculture.[120] Osiris taught men the common dialect and discovered writing for them.[121] Cyril thought it a sign that Hermes' activities were derived from those of Moses that he found it written in a Hermetic source that Hermes had provided Egypt with its ditches for irrigation, had given them laws (νόμοι) and had named the regions of the country νομοί after these laws.[122]

Cerfaux[123] also suggests a parallel in the fact that when Moses returned from the burning bush, where he had learned the name of God, he wrote it on a tablet and sealed it up. Cerfaux has recalled a law of Ptolemy Philopator requiring that the initiates into the mysteries of Dionysus must register the fact in the royal archives within a specified time by filing a sealed copy of the ἱερὸς λόγος of the mystery with the initiate's name. He suggests that the tablet of Moses was an imitation of this official tablet. The suggestion seems to me interesting but not quite warranted. For Moses does not file the tablet, he uses it only as a miraculous charm.

Moses the great miracle worker is thus in the Second Century B.C. specifically identified with Hermes, Musaeus, Orpheus, and given all the most recognizable and familiar functions of Isis and Osiris as well. Nothing more outright or blunt could have been composed to claim for the Jewish leader the prerogatives of paganism. Such a blanket identification meant to the reader that the writer was claiming for Moses that he was the mystic leader par-excellence, in whom all the virtues of the others were concentrated. The writer is so far from literal Judaism that he was willing to make Moses the founder of the cults of the other gods. Such a document can only be explicable to us as the expression of a crude early stage of syncretism, earlier, at least in spirit, than the adaptation by Aristobulus of the Orphic hymn.

At least mention should be made of another witness to the Mystery. In the account of Moses given by Clement of Alexandria[124] the author is drawing almost exclusively upon Philo's *De Vita Mosis*. But he is drawing upon other sources, for he quotes the poet Ezekiel and Artapanus. In addition he makes two references to "the Initiates" (οἱ μύσται) who had an account of Moses. From these we learn that Moses had three names: Joachim, given him by his

118. *Hymn of Ios*, z, 4–7 ἐγὼ νόμους ἀνθρώποις ἐθέμην καὶ ἐνομοθέτησα ἃ οὐδεὶς δύναται μεταθεῖναι. Cf. *Hymn of Andros*, v, 24. Oxyr. Pap. XI, 1380, ll. 119 f., 155 ff.
119. Diodor. Sic., I, xv, 19 (*Fontes*, I, 96).
120. Ib.; Albius Tibullus, I, vii, 29 ff. (*Fontes*, II, 148).
121. Diodorus Sic., I, 16. Augustinus, *Civ. Dei.*, XVIII, 39; Isidorus Hispalensis, *Etymolog.*, I, iii, 5; VIII, xi, 85; Mythographus Vaticanus III, VII, 4 (*Fontes*, I, 97; IV, 646; V, 723, 724; V, 746).
122. Cyril Alex., *Contra Julian.*, ap. Migne, PG, LXXVI, 547.
123. Pp. 49 f.   124. *Stromata*, I, xxiii.

mother at circumcision; Moses, given him by Pharoah's daughter; and Melchi, a name he had in heaven which was given him, apparently by God, after his ascension.[125] Again Clement tells us "the Initiates say that he slew the Egyptian by a word only."[126] One cannot conclude much from these references except that Clement knew a group of "Initiates" who had an elaborate spiritualization of the life of Moses, which made him a person with power to slay the Egyptian simply by his speech, and which included Moses' ascension and probably some important development of his career and saving influence after he got to heaven under the name Melchi. The significance of Melchi is not explained, but it at least suggests the eternal priesthood of Melchizedek. We do not know that these "Initiates" were Jews, but such, in view of the other sources Clement is using for the chapter, and in view of the fact that Moses is the hero, is the obvious assumption.

If it may be assumed that such representations of Moses were being commonly and openly made by Jews in Alexandria, we have again light upon the character of those detractions of Judaism answered by Josephus. For the extreme perversions of the syncretistic account of the Patriarchs there is little explanation. But Chaeremon makes Moses and Joseph scribes (γραμματεῖς) of the Egyptians, Joseph a sacred scribe (ἱερογραμματεύς). He gives them respectively the Egyptian names of Tisithen and Peteseph.[127] Manetho makes of Moses a priest of Heliopolis, named Osarseph, who led out a group of lepers in revolt and gave them a set of laws which were consistently the reverse of everything Egyptian: so all the kinds of animals sacred to the Egyptians were commanded by Moses to be killed in sacrifice.[128] The name Osarseph was taken from Osiris, Manetho explains.[129] Josephus adds that the fact is that the Egyptians think Moses a wonderful and divine person, and want in this way to claim him for themselves.[130] Strabo[131] gives the more natural picture that Moses was a priest of the Egyptians, but taught that the Egyptians were wrong in making animals gods. From the evidence before us it seems likely that the Egyptian attacks upon Moses did indeed contribute the detail of leprosy, but were actually counterattacks upon the Jewish attempts to claim all the best of Graeco-Egyptian culture for the Jews through precisely this identification of Moses with the gods of the Nile.

The tradition connecting Moses with Heliopolis reappears in Apion's attack.[132] Heliopolis is striking in its persistence, for the name appears also in Artapanus in connection with Moses.[133] It suggests precisely those solar aspects of Egyptian religion that went into the structure of the Jewish Mys-

125. Ib., xxiii, 151 (Stählin, II, 95).
126. Ib., xxiii, 154 (Stählin, II, 96, l. 6).
127. Cont. Ap., I, 290.
128. Ib., I, 238 ff., 261.
129. Ib., 265 f.
130. Ib., 279.
131. Geog., XVI, 35.
132. Josephus, Cont. Ap., II, 10.
133. Eusebius, Praep. Ev., IX, xxvii, 8.

294 BY LIGHT, LIGHT

tery. Certainly the pagans would not, and did not, originate such an identification, any more than they would have originated an identification of Moses with Osiris. It was perhaps not by chance that the Jewish temple of Onias was founded in Leontopolis in the nome of Heliopolis.

One interesting detail that has made little impression on the main stream of the Mystery as it finally appears in Philo, but which is worth mention, is the repeated indication that Joseph was identified with Sarapis. This identification is first met in the Christian Apology of Melito.[184] In a list of the gods of the various nations, he says: "The Egyptians worshipped Joseph the Hebrew, who is called Sarapis, since he furnished them with grain in the years of famine." The identification, appearing in a straightforward list of gods, seems not original with Melito, for he makes no other such identifications. He apparently repeats it as an accepted fact. So it appears also in Tertullian,[185] Firmicus Maternus,[186] Rufinus[187] and Suidas.[188] Some of the later writers are echoing Melito and Tertullian, but the Christian tradition indicates a Jewish original, and obviously an original of exactly the type of syncretistic and mystic Judaism we are studying. No further light can be thrown on the identification, and one must only guess at its origin and at the reason why no trace of it appears in the interpretations of Joseph by Philo. Perhaps it may be worth while to suggest that Sarapis was a deity of official manufacture by the early Ptolemies, one which as such would not be a part of the general religious thinking of the people as were Isis and Osiris in native Egyptian circles, or Musaeus and Orpheus among Greeks in Egypt. When Sarapis had become sufficiently important in current thinking to demand assimilation by Jews in Egypt Joseph may have been chosen as his Jewish type because Joseph had not been sufficiently esteemed to get an earlier identification, and because Joseph's official position in Egypt made him the natural one to choose for identification with the official cult. That is only a guess. But it is apparent that the Joseph-Sarapis identification gives us one more glimpse into the extraordinary Jewish syncretism that was of such long and important standing in Egypt.

It seems that there is enough material not only to prove the existence of Mystic Judaism, but to make possible a hypothetical reconstruction of the history of the movement.

Jews had always been sensitive to the religions of their neighbors. The whole history of Israel is a history of the struggle to make Jews into a people of an exclusive religion. The very pronouncements of the leaders in this

---

134. §5. Otto, *Corpus Apologet. Christ.* (3d edition), IX, 426.

135. *Ad Nationes*, ii, 8.   136. *De errore prof. rel.*, xiii, 1 f.

137. *Hist. Eccl.*, XI, 23 (*apud Griechische Christl. Schriftsteller*, Eusebius, *Kirchengeschichte*, II, ii, p. 1030, l. 4).

138. *S.v.* Sarapis. Much of the foregoing material is collected by Otto in his note to the Melito passage, IX, 466, n. 154.

slow movement make it only too apparent that they were all along in a minority in their struggles to prevent the mass of Jews from accepting the gods of Canaan and Philistia alongside the religion of Yahveh. Their greatest king, Solomon, had been notorious for his "idolatry," with none but the few purists to object. All the later reaction and development could not rob Solomon, because of his many cults, of his standing as the great founder of Jewish wisdom. It is clear from the legends of the captivity that the Jews who refused to follow the religious customs of their neighbors were very exceptional, while the mass of angelology and Babylonian mythology brought back by even the few loyalists who would return to rebuild Jerusalem indicates how much more extensive must have been the syncretism by Jews less devoted to their nation. The new legalism of Judaism after the return, and the new centering of Jewish worship in the Jerusalem temple was the great achievement of the Jewish priests for keeping Judaism exclusive in its cultus in Palestine. But the movement nearly collapsed when Jews even in Palestine were subjected to the rather remote Greek influence of the Seleucids in Antioch. If so remote a contact with Greek civilization thus affected the Judaism of Jerusalem, what was to be expected of Jews cut off from Jerusalem altogether and living in remote Alexandria surrounded by Hellenistic civilization in its very highest representation? The Pharisees themselves admitted that the Law could not be kept according to their standards outside Palestine itself.[139] Unquestionably many Jews would try to do so, and the persistence of the literalist-legalistic tradition, of the sort represented by the Hellenistic books *II* and *III Maccabees,* and by Philo's own address to ordinary Jews *On Blessings and Curses,* to name only a few works of this character, show that many Jews were sincerely trying to observe normative Judaism in the Greek world. In contrast some Jews seem to have left Judaism altogether for pagan cults. The last chapter of *III Maccabees,* Philo's violence toward apostates,[140] and the known career of Philo's own nephew Alexander are evidence for the existence of such a seepage from Judaism. How many thus apostatized we cannot even guess. Their loss only tended to strengthen the sense of separation and cohesion in the Jews that remained. The middle course that was open was one of syncretism, the adoption of religious concepts and values from the pagans into Judaism itself so that the Jews could have both paganism and a Jewish sense of separation at the same time. In an atmosphere where Greek mythological, mystical, and philosophic ideas were being freshly identified with the Egyptian concepts, Judaism struck up its claim in the same way. The Jews seem at the beginning to have been following Greek leadership rather than Egyptian, for the earliest syncretism

139. G. F. Moore, *Judaism,* I, 273; II, 71; III, 84, n. 42; II, 76, states "Outside the land of Israel most laws prescribing ritual purifications were not in force."

140. See my *Jewish Jurisprudence in Egypt,* pp. 33 ff.

of which we have any knowledge is with Orphism. Orphism, according to the one very important fragment adapted by Aristobulus, was teaching a monotheism headed by Zeus. He was apparently a solar deity, a source of radiation of light and life, and salvation consisted in leaving the material world to follow the true Road of Light that led to the welling source. From this the redeemed initiate finally drank. Judaism had itself been talking of the two roads, though in a different sense, and of the One God. Orpheus was thus easily identified with Moses, the great teacher of Judaism, just as Orpheus was the source of revelation of the true religion for his followers. Orphic literature was baldly rewritten to include references to Moses, and the Orphic form of hymns became a Jewish convention, which reappears repeatedly in the Sibylline books. Along with the Orphic syncretism there came into Judaism, as Aristobulus shows us, an eclectic Greek philosophy. The combination of Orphism with philosophy was probably not original with either Aristobulus or Judaism. The Pythagoreans and Plato show such large elements of Orphism that it is only natural that devotees of Orpheus should have borrowed many ideas from these schools at an early date. That they did so later is abundantly witnessed by such writers as Proclus. We can hardly read Proclus' details back into Hellenistic Orphism, but there is no antecedent reason for doubting that the Orphics might early have borrowed congenial philosophic ideas; the fact that Aristobulus shows the two in such definite union makes it highly likely that he found them already thus mingled, and that in taking over the Orphism of the day the Jews took over a mystery religion already well oriented with philosophy. Particularly is the presence of the θεῖος λόγος in the Orphic poem itself an indication of the early date of the philosophizing of the Orpheus mystery.

At this early stage there was still much to be worked out. Jewish claims to superiority could have made little impression so long as the books of the Old Testament remained unassimilated and uninterpreted in terms of the new conception. Aristobulus was making a beginning. But Judaism must rise to a place where it had forgotten the origin of its own interpretation of itself, cease identifying Moses with Orpheus or Musaeus, before it could pose as the supreme religion with any conviction to itself or others.

This process is largely lost to us. But the Jewish syncretism was so closely following Greek models that as the Greeks fused Orphism and the Isiac mysteries, Judaism at once followed by representing Moses as Osiris, and giving to him all the functions of Isis even to establishing the Egyptian cults for each nome of the country. He was also Hermes, a statement in Artapanus which Reitzenstein rightly regarded as of the greatest importance for showing the antiquity of the Hermetic development.

Already, then, by the middle of the Second Century B.C. there had long been in Egypt a movement to identify Judaism with the mystic schools about it. Sophia appeared in the Sibylline books, but the date of these books and their constituent parts is too uncertain to identify a date for Sophia as a link between Jewish and pagan thought. My own impression is that the passages from the Sibyl which we have discussed are probably from the early Second Century B.C., at least that that is the period of the conventionalization of their form. But later writers could so easily have tampered with details that the Sophia passage cannot be given any definite significance for the history of the movement. My impression is again that the Sophia passage is genuinely early. The native Hebrew Chochma was a conception too obviously serviceable for syncretism to have long missed the attention of early harmonizers. Just when it came into prominent use we cannot say, but since it probably was originally introduced according to the syncretistic technique we must assume a long history of the term before the mature presentation of the *Wisdom of Solomon,* where conscious syncretism has disappeared, and Sophia has come directly to mean the Light-Stream to Jewish writers and readers. *Wisdom* also shows another important fact—the Hebrew hero, here Solomon, has become the θεῖος ἄνθρωπος of paganism. He had had all the functions of the mystic saviors of the Gentiles, but he now has them of his own right, and not by virtue of identification with one of the pagan gods. This dropping of the identification, and emergence of the Hebrew hero himself as a θεῖος ἄνθρωπος, along with the forthright interpretation of Jewish texts as signifying mystic conceptions, is a long step from the primitive syncretism of perhaps two centuries earlier. But it was possible for Jews to write with the assurance of *Wisdom* and Philo only after such a long period, when the mystic and philosophic ideas of the Greek world could have become completely naturalized within Judaism for Jewish thinkers. Aristobulus was quite aware that he had got Zeus out from and Moses into the Orphic fragment only by changing the Greek verses. Philo and the author of *Wisdom,* writing with no sense of such syncretism, could think of Moses or Solomon as the mystic saviors without any sense that they were not speaking the idiom of Judaism. It will be recalled that Philo identified Jothar with the "Egyptian Proteus."[141] The identification was dubious in meaning, but is interesting as an atavistic survival from the early syncretistic stage, where such identifications were the whole basis of the interpretation of Judaism.

Some such appears the general history of the movement. At some time Iranian notions must have come into the Egyptian world and in turn been assimilated, as we have seen Sarapis came to be included through identification with Joseph. The Iranian syncretism is lost; we only infer the incident from the fact that Philo's "Powers" point so definitely in that direction.

141. See above, p. 212, n. 86a.

Jews were still Jews. Their separation had been preserved through this process by their clinging to the Torah. But the Torah was no longer necessarily Law in the sense of the "literalists" who had always fought the mystic development. To some it was simply the ἱερὸς λόγος of the Mystery. To others it was both a law to be practised and a Mystery. But to any who accepted the mystic interpretation the Torah was primarily a guide, through the great Saviors, to the Light-Stream and its Source, true Salvation. Yet by their insistence upon the Jewish formulation they kept alive their Jewish loyalty, and their Jewish distinctiveness, though they were making every effort to bring as many Gentiles as possible to join with them on the great journey of the true Road.

By this time, perhaps, Philo's Mystery seems not an isolated phenomenon in Jewish tradition. Before going on to the liturgical evidence, which must be given a chapter by itself, there is one more document which seems to me to be an important witness to the existence of mystic Judaism in the sense in which that term has been used. In 1925 I published in the *Harvard Theological Review* a study of the Pseudo-Justinian *Oratio ad Graecos.*[142] Except for Professor Harnack,[143] who gave it an extended review, the study was apparently overlooked. I had criticized in that article the interpretation of the document given earlier by Professor Harnack, and he was on the whole inclined to stand his ground. But he admitted that while my hypothesis was "eine blosse Möglichkeit," still it was definitely a "Möglichkeit." Professor Harnack was hardly a man who could write several pages of criticism without being very instructive, and in view of what he said and of my own subsequent studies I would like definitely to modify my position, though not essentially to change it, and to bring out some new points.

The thesis of the article was that the *Oratio* was not originally a Christian document at all, but the product of a Greek who had found satisfaction for his spiritual longings in a Philonic type of Judaism, and who was exhorting his people to do likewise. To this I originally added the suggestion that the document was one which Paul had definitely in mind when he wrote Galatians. This addition now seems to me to be untenable, as it seemed to Professor Harnack. The two passages where they have verbal similarities are of a nature to prove nothing. For one of them is a list of vices, which was fairly commonplace; the other, the exhortation "Become as I am, for I was as you are," though it is identical in verbal form in the two documents, is a phrase which may well have been a standardized exhortation of popular preaching. There would then have to be no direct literary connection between the two writings. But as to my main contention, that the *Oratio* was the product of a proselyte to Hellenistic Judaism, Harnack was not sure it

142. Vol. XVIII, pp. 187–200.
143. *Theologische Literaturzeitung,* 1925, pp. 442 f.

was wrong, and I still feel convinced that it was right. When the article was written I had not recognized the Mystery and its ramifications in Philo, and so missed a good deal of the implications of the *Oratio*. In spite of some duplication, it seems best to go over the ground again.

The *Oratio ad Graecos* is to be found in the third volume of Otto's *Corpus Apologetarum Christianorum,* and in Harnack's "Die pseudo-justinische Rede an die Griechen."[144] It represents itself as a defence for turning from the religion of the Greeks to the religion of the Logos, and presents its case most vigorously. The document opens with the traditional denunciation of the immoralities of the Greek gods and heroes, a purely Greek polemic which was begun at least as far back as Xenophanes. To this subject the author adds nothing, but presents an excellent epitome of the usual arguments. He then discusses the current way of living among the Greeks, and says that he rejected it with loathing; he justifies his opinion with a half-dozen vivid statements about Greek practices. From commenting upon the Greek religion and morality he turns in contrast to describe with equal pithiness the high moral and spiritual character of his new faith, exhorting his former associates to find the same peace and exaltation which the change has meant to him. The writer has remarkable power of going to the heart of what he discusses.

The document depends entirely upon its own testimony for its date and classification. Only one Greek manuscript came down to us, that in the Codex Argentoratensis (burned in 1870), in which the *Oratio* received an impossible ascription to Justin Martyr, corresponding to a work of similar title ascribed to Justin by Eusebius.[145] There is, indeed, in the statements of the *Oratio* about the Logos, a close resemblance to some of Justin's ideas; but that Justin was capable of saying so much to the point in so small a compass is inconceivable. With this evidence for authorship discredited, there is no further tradition whatever to help us in identifying or dating the document.

So far as the first four chapters of the *Oratio* are concerned, in which the immoralities of the Greek gods and of the Greek manners[146] are set forth, they might have been written by a Greek sceptic or rhetorician at any time after the Third Century B.C., and need not detain us. The last chapter, the

144. *Sitzungsberichte,* Berlin Academy, 1896, pp. 634 ff.
145. There is also a Syriac recension, a German translation of which is published by Harnack, *op. cit.*
146. The Christians, to be sure, inveighed proverbially against pagan immorality; but so did Philo, as in *Som.,* ii, 48 ff.; *Spec.,* i, 176; iii, 8 ff., 37–45. Philo was too discriminating to include all pagan life in these denunciations. But his sense of the contrast between the life of those in the Mystery and the darkened wretches who lived to the body is keen, as well as his general sense of Jewish superiority in morals.

fifth, is the only one in which positive remarks are made about the writer's own faith. It reads as follows:

Henceforth, ye Greeks, come and partake of incomparable Sophia, and be instructed by the divine Logos and learn the incorruptible King, and recognize His heroes who never slaughter with arms. For he, our captain, does not desire strength of bodies and beauty of forms, nor the haughtiness of high birth, but a pure soul fortified by holiness. And indeed the divine Logos has ceaseless care over us, and teaches us both the passwords of our King and divine acts. Oh thou soul which hast been permeated with the power of the Logos! Oh trumpet of peace in the soul torn by conflict! Oh city of refuge from terrible passion! Oh teaching that quenches the fire within the soul! This instruction does not make us poets, it does not train us as philosophers, or as skilful orators, but when it has been learned, it makes mortals become immortals, human beings gods, and from earth leads to the realms beyond Olympus. Come ye, and be instructed. Become as I am now, for I was like you. These things captured me, the divine inspiration of the instruction, the power of the Logos. For as a skilful snake-charmer makes the terrible serpent creep out of its hole, and puts it to flight, so the Logos drives from the recesses of the soul the terrible sensual affections: first lust, through which every horror is born, enmities, strifes, envy, intriguing, anger, and such like. So when lust has gone forth the soul becomes serene and calm. And when the soul is relieved from the evils that flow about its neck, it returns to him who made it. For it must be restored whence it departed.[147]

The first and most striking fact about this fine description of the power of the Logos to release the soul from the tyranny of the lower nature is that, like the rest of the document, it contains no hint of Christ, or any syllable that is distinctively Christian. And yet, so far as I have been able to ascertain, this obvious point has never been noticed. Found with Christian writings, its Christian character has gone unchallenged.

At first sight the Logos-passage, and with it the whole document, might well appear to be the product of any of the late Platonic or Eclectic mystics, for it fits in perfectly with the Logos idea of both Plutarch and Cornutus. But the general tenor of the *Oratio* is against this. The Philosophers never, to my knowledge, set off such an antithesis as is here made between the gods of Greece and the Logos. They rather sought to find the Logos in mythology by allegorizing the ancient myths. Even Plato, fiercely as he denounced the gods, and peremptorily as he banished Homer from his Republic, preserved in the *Timaeus* their purified replicas as intermediate deities.

The presumption, then, from the sharp contrast of the gods and the Logos is that the document did not come from the pen of a pagan philosopher. But another school of thought, Hellenistic Judaism, did scornfully reject the

147. The translation is made from the text as printed by Harnack.

mythology of the Greeks for a pure devotion to the Logos. To the Jews the legends of the immoralities of the gods were of course particularly distasteful. They preached openly that such mythology must be rejected before a true knowledge of God was possible. So, for instance, Josephus reproaches the Greeks for ascribing "sodomitical practices to the gods themselves," and representing that "the gods married their own sisters, contriving this apology for their own strange unnatural lusts."[148] In another passage Josephus refers to Plato's expulsion of the poets from the Republic for their teachings about the gods.[149] Such a denunciation of Greek gods is not found in Philo because of Philo's repeatedly avowed policy of treating with respect anything called a god by his neighbors. He can point out the error of calling such beings gods, but he cannot revile them. A Greek proselyte would obviously not need to be so careful as a Jew, and could freely have used the invectives of Greek sceptics and rhetoricians. So the presence of the invective in such a document as I am taking this to be is entirely natural.

More positive evidence for the nature of the *Oratio* is found in the Logos-passage itself. If the document is to have any point, this will prove to be an epitome of the new faith which the convert has found to be so superior to Greek religion. One turns for comparison to Athenagoras' elegant plea for Christianity. Athenagoras speaks as philosophically as possible, and as much as he can from the Greek point of view in making his criticisms of the Greeks. But when he contrasts their position with Christianity, the chapter (X) gives what was to him the most essential part of Christianity, its doctrine of the Father, Son, and Holy Spirit, which he prefaced with quotations from the prophets. One could not for a moment question the Christianity of the document, whatever the sources of much of his general argument. In the fifth chapter of the *Oratio,* similarly, the author must give us the fundamental features of the religion he is preaching or the address to outsiders will leave them, to say the least, completely at sea as to what in the world has so excited him. The paragraph is certainly not an epitome of Christianity as we know it from any other document. Except for the vague phrases which, we have recognized, were also used by Paul, and the words Logos and Sophia, there is not a word that suggests Christianity.

In contrast to its vagueness when viewed as a Christian document, the little section is as succinct a review of the essential features of Mystic Judaism as could be made.

The Greeks are exhorted to come and partake of the incomparable Sophia and be instructed by the divine Logos. This is precisely the paralleling of Sophia and Logos we have repeatedly met. "Learn the incorruptible king" (μάθετε βασιλέα ἄφθαρτον). If the reading μάθετε must stand it is very difficult: it would seem to mean that from the Logos or Sophia one can learn about God, the King; both the Logos as teacher of higher knowledge and God as King are obviously ideas familiar in the Mystery. "And come to recognize His heroes who do not slaughter with weapons" (οὐχ ὅπλοις . . . φόνον ἐργαζομένους). The Logos, or the King, is to be recognized through his peaceful heroes, that is demigods. The conception corresponds exactly to the mystic Patriarchs of Philo, who would in the Mystery be mentioned after the Logos as the way to the Logos. These heroes, who in contrast to the rulers and heroes of Greek tradition did not get their power by destructive warfare, recall that peace-making aspect of the Patriarchs which Philo loved to bring out. Philo tells kings whose titles are based upon conquest, however wide their sway, to regard themselves as private citizens in contrast with the great kings, the Patriarchs, who have received God as their portion.[150] Moses is particularly one who received his ἀρχὴ καὶ βασιλεία not by arms (ὅπλα, etc.), but on account of his virtue.[151] One is also strikingly reminded of the passage in *Wisdom* just discussed where Aaron as the Logos-Priest subdued the Death-Worker οὐχ ὅπλων ἐνεργείᾳ.[152]

"For he, our captain" is still the Logos. Philo is sparing about military figures for the Logos, though they are by no means absent. The Logos is the captain of the heavenly angels[153] and is recognizable as the χεὶρ καὶ δύναμις of God that fights with us as our ally (βοηθός).[154] Of course, in comparison to God, the Logos is only ὕπαρχος, lieutenant.[155] The captain's function is to be the guide and leader. For this it will be recalled that Philo more frequently uses the figure of the charioteer and pilot, who guide all things, including men, to their safety.[156]

This captain desires not bodily strength or beauty, or aristocratic birth, says the *Oratio*, but a pure soul fortified by holiness. The rejection of a physical qualification is natural enough in a Mystery which was primarily a running away from the body. True Philo frequently emphasizes the beauty of the Patriarchs, as for example the beauty of the boy Moses.[157] But these are qualities that went with the setting up of the ideal νόμος ἔμψυχος, in which, as *Wisdom* has it, a choice soul was joined to a beautiful body. The ordinary mystic ran away from the body. The rejection of aristocratic birth as a qualification recalls vividly Philo's insistence that the nobility of descent

150. *Plant.*, 66–68. Cf. *Praem.*, 87 where the peaceful character of the Jewish saints brings peace even between men and animals.
151. *Mos.*, i, 148.
152. *Wisd.*, xviii, 22. See above, p. 275.
153. Here ἡγεμών, *Conf.*, 174.   154. *Som.*, ii, 265–267.
155. *Som.*, i, 241.
156. E.g. ὁ κόσμος ἡνιοχεῖταί τε καὶ κυβερνᾶται σωτηρίως (*Praem.*, 34): cf. *Fug.*, 101: ὥσθ' ἡνίοχον μὲν εἶναι τῶν δυνάμεων τὸν λόγον κτλ. See above, p. 53. I would see a Hellenistic origin for ἀρχηγὸς τῆς σωτηρίας of Heb. ii, 10.
157. See above, p. 182.

from Abraham was in itself no qualification that put the Jew above a pious proselyte.[158] True εὐγένεια was to Philo "a mind purified by the perfect purifications."[159] Philo would have agreed with this statement of the *Oratio* in word and implication.

"The divine Logos," says the *Oratio*, "has ceaseless care over us, and teaches us both the passwords of our King and divine acts" (τὰ τοῦ βασιλέως ἡμῶν συνθήματα καὶ πράξεις θείας). This is a very difficult statement because of the variety of its possible meanings. Συνθήματα may mean collectively "covenants," like συνθῆκαι, and so the meaning here be that the Logos teaches the Covenant of our King, the Jewish Covenant, along with πράξεις θείας, divine actions, or the precepts of the Law. Or it may, as I think it does, have the mystical meaning I gave it in the first translation, and refer to passwords and "divine acts" in the sense of cultus. In either case the statement harmonizes perfectly with mystic Judaism. For if συνθήματα be read as "Covenant" it is still notably not to be learned from a scroll or code, but is the sort of covenant that must be learned directly from the Logos.

So the mystic's soul has become permeated with the δύναμις of the Logos, or filled with the Light-Stream.

The author of the *Oratio* now calls to mind several details of his new religion that are of significance. First he exclaims: "Oh trumpet of peace in the soul torn by conflict!" One has only to turn to Philo again to see that he is referring to the Hellenistic Jewish interpretation of the "feast of the trumpet." Philo says, after pointing out that the trumpet is ordinarily a symbol of conflict:

Wherefore, as a name of significance, the Law has called this the feast of the "Trumpet" an instrument of war, as token of thanksgiving to God who is the maker and guard of peace, etc.[160]

As a second detail he exclaims, "Oh city of refuge from the terrible passions!" One is struck, most forcibly of all the details, with the appearance of the φυγαδευτήριον as a term for the Logos in his capacity of being a city of refuge from the passions. The conception is so greatly elaborated by Philo,[161] and is connected so directly with the very heart of the Mystery that it would be sufficient in itself to establish a connection. It need hardly be said that the word is to be found in Greek only in passages dependent upon the Septuagint original.

The next detail to which he alludes is just as certainly Philonic. "Oh teaching that quenches the fire within the soul!" The notion of a teaching that stills the troubles of the soul is in itself definitely a reference to a doctrine

158. See especially the section on nobility in *Virt.*, 187–227.
159. Ib., 189.   160. *Spec.*, i, 192 (see 190).
161. See above, pp. 249 ff.

of mystical power. The last phrase, πῦρ ἔμψυχον, which I have translated "the fire within the soul" is more difficult. In the first place the translation is uncertain, for it would more naturally be read "the living, or animate, fire." In itself this would seem a reference to the Light-Stream, but as used here the words must refer to a kind of fire which has to be put out in order that the soul may be able to achieve its spiritual possibilities. It is obviously a reference to some type of sin or defect which is so vividly conceived as to be compared to fire. It is a fire which the "teaching" can put out. A few passages in Philo make the meaning clear. Philo explains that the passions, τὰ πάθη, are in themselves of an inflammable nature, which ἡ ἄλογος ὁρμὴ πυρὸς τὸν τρόπον, the irrational impulse (in the soul) after the manner of fire, makes burst into flames until it consumes all the soul's properties. For the irrational impulse, he continues, is a fire which kindles the passions but does not burn them up. What is consumed in the fire is the perfect virtue of the soul, its progress to that virtue, and even its original good disposition (ἀρετὴ τελεία, προκοπή, εὐφυΐα).[162] This conception is elsewhere variously applied.[163] This then is the fire which the "Teaching" quenches, the fire of the irrational impulse in the soul or the fire which that impulse kindles within the πάθη to the utter destruction of the better nature and hope of the individual.

This instruction, continues the Oratio, does not make us poets, philosophers, or skilful orators, but it makes mortals immortals, human beings gods, and leads from earth to the realms beyond Olympus. Professor Harnack doubted that in Hellenistic Judaism one could so belittle philosophers as to class them with rhetoricians. It is quite true that Philo uses the term "philosopher" as meaning the Mystic, and as such he would never have used the term in this connection. For rhetoric and poetry belonged to the studies of youth, as Philo thought, along with geometry and the whole of encyclical learning.[164] In this Philo did not include philosophy, which began only when these studies ended, and was really concerned with metaphysics and mysticism only. Yet he is acquainted with a use of the term which puts it on exactly this level. In one place he has been speaking of the Royal Road of the Mystery, and continues:

This Road you must understand to be philosophy, not the philosophy that is pursued by the present day sophistic group of men. For these have practised the arts of words against the truth, and then called their villainy "sophia," giving a wicked work a divine name.[165]

Sophia and philosophy are indeed divine names to Philo. But he would entirely have understood what the writer meant when he spoke of a philoso-

162. LA, iii, 248 f.
164. Agr., 18.

163. Ib., 234 f.; Mig., 100; Cong., 55.
165. Post., 101.

phy that was on the level of poetry and rhetoric, and so ought Harnack to have understood him. Philo would have agreed entirely that the instructions of the Mystery did not make men into that kind of philosophers.

And Philo would have agreed that the Mystery made human beings into gods, mortals into immortals, and led the initiate from earth into the immaterial realm beyond Olympus, the highest heaven. And though he does not use the figure he would have highly approved of speaking of the Logos as a snake-charmer which lures out the snake, the πάθη of the soul, and drives it away, so that the soul will be pure to mount the blinding ascent to God.

The last figure of the snake-charmer is in some ways the most interesting of all. The others have abundantly demonstrated that the closing paragraph, in which the *Oratio* should give an epitome of the religion of its author, does give an excellent epitome of the salient points of Philo's Mystery. But without the last figure, so closely has the author followed Philo that one might have been justified in saying that it was a literary compilation made from Philo's writings without giving evidence of being what it purported to be, the triumphant testimony of a Greek to the existence and power of a Jewish mystery doctrine.[166] But with the appearance of the snake-charmer we see that the author, though he has given a splendid summary of the valuable points of the Mystery Philo has described at greater length, is still drawing upon another source than Philo himself, at least other than the writings of Philo which have come down to us.

One turns from this analysis to try to find reasons for calling the *Oratio* Christian, and frankly I can find not one. No one, then or since, would have recognized Christianity or known what the author was meaning by this description of mystic achievement. True so much of the ideology of the Mystery did go over into Christianity that many of its ideas are also found in Christian writings. But this religion of the Logos-Sophia, the King with peaceful heroes, the teacher of passwords and "divine practices," who is our trumpet of peace, our city of refuge, our teaching that quenches the fire of the irrational impulse—this is not Christianity. What Harnack never noticed was that when the Syriac translator wanted to pass the document off as Christian, as he could easily do considering the number of elements Christianity had taken from the Mystery, he had to *insert in the text a statement presumably by the author that his conversion was to the "Wisdom of the Christians."*[167] The fact is that without such an insertion the parallelism of the document to Philo is flawless. The *Oratio* stands as an independent witness of the thriving existence of the Jewish Mystery-teaching.

166. Not to press the possibilities of cult reference in the θεῖα ἔργα already discussed.
167. See Harnack's article in the *Sitzungsberichte* of the Berlin Academy 1896, p. 629, l. 4.

CHAPTER XI

THE MYSTIC LITURGY

In 1915 W. Bousset published an amazing collection of fragments of Jewish liturgy.[1] He pointed out the slight interpolations by which Christians had adapted them for their own purposes, and thus brought to light a body of liturgy in the *Apostolic Constitutions* that was unmistakably Jewish, though obviously from a Judaism strongly Hellenized. Indeed the first prayer turned out to include the Kedusha still used in Jewish liturgy. With fine methodology Bousset selected the material of Jewish origin, analyzed it sufficiently to prove its Judaism and Hellenism alike, but had no suggestion as to the milieu that would have produced such a liturgy, and of course left many other points still to be discussed. So far as I know nothing has since been done with this material. In the posthumous third edition of Bousset's own *Die Religion des Judentums* the editor made no use of it, and the original study remains, I believe, little known.[2] The Fragments are so strikingly appropriate to the thesis of this book that, with minor changes from Bousset's presentation, they must be reproduced here entire. I shall first give a translation of the texts, with incidental comment, and when they are all before the reader discuss their total implications.[3]

The first fragment to be considered is the one first presented by Bousset:

FRAGMENT I

Constitutiones VII, xxxv, 1–10.

I 1. Great art Thou, O Lord Almighty, and great is Thy power, and of Thy understanding there is no number.[4] Our Creator and Savior, rich

1. "Eine jüdische Gebetssammlung im siebenten Buch der apostolischen Konstitutionen," in *Nachrichten von der K. Gesellschaft der Wissenschaften zu Göttingen*, Philologische-Historische Klasse, 1915 (1916), pp. 435–485. Hereafter referred to by author and page. Actually some of the material comes from the eighth book.

2. I am indebted for knowledge of it to the all-seeing eye of Professor A. D. Nock of Harvard.

3. The fragments are given fundamentally after the translation of James Donaldson which appeared in his edition of the *Apostolic Constitutions* in the *Ante-Nicene Christian Library* (Edin., 1870). Donaldson says that his version is only a close revision of an earlier translation by Whiston. I have revised again carefully according to Funk's text (*Didascalia et Constitutiones Apostolorum*, Paderborn, 1905). Each Fragment is numbered here in series, with indication of the passage in the *Constitutiones* whence it is taken, and I have retained the paragraph enumeration as made by Funk for the original chapters. Christian interpolations are retained but indicated by italics.

4. Ps. cxlvii, 5.

in grace, long-suffering, and the bestower of mercy, who dost desire the salvation of Thy creatures: for Thou art good by nature, and sparest sinners, and invitest them to repentance; for admonition is the effect of Thy bowels of compassion. For how should we have survived if we had been required to come to judgment immediately, when, after so much long-suffering, we hardly get clear of our weakness? 2. The heavens declare Thy dominion,[5] and the earth shakes with earthquakes, and, hanging upon nothing, declares Thy unshaken steadfastness. The sea raging with waves, and feeding a flock of ten thousand creatures, is bounded with sand, as trembling at Thy will, and compels all men to cry out: "How great are Thy works, O Lord! in wisdom hast Thou made them all: the earth is full of Thy creation."[6] 3. And the bright host of angels and the intellectual spirits say, "There is but one holy Being to Phelmuni";[7] and the holy seraphim, together with the six-winged cherubim, who sing to Thee their triumphal song, cry out with never-ceasing voices, "Holy, holy, holy, Lord of Sabaoth! heaven and earth are full of Thy glory";[8] and the other multitudes of the orders, archangels, thrones, dominions, principalities, authorities, and powers[9] cry aloud, and say, "Blessed be the glory of the Lord out of the very place."[10] 4. But Israel thy church on earth, *taken out of the Gentiles,* emulating the heavenly powers night and day, with a full heart and a willing soul sings, "The chariot of God is ten thousand fold thousands of them that rejoice: the Lord is among them in Sinai, in the holy place."[11] 5. The heaven knows Him who fixed it as a cube of stone,[12] in the form of an arch, upon nothing, who united the land and water to one another, and scattered the vital air all abroad, and conjoined fire therewith for warmth, and as a comfort against darkness. The choir strikes us with admiration, declaring Him that numbers them, and showing Him that names them;[13] the animals declare Him that puts life into them; the trees show Him that makes them grow: all which creatures, being made by Thy Logos show forth the greatness of Thy power. 6. Wherefore every man ought to send up an hymn from his very heart to Thee, through *Christ,* in the name of all the rest, since man has power over them all by Thy appointment. 7. For Thou art

5. Ps. xviii, 2.   6. Ps. civ, 24.   7. Dan. viii, 13.
8. Is. vi, 3.
9. This list recalls Col. i, 16, but seems independent of that list since ἀρχάγγελοι and δυνάμεις are here additional.
10. Ezek. iii, 12.   11. Ps. lxviii, 17.   12. Job. xxxviii, 38.
13. Ps. cxlvii, 4.

kind in Thy benefits, and beneficent in Thy bowels of compassion, who alone art almighty: for when Thou willest, to be able is present with Thee; for Thy eternal power both quenches flame,[14] and stops the mouths of lions, and tames whales, and raises up the sick, and overrules the power of all things, and overturns the host of enemies, and casts down a people numbered in their arrogance. 8. Thou art He who art in heaven, He who art on earth, He who art in the sea, He who art in finite things, Thyself unconfined by anything. For of Thy majesty there is no boundary,[15] for it is not ours, O Lord, but the oracle of Thy servant, who said, "And thou shalt know in thine heart that the Lord thy God He is God in heaven above, and on earth beneath, and there is none other besides Thee":[16] 9. for there is no God besides Thee alone,[17] there is none holy besides Thee, the Lord, the God of gnosis,[18] the God of holy men, holy above all holy beings; for they are sanctified by Thy hands.[19] Thou art glorious, and highly exalted, invisible by nature, and unsearchable in Thy judgment;[20] whose life is without want, whose duration can never alter or fail, whose operation is without toil, whose greatness is unlimited, whose excellency is perpetual, whose habitation is inaccessible,[21] whose dwelling is unchangeable, whose gnosis is without beginning, whose truth is immutable, whose work is not one of mediation, whose dominion cannot be taken away, whose monarchy is without succession, whose kingdom is without end, whose strength is irresistible, whose army is very numerous: 10. for Thou art the Father of Sophia, the Creator, as the cause, of the creation, by a Mediator; the Bestower of providence, the Giver of laws, the Supplier of want, the Punisher of the ungodly, and the Rewarder of the righteous; *the God and Father of Christ, and the Lord of those that are pious towards Him, whose promise is infallible, whose judgment is without bribes, whose sentiments are immutable, whose piety is incessant, whose thanksgiving is everlasting, through whom adoration is worthily due to Thee from every rational and holy nature.*

Bousset began with this prayer because its Judaism, of all the fragments, had the best external attestation. For, as he points out,[22] §3 corresponds so closely to the Kedusha, in the form in which it appears, with slight variation, in three places in contemporary Jewish liturgy, that there can be no doubt

14. Dan. iii, 24 ff. 15. Ps. cxlv, 3. 16. Deut. iv, 39.
17. Is. xlv, 5. 18. I Sam. ii, 3. 19. Deut. xxxiii, 3.
20. Rom. xi, 33. 21. I Tim. vi, 16. 22. Bousset, pp. 436 f.

that we have here a very early form of the Jewish prayer. That the Jews took the prayer from Christian liturgy could not be suggested. The only possible conclusion was that the prayer, as a Jewish prayer, was at least as old as the Second Century of our Era,[23] and that the Christians had taken it from the Jews. There was some difficulty, in the parallel passages, in the classes of the angels named, for while the present Jewish text names ophanim and chajjot with the seraphim, the text before us names besides the seraphim and cherubim the six classes of angels named in the New Testament. This may be a Christian alteration, Bousset says, but it may also represent the earlier Jewish form, since we cannot be sure that the prayer as now used in synagogues has not gone through many changes in seventeen centuries, and since the angel classes given here and in the New Testament are all Jewish orders of angels. Bousset further pointed out that the sort of petition which in the Jewish liturgy today follows the Kedusha is the same sort of exhortation to Israel as that in the text given above (§4).

Bousset thinks that 'Ισραὴλ δὲ ἡ ἐπίγειός σου ἐκκλησία is a Christian alteration from 'Ισραὴλ ἡ ἐξ ἐθνῶν. This is of course possible. But a glance at Leisegang's *Index*, s.v. ἐκκλησία, will show how commonly that word was applied by Philo to the Jewish race. We have already encountered a passage where the migration, the moving of the race out from Egypt into the Mystery, was the transformation of the race into an "ecclesia."[23a] Indeed it seems highly likely that early Christianity took that word for its collective community directly from Greek Judaism. The next phrase "taken out of the Gentiles" would most obviously seem to be a Jewish reference to the separation of the race away from the Gentiles. When Bousset examined the rest of the prayer its general Jewish character became quite clear, as well as the awkward way in which the Christian liturgists had adapted it to their purposes by inserting "Christ" in §6, and appending the Christian termination.

There may be some question as to whether the phrase "made through thy Logos" (§5) should be regarded as Christian. At first sight one would be tempted to italicize it as non-Jewish. But the certainly non-Christian "The Creator of creation by a Mediator, as the cause" (for why thus avoid mentioning Christ?), and the general theology of the fragments as it will emerge from the total collection, make it seem that the Logos reference was not Christian, and so was probably part of the original Jewish prayer.

In spite of the fact that the Kedusha appears in this prayer, and God is the "Giver of Laws" (§10), there is nothing in the rest of the prayer so specifically Jewish that a Christian *could not* have written it, though it is not the sort of prayer one can imagine a Second or Third Century Christian as

---

23. Bousset, p. 438, is indeed able to trace the prayer back in Judaism to the middle of the Fourth Century.

23a. See above, p. 205.

spontaneously writing. What this prayer, by the fact that it embodies the
Kedusha, does do is to make it certain that the Christians of the time were
borrowing from Jewish liturgy. Once this most difficult point is definitely
established, one can go on to investigate the extent of that borrowing with
a freer hand.

The next fragment is an even more idiomatically Jewish expression.

FRAGMENT II

Constitutiones VII, xxxvi, 1–6.

II 1. O Lord Almighty, Thou hast created the world by *Christ,* and hast
appointed the Sabbath in memory thereof, because that on that day
Thou hast made us rest from our works, for the meditation upon Thy
laws. Thou hast also appointed festivals for the rejoicing of our souls,
that we might come into the remembrance of that Sophia which was
created by Thee;[24] 2. *how he submitted to be made of a woman on our
account; He appeared in life, and demonstrated Himself in His baptism; how He that appeared is both God and man; He suffered for us
by Thy permission, and died, and rose again by Thy power: on which
account we solemnly assemble to celebrate the feast of the resurrection
on the Lord's day, and rejoice on account of Him who has conquered
death,*[25] *and has brought life and immortality to light.* For by Him
Thou hast led *the Gentiles* to Thyself for a peculiar[26] people, that is, the
true Israel,[27] beloved of God, the one that sees God.[28] 3. For Thou, O
Lord, broughtest our fathers out of the land of Egypt,[29] and didst deliver them out of the iron furnace, from clay and brick-making, and
didst redeem them out of the hands of Pharaoh, and of those under
him, and didst lead them through the sea as through dry land,[30] and
didst bear their manners in the wilderness,[31] and bestow on them all
sorts of good things. 4. Thou didst give them the Law or Decalogue,
which was pronounced by Thy voice[32] and written with Thy hand.
Thou didst enjoin the observation of the Sabbath, not affording them
an occasion of idleness, but an opportunity of piety, for their knowl-

24. Variant reading in d, θεοῦ γενηθείσης, shows Christian redaction in the interest of
orthodoxy. Sophia as "created" comes from Prov. viii, 22.
25. I Cor. xv, 55; II Tim. i, 10.   26. Deut. vii, 6.
27. Gen. xxxv, 10.
28. So the text as in Funk. For suggested emendation see the discussion below.
29. Deut. iv, 20.   30. Exod. xiv, 29.
31. Acts xiii, 18: a paraphrase of Deut. i, 31, which may have been a proverbial formula.
32. Exod. xx, 18.

edge of Thy power, and the prohibition of evils; having limited them as within an holy precinct for the sake of teaching them the joy of the hebdomad. On this account was there appointed one hebdomad,[33] and seven hebdomads,[34] and the seventh month, and the seventh year, and the cycle of these, which is the fiftieth year for remission,[35] 5. that men might have no occasion to pretend ignorance. On this account He permitted men every Sabbath to rest, that so no one might be willing to send one word out of his mouth in anger on the day of the Sabbath. For the Sabbath is the ceasing of the creation, the completion of the world, the inquiry after laws, and the grateful praise to God for the blessings He has bestowed upon men. 6. *All which the Lord's day excels, and shows the Mediator Himself, the Protector, the Lawgiver, the Cause of the resurrection, the First-born of the whole creation,[36] God the Logos, and man, who was born of Mary alone, without a man, who lived holily, who was crucified under Pontius Pilate, and died, and rose again from the dead. So that the Lord's day commands us to offer unto Thee, O Lord, thanksgiving for all. For this is the grace afforded by Thee, which on account of its greatness has obscured all other blessings.*

Bousset has called this a "Sabbatgebet." A Christian who would have written it *de novo* as it stands is inconceivable. The two main sections marked as Christian are obviously insertions. The latter one, after the praise of the Sabbath, weakly asserts that the Lord's Day is more important than the Sabbath. But only one quarter as much space as is devoted to the Sabbath is given to the Lord's Day, and of this small portion more than half is devoted to a brief creed. To say the least, the passage on the Lord's Day is an anti-climax, quite intelligible as a Christian appendix to the Jewish "Sabbatgebet," but unintelligible as the originally planned objective of the prayer.

The first large insertion is just as clearly extraneous to the original. The original prayer has referred to the creation of Sophia, and by identifying Christ with Sophia the Christian redactor has an opportunity again to put in some lines from the Creed and to mention the Lord's Day. The Christian has not noticed what Bousset has pointed out, that in identifying Christ with

33. That is a week of seven days. Cf. Lev. xxiii, 39 ff.; xxv.
34. The cycle of seven weeks.
35. This apparently represents the cycle of seven seventh years, that is forty-nine years, plus the previous cycles, seven months, seven weeks, seven days, which makes approximately fifty years.
36. Col. i, 15.

Sophia, specifically here a created being, he has fallen into a heresy, the representation of Christ as a created being, which he himself elsewhere is careful to deny. He certainly would not himself have spoken of κτισθεῖσα σοφία who was Christ, and one manuscript, written by a more observant Christian, has changed the κτισθείσης to γενηθείσης.

There is some problem in judging how much of the sentence given immediately after the first longer insertion (§20) is in its original form. The problem cannot be resolved finally, for we have no way of knowing whether this sentence went on immediately after the last Jewish sentence before the Christian insertion, or there were some other Jewish statements which originally stood between. Bousset suggests that by changing the αὐτοῦ to αὐτῆς, and so making the sentence refer to the Sophia just mentioned, there would be no need of supplying any intermediate material. But he also would change τὰ ἔθνη to ἡμᾶς, τὸν ἀληθινὸν Ἰσραήλ to τὸν Ἰσραήλ. That is, granting the change which makes the first phrase a reference to Sophia, he would make the section read: "For through her he has led us to Himself to be a peculiar people, Israel, the race beloved by God, the one that 'sees God.'" The last phrase is, however, so thoroughly Philonic,[37] indeed so reminiscent of the very heart of the Mystery, that I would keep the ἀληθινόν which he rejected, and make the sentence read: "For through her he has led us to Himself to be a peculiar people, the *true* Israel, that is the group that is beloved by God and 'sees God.'" For I see the passage as an expression of the inner mystic joys of Judaism. But this reading will depend for its justification upon the type of Judaism which the fragments as a whole are seen to reflect, and hence judgment must wait for the rest of the material.[38]

FRAGMENT III

Constitutiones VII, xxxvii, 1–3.

III 1. Thou who hast fulfilled Thy promises made by the prophets, and hast had mercy on Zion, and compassion on Jerusalem, by exalting the throne of David,[39] Thy servant, in the midst of her,[40] *by the birth of Christ, who was born of his seed according to the flesh,*[41] *of a virgin alone;* do Thou now, O Lord God, accept the prayers which proceed

37. Bousset recognized that this phrase was Philonic (p. 444, n. 2), but without the conception of the Mystery of the True Israel he did not see that it was intimately connected with the idea of the sentence as a whole. The phrase reappears below in Fragment X.

38. See below, p. 353.   39. Is. ix, 7.

40. Perhaps the words: "by exalting . . . her" are part of the Christian insertion, since, as Bousset points out (p. 446, n. 2), this is not a familiar expression in Jewish prayers. But on the whole I agree with him that it is Jewish.

41. Rom. i, 3.

from the lips of Thy people *which are of the Gentiles,* which call upon Thee in Truth,[42] as Thou didst accept of the gifts of the righteous in their generations. 2. In the first place Thou didst respect the sacrifice of Abel, and accept it as Thou didst accept of the sacrifice of Noah when he went out of the ark; of Abraham, when he went out of the land of the Chaldeans; of Isaac at the Well of the Oath; of Jacob in Bethel; of Moses in the desert; of Aaron between the dead and the living;[42a] of Joshua the son of Nun in Gilgal; of Gideon at the rock, and the fleeces, before his sin; of Manoah and his wife in the field; of Samson in his thirst before the transgression; of Jeptha in the war before his rash vow; of Barak and Deborah in the days of Sisera; of Samuel in Mizpah; 3. of David on the threshing-floor of Ornan the Jebusite; of Solomon in Gibeon and in Jerusalem; of Elijah on Mount Carmel; of Elisha at the barren fountain; of Jehoshaphat in war; of Hezekiah in his sickness, and concerning Sennacherib; of Manasseh in the land of the Chaldeans, after his transgression; of Josiah in Phassa; of Ezra at the return; of Daniel in the den of lions; of Jonah in the whale's belly; of the three children in the fiery furnace; of Hannah in the tabernacle before the ark; of Nehemiah at the rebuilding of the walls; of Zerubbabel; of Mattathias and his sons in their zeal; of Jael in blessings. Now also do thou receive the prayers of Thy people which are offered to Thee with gnosis, *through Christ in the Spirit.*

As Bousset remarks,[43] it is incredible that a Christian of the time when the *Apostolic Constitutions* was written could have based all his precedents for prayer upon this list of the Patriarchs down to the Maccabees, the last Jewish period of grace, and not gone on to mention the prayer or sacrifice of Christ or the achievements of the Apostles.

FRAGMENT IV

Constitutiones VII, xxxviii, 1–8.

1. We give Thee thanks for all things, O Master Almighty,[44] that Thou hast not taken away Thy mercies and Thy compassions from us; but in every succeeding generation Thou dost save, and deliver, and assist, IV

42. Ps. cxlv, 18.
42a. Numb. xvi, 48. On the mystic interpretation of this incident see *Wisd.,* xviii, 22–25; *Heres,* 201, and above, pp. 275 f.
43. p. 446.
44. For the Jewish origin of this phrase see Bousset's elaborate note, p. 446, n. 4.

and protect: 2. for Thou didst assist in the days of Enos and Enoch, in the days of Moses and Joshua, in the days of the judges, in the days of Samuel and of Elijah and of the prophets, in the days of David and of the kings, in the days of Esther and Mordecai, in the days of Judith, in the days of Judas Maccabeus and his brethren, 3. *and in our days Thou didst assist us through Thy great High-Priest, Jesus Christ Thy Son.* For He[45] has delivered us from the sword, and hath freed us from famine,[46] and sustained us; has delivered us from sickness, has preserved us from slander.[47] 4. For all which things do we give Thee thanks through *Christ,* who has given us an articulate voice to confess withal, and added to it a suitable tongue to be an instrument like a plectrum, and a proper taste, and an appropriate touch, and a sight for contemplation, and the hearing of sounds, and the smelling of vapours, and hands for work, and feet for walking. 5. And all these members dost Thou form from a little drop in the womb; and after the formation dost Thou bestow on it an immortal soul, and producest it into the light as a rational animal, even man. Thou hast instructed him by Thy laws, improved him by Thy statutes; and when Thou bringest on a dissolution for a while, Thou hast promised a resurrection. 6. Wherefore what life is sufficient, what length of ages will be long enough, for men to be thankful? To do it worthily is impossible, but to do it according to our ability is just and right. For Thou hast delivered us from the impiety of polytheism, 7. *and from the heresy of the murderers of Christ;* Thou hast freed us from erring ignorance; *Thou hast sent Christ among men, being the unique God; Thou hast made the Comforter to inhabit among us;* Thou hast set angels over us; Thou hast put the devil to shame; Thou hast brought us into being when we were not; Thou takest care of us when made; Thou measurest out life to us; Thou affordest us food; Thou hast proclaimed repentance. 8. Glory and worship be to Thee for all these things, *through Jesus Christ,* now and ever, and through all ages. Amen.

Here again is the series of heroes of old, ending precisely with the Maccabees, though in this case the Christian has not left it without the reference to Christ which the preceding prayer lacked. Bousset, as indicated in the

45. With the Christian interpolation out, "He" is naturally Judas Maccabeus. So Bousset takes it (p. 447). I suspect that the text was originally "they" with reference to the whole patriarchal succession, or "Thou" with reference to God.

46. Ps. xxxiii, 19.

47. Literally, "from an evil tongue." Cf. Ps. xxxi, 20.

text, thinks that the "He" who also delivered us from the sword, etc. (§3) is Judas Maccabeus. His reasoning seems not fully convincing on that detail. For an understanding of the passage the Christian interpolation is suggestive. In the list of heroes, though the text simply states that "Thou," that is God, "assisted us *in the days*" of each hero, the implication is that God "assisted us" *through the instrumentality* of each, a thought that is made clear by the interpolation, when the assisting "in our days" is done through the instrumentality of "the great High-Priest, Jesus Christ." If the original Jewish prayer did not specifically state that the assistance of old came through the priestly mediation of these men (who were or could be priests only in the mystic sense), the reader of the day so much understood the prayer that way that the Christian interpolator felt he was only carrying on the thought in bringing in the High-Priesthood of Christ. It will be seen that these heroes are many of them included in a list of "priests" in Fragment XI. If a definite reference to the priesthood of these heroes of old has been taken out by the Christian from the Jewish prayer, it may be that the Savior there was the Logos, and that that Logos was working to save Israel through the heroes. In that case the "He" (of §3) who "delivered us from the sword" etc., is the Logos, and the text would not need to be changed. Otherwise, instead of "He has delivered" the original probably read "Thou hast," etc.

A more tangible passage follows (§4) in which God is praised for having given men the different senses and the hands and feet. Bousset[48] follows Wendland in connecting this part of the prayer with a description of the proper way to pray given by Philo:

When thou givest thanks for an individual man, distribute thy thanksgiving in a rational way, not taking up the least and last details, but the main divisions, first body and soul out of which the man is constituted, then his logos, mind (νοῦς) and sense perception. For a thanksgiving for each of these individually it would not be unworthy for God to hear.[49]

It is apparent at once that the thanksgiving in the prayer before us would have seemed to go into somewhat too great detail for Philo, but it is precisely the sort of prayer he was accustomed to hear, and which he thought could be better composed as he suggested.

Bousset[50] has compared §7 with the following prayer from the Jewish Liturgy, one that comes immediately before the Kedusha de Sidra:

Blessed art Thou, our God, who hast made us to Thy honor, and hast separated us from the erring, and hast given us the Teaching of Truth, and hast planted within us eternal life.

48. p. 448.
50. p. 448.

49. *Spec.*, i, 211. See above, pp. 111 f.

The similarity is obvious and striking. Yet I find in the πεπλανημένη ἄγνοια a slight but definite indication of Hellenistic thought as contrasted with the normative Judaism of the modern prayer. "Thou hast separated us from the erring" is something quite different from "Thou hast freed us from erring ignorance." Philo has not exactly this phrase in combination, but does say that ἄγνοια is the cause of all sin,[51] the cause of halting progress and confusion in contrast to the knowledge which shows the mystic "way of Salvation."[52] Ignorance is the thing that maims the part of the soul which sees and hears.[53] Similarly Philo uses πλανᾶσθαι in various forms with reference to wandering from the mystic Road.[54] "Ignorance which makes us wander" is then specifically the phraseology for the type of reprobation distinctive, in Judaism, of the Mystery.

In some ways the most interesting Fragment of all is the following:

FRAGMENT V

Constitutiones VII, xxxiii, 2–7.

V 2. Our eternal Savior, the King of gods,[55] who alone art almighty, and the Lord, and God of all beings, and the God of our holy and blameless fathers,[56] and of those before us; the God of Abraham, and of Isaac, and of Jacob; who art merciful and compassionate, long-suffering, and abundant in mercy; to whom every heart is naked, and by whom every heart is seen, and to whom every secret thought is revealed: to Thee do the souls of the righteous cry aloud, upon Thee do the hopes of the godly trust, Thou Father of the blameless, Thou hearer of the supplication of those that call upon Thee with uprightness, and who knowest the supplications that are not uttered: for Thy providence reaches as far as the inmost parts of mankind; and by Thy knowledge Thou searchest the thoughts of every one, and in every region of the whole earth the incense of prayer and supplication is sent up to Thee. 3. O Thou who hast appointed this present world as a race course[57] in righteousness, and hast opened to all the gate of mercy, and hast demonstrated to every man by implanted knowledge, and natural judgment, and the admonitions of the Law, how the possession of riches is not everlasting, the ornament of beauty is not perpetual, our

51. Ebr., 160. 52. Jos., 183. 53. Ebr., 157.

54. E.g., Det., 10, 21; Cong., 108; Fug., 131. On the contrary it must be noted that the doctrines of a resurrection and of a personal devil in the prayer, while sufficiently Jewish, are not Philonic, though they were familiar in Hellenistic Jewry. IV Maccabees is sufficient evidence for the former, Wisd., ii, 24 for the latter.

55. Esther xiv, 12, LXX. 56. Exod. iii, 16. 57. I Cor. ix, 24.

strength and force are easily dissolved; and that all is vapour and vanity; and that only the good conscience of faith unfeigned passes through the midst of the heavens, and returning with truth, takes hold of the right hand of the joy which is to come. And withal, before the promise of the regeneration[58] is accomplished, the soul itself exults in hope, and is joyful. 4. For from the beginning when our forefather Abraham laid claim to the way of truth[59] Thou didst guide him by a vision, and didst teach him what kind of state this world is; and gnosis was the forerunner of his faith; and faith was the consequence of his gnosis.[60] For Thou saidst: "I will make thy seed as the stars of heaven, and as the sand which is by the sea-shore."[61] 5. Moreover, when Thou hadst given him Isaac, and knewest him to be like him in his character, Thou wast then called his God, saying: "I will be a God to thee, and to thy seed after thee." And when our father Jacob was sent into Mesopotamia, Thou showedst him *Christ,* and by him speakest, saying: "Behold, I am with thee, and I will increase thee, and multiply thee exceedingly."[62] 6. And so spakest Thou to Moses, Thy faithful and holy servant, at the vision of the bush: "I am He that is; this is my name for ever, and my memorial for generations of generations."[63] 7. O Thou great protector of the posterity of Abraham, Thou art blessed for ever.

Except for the identification of Christ with Jacob's dream of the Logos, an identification which Justin Martyr[64] shows was early made by Christians from Hellenistic Judaism, there is not a Christian syllable in this prayer. Christian authorship is unthinkable.

Bousset has discussed the prayer at length, but I find myself here disagreeing with him on many points. "The consciousness of faith unfeigned" (συνείδησις πίστεως ἀνύπουλος, §3) must, according to him,[65] be either a Christian interpolation or else faith in the "Stoic" sense. That it might be, as I think it is, faith in the Hellenistic Jewish sense has not occurred to him.

At the suggestion of Rahlfs he has pointed out that several words in this prayer reflect the terminology of the Aquila translation of the Old Testa-

58. παλιγγενεσία, the mystic transformation with which initiation culminates. See Frag. IX, 6.
59. τοῦ προπάτορος ἡμῶν Ἀβραὰμ μεταποιουμένου τὴν ὁδὸν τῆς ἀληθείας. The text is dubious.
60. This translation, "gnosis . . . gnosis," follows ms. a rather than the text as given by Funk, for reasons given below, p. 356.
61. Gen. xiii, 16; xxii, 17.
62. A composite of Gen. xxviii, 15 and Gen. xlviii, 4.
63. Exod. iii. 14, 15.
64. *Dialogue,* 58. See my *Theology of Justin Martyr,* Jena, 1923, pp. 142 ff.
65. p. 464.

ment.[66] Yet an investigation of the direct citations in the Fragment showed that in all but this one case, and that a paraphrase only reflecting Biblical terminology, the Septuagint was exclusively followed. Bousset and Rahlfs think then either that the Septuagint citations must have been put in later by the Christian redactor, or that the direct citations originally were given in the Aquila version, but were corrected by Jews or Christians after the composition of the prayer to make them accord with the Septuagint. Each of these suggestions has serious difficulties. The citations are too organically parts of the prayer to have been put in by a *Christian* who had altered the prayer as slightly as this prayer has been altered. Alterations of the direct citations from Aquila back to the Septuagint would seem to have been made by a Jew, since the prayer shows such slight evidence of Christian redaction. But what type of Jew would have been interested in turning back to the Septuagint? Obviously only a thoroughly Hellenized Jew. As a mere possibility I should suggest that the prayer originated in a normative Hellenistic milieu, from Jews using the Aquila translation. This normative prayer was then retouched by mystic Jews. The direct citations were put back into the Septuagint and the notion introduced that Jacob's vision was one of the Logos, along with other mystic notions. The language that came into the prayer from Aquila but not in the form of direct citation escaped the redactor. The Christians took the prayer from mystic Jews, as they seem to have taken the others in this group, and only changed the Logos to Christ.

Bousset goes on to a very interesting discussion of the ideas of the prayer, which he finds distinctly those of Hellenistic Judaism. To this we shall return in the general discussion of the prayers.

There is one more Fragment in this group, a group distinct in the *Constitutions,* which like the others is of Jewish origin.

FRAGMENT VI

Constitutiones VII, xxxiv, 1–8.

VI 1. Thou art blessed, O Lord, the King of ages,[67] who by *Christ* hast made the whole world, and by Him in the beginning didst reduce into order the disordered parts; who dividest the waters from the waters by a firmament, and didst put into them a spirit of life; who didst fix the earth, and stretch out the heaven, and didst accurately dispose the order of every creature. 2. For by Thy taking thought, O Lord, the world is beautified, the heaven is fixed as an arch over us, and is rendered

---

66. For details see Bousset, pp. 465 ff., and Lütkemann and Rahlfs in *Nachrichten von der k. Ges. d. Wissenschaft zu Göttingen,* Philol.-Histor. Klasse, 1915, Beiheft, pp. 29 ff.
67. I Tim. i, 17.

illustrious with stars for our comfort in the darkness. The light also and the sun were begotten for days, and the production of fruit, and the moon for the change of seasons, by its increase and diminutions; and one was called Night, and the other Day.[68] And the firmament was exhibited in the midst of the abyss, and Thou commandest the waters to be gathered together, and the dry land to appear.[69] 3. But as for the sea itself, who can possibly describe it, which comes with fury from the ocean, yet runs back again, being stopped by the sand at Thy command? For Thou hast said: "Thereby shall her waves be broken."[70] Thou hast also made it navigable for little and great creatures, and for ships. 4. Then did the earth become green, and was adorned with all sorts of flowers, and the variety of several trees; and the shining luminaries, the nourishers of those plants, preserve their unchangeable course, and in nothing depart from Thy command. But where Thou biddest them, there do they rise and set for signs of the seasons and of the years, compensating the work of men. 5. Afterwards the kinds of the several animals were created—those belonging to the land, to the water, to the air, and both to air and water; and the creative Sophia of Thy providence does still impart to every one a suitable providence. For as she was not unable to produce different kinds, so neither has she disdained to exercise a different providence towards every one. 6. And at the conclusion of the creation Thou gavest direction to Thy Sophia, and formedst a reasonable creature as the citizen of the world, saying, "Let us make man after our image, and after our likeness";[71] and hast exhibited him as the ornament of the world,[72] and formed him a body out of the four elements, but hadst prepared a soul out of not-being (ἐκ τοῦ μὴ ὄντος), and bestowedst upon him his five senses, and didst set over his sensations a mind as the conductor of the soul. 7. And besides all these things, O Lord God, who can worthily declare the motion of the rainy clouds, the shining of the lightning, the noise of the thunder, in order to the supply of proper food, and the most agreeable temperature of the air? 8. But when man was disobedient, Thou didst deprive him of the life which should have been his reward. Yet didst Thou not destroy him for ever, but laidst him to sleep for a time; and Thou didst by oath call him to a resurrection, and loosedst

68. Gen. i, 5.   69. Gen. i, 9.   70. Job xxxviii, 11.
71. Gen. i, 26.
72. κόσμου κόσμον. See Fragm. VII, 16. The phrase may well be an expression which we do not have elsewhere, meaning that man is created the microcosm.

the bond of death, O Thou reviver of the dead, *through Jesus Christ, who is our hope.*[73]

With this prayer Bousset elaborately compares the great "It is very meet and right" prayer of *Constitutions* VIII, which must be quoted at once:

FRAGMENT VII

Constitutiones VIII, xii, 6–27.

VII

6. It is very meet and right before all things to sing an hymn to Thee, who art the true God, who art before created things; from whom the whole family in heaven and earth is named;[74] who only art unbegotten, and without beginning, and without a ruler or a master; who alone standest in need of nothing; who art the bestower of everything that is good; who art beyond all cause and generation; who art alway and immutably the same; from whom all things came into being,[75] as from their origin. 7. For Thou art Gnosis, which hath no beginning, everlasting sight, unbegotten hearing, untaught Sophia, the first by nature, alone in being, and beyond all number; who didst bring all things out of not-being (ἐκ τοῦ μὴ ὄντος)[76] into being by Thy only[77] Son, but didst beget Him before all ages by Thy will, Thy power, and Thy goodness, without any agency, the only Son, God the Logos, the living Sophia, the first-born of every creature,[78] the angel of Thy great counsel,[79] and Thy High-Priest, but the King and Lord of every intellectual and sensible nature,[80] who was before all things, by whom were all things.[81] 8. For Thou, O eternal God, didst make all things by Him, and through Him it is that Thou vouchsafest Thy suitable providence over the whole world; for by the very same that Thou bestowedst being, didst Thou also bestow wellbeing: the God and Father of Thy only Son, who by Him didst make before all things the cherubim and the seraphim, the aeons and hosts, the powers and authorities,[82] the princi-

---

73. I Tim. i, 1.

74. Perhaps this is a Christian interpolation, but it is just as likely the source of the words in Ephesians iii, 15.

75. Cf. I Cor. viii. 6.　　　　　　　　　　76. See above, Frag. VI, 6 and below, §17.

77. Μονογενής *may* have come from John i, 14, 18. See below, p. 342.

78. Col. i, 15.　　　　　　　　　　79. Is. ix. 6, LXX.

80. A fairly frequent expression in this liturgy (see Bousset 435, n. 1) which vividly recalls Philo's distinctions in φύσις. See above, pp. 50 ff.

81. Cf. Col. i, 17.

82. Col. i, 16 is similar but not an exact parallel.

palities and thrones, the archangels and angels; and after all these, didst
by Him make this visible world, and all things that are therein. 9. For
Thou art He who didst frame the heaven as an arch,[83] and stretch it
out like the covering of a tent,[84] and didst found the earth upon nothing[85] by Thy will; who didst fix the firmament, and prepare the night
and the day; who didst bring the light out of Thy treasures, and on its
departure didst bring on darkness, for the rest of the living creatures
that move in the world; who didst appoint the sun in heaven to rule[86]
over the day, and the moon to rule over the night, and didst inscribe
in heaven the choir of stars to praise Thy glorious majesty; 10. who
didst make the water for drink and for cleansing, the life-giving air
for inhalation and exhalation, and for the affording of sounds, by
means of the tongue, which strikes the air, and the hearing, which co-
operates with the air, so that when speech comes into the hearing and
falls upon it, the hearing perceives it; 11. who madest fire for our consolation in darkness, for the supply of our want, and that we might be
warmed and enlightened by it; 12. who didst separate the great sea
from the land, and didst render the former navigable and the latter fit
for walking, and didst replenish the former with small and great living
creatures, and filledst the latter with the same, both tame and wild;
didst furnish it with various plants, and crown it with herbs, and beau-
tify it with flowers, and enrich it with seeds; 13. who didst establish
the great deep, and on every side madest a mighty cavity for it, which
contains seas of salt waters heaped together,[87] yet didst Thou every way
bound them with barriers of the smallest sand;[88] who sometimes dost
raise it to the height of mountains by the winds, and sometimes dost
smooth it into a plain; sometimes dost enrage it with a tempest, and
sometimes dost still it with a calm, that it may be easy to seafaring men
in their voyages; 14. who didst encompass this world, which was made
by Thee through *Christ,* with rivers, and water it with currents, and
moisten it with springs that never fail, and didst bind it round with
mountains for the immovable and secure consistence of the earth: 15.
for Thou hast replenished Thy world, and adorned it with sweet-smell-
ing and with healing herbs, with many and various living creatures,
strong and weak, for food and for labor, tame and wild; with the noises
of creeping things, the sounds of various sorts of flying creatures; with
the circuits of the years, the numbers of months and days, the order of

83. Is. xl, 22.   84. Gen. i; Ps. civ, 2.   85. Job xxvi, 7.
86. Gen. i, 16.   87. Job xxxviii.   88. Job xxxviii, 8; Jer. v, 22.

the seasons, the courses of the rainy clouds, for the production of the fruits and the support of living creatures. Thou hast also appointed the station of the winds,[89] which blow when commanded by Thee, and the multitude of the plants and herbs. 16. And Thou hast not only created the world itself, but hast also made man for a citizen of the world, exhibiting him as the ornament of the world (κόσμου κόσμον); for Thou didst say to Thy Sophia: "Let us make man according to our image, and according to our likeness; and let them have dominion over the fish of the sea, and over the fowls of the heaven."[90] 17. Wherefore also Thou hast made him of an immortal soul and of a body liable to dissolution—the former out of not-being (ἐκ τοῦ μὴ ὄντος), the latter out of the four elements—and hast given him as to his soul rational knowledge, the discerning of piety and impiety, and the observation of right and wrong; and as to his body, Thou hast granted him five senses and progressive motion: 18. for Thou, O God Almighty, didst by *Christ* plant a paradise in Eden, in the east, adorned with all plants fit for food, and didst introduce him into it, as into a rich banquet. And when Thou madest him, Thou gavest him a Law implanted within him, that so he might have at home and within himself the seeds of divine knowledge. 19. And when Thou hadst brought him into the paradise of pleasure, Thou allowedst him the privilege of enjoying all things, only forbidding the tasting of one tree, in hopes of greater blessings; that in case he would keep that command, he might receive the reward of it, which was immortality. 20. But when he disregarded that command, and tasted of the forbidden fruit, by the deceit of the serpent and the counsel of his wife, Thou didst justly cast him out of paradise. Yet of Thy goodness Thou didst not overlook him, nor suffer him to perish utterly, for he was Thy creature; but Thou didst subject the whole creation to him, and didst grant him liberty to procure himself food by his own sweat and labors, whilst Thou didst cause all the fruits of the earth to spring up, to grow, and to ripen. But when Thou hadst laid him asleep for a while, Thou didst with an oath call him to a restoration again, didst loose the bond of death, and promise him life by resurrection. 21. And not this only; but when Thou hadst increased his posterity to an innumerable multitude, those that continued with Thee Thou didst glorify, and those who did apostatize from Thee Thou didst punish. And while Thou didst accept the sacrifice of Abel as a holy person, Thou didst reject the gift of Cain the murderer of his

89. Job xxviii, 25.   90. Gen. i, 26.

brother, as an abhorred wretch. And besides these, Thou didst accept Seth and Enos, and didst translate Enoch: 22. for Thou art the creator of men, and the giver of life, and the supplier of want, and the giver of laws, and the rewarder of those that observe them, and the avenger of those that transgress them; who didst bring the great flood upon the world by reason of the multitude of the ungodly, and didst deliver righteous Noah from that flood in an ark, with eight souls,[91] the end of the foregoing generations, and the beginning of those that were to come; who didst kindle a fearful fire against the five cities of Sodom, and didst turn a fruitful land into a salt lake for the wickedness of them that dwelt therein,[92] but didst snatch holy Lot out of the conflagration. 23. Thou art He who didst deliver Abraham from the impiety of his forefathers, and didst appoint him to be the heir of the world, and didst discover to him Thy *Christ;* who didst aforehand ordain Melchizedek an high-priest for Thy worship; who didst render Thy patient servant Job the conqueror of that serpent who is the patron of wickedness; who madest Isaac the son of the promise, and Jacob the father of twelve sons, and didst increase his posterity to a multitude, and bring him into Egypt with seventy-five souls. 24. Thou, O Lord, didst not overlook Joseph, but grantedst him, as a reward of his chastity for Thy sake, the government over the Egyptians. Thou, O Lord, didst not overlook the Hebrews when they were afflicted by the Egyptians, on account of the promises made unto their father; but Thou didst deliver them, and punish the Egyptians. 25. And when men had corrupted the Law of Nature, and had sometimes esteemed the creation to be self-caused (αὐτόματον), and sometimes honoured it more than they ought, and made it the equivalent of Thee, the God of the universe, Thou didst not, however, suffer them to go astray, but didst raise up Thy holy servant Moses, and by him didst give the written Law for the assistance of the Law of Nature,[93] and didst show that the creation was Thy work, and didst banish away the error of polytheism. Thou didst adorn Aaron and his posterity with the priesthood, and didst punish the Hebrews when they sinned, and receive them again when they returned to Thee. 26. Thou didst punish the Egyptians with a judgment of ten plagues, and didst divide the sea, and bring the Israelites through it, and drown and destroy the Egyptians who pursued after them. Thou didst sweeten the bitter water with wood; Thou didst bring water out

91. Cf. I Pet: iii, 20. 92. Gen. xix; *Wisd.,* x, 6; Ps. cvii, 34.
93. Is. viii, 20, LXX.

of the sharp-hewn rock; Thou didst rain manna from heaven, and quails, as meat out of the air; Thou didst afford them a pillar of fire by night to give them light, and a pillar of cloud by day to overshadow them from the heat; Thou didst declare Joshua to be the general of the army, and didst overthrow the seven nations of Canaan by him; Thou didst divide Jordan, and dry up the rivers of Etham; Thou didst overthrow walls without instrument or the hands of man. 27. For all these things, glory be to Thee, O Lord Almighty. Thee do the innumerable hosts of angels, archangels, thrones, dominions, principalities, authorities, and powers, Thine everlasting armies, adore. The cherubim and the six-winged seraphim, with twain covering their feet, with twain their heads, and with twain flying, say, together with thousand thousands of archangels, and ten thousand times ten thousand of angels, incessantly, and with constant and loud voices, and let all the people say it with them: "Holy, holy, holy, Lord God of Sabaoth, heaven and earth are full[94] of His glory: be Thou blessed for ever.[95] Amen.

Here ends the Jewish prayer, or hymn, of Praise. It comes to a full stop with the Jewish Trishagion, and the Christian ritual of the *Constitutions* begins afresh to hymn the Christian story of redemption, culminating in the consecration of the Eucharistic elements.[96] The theme of this great Jewish prayer has been to hymn the giving of Natural Law to the Patriarchs, their great achievements in living according to it, and then the necessity of giving the written Law to assist Natural Law with ordinary men, that is to assist ordinary men in living according to Natural Law. It is interesting that the Christian hymn or prayer begins with what the Jewish prayer has not hinted, the failure of the Law of Moses as a supplement to Natural Law, which necessitated the incarnation of the Lawgiver, the source of Nature and Nature's Law, if man was to be saved. The Christian redaction of the original Jewish prayer has not included this idea, however, but has been content with representing Christianity with only an occasional διὰ Χριστοῦ, which may be outright insertion or, more probably, as throughout these prayers, the slight alteration of an original διὰ λόγου. It is clear that in §23 Abraham was in the original given a vision of the Logos, which here appears as Christ.[97]

94. Is. vi, 3.   95. Rom. i, 25.
96. In pp. 471–478 Bousset carefully analyzes this piece and finds it rather a compilation of Jewish prayers than a single prayer. His reasoning is to me not conclusive, but since he admits that all the material is Jewish it would take us too far afield to go into the matter. I have printed the prayer as a unit, not as begging, but as avoiding, a question at present irrelevant.
97. Justin Martyr shows how this conception of Hellenistic Judaism, the revelation of the Logos to Abraham, like that already found with Jacob (see above, p. 317, n. 64), was thus adapted by early Christianity. See my *The Theology of Justin Martyr*, pp. 29 ff.

According to the Jewish prayer, then, the Law of Moses supplemented the Law of Nature, which in itself was enough for the Patriarchs, in whom Natural Law was νόμος ἔμφυτος, obviously a verbal variant of Philo's νόμος ἔμψυχος.[98] Beyond this combination of implanted Law and written Law, according to the Jewish prayer, neither men nor the great choir of heaven felt obliged to look. With the giving of the Law of Moses and the settling of the Tribes in the Promised Land all the problems of creation seem to have been solved, so that everything can unite in the great Song of Triple Glory.

In his analysis of Fragments VI and VII Bousset[99] has published the Greek text of the two in parallel columns with the common words underlined. The similarities thus revealed make it beyond question that a common original lies behind the two. Yet it is clear that both prayers, as preserved in the *Constitutions* and translated above, while redactions of an original, are still Jewish redactions. In both of them the Christian element is, except possibly for the phrases which echo Pauline letters, the same wooden type of insertion that we have become accustomed to. Personally I am convinced, with Bousset,[100] that these or similar prayers are rather the source of Pauline phraseology than *vice versa*. To this question we must return. Both prayers seem longer and shorter recensions of the same type of prayer, to be used by Jews in more or less elaborate ceremonies. What the type of prayer is Bousset[101] has gone on to analyze, and discovered that it corresponds amazingly to another formula of prayer given by Philo himself:

When thou wishest, Oh mind (διάνοια), to give thanks to God for the creation (γένεσις) of the world, make your thanksgiving both for the whole and for its most important parts, as for the bodily members of a most perfect animal, such as for the heaven, sun, moon, planets, and fixed stars; then for the earth and animals and plants upon it; then for the sea and the rivers, those that rise from springs and those from the snow of the mountains, as well as for the things in the waters; then for the air and its changes.[102]

The pertinence of the parallel is at once apparent. Philo is giving the Gentiles instructions, both here and in the foregoing passage,[103] as to how

98. Literally the two terms express the same notion from slightly different angles. The Law could be said to have been "implanted" within the Patriarchs, or they themselves could be regarded as that Law become animate.
99. pp. 451 ff.   100. p. 469.
101. P. 461. Bousset took the suggestion from Wendland, in "Zwei angeblich christliche liturgische Gebete," by Reitzenstein and Wendland in *Nachrichten von d. Ges. d. Wissenschaften zu Göttingen* (Phil. Hist. Klasse), 1910, p. 332.
102. *Spec.*, i, 210. Cf. (with Wendland) *Spec.*, i, 97. This last seems to me not in point as a parallel. The priest is beseeching and thanking God in *behalf* of, *in the name* of, men and the parts of the cosmos: he is not thanking God for having created the world or its parts as in these prayers.
103. See above, p. 315.

to pray according to the standards of Greek Jewish usage, a usage which both these prayers clearly have preserved to us.

Bousset[104] has further discussed the references to the resurrection at the end of Fragment VI and in §20 of Fragment VII, and shown them to be Jewish statements of the sort quite to be expected from Jewish apocryphal tradition about Adam,[105] and the general belief of Jews in the resurrection. It is hard to think that a Christian could thus have discussed the resurrection without a reference to Christ other than the conventional Christian termination of Fragment VI.

The Christian who compiled the *Constitutions,* as Bousset has recognized,[106] lived in an environment where the Jewish baptism of proselytes was a vivid memory, if not a familiar practice. For the Christian compiler insists[107] that unless the prayer formula be said in baptizing a Christian, a formula which connects the rite with Christ's death and resurrection, Christian baptism is no more regenerative than Jewish baptism. With this fact before us, Bousset seems rather to understate than exaggerate the claims of the following to be taken from the rules for instructing a Jewish catechumen in preparation for initiation into the Jewish Mystery.

FRAGMENT VIII

Constitutiones VII, xxxix, 2–4.

VIII 2. Let him, therefore, who is to be taught the truth in regard to piety be instructed before his baptism in the Gnosis of the unbegotten God, *in the additional Gnosis*[108] *of His only begotten Son, in the assured acknowledgment of the Holy Ghost.* Let him learn the order[109] of the several parts of the creation, the sequence of providence, the tribunals of diverse legislation. Let him be instructed why the world was made, and why man was appointed to be a citizen therein; let him also know his own nature, of what sort it is; 3. let him be taught how God punished the wicked with water and fire, and did glorify the saints in every generation—I mean Seth, and Enos, and Enoch, and Noah, and Abraham and his posterity, and Melchizedek, and Job, and Moses, and Joshua, and Caleb, and Phineas the priest, and those that were holy in every generation; and how God still took care of and did not reject mankind, but called them from their error and vanity to the knowl-

---

104. p. 462.
106. p. 471.
105. See below, p. 349, n. 235.
107. *Constitutiones,* VII, xliv, 3.
108. It is interesting that the Christian redactor has shown that his addition is really such by using ἐπίγνωσις for the new material.
109. For Philo's emphasis upon the τάξις of creation, see *Opif.,* 13 ff.

edge of the truth[110] according to various seasons, reducing them from bondage and impiety unto liberty and piety, from injustice to righteousness, from death eternal to everlasting life. 4. Let him that offers himself to baptism learn these and the like things during the time that he is a catechumen.

Certainly no Christian ever wrote this as a program for catechetical instruction. Aside from the trinitarian embellishment at the first, the important thing set forth to be learned is the unbegotten God, His order of creation, and the judgment-seats of legislation. The catechumen is to learn how God glorified the Patriarchs and their spiritual successors. The whole body of specifically Christian teaching is represented only by "the like things," which phrase the Christian wrote, or understood, as a reference to the Christian Mysteries. But if Christian authorship is unthinkable, the type of Judaism from which the piece arose is obvious. Reference has frequently been made to Philo's care in instructing the Gentiles. Indeed the *Exposition* of Philo written for Gentiles is built up exactly on the outline of instruction given in this fragment. It begins with the account of the creation, whose purpose is to explain the nature of the unbegotten God, "the order of creation," and how God rules the world. Philo then goes on to the various forms of law-giving:[111] Natural Law to creation in the *De Opificio,* the same Law given immediately to the Patriarchs who were thereby "glorified," as described in the Lives of the Patriarchs; the giving of the Ten Commandments, and then the Special Laws. Through all this the other aspects of this program of catechetical studies are prominently stressed: the purpose of all creation in man's formation, and man as the Citizen of the World; the nature of man, psychologically and spiritually, and the character of his problem because of this nature; how we are called from error and vanity to knowledge of the truth, from slavery to liberty, from impiety to piety, from injustice to justice, and from eternal death to eternal life. The Patriarchs selected as "glorified" are, except Job, precisely those of Philo. How much the Christian has toned down the original we cannot say. But what is here is unmistakably the Judaism of the Mystery.

Another bit gives us a further glimpse into the initiation of the catechumen:

111. The phrase νομοθεσίας διαφόρου δικαιωτήρια is very obscure. Donaldson took it to mean, "The different dispensations of Thy laws." Possibly it refers to the different stages in the mystic ladder of legislation by each of which a man could be judged. That is, in Philo's group of Cities of Refuge, each city might be conceived as a δικαιωτήριον νομοθεσίας, a judgment seat, for to get the protection possible from each city the fugitive must conform to the standards of that city. A simpler explanation is that it refers to the two types of Law, the written and the natural implanted Law. See below, p. 350.

FRAGMENT IX

Constitutiones VIII, vi, 5–8.

IX 5. Let us all pray fervently unto God for the catechumens, that He who is good, He who is the lover of mankind, will mercifully hear their prayers and their supplications, and so accept their petitions as to assist them and give them those desires of their hearts[112] which are for their advantage, and reveal to them *the gospel of His Christ;* give them illumination and understanding, instruct them in the knowledge of God, teach them His commands and His ordinances,[113] implant in them His pure and saving fear, open the ears of their hearts, that they may exercise themselves in His Law day and night; 6. strengthen them in piety, unite them to and number them with His holy flock; vouchsafe them the laver of regeneration,[114] and the garment of incorruption, which is the true life; and deliver them from all ungodliness, and give no place to the adversary against them; and cleanse them from all filthiness of flesh and spirit,[115] and dwell in them, and walk in them,[116] by His *Christ;* bless their goings out and their comings in, and order their affairs for their good.[117] 7. Let us still earnestly put up our supplications for them, that they may obtain the forgiveness of their transgressions by their initiation, and so may be thought worthy of the holy Mysteries, and of permanent duration along with the saints. 8. Rise up, ye catechumens, beg for yourselves the peace of God through His *Christ,* a peaceable day, and one free from sin, and the like for the whole time of your life, *and your Christian death;* a compassionate and merciful God; and the forgiveness of your transgressions. Dedicate yourselves to the only unbegotten God, through his *Christ.* Bow down your heads and receive the blessing.

Bousset (p. 484) recognized the kinship of §5 with Fragment VIII, 6, and saw that all might well have been said to a Jewish initiate. But he did not claim the entire Fragment for Judaism as I am doing, probably because he had not the conception of the Jewish Mystery as I have expounded it. In view of that Mystery the Judaism of the Fragment as printed above is apparent. For the piece centers its thought in obedience to the commands and ordinances, the exercising of oneself in the Law day and night, while the refer-

112. Ps. xxxvii, 4.   113. Ps. cxix, 12.
114. Tit. iii, 5.   115. II Cor. vii, 1.
116. II Cor. vi, 16; Lev. xxvi, 12. On this section see below, p. 351.
117. Ps. cxxi, 8.

ences to Christ throughout are the wooden interpolations by now thoroughly familiar. On the whole I do not regard the phrase "laver of regeneration" as an insertion.[117a] "The garment of incorruption," suggests I Cor. xv, but this is different, for it is a garment put on, not at death, as in Corinthians, but at initiation. Certainly we are here presented with a formula for introducing initiates into a Jewish legalism, a process which is only possible by the "opening of the ears of their hearts"; in it they aspire to the garment of incorruption, true life. They are cleansed from the filth of body and spirit, obtain forgiveness for past sins, get illumination and understanding and permanent duration along with the saints. Such it is to be admitted to the Holy Mystery. It is notable that the blessing which is given following this Fragment is as thoroughly Christian as the preceding was Jewish. So, since the thought is throughout Jewish-Mystic, and we know that such Jews used baptism, I see no reason for regarding the "laver of regeneration" as a phrase foreign to them.

Another prayer is identified by Bousset[118] as Jewish and shown to be so close to parts of Fragment I as to require the assumption that both spring from a common Jewish original. But this prayer is no less clearly Jewish than the other Fragments:

FRAGMENT X

Constitutiones VIII, xv, 7–9.

7. O God Almighty, the true God, to whom nothing can be compared, who art everywhere, and present to all things, but art in nothing as a thing contained; and art not bounded by place, who art not grown old by time, nor bounded by ages; who art not deceived by words; who art not subject to generation, and wantest no guard; who art above all corruption, free from all change, and invariable by nature; who inhabitest light inaccessible;[119] who art by nature invisible, and yet art known to all reasonable natures who seek after Thee with a good mind, and art comprehended by those that seek after Thee with a good mind; the God of Israel, Thy people which truly see, *and which have believed in Christ:* 8. Be gracious to me, and hear me, for Thy name's sake, and bless those that bow down their necks unto Thee, and grant them the petitions of their hearts, which are for their good, and do not reject any one of them from Thy kingdom; but sanctify, guard, cover, and assist them; deliver them from the adversary and every enemy; keep

X

117a. See below, p. 351.
119. I Tim. vi, 16.

118. pp. 478 f.

their houses, and guard their comings in and their goings out.[120] 9. For to Thee belongs the glory, praise, majesty, worship, and adoration, *and to Thy Son Jesus, Thy Christ, our Lord and God and King, and to the Holy Ghost,* now and always, for ever and ever. Amen.

The Philonic character of this address to God needs no further exposition. It is interesting to note that Israel as the race that "sees God" reappears here as in Fragment II. God is here specifically conceived as "dwelling in unapproachable light." But again the expression is so essential a part of the type of deity being described that I feel like Bousset disinclined to regard it as a phrase from I Tim. vi, 16.

Bousset has rightly recognized the Jewish origin of the following prayer in view of its general parallels to the fragments already given, and especially to Fragment VII, 6 f. It is part of the prayer given in the *Constitutions* for the consecration of a Bishop:

FRAGMENT XI

Constitutiones VIII, v, 1–4.

XI 1. O Thou the great Being, O Master, Lord, God, the Almighty, who alone art unbegotten, and ruled over by none;[121] who always art, and art before the world; who standest in need of nothing in any way, and art above all cause and beginning; who only art true, who only art wise; who only art the most high; who art by nature invisible; whose gnosis is without beginning; who only art good, and beyond compare; who knowest all things before they are; who art acquainted with the most secret things; who art inaccessible, and without a superior; 2. the God and Father of Thy only Son, our God and Saviour; the Creator of the whole world by Him; whose providence provides for and takes the care of all; the Father of mercies, and God of all consolation;[122] who hath His seat on high[123] and yet lookest to the things below: 3. *Thou who didst appoint the rules of the church, by the coming of Thy Christ in the flesh; of which the Holy Ghost is the witness, by Thy apostles, and by us the bishops, who by Thy grace are here present;* Thou who hast foreordained priests from the beginning for the government of Thy people—Abel in the first place, Seth and Enos, and Enoch and Noah, and Melchizedek and Job; 4. who didst appoint

120. Ps. cxxi, 8.
121. I Tim. i, 17, ideological parallel; also Mat. xix, 17.
122. II Cor. i, 3.   123. Ps. cxiii, 5.

Abraham, and the rest of the patriarchs, with Thy faithful servants Moses and Aaron, and Eleazar and Phineas; who didst choose from among them rulers and priests in the tabernacle of Thy testimony; who didst choose Samuel for a priest and a prophet; who didst not leave Thy sanctuary without ministers; who didst delight in those whom Thou chosest to be glorified in.

The list of saints given here has become familiar from the foregoing Fragments. Here a new and striking element is added, that they all, including Abel, Seth, Enos, Enoch, Noah, Job, Abraham and the succeeding Patriarchs, and Moses, were *priests*. This is a list of *priests* that could have come only from the Mystery, by whose Judaism alone they were accounted such. I may hazard the suggestion that this prayer is taken from the consecration of a "priest," Presbyter, or hierophant in the Jewish Mystery. A more fitting prayer for such a consecration could hardly have been framed.

The following brief prayer is one for use in the cases of post-baptismal sinners who present themselves as penitents:

FRAGMENT XII

Constitutiones VIII, ix, 8–9.

8. Almighty, eternal God, Master of the whole world, the Creator and Governor of all things, who hast exhibited man as the ornament of the world,[124] *through Christ,* and didst give him a Law both naturally implanted and written, that he might live according to Law, as a rational animal; and when he had sinned, Thou gavest him Thy goodness as a pledge in order to repentance: Look down upon these persons who have bended the neck of their soul and body to Thee; for Thou desirest not the death of a sinner, but his repentance, that he turn from his wicked way and live.[125] 9. Thou who didst accept the repentance of the Ninevites, who willest that all men be saved, and come to the acknowledgment of the truth;[126] *who didst accept of that son who had consumed his substance in riotous living,*[127] *with the bowels of a father, on account of his repentance;* do Thou now accept of the repentance of

XII

---

124. κόσμου κόσμον, see Frag. VI, 6.   125. Ezek. xxxiii, 11.

126. We have met this phrase frequently. I Tim. ii, 1–5a is a liturgical call to, and instruction for, prayer quite in accord with these Jewish Prayers. The Christian element there begins at the identification of Christ with the μεσίτης θεοῦ. The preceding part seems a rehearsal of the typical Jewish Hellenistic call to prayer such as is here made familiar. Hence it seems that this statement is as likely to be original here as in I Tim.

127. Luke xv, 13, 20.

Thy supplicants: for there is no man that will not sin;[128] for if Thou,
O Lord, markest iniquities, O Lord, who shall stand? For with Thee
there is propitiation.[129]

Again we are struck by the fact that this prayer is thoroughly Jewish in
its philosophy of repentance rather than Christian. God, who revealed Himself to man through the two-fold giving of the Law, the νόμος ἔμφυτος and
the νόμος γραπτός, gave in addition, for the benefit of those who might slip
into sin, his ἀγαθότης. To this ἀγαθότης the penitents come as supplicants.
Of course this ἀγαθότης may be a reference to Christ, but it is in a strange
context, and is a still stranger form of reference to Christ for a Christian
to use. The mention of the two-fold Law so definitely points to the Mystery
that it is natural to look there for an explanation of the ἀγαθότης. Here at
once comes to mind the third City of Refuge, the Power of Divine Mercy,
the refuge that is next highest after the two cities of negative and positive
commands.[130] This conception is also based upon the mercy seat of the ark.
Is not the Goodness of God here the Power of Mercy of the Mystery? Read
in this sense the prayer is, except for the Christian interpolations, a consistent
document, consistent both with itself and with a known Jewish philosophy
of life.

Bousset[131] goes on to analyze a series of short morning and evening prayers
found in Constitutions, VIII, xxxv–xxxix. I quite agree that they are Jewish,
but they add so little to the foregoing that I do not print them. It is to be
noticed that in the prayer at VIII, xxxvii, 5, God again is represented as
creating man a reasonable animal (λογικὸν ζῷον) through His Sophia.

Other interesting material is still left, however. Of the following Fragment Bousset[132] prints as Jewish only the prayer of the "bishop" (§§4 f.). The
preceding exhortation of the "deacon" seems to me quite as Jewish as the
other, and I print both together:

FRAGMENT XIII

Constitutiones VIII, xli, 2–5.

XIII 2. Let us pray for our brethren that are at rest in Christ, that God, the
lover of mankind, who has received his soul, may forgive him every
sin, voluntary and involuntary, and may be merciful and gracious to
him, and give him his lot in the land of the pious that are sent into the
bosom of Abraham, and Isaac, and Jacob, with all those that have

128. I Kings viii, 46.
130. See above, pp. 252 f.
132. pp. 485 f.

129. Ps. cxxx, 3, 4.
131. pp. 483 ff.

pleased Him and done His will from the beginning of the world, whence all sorrow, grief, and lamentation are banished.[133] Let us arise, let us dedicate ourselves and one another to the eternal God, through that Logos which was in the beginning.[134] 3. And let *the bishop* say: 4. O Thou who art by nature immortal, and hast no end of Thy being, from whom every creature, whether immortal or mortal, is derived; who didst make man a rational creature, the citizen of this world, in his constitution mortal, and didst add the promise of a resurrection; who didst not suffer Enoch and Elias to taste of death; the God of Abraham, the God of Isaac, and the God of Jacob,[135] who art the God of them, not as of dead, but as of living persons:[136] for the souls of all men live with Thee, and the spirits of the righteous are in Thy hand, which no torment can touch;[137] for they are all sanctified under Thy hand:[138] 5. do Thou now also look upon this Thy servant, whom Thou hast selected and received into another state, and forgive him if voluntarily or involuntarily he has sinned, and afford him merciful angels, and place him in the bosom of the Patriarchs, and prophets, *and apostles,* and of all those that have pleased Thee from the beginning of the world, where there is no grief, sorrow, nor lamentation; but the peaceable region of the godly, and the land of the upright that is dedicated to Thee, *and of those that therein see the glory of Thy Christ; by whom glory, honor, and worship, thanksgiving, and adoration be to Thee, in the Holy Spirit, for ever. Amen.*

This material seems to me thoroughly Jewish. The emphasis upon the distinction between voluntary and involuntary offences against the law is one of the outstanding points which Philo has in common with normative Judaism,[139] but it was not a distinction that could have meant much to, or been useful for, a Christianity which had abandoned legalism. So I cannot imagine a Christian as the author of the prayer. For the character of the Judaism whence the Fragment came the quotation from *Wisdom* is significant.

This is the last of the Fragments which Bousset has selected as being defi-

---

133. Is. xxxv, 10.   134. John i, 1.   135. Ex. iii, 6.
136. Mat. xxii, 32. For my reasons for not indicating this as a quotation from Matthew, see below, p. 355.
137. *Wisd.,* iii, 1.
138. Deut. xxxiii, 3. Bousset stops here. The rest seems to me just as Jewish as the preceding.
139. On the distinction as made in normative Judaism see G. F. Moore, *Judaism,* I, 463. For Philo see *Fug.,* 85 f., where it is a distinction known only to initiates in the Mystery, together with the mystic salvation for *inadvertent* sinners offered by the Cities of Refuge as Powers (see above, p. 251).

nitely of Jewish origin. He has been very conservative, and left some room for doubt about a few, especially about Fragment XIII. He warns that all this liturgy in its Christian form may be a privately constructed liturgy of arbitrary character, and so be quite misleading if one leaps too quickly to generalizations about the influence of Jewish liturgy upon the Christian cultus. Into that problem we shall go more thoroughly in a later study. Here that question is of slight importance compared with the fact that, whether the *Christian* liturgist was working privately or officially, he has actually preserved for us very large remains from a Hellenistic Jewish liturgy, a liturgy which is inconceivable without an established sect that produced it for use.

Before going on to a closer study of the ideology of the Fragments three more must be quoted which seem to me to belong in the collection, but which Bousset, in his cautious first statement, did not consider.[140]

First is the prayer to be offered, according to the Christian order, immediately after participating in the Eucharist.

FRAGMENT XIV

Constitutiones VII, xxvi, 1–3.

XIV   1. *After the participation, give thanks in this manner:* 2. We thank Thee, O God and Father *of Jesus our Savior,* for Thy holy Name, which Thou hast made to inhabit among us; and that knowledge, faith, love, and immortality which Thou hast given us through Thy Son *Jesus.* 3. Thou, O Almighty Master, the God of the universe, hast created the world, and the things that are therein, by Him; and hast planted a Law in our souls, and beforehand didst prepare things for the convenience of men. O God of our holy and blameless fathers, Abraham, and Isaac, and Jacob,[141] Thy faithful servants; Thou, O God, who art powerful, faithful, and true, and without deceit in Thy promises.

In view of the other Fragments, the Jewish origin of this part of the prayer is as clear as the Christian inspiration of the rest, which I have not printed. The thanks to the God of Abraham, Isaac, and Jacob are here offered because He has given men his holy Name, has created the world, and planted a Law in men's souls, and is faithful in His promises. This was certainly a

140. Like Bousset (p. 488) I shall be content with merely mentioning the possibility that the great prayer of Manasseh (*Ap. Const.* II, xxii, 12–14) is a real Jewish prayer. It may also, from the context, be a free composition, so it is not here included.
141. Exod. iii, 16.

Jew's approach to God. The whole of the remainder of the prayer seems to me a Christian development built upon this typically Jewish opening.

The following is another Jewish *incipit* to a prayer. Its Judaism seems sufficiently attested by the fact that all the provision it knows for the soul is the Laws of God:

FRAGMENT XV

Constitutiones VIII, xvi, 3.

O Lord Almighty, our God, who hast created all things by *Christ,* and dost appropriately take care of the whole world by Him; for He who had power to make different creatures,[142] has also power to take care of them, according to their different natures; on which account, O God, Thou takest care of immortal beings simply by protecting them, but of those that are mortal by subordinate agency[143]—of the soul by the provision of Laws, of the body by the supply of its natural wants.

The whole reads perfectly as a Jewish prayer if one supply "Logos," in place of the "Christ" or, changing the genders, "Sophia."

The following, the last, seems again Jewish for its address to the God of Abraham, Isaac, and Jacob, and its general tone. It is interesting as one of the few cases where the original reference to creation through the Logos has not been changed by the Christian redactor to "Christ."

FRAGMENT XVI

Constitutiones VIII, xl, 2-4.

2. We give thanks to Thee, O Lord Almighty, the Creator of the whole world, and its Preserver, *through Thy only Son Jesus Christ our Lord* for the first-fruits which are offered to Thee, not in such a manner as we ought, but as we are able. 3. For what man is there that can worthily give Thee thanks for those things Thou hast given them to partake of? The God of Abraham, and of Isaac, and of Jacob, and of all the saints, who madest all things fruitful by Thy Logos, and didst command the earth to bring forth various fruits for our rejoicing and our food; who hast given to the duller and more sheepish sort of creatures food—herbs to them that feed on herbs, and to some flesh, to others seeds, but to us corn, as advantageous and proper food, and many other things—

---

142. *Wisd.,* vi, 8.   143. διαδοχῇ, literally "by succession."

some for our necessities, some for our health, and some for our pleasure. 4. On all these accounts, therefore, art Thou worthy of hymns of praise for Thy beneficence to all, *by Christ, through whom glory, honor, and worship be to Thee, in the Holy Spirit, for ever. Amen.*

The Jewish origin of these Fragments was made certain by Bousset's analysis, as well as their strong Hellenization. We have seen that Hellenistic Judaism was not a unit, for it was divided between the normative literalists and the allegoristic or mystic Jews. In the few comments on the Fragments made up to this point it is clear that they seem to me to be the product of specifically mystic Judaism, a conclusion which can be justified only by an analysis of the theology and general ideology of the Fragments themselves.

The doctrine of God is the one most fully represented. In as much as mystic Judaism was still Judaism, there were many conceptions of Deity, and terms of address to Him, that it had in common with normative Judaism. That God is the Almighty (παντοκράτωρ),[144] that he dwells on high,[145] that He is the Creator,[146] is holy,[147] the giver of Laws,[148] the only True, the only Wise, the only Good, the only Most High;[149] that He is compassionate,[150] cares for man,[151] hears supplications,[152] is without a superior,[153] knows the future,[154] and all secret things,[155] is omnipresent,[156] is ruled by no one,[157] —this is the God of Judaism of all kinds and ages. So Jews have from time immemorial prayed to "the God of our holy and blameless fathers, and of those before us; the God of Abraham, and of Isaac, and of Jacob."[158] But other descriptions of God than these are represented.

Fragment X, for example, addresses God as normative ritual cannot be conceived as doing. That address begins with the familiar "Oh God Almighty, the true God, to whom nothing can be compared," but goes on to phrases of quite a different sort. "Who art everywhere and present to all things, but art in nothing as a thing contained, who art not bounded by place."[159] This is an orientation of the Jewish doctrine of divine omnipres-

---

144. Frag. I, 1; V, 2; XVI, 2; etc. On this conception in normative Judaism, see G. F. Moore, *Judaism*, I, 374–380.

145. Frag. XI, 2.
147. Frag. I, 9.
149. Frag. XI, 1.
151. Frag. IV, 7; XIII, 2.
153. Frag. XI, 1.

146. Frag. I, 10; XI, 2; XII, 8; XV, 3.
148. Frag. I, 10; II, 4; XII, 8; XV, 3.
150. Frag. IX, 8; XI, 2.
152. Frag. V, 2.

154. Frag. XI, 1. God's knowledge of the future is the presupposition of all prophecy.
155. Ib., Frag. V, 2. Cf. G. F. Moore, *Judaism*, I, 373 f.
156. Frag. X, 7. On God's omnipresence in normative Judaism, see G. F. Moore, *Judaism*, I, 370.
157. Frag. XI, 1.
158. Frag. V, 2. Cf. XVI, 3; XIV, 3.
159. τοῖς πᾶσι παρὼν καὶ ἐν οὐδενὶ ὡς ἐνόν τι ὑπάρχων, ὁ τόποις μὴ περιγραφόμενος, §7.

ence with philosophical conceptions of space, primarily of the sort that distinguishes Philo from normative thought. G. F. Moore was quite right in denying any trace of philosophical interest in the normative doctrine of omnipresence.[160] But Philo would say:

God is not somewhere (που), for He is not contained (περιέχεται), but contains the universe (τὸ πᾶν); but that which came into being is in a place (ἐν τόπῳ), for it must itself be contained but not contain.[161]

The author of this Fragment was thus thinking, at least at this point, of the hellenized Deity of Philo. After denial of God's spatiality, the liturgist goes on to deny His temporality. "Who art not made old by time nor bounded by the ages" (ὁ αἰῶσιν μὴ περατούμενος). Philo also stresses the fact that, while God is the grandfather of time (since time is the son of the cosmos, and the cosmos of God), the category "future" has no application to God.

God has put the bounds (πέρατα) of the ages (τῶν χρόνων) beneath Himself. For the Life (βίος) of God is not time (χρόνος) but is the archetype and eternal pattern of time. And in eternity (ἐν αἰῶνι) there is no past nor future, but only present existence.[162] It is forbidden to say that God was not antecedent, or that He came into being at any time (ἀπό τινος χρόνου γενόμενον) or that He does not continue through all ages (διαιωνίζοντα).[163]

The next phrase of Fragment X explains that God is "not deceived by words," which does little to help identify the kind of Judaism implied. But immediately God is definitely hellenized again: "Who art not subject to generation, and wantest no guard." The contrast of God to everything that came by generation is too familiar in Philo to need elucidation.[164] It is because of this contrast that God is constantly ὁ ἀγένητος in Philo. That God is so self-sufficient as to need no guard seems only a fanciful variant of Philo's oft-repeated assertion that He is so self-sufficient that He needs nothing whatever.[165] The Philonic form of statement appears elsewhere three times in the Fragments.[166]

"Who art above corruption" (ὁ φθορᾶς ἀνώτερος), Fragment X continues. This description is likewise in the main line of the Mystery. The notion that this life because of its material associations, is corruption, and that salvation is putting off the corruptible to put on incorruption has appeared as one of the earliest Orphic motifs carried on in Hellenistic Judaism unbrokenly through Philo.[167]

160. *Judaism*, I, 371.
161. *LA*, iii, 51.
162. *Immut.*, 31 f.
163. *Dec.*, 58.
164. See e.g., *LA*, iii, 7, θεὸν καὶ γένεσιν, ἀντιπάλους φύσεις; *Heres*, 45.
165. See Leisegang's *Index*, p. 366, b, ll. 17–30.
166. Fragments, I, 9: οὗ ἀνενδεὴς ἡ ζωή; VII, 6: τὸν ἀνενδεῆ; XI, 1: ὁ παντὶ ἀνενδεής.
167. Cf. *Sib. Orac.*, Frag. 3, ll. 17, 34: ὃς δ' ἔστιν ζωή τε καὶ ἄφθιτον ἀέναον φῶς;

"Free from all change (ὁ τροπῆς ἀνεπίδεκτος) and invariable by nature (ὁ φύσει ἀναλλοίωτος)" are the next apostrophes. This is by no means a conception derived from the normative Judaism of the time, which has no hint in its tradition of the philosophic conception of God as "unchanging."[168] The conception does appear in such statements as that in James i, 17, "The Father of lights, with whom can be no variation (παραλλαγή), neither shadow cast by turning (τροπῆς ἀποσκίασμα)," but this, from the material discussed, is obviously a reflection of the Mystic Deity of Hellenistic Judaism.[169] Indeed the idea of "unchangeableness" is essentially foreign to the strongly personalized God of Palestine. But it appears again in the Liturgy,[170] and is one of the constants of the Mystery. According to Philo God is πρὸς ἀλήθειαν ἑστώς, while the beings "after Him" are subject to τροπὰς καὶ μεταβολὰς παντοίας.[171] No greater blasphemy could be committed than to suppose that the Unchanging changes (ἄτρεπτον τρέπεσθαι).[172] While unchangeableness is God's peculiar attribute, it also is the reward of the ultimate mystic attainment for man.[173]

The prayer continues with the phrase familiar in I Tim. vi, 16, "Who inhabitest light inaccessible" (ὁ φῶς οἰκῶν ἀπρόσιτον). The foregoing phrases about the immutability of God appeared very close to James i, 17. Yet it is a more likely hypothesis that James drew upon a source similar to this prayer than that the author or redactor of the prayer had paraphrased the New Testament passage.[174] Immediately after it in the Prayer comes this phrase which is exactly similar to a phrase in quite another New Testament writing. Possibly both are the work of the Christian editor, who paraphrased one passage and quoted the other exactly. But that is not a necessary conclusion. For myself I would see the Timothy passage as a reflection of this very

V, 497: θεὸν ἄφθιτον ἐξυμνοῦντες. See also *Wisd.*, ii, 23: ὅτι ὁ θεὸς ἔκτισεν τὸν ἄνθρωπον ἐπ' ἀφθαρσίᾳ. Philo protests that it is a travesty to represent the material world as ἄφθαρτον and ἀγένητον, *Som.*, ii, 283. Ἀφθαρσία is ἀδύνατον ανθρώπῳ, at least for the herd, though the rare men in the Mystery may attain it: *Mut.*, 210, 213. Yet it is a quality of the soul which the soul regains when freed from the body and restored to its original condition, *Som.*, i, 181. Such was Abraham's experience at death, *Sac.*, 5. Sophia, the Mystery, further teaches that those who cleave to God have ἀφθαρσία here and now, while all other men are dead, *Fug.*, 56. So ἀφθαρσία is the mystic goal, *Som.*, i, 218. For Philo's extensive use of the word in these ways see Leisegang's *Index, s.vv.* ἀφθαρσία and ἄφθαρτος. The Hellenistic Jewish treatment of ἀφθαρσία is so consistently Orphic that it is not surprising to find it attributed to God in the Orphic fragment quoted by Clem. Alex., *Stromata*, V, xiv (ed. Stählin, II, 410, 19 ff.) (Kern, *Orph. Frag.*, Frag. 248): ἄφθιτον, ἀθάνατον, ῥητὸν μόνον ἀθανάτοισιν.

168. Such passages as Ps. xv, 4, Mal. iii, 6, are not philosophical in their import.

169. Neither can this particular prayer be represented as the direct literary source of James, nor James of the prayer. Yet the ideas are so closely parallel that the most likely assumption is that the phrase came to James from another such piece of Hellenistic Jewish Liturgy.

170. Frag. VII, 6: God is ὁ πάντοτε κατὰ τὰ αὐτὰ καὶ ὡσαύτως ἔχων.

171. *Mut.*, 57. Cf. *Opif.*, 22, 151.

172. *Immut.*, 22.

173. *Post.*, 28.

174. See note 169.

prayer, or of a similar one, since the ideology is not essentially Christian in Timothy, while it is entirely in place as a part of the prayer's general reproduction of the ideology of the Mystery. True, God as Light does appear in the New Testament. But the conception there is definitely Hellenistic, no part of normative Judaism or Palestinian Christianity. Yet granted for the moment that the phrase in Timothy did not itself come from such a piece of Hellenistic Jewish liturgy as this, it is hard to think that the expression in the Fragment has come from Timothy. The general method of the Christian redactor is obvious and clumsy enough. There is no attempt to alter the fundamental Judaism of the prayers by any method other than the crudest sort of casual insertion of references to Christ or bits of Christian creed. Had the redactor wanted to make the God here being addressed into the Christian God he certainly would not have done so simply by inserting such phrases as that God inhabits light inaccessible. On the other hand the phrase is entirely appropriate and germane as a part of the context, an apostrophe of God in purely Hellenistic Jewish concepts, concepts in which we have seen that the light figure for God played not only an important but an essential part. However the phrase came to Timothy, then, I think it a definite part of the original Jewish prayer here.

Fragment X goes on to state that while God is τῇ φύσει ἀόρατος, yet He can be known (ὁ γνωστός) and mystically apprehended (ὁ καταλαμβανόμενος) by reasoning natures (λογικαῖς φύσεσιν) who seek Him μετ' εὐνοίας. The invisibility of God is a concept found three times in the New Testament,[175] not once in our records of normative Judaism up to that time. According to the Old Testament a direct view of God was an experience so overpowering that it would be fatal to a human being; but that is a very different thing from φύσει ἀόρατος. It appears twice in other Fragments[176] and Philo is full of the notion.[177] God is ὁ ἀόρατος,[178] and the phrase so prevalent from the Orphic mystery, "Himself invisible He yet sees all things,"[179] is itself found in Philo.[180] That this invisible God is to be apprehended by reason or reasonable beings is again Philonic, though probably originally Orphic. Philo has a detailed explanation for the benefit of the mystic initiates, οἱ Μωϋσέως γνώριμοι, of how man can get the apprehension (ἔννοιαν ἔλαβεν) of the invisible God. The explanation is in the fact that man is created in the image of God, that is that the human mind (νοῦς) is an undivided part, an extension, of the divine soul (ψυχή).[181] Such a vision as he here describes is not, of course, possible for all men, but only for one

175. Col., i, 15; I Tim. i, 17; Heb. xi, 27.   176. Frags. I, 9; XI, 1.
177. Post., 15; Mig., 183; Som., i, 72; Dec., 120; Spec., i, 46; iv, 31; Legat., 290, 318.
178. Sac., 133; Mut., 139; Spec., i, 20.
179. See above, pp. 280, 284.
180. Opif., 69.   181. Det., 86–89.

who has made the great change from τὸ κακόνουν εἰς εὔνοιαν.[182] The phrase here is only one of many to express repentance, and Philo does not elsewhere use the word εὔνοια to describe the state of mind prerequisite for mystic achievement: But it is clear that the term was acceptable to him to express that prerequisite, as here in the Liturgy.

The apostrophe of Fragment X closes with calling upon God as "The God of Israel, Thy people who truly see," that is, the God of the Mystery.

Discussion of this one Fragment's address to God has been thus extended to show that the thought of God in terms of the Mystery is not sporadic, but is the fundamental approach to God. Conceptions common to normative Judaism and the Mystery are found, but none that are distinctively normative, while whole prayers are based upon purely mystic notions, and at least some distinctively mystic elements are absent from none of them. God is ὁ μόνος ἀγέννητος,[183] ὁ πάσης αἰτίας καὶ γενέσεως κρείττων,[184] "the Lord God of γνῶσις," "whose γνῶσις is without beginning,"[185] "The Father of Sophia,"[186] "inaccessible" (ἀπρόσιτος).[187] One Fragment has it: "For Thou art Gnosis which hath no beginning, everlasting sight, unbegotten hearing, untaught Sophia, the first by nature, alone in being, and beyond all number."[188]

The God of these prayers is thus the God of Philo and the Mystery.

With God the Fragments give us two formulations of His radiating powers, the Logos and the Sophia. That the two are ultimately identical appears in the following, the fullest passage describing the conception:

Thou didst beget Him, Thy only Son, before all ages by thy will, Thy power, and Thy goodness, without any agency, the only Son, God the Logos, the living Sophia, the first born of every creature, the angel of Thy great counsel, and Thy High-Priest, but the King and Lord of every intelligible and sensible nature, who was before all things, by whom are all things.[189]

The hymn goes on to describe creation by the Logos, but we must stop to examine this passage. The Philonic character of each phrase cannot be attested by exact parallels, though many of them are Philonic. So there is no

---

182. *Som.,* ii, 108. See the context.   183. Frag. VII, 6. Cf. VIII, 2; XI, 1.
184. Frag. XI, 1.
185. Frag. I, 9. The "Lord God of knowledge," κύριος θεὸς γνώσεων (I Sam. ii, 3), meant something to the Greek reader, as this passage shows, that the Hebrew original did not suggest. The original psalm meant simply that God knows all things. The change of meaning, like so many in the LXX, seems a deliberate attempt to put mystic meaning into the original text.
186. Frag. I, 10.
187. Frag. XI, 1. Cf. Philo, *Post.,* 169. The conception, if not the term, is originally Orphic, for the Orphic original of Aristobulus (see above, pp. 279 f.) enlarges at considerable length on how God is shut off from men on His throne.
188. Frag. VII, 7.   189. Frag. VII, 7.

exact parallel to the statement that God begat the Logos, though Philo frequently calls the Logos the "first begotten Son,"[190] and God the "Begettor of all things."[191] Philo does not state, since he does not describe the begetting of the Logos, that God begat Him without a mediator. But since to him the Logos is the great mediator by which or whom God began creation and then created everything else, it is quite in harmony with his thought that the first begetting, the projection of His power in the form of the Logos, should be "without mediation." True in some passages of Philo the Logos follows Female Principle mythology and is the son of God by Sophia. But we have seen that this is not an essential part of Philo's thinking, since Sophia and the Logos were for him only different formulations of the same concept, and were really identical.[192] That the Logos was begotten before all things, and before all ages, is implied in the fact that according to Philo the Logos was πρωτόγονος υἱός, and that all things were created by the instrumentality of the Logos, who must thus have been begotten before them. Since time began only with the creation of the world, was a "son" of the material world, the Logos must have been begotten in the "time" or eternity before time, that period which Philo calls, as here, ἐν τῷ πρὸ αἰῶνος.[193] The phrase πρωτότοκος πάσης κτίσεως seems only a variant of Philo's πρωτόγονος.

The Logos as θεός without the article is familiarly Philonic.[194] He is the "angel of thy great counsel," a phrase from the Septuagint of Is. ix, 6. Philo frequently calls the Logos the Angel or Archangel of God,[195] so that the conception is quite in harmony with his thinking. But the phrase here, if it is not a Christian interpolation to link the passage with one of the favorite "Messianic" statements, comes from a Hellenistic Jew who drew upon the prophets for phraseology as Philo preferred not to do. The Logos as the High-Priest in Philo has been so much discussed that further demonstration of its place in his thinking is unnecessary. The Philonic character of the thought of the Logos in the Fragment is fully attested by the statement that the Logos is "King and Lord of every intelligible and sensible nature." The division of reality into ἡ νοητὴ φύσις and ἡ αἰσθητὴ φύσις is conspicuously in accordance with his thought,[196] and the Logos as King and Lord is likewise familiar.[197]

190. E.g., *Agr.*, 51; *Conf.*, 146: πρωτόγονος.

191. *Heres*, 36, 157. God is ὁ γεννήσας πατήρ (*Cher.*, 23) (see Leisegang's *Index, s.v.* γεννᾶν, 1, ὁ θεὸς γεννᾷ).

192. ἡ [σοφία] δέ ἐστιν ὁ θεοῦ λόγος, he flatly says in one passage, *LA*, i, 65. Philo says that the Logos is the source of Sophia, ὁ λόγος σοφίας ἐστὶ πηγή (*Fug.*, 97) and again that the Logos flows from Sophia, its source, like a river (*Som.*, ii, 242). Both of these statements are only figurative, since Sophia was identical with the Logos. So more accurately Philo says ὁ θεὸς πηγὴ λόγου (*Post.*, 69; *Det.*, 82).

193. *Mut.*, 12.   194. See the often quoted passage, *Som.*, i, 229.

195. As in *Mut.*, 87; *QE*, ii, 13.   196. See above, pp. 50 ff.

197. ποιμὴν ⟨καὶ⟩ βασιλεύς, *Mut.*, 116; ὁ δίοπος καὶ κυβερνήτης τοῦ πάντος λόγος θεῖος, *Cher.*, 36; cf. *Mig.*, 67.

The impression that the passage leaves as a whole is that it is definitely in accord with the thought of Philo, but shows no signs of being drawn from Philo himself, since the phraseology is so often different from his. It is the product of other Jewish "initiates." The impression grows as one goes on to the description of creation through the Logos. The grades of angels, as will be seen,[198] appear there in a way impossible for Philo. Thus far Isaiah has been drawn upon, and πρωτότοκος substituted for Philo's πρωτόγονος. Have we then a Jewish statement at all, or a Christian one, since the Logos is here also μονογενής as in John i, 18, is the High-Priest as in Hebrews, is ὁ πρὸ πάντων as in Col. i, 17, πρωτότοκος πάσης κτίσεως as in Col. i, 15, is δι' οὗ τὰ πάντα as in I Cor. viii, 6? Any of these phrases, it must at once be admitted, may have been introduced by the redactor. Indeed the phrase μονογενὴς υἱός may come from the Fourth Gospel, since that was a common reading of the passage in the Fourth Century,[199] and Funk may be right in regarding υἱὸν μονογενῆ, λόγον θεόν as a direct reflection of the Johannine Logos passage. There is no part of the Jewish liturgy that would be so apt to be "adapted" by the Christian redactor as the Logos passages. We have seen that many of the Logos references, διὰ λόγου or λόγῳ have been changed to διὰ Χριστοῦ or Χριστῷ. The Logos passage we are considering escaped with at least relatively slight emendation perhaps because the incarnation was to be described in the prayer intended immediately to follow this one. The other terms which have New Testament parallels are all thoroughly Philonic in meaning, and except for the two phrases in Colossians, represent a wide scattering of sources. Yet while Christian editing of the Logos passage is to be expected, the sort of editing before us is not what we should have anticipated from a Christian. For if these phrases are additions or substitutions (as of μονογενής for an original πρωτόγονος) it is amazing that an editor has done so much without putting in a single phrase that would make the passage distinctively Christian, particularly since the editor (or editors) has shown no finesse at all in his blunt insertion of Christian material elsewhere. For even μονογενής simply describes the Logos as a unique being, and we have seen that the word was used in *Wisdom,* apparently from the original Orphic usage.[200] With μονογενής in its proper sense Philo, like *Wisdom,* could have had no difficulties whatever. Whether the passage stands now as it was originally written cannot, it seems, be positively affirmed or denied. But this much can be said: the Logos as here presented is still quite in accord with the Jewish Mystic Logos, and for all the possibility of

198. See below, p. 344.
199. See note to John i, 18 by W. Bauer in *Handbuch zum Neuen Testament* (1912). On μονογενής see J. Grill, *Untersuchungen über die Entstehung des vierten Evangeliums,* I (1902), pp. 77 f.; A. Aall, *Geschichte der Logosidee,* II (1899), pp. 120 f.
200. *Wisd.,* vii, 22. See above, pp. 18, 272 f.

insertion of phrases from Christian documents, has not in any way been Christianized. The more natural assumption seems then to be that the Christian redactor has not altered the original Hellenistic Jewish Logos passage, and that the New Testament parallels are to be more easily understood as drawn from such a source as this, than as themselves the source of the statements here.

Other passages on the Logos are of less significance. Fragment I, 5 f., speaks of the Logos as the Creator, and apparently went on to say, though "Logos" becomes "Christ," that as a result one should pray to God through the Logos. Of this last we cannot be certain. Fragment XIII, 2, speaks of dedicating oneself to God through the Logos which was in the beginning (διὰ τοῦ ἐν ἀρχῇ λόγου). Again there is the difficult problem of knowing whether this is an originally Hellenistic Jewish phrase, or a reflection of the Fourth Gospel. There is no reason why it could not have been Jewish, since Harris is certainly right in seeing the Sophia who was ἐν ἀρχῇ as the ultimate ancestor of the language of the Prologue,[201] and the similarity to Philo's use of ἀρχή has been long familiar.[202] Yet the fact that the prayers have undergone a Christian revision makes it always possible that such a phrase is a later insertion.

On the whole, then, the Logos passages are for our purpose quite disappointing. Nothing is said of the Logos to which Philo would not have agreed. There is no hint, except in credal insertions, of anything resembling a trinitarian treatment of the conception, or of any personalizing of it beyond what Philo could himself have allowed. Yet it must be said that there is nothing about the Logos that any Christian might not have written, while New Testament phrases are quite abundant. What makes me confident that the Logos passages are almost entirely in the form in which a Hellenistic Jew originally wrote them is the fact that their meaning for Christianity is as indirect, their vagueness as strange, as their meaning and formulation are direct and natural for the Mystery. But more distinctive material will again appear in connection with other aspects of the theology of the prayer.

Sophia in the Fragments is the daughter of God.[203] She is "creative" (ἔντεχνος), and dispenses, like the Logos,[204] the Providence of God, giving to each type of created being the right sort of providence. In the creation of man, when God said, "Let us make," he was addressing Sophia.[205] She was herself "created" (κτισθεῖσα) by God, and knowledge of her is the objective of the Jewish festivals.[206]

These statements suggest the Mystery. To call Sophia the daughter of God

201. Prov. viii, 22. R. Harris, *The Origin of the Prologue to Saint John's Gospel*, 1917, p. 4.
202. J. Grill, *Untersuchungen über die Entstehung des vierten Evangeliums*, I (1902), p. 106.
203. Frag. I, 10.   204. Frag. VII, 8.
205. Frag. VI, 5 f.; VII, 16.   206. Frag. II, 1. Cf. Prov. viii, 22.

goes further than Proverbs, while that she is the vehicle of God's providence and the objective of the festivals goes quite beyond what we find about her in normative Judaism. The fact that Sophia and the Logos were both so important as to appear in the very prayers of the group shows that much more must lie behind these scattered phrases than one would dare to try to formulate. The thinking of a group must very thoroughly have solidified around an idea before it can find its way into formal liturgy like this.

Beneath the Logos-Sophia, the liturgy makes clear, were the angelic hosts. The Logos[207] or the Sophia,[208] as Creator, began, before actual creation (πρὸ πάντων) to act as the medium for the making of cherubim and seraphim, the aeons and hosts, the powers and authorities, the principalities and thrones, the archangels and angels.[209] This statement follows the somewhat detailed description of the Logos that has been discussed, where New Testament phraseological parallels, especially parallels to Colossians i, 15, 17, appeared.[210] It is therefore of interest to note that Funk marks "authorities, principalities, and thrones" (ἐξουσίας, ἀρχάς τε καὶ θρόνους) as a quotation from Col. i, 16: ἐν αὐτῷ ἐκτίσθη τὰ πάντα ἐν τοῖς οὐρανοῖς καὶ ἐπὶ τῆς γῆς, τὰ ὁρατὰ καὶ τὰ ἀόρατα, εἴτε θρόνοι εἴτε κυριότητες εἴτε ἀρχαὶ εἴτε ἐξουσίαι. The similarity of the two is admittedly great. But if the Prayer is here an expansion of the Colossians passage, why did the author omit the κυριότητες, since he was not content with the Colossians list anyway, and more than doubles the number of types of heavenly beings named by the author of the Epistle? Furthermore it is obvious that the liturgical list is definitely graded by rank downwards, while the list in Colossians reverses the order. It is clear that the liturgist had another list of the heavenly beings which he is following, one that did not contain the κυριότητες, but did contain the other three which also appear in Colossians. The same conclusion seems to me to be true for two other lists. The list in Fragment I, 3, after the cherubim and seraphim of the Kedusha, names archangels, thrones, dominions, principalities, authorities, and powers. The orders named between the archangels and powers are exactly those of Colossians, yet the list as a whole is not from Colossians. The complete list appears, in ascending order, in Fragment VII, 27. Obviously the Colossians list is only an excerpt from the accepted angelic hierarchy of Hellenistic Judaism. Such a list is preserved, in the order of Colossians, but complete, in II Enoch xxi, 1.

The presence of these heavenly beings in the liturgy presents one of the most interesting divergencies from Philonic Judaism. Philo, from his Sadducean background, conspicuously omits all this type of angelology,[211] and

---

207. Frag. VII, 8; I, 5.   208. Frag. VI, 5.

209. Frag. VII, 8. Unfortunately the fragments give us no indication of the function of these beings other than to act as a heavenly choir singing praises.

210. See above, p. 342.   211. See above, p. 79.

simplifies the Light-Stream by restricting it to the Logos and the Powers. Angels do appear casually, but only as logoi, temporarily specific manifestations of the Stream. Τὰ ἀόρατα are to him τὰ νοητά, not specifically an angelic choir. It is of great interest to see that the Mystery had apparently great variety of details. The fundamental conceptions of God, the Logos, Sophia, and the Stream, of man, the world, and salvation, of the Law and the Patriarchs, will appear quite the same in the Liturgy as in the Hellenistic Jewish sources we have been discussing. But as Philo so definitely follows what we know of the Sadducean tradition about angels, personal immortality, personal liberty, and the unique authority of the Pentateuch, it is highly likely that other Jews would conform just as closely to the peculiar Pharisaic positions, without being in general restricted to the Pharisaism of Palestine for their ideology any more than Philo was restricted to the thought world of the Palestinian Sadducee. From this point of view what we may call "Pharisaic" Hellenistic Judaism would use the Psalms and Prophets as Philo did not, would accept the Pharisaic angelology, determinism, and aspiration for personal immortality, while still, like Philo, taking these peculiar sectarian doctrines and incorporating them within Mystic Judaism. The doctrine of determinism does not happen to appear in the liturgical fragments we have, possibly because determinism was not, in spite of Paul's authority, generally popular in the Church before Augustine (or after him either for that matter), and so such possible passages of the original liturgy would not have been preserved by the Christian excerptor. But whether the Jewish liturgy originally reflected determinism or not, it is clear that, in distinction to Philo's Sadducean formulation of the Mystery, the liturgy has the other Pharisaic points of view. Here we may learn then, I believe, something of what it meant for a Hellenistic Jew to be a Pharisee.

After the creation of the heavenly choir, God through the Logos[212] went on to create the visible world. In the long passage describing this event, Fragment VII, 9–15, the order of creation is: Heaven is stretched as a tent; the earth is made and founded upon nothing; then come the firmament, night and day, light and shade, the sun, the moon, and the choir of stars to hymn God's majesty. So far the Fragment is in general following the first chapter of Genesis. But there are interesting departures. That creation should begin with heaven, then earth, then the "firmament," which in Genesis is itself heaven, and here is apparently a Biblical echo without meaning, is itself interesting. But the Greek cosmologies have already shown their influence in that light and darkness, day and night, are created after the heaven and earth, and not before, as in Genesis. Obviously night and day, light and dark, are in the author's mind only to be conceived in connection with what is next named, the creation of sun, moon, and stars. Also it is interesting that

212. Frag. I, 5: "All which creatures are made by Thy Logos."

there has entered the Platonic notion of the stars as a choir, a reflection of the music of the spheres described in the Timaeus.[213] There are other phrases, as indicated in the footnotes to the text above, from Job and the Psalms.

The story of creation in Fragment VII now takes a new turn. Creation of the earth seems to have satisfied the author for the element that goes by that name. So he goes on to describe the creation of the other three elements, water, air (§10) and fire (§11). The purpose of each is explained from an anthropocentric point of view. Water is for drink and cleansing; air to give life by breathing and to be the vehicle of sound in speech; fire to give men warmth and light. With the creation of the four elements described, the first stage in almost all Greek accounts of material creation, the author can now return to the Biblical separation of land from sea. Then land is given its vegetation, and water is distinguished into two types, the salt sea and the fresh water of the springs and rivers (§§13 f.).[214] The story of creation closes with pointing out the importance for man of all the animal and vegetable creatures of the earth (§15).

Another Fragment[215] explains briefly that the heaven was made as an arch upon nothing, and mentions the four elements, the choir of stars, the animals and trees. These were all made, or came into existence, "at the instrumentality of thy Logos" (τῷ σῷ λόγῳ), but here exist to give praise to God. The plan of creation assumed is definitely that of the longer passage in Fragment VII we have been discussing. Further on God is "the Creator, as the cause, of the creation, by a mediator" (§10).

Another passage on creation appears again in Fragment VI, 1–5. Here the story is only a paraphrase of the creation story of Fragment VII, but much less hellenized. The four elements are not included, and the story is rather geocentric than anthropocentric in its aetiology. It is interesting, as further evidence of the lesser degree of hellenization, that the creative agent is here not the Logos but Sophia. Creation, in the first sentence, is done "by Christ," which would seem here to represent an original διὰ σοφίας, since Sophia is so sharply emphasized in §§5, 6. The angelic hosts are not mentioned as a part of the story of creation, nor indeed at all in the Fragment, and the stars are not a choir. At the beginning of the creation story of Fragment VII (§7) it is stated that creation was made, by the mediation of the Logos, "out of not-being" (ἐκ τοῦ μὴ ὄντος). Fragment VI, 6, like VII, 17, has this phrase

213. The source of the notion may, of course, be the Pythagoreanism whence Plato himself learned it. See Aristotle, *De Caelo*, II, 290b 12 ff.

214. This distinction may well be a reflection of the *Logos Tomeus* theory of creation which I have elsewhere discussed, a Pythagorean theory which described land as divided into islands and mainland, water into fresh and salt. The notion is, as a whole, and in this detail, accepted by Philo. See my "Neo-Pythagorean Source," p. 154. Philo, *Heres*, 136; Ps.-Aristotle, *De Mundo*, 392b, 14 ff.; 393a 5 ff.

215. Frag. I, 5.

for the creation of the soul of man, but the universe in Fragment VI, 1, was made by the "ordering of disordered parts." The phrase τὸ μὴ ὄν is a famous one in Greek philosophy. The existence of not-being had been a favorite logical debate before Greek logic had finally learned to distinguish between the copulative and the existential uses of the verb "to be." So Plato, against Parmenides, could assert the existence of τὸ μὴ ὄν as a result of the presence of τὸ θάτερον in every quality.[216] But it is difficult to take Plato seriously in this. Leucippus and Democritus made a more positive use of the conception when they asserted that τὸ κενόν, space, existed, but as τὸ μὴ ὄν.[217] The use of the phrase for unformed matter is, so far as I know, first clearly attested in Plotinus, where matter is τὸ μὴ ὄν, not absolutely, for it exists, but in the Platonic sense of its being ἕτερον τοῦ ὄντος, only an εἰκὼν τοῦ ὄντος.[218] Philo speaks of a γένεσις ἐκ τοῦ μὴ ὄντος εἰς τὸ εἶναι[219] which plants and animals follow, and anticipates Plotinus in stating that the contrast between the existence of God and of other things is the διαφορὰ ὄντος τε καὶ μὴ ὄντος.[220] Logically, then, matter in its unformed condition would have been for him τὸ μὴ ὄν. Yet he quotes with approval Empedocles' denial of the impossibility of generation ἐκ τοῦ μὴ ὄντος,[221] and describes the material cause, ὕλη, of creation as being τὰ τέσσαρα στοιχεῖα.[222] Bréhier asserts that Philo could have known nothing of a creation *ex nihilo*,[223] but to come to this conclusion Bréhier gallantly refuses to consider the statement in the Armenian *De Deo* (§6): *creatur formaturque materia*. The confusion in all this is apparent, and further documentation would only add to the confusion. For the problem of what the Fragment could have meant by creation ἐκ τοῦ μὴ ὄντος is obviously not being clarified. Was the phrase only a description of formless matter, so that the Fragments which talk of creation from τὸ μὴ ὄν are only using a Platonic jargon for what the other Fragment calls "the ordering of disordered parts"? Or was there a real change of thought between the two, so that here more philosophical language is referring to a creation *ex nihilo*? Judgment on such a matter can be little more than personal opinion. I should guess that the thought has not changed, and that in both passages the liturgist had in mind an ordering of unformed matter. But definitely the philosophic form of statement in Fragment VII about the character of creation shows a greater hellenization than that in Fragment VI, just as has appeared to be the case in other details.[224]

216. *Sophist*, 255e–259d.   217. Diels, *Frag. Vorsok.*, 54A 8; 55A 38.
218. *Enn.*, I, viii, 3. Cf. Arist., *Metaph.*, 1089a 16.
219. *Immut.*, 119.   220. *Mos.*, i, 75.
221. *Aet.*, 5.
222. *Cher.*, 127. Cf. Albinus (Alcinous), *Introduction*, 12.
223. *Les Idées*, pp. 81 f.
224. My impression is that τὸ μὴ ὄν as a description of unformed matter was a Neo-Platonic, certainly post-Philonic, invention, for had it taken on this meaning in Philo's day it is incon-

The liturgy as we have it seems then to show definite stages of development. It would appear that creation, for liturgical purposes, very early became a fairly standardized story, made up as much out of phrases from the Psalms and Job as from Genesis, though the Genesis account is clearly basic. Sophia herself as the agent may be a later addition. Certainly the change of the account as found in Fragment VI to include in Fragment VII the formation of the four elements, the making of the distinction between salt and fresh water, the change of the stars into the Platonic or Pythagorean choir, the inclusion of the angelic hosts, the alteration of Sophia into Logos, and the introduction of creation ἐκ τοῦ μὴ ὄντος, all suggest the influence of later currents in Judaism, currents for the most part Hellenistic, while the form of the story without these insertions suggests just as definitely an earlier stage of Judaism. Since one can hardly visualize a motive for omitting these elements to reduce the form of the creation story in Fragment VII to that in Fragment VI, it seems right to conclude that Fragment VI has actually preserved an earlier form of the prayer.

Fragment VII, which is proving our best guide to the theology and philosophy of the Fragments, now goes on in §§16 and 17 to man, his creation and nature.[225] Man was made a citizen of the world, κοσμοπολίτης; he was the κόσμου κόσμος which probably means that he was, as the ornament, the objective of creation, but may imply that he was the microcosm. So he was, after consultation with Sophia, made in the image of God. He was made of two parts, a soul that was immortal, formed ἐκ τοῦ μὴ ὄντος,[226] and a body that was subject to dissolution (σκεδαστόν) as made up from the four elements. Without attempting to justify the inconsistency, I may state that my impression is here that the creation of soul, in contrast to that of the world, is *ex nihilo*. However that may be, the statement is clear as to the complete dissimilarity of soul and body. Gifts are made to each: to the soul rational knowledge, the discovering of piety and impiety, and the observation of right and wrong (δίκαιον καὶ ἄδικον); to the body the five senses and the power of motion. That is, to the soul is given, in Greek terms, implanted reason and power to fulfil the prime requirements of Judaism, piety to God and righteousness to men. Indeed the treatise goes on in §18 to describe how when Adam was formed in Eden God gave him νόμος ἔμφυτος,[227] that he might have within and for himself the seeds of θεογνωσία.

This brief outline is echoed and expanded in other Fragments. That man was a citizen of the world is stressed in the highly abbreviated syllabus for catechetical instruction.[228] In one place the formation of the body and its

ceivable that he would not have used it. It was precisely the phrase he appears to have been looking for.

225. Cf. the similar passage in Frag. VI, 6–8.   226. Cf. Frag. VI, 6.
227. Cf. Frag. XIV, 3.   228. Frag. VIII, 2. Cf. XIII, 4.

senses from the seminal drop is described, with the statement that an immortal soul is given it, so that man emerges as a rational creature. When the dissolution comes, a resurrection is promised.[229] Again the mind is given, in true Philonic sense, to be the charioteer of the soul.[230] For man this life is a race course in righteousness (στάδιον δικαιοσύνης), for which he is provided with γνῶσις ἔμφυτος, κρῖσις φυσική, and the admonitions of the Law. From all of these alike he learns that this world, with its riches, beauty, and strength, is but vapor and vanity, and that only one's faith can soar to heaven, and, returning with truth, seize in anticipation the joy to come, and so make, even in our present state, the soul full of joy.[231] The νόμος ἔμφυτος, in contrast here to the γραπτός, also reappears as an original endowment of man.[232]

The very constitution of man is thus pictured in terms of the Mystery. The history of man is similarly regarded. In spite of the original νόμος ἔμφυτος given to him, and the additional revelations made to the early Patriarchs, man was found unable to accomplish his destiny. As man was first made, he had only to obey to be immortal. Because of Adam's disobedience death came upon man. But God could not allow even a disobedient creature to suffer utter destruction, so he instituted the resurrection.[233] In two passages[234] the resurrection was instituted by an oath of God, an interesting statement for which, as to the oath, I can find no parallels. Bousset showed that the prophecy of the resurrection to Adam was a part of Hellenistic Jewish teaching by his reference to the tradition recorded in the Books of Adam.[235]

After this mention of the beginnings of the hope of resurrection, Fragment VII goes on to describe the careers of the Patriarchs, to which we shall return, and then states that by the time of Moses it had become clear that the Law of Nature (ὁ φυσικὸς νόμος), apparently the same as the νόμος ἔμφυ-

---

229. Frag. IV, 4 f. Frag. VII, 20 tells how this was given after the Fall.
230. Frag. VI, 6. See the Appendix.   231. Frag. V, 3.
232. Frag. XII, 8.
233. So in Frag. VII, 20 and VI, 8. But Frag. XIII, 4, represents man as originally made mortal, then given the promise of the resurrection.
234. Frag. VI, 8; VII, 20.
235. Bousset, p. 462. *Apocalypse of Moses*, xxviii, 4; xxxvii, 3; xli, 3; xliii, 1; *Vita Adae et Evae*, li, 2. The parallels are very interesting for the origin of the complicated Adam literature. It has been generally recognized as Hellenistic, though its angelology and general mythological treatment make it impossible to associate much of it with Philo. When in *Apoc. Mos.*, xxxvii, 3, the soul of Adam is snatched to heaven and washed in the Acherusian Lake, if the text is right, the conception is certainly that of the Orphic purification, by which the good soul is purified by being washed in Acheron (Kern, *Orph. Fr.*, 222; Procl., *In Plat. Rempubl.*, II, 340, 11, Kroll). In this literature God is strikingly described as Light-Life (*Vita Adae et Evae*, xxviii, 2; *Apoc. Mos.*, xxxvi, 3). The Angels come to Eve in a peculiar way, twelve of them, while two "Powers" stand one on either side of her (*Vit. Adae et Evae*, xxi, 1). The lore which Adam receives is a Mystery not to be revealed to Cain (*Apoc. Mos.*, iii, 2). Apparently a complete picture of the Mystery would include most of this material. But it is difficult to include it with the other evidence now at hand.

τος, had itself become corrupted. The great sin of men was that they had come to think of creation as self-caused, and indeed had made the created world itself the equivalent of the God of the universe. Here is precisely the arch-heresy against which Philo directs his constant denunciation.[236] Apparently the attraction of Stoic pantheism was so great a danger as to be recognized thus corporately by the Hellenistic Jewish liturgy. It was this type of heresy, the passage goes on to tell us, which necessitated the Mosaic legislation, a written (γραπτός) law which was given to assist the Natural (φυσικός) Law, and which declared that God was the creator, and denounced polytheism.[237] This secondary Law, or Decalogue, was pronounced by God and written by His hand.[238] Man could now be called "instructed by Thy laws, improved by Thy statutes."[239] Thus, living by the Law both as implanted and as written, man could "live according to Law as a rational animal,"[240] that is fulfil his original destiny, for he was created a "rational animal."[241] It is with the idea of the two stages of legislation, the Natural Law implanted in man, and its assistant, the written Law, that I connect the cryptic phrase from the brief catechetical syllabus, "Let him learn . . . the tribunals of Thy legislation."[242] The two types of legislation again strongly suggest the Mystery. Sin is, from the legal point of view, conceived of as taking two forms, the voluntary and the involuntary.[243] Even God's providence for the spiritual welfare of man is described as being done by a subordinate agency, that is by the provision of Laws.[244] The Sabbath is, among other things, a divine institution to give men time to meditate upon (εἰς μελέτην), or to make investigation (ζήτησις) of, the Laws.[245]

Man has nevertheless continued to sin. So there is further preparation made for him. When the implanted and written Laws together had still not kept him from sin, he was given the goodness of God "as a pledge in order to his repentance,"[246] and God is exhorted to forgive the penitent sinner.[247] Man is to share in the experience of Abraham, and by the good conscience of faith is to pass through the midst of heaven and return with truth and a firmer hold upon the joy to come.[248] The similarity of the gift of the "goodness" of God to Philo's Power of Mercy has already been pointed out.[249] The faith unfeigned which permits what is obviously the Greek "flight of the mind" through the universe to God is also an unmistakable echo of the Mystery.

236. See above, pp. 137 f.
237. Frag. VII, 25.
238. Frag. II, 4.
239. Frag. IV, 5.
240. Frag. XII, 8: πρὸς τὸ ζῆν αὐτὸν ἐνθέσμως, ὡς λογικόν.
241. Frag. IV, 5: προάγεις εἰς φῶς τὸ λόγικον ξῶον.
242. Frag. VIII, 2. See above, p. 327, n. 111.
243. Frag. XIII, 2, 5. See above, p. 333.
244. Frag. XV, 3.
245. Frag. II, 1, 5.
246. Frag. XII, 8.
247. Ib., 9.
248. Frag. V, 3 f.
249. See above, p. 332.

The joy "to come" which the mystic apprehends is here more eschatologically described than Philo would have done, but that is of a piece with the whole orientation of the Fragments in an active expectation of the resurrection, and emphasis upon the future life, essentially foreign to Philo's Sadducean point of view. Yet the conception is none the less mystical or Jewish for this discrepancy.

Another passage which describes the goal of pious aspiration is in Fragment IX, in the *Constitutions* preserved as a prayer for catechumens. The extreme similarity of this Fragment to early Christian points of view, and yet its almost complete accord with the Jewish Mystery, portend the importance of the Mystery for an understanding of the origin of much of early Christian thought. My reasons for regarding the Fragment as Jewish have been stated already.[250] The candidate for admission is, it is prayed, to get illumination and understanding (φωτίσῃ αὐτοὺς καὶ συνετίσῃ). The first word has no reference to the Christian baptism, for in the *Constitutions* the prayer has no connection with baptism. The second word is taken from the Psalms, for in the context we are reminded at once of Ps. cxix, 34. "Give me understanding and I shall keep Thy Law." God is besought to give the catechumens θεογνωσία. All this, the Fragment makes clear, is to result in their better understanding and keeping the Law. As the prayer goes on it is apparent that salvation involves not only the achievement of divine γνῶσις, but includes a definite initiation into a group, and specific rites. In §6 the aspirant is to be "united to and combined with God's flocks"; is to be granted the laver of regeneration. This expression, found also in Titus iii, 5, would at first suggest a Christian interpolation, but I see no reason to call it so. We know that the Jews were using baptism within the circles familiar to the compiler of the *Constitutions*. Baptism is to be followed in the Fragment, by the "garment of incorruption," something not known in Christian cultus, but a notion to which all the symbolism of the Mystery has been pointing. Putting the two together, I see no reason for supposing that we have gone out from Jewish Mystic initiation. By this initiation, we see in §7, candidates obtain forgiveness for their transgressions, and so become worthy of the holy mystic teachings (μυστήρια), and of permanent duration along with the saints (μετὰ τῶν ἁγίων διαμονή). The candidate is to pray to be kept from sin through all his life and to receive Christian death (what the original of this last phrase could have been I shall not guess). He is to dedicate himself to the only unbegotten God through His Logos (the probable original of the "Christ" here). All of these phrases were given Christian content by the Church, but as they stand there is no indication that a Christian originally conceived them. Nor are the "saints" (ἅγιοι) an indication of Christianity.

250. See above, p. 331. The Power of Mercy seems suggested again in another connection. See below, p. 352.

By entrance into the "Mysteries," the Fragment says, one comes to partake in the "duration," διαμονή, along with the saints. This experience is in the present, not eschatological. Who are these saints? For the answer to this we must look to the Fragments. In one passage God is God of the saints, who are sanctified by His hands.[251] This sounds like the God of the Patriarchs, a suspicion that is confirmed by the fact that it is specifically the Patriarchs and their successors who were according to another passage, "sanctified by Thy hand."[252] Further we notice that Moses is God's ἅγιος θεράπων,[253] while the "saints in every generation" are in the catechetical syllabus listed by name as the great Patriarchs and their successors.[254] The saints then are the Patriarchs who partake in a διαμονή, a "duration." This term is peculiar, but its meaning seems to me to be clear from a striking passage in Philo where he speaks of the duration of virtue.

Let us pray then that, like a central pillar in a house, there may constantly remain (διαμένειν) for the healing of our maladies the righteous mind in the soul, and in the human race the righteous man; for while he is sound and well, there is no cause to despair of the prospect of complete salvation, for our Saviour God holds out, we may be sure, the most all-healing remedy, His Power of Mercy, and commits it to His suppliant and worshipper to use for the deliverance of those who are sickly, that He may apply it as an embrocation to those soul-wounds which were left gaping by the sword-edge of follies and injustices and all the rest of the horde of vices. The most patent example is righteous Noah, who, when so many parts of the soul had been swallowed up by the great Flood, valiantly riding upon the waves that buoyed him up, stood firm high above every peril, and when he had come safe through all, put forth from himself fair roots and great, out of which there grew up like a plant wisdom's breed and kind; which, attaining goodly fertility, bore those threefold fruits of the seeing one, even of "Israel," that mark the threefold divisions of eternity, Abraham, Isaac, Jacob; for in the All virtue is, shall be, has been:[255]

The Power of Mercy is here depicted as a constant, a διαμονή, extended into mankind as a saving force in the form of the lives of the virtuous men in each generation. The Power of Mercy appeared already in the Fragments as the gift of God after the Law. The outstanding examples of this διαμονή given by Philo are the Patriarchs. They are great Saviors, but in a sense types of the mystic salvation which comes to every generation through their successors. The great διαμονή of the Fragment would seem to be the duration of saving virtue projected by the Power of Mercy through the Patriarchs and their successors, and the initiate comes into the condition of himself being one of the contemporary manifestations of that διαμονή, a part of the

251. Frag. I, 9. 252. Frag. XIII, 4.
253. Frag. V, 6. 254. Frag. VIII, 3.
255. *Mig.*, 124–125, translated by Colson and Whitaker.

great succession. The idea is familiarly Jewish, and is found in several other Fragments.[256] Its counterpart in Christianity is the notion that God saves the race because of the presence in it of the few saints, "the seed of the Christians, which God recognized as a cause in nature."[257]

If this Fragment is originally Jewish, as seems indisputable, the implication is inevitable that there was an actual initiation into a Jewish Mystery, as certain passages of Philo indicated,[258] the initiation which the Pseudo-Justinian convert celebrated.[259] The initiation involved a baptism, or a φωτισμός, a putting on of a garment of incorruption, a "flight of the mind" through the heavens to God, and a return with a new and superhuman grasp of truth and life which made the initiate a member of that inner group of saints which, from the Patriarchs down, was the source of racial and personal διαμονή. The legalism which they have is taught them directly by God, and they become members of God's holy flock.

It is a short step indeed to regarding the initiates as having become Israelites of the type which "truly see." A passage, already discussed in part, may now be again considered.[260] It seemed that the most natural reading of a sentence in Fragment II (§2) was: "For by Him [the Logos or Sophia] Thou hast led ⟨us⟩[261] to Thyself for a peculiar people, that is, the true Israel, beloved of God, the one that sees God." Bousset regarded the word ἀληθινόν of the phrase "the true Israel" as a Christian interpolation. But the very fact that the fragment mentions Israel as "seeing God" shows that we are in the world of the Mystery, which has throughout appeared to be an esoteric group within Judaism. Philo nowhere calls this group the "true" Israel, but he obviously thought of it as such. For he insists that "nobility" is a matter of mystic initiation into the lives of the Patriarchs rather than of blood descent from them,[262] so that many of the Patriarchs' own children were not of the elect race[263] while Gentiles who have this "nobility" are the ones who will get the reward.[264] Hence it is clear that he really thought of the initiates as the "True Israel." "For besides the fact that the wicked are not members of the nobility, I see further that they are all actually its irreconcilable enemies, since they have cancelled their ancestral rank (τὸ προγονικὸν ἀξίωμα) and have dimmed and extinguished whatever was brilliant in their race."[265] Philo could hardly have more plainly implied that there were Jews and

---

256. Frag. III; IV, 1 ff.; VIII, 3; XI, 3.

257. Justin Mart., *Ap.*, II, 7, 1. Justin derives this from the concept that Sodom was not to be destroyed if it contained a nucleus of just men. To Philo this incident was also a suggestion of ὑγείας σπέρμα (*Sac.*, 122 f.). Justin has probably rightly indicated the Scriptural passage with which the notion was connected by the Jews.

258. See above, pp. 259 ff.   259. See above, pp. 298 ff.

260. See above, p. 312.

261. Bousset's suggestion for "the Gentiles."

262. *Virt.*, 188–191.   263. Ib., 206–210.

264. Ib., 211, 227.   265. Ib., 191.

Jews, some of the promise (in the Mystery) and some not. Those who "saw God," shared the Mystery, whether Jew or Gentile by birth, were to Philo really the "True Israel." In Fragment X, 7, the God of the group is again addressed as "the God of Israel, Thy people which truly see." So the initiate into this inner group becomes one of the Jews who were the guardians of the true mystic teaching which other Jews did not understand.

The significance of the Patriarchs for this type of Judaism has already been suggested by the doctrine of the initiate's entering into their saving succession. But there are other important details suggested about them. One long list is of the "righteous" (οἱ δίκαιοι) whose gifts were accepted by God in their several generations. It runs from Abel through the usual names, but adds many not included by Philo from later Judaism, such as Ezra, Daniel, Jonah, the three children, and down to Mattathias, and Joel. It closes with the petition: "Now also do thou receive the prayers of Thy children which are offered to Thee with knowledge (μετ' ἐπιγνώσεως).[266] The word ἐπίγνωσις is familiar in the New Testament, especially in Paul, for an apprehension of the inner significance of divine truth. So the Jews have a zeal for God, Paul says, but not κατ' ἐπίγνωσιν.[267] Paul prays that the Christians may be given the πνεῦμα σοφίας καὶ ἀποκαλύψεως ἐν ἐπιγνώσει αὐτοῦ πεφωτισμένους τοὺς ὀφθαλμοὺς τῆς καρδίας ὑμῶν.[268] Again it is prayed that they may come εἰς ἐπίγνωσιν τοῦ μυστηρίου τοῦ θεοῦ.[269] The word is one of Paul's most strongly mystical terms. Philo uses the term less extensively, as in general he seems avoiding the language of gnosticism. But his occasional passages where the word appears show that it had the same meaning for him, and that Paul's usage was by no means a peculiar one. Especially applicable to our case is Philo's description of the mystic race: "The good man runs away from himself as he turns back to the ἐπίγνωσις τοῦ ἑνός."[270] The implication of the prayer is then obvious. The Patriarchs have in generation after generation been accepted by God. Do Thou also, is the prayer, receive us who pray with the mystic knowledge.

The list in Fragment III has not been Christianized at all to bring the succession down to Christ. In Fragment IV, 2 f., a shorter list is given, but one that runs on down to Judas Maccabaeus, and then includes Christ, and the succeeding text, as it now stands, makes the benefits which came from God or the Patriarchs come now from Christ. The section has then little to tell us of the thought of Judaism about the Patriarchs without purely conjectural change of text.

It is significant for the importance of the Patriarchs in the type of Judaism represented by the Fragments that in the brief outline for catechetical instruction great stress is laid upon the careers of the Patriarchs:

266. Frag. III, 2–4.   267. Rom. x, 2.   268. Ephes. i, 17.
269. Col. ii, 2.   270. *LA*, iii, 48.

How God did glorify the saints in every generation, I mean Seth, and Enos, and Enoch, and Noah, and Abraham and his posterity, and Melchizedek, and Job, and Moses, and Joshua, and Caleb, and Phineas the priest and those that were holy in every generation.[271]

The great prayer which has afforded the main outline for the theology of the Fragments has these same Patriarchs, though adding Abel, Lot, and Aaron, and omitting Phineas, Joshua, and Caleb; it gives a note upon each for his special significance.[272] The list in Fragment IX makes them all priests appointed for the government of God's people, a conception impossible in normative Judaism. Fragment XIII shows how this Judaism, with its vivid belief in heaven, has connected the Patriarchs with their eschatology. Heaven can be described in no more rapturous terms than by the figure that the pious soul is received into the bosom of Abraham, Isaac, and Jacob. God is the God of these Patriarchs not as of dead men but as living. The fragment is too thoroughly Jewish for these statements not to seem a part of the Jewish tradition whence Jesus drew the same way of speaking about heaven. It is not just the bosom of Abraham, as in Jesus' parable, but also of Isaac and Jacob. Jewish tradition is strongly insistent upon the fact that God, as God of the Patriarchs, was God of them *after* they had died to the flesh, but were living with Him.[273]

The different Patriarchs or heroes in the line of διαμονή of the saints, present some interesting details.

Abel was the man whose sacrifice was accepted because he was holy (ὅσιος) in contrast with the wicked Cain.[274] Noah was, as in Philo, ὁ δίκαιος.[275] Lot was also ὅσιος.[276] Abraham was, if the text is correct, one who "laid claim to the way of truth,"[277] that is, took the mystic Road. God guided him by a vision.[278] What this vision was we learn from another Fragment, where it is stated that Abraham was made the heir of the world (κληρονόμος τοῦ κόσμου), that is the man who was given the cosmos to be his own possession, and God revealed to him "Thy Christ." This, as I have already indicated,[279] was the familiar Christian adaptation of the Mystic Vision of the Logos which Philo describes as marking the supreme achievement of Abraham's experience. The effect of this vision was γνῶσις, mystic knowledge, which in turn resulted in πίστις, and as a consequence Abraham was given the great συνθήκη by which Abraham's seed was consecrated.[280] Here is a very interesting sketch of the mystic Road, which exactly follows Philo's

271. Frag. VIII, 3.   272. Frag. VII, 21–26.
273. Strack-Billerbeck have collected a great number of parallels in their commentary to Mat. xxii, 32.
274. Frag. VII, 21.   275. Ib., 22.   276. Ib.
277. Frag. V, 4.   278. Ib.
279. Frag. VII, 23. See also above, p. 324, n. 97.
280. Frag. V, 4.

schematization. Abraham was first delivered out from the impiety of his fathers and began upon the Road. The first step was the Cosmic Mystery by which he became "heir of the cosmos." Then came the vision of the Logos, which resulted in a mystic γνῶσις of "what this world is," in contrast, we understand, to the higher reality revealed to him. Gnosis produced faith, and the reward of faith was the covenant. Now it is interesting that this last series of steps has been changed in the manuscript tradition followed by Funk to make faith precede Gnosis. The difference is significant. In Hellenistic Judaism, as represented by Philo, faith is the crown of the mystic ascent, not its condition as in Paul. The contrast has often been pointed out.[281] The two texts, then, the one accepted by Funk giving the Christian order, the one in Ms. A, the oldest manuscript, giving the Hellenistic Jewish order, seem to me to represent respectively a Christian correction and the original text. The whole picture of Abraham is thoroughly Philonic, quite the Abraham of the Mystery.

Of Isaac we have less satisfactory information. But it is clear that Isaac was also of great importance in the tradition since it was only after Isaac had been born, and God saw that Isaac was like Abraham τῷ τρόπῳ, in his character, that God made the full promise to Abraham: "I will be a God to thee, and to thy seed after thee." There is room here for the Philonic notion that Isaac was born already the "Self-Taught," the complete mystic, who from his birth had the perfection which Abraham only gradually achieved. It seems suggested in the fact that at birth God recognized in Isaac the τρόπος of Abraham. But less extreme interpretations are possible, so that this one cannot be pressed.

Jacob, again as in Philo, is given the vision of the Logos (Christ).[282]

Melichizedek is frequently mentioned in the list, but with nothing distinctive said of him.

Job appears in various lists as a contemporary of Abraham. His great achievement was the conquering of "that serpent who is the patron of wickedness,"[283] which seems to me intelligible only in view of Philo's association of the serpent with physical pleasure. Philo's dependence upon the Pentateuch has deprived us of knowing the use made of Job, who appears to have been one of the favorite great heroes of the Mystery.

Joseph is the type of chastity, as in all Jewish tradition to the present.

Moses was God's "holy servant" by whom the written Law was given to assist Natural Law, to demonstrate God as the Creator, and to abolish polytheism.[284] The incident of the bush is brought forward in another passage

---

281. See especially A. Schlatter, *Der Glaube im neuen Testament*, pp. 84–105. The distinction is helpful here in contrasting the Hellenistic Jewish original with the Christian alteration. But in the Appendix (p. 401) it will appear to represent no essential change of conception.

282. Frag. V, 5.　　　　283. VII, 23.　　　　284. Frag. VII, 25.

to show how Moses was also in the succession of the greatest leaders in the Mystery.[285] Moses' vision then was apparently, to the author of the Fragment as to Philo, parallel to the vision of Abraham and Jacob already discussed, a vision of the Logos.

Finally the play with the number seven in Fragment II is clearly a part of that mystic numerology that went back at least as far as Aristobulus.

The analysis of the Fragments has led us back so repeatedly to Judaism, to Hellenistic Judaism, and specifically to the Mystery, that it would seem that they must have come from the Mystic Judaism of which we have elsewhere found elaborate indication. The conclusion is of great importance. Hellenistic Judaism, or one wing of it, must have been so oriented in the Jewish Mystery that the language of its prayers was the language of the Mystery. The people who thus expressed their aspirations to God through the Logos or Sophia, who looked to the Patriarchs with their Mystic Vision of the Logos, who felt themselves as the True Israel that sees God, as initiated into the great διαμονή; the people who trained their catechumens in the doctrine of the double law and in gnosis of God as first achieved by Abraham and the Patriarchs; these were a strange Jewish group. But an actual Jewish group! We cannot say how representative of Hellenistic Judaism in general this group was, for we must always remember the non-mystical "literalists" whose existence and tradition is as unmistakable, though not attested by so many literary remains, as Mystic Judaism. But the existence of the mystic sect seems indisputable, as well as its great importance for Christian origins in the Hellenistic world.

There is no way of guessing at what may have been the destiny of the group. The Fragments themselves seem to me to be post-Philonic, if only for the single detail of creation ἐκ τοῦ μὴ ὄντος. There is no trace, as has been pointed out, of the use of the term in this way before Plotinus, and I do not think it could have been invented to express the conception of primitive, unformed matter by Philo's day or he would have used it, since it so obviously would have expressed his thought better than he was able to do without it. But how much later than Philo the term must be put cannot be stated with certainty. It is to me hard to believe that relations between Christians and Jews of even this type were sufficiently cordial after the middle of the Second Century after Christ to have made it possible for Christians to have taken the liturgy over for their own use. It is of course possible that the borrowing was early, and that such a detail as τὸ μὴ ὄν may have come from later redaction. So there is really nothing that I can see from which we may date the composition of the Jewish original, or its Christian adoption.

285. Frag. V, 6. See the whole Fragment.

But these questions, interesting as they are do not need to concern us. The purpose of this work as a whole will have been fulfilled if it has made clear the existence of the Mystery, and given an acceptable presentation of its points of view.

One word should be added in closing. The Mystery has been found on the whole to have had no more sense of credal orthodoxy than any other type of Judaism. True Philo has come much nearer a creed than Judaism in general has done. But the points in the creed were remarkably general—monotheism, God the Creator, the κόσμος νοητός—and other Mystic documents have with perfect freedom developed notions not found in Philo. The points of dispute between Pharisees and Sadducees in Palestine were obviously not agreed upon also among the Mystics. The Laws as statutes seem in the Fragments to be more important than to Philo, but were to him more important than to the "Allegorists." The Bible was the Pentateuch to Philo, but was the whole "Law, Prophets, and Writings" to the author or authors of the Fragments. Abraham, Moses, Isaac, Jacob, or Solomon might for any individual be the outstanding inspiration.

Yet they had in common in the Mystery the Streaming Light from God which was Sophia or Logos at convenience; they had the Patriarchal Hierophants with whom they could share the Mystic Vision, and come to live by the higher Law, besides the many other details which need not be repeated. All alike were trying to become Jews in the highest sense by repeating the mystic experience of the Jewish Saints, that is by racing like them from matter toward God along His Royal Road, the great Stream. This is throughout the touchstone of the Mystery.

οἱ τὸν θεὸν θεῷ φαντασιωθέντες, φωτὶ φῶς.

EPILOGUE

TRACES OF THE MYSTERY IN THE KABBALAH

Only a profound Jewish scholar can speak of the Kabbalah without the greatest hesitation.[1] Yet one who knows the Kabbalah even slightly must, in reading this description of the Hellenistic Jewish Mystery, have been struck with the amazing number of similarities between the two schools. The best analysis to date of the points of resemblance between Philo and the *Sohar* is by Karppe,[2] but, useful as his analysis is, he has given similarities of detail rather than the more fundamental resemblances. His most useful section is his discussion of the likenesses and differences in the matter of the allegorical technique of the two.

The general differences are of course as striking as the similarities. The most obvious difference is in the technique of allegory. Kabbalists, writing in Aramaic and Hebrew, used a system of turning the Hebrew letters of a given word into numbers, and then rearranging the numbers to produce other words, a system of which Philo never dreamed. This technique of allegory, with its many subsidiary rules, was perhaps more than anything else the peculiar contribution of Kabbalistic thinkers, and it would seem to have been the development of this interpretative art which gave the Kabbalistic system its distinctive form. One is impressed, however, by the fact that the whole might well have been influenced, like Philo, by Neo-Pythagorean numerology as well as by oriental magic. Karppe has indicated a great many resemblances of detail in allegorical method which need not here be repeated.

Second it is clear that the ten *Sephiroth* are not the seven Powers of Philo (although Kabbalistic tradition knew of seven *Sephiroth* also) either in number or name; yet there are many similarities, as we shall see, between them. Third *En Soph*, if it is really the Hebrew equivalent of the ἄπειρον of Greek Philosophy, as Ginsburg thinks, is a name which Philo could not possibly have countenanced for Deity. Actually I question the notion that they are equivalent. The ἄπειρον was to a Greek the "undefined," not in the sense that it was above description, but beneath it. The ἄπειρον had not such specific qualities that they could be indicated by terms. The Absolute of Philo and Neo-Platonism was on the contrary above description, ἀκατάληπτος, not ἄπειρον. Qualities such as men could name belonged to human categories, it was argued, and none of these applied to τὸ ἕν, or τὸ ὄν. That did

---

1. For the present purpose, which is rather suggestion than demonstration, I have used only the close analyses of C. D. Ginsburg, *The Kabbalah* (1920), and S. Karppe, *Étude sur les origines et la nature du Zohar* (1901). It is for an expert to use the sources of Jewish mysticism at first hand.

2. *Op. cit.*, pp. 527–581. The section, pp. 413–419, is also very important.

not imply lack of form or definiteness, however, but superiority to human definition. The *En Soph,* as it is described in the Kabbalistic books, is the undefined in exactly this higher Greek sense. It is notable that Karppe was quite aware of the similarity of Philo and the *Sohar* as to the ultimate nature of God.[3] Fourth there is a striking difference from Philo in the extensive use made throughout Kabbalistic literature of Iranian-Jewish angelology, and in the eschatological elements which looked to the ultimate restoration of the Good Order as all is restored to the Light.

There are many other points of contrast. But the points of similarity must not be lost in these points of difference. Both the Kabbalah and Philo have fundamentally the identical conception that the Absolute and Unrelated God is related to the lower world or worlds through a series of emanations which are as a whole to be conceived by the figure of a single Stream of Light from the Source. "By Light, Light" is as descriptive of the kernel of the thought of the one as of the other. The following might well be taken, except for the technical Kabbalistic terms, as Philo's own statement:

The Aged of the Aged, the Unknown of the Unknown, has a form and yet has no form. He has a form whereby the universe is preserved, and yet has no form, because He cannot be apprehended. When He first assumed the form [of the first *Sephira*],[4] He caused nine splendid lights to emanate from it, which, shining through it, diffused a bright light in all directions. Imagine an elevated light sending forth its rays in all directions. Now if we approach it to examine the rays, we understand no more than that they emanate from the said light. So is the Holy Aged an absolute light, but in Himself concealed and incomprehensible. We can only comprehend him through those luminous emanations [*Sephiroth*] which again are partly visible and partly concealed.[5]

From the identity of this basic concept many similar details are developed within the two systems. It is this fundamental similarity which is Karppe's most serious oversight. Of the similar details derived from the identical foundation the following may be noted:

First the *Sephiroth* as a group are the Heavenly Man, just as in Philo the

3. It is perhaps worth suggesting that the "Endless" or "Limitless" as a name for the Ultimate Principle may have come into Kabbalistic tradition from Zarvanism, whose Ultimate Principle was "Boundless Time," or from the "without beginning" Light of Ahura Mazda in Zoroastrianism: see H. Lommel, *Der Religion Zarathustras,* pp. 22–28. The Greek ἀγένητος is by this suggested as a possible original for *En Soph*. But in later Greek tradition some such oriental idea came so to affect the Greek word ἄπειρον, that, for example, ὁ ἀπέραντος is a frequent term (used twenty-five times) for the Ultimate in the Gnostic treatise published by C. A. Baynes (*A Coptic Gnostic Treatise,* 1933; see Index I, s.v.). Its meaning in this treatise is difficult to determine since it is used only as a title for God, not defined or discussed. The term *En Soph* may have come to the Kabbalistic writers from any such sources as these, directly or indirectly.

4. That is the Logos of Philo.

5. *Idra Suta, Sohar,* iii, 288a; quoted by Ginsburg, p. 96.

Logos as a totality is the οὐράνιος ἄνθρωπος, the υἱὸς τοῦ θεοῦ. The Kabbalah makes use of this concept to an extent far beyond what Philo does. It is recognizably Iranian in origin in Philo, and the elaborations of the Kabbalah only bring out the Iranian elements more strongly. But the distinctive contribution of Hellenistic Judaism was to identify the Gayomart—Heavenly Man—Adam of the East with the Greek Logos, and thereby with the κόσμος νοητός of Platonism. The Logos as the υἱὸς τοῦ θεοῦ, or Primal Man, in Philo becomes the prototypal man in the Platonic sense. This element, that the Heavenly Man—*Sephiroth* is the prototypal Form or the κόσμος νοητός in general, but especially the Form of Man, is developed in the Kabbalah in that same peculiar combination with Iranian ideas which Philo shows Hellenistic Jews were making.

Second the tendency to group the *Sephiroth* in triads is exactly that of Philo, whose Powers are similarly grouped, though the Kabbalah has as a rule one triad more than Philo.

This extra triad, in the third place, which makes the Kabbalah often have ten *Sephiroth* as compared with Philo's sacred Seven, has been indicated as one of the important distinctions between Philo and the Kabbalah. But it is notable that the change is only from the sacred Seven to what Philo himself regarded as the still more sacred Ten. Philo seems to have kept the Seven because he was closer than the Kabbalah to the Iranian *Amesha Spentas,* whose six members, together with the *Ahura Mazda,* made a number sufficiently sacred to Judaism and Pythagoreanism alike to satisfy him. The advance to the Ten was probably quite early, as the report of the teaching of the Gnostic Monoimus indicates,[6] but compelled a complete rearrangement of the specific members of the group. There had always been, apparently, considerable freedom for the imagination in the naming of the individual emanations. Philo is so close to the *Amesha Spentas,* it is recalled, that Darmesteter erroneously thought the *Avestas* must have the conception from him. Yet Philo's names, for all the occasional resemblances, are not the Persian names. He was chiefly trying to express the fundamental unity of the two chief functions of God, the creating, merciful function and the ruling, legalistic, and punitive function. Now the outstanding point is that for all the rearrangment and renaming of the Kabbalistic emanations it is precisely the formulation and reconciliation of the same two functions of divine relation with the world which the *Sephiroth* are fundamentally designed to exemplify.

Fourth, in rearranging the emanations and expanding their number the Kabbalists could work out a reconciliation between two mystic formulations which have abundantly appeared as parallels within Philo's Mystery. Philo

6. Hippolytus, *Refutatio*, VIII, xii–xv.

has used a sexual formulation of ascent through the Female Principle, a formulation which came to Philo apparently ultimately from Isis, but which had been taken in by the Orphics along with other female mystic deities long before his time. It appears in Hellenistic Judaism as the Sophia, the daughter and spouse of God. Alongside the Sophia formulation Philo used the ascent through the Powers. Both these formulations were used interchangeably by Philo for the Light-Stream according as the exigencies of allegory required a male or female counterpart. But the two were always parallel formulations in Philo and never properly integrated. In the Kabbalah the sexual and female element is introduced directly into the *Sephiroth,* as it was used by the Gnostics in their schemes of emanations. The two schemes of Philo appear thus united in the single scheme of the Kabbalah.

Fifth, in comparing the two schemes one is struck by the fact that the names of the *Sephiroth* are closer to Philo's Powers than are Philo's Powers to their Iranian prototype.[7] A glance at the accompanying chart shows the similarity of the general structure of the two. Both are the Light-Stream from the Absolute Source. The "Pillar of Mercy," made up of numbers 2, 4, 7, in the *Sephiroth,* corresponds to the Creative Power and Merciful Power of Philo. This vertical pair and the "Pillar of Mercy" represent the right hand of God in each case. The "Pillar of Rigor," numbers 3, 5, 8, of the *Sephiroth,* has the same collective function as Philo attributes to the Royal and Law-making Powers, the avenging and rigorous expression of God's left hand. Each of the *Sephiroth* which do not, like Mercy and Justice, correspond exactly to Philo's nomenclature can be traced to familiar Philonic attributes of God. Νοῦς, σοφία, τὸ καλόν, δόξα, βεβαιότης, βασιλεία are familiar to any superficial reader of Philo as mystic approaches to God or derivative expressions of His nature. "Foundation" is not so easily recognizable until one turns to *Plant.,* 5–8, where the function of the Logos as the foundation, ἔρεισμα, of the universe is expounded as a part of the creative or cosmic function of the Logos, and so becomes a natural member of the creative and merciful "Pillar." Sophia is of course a creative power throughout Jewish tradition. The highest *Sephira,* the "Crown," is likewise Philonic, though not obviously so. At the highest point of ascent in mystic experience Philo, like Paul, speaks of receiving the "Crown," which, in Philo, is the Vision of God.[8] The thoroughly Philonic character of the different *Sephiroth* is thus as plain as the similarity of the two conceptions as a whole. Karppe has not fully understood the Powers of Philo, so that some of his remarks are not accurate, and as a whole they are inadequate. The lower triad of Philo is, to Karppe,[9] made up of names that are mere doublets to fill out the number Seven. This

7. So close are the *Sephiroth* to one passage on the Ten in Philo (*Cong.,* 104 f.) that Karppe, p. 574, thinks that the very term is derived from the *Spheres* there described.
8. *LA,* ii, 108; *Praem.,* 27.   9. p. 563.

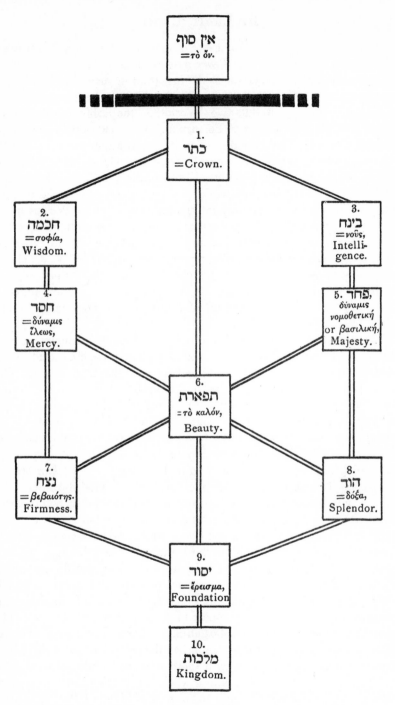

PLATE III. GOD AND THE SEPHIROTH OR HEAVENLY MAN
OF THE KABBALAH. COMPARE PAGES 24 AND 29

is because he has missed the significance of the contrast Philo makes between the upper and lower triads. The lower triad is actually, as we have seen, an extension or lower representation of the first triad in such natures that they could have relationship with the created realm. They lie between the created and uncreated as do the middle two "Worlds" of the Kabbalah, the "World of Creation" and the "World of Formation," each made up of a group of ten lower *Sephiroth*. These are the "Worlds" which actually did the creating of the material "World," the lowest, after the model of the "World of Emanations" or "Heavenly Man," the first Sephiric World. The lower triad of Philo can affect the material world directly, and be represented in it, as the higher triad cannot. The very multiplication of Sephiric Worlds in the Kabbalah is again and clearly an expansion of Philonic thought. The first Sephiric World, the one represented in the diagram, is really an expansion of the first triad of Philo by bringing in other notions all of which are recognizably familiar in Philonic thought. The second and third Sephiric Worlds are based upon the lower Philonic triad, but are almost unrecognizable because of the large amount of Iranian demonology which is also there.

Philo's first triad is made up of the notion of the two attributes of God, Creation or Mercy and Royalty, Law, or Discipline, these connected by the Logos as the primal and undistinguished form of the Light-Stream. This concept finds other striking analogies in the Kabbalah. For the two Powers of Creation and Royalty are read by Philo into the Old Testament, it has been repeatedly indicated, by the contrast between κύριος and θεός, the Septuagint version of *Yahveh* and *Elohim*. It is proverbial in the Kabbalah that the two "Pillars" are likewise representations of the two aspects of Mercy and Discipline of which the two terms *Yahveh* and *Elohim* are the fixed symbols. Not only are these identical attributes of God thus identically connected with Scripture: the two attributes are themselves in both systems but complimentary manifestations of the single primal emanation from God. In Philo this primal emanation is the Logos which, we have seen *in extensu* in Chapter I, appears as the middle third principle when the upper triad is viewed by men. Men who have this vision from below, and do not understand, think that the three they see are really three. But to one who has ascended mystically to the Logos, and so can view the three from above, the divisions disappear and the three appear to be what they truly are, one. The "Crown" takes the place in the Kabbalah of the Logos in this sense of being the first emanation, and in it is accomplished the reconciliation of the divine properties expressed by *Yahveh* with those subsumed under *Elohim*. It is true that considering the *Sephiroth* as a whole this uniting function is often ascribed to the last *Sephira*, "Kingdom," or to the "Middle Pillar" in general as contrasted with the *Yahveh* and the *Elohim* "Pillars." The *En Soph* itself "is united by the number three."[10] The "Crown" is the uniting factor between "Intelligence" and "Wisdom," making them into a unit. "Beauty" unites "Mercy" with "Justice," "Kingdom" unites the other *Sephiroth*, making three triads, which are themselves united and One, so that the "Heavenly" or "Primal Man," the first Sephiric World, is one. This playing with triads or trinities made up of a member from each outer "Pillar" united in a member of the inner "Pillar" is used a great deal by the Kabbalists. Ginsburg, with apparently no Philonic background, quotes some of these passages as instances of Christian influence. There are the passages in which the trinity of the *Shema* is discussed. The phrase, *"Yahveh is our Elohim; Yahveh is one"* gave rise to frequent question. In one passage the *Sohar*[11] says of this expression in the *Shema:*

These three constitute together a unity, and for this reason He [*Yahveh*] is said to be one. But there are three names, and how can they be said to be one? . . . Now this is revealed by the vision of the Holy Ghost [that is the mystic vision by which Philo said the oneness of the trinity was to be apprehended], and when the eyes are closed we get to know that the three are only one.

The passage goes on to adduce the analogy of the voice, which is a single entity though it involves, besides air, fire in its warmth and water in its moisture. "These also, *Yahveh, Elohenu,* and *Yahveh,* constitute one, three forms which are one." The author is not inclined to be too insistent upon the analogy of the voice: if another figure is more helpful, use it, he advises. But the fact of the unity in the trinity of the three names remains. Another passage which Ginsburg quotes refers to the fact that *Yahveh,* the tetragram, is in the Hebrew text sometimes pointed and read as *Adonai* and sometimes as *Elohim.* How can these be confused when the one represents Mercy the other Justice in the rigorous sense? The answer is that the true mystic meaning is not only that the justice of God is tempered with mercy, and *vice versa,* but that

There are three degrees in God, and each degree exists by itself [i.e. in the Deity], although the three together constitute one; they are closely united into one and are inseparable from each other.[12]

One has only to compare these statements, for form and objective, with the Christian Trinity which did get into a single codex of the *Sohar*[13] to see that

10. *Sohar,* iii, 288b; Ginsburg, p. 101.
11. *Sohar,* ii, 43b; Ginsburg, pp. 138 ff.
12. *Sohar,* iii, 65a; Ginsburg, pp. 139 f. See also *Sohar,* iii, 262a; Ginsburg, p. 140.
13. Ginsburg, p. 140: In the trishagion "the first holy refers to the Holy Father, the second to the Holy Son, the third to the Holy Ghost."

the true Kabbalistic notion of trinity is as far from Christianity as it is close to Philo.

The processes of creation in the Kabbalah and in Philo are much less alike than are the two conceptions of Deity. That the material world is created after the heavenly model is common to the two schools, but the Kabbalah, in making the material world the lowest emanation from God, has advanced with Neo-Platonism beyond the dualism of God and matter which Philo shares with earlier Orphic, Pythagorean, and Platonic thought. It has been seen that as the Neo-Platonist emanation doctrine is recognizably a development out of the Platonism and mystic philosophy of Philo's day and thought, so the "Worlds" of *Sephiroth* are an elaboration of Philo's notion of the higher and lower triads of emanations; but there is nothing in Philo to suggest the four "Worlds" of the Kabbalah. Ginsburg parallels this four with the four grades of reality in Neo-Platonism, and the evidence shows that as philosophy developed through the succeeding four or five centuries after Philo some Jews, at least, were going on with the process of making their Scriptures teach the most advanced ideas of the day.

At the same time it is clear that as Iranian Judaism developed, and Jews, now all united in Hebrew or Aramaic as they were not in Philo's day, were reading much the same books, the angelology and demonology which Jews in the East had been working out for Judaism on Iranian lines were being accepted as a part of the Mystery tradition. The beginning of this is clearly reflected in *II Enoch* and the Mystic Liturgy. Hence Metatron and Samaël and their hosts haunt the thought of the Kabbalists in a way utterly foreign to Philo. Yet even in these realms there are still traces of Philonic thought. Metatron is recognizably the Cosmic Logos of Philo, that aspect of his thinking which is most akin to Stoicism. It has been pointed out that the conception is not Stoic in Philo, for the Cosmic Logos is for him the presence of the immaterial form-force of God within the material world; it is not the ultimate form and force of matter itself as in Stoicism. Metatron in the Kabbalah would seem to have the same resemblance to and difference from the Stoic Logos as does Philo's Logos.

The creation of man as described in the Kabbalah is strongly reminiscent of Philo in the matter of man's being a copy of the Heavenly Man. The Heavenly Man in Philo is the Logos, but not the Logos as the first emanation in contrast to the other emanations, nor is it the Cosmic Logos as the lowest emanation. It is the Logos as the whole Stream from God in its unity. Such is the Heavenly Man of the Kabbalah, though much more elaborated. But in the Kabbalah one feels more clearly than in Philo the influence of Adam-Gayomart speculation from the East of the sort revealed in the Adam literature. As in that literature the Protoplast of the Kabbalah was not of gross matter: he was clothed in the celestial garment, which is a garment of heavenly light. But when he was expelled from the garden of Eden, and became subject to the wants of this world, what is written? "The Lord God made coats of skins unto Adam and to his wife, and clothed them"; for prior to this they had garments of light, light of that light which was used in the garden of Eden.[14]

In view of his being a copy of the whole first Sephiric World, the Heavenly Man, man is the summation of all forms and so the microcosm, as Philo insisted. In spite of his losing the garment of light, man still is the microcosm in his soul, the Kabbalists taught. It is notable that at death man throws off the garment of skins and is given back the garment of light. One is strikingly reminded of the "resurrection body" of Paul. Was the idea a current one among mystic Jews in Paul's day, and did he have it as part of his large borrowings from the Mystery? Certainly in the Adam literature the tradition of the garment of light for the Protoplasts is sufficiently familiar. It is much more natural to take Paul as evidence for the existence of the notion in the Judaism of his day than to derive the Jewish doctrine as it appears in the Adam literature and the *Sohar* from Paul. The ideas are too strikingly similar to be without some connection. Paul's very casualness in referring to the resurrection body would imply readers to whom the passage would carry more meaning than it has done to later generations. As to the Kabbalistic doctrine of man in general, with its notions of preëxistence, incarnation, and of man's release at death to return to the Light, the whole is as fundamentally Orphic as it is in disagreement with the normative tradition of the bodily resurrection. On this point the Kabbalah, because it goes into the problem of life after death much more fully than Philo does, outdoes Philo himself in Orphism. The additional elements, however, only throw us back more directly on the sources of Philo's own thinking, and strengthens the impression that the Kabbalah has its resemblances to Philo not from being a teaching worked out of Philo's writings by later generations, but from having its basis in a great tradition which began in an originally large and varied movement in Hellenistic Judaism of which Philo is only our greatest extant representative.

Like Philo the Kabbalists thought that love was a much higher motive for serving God than fear. Both motives are recognized as legitimate by both schools, but, in each, love is the motive of all higher worship.

In regard to the patriarchs there are striking reminiscences of Philo in the Kabbalah. It will be recalled that according to Philo all the virtues were represented in each great patriarch, yet each represented one virtue predominantly. In the Kabbalah this takes the form of saying that all the *Sephiroth* abide within each of the great patriarchs but that in every case

14. *Sohar*, ii, 229b; Ginsburg, p. 112.

there is one *Sephira* predominant: Mercy in Abraham, Rigor in Isaac, Mildness in Jacob, Firmness in Moses, Splendor in Aaron, Foundation in Joshua, Kingdom in David. The Kabbalah has had to include other patriarchs than Philo's favorites to make the Ten. Philo does not develop an equation of the patriarchs with the Powers in any extant writing, but he apparently had the notion none the less. It will be recalled that he had two triads of patriarchs, Enos, Enoch, and Noah, then Abraham, Isaac, and Jacob. He nowhere explains the selection of these triads, but their correspondence to the triads of Powers is too obvious to be unintentional.[15] The Seventh of Philo stands out all over his writings as Moses. Furthermore Abraham, Isaac, and Jacob "mark the threefold division of eternity" to Philo,[16] and one passage has twice been discussed where these three Patriarchs are obviously being regarded as equivalent to the three highest Powers.[17] So the identification of *Sephiroth* with the patriarchs in all probability goes back to the Mystery of Philo's day.

Along with these similarities goes a very similar use of the Old Testament and attitude toward the Law in the two schools. The Kabbalah, like Philo, draws all its ideas from the Pentateuch. For both, the true Law was a spiritual immaterial reality which put on an earthly garment in descending to earth and representing itself through the medium of the written word. For Philo the contrast between the literal and inner meanings, the latter to be educed by allegory, was the contrast between body and soul. The Kabbalists likewise wanted to strip off the outer wrap to get to the true Spirit-Law beneath. Again the Kabbalists elaborated the notion beyond Philo, and called the narratives in the Bible the clothing, the commandments the body, the mystic doctrine the soul. And as has been stated the whole technique of allegory was enormously developed in the later school beyond what appears in the earlier. But again their notion is obviously an expansion of an idea whose original spermatic form appears in the Mystery. The Kabbalists seem often akin to the extreme allegorists of Hellenistic Judaism in their denunciation of the whole legal tradition of Judaism in the interest of the "spiritual meaning."

The question has often been asked, "What became of Hellenistic Judaism?" Answers have been various. Those who believe that Hellenistic Judaism was a creation of Philo's unique imagination say, of course, that it died, as it was born, with him. Others have suggested that it perished with the other schools of Judaism before the triumphant advance of the normative legalism of the Pharisees, while those who kept the Hellenistic point of view moved over into Christianity. It is likely that many believers in the Jewish Mystery did become Christians. The believers in the Kabbalah have like-

15. See above, p. 129.　　16. *Mig.*, 125.
17. *Abr.*, 51–55. See above, pp. 136, 203.

wise, of all the schools of Judaism, been most susceptible to Christian propaganda. But it would seem that one who wants to know what became of Hellenistic Judaism must begin by recognizing that the spirit and a host of the most important details of the Mystery which Philo described have survived among Jewish mystics and come to full flower again in the Kabbalah, and that in that form it is still a familiar branch of Judaism. To trace the process by which the ideas of Philo survived for a thousand years and reappeared in the Kabbalah is a task for a Jewish scholar. It is doubtful if any one can recover from the vague tradition of the *Maaseh Bereshith* and the *Maaseh Merkabah,* as they appear occasionally mentioned in the Talmud and in the writings of the Gaonim, enough to trace the story satisfactorily. As one reads the illuminating history of this mysticism by Karppe striking reminiscences of detail keep emerging. It can be seen how the teaching steadily developed to make increasing the use of the Ten as over against the Seven, and how the numerological treatment of the text of the Pentateuch became more and more popular. A relatively late pre-Kabbalistic mystic, Saadyeh, suddenly emerged with the forgotten allegory of the Temple as a symbol of the cosmos. The mystic patriarchs were described in the most varied connections. Either the Mystery was never entirely forgotten among Jews, and had a consecutive, if now lost, history, or else Hellenistic Jews so deeply and truly expressed the mystic life of the race that as Jews went on with their Scriptures in a pagan and philosophic world they over and again produced fundamentally the same kind of a mystic union of Judaism with pagan philosophy and mysticism. Whichever of these was the case, there is no more reason for thinking that Jews in Alexandria could not have produced a very popular and widely accepted Mystery of the type we have been describing than for denying the historical reality of Kabbalistic Judaism since the eleventh or twelfth centuries.

APPENDIX

LAW IN THE SUBJECTIVE REALM

An examination of the conceptions which Philo associated with the words νόμος, δικαιοσύνη, and their cognates would lead into many fields. It would appear that his cosmogony and his ideals for society were alike ultimately based upon the notion that the cosmos was, and human relations ultimately ought to be, an expression of justice, by the fact that they are founded upon true Law. In practice there was one Law of Nature and another of society. But the ideal was that all men in political power, from the king down, should be in their own characters copies of τὰ φύσεως ἔργα in order that others might imitate them. Every magistrate's business was the dispensation of δικαιοσύνη, and as fire must be hot before it can give out heat, snow cold before it can chill, the governor or judge must be δίκαιος before he can give out δικαιοσύνη, or, what amounts to the same thing, be a potable stream of εὐνομία for thirsty humanity.[1]

The study of Philo's political thinking must be left to another publication. The present task is to follow Philo's νόμος and δικαιοσύνη into the subjective realm, where, in the Hellenistic Age, the great longing for peace and σωτηρία was quite as strong as in the realm of political and social relations. The use by Paul of the term δικαιοσύνη for the ideal inner state of man has led to more fundamental confusion than any word in the Bible. Because "justice" is a social conception with us, δικαιοσύνη has been translated "justification," and explained as the stage in which, by the merit of Christ, we are "made" just, or "accounted" just. As a matter of fact the social virtues, important as they were to Paul and to all early Christianity, were secondary manifestations, inevitable concomitants, but still concomitants, of the single primary experience, the individual's achievement of right relations with God, as a result of which he first gained subjective balance and order. Not until one had had this experience could he do the good he had always seen and desired, but had been unable to do. He could enjoy a settled peace with God and man only as long as he was at peace with himself. Not the aiming at this state of inner adjustment, but the state itself, was δικαιοσύνη. It might just as well have been called σωτηρία, or εἰρήνη. Each of these and other terms only bring out distinct aspects of a single experience which δικαιοσύνη most accurately characterizes as a whole.

The word need not be confusing to anyone who has the Greek, and espe-

---

1. *Spec.*, iv, 55–58. This whole passage on the character of the just judge I have discussed more fully in my *Jewish Jurisprudence*, pp. 189 ff.

cially the Pythagorean-Platonic, point of view in mind. The cosmos, by that point of view, has been filled with ἰσότης, or has been δίκαιος, according as its various parts act in the balanced relation determined by the principles of the Law of Nature or God, by which the lower parts must be obedient to the higher, and the higher must fulfil their obligations to the lower. In turn the state is filled with εὐνομία or δικαιοσύνη or ἰσότης as the balance of its various parts have conformed to the ideal law of society, which is again a reflection or part of the Law of God or of Nature, with the higher members of society properly caring for the obedient lower members. Δικαιοσύνη, in cosmos and society alike, is a matter of what Plato called each member's doing his part, and only his part.[2] Ὁ δίκαιος is always ὁ νόμιμος, for the function of law in society, or in the universe, is to put and keep every man and his activity in his place.

The term in no sense changes in meaning when it is applied to the subjective realm. The Greeks thought of personality literally as a realm, with various parts and members, and by no means with a common origin or nature between them. There was that divine part which the Stoics called the ἡγεμονικόν, the ruling and guiding part, and which corresponds in some ways with Aristotle's higher νοῦς, and Plato's ἐπιστήμη. There was the θυμός, a collective term for many types of impulses and emotions; there were the various sensory organs with their almost independent power of action and compulsion; there was the ψυχή, usually comprised of the latter two classes plus the actual material of the blood; and then there was the body itself, by its illnesses and necessities often regarded as another, and in itself highly complicated, member in the personality. Even the mind was not single. Beside the ἡγεμονικόν there was often conceived a human mind, thinking largely on the basis of inference from sense perceptions. The Greek did not discuss these as only figurative entities, having their reality only as parts of a whole which we would call the personality. For, for all the psychological acumen of the Greek, he was surprisingly content to talk of the component parts of the personality with little concern for the personality itself.

A careful reading of Aristotle's *De Anima* might have suggested that the personality was ultimately a μῖξις. Man, ὁ ἄνθρωπος, is not the soul, but "pities, learns, and thinks" by means of the soul.[3] And such powers perish at the dissolution of the individual, who is a κοινόν.[4] The soul cannot be described as an added principle in addition to the material μῖξις, but is itself one aspect of the μῖξις, and perishes with the destruction of the μῖξις.[5] Aristotle is not content with so crude a statement, and goes on to his famous

---

2. On this familiar doctrine, that each man is "to fulfil his own function" (τὸ αὑτοῦ πράττειν) in the state, and on its psychological concomitant in Plato, see E. Barker, *Greek Political Theory*, 150 ff., 164 ff.

3. 408b 12 ff.   4. Ib., ll. 25 ff.   5. 408a 24 ff.

definition of the soul as the ἐντελέχεια of the body.[6] But the question of the constituting element of personality itself is not raised, beyond the inference that a man from the point of view of matter and form is still a μῖξις.[7] The Stoics after Posidonius tended increasingly to feel the influence of that tendency in Greek thought which had its ultimate roots in Orphism, the tendency to identify the personality with the soul, which is a sojourner, prisoner, in the tomb of the body.[8] Such a dualism had become almost proverbial in the Hellenistic world, and was irresistible to men in sympathy with the religious feeling of the period.

But though there was a tendency implicitly to identify the personality with the soul, nothing was made of this identification in a practical way. When a Greek or Hellenized Roman began to talk of the problem of his inner life he did so in a manner quite suggestive of the modern psychiatrist's notion of the problem of life as one of "adjusting" the various impulses and tendencies in the ego with each other. The ego was actually a little city; the ideal situation which meant peace and security was just as properly described as εὐνομία and δικαιοσύνη in that realm as in any other. Paul and Philo meant literally that δικαιοσύνη in the soul itself, in the sense of a city, is its highest state and best happiness. It was precisely the aspiration of Plato, and of thoughtful Greeks always.

A brilliant, but little read, study by Freudenthal[9] threw a searching light upon the manifold character of Philo's psychological teaching. Philo was a person of his age in at once being much interested in psychology and being inconsistent in his remarks about it. To Philo, too, man was a σύγκριμα,[10] made up of σῶμα, αἴσθησις, γαστὴρ καὶ αἱ μετὰ γαστέρα ἡδοναί, and πάθη τὰ ἄλλα, γλῶττη, and συνόλως ἅπαν τὸ σύγκριμα,[11] which σύγκριμα was a πόλις ἢ χώρα over which the higher part, in this passage the νοῦς,[12] ruled. To Philo as to Plato the πόλις of society is only an imitation of the real πόλις in the soul of each individual.[13] All material existences were divided by Philo, in Stoic fashion, into four groups. The first type of existence has only ἕξις, cohesion, or that primary manifestation of the Stoic universal πνεῦμα

6. 412a 21.

7. In *Eth. Nic.*, 1177b 26 ff. Man is apparently a σύνθετος, one of whose ingredients is νοῦς, a divine thing, according to which the σύνθετος should try to live. But Aristotle goes on to say that in the proper sense each man is (that is the seat of personality is identified with) this divine part, small a part of man as it is (1178a 2).

8. Heinemann, *Poseidonios*, I, 56. I cannot agree that this was a case of the ethical wine of Posidonius breaking the old Stoic wine-skins (ib., p. 58).

9. Max Freudenthal, *Die Erkenntnislehre Philos von Alexandria*, Berlin, 1891 (*Berliner Studien für classische Philologie und Archaeologie*, XIII, 1).

10. *Det.*, 52, 103, 139; *Sac.*, 105; *LA*, iii, 191; *Gig.*, 62; *Immut.*, 111.

11. *Sac.*, 49.   12. *Ib.*, 45.

13. *Conf.*, 107. The notion is familiar from Plato's search for δικαιοσύνη in the individual by examining the magnified individual, the πόλις.

in which a particle of πνεῦμα has definite physical limits. It extends from the center of the object to the circumference, then back to the center.[14] This it is which makes the material object into an identity, and would seem to be the Stoic notion of the origin of individual existence (πέρας) in the otherwise indefinite extension of undifferentiated indetermination (ἄπειρον), as other schools expressed the problem.

The next order of existence, φύσις, is that to which the powers of taking nourishment, of growing and changing, are added to the ἕξις, a type represented by the plants, hair, and nails.[15] Nothing is said of the πνεῦμα in this connection, but in view of his general acceptance of the Stoic notion, this would be only a higher manifestation of πνεῦμα.[16]

In ψυχή, the characteristic possession of animals (including man), φαντασία and ὁρμή are added to φύσις;[17] or as he elsewhere explains, ψυχή is distinguished from φύσις by having (in addition to the qualities of φύσις) αἴσθησις, φαντασία, and ὁρμή.[18] Philo defines these: αἴσθησις means sense experience, or the faculty by which the outer world may come into the mind, and be kept there;[19] φαντασία means that faculty by which these impressions, more than just being inside us, get stamped upon the soul. Hicks[20] thinks that "presentation" is a better term than "perception" or "impression" for this notion. As to ὁρμή Philo says:

The object which has appeared and stamped itself [τὸ φανὲν καὶ τυπῶσαν, i.e., the object present to the soul by the first two of these faculties] disposes the soul sometimes toward and sometimes away from the object.[21] This condition of the soul is called ὁρμή (impulse), which has been defined as the primary movement of the soul.[22]

Repulsion, which Philo includes under ὁρμή along with its proper meaning of "impulse toward" a thing, was by the Stoics properly called ἀφορμή.[23] From all of this what Philo meant by ψυχή has appeared in careful outline. It is that (form of πνεῦμα ?) which when present in a material object gives power of sensation, perception, reaction and impulsion, in addition to the

14. *Immut.*, 35.   15. Ib., 37.
16. Cf. Galen's *Comm. 5 in Hippocr. epid. 6, ap. SVF*, II, 715. See also ib., 716.
17. *LA*, ii, 23.   18. *Immut.*, 41.
19. αἴσθησις = εἴσθεσις.
20. Note to his translation of Diogenes Laertius, II, p. 152 (Loeb). Quoted by Colson and Whitaker, note *ap. Immut.*, 41.
21. These words are a very free paraphrase of τοτὲ μὲν οἰκείως τοτὲ δὲ ὡς ἑτέρως διέθηκε τὴν ψυχήν. I do not understand the meaning of Colson and Whitaker's translation, "has an effect upon the soul sometimes of an appropriate kind, sometimes the reverse." See the quotation from Plutarch in their note to this section, iii, 484, i.e., Plutarch, *Adv. Coloten*, 1122c: τὸ δὲ ὁρμητικὸν ἐγειρόμενον ὑπὸ τοῦ φανταστικοῦ πρὸς τὰ οἰκεῖα πρακτικῶς κινεῖ τὸν ἄνθρωπον.
22. *Immut.*, 44.
23. As Colson and Whitaker point out in their note, iii, 484.

quality of individual identity, and the power of taking nutrition, and of growing and altering in form, characteristic also of lower forms of existence.

All of these qualities and powers man shares with the higher animals; he is set off from other ζῷα by his διάνοια or νοῦς, which is not a part of the ψυχή in its lower manifestations, though like those other parts it is called an εἶδος τῆς ψυχῆς. Rather, as he says, νοῦς "has gained possession of the better and purer οὐσία out of which the divine φύσεις were made."[24] This νοῦς is the "eye of the soul" by which the darkness of ignorance is scattered. By virtue of it man alone is free. The ψυχή of animals is thus regarded in Stoic fashion as typifying that inevitability of natural causation with which Philo does not want to associate man too closely because he sees that moral responsibility and materialistic determinism are quite incompatible. So he points out the moral irresponsibility of plants and animals, because they had not this higher gift of an immediate share in the divine substance.

Philo can easily abandon the Stoic psychology to describe the constitution of man in Aristotelian language:[25]

There are three parts of the soul, the θρεπτικόν, the αἰσθητικόν, and the λογικόν. The divine πνεῦμα is, according to the Theologian [Moses], the οὐσία of the λογικόν, for he says that God breathed into man's face the breath of life. The οὐσία of the αἰσθητικὸν καὶ λογικόν is the blood. . . . Blood is most correctly called the soul of the flesh.[26] Sense and emotion are concerned with flesh, not mind and reason. Yet of a truth even the expression "in the blood of the soul"[27] indicates that the soul is one thing and the blood another; so that πνεῦμα is really the οὐσία of the soul, yet the πνεῦμα is not separated off by itself in a place apart from the blood, but is contained within the blood and mixed (συγκεκρᾶσθαι) in it.

It is obvious that the Stoic or the Aristotelian formulations were as such equally indifferent to him. Either could be advanced according to the exigencies of a given allegory. What did matter to Philo was that the total personality was made up of diverse elements dominated by the reasoning faculty. The classification and characterization of the lower elements was neither fixed nor important. For the personality, or the individual, seems to consist in none of the specific parts of the σύγκριμα, however those parts may be described, but in the σύγκριμα itself.[28] In a passage where Philo has described the universe as made up of a series of opposites held together in

24. *Immut.*, 46. In §35 the distinction is between the ψυχή of animals, and the λογικὴ ψυχή of man.

25. *QG*, ii, 59; Harris, *Fragments*, pp. 25 f.; Freudenthal, *Erkenntnislehre Philos*, 40, n. 2. Cf. *Opif.*, 69; *QG*, iv, 186. See Arist., *De Anima*, 413b 11 ff.: ἡ ψυχὴ . . . τούτοις ὥρισται, θρεπτικῷ, αἰσθητικῷ, διανοητικῷ, κινήσει.

26. Lev. xvii, 11. 27. Gen. ix, 4, LXX.

28. Philo's remarks recall on many points the following: καθ' οὓς δὲ μία ζωὴ τῆς ψυχῆς

harmony by love[29] he goes on to show that by causing this sort of cohesion God keeps His rulership over all things, while each individual constituent of the universe has the use of other parts, but no permanent ownership of, or domination over, any of them. He says:[30]

> We have ourselves, and all that goes to make these selves, as a loan.[31] I, indeed, am a combination of soul and body, seeming to have mind, reason (or speech) and sense perception, yet I find that none of these is my own property. For where was my body before I was born, and whither will it go when I have died? And what has become of the distinct life-periods of this "self" which appears to be a constant? Where is the babe that once I was, the little boy, the stripling, the young adolescent, the youth, the young buck, the young man, and the adult? Whence came the soul and whither will it go, and how long will it live with us? Can we tell what is its essential nature? And when did we come to possess it? Before birth? But then we did not exist. After death? But then we, who, in our junction with our bodies, are mixtures (σύγκριτοι) and have qualities, shall not exist, but shall be brought into the rebirth, by which, becoming joined to immaterial things, we shall become unmixed (ἀσύγκριτοι) and without qualities.[32]

Here it is specifically stated that the ego is a mixture of soul and body, and consists of neither the soul nor the body by itself. The body did not exist until "I" was born: the soul is ἡμῖν ὁμοδίαιτος, a thing of which the ego never got full possession. This is all clear. The soul existed before our birth, but "we" did not.[33] The last quoted sentence confuses the matter. For instead of logically concluding that after death we shall cease to exist, he says that we who are a mixture shall not exist. After death "we" shall be pushed into palingenesis, when "we" shall be joined with immaterial things. The text of this last phrase is impossible as preserved in·the manuscripts, and sense can be made only by arbitrary emendation. But it is quite apparent that whatever the future relation of the "ego" to immaterial existences, the text clearly made the "ego" survive the dissolution of that σύγκριμα in which it had apparently solely consisted, and whose destruction should have put an

---

ἐστιν ἡ τοῦ συνθέτου, συγκεκραμένης τῆς ψυχῆς τῷ σώματι, ὡς οἱ Στωϊκοὶ λέγουσιν. κατὰ τούτους εἰς ἐστιν ὁ τρόπος τῆς παρουσίας αὐτῶν, ὁ ἐν τῷ μετέχεσθαι ἢ ἐν τῷ κεκρᾶσθαι τῷ ὅλῳ ζῴῳ. Iamblichus, ap. Stob., I, p. 368, 6 f., SVF, II, 826.

29. A Pythagorean motif in Philo which I have discussed at length in my "Neo-Pythag. Source," pp. 120 ff.

30. Cher., 113 ff.

31. ἑαυτοὺς καὶ ὅσα περὶ ἡμᾶς χρῆσιν ἔχομεν.

32. Cf. Ebr., 101. "Man" is defined as τὸ ψυχῆς καὶ σώματος ὕφασμα ἢ πλέγμα ἢ κρᾶμα ἢ ὅ τι ποτὲ χρὴ καλεῖν τουτὶ τὸ σύνθετον ζῷον. In contrast is νοῦς εἰλικρινέστατος καὶ καθαρώτατος, dragged down and imprisoned in our bodies. Cf. ib., 144.

33. Philo goes on in §115 to a further contrast between "us" and our souls. The soul knows "us," but "we" do not know it. It commands, "we" obey. It secures a divorce from us when it wishes and leaves "our house" bereft of life. Its nature is so subtle that it gives the body no grip upon it. Philo is so anxious to deny the identity of the ego with the soul that he temporarily almost confuses the ego with the body.

end to it altogether. It would appear that the passage is a syncretistic or eclectic combination of a notion of personality originally that of Heracleitus, through whatever channels it may have come to Philo,[34] with an Orphic, Neo-Pythagorean, mystic notion that the personality survives death and achieves a new and immaterial existence.[35] By the one, personality is a function of the temporary pattern produced by the combination of soul and body, or of the elements out of which each of these is composed; by the other, personality is an immortal thing, now identified with this pattern, now to be transferred to another and quite different pattern, so that logically the personality was for its existence independent of each alike. The latter can only have meaning if the personality was thought of as a permanent principle distinct from both soul and body. But this notion is to be used only in connection with the problem of life after death. From the ethical and temporal point of view, man is essentially the σύγκριμα of body and soul.

The picture of man as a composite is again made clear in the frequently repeated Stoic description of man as made up of two parts, the ἡγεμονικόν, called also the πνεῦμα, νοῦς, or λόγος, and the unreasoning part, itself consisting of seven subdivisions, the five senses plus powers of speech, and reproduction. All of these seven parts are but the extensions of the ἡγεμονικόν.[36] The Stoic conception should logically have implied a unity of personality. The senses are by this theory not self-existent entities but only

34. L. Cohn connected this passage with the *Jos.*, 127, at the translation of which passage (in *Philos Werke*) he refers to the investigation of H. von Arnim, *Quellenstudien zu Philo von Alexandria*, Berlin, 1888, pp. 94 ff. Von Arnim thinks the *Jos.* passage (he overlooked the passage in *Cher.*) is of Heraclitean origin, and that it came to Philo through a Cynic writer, probably Aenesidemus. Since the *Cher.* passage is already combined with a mystical belief in immortality, and since in the Plutarch parallel (*E ap. Delphos*, 18) which von Arnim adduced, the idea is used for the non-Heraclitean, but quite Pythagorean, contrast between τὸ γιγνόμενον and τὸ ὄντως ὄν, it seems to me that the combination of ideas of personality was made not by Philo but by the Neo-Pythagoreans. But the fact that the combination was made by a source of Philo's and not by Philo himself does not remove the essential contradiction in the psychology.

35. The παλιγγενεσία here, as L. Cohn suggested (note to *Cher.*, 114), is certainly the mystic one, more fully described in *QE*, ii, 46: "prior nativitas . . . commixta per carnem et corruptibiles habebat parentes; secunda nativitas . . . incommixta simplexque anima principalis (vel spiritus principis), mutata a genita ad ingenitam cuius non est mater, sed pater solus, qui et universorum." The suggestion in Colson and Whitaker (*ad loc.*) that it might be connected with the Stoic παλιγγενεσία seems beside the point. It is quite in keeping with such remarks as *Corpus Herm.*, XIII, 3, 14. Cf. Angus, *Religious Quests of the Graeco-Roman World*, pp. 368 ff.; Kroll, *Lehren des Hermes Trismegistus*, pp. 363 f. It would appear that the Stoics had the term from Orphics and Pythagoreans: Rohde, *Psyche* (English), p. 356, n. 47; p. 361, n. 84.

36. For the divisions of the irrational part of the soul the best passages are *Heres*, 230–236; *Agr.*, 30 ff.; see also *Opif.*, 117; *LA*, i, 11; *Det.*, 168; *QG*, i, 75; ii, 12; *Mut.*, 110 f. For Stoicism see the passages quoted in *SVF*, II, 827–831. For these divisions as all being extensions and δυνάμεις of the ἡγεμονικόν see *Fug.*, 182: τὸ ἡγεμονικὸν ἡμῶν ἐοικὸς πηγῇ δυνάμεις πολλὰς οἷα διὰ γῆς φλεβῶν ἀνομβροῦν, τὰς δυνάμεις ταύτας ἄχρι τῶν αἰσθήσεων [ὀργάνων], ὀφθαλμῶν, ὤτων, ῥινῶν, τῶν ἄλλων, ἀποστέλλει. κτλ.

δυνάμεις of the ἡγεμονικόν, while the ego is definitely located in this dominant διάνοια.[37] But Stoic ethics was notoriously based upon the struggle for independence, achieved only by the σοφός, which the διάνοια had to carry on against its own δυνάμεις as well as against the external world. So if the personality was theoretically unified, practically it was a medley of warring factions and tendencies. Philo had obviously little scientific interest in psychology, as is shown by his using such divergent theories, as well as by his tampering with the theories as he got them. So in one place he refers obviously to the Stoic division, but makes the total seven instead of eight parts by leaving out the sexual function, merely to get the right number for the allegory immediately at hand.

Again Philo describes the soul and its parts as being the result of the dividing action of the undivided higher mind (here the λόγος τομεύς) upon the lower ἄλογον ψυχῆς μέρος. The human soul is thus like the κόσμος in being made up of the circles of the planets, seven in all, plus the undivided region of the οὐρανός, the sphere of the fixed stars.[38] The νοῦς is itself a copy of the universal Logos, as that is a copy of God. With this talk of a παράδειγμα and an ἀπεικόνισμα, as well as of the λόγος τομεύς, we are in a Neo-Pythagorean milieu.[39] It is true that the seven divisions are sometimes μοῖραι[40] and sometimes δυνάμεις[41] of the soul or of τὸ ἄλογον τῆς ψυχῆς, but in either case Philo thought vividly of the reality of the divisions. The senses, like the body, are only vessels of the mind which lives in them, and should support them and all the activities of the soul as a pillar does a house.[42] The senses are indeed passive in themselves, as sight and hearing are in a passive relation to their objects, but are activities of the νοῦς, for sense perception is a high development of one of the many δυνάμεις of the νοῦς.[43] Yet not only is the mind bare without these faculties: Philo states specifically that without these faculties the mind cannot be said even to exist,[44] by which we are again thrown back upon the notion of the σύγκριμα as the seat of personality.

It has been seen that one of the approaches to the problem of the psychological constitution of man is through speaking of two or three souls—the one the αἰσθητική, the other the λογικιή, a third the θρεπτική.[45] The two-

37. See Zeller, *Phil. d. Gr.*, III, i (4th ed.), pp. 200 ff., esp. 203, n. 2.
38. *Heres*, 230 ff.
39. Philo connects the tripartite division of the soul proper with this material in *Heres*, 225.
40. As in *Det.*, 168.
41. As in *Mut.*, 110. See Freudenthal, *op. cit.*, pp. 36 ff.
42. *Mig.*, 124: εὐχώμεθα οὖν τὸν ὡς ἐν οἰκίᾳ στῦλον νοῦν ἐν ψυχῇ. Freudenthal's passages do not justify his calling the νοῦς in this connection "die eigentliche Seele" (p. 38).
43. *LA*, ii, 35 ff.
44. *LA*, iii, 49: ἄνευ τῶν δυνάμεων ὁ νοῦς καθ᾽ ἑαυτὸν γυμνὸς καὶ οὐδὲ ὢν εὑρίσκεται. In *Cong.*, 59 Philo says: λογισμοῦ ἡ ὅλη ψυχὴ καθάπερ ἀστὴ σύμβιος.
45. See above, p. 374.

fold soul, more common than the three-fold, Philo justified by the fact that in one passage of Scripture the ψυχή was identified with blood,[46] in another with πνεῦμα.[47] In the passage quoted these are combined into a σύγκριμα, the πνεῦμα type of ψυχή being interfused into the blood. The same scriptural passages appear again when he says:

The word soul is used in two senses, with reference either to the soul as a whole or to its dominant (ἡγεμονικόν) part, which latter is, properly speaking, the soul of the soul (ψυχὴ ψυχῆς). . . . Therefore the Lawgiver held that the οὐσία of the soul is likewise twofold, blood being the οὐσία of the soul as a whole, and the divine πνεῦμα of the dominant part.[48]

The mixture here is quite the same as in the passage based upon Aristotle quoted from the *Quaestiones in Genesin*.[49] The idea appears elsewhere in Philo.[50] In the passages quoted the "two souls" have been quite obviously worked out on the basis of the Stoic ἡγεμονικόν, which is a unique part, but still a part, of the soul.

Philo has here hopelessly confused two very distinct types of doctrine. The notion that the soul is essentially the πνεῦμα or διάνοια, with the radiating δυνάμεις, should lead logically to the conclusion that the soul is a unit. This conclusion many, including Posidonius, took.[51] Philo followed the traditions of the Pythagoreans,[52] as well as of Hippocrates, and Plato, in talking literally of "parts" of the soul, or of distinct souls. This he did, apparently, to maintain his notion of the personality as a mixture of various elements, not a single entity like Posidonius.[53]

In another passage Philo uses the same Old Testament texts with Platonism, especially the Timaeus, in mind.[54] Here the fact that ψυχή is identified in one scriptural passage with blood, in another with πνεῦμα shows that

46. Lev. xvii, 11.   47. Gen. ii, 7.   48. *Heres*, 55.
49. See above, p. 374.
50. See also *Spec.*, iv, 123. The οὐσία ψυχῆς νοερᾶς καὶ λογικῆς is πνεῦμα θεῖον, while blood is the οὐσία ψυχῆς τῆς αἰσθητικῆς, καθ' ἣν ἡμῖν τε καὶ τοῖς ἀλόγοις κοινὸν τὸ ζῆν συμβέβηκεν.
51. See the long discussion of Galen, *de Placitis Hipp. et Plat.*, p. 501, 10 ff. by Schmekel, *Philosophie der Mittleren Stoa*, p. 259, n. 2; also the many passages in Zeller, *Phil. d. Gr.*, III, i (4th ed.), p. 202, n. 3.
52. Diog. Laert., VIII, 30.
53. There was a confusion similar to Philo's among the ancients as to the relations of the soul and the blood. Empedocles and Critias identified soul and blood. The Stoic tradition identified soul with πνεῦμα, but said it was nourished by the blood. But some Stoics, notably Diogenes of Babylon, were uncertain. Cf. *SVF*, III, p. 216, ll. 26–31: καὶ αὐτὸς ἐπιλανθανόμενος τῶν οἰκείων δογμάτων αἷμά φησιν εἶναι τὴν ψυχήν, ὡς Ἐμπεδοκλῆς καὶ Κριτίας ὑπέλαβον. εἰ δέ γε ἕποιτο Κλεάνθει καὶ Χρυσίππῳ καὶ Ζήνωνι, τρέφεσθαι μὲν ἐξ αἵματος φήσασι τὴν ψυχήν, οὐσίαν δ' αὐτῆς ὑπάρχειν τὸ πνεῦμα, πῶς ἔτι ταὐτὸν ἔσται τὸ τρέφον καὶ τὸ κινοῦν, εἴπερ τρέφει μὲν τὸ αἷμα, κινεῖ δὲ τὸ πνεῦμα; Cf. Diog. Laert., VIII, 30. I have not been able to find any philosopher, who taught the doctrine of two souls, one the blood, the other the πνεῦμα.
54. *Det.*, 79 ff.

each of us is two in number, an animal and a man. To each has been allotted a δύναμις akin to the δυνάμεις of the soul, to the one power of life, by virtue of which we live, and to the other the reasoning power, by virtue of which we are rational beings. The irrational beings, also, have a share in the life-power, but of the reasoning power, God is, not indeed the partaker, but the originator, the fountain of the primal Reason.[55]

Blood is thus properly the οὐσία of the ζωτικὴ δύναμις, πνεῦμα the οὐσία of the λογική. This πνεῦμα is not (as elsewhere in Philo) moving air, but is τύπος τὶς καὶ χαρακτὴρ θείας δυνάμεως, or εἰκών,

showing that God is the archetype of the logical nature, and that man is an imitation and copy. But by "man" is meant not the double-natured animal, but that best part (εἶδος) of the soul which is called νοῦς and λόγος. . . . And He called πνεῦμα the soul of man, meaning by "man" not the σύγκριμα, as I said, but that God-like creation by which we reason, whose roots He stretched up to heaven and bound to the last circle of the fixed stars.[55a]

The passage, as has frequently been pointed out, is obviously based upon the *Timaeus* of Plato (90a ff.). For our immediate purpose it is notable that while Philo has seemed to contradict his conception that the personality of the individual consists in the σύγκριμα, he has in reality kept to it clearly. For it is notable that the ego (ἕκαστος ἡμῶν) is made up of the double-natured compound. True only the higher nature is properly "human," and we are "human" not by virtue of the mixture, but only of the god-like reason in us. But "we" are not identified exclusively with the human part, for we "use" this part of "us" when we think. The ego is still the σύγκριμα, and the "man" and the "animal" in us are each alike parts of "us."[56]

Philo frequently uses the Platonic divisions of the human soul into reason (νοῦς, τὸ λογικόν, etc.), θυμός, and ἐπιθυμία, assigned respectively to the head, chest, and abdomen.[57] In one passage he uses the distinctively Platonic expression that the soul has a τριττὸν εἶδος,[58] but he more frequently talks of the three divisions as μέρη of the soul, as does Plato also.[59]

It is apparent that Philo will use any psychological scheme that fits the immediate necessities of his allegory. The one constant, which he brings out in all the theories, is the conception of the ego as a σύγκριμα, however the

55. Ib., 82.   55a. Ib., 83.
56. It is in this sense that he speaks of τὸν ἐν ἡμῖν πρὸς ἀλήθειαν ἄνθρωπον, τουτέστι τὸν νοῦν; that is, "the real man," the νοῦς, is ἐν ἡμῖν, the totality: *Plant.*, 42.
57. A frequent idea in Plato. See especially *Timaeus*, 69c ff.
58. *Spec.*, iv, 92. Cf. Plato, *Repub.*, 580d: ὥσπερ πόλις διῄρηται κατὰ τρία εἴδη, οὕτω καὶ ψυχὴ ἑνὸς ἑκάστου τριχῇ.
59. *Conf.*, 21; *Heres*, 225; *LA*, i, 70, iii, 115; cf. *Repub.*, 442b f. In *Virt.*, 13, Philo calls them δυνάμεις τῆς ψυχῆς. Philo also speaks of the divisions "in us" as *caro, sensus, et ratio: QG*, iii, 3; cf. iv, 117.

ingredients of the mixture may be defined.[60] Philo's emphasis upon the personality is quite a departure from his Greek sources for psychology. In handling all of these the notion of the σύγκριμα, indeed the word itself, is superimposed upon the Greek ideas. It is true that Antiochus taught a doctrine of man as made up of soul and body,[61] while Plutarch records that οἱ πολλοί thought of man (ὁ ἄνθρωπος) as a σύνθετον.[62] Philo may then simply be reproducing popular Greek thought. But his notion of the σύγκριμα as the total man is given an entirely new prominence even over against his Orphic mysticism. So consistent an importation of a new idea into the Greek source must have had some definite motivation, and the motive is not far to seek. The Jews of Philo's day, and for long into the past as we know them, had thought of man as body plus soul. The Jewish resurrection of the body was elaborately explained as necessary because if there is to be punishment after death neither the body nor the soul could properly be blamed for the sins committed by the two in conjunction.[63] That is, the personality is definitely made up of what Philo calls the σύγκριμα. This much Philo has from Judaism. It is true that his mind is so filled with the Orphic-Pythagorean point of view that salvation after death is a release from the body and restoration of the immaterial διάνοια to the source. Yet he never lost his Judaism so completely that he ceased to think of man in the practically wholesome way of being a combination of body and soul, into whatever logical difficulties it might lead him with the Orphic point of view.[64]

The total impression from his most varied remarks on the subject is that Philo's own approach was that of a man primarily with a religious problem,[65]

60. In describing a man of ordinary human nature as contrasted with the ideal man Philo says that since he has a greatly mixed and earthly body, he has no share in single and uncompounded nature (as does the ascetic), for his state is one that is πολύτροπος καὶ ἐκ παντοίων συνηρημένη καὶ πεπλασμένη (Plant., 44).

61. See the report of Antiochus in Cicero, De Finibus, V, xii, 34: "Atqui perspicuum est hominem e corpore animoque constare, quum primae sint animi partes, secundae corporis." But Antiochus does not seem to have used this in a way at all like Philo.

62. De Facie in Orbe Lunae, 943a. And we recall Aristotle's μίξις. See above, p. 371.

63. See the material collected by G. F. Moore, Judaism, I, 486 ff.

64. This point is clearly brought out in Cong., 97, a passage which Heinemann quotes (Poseidonios, I, 62, n. 5) as indicating that Philo followed Posidonius in identifying the personality with the νοῦς. Philo says: ὁ νοῦς, ὃς κυρίως εἰπεῖν ἄνθρωπός ἐστιν ἐν ἀνθρώπῳ, κρείττων ἐν χείρονι καὶ ἀθάνατος ἐν θνητῷ. This statement has no absolute value, for it is a part of an allegory of the command to offer first fruits, which involves, Philo says, not only the first fruits of the farms and animals, but also the first fruits of the body, and of man in the sense of reason. That Philo does not mean the statement literally appears a few lines below in §98, where he says, τὸ γὰρ πρῶτον καὶ ἄριστον ἐν ἡμῖν αὐτοῖς ὁ λογισμός ἐστι, by which ὁ λογισμός is plainly restored to its normal place in Philo's thinking as a part of "ourselves," a larger totality. The other passage adduced by Heinemann, Agr., 9, is also a product of the allegory. Posidonius seems to have taught, on the contrary, a doctrine paraphrased by Cicero: "Mens cuiusque is est quisque": Rep., VI, 26. See Heinemann, op. cit., I, 61 f., 181; II, 22.

65. Freudenthal prefers to call this "ethical" rather than "religious," Erkenntnislehre Philos,

the warfare of the "lower" against the "higher" elements of his nature. Without going into too great detail, it will be necessary to define more exactly how Philo thought of these two main divisions.

By whatever philosophy Philo was being guided at a given time, it has already appeared that he thought always of the highest part of a man as being essentially an intellectual force. Even concerning the intellect, Philo has no theory to which he adheres consistently. The νοῦς ἡγεμών is in the first place quite incomprehensible.[66]

What do we suppose its substance (οὐσία) to be? Is it πνεῦμα or blood or matter at all (σῶμα συνόλως)? It is not matter, for it must be called ἀσώματος. Or is it limit (πέρας) or form (εἶδος) or number, or ἐνδελέχεια,[67] or attunement (ἁρμονία), or any existing thing whatever?

Except for its immateriality, then, Philo is quite at a loss what to call its essential substance. He does not know, he goes on to point out, whether it is infused into us from without or is the warm principle within us (ἡ ἔνθερμος ἐν ἡμῖν φύσις) hardened like steel by contact with the cold air about us. He cannot say whether it perishes with the body, continues to live after the death of the body for only a period of time, or is permanently indestructible. He will not say whether it is situated in the head or in the heart. Philo's theoretical skepticism about the soul would seem to be thorough and complete, and one might infer that the passages where he makes more positive statements about the soul are of a tentative character. Yet if Philo despaired of any critically exact knowledge of the νοῦς ἡγεμών, he says many instructive things about it. At one time the νοῦς or διάνοια seems quite a part of the man's own personality. It is itself a human affair, and stops short of apprehending divine nature. For the fact that the νοῦς ἡγεμών is in the image of God by no means indicates, he says, that it is upon an equality with God. It is not even upon an equality with the "heavenly man," who was "stamped after the image of God," while the earthly man, i.e., the human being, was

39, n. 1. I am deeply in sympathy with an important remark of Kennedy (*Philo's Contribution to Religion,* 1919, p. 89, n. 1). Kennedy says that when Lietzmann contrasts Paul's and Philo's psychology, he is in error in saying that Philo is looking from the intellectual standpoint, Paul from that of pure religion. "In our judgment," says Kennedy, "Philo is here far more directly influenced by religious experience than by any philosophical theory." The statement could be improved only by omitting the word "here," and so making it perfectly general. Indeed, in view of Philo's obvious lack of any fixed notion of psychology, the fact that Paul expresses himself differently from Philo means not at all that Paul's remarks would not have been as acceptable to Philo as any one of the half dozen notions Philo reflects. Kennedy is in this section especially sound in his conclusions.

66. *Som.,* i, 30–33. Cf. *Opif.,* 69.

67. Philo was probably making the common Hellenistic confusion, using ἐνδελέχεια in the sense of ἐντελέχεια. See Liddell and Scott, s.v. ἐντελέχεια. So he should be understood here as meaning that the soul is the Aristotelian "actuality" rather than "continuity."

"made, but not begotten."[68] Man is not a direct copy of God, but only secondarily so as a copy of the Logos.[69] And yet for the human νοῦς to be a copy of the Logos is to have συγγένεια with it.[70] Philo asserts that the νοῦς ἡγεμών, by virtue of its having been created in God's image, has a substance as inscrutable as God's. It is able, like God, while itself invisible, to see all things; it works out all the sciences, traverses land and sea and the universe itself, and even goes on beyond the material into ἡ νοητὴ οὐσία, where the visions it gets inspire it to go even on to God Himself. But to get up to God Himself is ultimately impossible for the human mind, for at the last step the eye of διάνοια is suddenly dazzled and blinded by streaming rays of concentrated light (φῶς ἀθρόον).[71] The idea that ὁ ἀνθρώπινος νοῦς could be the μέτρον πάντων χρημάτων seems to Philo the most impious of notions —typified by so low a person as a woman who would become Cain's wife.[72] Likewise he considered the Stoics utterly wrong in thinking that the universe goes along in an automatic process guided by no personal Director, with the inference that the human mind has created the arts, professions, laws, and customs and the πολιτικὰ καὶ ἴδια καὶ κοινὰ δίκαια. One who could think such extravagances of man's mind seems to Philo to have reversed the whole aim of the Mystery. He has run away from the divine mind and is living in his own mind. ὁ γὰρ ἀποδιδράσκων θεὸν καταφεύγει εἰς ἑαυτόν. From this the human mind would seem to be almost the complete antithesis of the divine mind.[73]

The same contrast is frequently brought out in Philo's explanation of ecstasy and prophetic inspiration. "Our" minds are, like God's, light-centers, sending νοητὰς αὐγάς through "us" as the sun illumines the material universe. So long as this is going on we are "in ourselves" and so cannot be possessed. But when the light of our minds "sets" there naturally then comes the state of ecstasy, enthusiasm, possession, mania. For when the divine light shines, the human light sets, and when the divine light sets, the human rises.[74]

When talking in this vein Philo has obviously a very high opinion of the

68. LA, i, 31.
69. Opif., 25; Plant., 19 f. See J. Cohn's note to Opif., 25 in Philos Werke; G. F. Moore, Judaism, I, 446 ff.; III, 136, n. 177. When Philo says that man is ἀντίμιμον θεοῦ δυνάμεως, εἰκὼν τῆς ἀοράτου φύσεως ἐμφανής ἀιδίου γεννητή (Mos., ii, 65) he is saying the same thing, though not distinguishing that this is true only with respect to the νοῦς.
70. Exs., 163.
71. Opif., 69–71. In the illuminating essay by R. M. Jones, "Posidonius and the Flight of the mind through the Universe," Classical Philology, XXI (1926), pp. 104–113, this type of argument is examined as a phenomenon in Greek Philosophy. Jones proves conclusively that it is not uniquely to be classed as a Posidonian contribution. His discussion of the matter in Philo is very thorough. Philo is fond of describing the power of the mind as being based upon its ability to see the higher truth: See Opif., 53; LA, iii, 110; Sac., 78; Abr., 57; Virt., 11 ff.; such I take to be ὁ βλέπων λογισμός in LA, iii, 110.
72. Post., 34–39.   73. LA, iii, 28–31.   74. Heres, 263 f.

possibilities of the human reason, though he thinks that to dwell in it too much is eventually to be led into some philosophical absurdity. Yet even at its very highest, the human mind is utterly different from the divine mind. Man must go out of himself altogether to have communion with the mind of God.

In sharp contrast with this notion of the human νοῦς is another, just as common in Philo, that the mind of man is a bit of God, or what is ultimately the same thing, of the Logos of God, dwelling in him. "Every man," he says, with a shrug of the shoulders at too close psychological theory, "is in respect of his mind closely assimilated to (ᾠκείωται) the divine Logos, for he has come into being [in that respect] as a copy, or fragment, or emanation of that blessed nature."[75] The λογισμός in man may be called an ἀπόσπασμα (fragment) of the soul of the Universe, but it is more pious for a student of the philosophy of Moses to speak of it as an impression (ἐκμαγεῖον) of the divine likeness.[76] Important as are the philosophical implications of this distinction, to Philo it is a mere matter of terminology.

For Philo makes the distinction at all only when he has in mind the verse: "God created man in his own image." By that verse he may understand a reference to the "heavenly man," but he understands one also to the "earthly man," the human being,[77] or rather to his νοῦς,[78] which is itself in some sense like God. For God made this νοῦς, and then breathed the πνεῦμα into it.[79] But this same notion of the inbreathing of the πνεῦμα may to him betoken also God's giving to man ἡ λογικὴ ψυχή,[80] whose "priest," that is, whose link with God, is "the true man," the νοῦς.[81] So again, because God is said to have breathed in the πνεῦμα, Philo says that in man is νοῦς, ἀπόσπασμα θεῖον ὤν, precisely the word which in the passage just quoted he thought ill-advised.[82] Indeed he goes all the way to a·complete contradiction of the notion of the limitation of the human mind when he describes again how the mind of man can go over the whole universe, and aim at going on to apprehend ἡ ἀκατάληπτος θεοῦ φύσις.[83] But whereas before he said that being only in the image of God it could not stand the rays coming out from God, now he identifies the mind of man with these divine rays. For how could the mind of man have comprehended this universe, he asks,

if it had not been an inseparable ἀπόσπασμα of that divine and blessed soul?[84]

75. *Opif.*, 146: τῆς μακαρίας φύσεως ἐκμαγεῖον ἢ ἀπόσπασμα ἢ ἀπαύγασμα. Cf. *Opif.*, 135.
76. *Mut.*, 223; the idea is the familiar stamp of the Seal, the Logos. See also *Mos.*, ii, 128.
77. *Plant.*, 19.
78. *LA*, i, 32. See below, p. 385.
79. Ib., 37.   80. *Plant.*, 18 f.
81. *Som.*, i, 215; on understanding ὁ πρὸς ἀλήθειαν ἄνθρωπος as νοῦς, see *Plant.*, 42.
82. *Som.*, i, 34.   83. *Det.*, 89 f. See above, n. 71.
84. It would seem here that God is identified with ἡ τοῦ παντὸς ψυχή.

For no part of the divine existence is cut off into something separate, but only is extended.

So the human mind has a share in the perfection manifest in the universe.[85]

On the other hand Philo has one striking description of the human mind in its condition before it was united with the other "half of the soul," αἴσθησις. In that state it was utterly blind and deaf, completely dissociated from the realm of matter, and hence entirely ἀδύνατος. The soul as a whole (ἡ ὅλη ψυχή) was not made until the νοῦς was woven into a single fabric with αἴσθησις.[86] Nothing could be more complete a contrast to the notion that the mind is an ἀπόσπασμα of the divine mind, which is regarded as seeing and knowing all things, and itself not only forming, but ruling, the material world.[87] True Philo goes on at length to point out the folly of thinking that man's own perceptions and notions on the basis of his sense experiences are his own creation; for all things are of God.[87a] But nothing is said here to controvert the impression that the mind put into man was as different as possible from the divine mind.

Yet again in complete contrast he describes νοῦς and its relation to the rest of the soul as follows:

Νοῦς imparts to the unreasoning part of the soul that of which it has received a share from God, so that the νοῦς is ensouled from God, but the unreasoning part by νοῦς. For νοῦς is in a sense God of the unreasoning part. . . . For some of the things which come into existence do so from God acting as both cause and agent (καὶ ὑπὸ θεοῦ καὶ δι᾽ αὐτοῦ), while some things do so with God as cause but not agent. The best things come in with God in both relations, . . . and νοῦς is one of them. But the unreasoning part, while ultimately caused by God, did not come into existence through God's immediate agency, but through the agency of the reasoning part, the ruler and king in the soul.[88]

It seems useless to try to reconcile this statement with the description of the soul as blind and deaf, impotent, before it was combined with αἴσθησις. The only possible reconciliation might be found in the indications that Philo believed in a double νοῦς, and might be speaking of one or the other at any

---

85. Posidonius had probably the same notion (see Heinemann, *Poseidonios*, i, 62, 185), but since it was found also in Plato and Aristotle, as Heinemann himself recognizes (ib., 65 f.), and in the Pythagoreans as well, it might have reached Philo through some other source than Posidonius.

86. *Cher.*, 58–60. In §58 I would accept the suggestion of Markland, and read σώματος οὐκ ἐφήπτετο ἀθρόως, ⟨οὐκ⟩ ἔχων.

87. For example *Heres*, 235: ὅ τε γὰρ θεῖος λόγος τὰ ἐν τῇ φύσει διεῖλε καὶ διένειμε πάντα, ὅ τε ἡμέτερος νοῦς, ἅττ᾽ ἂν παραλάβῃ νοητῶς πράγματά τε καὶ σώματα, εἰς ἀπειράκις ἄπειρα διαιρεῖ μέρη καὶ τέμνων οὐδέποτε λήγει. It is impossible to reconcile such a statement with the notion that νοῦς, without αἴσθησις, is now, and was always, entirely without contact with, or knowledge of, σώματα.

87a. *Cher.*, 61 ff.   88. *LA*, i, 40.

given time. And there are quite clear indications that Philo did believe in a two-fold mind. He tells how God made the earthly mind as a part of earthly man, who is defined as νοῦς εἰσκρινόμενος σώματι, οὔπω δ' εἰσκεκριμένος. This νοῦς is γηγενὴς καὶ φιλοσώματος.[89] It would appear, from *Immut.*, 41 ff., that this type of mind was a part of the soul, the part which had to do with sense-perception, having memory, and reacting in impulse (ὁρμή). But it is notable that it is a νοῦς, if it is right to associate these two passages. The νοῦς which Philo often has in mind is that higher thing, to which in this passage he gives the name νοῦς or διάνοια exclusively. Τοῦτο τῆς ψυχῆς τὸ εἶδος, as he also calls it, was not created out of the material elements, but received a share in that purer and better οὐσία out of which the divine natures were made. So it alone of our constituting parts is indestructible. It has a share in the distinguishing characteristic of God, His freedom. The οὐσία to which Philo refers is obviously the πνεῦμα of God mentioned in other passages, but is also the πέμπτη οὐσία, the ether, of which mind is a fragment.[90] Much of Philo is made clearer if we might, as I think we may, assume that he was frequently thinking of this double sort of mentality.[91] So in his warfare between opinion (κενὴ δόξα) and the higher reason,[92] it is hard to know whence this opinion can come if not from a lower mind. In the *Legum Allegoria*, iii, 228 ff., opinion corrupts νοῦς in us, and our νοῦς is very corruptible; the only safe thing is to believe in God. Philo is rationalizing Abraham's "believing God," but seems clearly to indicate a human mind as over against a higher source of truth, an immediate presence of God, to which we have access, and which would appear to be the ὀρθὸς λόγος encountered elsewhere. Σοφία, ἐπιστήμη ὀρθοῦ λόγου, is possible for us, but we can achieve it only by banishing δόξα and the νοῦς,[93] and keeping our διάνοια fixed upon the φαντασία τοῦ θεοῦ.[94] He can speak of the νοῦς as utterly unable "in itself" to come to sound judgment; he discusses

89. *LA*, i, 31 ff.

90. *Heres*, 283. See Colson and Whitaker, III, 485. See also *LA*, iii, 161: τὸ μὲν οὖν σῶμα ἐκ γῆς δεδημιούργεται, ἡ δὲ ψυχὴ αἰθέρος ἐστίν, ἀπόσπασμα θεῖον, κτλ. Ψυχή is here the πνεῦμα of God, and obviously equals νοῦς. Similarly *Decal.*, 134: ἄνθρωπος δέ, ζῷον ἄριστον κατὰ τὸ κρεῖττον τῶν ἐν αὐτῷ, τὴν ψυχήν, συγγενέστατος τῷ καθαρωτάτῳ τῆς οὐσίας οὐρανῷ, ὡς δ' ὁ τῶν πλείστων λόγος, καὶ τῷ τοῦ κόσμου πατρί, τῶν ἐπὶ γῆς ἁπάντων οἰκειότατον ἀπεικόνισμα καὶ μίμημα τῆς ἀιδίου καὶ εὐδαίμονος ἰδέας τὸν νοῦν λαβών. The more typically Stoic notion is just as plainly stated when he says that the soul has from a single root put out two shoots, the one undivided, the mind, the other cut up into the seven divisions of five senses, speech, and generation: *Agr.*, 30.

91. The probability of an ultimate Aristotelian origin of Philo's double mind need only be suggested. A comparison of Philo's remarks with Aristotle's would here be a considerable and needless digression.

92. E.g., *Som.*, ii, 95. In *LA*, iii, 79 f., νοῦς is a tyrant leading men to lawless acts of the body, in contrast with the true king which gives laws, ὁ ὀρθὸς λόγος, here at once divine and a part of man.

93. *Cher.*, 9 f.   94. Ib., 13.

at length the causes of human illusion, and the resulting confusion of philo-sophical systems.[95] In every man there are two tribunals, that of his λογισμός, which judges all things by the canon of τὰ νοητά, and that of αἴσθησις, which judges by τὰ ὁρατά; the former leads man into ἀλήθεια, the latter to δόξα.[96] Each of these is obviously a mentality, in that each can form judg-ments. Again the sin of the tower of Babel represents the sin of trying by means of the αἰσθήσεις to reach the border of heaven, our own νοῦς; that is, the people at Babel preferred αἴσθησις to διάνοια, and presumed to think that they could apprehend τὰ νοητά by means of the senses, enslaving the ruling things and violently putting up slaves as rulers.[97] Philo's remarks can be harmonized only by thinking that he, at least in some moods, thought of νοῦς as double, the one νοῦς properly our own, the other νοῦς a higher principle within us, sometimes thought of as almost fully divine, an ἀπό-σπασμα θεῖον within us, and sometimes as a part of our earthly creation.

Corresponding to these two minds are the two approaches to mystical ex-perience, represented in the Mystery by the Higher and Lower Mysteries. The better way is by direct revelation of God to man, whereby man "per-ceives God by means of God," which can only mean that the ἀπόσπασμα of God within him perceives the revealed totality, though here the ἀπόσπασμα is not normally a constant part of the human constitution, at least in measure adequate for the vision. The mystic apprehension of God is also described as an experience of apprehending light by means of light. Another mystic method, not so good as the first, but still a method, is to come to a knowledge of God, as Philo says, "from below," that is by physical research, a cosmologi-cal approach in which the world is found to be a great πόλις with its laws, and so the mind goes on to infer the Creator and Ruler behind the cosmos.[98] This is of course based upon a conception of the mind as operating primarily through, or on the basis of, sense perception. The double approach to the problem of mental operations, though found in Plato,[99] would seem ulti-mately to be Pythagorean. For from Pythagoreanism came simultaneously two things: first the inspiration to scientific cosmology based upon geometry and proportion, as reflected in Plato's Timaeus, whose aim was to "save the appearances"; and second that Orphic type of mysticism which despised all sense, and sought liberation of the fragment of the divine Mind from the body. Philo could hardly be expected to be more consistent than the schools themselves.

The proper way to live, corresponding to each conception of νοῦς, would

95. Ebr., 166–205.   96. Praem., 28.   97. Conf., 133.
98. Praem., 37–46: ἀλήθειαν δὲ μετίασιν οἱ τὸν θεὸν θεῷ φαντασιωθέντες, φωτὶ φῶς (§46). In these two approaches we recognize at once the distinction between Philo's two "Mys-teries."
99. One recalls especially the double method of thought at the close of the sixth book of the Republic.

be the complete mastery of the divine portion over the lower portions. When the human mind is thought of as base and earthly, Philo looks for its "setting," and the rising in its place of the divine mind. When the mind is a copy of the divine, it is good to develop it by every discipline, though holding it subordinate to God. When the human mind is itself divine, its destiny is to be constantly nourished and developed by influx of more of the divine principle, while it holds strict rule over the rest of man's constitution. In any case, man is only to achieve his proper destiny when the "city" of the soul, with its varied inhabitants, are benevolently but firmly ruled by the divinely appointed king of the "city," however the "king" itself might be described.

Philo has several descriptions of the kingship of the mind. In one passage[100] he has been allegorizing the notion of the shepherd or herdsman (a royal figure), in which the impulses of the senses toward pleasure are described as cattle who must be tamed. These ἄλογοι δυνάμεις τῆς ψυχῆς,[101] the ἄλογον στῖφος ψυχῆς, try to get the mastery over ὁ λογισμός, ὁ ἡγεμὼν νοῦς. When the herd is stronger than the herdsman, instead of τάξις everything is filled with ἀταξία, or with ἀκοσμία instead of εὐκοσμία, with tumult and confusion instead of order and clarity, because of all lack of legally (νόμιμος) constituted rulership. Νοῦς is βασιλεύς, and when it is weak, the subjects are open to attack by any invader. For lack of rulership (ἀναρχία) is treacherous, but rulership is σωτήριον, especially that in which νόμος and δίκη are honored. Such a rulership is rule σὺν λόγῳ. The mind in us is quite analogous to the great Mind of the universe in that both of them rule and shepherd their subjects down to the least details according to νόμος and δίκη. This rulership is set up when "we" abandon the life of δόξα and go into the region (or state) where we become the σωματικὸς οἶκος διανοίας.[102] Philo is, as usual in technical philosophy, inconsistent here. He goes on to explain in this passage that we become thus under the rulership of the mind when we close our eyes and ears to the life of the senses in complete ascetic withdrawal;[103] in other passages he describes the rulership as one not of abandoning the senses, but, in the more proper sense of the figure, of guiding them. Whatever the senses perceive when working under the direction of νοῦς is perfect (τέλεια), and such a functioning is κατὰ θεόν: their unguided operation is characteristic of "ourselves."[104] The Sophos, under the rulership of reason, has purified all his senses, has reduced them under such control that

---

100. *Som.*, ii, 15 ff.; cf., *QG*, iv, 216, where the Greek must have been very similar to this passage. The lower princes destroy that which is *justum et utile* (cf. *Som.*, ii, 154 where the herdsman rules ἐνδίκως καὶ συμφερόντως). See also *QG*, iv, 218; *Spec.*, iv, 95; *Sac.*, 49.

101. This peculiar use of δυνάμεις recalls Antiochus (*ap.* Cicero, *De Finibus*, V, xvii, 46): "cuiusque partis naturae et in corpore et in animo sua quaeque vis sit"; cf. xii, 361 "atqui in sensibus est sua cuiusque virtus"; Heinemann, *Poseidonios*, I, 49.

102. *Mig.*, 186 f.   103. See also *Mig.*, 7–15.

104. *Sac.*, 104–106.

they are never spontaneously active, but are entirely passive to the prompt-ings of reason.[105]

With this contrast the notion appears to be introduced that to live accord-ing to "ourselves" is the life of sin and disorder, while the only true life is that κατὰ θεόν. The notion becomes clearer when it appears that Philo also described the state where mind rules over the lower members as one which is in accordance with the Law of Nature,[106] and the state of anarchy as παρὰ φύσιν, a state of disease.[107] It is accordingly not surprising that King Reason should also be called by that highly inclusive term, ὀρθὸς λόγος. It has already appeared that while this term is used of the human mind when it is "think-ing straight," it is also used to bring out the legal aspect of the universal Logos.[108] Ὁ ὀρθὸς λόγος always suggested, even when used of the subjec-tive realm, the universality of the legal force of the divine Logos, represent-ing itself in many ways, not least importantly as the human mind in its highest sense. In one passage the ὀρθὸς λόγος is equivalent to God Him-self, for Philo says that the good man is a friend to God (θεῷ) but the bad man is an enemy of the ὀρθὸς λόγος, and as such is concealed from God.[109] In other passages, where honoring the ὀρθὸς λόγος is described as bringing the ideal state of peace and order, it is impossible to know whether it is the cosmic or the subjective ὀρθὸς λόγος to which Philo is referring.[110] That Philo has both the subjective and cosmic principles in mind is clear from the following, where the same imagery is used:[111]

Souls, when they cleave to God, from being women become virgins; they cast off the womanly destruction which is latent in sense and feeling, and follow after the true and untampered Virgin, namely that which is pleasing to God. Such souls then have by definition become widows; they take to themselves now in addition the ὀρθὸς νόμος of nature as a husband, but also as a father, for with the greatest concern the ὀρθὸς λόγος tells to the individual as to an offspring what things must be done.

One wonders whether the text read here originally νόμος or λόγος but it would have meant quite the same thing in either case. It is possible to think of the ἡγεμών as the νοῦς ἀπόσπασμα in the individual, as his ὀρθὸς λόγος, or as the indwelling νόμος τῆς φύσεως. They are all only different terms

---

105. *Det.*, 171 ff.   106. *Agr.*, 31.

107. *Decal.*, 142, 150.   108. See above, pp. 54 ff.

109. *LA*, iii, 1. The ὀρθὸς λόγος as Father is the Universal Principle in *Ebr.*, 33 ff.; it would also appear universal when Philo says that what man has in his soul must be judged κανόνι ὀρθοῦ λόγου: *Agr.*, 130.

110. E.g. *Conf.*, 43. See also *Plant.*, 60; *Post.*, 32. The Stoics were also aware that to live according to nature was to live by the ὀρθὸς λόγος, identical in us and in the universe, since μέρη εἰσὶν αἱ ἡμέτεραι φύσεις τῆς τοῦ ὅλου: Diog. La., VII, 87-89. Cicero had the same idea, probably from Posidonius, *De Legibus*, I, vi, 18.

111. *QE*, ii, 3. Greek in Harris, *Fragments*, p. 51.

for the same thing. The ὀρθὸς λόγος of the universe is the ὀρθὸς λόγος of the individual. It is the προστάτης ἢ ἐπίτροπος ἢ πατὴρ ἢ ὅ τι φίλον καλεῖν τοῦ συγκρίματος ἡμῶν, and when it is not honored it goes away from us to the destruction of its rebellious subjects.[112] Or in other words, when the soul resorts to evil passions it forsakes its legal husband, the ὀρθὸς λόγος, who is also σπερματικὸς καὶ γεννητικὸς τῶν καλῶν,[113] the husband which can as well be called νοῦς.[114] Those who honor the ὀρθὸς λόγος, abandoning everything else, may be hated by men, but get infinite rewards from God.[115] When the soul loses λογισμός it loses laws as well, for λογισμός is like all rulers in being the living inscription of laws.[116]

We begin to understand the sense in which a man may obtain salvation by following the Law of Nature. A man lives according to nature, he explains, when his νοῦς "enters upon the path of virtue and walks in the footsteps of the ὀρθὸς λόγος, that is, follows God."[117] Virtue and the Sophos are alike founded upon the ὀρθὸς λόγος.[118] So in allegorizing democracy Philo may use the democratic variant of the βασιλεύς as the living Law, in which νόμος καὶ δίκη are together the king and ruler of the democratic state. When he speaks of the soul as a democracy of this kind, he says that the soul can be a true democracy, rather than an ochlocracy, only when the subjective πόλις honors νόμος καὶ δίκη as the ruler.[119] The rule of reason is the rule of the Law of Nature, by the fact that the ὀρθὸς λόγος within us, or properly within us if we have not renounced it, is indeed the cosmic Law of Nature itself. The same notion may be used equally well as Philo feels more or less ascetically inclined. For the rule of the ὀρθὸς λόγος within us may mark the complete development of the lower powers of man, or their destruction. In any case it is the full identification of the "self" with the great ordering force of the universe, whether that force is conceived as objective or subjective, and the domination of every other part of the "self" by it.

To live according to nature is then not just a pretty phrase Philo brings in from Greek Philosophy. It is only another way of describing his highest aim in life. To follow nature is the mark of a strong and truly masculine reason.[120] Again and again the notion reappears.[121] Virtue is not only built

112. *Post.*, 68. Ὀρθὸς λόγος is the father again in *Som.*, ii, 135; *Ebr.*, 33 ff.

113. *LA*, iii, 148, 150; *Det.*, 149; *QG*, iv, 38.

114. *LA*, iii, 221. But in §222 it is again ὀρθὸς λόγος which is the proper guide of νοῦς, as νοῦς is of αἴσθησις.

115. *Ebr.*, 65 ff. It will be noticed that in §§80 ff. Philo puts as a higher type of man the person who combines this with a deep sense of obligation to the state.

116. *Det.*, 141. See also *LA*, iii, 222 ff.

117. *Mig.*, 128. The καί here, as frequently in Philo, adds an explanation rather than a parallel conception.

118. *Gig.*, 48. Cf. Cicero, *De Legibus*, I, 42.

119. *Conf.*, 108.   120. *Ebr.*, 55; cf. 151.

121. See, besides other passages quoted, virtue as ὁ κατὰ φύσιν βίος, *Mos.*, ii, 181.

upon the ὀρθὸς λόγος; it is itself the Law of Nature, and to follow it is ι͵ get happiness and length of life.[122] Since Law is the great harmonizing force of the universe, the ideal for the lawful man is that he fit his acts to the will of nature by which the world is ordered.[123] Just as law is the sole guarantee of civic liberty, so with the individual it is the lawful balance of his inner life which alone can set man free.

It is in this sense that virtue is itself a law, or the virtues are laws,[124] a fact of such capital importance to Philo that he put the Greek virtues along with the Decalogue as foundation laws under which he could classify the specific commands of the Torah.[125] As τὸ ἴσον and τὸ εὔνομον are the cosmic seeds of peace, the source of universal security and permanence,[126] so by honoring the ὀρθὸς λόγος, the perfect blending of the virtues, one can have a life εὔδιον καὶ γαληνόν.[127] The soul of such a man is a copy of heaven, indeed a heaven on earth (οὐρανὸν ἐπίγειον), with perfection similar to the cosmos in the matter of his motives, revolutions, and in his power to radiate virtue.[128] Such a man is indeed sustained by a food which God rains down upon him from heaven, possible for only the pure to eat, the "cibum voluntariae legis purae sapientiae ab invitatore deo."[129] The Powers of God come to man bringing νόμους καὶ θεσμοὺς ἀπ' οὐρανοῦ for the sake of sanctifying and purifying the souls of man, and sowing in them the seeds of happiness.[130] The spirit of God, whether the external thing or as represented in the minds of good men, remains with them only so long as they abide by νόμος καὶ δίκη, and forsakes them when they renounce this higher Law.[131] In connection with the ideal character of the high-priest Philo becomes more specific as to just what following the higher Law implies. The high-priest, to be fit to make the sacrifice, must himself be in harmony with τῆς φύσεως νόμοι καὶ θεσμοί. This means that he must be able to say as he puts his hands on the victim:

These hands have never taken a bribe for unjust actions nor any division in the spoils of rapine or "graft" (πλεονεξία); they have never touched innocent blood, or committed any of the aggravated types of assault (πήρωσις, ὕβρις, τραῦμα,

---

122. *Post.*, 185.
123. *Opif.*, 3. Cf. *Abr.*, 61. Of course we all must follow the Law of Nature, if not by obeying the precepts, then in paying the legal penalty. This is what Stoics meant when they said: "Ducunt volentem fata, nolentem trahunt," Cleanthes (see *SVF*, I, 527; cf. Heinemann, *Poseidonios*, I, 3, n. 2; P. Wendland, *Philos Schrift über die Vorsehung*, p. 24, n. 4). For natural law is with Philo guarded by Δίκη, whom he freely personifies. See above, pp. 59 ff. Cf. *Spec.*, i, 155; iii, 19; *Som.*, ii, 292.
124. *QG*, i, 99; *LA*, iii, 245.
125. See L. Cohn's introduction to the *Virt.* in *Philos Werke*, II, 315 ff.
126. *QE*, ii, 64 (Harris, *Fragments*, 64): σωτηρίας αἴτια καὶ τῆς εἰσάπαν διαμονῆς.
127. *Conf.*, 43.
128. *Heres*, 88.
129. *QG*, iv, 8.
130. *Cher.*, 106.
131. *Gig.*, 21–23.

βία),[132] nor done anything else reprehensible or blameworthy. Rather have they been the servants of all τὰ καλὰ καὶ συμφέροντα which are honored by wisdom and the laws, by wise and law-abiding men.

This the ideal priest can say only as he has kept his mind consecrated to γνῶμαι ἀγαθαὶ καὶ συμφέρουσαι, and as a consequence (ἔπειτα) built his life up out of the noblest actions.[133] Such is a life according to Natural Law. Its external manifestations are only corollaries of an inner assimilation of the Law of Nature which is itself achieved by the mystical apprehension of the higher truth by the νοῦς, and then by the subjugation of the other parts of one's personality to the νοῦς thus properly fulfilling its highest function.

Philo indeed hints at a higher experience achieved by ὁ σοφὸς τέλειος, a title he seems to reserve exclusively for Moses. In him the orientation of life in God is so complete that he has actually transcended any appeal or force in the passions. He has cut off the hand and foot, etc., which offended him. The priests, as being in the lower Mystery (οἱ ἀσκηταί), use Logos to keep the passions subdued, for obedience to Logos is a noble thing. But the man in the highest state has transcended the guidance of the Logos.[184] For although one must follow the Logos in the preliminary stages, when he has arrived at the height of perfect ἐπιστήμη the perfect man walks not after, but along with the divine Logos as both together attend God.[185] Philo does not describe the exscinding of the lower life like Paul as "death to the body,"[186] but uses the figure of "cutting off" offending members which is found in the Sermon on the Mount. It seems clear that both figures express the same ascetic ambition. Philo himself lived on the plane where reason was trying to rule the impulses. When he went to a banquet he had to take logos along to keep himself in control, and this is the level of experience he is ordinarily assuming in others.[187]

Man, the "personality as a whole" thus obeys the higher Law according as his νοῦς is properly developed and dominant. But there is, in the language of Paul, "another law in his members" which is as destructive for the total personality as the higher Law is salutary. For just as the lower part, or αἴσθησις, may itself be represented as a tribunal or mentality of a sort, producing δόξαι, so it can be represented as a legal principle of its own. The true king, Melchizedek, is at enmity with the tyrant, mind, which decrees for both soul and body violent and injurious commands (ἐπιτάγματα, king-made laws). But Melchizedek, the good pilot, the λόγος, gives laws which

---

132. On these terms see my *Jewish Jurisprudence*, pp. 137, 232 ff.
133. *Spec.*, i, 202–204.   134. *LA*, iii, 144, see 140 ff.
135. *Mig.*, 174 f.
136. Though of course he does speak of a man's slaying his lower powers for the sake of the higher: *Ebr.*, 66–70.
137. *LA*, iii, 153–159.

bring peace and happiness to the soul.[138] The tyrant is a natural enemy, he says again;[139] the tyrant of a city is a man, but the tyrant over body and soul and their affairs is the most bestial mind (ὁ θηριωδέστατος νοῦς), who fortifies the citadel against one's own self. In place of this comes the shepherding, in this case, of God Himself.[140] But shortly it is νοῦς which is the herdsman of the soul, and who uses the Law of Nature as his teacher in the art of ruling.[141] Mind in the lower sense is represented as folly,[142] or as a bodily principle attempting to lord it over the truly royal nature which temporarily dwells in the body. This is brought out in an allegory of the brothers of Joseph, true kings, becoming subject to the king of Egypt, that is to the king of the body.[143] The king of Egypt forces the true kings and their children to make bricks, and in so doing "the [lower] mind which appears to occupy the place of king" wishes to indicate the enslavement of the virtues to the passions. That is, Pharaoh's decrees are laws issued by the lower mentality, from which one must have recourse to God to be saved.

Lot came into Sodom and tried to overturn the customs of the inhabitants by prohibiting sodomy. This is Mind going into the bodily constitution from the outside and attempting to overthrow the law of that region to put a higher Law in its place. The inhabitants protest: "Nostra enim regio est libido, et lex legitimaque voluntas concupiscentia."[144] Again Noah, though he was ὁ δίκαιος, "non est exemptus a corporeis legibus."[145] The soul is a city which lays down laws and customs for the individual (τὸ ζῷον), and this city must be abandoned as the mind goes out to God.[146] A man may be yoked to a chariot of the passions whose driver is not νοῦς or ἐπιστήμη, but ἀφροσύνη. Such a man becomes a slave of harsh and unbearable masters which are within himself, and which have the law (νόμος) that they will never let any one be emancipated. The only hope is to escape to the good mind in contrast to the foolish one.[147] Pleasure commands what it wants.[148] The law of the lower realm comes out strikingly when Philo says:

When the prudence of the acute and seeing nature (i.e., God's in-streaming Logos) enters the soul as though it were coming into a country, all the racial laws that are in it grow insanely angry and withdraw from worthy thinking, since bad things cannot live and stand along with good things.[149]

138. *LA*, iii, 79–82.   139. *Agr.*, 46.
140. Ib., 49, 54.
141. Ib., 66. He goes on to use the Platonic comparison of the insurgency of the lower over against the higher with a man carried by an unruly horse, or a ship out of the pilot's control (§§67–94). Νοῦς is the horseman of the soul, §73.
142. *Conf.*, 54.   143. Ib., 88 ff., espec. 91.
144. *QG*, iv, 39. See also §38.   145. *QG*, ii, 45.
146. *LA*, iii, 43 f.   147. Ib., 189 ff., especially §194.
148. *Ebr.*, 102: τὰ ἑαυτῇ φίλα εἴωθε προστάττειν. The legal form of the last word is striking.
149. *QE*, ii, 22.

Here the "racial laws" of the "country" are clearly the laws "of the members," or of the lower parts or functions of the soul. That is again whether from the ascetic or more ethical point of view, the personality is confronted by a duality of laws, and the lower must be ascetically abandoned, or conquered in the interest of ethics, if one is to achieve his highest possible type of living.

A suggestion of a metaphysical background for this law of the lower constitution, whether it be the body, or the bodily principle, the lower mind, or αἴσθησις, may be found in the statement that

The good (τὸ ἀγαθόν) of the flesh is irrational pleasure, but the good of the soul and of the individual as a whole is ὁ νοῦς τῶν ὅλων, ὁ θεός.[150]

Τὸ ἀγαθόν here is used in the Aristotelian sense of the object of strivings.[151] That is, it is quite inevitable that the flesh should seek pleasure, since pleasure is the natural aim of the flesh as such. Hunger, thirst, cold and heat are the "necessities of nature (τὰ τῆς φύσεως ἀναγκαῖα) which are in the habit of reducing persons to slavery and subduing them with an exuberance of strength,[152] so that it is pleasant (ἡδύ) to commit injustice, laborious to act justly. This is "the most infallible law," he says, inherent in our lower parts and functions.[153] It is the natural law of what Paul calls our "members," the total unreasoning part of our constitution.

The higher goods are goods only of a principle within man higher than mere sensuous experience. But this "good" or objective of the flesh is itself probably ultimately to be connected with the fact that matter is itself ἀνάγκη, and hence a sort of law.[154] For while "God is peace, ἡ δὲ γενητὴ καὶ φθαρτὴ οὐσία πᾶσα is constant war." God is the principle of the voluntary, while matter (οὐσία) is ἀνάγκη.[154a] Concupiscence itself, he says, is something quite in accordance with the Law of Nature, for by it our bodies are preserved.[155] That is, it is a law of the nature of the flesh to seek its own gratification. The law is quite inevitable, because it is only by thirst and hunger that the body is able to express and gratify its needs. The other impulses are similarly of quite a utilitarian and necessitous nature. They are natural laws for the body. The difficulty is that as all material nature should be subject to the Law of Nature in its larger and immaterial sense, as viewed from the

---

150. *Gig.*, 40.
151. As in the famous definition: διὸ καλῶς ἀπεφήναντο τἀγαθόν, οὗ πάντ' ἐφίεται: *Eth. Nic.*, I, i (1094a 2).
152. *Cong.*, 165.   153. Ib., 163.
154. On the interchangeability of ὀρθὸς λόγος, World-Soul, God, Pronoia, ἀνάγκη, and τύχη, see Antiochus *ap.* Cicero, *Acad.*, I, 28 f.; Heinemann, *Poseidonios*, I, 51.
154a. *Som.*, ii, 253.
155. *QG*, ii, 46: "concupiscentia, qua illud [corpus nostrum] servatur ac durat, moderate nimirum et iuxta legem naturae."

point of view of God or the totality, the impulses of any member must often
be restrained. In a sense there is conflict within nature itself between the law
of the nature of the part, and the law of the nature of the whole, and the
ultimate solution is made more by a tuning together of conflicting tendencies
than by a reduction to a monotone. In man these two aspects of natural law
clash—the law of the whole and the law inherent in each individual member.
As the harmony of nature is only kept by the subordination of the natures
of the particular, so in man the higher Law, represented by his reason as the
Logos within him, is in conflict with the law of the senses and body, and
mutual attunement can result only from the victory of the higher Law. So
long as the flesh is dominant, the higher Law is automatically impotent,
exiled from the individual. The unchecked assertion of the law or laws of
the members must mean anarchy for the individual as a whole, for only the
mind has a law that can dominate all the others successfully. On this basis,
he says, one's aspiration should be to abandon war, necessity, what comes
into existence and passes away, so that one can go over to the unbegotten
and voluntary.[156] Kennedy[157] is quite right in denying that Philo's remarks
about abandoning one's material nature can be taken as indicating a settled
conviction on Philo's part that matter is a principle of evil distinct from God,
the principle of Good. However it is clear that the Platonic contrast between
the realm of settled being and the world of becoming was carried out by
Philo to the place where he thought of the lower world as by its very nature
having tendencies frequently at variance with the good of the totality, or of
the higher world, a set of tendencies which could well be expressed as the
indigenous laws of the lower realm in contrast to the Laws of God, or of the
ἀπόσπασμα of God in man.

No better summary of this notion could be written than Paul's much de-
bated words:

I find then the law, that, to me who would do τὸ καλόν evil is present. For "I"
delight in the law of God after the inward man: but I see a different law in my
members, warring against the law of my νοῦς, and bringing "me" into captivity
under the law of sin which is in my members.[158]

Paul assumes a knowledge of the sort of treatment of law in the inner man
preserved to us only by Philo, a knowledge which his readers most probably
had, but whose absence has obscured his remarks ever since for later readers.
Only one who has not read in full the passages here abbreviated can say that
Philo's interest in the subject is academic or metaphysical in contrast to
Paul's. Christian scholars will probably always cling to the belief that Paul's

156. *Som.*, ii, 253.
157. *Philo's Contribution to Religion* (1919), p. 73.
158. *Rom.* vii, 21-23.

religious experience was a greater thing than Philo's, and probably they are right, though an absolute criterion for such a judgment is hardly at hand. Philo was obviously so much interested alike in practical, religious, and metaphysical problems that religious problems in themselves never became the single concern of his life as they did of Paul's. But the struggle for Philo between the law of the members and the law of the mind was the great struggle of his religious life, one that was resolved only in the Mystery, and which explains his devotion to the Mystery. If his words give the impression of coming from less a religious genius than Paul, the spirit reflected is one less than Paul's alone.[159]

As with Paul sin is described by Philo in many other ways, just as he has many parallel schemes of psychology. The sinfulness of the flesh,[160] sin as a yielding to pleasure,[161] as estrangement from God,[162] as death of the higher part,[163] as honoring matter rather than the Creator,[164] are all freely developed notions. Sometimes the mind is regarded as pure and good, but, by being engulfed in the body and pleasure, we understand, is in a fallen state;[165] but again the mind is at the beginning morally indifferent, capable of development in virtue or vice,[166] and it is the influence of environment which pulls it down.[167] The breaking of law is thus only one of his many approaches to the problem of sin, but historically, in view of the use of the conception by Paul and later Christians, the fact that it occupies so large a place in Philo's thinking is of the greatest importance.

It is from this point of view that Philo's notion of conscience becomes most intelligible. It has frequently been pointed out that in his writings the conception of conscience appears for the first time to occupy a conspicuous place.[168] The Logos or Higher Law, dwells in man, among other things, as conscience.[169] Kennedy has recently expounded Philo's notion of conscience

159. See Kennedy, *op. cit.*, p. 89, n. 1.

160. *Gig.*, 12–15; *Immut.*, 142 f.; *Agr.*, 89; *Heres*, 239 f. See also the great collection of passages in Leisegang, *Index* s.vv. σῶμα, 7 (pp. 756 f.) and σάρξ (p. 703). Drummond's discussion of Philo's notion of sin is very valuable on this and many of the following points. See his *Philo Judaeus*, II, 289 ff.

161. *Opif.*, 152; *LA*, ii, 107. The idea is Cynic, as Bréhier has pointed out in his note to §§88 ff., and *Les Idées*, 262–264. Leisegang, *Index*, s.v. ἡδονή, 6 (p. 345).

162. See Bréhier's *Les Idées*, pp. 297 ff., with the passages there adduced. See also *Opif.*, 149 ff.

163. *LA*, i, 107; *Det.*, 48.

164. *Spec.*, iii, 180. Under this comes sin as presumption, described by Bréhier, *Les Idées*, p. 298.

165. *Mut.*, 56.   166. *LA*, iii, 246.

167. *Heres*, 295. Cf. Cleanthes, *ap.* Diog. La., VII, 89.

168. See especially Gfrörer, *Philo und die jüdisch-alex. Theosophie*, I, 207 ff.; Bréhier, *Les Idées*, pp. 299 ff.; Kennedy, *Philo's Contribution to Religion*, 106 ff. These authors furnish abundant documentation.

169. See for example, *Det.*, 146.

so well that it need not here be explained more than to point out that the very term by which he calls it (ὁ λόγος ἔλεγχος) is a legal term. Knowledge of the higher right or morality stands in eternal opposition to the tendencies of the lower impulses, and their warfare must result in the victory of the higher principle, the true King Abraham, over the kings of the lower realms.[170] Indeed Philo is like Paul in insisting that the tendencies of the senses could not in themselves be considered sinful if a knowledge of the higher Way or Law did not make them out to be such, though also like Paul Philo protests that it is not the Law itself which makes a sinner, but his perverse refusal to obey.[171] Philo is less obviously than Paul referring to the Jewish Law in this connection. The higher right, as represented in every individual by this higher element of his composite nature, when not heeded transforms the inherently amoral impulses into sins without itself being in any sense the cause of sin.

The ideal state of every man is thus εὐνομία, ἁρμονία,[172] by the fact that his higher nature dominates the lower, a condition that can just as well be described as the rule of God in him, or as his following the Law of Nature. One's difficulty appears in the fact that the lower nature puts up a ceaseless resistance to any domination, and the usual state of a man is one of sin. Only the very rare individual fulfils the ideal. Yet God the Savior is always working for our salvation,[173] and the means of grace are at hand for every man. The psychology of the process of salvation is a subject, like that of sin, too extensive for development here.[174] It need only be pointed out that salvation is, among other things, treated as a matter of restoration to attunement and lawfulness. Salvation is never achieved by an effort of will which can be credited in any sense to the man himself. If the λογισμός is to be brought up into a dominating position over the lower powers, in so far as it is the man's own λογισμός it is to be distrusted. Only a λογισμός trusting in the power of God for its insight into the higher truth, and for its stability, is functioning properly and fully.[175] The man who has achieved the ideal life lives to God rather than to himself (ζῆσαι θεῷ μᾶλλον ἢ ἑαυτῷ), and does this when he exercises the senses to find the truth, the soul to find τὰ νοητά, and his voice to hymn the universe and its Creator.[176] That is, the full life, often as it is described as ascetic renunciation of the body and the senses, is

170. *Abr.*, 244. Gfrörer, *loc. cit.*, rightly connects this passage with conscience, though here λόγος is used without ἔλεγχος.
171. *Immut.*, 134 ff. Kennedy, *op. cit.*, 109 ff. *Provid.*, ii, 82: "violentiae vero et rapinae ac consimilium non lex in causa est, sed iniquitas incolarum legem contemnentium."
172. On ἁρμονία as this sort of adjustment in man see *Ebr.*, 116.
173. *Virt.*, 185; *QG*, iii, 27; iv, 234.
174. It is on this point that the brief but penetrating study of Kennedy is most useful.
175. *Praem.*, 28–30; *Mut.*, 216 f.; *LA*, iii, 228.
176. *Heres*, 111.

quite as much to be understood as a complete functioning of all parts of the σύγκριμα. But even in such a case, the focus is rather in God than in the individual as such. We are saved from lawlessness (παρανομία) as we have hope and faith in God the only Savior,[177] who judges us to be worthy of full salvation.[178]

It is the man who is νόμιμος in this sense who is the citizen of the universe, regulating his actions by the will of nature,[179] and though the primal man[180] and God[181] are each described as citizens of the universe in a way impossible for men, still the mystic sage is repeatedly called such.[182]

And yet the higher life for man, much as it is to be described in terms of legality, is not to be thought of as obeying laws. For it has frequently appeared that, like all thoughtful Greeks, Philo distinctly contrasted νόμος with νόμοι. Law was essentially πνεῦμα, a force emanating from the mind of God, or the dynamic operation of Nature herself, not a series of commands. Specific laws were matters of inference from the great Law, the direction the πνεῦμα would take under a given set of circumstances, and did not in themselves have any independent existence or inherent value. The man who had no better guide should be νόμιμος by the laws of the realm, or by the unwritten traditions of his group. But the man who would be νόμιμος in the higher sense would have found the πνεῦμα—νόμος itself, and be guided thereby, while the νόμος γεγραμμένος, the γράμμα, would be as little the object of his concern as the rules in books on rhetoric for an accomplished stylist, and might often be an impediment rather than a help. The conception of the νόμος ἄγραφος in the ancient world has been brilliantly expounded by Hirzel.[188] Philo, as has appeared, used the notion most importantly in connection with Jewish Law. Much as Law is the vehicle or norm according to which, and by which, man is saved, the higher development is impossible to one who clings exclusively to written laws. Man will have God for his inheritance, Philo says, according as he avoids all laws made by hand, for these are all arbitrary derivations, at best only approximations of the higher Law.[184] The long discussion already mentioned, in which Philo treats of the figure of the universal Father and Mother and their children, is, among many applications, interpreted as a contrast between the ὀρθὸς λόγος, the Father, and the Mother who enjoins obedience to what

177. Ib., 60.
178. *Ebr.*, 69–72; §72: σωτηρίας ἠξιώθη παντελοῦς.
179. *Opif.*, 3.   180. Ib., 142 ff.
181. *Cher.*, 121.
182. *Mos.*, i, 157; *Mig.*, 59; *Conf.*, 106; Harris, *Fragments*, p. 103.
183. Rudolph Hirzel, " Ἄγραφος Νόμος," in *Abhandlungen der sächsischen Gesellschaft*, Philol.-Hist. Classe, XX. See above, pp. 86 f.
184. *Mut.*, 26. Such I take to be the implication of the rather cryptic Greek, which says— you will become so ἂν τοὺς χειροποιήτους καὶ ἐκουσίους ἅπαντας νόμους ἐκφύγῃς.

is θέσει δίκαιος according to the legal enactments of cities and races.[185] The νόμοι ἄγραφοι appear also as the ἔθη of a people, as distinguished from their written statutes; in that sense they too are specific, and hence are as inferior to the Law of Nature as the statutes themselves.[186] True, obedience to the unwritten law in even this sense is a higher act than that to the written, for the former carries with it no statutory penalty, and hence is much more an act of free will on the part of one who obeys it.[187] Yet that perfect law, the Law of Nature or of God, by which the Patriarchs lived before the giving of the Torah, is also called the Unwritten Law.[188] So those who live according to the Law are free, while those under the power of the impulses are slaves. But the Law which really will set us free, he says, is the νόμος ἀψευδής, ὁ ὀρθὸς λόγος, not a law whose source and sanction is force, or something written on papyrus or slabs of stone, an inanimate object upon an inanimate medium, the perishable product of a mortal man. In contrast, we assume, the true law is unwritten, sanctioned by voluntary choice of the man who follows it, for it is an imperishable stamp put upon our immortal minds by immortal nature.[189] This is the Law which is really release from lower types of law, and the source of spiritual liberty. By simply omitting the reference to Jesus Christ in Paul's Romans viii, we have all been familiar from childhood with a description of the higher spiritual Law which can set one free from the law of the flesh and of sin, a description with which Philo would heartily have agreed.

It is interesting that this higher state, a legal formulation of the goal of the Mystery, is for Philo quite as much as for Paul to be characterized by the word δικαιοσύνη. The meaning and importance of the term for Philo's cosmic system has already appeared. Δικαιοσύνη is primarily the virtue of obedience to law, whether in the state[190] or in the cosmos. That blessed state which a man achieves when he turns from sin to a life in harmony with God's Spirit or Law is the state of δικαιοσύνη, specifically explained as the voluntary following of the Laws of Nature.[191] To say that a man has acted unjustly, has broken the higher Law, or has committed impiety, these are but three ways of saying the same thing, according to Philo and Paul alike.[192]

---

185. *Ebr.*, 34.   186. *Heres*, 295; *Spec.*, iv, 149; *Legat.*, 115.

187. *Spec.*, iv, 150. Hirzel shows how close this is to Aristotle. See *Rhet.*, I, 1375a 15, 1374a 21. Cf. Dio Chrys., *Orat.*, 76 (ed. Budé, II, p. 257); Dionysius Hal., *Ant. Rom.*, VIII, 60.

188. *Abr.*, 5 f.   189. *Prob.*, 45 f.

190. Justice, the civic virtue, is frequently defined in Aristotelian form as a giving to each according to his deserts: *QG*, iii, 24; *LA*, i, 65; *Sob.*, 40; *Spec.*, i, 118 ff. This is a dispensation of a copy of the works of nature, *Spec.*, iv, 55.

191. *Som..* ii, 174: ἑκουσίῳ γνώμῃ φύσεως νόμοις καὶ θεσμοῖς ἑπόμενον. The notion that δίκη was fundamentally contrasted with βία, compulsion, was a constant in Greek thought at least from Hesiod's time: καί νυ δίκης ἐπάκουε, βίης δ' ἐπιλήθεο πάμπαν, *Works and Days*, 275.

192. *Decal.*, 89.

As such Justice is an all-inclusive virtue, interchangeable with ἀρετή itself.[193] It is in explaining the nature of the just man that Philo describes his state thus:

The man to whom it is granted to see beyond and to transcend all material and immaterial existences, and to build and found himself upon God alone with strong-minded reason and fixed and inflexible faith, he is in truth the happy and thrice blessed man.[194]

When a judge gives out justice to the litigants he is giving them a copy of the works of nature, and so satisfying their thirst for εὐνομία.[195] But justice can as well be described as the rule of reason over the lower faculties,[196] since it has appeared that this is only another approach to describing a man's following Natural Law. Indeed so much does Philo associate justice with reason that he boldly says that storks must possess reason since they practice justice in honoring their parents. For while aequum (ἰσότης) is in all parts of the world, yet only by reason can justice and injustice be observed, for both belong to reason.[197] Δικαιοσύνη is at once the following of the higher Law, and the rule of reason, and is thereby the supreme purification of the soul, for Philo says that τὸ ἄριστον τῆς καθάρσεως καὶ τελειώτατον is not to take to heart anything out of the way, but to govern oneself with peace and εὐνομία, whose guide is δικαιοσύνη.[198]

There is no delight more exquisite than to have the soul filled in every part with δικαιοσύνη, when the soul dwells upon its eternal teaching and propositions, and has no empty place into which ἀδικία can penetrate.[199]

Noah is explained as the type of the just man who finds supreme happiness through δικαιοσύνη, for it gives rest from labor, destroys pain, and in destroying sin, for which it is a panacea, fills him with joy. For δικαιοσύνη begets in him ὁ δίκαιος λογισμός.[200] Δικαιοσύνη seems here an active and self-existent principle which can beget the specific virtues in the soul. One need not be surprised to find such a touch of Platonism in Philo. The virtues are carefully explained as self-existing principles in contrast with the human virtues which would normally die with the individual. But to attain to the virtues fully is to get by God's gift the eternal principles themselves, exchange the

193. The vacillation between justice and virtue is constant throughout the discussion of Noah, ὁ δίκαιος, in QG, ii, 36 ff. Τὸ δίκαιον seems equivalent to ἀρετή also in Praem., 93.
194. Praem., 30. Cf. Heres, 94 f., where Philo discusses the relation of δικαιοσύνη and πίστις. In discussing justice Philo has a similar description of the perfect man in Spec., iv, 140 f.
195. Spec., iv, 55 f.
196. LA, i, 72 f., Abr., 31–33; Conf., 108 ff., esp. §112.
197. Animal., 61.
198. Mut., 240.
199. Spec., iv, 141.
200. Det., 121–123.

part for the whole, the species for the genus, the corruptible for the incorruptible. This is to attain to the highest type of spiritual joy, the real objective in the mystical aspiration.[201] Philo would seem to have in mind much that Paul did in his contrast between the δικαιοσύνη ἡ τοῦ νόμου and that τῆς πίστεως.[202] For the lower type of virtue according to both Paul and Philo is one based upon human effort to follow an ideal, as contrasted with the virtue as God could give it. Paul could say for both: ἀγνοοῦντες τὴν τοῦ θεοῦ δικαιοσύνην, καὶ τὴν ἰδίαν ζητοῦντες στῆσαι, τῇ δικαιοσύνῃ τοῦ θεοῦ οὐχ ὑπετάγησαν.[208] The single virtue of δικαιοσύνη does not emerge so sharply in Philo as in Paul as the one unique virtue, though Philo does say that it is the leader of the virtues.[204] He can frequently praise other virtues or virtue as the supreme objective, and represent δικαιοσύνη as only one of the four or five virtues.[205] He can praise σωφροσύνη for being identical with σωτηρία,[206] but since he described σωφροσύνη as the state when λόγος in the soul rules like a charioteer over θυμός and ἐπιθυμία, he might as well, or with greater consistency, have called it δικαιοσύνη, and indeed is attracted to use the term σωφροσύνη here only by a pun (σωφροσύνη, σωτηρίαν τῷ φρονοῦντι . . . ἀπεργαζομένη).[207] For to Philo the state of salvation is ultimately that inner mastery of desires, and attunement with God's supreme order, which appears most fittingly characterized by him, as well as by Paul, as δικαιοσύνη.[208] Σωτήριον ἐν τοῖς μάλιστα δικαιοσύνη, καὶ ἀνθρώπων καὶ τῶν τοῦ κόσμου μερῶν, γῆς καὶ οὐρανοῦ.[209] This, we have learned to see, is not adventitious, but founded deeply upon the belief: τὸ ἔννομον καὶ τὸ ἴσον εἰρήνης σπέρμα, καὶ σωτηρίας αἴτιον καὶ τῆς εἰς ἅπαν διαμονῆς. Ἀνισότης δὲ καὶ πλεονεξία ὁρμητήρια πολέμου καὶ λυτικὰ τῶν ὄντων.[210] For ἰσότης is itself the μήτηρ δικαιοσύνης.[211]

It would lead into a large digression to consider the relation of πίστις to δικαιοσύνη, for πίστις itself would have to be defined as Philo thought of it. Fortunately that has already been adequately done.[212] To Philo πίστις was in brief that ultimate trust and dependence upon God that marked the achievement of the life completely oriented in God. In contrast to Paul, πίστις was

---

201. *QG*, iii, 53.
202. Rom. x, 5 f.
203. Ib., 3.
204. *Abr.*, 27.
205. See the large collection of references to such usage in Leisegang, *Index*, p. 193, the last 16 lines of column b and following. A typical statement is: χαρᾶς αἴτιον, ὃ πέφυκε γεννᾶν δικαιοσύνη καὶ φρόνησις καὶ αἱ σύνθρονοι ταύτης ἀρεταί: *LA*, iii, 247.
206. *Virt.*, 13 f.
207. For this is precisely the definition of δικαιοσύνη given in *LA*, i, 72.
208. Even as penalty, δίκη is described as πάντα μοχθηρὸν ἐκκαθαίρουσα διανοίας, *Ebr.*, 28.
209. Fragment, *ap.* Harris, *Fragments*, p. 101.
210. Fragment, *loc. cit.*
211. *Spec.*, iv, 231. Cf. *Legat.*, 85; *Cont.*, 17; *Aet.*, 108.
212. A. Schlatter, *Der Glaube im neuen Testament* (1885), pp. 55–101.

the goal, not the first step in achieving the goal. It is easy to exaggerate the differences between Paul and Philo, and so to forget that for both the word meant an abandoning of trust in one's own strength, and a conscious commitment of the management of one's life to God. Paul believed as much as Philo that as the spiritual life developed one "grew in faith," that is learned how to make the orientation in God more complete. Philo reserves the term for the completed stage, but he would begin exactly as Paul by despairing of efforts to save himself, and looking to God the Savior, or the Logos, to make that orientation which was impossible for his human efforts. Paul calls the first look, as well as the final achievement, πίστις. But in view of the fundamental similarity of conception, the point at which the term πίστις was applied to the process seems relatively unimportant. In any case it is clear that to Philo as to Paul the association of δικαιοσύνη and πίστις was very close. In one passage he discusses the magnificent πίστις of Abraham, who believed God and left his kindred (his lower nature) to "anchor firmly and unchangeably on the only living God." This is an incredible step in the minds of men who themselves lack faith. But the act of faith is itself δίκαιον καὶ ἀκόλουθον τῇ φύσει, is the μόνον ἔργον τῆς δικαιοσύνης.[218]

Νόμος would then appear to be the pole of Philo's inner life as well as of his metaphysics and political theory. Even in the mysticism of faith he assures himself that he is acting ἀκόλουθον τῇ φύσει, which is itself νόμος. His inner struggle is a conflict of natures to be described as a conflict of the laws of those natures. The resolution of the struggle must be the enlarging of the original ἀπόσπασμα, by the mercy of God, so that it will have strength to subdue its adversaries, or may be described as the abandoning of the lower parts, their destruction, while the higher man lives in the heavenly city, in God Himself. The man who can, by God's help, rise to this achievement has fulfilled the Law of Nature in its highest sense. The wicked man is of course living according to the Law of Nature, for the desires he is following are natural laws of his αἴσθησις. But he only demonstrates the inadequacy of the part as compared with the whole. Not the law of the arm or the belly, but the law embracing all nature can alone give him that attunement and security which the Graeco-Roman world was coming to call σωτηρία.

In the foregoing discussion occasional parallels have been drawn between Philo's statements and those of other teachers of antiquity, but the subject of the direct source of Philo's writing has not been touched. The first impression one receives is that in so highly eclectic a formulation the best that can be done is to identify the sources of various details. But what of his general point of view? We have here a view that man is primarily a σύγκριμα, whose problem is the harmonious interadjustment of the parts. This can only be

213. *Heres,* 95; see the previous context.

done if the dominant part, the νοῦς ἡγεμών, is truly the ruler of all the rest of the man, whether that rest be called the unreasoning part of the soul, or the sense-perception, or the body. Such a balance in man is called δικαιοσύνη, and the term itself implies that the rule of reason is a rule of law. But what law? All true law, the law of the state as well as the law used by the νοῦς βασιλεύς, is only a reflection of the νόμος τῆς φύσεως, so if the νοῦς is to be truly correct in its ruling, it must know and appropriate the Law of Nature, and apply it as a whole to the subject parts. Philo bows to the law of the state, but here only in passing. Such law does not lie in the center of importance for a soul which has gone beyond the most rudimentary development. The νοῦς must then seek the Law of Nature, or of God, and live by it and in it. This search turns out to involve in its elementary stages, the mastery of the learning of the schools, but must get beyond this into a mystic state where God gives the Law to man, and man finds it in God.

In looking for the sources for Philo's doctrine of the rule of mind over the lower faculties, and the following by the mind of natural Law as the guide in controlling its subjects, I confess myself unable to see any one source as demonstrably the one on which Philo was directly drawing. It is true that Cicero gives a doctrine similar at many points. For him too the ὀρθὸς λόγος is at once the Law of Nature and the right reasoning of the human mind.[214] This must have been a Stoic commonplace, and I can see no reason for Heinemann's statement that Posidonius introduced it into Stoicism, and hence that its appearance is always a symptom of Posidonian influence.[215] Panaetius,[216] as well as Posidonius,[217] seems to have taught that mind must rule the body and ὁρμή, and Posidonius is drawing directly upon Plato for the notion and its formulation. The notion is taken for granted in the Pseudo-Heraclitean Letter IX.[218] On one point Philo does seem distinctly to be in the path of Posidonius. When he makes the Platonic ruling of mind over the lower parts the way in which one may follow nature he is doing what

214. *De Legibus,* I, 18.

215. Heinemann, *Poseidonios,* ii, 230. Schmekel (*Philos. d. mittel. Stoa,* 268, n. 1) thought that Posidonius was the first to take the ὀρθὸς λόγος in the technical sense of the κριτήριον, and Heinemann goes on still further to declare that Posidonius introduced the ὀρθὸς λόγος itself into Stoicism. Schmekel seems to me unconvincing in view of our evidence, for Posidonius himself says that the term was used as he used it by his Stoic predecessors (*SVF,* I, 631). Heinemann's enlargement of Schmekel's already dangerous generalization is quite in the teeth of such evidence as Diogenes' (VII, 128) direct quotation from Chrysippus: φύσει τε τὸ δίκαιον εἶναι καὶ μὴ θέσει, ὡς καὶ τὸν νόμον καὶ τὸν ὀρθὸν λόγον.

216. *Apud* Cicero, *De Officiis,* I, xxviii, 101; xxx, 105.

217. *Apud* Galen, *De Hipp. et Plat. Placitis,* 470: πρῶτόν ἐστιν ἐν αὐτῇ [εὐδαιμονίᾳ] τὸ κατὰ μηδὲν ἄγεσθαι ὑπὸ τοῦ ἀλόγου τε καὶ κακοδαίμονος καὶ ἀθέου τῆς ψυχῆς. See the whole fragment and 466 f.; Heinemann, *Poseidonios,* i, 97 ff.

218. Ed. Bywater, p. 78, ll. 24 f.: σῶμα δοῦλον ψυχῆς συμπολιτεύεται ψυχῇ, καὶ οὐ χαλεπαίνει νοῦς ἰδίοις συνοικῶν ὑπηρέταις.

Galen tells us Posidonius did in distinction to Chrysippus.[219] Galen's chief criticism of Chrysippus is that he reviles Plato, and I see no reason why any eclectic who tried to cling to both Platonism and Stoicism, whether primarily from the point of view of one school or the other, would not have made much the same combination on this point. At least there is no reason for thinking that Philo is largely and directly influenced by Posidonius because of this one similarity which might well have been popularized by Philo's time.

For all the details that have clearly arisen from Stoic, Platonic, or Aristotelian sources, Philo has often appeared to have been deriving his fundamental positions from Pythagoreanism. As in his theories of the Law of Nature and of the law of the state, a review of the Pythagorean teaching of his day, itself strongly eclectic, will show that his psychology is even more thoroughly Pythagorean than detached parallels have revealed. Indeed Philo's very eclecticism seems to me to follow the pattern of the Pythagorean borrowings, and not to be any contribution of his own.

In histories of Hellenistic thought the Pythagoreans have been given very little attention. This is probably because the Romans seem to have been little interested in them, for Stoicism, Epicureanism, and the various Eclectic schools appealed to Romans much more than the teachings of a school which, if we may believe Justin Martyr, was even in the second century making rigid requirements of mathematical and scientific training a prerequisite for admission to its philosophical discussions.[220] Cicero seems to have picked up much of their moral and political point of view, but probably did so through his eclectic predecessors. But fragments of the Neo-Pythagorean writings are quite extensive, and we are in an excellent position to form an adequate estimate of many aspects of their teaching, especially in the ethical, psychological, and political realms. A study of the teachings of the school as a whole, much as such a study is needed, is beyond our present scope. But the fragments are so little read, and yet so illuminating for Philo's point of view, that it will be in point to give a few samples of their teaching.

219. Galen, *op. cit.*, 469 ff.

220. Justin Martyr, *Dialogue with Trypho*, 2, 4 (Ed. Goodspeed, p. 92). When Justin applies to the Pythagorean for admission to his school, the Pythagorean replies: Τί δαί; ὡμίλησας μουσικῇ καὶ ἀστρονομίᾳ καὶ γεωμετρίᾳ; ἢ δοκεῖς κατόψεσθαί τι τῶν εἰς εὐδαιμονίαν συντελούντων, εἰ μὴ ταῦτα πρῶτον διδαχθείης, ἃ τὴν ψυχὴν ἀπὸ τῶν αἰσθητῶν περισπάσει καὶ τοῖς νοητοῖς αὐτὴν παρασκευάσει χρησίμην, ὥστε αὐτὸ κατιδεῖν τὸ καλὸν καὶ αὐτὸ ὅ ἐστιν ἀγαθόν; so, lacking these preliminaries, Justin was refused admission. On this contact of Justin with Greek philosophy, see my *The Theology of Justin Martyr*, pp. 57 ff. The emphasis upon the necessity for such training in the Pythagorean fragments and in Philo himself entirely bears out Justin's description. See for example a fragment ascribed to Archytas *ap.* Stobaeus, III, iii, 65 (Wachs., III, 217 ff.).

The first is from Theages, of whom we know nothing beyond the fact that Stobaeus quotes the following from his book *On Virtue:*[221]

There are three fundamental principles (ἀρχαί) underlying all virtue: knowledge (γνῶσις), power (δύναμις), and choice (προαίρεσις). Knowledge is a sort of sight by which we examine and pass judgment upon phenomena; power is a sort of strength (ἀλκά) of the bodily tabernacle[222] by which we are subject and are faithful to phenomena: and choice is in a sense the hands of the soul by which we impel and grasp phenomena. And the organization of the soul is as follows: one part of it is the reason (λογισμός), the second is the spirited part (θυμός), and the third desire (ἐπιθυμία); reason is the part which rules over knowledge, the spirited part is the part which rules over passion (μένος), and desire is the part which rules the desires. When these three pass into one by manifesting a single attunement to each other,[223] then virtue and concord (ὁμολογία) come into being in the soul. But when these strive and are detached from each other, then vice and the out-of-tune come into being in the soul. And when the reason rules over the unreasoning parts (τὰ ἄλογα μέρεα) of the soul, then endurance and continence come into being, endurance in the domination (κατοχά) of pain, and continence in the domination of pleasures. But when the unreasoning parts of the soul rule over the reason, then weakness and incontinence come into being in the soul, weakness in that one flees from pains, and incontinence in that one is conquered by pleasures. But when the better part of the soul rules, and the worse is ruled, and the one leads and the other follows, and each consents to and agrees with the other, then virtue and complete goodness come into being throughout the whole soul. And when the desirous part of the soul follows the reasoning part, self-control (σωφροσύνα) comes into being; and when the spirited part [follows the reasoning part] courage [comes into being]. And when all the parts [follow the reasoning part] justice (δικαιότας) [comes into being]. For it is justice which separates all the virtues and evils of the soul from each other. Justice is a sort of organization (σύσταμα) of the attunement of the parts of the soul, and is virtue perfect and supreme. For all things are included under justice, and the other goods of the soul do not [exist] apart from it. Wherefore justice has great force among gods and men alike. For this virtue holds together the commonwealth (κοινωνία) of the All and the Whole, as found among both gods and men.[224] So Themis is spoken of among the heavenly gods, Dike among the

221. Stobaeus, III, 117, 118 (Wachs., III, 76 ff.). See Mullach, *Fragmenta Philosophorum Graecorum,* II, 18 ff.

222. The Pythagoreans were fond of using the word σκῆνος for the body since it described the body as the temporary dwelling place of the soul. It is used in this Pythagorean sense in John i, 14: ὁ λόγος . . . ἐσκήνωσεν ἐν ἡμῖν.

223. Συναρμογά; ἀρμογά was used interchangeably with ἁρμονία, which means in English not harmony, but attunement. The Greeks seem to have been very conscious of variations from the fixed intervals of their scale, and to have had indescribable delight at musical progression in exact intervals. The much discussed ἁρμονία of the lyre was its being in perfect tune with itself. It is from this point of view that ἁρμονία and mathematical proportion and ratio were synonymous.

224. Plato, *Gorgias,* 508a, is witness to the antiquity of this thoroughly Pythagorean notion. Plato has it from οἱ σοφοί who are with him always the Pythagoreans.

chthonic gods, and Law among men. These are signs and symbols of the fact that justice is the supreme virtue.[225]

Theages goes on to a classification of the virtues by another scheme, which he now summarizes:[226]

And in general what is not in tune with the ὀρθὸς λόγος[227] is vice. . . . But the alignment (σύνταξις) of the soul with the ὀρθὸς λόγος, which manifests itself in the act of examining and passing judgment, is called intelligence (φρόνασις); when it manifests itself in the enduring [of pains and the resisting of][228] pleasures, it is called self control; when in eschewing gain and injury of ones neighbor, justice. Alignment of the soul with the ὀρθὸς λόγος, as well as departure from it, is a matter of endeavor for what is necessary (τὸ δέον) and of shunning what is not necessary. The necessary is what needs must be; and this allows no adding or taking away, for it is itself what needs must be. There are two forms of the unnecessary, namely excess and lack. And excess is more than is necessary, lack is less than is necessary. But virtue is a state of the necessary (ἕξις τις τῶ δέοντος), wherefore it is immediately a state of the extreme and the mean. It is a state of the extreme in that it contains what is necessary; and of the mean by the fact that it lies between excess and lack. . . . But[229] since ethical virtue concerns the passions (πάθεα), and pleasure and pain are the highest forms of sensation, virtue would lie not in the eradication of sensation, pleasure, and pain from the soul, but in the tuning of these together (συναρμόζασθαι). For health, which is a proper mixture (εὐκρασία)[230] of the faculties (δυνάμεις) of the body consists not in the eradication of the hot, cold, wet, and dry, but in their blending, since it is a sort of symmetry of these. Similarly in music concordance (σύμφωνον) consists not in the eradication of the high and low tones, but in their somehow being tuned to each other. For when the high and low are attuned, concordance is achieved and discord banished; and when the hot, cold, wet, and dry are tuned together health arises and illness perishes. So when the spirited part and the desire have been tuned together, vices and passions (πάθεα) disappear, while virtues and good dispositions (τὰ ἤθεα) arise.[231] The distinguishing characteristic (ἰδιαί-

225. The Aristotelian character of this treatment of justice need only be mentioned. See the Fifth Book of the *Ethics, passim,* especially its definition as ἀρετὴ τελεία, and αὕτη μὲν οὖν ἡ δικαιοσύνη οὐ μέρος ἀρετῆς ἀλλ᾽ ὅλη ἀρετή ἐστιν, *Eth. Nic.,* 1129b 25–1130a 10. Did Aristotle himself have it from Pythagoreans?

226. P. 80, ll. 1 ff. (Wachs).

227. On the Pythagorean use of ὀρθὸς λόγος cf. Euryphamus *ap.* Stobaeus, IV, xxxix, 27 (Wachs., V, 918, 5); Praechter, "Metopus, Theages, and Archytas," in *Philologus,* L (1891), p. 52, ascribes the Pythagorean notion to Aristotelian origin, *Eth. Nic.,* 1119a 20, 1138b 25.

228. The text must have contained these words.

229. §118, Wachs., III, 81.

230. A familiar definition of Greek medicine which Galen attributes to Zeno, Plato, and Aristotle: *SVF,* I, 132. See Aristotle, *De Partibus Animalium,* 673b 25.

231. This sort of reasoning is familiar in Aristotle, and raises the question whether Aristotle borrowed from Pythagorean ethical teaching, or these fragments are drawing upon Aristotle. In the absence of adequate evidence for Pythagorean ethics before Aristotle, the latter cannot be denied, though I am inclined to think that Aristotle's ethics owed more to Pythagoreans than we can now demonstrate. His doctrine of the two approaches to personality, first the σύνθετον,

τατον) of the virtue of the good disposition is choice exercised in noble matters. For it is possible to use reason and power (δύναμις) even without virtue, but it is impossible to use choice. For choice indicates the worth of the disposition. Wherefore the reason, by forceful domination of the spirited and desiring parts, introduces continence and endurance, but when reason itself is on the contrary forcefully dominated by the unreasoning part, it introduces incontinence and weakness. Such states of the soul are only half perfect either as virtues or vices. For the reason is in the one case healthy, but the unreasoning parts of the soul are ill. And in so far as the spirited and desiring parts are ruled and led by the part of the soul that has reason, continence and endurance can be regarded as virtues; but in so far as this happens to them forcibly rather than by their own volition, continence and virtue are evils. For virtue ought to do the necessary things not painfully but with pleasure. And again, in so far as the spirited and desiring parts dominate the reason, and so introduce weakness and incontinence, they are to be regarded as evils; but in so far as along with the [endurance of] pains they gratify the passions, yet recognizing that they are in error because the eye of the soul is still functioning properly, in this they are not evils. So again the same thing is clear, that virtue must do the necessary things voluntarily. The involuntary is never without pain and fear, but the voluntary is never without pleasure and good cheer. . . .[232] For knowledge and vision of matters is the prerogative of the reasoning part of the soul. But power (δύναμις) is the prerogative of the unreasoning part. For the power to endure pain and control pleasure is the property of the unreasoning part of the soul. But choice involves both of these, both the reasoning and unreasoning parts of the soul. For choice is made up out of the combination of intelligence and impulse (ὄρεξις), and of these intelligence belongs to the reasoning part, impulse to the unreasoning. Wherefore every virtue consists in a tuning together of the parts of the soul, and virtue involves altogether the voluntary and the power of choice.

This is Philo's reasoning exactly. Virtue is a matter of the whole man perfectly in tune, with the lower parts of one's nature voluntarily taking their pitch from the dominant reason, while reason itself is in tune with the infinite pitch of God Himself.[233] The author of the little fragment ascribed to Clinias[234] writes in the same terms, as well as Metopus,[235] who adds the

and then the true man who is a particle of divinity in the σύνθετον (*Eth. Nic.*, 1177b 26–1178a 4) sounds much more like Pythagoreanism than the type of anthropology Aristotle could possibly have derived from his own notion of Deity. This contrast between ἤθεα or ἦθος and πάθος is frequent in Aristotle. See for example ib., 1179b 26–31. And the treatment of virtue as the mean between extremes, while found also in Plato, suggests by its very terminology that it was the sort of formulation likely to have arisen among Pythagoreans. In any case Philo's Aristotelian touches in matters of ethics are adequately accounted for by considering that he was following a predecessor of Theages.

232. A sentence here is so corrupt as to be unintelligible.
233. Hippodamus has worked this latter out in a little more detail. Stobaeus, IV, xxxix, 26 (Wachs., V, 910, 15 ff.).
234. Stobaeus, II, i, 75 f. (Wachs., III, 30 ff.).
235. Stobaeus, II, i, 115 (Wachs., III, 66 ff.).

detail that the unreasoning part of the soul is the δορύφορος καὶ σωματοφύ-
λαξ of the reasoning part, which is itself the οἰκονόμος καὶ οἰκουρός.[236]
Metopus also throws light upon Philo's "bestial mind." For he says that
bestiality is a matter of the spirited part of man, or of the unreasoning part
of the soul: while actual vice always involves the understanding, if a man
follows his lower nature he is just bestial.[237] According to Polus, justice is
the mother of all the other virtues, because it is itself the attunement of the
soul.[238] Bryson[239] adds the notion familiarly associated with Stoicism that
slaves are of three types, those made slaves by law, by nature, and by the
fact that their passions rule in the soul. But these last are not properly to be
called slaves, only evil men, since the natural slave is outside the moral categories as receiving all his motivation from his master. In this, Philo is more
Stoic than Bryson. Callicratides also treats of the soul as the governor of the
body, and adds a new element in saying that as ὁ βίος is a tool (ὄργανον) of
the human ζωή, so the body is a congenital tool of the ψυχή. Like Philo he
goes from the rule of the body by the soul to the ideal rulership of God in
the universe, and the prince in the state.[240]

A fragment attributed to Archytas[241] has so many parallels to Philo that
it must be quoted in part. Happiness has just been defined as the use of
virtue in fortunate circumstances. The author goes on:

We are talking now of human happiness. Man is not soul alone, but body as
well. For the living creature is made of both these, and man is a living creature
composed of such ingredients. For if the body is the tool of the soul, yet it is a
part of the man, and soul is part also. Wherefore there are some goods of the man
as a whole, and some goods of the parts. The good of the man as a whole is
happiness. The goods of the parts of a man are: of the soul the goods are intelligence, courage, justice, and self-control; of the body, beauty, health, good physical
condition, and keen sense perception. The external goods, wealth, fame, honor,
and good birth, are human by-products, and are secondary to those goods which
are primary by nature. The lesser goods are attendants (δορυφορεῖ) of the
greater:[242] friendship, glory, and wealth attend the body and the soul; health,
strength, and keenness of perception attend the soul; intelligence, courage, self-
control, and justice attend the mind of the soul; and the mind attends God. For
He is the most powerful and the Leader. The other goods must be there for His
sake. For the general directs the army, the pilot directs the ship, God directs the
world, mind directs the soul, and intelligence directs happiness in the life. For

236. Stobaeus, II, i, 115 (Wachs., III, p. 72, ll. 13 ff.).
237. Stobaeus, II, i, 115 (Wachs., III, p. 70 f.).
238. Stobaeus, III, ix, 51 (Wachs., III, 362 f.).
239. Stobaeus, IV, xxviii, 15 (Wachs., V, 681).
240. Stobaeus, IV, xxviii, 16, 17 (Wachs., V, 683 f.).
241. Stobaeus, III, i, 112 (Wachs., III, 61 ff.).
242. Philo reproduces this exactly: δορυφόροι σώματος πλοῦτος, εὐδοξία, κτλ. δορυφόροι ψυχῆς ἀκοαὶ καὶ ὄψεις, κτλ., Conf., 17 ff.

intelligence is nothing but an understanding of happiness in life, or of the natural goods of man.

Here is unmistakably the σύγκριμα of Philo, and the sense of the gradations of goods.[243] In even stronger terms a fragment ascribed to Hippodamus describes attunement as the virtue of the whole. In an organism, the writer insists, the whole is always antecedent to the parts. Without the body as a whole there could be no ear or eye. And the virtue of the part is a derivative from the virtue of the whole. So happiness and virtue are matters of the soul as a whole, and the individual members can get virtue only through the virtue of the whole. The discussion began with the city to show that the individual could be happy only as part of a well-lawed commonwealth; but the course of the argument shows that the same analogy is applicable within the subjective realm.[244] There is nothing in this fragment to contradict the general impression from the Neo-Pythagorean fragments that man is a combination of parts with individual tendencies which must be aligned with the good of the totality as represented by the soul or mind. Quite the reverse. The comparison of the subjective realm to a city in which the impulses of the individual citizens would be aligned with the εὐνομία of the state is precisely what the other fragments and Philo have in mind.

On the basis of these descriptions the goods of the members might very well be imagined, as Philo does, as being laws of their own, and at warfare with the law and good of the whole and so destructive of Philo's ultimate happiness. It seems that Philo intensified the importance of the σύγκριμα under the inspiration of Jewish teaching, which could so little separate the soul from the body in its thought that it usually required a bodily resurrection and the reunion of soul and body to conceive of a continuation of personality after death. Yet Philo is like the Pythagoreans in alternately insisting upon the personality as a σύγκριμα, and thinking that life after death, while a continuation of the personality, would be free from the body altogether.

The fragments which happen to have survived also show that like Philo

243. On Goods used in this sense in Philo see above, p. 393. It need hardly be pointed out that the notion of the σύγκριμα is a doctrine of the older Pythagoreans. Aristotle tells us that the Pythagoreans say that the soul is a ἁρμονία. Καὶ γὰρ τὴν ἁρμονίαν κρᾶσιν καὶ σύνθεσιν ἐναντίων εἶναι, καὶ τὸ σῶμα συγκεῖσθαι ἐξ ἐναντίων (De Anima, I, 407b 30). In Politics, VIII, 1340b 18, he adds: διὸ πολλοί φασι τῶν σοφῶν οἱ μὲν ἁρμονίαν εἶναι τὴν ψυχὴν, οἱ δ' ἔχειν ἁρμονίαν. Aëtius tells us (I, 3, 8, Diels, Doxogr., 280) that the Pythagoreans taught that ἡ ἡμετέρα ψυχὴ ἐκ τετράδος συγκεῖται, εἶναι γὰρ νοῦν, ἐπιστήμην, δόξαν, αἴσθησιν. Aristoxenus, speaking of man, says that the Pythagoreans rightly assert that ὑβριστικὸν φύσει τὸ ζῷον εἶναι, καὶ ποικίλον κατά τε τὰς ὁρμὰς καὶ κατὰ τὰς ἐπιθυμίας καὶ κατὰ τὰ λοιπὰ τῶν παθῶν (Iambl., Vit. Pythag., 174, Diels, Frag. Vorsok., 45D 3; cf. 205–207. See Stob., III, x, 66 (Wachs., III, p. 424).

244. Stobaeus, IV, xxxix, 26 (Wachs., V, 912, ll. 12 ff.).

the Neo-Pythagoreans emphasized law as the organizing force in the inner life. Some traces of it have already appeared. Another fragment begins:

Law is to the soul and life of man what attunement is to hearing and sound. For law educates the soul and organizes the life, while attunement makes the hearing intelligent and the sound unified.[245]

The fragment goes on to apply this to the rule of a king in the city, and of reason in the soul.

A fragment which Stobaeus did not know whether to ascribe to Criton or Damippus says that the rule of reason is the mother of all the other virtues because it brings about the attunement of the soul; "for all virtues are attunements and alignments [of the parts of the soul] in relation to the λόγος and the νόμος of reason."[246] Another fragment ascribed to Criton alone distinguishes between the ordinary goods of which man can be the cause, and the aspiration κατ᾽ ὀρθὸν λόγον which only God can put into man.[247] A fragment ascribed to Euryphamus[248] is eloquent in comparing the perfect life to the well-tuned lyre, and, after describing the parts of life as the goods respectively of body, money, fame, and friends, he insists that these have their musical arrangement (ἐξάρτυσις) in their fulfillment, and their attunement in being aligned κατ᾽ ἀρετὰν καὶ νόμως. With him too the ὀρθὸς λόγος is the norm.

A very important fragment in this connection is the one ascribed in the better manuscripts to Aisara of Lucania, a daughter of Pythagoras, in some manuscripts to Aresas of Lucania, one of the heads of the early Pythagorean school.[249] The ascription, like all the Neo-Pythagorean ascriptions, cannot be relied upon, but the fragment itself is here of great importance. It reads:

Human nature seems to me to be the norm (κανών) of law and justice, as well as of the household and the city. For if any one should track out and seek the traces in himself, he would find them. For there is law in himself, as well as justice, the orderly arrangement (διακόσμασις) of the soul. For as the soul is itself triple, it engages in a threefold activity: there is mind which produces knowledge and intelligence, and the spirited part which produces courage and impulse, and desire which produces love and friendliness. And all these are so aligned with reference to each other that the strongest directs them, the weakest is ruled, and the one of medium strength takes a medial position, and both rules and is ruled. And in the process of forming and working out the human taber-

---

245. The fragment is from a treatise περὶ νόμου καὶ δικαιοσύνης *ap.* Stobaeus, IV, i, 135 (Wachs., IV, p. 82). Cf. Diotogenes' description of justice, Stobaeus, IV, vii, 62 (Wachs., IV, 268, ll. 17 ff.).

246. Stobaeus, III, iii, 64 (Wachs., III, 217, 6 ff.).

247. Stobaeus, II, viii, 24 (Wachs., II, 157 f.).

248. Stobaeus, IV, xxxix, 27 (Wachs., V, 916).

249. Stobaeus, I, xlix, 27 (Wachs., I, p. 355–357).

nacle God so contrived (ἐμάσατο) these in accordance with reason that only man did he ordain to be receptive of law and justice, and none of the other mortal animals. For an organization based upon mutual relationships (σύσταμα κοινωνίας) would never be made out of one thing, nor out of many, but out of similar things (for it is necessary, since their concerns are different, that the parts of the soul in us should be different; just as in the case of the body, the organs of touch, sight, hearing, taste, and smell are different, for they all do not have the same attunement to all things). Nor is this organism made out of many and dissimilar things that are selections of chance, but out of things which produce fullness, order, and mutual attunement with reference to the total organism. And such an organism must be constituted not only out of many dissimilar things which make for a totality and completion, but also of these same things organized not casually or at random, but in accordance with some law and intelligent authority (ἐπιστασία). For if the dissimilar parts, some better, some worse, and some lying between the better and worse, had an equal portion of power and honor, the mutual relationship (κοινωνία) of the parts in the soul could not be attuned together. But if they have an unequal share in them, yet not the better but the worse has the greater portion, it would make great folly and disorder in the soul; and if the better part has the greater portion of power and honor, the worse part the lesser portion, and each of them is not proportionally (ποτὶ λόγον) allotted, there could be no agreement (ὁμόνοια), friendship, or justice in the soul, since I mean by perfect justice that state in which each part is aligned according to the attuning principle, proportion. And agreement and single-mindedness (ὁμοφρασύνα) follows upon such an alignment. Such a condition would rightly be called a well-lawed organization (εὐνομία) of the soul, which, from the fact that the better part is being the ruler, and the worse part is being ruled, introduces into the soul the power of virtue.[250]

Many of the ideas of these fragments and of Philo are of course to be found in the Stoics, especially in the later Stoics. But though later Stoics frequently adopted the Platonic three-fold division of the soul, as Posidonius did,[251] still in so far as they kept by Stoic teaching at all they retained (Posidonius especially) the distinctive Stoic notion that the soul was of a unified material, and regarded the parts of the soul as functions of the νοῦς or λόγος rather than as entities in any sense independent.[252] Galen tells us that while Posidonius agreed with Aristotle in making a threefold division of the soul,

yet the separation of these parts from each other in their positions, and the representing of one soul as having in it not only many δυνάμεις but as being a σύνθε-

250. The fragment goes on a dozen lines further to discuss the place of pleasure in the perfect adjustment.

251. *Ap.* Galen, *De Placitis Hipp. et. Plat.*, pp. 448 ff. (ed. Müller).

252. This is true in spite of the tendency of Stoic ascetic writers, like Epictetus, to describe the relations between the λόγος or λόγισμος and the lower functions as one of eternal warfare in which the only solution was the complete suppression to the point of annihilation of the lower.

τον out of heterogenous parts which were distinct in their natures, this is the teaching of Hippocrates and Plato.[253]

We may add to this statement that it was also a teaching of the Pythagoreans, or at least of the Neo-Pythagoreans. Here was, in psychological doctrine, the essential contrast between the Stoics, including ultimately Posidonius, and the position occupied by the Platonists and Aristotelians, as well as by the Neo-Pythagoreans and Philo. Their notion of the σύγκριμα or σύνθετον, which necessitated a legal regimentation in the soul, was essentially different from the Stoic notion of the lower parts as δυνάμεις of the greater part, by which the νοῦς ἡγεμών was really more the cause and source of the lower parts than their ruler in a proper sense.[254] So it is in Pythagorean, not in Stoic, teaching that we find parallels to the notion that each of the senses and parts of the soul have "goods" or "ends" peculiar to themselves. And it would only be in this philosophic environment that the "goods" could be considered as "laws" of the members, for the parts of the soul in Stoicism, as mere extensions, or functions, of the ἡγεμονικόν, could not be treated thus as having an independent relation with the universal nature.

Accordingly the Stoic aspiration was not for ἁρμονία of the lower parts with the higher, but συμμετρία of the whole.[255] That is, the aspiration is not for the attunement of fundamentally different ingredients in the soul, but for proportional development of the single soul stuff, as it flows out from the λογισμός into the various forms in which that dominating principle and source expresses itself. Practically the two forms of expression would result in much the same sort of adjustment to life. Reason was in either case to predominate over all the lower aspects of man's nature. Galen points out that Chrysippus and Plato agreed in describing beauty of soul as a matter of συμμετρία,[256] though he finds difficulty in Chrysippus' description of the soul. The Stoic was really looking for such a health of the logos that as it reached out to function in the various lesser manifestations it would do so keeping a due sense of proportion. It is true that this health was a matter of keeping the individual's logos in harmony with the Logos-Nomos of the universe,[257] but such a conception never, so far as I can ascertain, led the

253. *De Placitis Hipp. et Plat.*, p. 432 l. 11 ff. (ed. Müller).
254. Galen, *op. cit.* (p. 433) goes on to quote Chrysippus as saying that πᾶσαν ἐνέργειάν τε καὶ πάθος ἐν τῷ λογιστικῷ μόνῳ συνίστασθαι.
255. Galen, *op. cit.*, pp. 338 ff.
256. *Op. cit.*, pp. 424, 431. Galen quotes Plato, *Sophist,* 227d ff.
257. So the ὁμολογία of the Stoic was an inner "harmony" only secondarily. Virtue was primarily a διάθεσις ὁμολογουμένη but the context shows it is "agreement" with universal nature: so Cleanthes. Chrysippus included "agreement with the individual nature of man." But this phrase is unfortunately not explained, Diog. Laert., VII, 87–89. This is the sense in which is to be taken the fragment in Plutarch, *De Stoicorum Repugn.*, 9, 1035c (*SVF*, III, 326). See Schmekel, *Philosophie der mittleren Stoa* (1892), p. 357.

Stoics to talk of a legal regimentation of the mind as over against the lower members. Such a description could have originated and been accurate only in a school, like the Pythagoreans, Platonists, or Aristotelians, which thought fundamentally of the lower members as being of independent nature and origin, not as being extensions of the individual's logos itself. It is true that the Stoics did speak of the disobedience of the lower parts of the soul, but Galen, in quoting Stoics in that connection, points out the fundamental absurdity of such language from philosophers who saw the lower parts as aspects of the logos itself. He asks, pertinently, πῶς γὰρ ἂν ἢ ἀπειθεῖν ἑαυτῷ τι δύναιτο ἢ ἀποστρέφεσθαι ἑαυτὸ ἢ μὴ ἕπεσθαι ἑαυτῷ;[258] That is, the whole notion of reason as ruler in the soul had no proper place in Stoicism, because the ruler had no real subjects, and when the Stoics used such language they were only borrowing a terminology that was practically useful but fundamentally inconsistent with their postulates.[259] There are no Stoic elaborations of law and rulership in the soul comparable to those of Philo and the Pythagoreans because there could not be. Philo's frequent description of the Law of Nature is often Stoic in its terminology, as well as the way in which he describes the harmony of the individual logos with the cosmic Logos. But again that cosmic Law of Nature lacks the distinctive Stoic feature of being itself the ultimate, and of being a fatalistic and deterministic force. Philo's insistence upon individual freedom, and upon the cosmic Law as being an expression of the will of God, whose nature transcended even His Law, is as Pythagorean as it is definitely a contradiction of Stoicism.

That the Jews of the Diaspora should have found in Pythagoreanism the most congenial classical presentation of ethics is not at all strange. Here is a doctrine which puts man over against God, and yet in intimate relation with Him, in a way quite sympathetic to their religion. The Pythagoreans themselves were full of the type of mysticism popular among devout people of the day, and it was their thinking that was always predominant in philosophical explanations of the Mysteries. Hellenistic Jews would then probably have found Orphic thought already fused with Pythagoreanism, as the early writings of Aristobulus have suggested. Not the least adaptable feature for Jewish thinking was this legalistic psychology, even though it involved the ultimate transcending of the written Code.

Further the Pythagoreans presented a notion of man as being both body and soul which a Jew would have found most acceptable. Here too was an explanation of life in terms of a great Natural Law which came from God, and which must be expressed alike in the state and in the individual life. It is true that Philo and Paul show that Jews developed this aspect of the

---

258. *De Placitis Hip. et Plat.* (ed. Müller), p. 343, ll. 10 f.
259. As in the argument generally ascribed to Panaetius in Cicero's *De Officiis*, I, xxviii, 101 f.

teaching for the subjective realm more in detail than we can prove the Pythagoreans to have done, but it was Pythagoreanism which offered them an explanation of life in which their own great devotion to the Law of a personal God could find a place. While the Pythagorean conception is elaborated in Philo, it is still thoroughly Pythagorean in its point of view. It is interesting to recall that the Pythagorean fragments I have quoted seemed so much like Philo that Gruppe[260] thought they must themselves have been written by Hellenized Jews. The frequent inclusion of polytheistic elements and the total absence of any trace of the Jewish Law made this theory impossible. But it seems not to have occurred to the people who rejected Gruppe's suggestion that the similarity of the point of view which he pointed out was still there, and indicated that if the fragments were not Hellenistic Jewish, much of what we have of Hellenistic Judaism is thoroughly Pythagorean, at least in its political, ethical, and mystical aspects. The Pythagoreanism of the day was of course an eclectic affair, and left the door open for convenient borrowings of details from other schools, when it had not itself done the borrowing. Had we the treatises which lie behind the fragments in Stobaeus we might come to some conclusion as to how much the eclecticism of Philo was already worked out for him by the Pythagoreans. Even from what we have it is obvious that the essential Platonic and Aristotelian elements of ethics which appear in Philo, if not originally Pythagorean, were already fused by the Pythagoreans with their own thinking, as well as many details from Stoicism. It seems definitely a step toward the understanding of Philo to recognize that, fundamental for his systematic thinking and religious spirit as were the Torah and the mystery religions, equally so was the point of view of the Pythagorean school for the philosophical and psychological foundations of his ethical and mystical thought.

260. Gruppe, *Fragmente des Archytas*, 123 ff. Lutterbeck, *Neutestamentliche Lehrbegriffe*, I, 271, ascribes them to the Essenes. Zeller, *Philos. der Griechen*, III, ii (1903), 122 f., properly rejects both suggestions.

INDEX I

SUBJECTS AND NAMES

FOR names of classical authors and of Biblical and Apocryphal books see also Index IV.

INDEX II

GREEK WORDS

WORDS are given as they appear in the text unless they appear in a variety of forms, in which case they are given in the primary form only.

PHILONIC PASSAGES

245, 195; 237, 61; 246–257, 195; 249, 50; 258–269, 195; 263, 50; 270–287, 195; 279, 61; 288–292, 195

Fragments: *ap.* Harris, *Fragments,* pages, 8, 36; 47, 66; 53, 70; 69, 260; 72, 151, 238; 75, 261; *101,* 64, 400; *103,* 397; *109,* 35; *110,* 69; *ap.* Eusebius, *Praeparatio Evangelica, VIII, xiv, 3,* 53; *VIII, xiv, 23,* 70; *ap.* Cohn, *Philonis Opera, edit. maior., IV, 212,* 60

INDEX IV

NON-PHILONIC PASSAGES

ITALIC figures indicate passages of sources, roman figures the pages of this book. A dash indicates that the preceding chapter reference is unchanged. *E.g., iii, 6,* 333; ——, *14, 15,* 317 would mean that chapter iii, verse 6 is to be found on page 333 of this book; chapter iii, verses 14, 15, on page 317.